Rave reviews for
Bed & Breakfast U.S.A.:

"One of the bibles of the business."—*Chicago Tribune*

"There must be a dozen B&B guidebooks published by my company and numerous others. The one that I wish I had published is the acknowledged leader among them, *Bed & Breakfast U.S.A.* by Betty Rundback."—*Arthur Frommer, "The Travel Almanac"*

"A best-selling travel book."—*Reader's Digest*

"An excellent, readable travel guide."—*Washington Post*

"A valuable source of information."—*New York Times*

"Extremely useful, well-organized guide."—*ALA Booklist*

"Many a first-time B&B guest vows never again to stay in a motel . . . business travelers—particularly women traveling alone—have found this personal touch just the ticket."—*Karen Bure, TWA Ambassador*

"The best overall view . . . Betty Rundback is so enthusiastic that she even gives readers pointers on how to start their own B&Bs."—*Detroit News*

"Squeezed budgets get relief at B&Bs. . . . *Bed & Breakfast U.S.A.* [is] an extensive list of establishments."—*United Press International*

"Especially helpful . . . especially valuable."—*New York Daily News*

"The most comprehensive B&B guide."—*Savvy*

Bed
&
Breakfast
U.S.A. 1995

*Betty Revits Rundback
and Peggy Ackerman*

Tourist House Association of America

A PLUME BOOK

With great pride, our entire family remembers the love and enthusiasm Betty Revits Rundback put into this book every year. She touched many hearts. May her warmth and wisdom never be forgotten.

PLUME
Published by the Penguin Group
Penguin Books USA Inc., 375 Hudson Street, New York, New York 10014, U.S.A.
Penguin Books Ltd, 27 Wrights Lane, London W8 5TZ, England
Penguin Books Australia Ltd, Ringwood, Victoria, Australia
Penguin Books Canada Ltd, 10 Alcorn Avenue, Toronto, Ontario, Canada M4V 3B2
Penguin Books (N.Z.) Ltd, 182–190 Wairau Road, Auckland 10, New Zealand

Penguin Books Ltd, Registered Offices:
Harmondsworth, Middlesex, England

Published by Plume, an imprint of Dutton Signet,
a division of Penguin Books USA Inc.

First Printing, January, 1995

10 9 8 7 6 5 4 3 2 1

Permission to use photographs on the back cover is gratefully acknowledged to Grand Avenue Inn, Missouri (page 338), and Gingerbread Mansion Inn, California (page 85).

 REGISTERED TRADEMARK—MARCA REGISTRADA

LC card number: 86-649303

Printed in the United States of America

Set in Palatino and Optima
Designed by Stanley S. Drate/Folio Graphics Co. Inc.

If you want to be listed in future editions of this guide, DO NOT WRITE TO PLUME OR PENGUIN. See page 735 for a membership application, or write to:
Tourist House Association
RD 1, Box 12A
Greentown, PA 18426
Applications will be accepted until March 31, 1995.

Contents

Reservation service organizations appear here in boldface type.

Reservation service organizations appear here in boldface type.

Reservation service organizations appear here in boldface type.

Reservation service organizations appear here in boldface type.

Reservation service organizations appear here in boldface type.

Reservation service organizations appear here in boldface type.

Reservation service organizations appear here in boldface type.

Reservation service organizations appear here in boldface type.

Reservation service organizations appear here in boldface type.

Reservation service organizations appear here in boldface type.

Reservation service organizations appear here in boldface type.

Reservation service organizations appear here in boldface type.

MASSACHUSETTS

Reservation service organizations appear here in boldface type.

Reservation service organizations appear here in boldface type.

Reservation service organizations appear here in boldface type.

Reservation service organizations appear here in boldface type.

Reservation service organizations appear here in boldface type.

Reservation service organizations appear here in boldface type.

Reservation service organizations appear here in boldface type.

Reservation service organizations appear here in boldface type.

Reservation service organizations appear here in boldface type.

Reservation service organizations appear here in boldface type.

Reservation service organizations appear here in boldface type.

Reservation service organizations appear here in boldface type.

Reservation service organizations appear here in boldface type.

Reservation service organizations appear here in boldface type.

Reservation service organizations appear here in boldface type.

Reservation service organizations appear here in boldface type.

Reservation service organizations appear here in boldface type.

Reservation service organizations appear here in boldface type.

Reservation service organizations appear here in boldface type.

Reservation service organizations appear here in boldface type.

Reservation service organizations appear here in boldface type.

Preface

If you are familiar with earlier editions of *Bed & Breakfast U.S.A.*, you know that this book has always been a labor of love. It is personally gratifying to see how it has grown from the first sixteen-page edition, titled *Guide to Tourist Homes and Guest Houses*, which was published in 1975 and contained 40 individual listings. Nineteen years later, the eighteenth revised edition lists 1,154 homes and 111 reservation agencies, giving travelers access to over 11,000 host homes. This spectacular success indicates how strongly the revived concept of the guest house has recaptured the fancy of both travelers and proprietors.

On the other hand, what was welcomed as a reasonably priced alternative to the plastic ambience of motel chains has, in some instances, lost its unique qualities. Our mailbox is crammed with letters from grand hotels, condominium rental agencies, campground compounds, and chic inns with nightly tariffs topping the $100 mark. All share a common theme—they all serve breakfast and they all want to be listed in *Bed & Breakfast U.S.A.* Who can blame them? Since 1976, over half a million people have bought this best-selling guide.

We also receive a substantial amount of mail from our readers and we have tailored our book to meet their needs. We have given a great deal of thought to what we feel a B&B should be and are again focusing on our original definition: an owner-occupied residence with breakfast included at a fair rate, where the visitor is made to feel more like a welcome guest than a paying customer.

Because of personal experience, and comments from our readers, *Bed & Breakfast U.S.A.* will go back to the basics. We will no longer accept any bed & breakfast over $85 for a double occupancy (this does not include reservation services, suites, cottages, apartments, or qualified inns) or with rates exceeding $40 when there are five guests sharing one bath; or if they do not offer breakfast (when paying $35–$40, no one wants to go out to a restaurant for breakfast—no matter how close it may be, it's just not the same as breakfast "at home.") For those of you who do not mind paying a higher rate, the reservation services listed in *B&B U.S.A.* will gladly help you.

As a result of these new guidelines, we will regretfully have to delete a great number of listings that have been on our roster for years. This does not imply in any way that these B&Bs aren't nice; it simply means that, in our opinion, they do not fit the traditional

B&B experience. I'm sure we will be receiving hundreds of letters from irate members disputing our opinion and pointing out that rising operating expenses must be reflected in their charges. New-comers to the business decry our stand and tell us of the high costs that must somehow be recouped. While we sympathize and fully understand their positions, we must, in all fairness, be firm.

This is not a project for which listings have been compiled just for the sake of putting a book together; bigger isn't necessarily better. *Bed & Breakfast U.S.A.* is a product of a membership organization whose credo is "Comfort, cleanliness, cordiality, and fairness of cost." We solicit and rely on the comments of our readers. For this purpose, we include a tear-out form on page 745. If we receive negative reports, that member is dropped from our roster. *Bed & Breakfast U.S.A.* is looking for B&Bs set up to accommodate disabled guests. See page 745 for more information. We genuinely appreciate comments from guests—negative if necessary, positive when warranted. We want to hear from you!

All of the B&Bs described in this book are members of the Tourist House Association of America, RD 1 Box 12A, Greentown, Pennsylvania 18426. THAA dues are $35 annually. We share ideas and experiences by way of our newsletter and sometimes arrange regional seminars and conferences. To order a list of B&Bs that joined after this edition went to press, use the form in the back of this book.

PEGGY ACKERMAN
Tourist House Association of America

January 1995

Even after careful editing and proofreading, errors occasionally occur. We regret any inconvenience to our readers and members.

Acknowledgments

A special thanks to all the travel writers and reporters who have brought us to the attention of their audiences.

To my family, Mike Ackerman, Travis Kali, and Justin Ackerman, the three men in my life—thank you for all the encouragement and support you have shown; to Mary Kristyak Donnelly, a superb mother, grandmother, and best friend—I admire you so; to Bill Donnelly, dad and joke teller; to the grandmothers, Ann Revits and Helen Kristyak.

Deep appreciation goes to very eager and very patient staff members: Grace and Sheri Schweisguth, Venice Anns, and Courtney Sears.

A final note of thanks to my editor, Leslie Jay, for her deeply appreciated assistance. Never too much, always a smile.

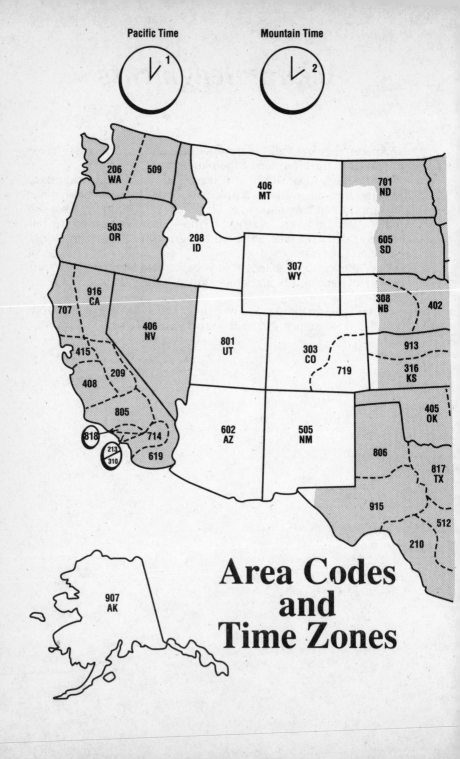

Pacific Time

Mountain Time

Area Codes and Time Zones

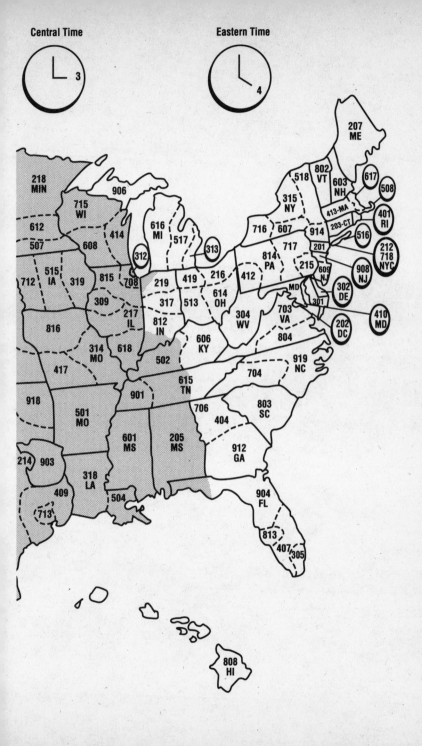

Central Time

3

Eastern Time

4

1

Introduction

Bed and Breakfast is the popular lodging alternative to hotel high-rises and motel monotony. B&Bs are either private residences where the owners rent spare bedrooms to travelers, or small, family-operated inns offering a special kind of warm, personal hospitality. Whether large or small, B&Bs will make you feel more like a welcome guest than a paying customer.

The custom of opening one's home to travelers dates back to the earliest days of Colonial America. Hotels and inns were few and far between in those days, and wayfarers relied on the kindness of strangers to provide a bed for the night. Which is why, perhaps, there is hardly a Colonial-era home in the mid-Atlantic states that does not boast: "George Washington Slept Here!"

During the Depression, the tourist home provided an economic advantage to both the traveler and the host. Travelers always drove through the center of town; there were no superhighways to bypass local traffic. A house with a sign in the front yard reading "Tourists" or "Guests" indicated that a traveler could rent a room for the night and have a cup of coffee before leaving in the morning. The usual cost for this arrangement was $2. The money represented needed income for the proprietor as well as the opportunity to chat with an interesting visitor.

In the 1950s, the country guest house became a popular alternative to the costly hotels in resort areas. The host compensated for the lack of hotel amenities, such as private bathrooms, by providing comfortable bedrooms and bountiful breakfasts at a modest price. The visitors enjoyed the home-away-from-home atmosphere; the hosts were pleased to have paying houseguests.

The incredible growth in international travel that has occurred over the past 30 years has provided yet another stimulus. Millions of Americans now vacation annually in Europe, and travelers have become enchanted with the bed and breakfast concept so popular in England, Ireland, and other parts of the Continent. In fact, many well-traveled Americans are delighted to learn that we "finally" have B&Bs here. But, as you now know, they were always here—just a rose by another name.

Bed and breakfasts are for:

- **Parents of college kids:** Tuition is costly enough without the added expense of Parents' Weekends. Look for a B&B near campus.
- **Parents traveling with children:** A family living room, playroom, or backyard is preferable to the confines of a motel room.
- **"Parents" of pets:** Many proprietors will allow your well-behaved darling to come, too. This can cut down on the expense and trauma of kenneling Fido.
- **Business travelers:** Being "on the road" can be lonely and expensive. It's so nice, after a day's work, to return to a home-away-from-home.
- **Women traveling alone:** Friendship and conversation are the natural ingredients of a guest house.
- **Skiers:** Lift prices are lofty, so it helps to save some money on lodging. Many mountain homes include home-cooked meals in your room rate.
- **Students:** A visit with a family is a pleasant alternative to camping or the local "Y."
- **Visitors from abroad:** Cultural exchanges are often enhanced by a host who can speak your language.
- **Carless travelers:** If you plan to leave the auto at home, it's nice to know that many B&Bs are convenient to public transportation. Hosts will often arrange to meet your bus, plane, or train for a nominal fee.
- **Schoolteachers and retired persons:** Exploring out-of-the-way places is fun and will save you money.
- **History buffs:** Many B&Bs are located in areas important to our country's past. A number have the distinction of being listed on the National Register of Historic Places.
- **Sports fans:** Tickets to championship games are expensive. A stay at a B&B helps to defray the cost of attending out-of-town events.
- **Antique collectors:** Many hosts have lovely personal collections, and nearby towns are filled with undiscovered antique shops.
- **House hunters:** It's a practical way of trying out a neighborhood.
- **Relocating corporate executives:** It's more comfortable to stay in a real home while you look for a permanent residence. Hosts will often give more practical advice than professional realtors.
- **Relatives of hospitalized patients:** Many B&Bs are located near major hospitals. Hosts will offer tea and sympathy when visiting hours are over.
- **Convention and seminar attendees:** Staying at a nearby B&B is less expensive than checking into a hotel.

And everyone else who has had it up to here with plastic motel monotony!

What It Is Like to Be a Guest in a B&B

The B&B descriptions provided in this book will help you choose the places that have the greatest appeal to you. A firsthand insight into local culture awaits you; imagine the advantage of arriving in New York City or San Francisco and having an insider to help you sidestep the tourist traps and direct you to that special restaurant or discount store. Or explore the countryside, where fresh air and home-cooked meals beckon. Your choice is as wide as the U.S.A.

Each bed and breakfast listed offers personal contact, a real advantage in unfamiliar environments. You may not have a phone in your room or a TV on the dresser. You may even have to pad down the hall in robe and slippers to take a shower, but you'll discover that little things count.

- In Williamsburg, Virginia, a visitor from Germany opted to stay at a B&B to help improve her conversational English. When the hostess saw that she was having difficulty understanding directions, she personally escorted her on a tour of Old Williamsburg.
- In Pennsylvania, the guests mistakenly arrived a week prior to their stated reservation date and the B&B was full. The hostess made a call to a neighbor who accommodated the couple. (By the way, the neighbor has now become a B&B host!)
- In New York City, a guest was an Emmy Award nominee and arrived with his tuxedo in need of pressing. The hostess pressed it; when he claimed his award over nationwide TV, he looked well groomed!

Expect the unexpected, such as a pot of brewed coffee upon your arrival, or fresh flowers on a nightstand. At the very least, count on our required standard of cleanliness and comfort. Although we haven't personally visited all of the places listed, they have all been highly recommended by chambers of commerce or former guests. We have either spoken to or corresponded with all of the proprietors; they are a friendly group of people who enjoy having visitors. They will do all in their power to make your stay memorable.

Our goal is to enable the traveler to crisscross the country and stay only at B&Bs along the way. To achieve this, your help is vital. Please take a moment to write us of your experiences; we will follow up on every suggestion. Your comments will serve as the yardstick by which we can measure the quality of our accommodations. For your convenience, an evaluation form is included at the back of this book.

Cost of Accommodations

Bed and Breakfast, in the purest sense, is a private home, often referred to as a "homestay," where the owners rent their spare bedrooms to travelers. These are the backbone of this book.

However, American ingenuity has enhanced this simple idea to include more spectacular homes, mansions, small inns, and intimate hotels. With few exceptions, the proprietor is the host and lives on the premises.

There is a distinction between B&B homestays and B&B inns. Inns are generally defined as a business and depend upon revenue from guests to pay expenses. They usually have six or more guest rooms, and may have a restaurant that is open to the public. The tariff at inns is usually higher than at a homestay because the owners must pay the mortgage, running expenses, and staff, whether or not guests come.

Whether plain or fancy, all B&Bs are based on the concept that people are tired of the plastic monotony of motels and are disappointed that even the so-called budget motels can be quite expensive. Travelers crave the personal touch, and they sincerely enjoy "visiting" rather than just "staying."

Prices vary accordingly. There are places listed in this book where lovely lodging may be had for as low as $25 a night, and others that feature an overnight stay with a gourmet breakfast in a canopied bed for $85. Whatever the price, if you see the sign ○ , it means that the B&B has guaranteed its rates through 1995 to holders of this book, so be sure to mention it when you call or write! (If there is a change in ownership, the guarantee may not apply. Please notify us in writing if any host fails to honor the guaranteed rate.)

Accommodations vary in price depending upon the locale and the season. Peak season usually refers to the availability of skiing in winter and water sports in summer; in the Sunbelt states, winter months are usually the peak season. Some B&Bs require a two-night weekend minimum during peak periods, and three nights on holiday weekends. Off-season rate schedules are usually reduced. Resorts and major cities are generally more expensive than out-of-the-way places. However, B&Bs are always less expensive than hotels and motels of equivalent caliber in the same area. A weekly rate is usually less expensive than a daily rate. Special reductions are sometimes given to families (occupying two rooms) or senior citizens. Whenever reduced rates are available, you will find this noted in the individual listings.

Meals

Breakfast: *Continental* refers to fruit or juice, rolls, and a hot beverage. Many hosts pride themselves on home-baked breads, homemade preserves, as well as imported teas and cakes, so their Continental breakfast may be quite deluxe. Several hosts have regular jobs outside the home, so you may have to adjust your schedule to theirs. A "full" breakfast includes fruit, cereal and/or eggs, breakfast meats, breads, and a hot beverage. The table is set family-style and is often the highlight of a B&B's hospitality. Either a Continental breakfast or full breakfast is included in the room rate unless otherwise specified.

Other Meals: If listed as "available," you can be assured that the host takes pride in his or her cooking skills. The prices for lunch or dinner are usually reasonable but are not included in the quoted room rate unless clearly specified as "included."

Making Reservations

- Reservations are a MUST or you may risk missing out on the accommodations of your choice. Reserve *early* and confirm with a deposit equal to one night's stay. If you call to inquire about reservations, please remember the difference in time zones. When dialing outside of your area, remember to dial the digit "1" before the area code.
- Many individual B&Bs now accept charge cards. This information is indicated in the listings by the symbols MC for Master-Card, AMEX for American Express, etc. A few have a surcharge for this service, so inquire as to the policy.
- Cash or traveler's checks are the accepted method of paying for your stay. Be sure to inquire whether or not tax is included in the rates quoted so that you will know exactly how much your lodging will cost.

- Rates are based on single or double occupancy of a room as quoted. Expect that an extra person(s) in the room will be charged a small additional fee. Inquire when making your reservation what the charge will be.
- If a listing indicates that children or pets are welcome, it is expected that they will be well behaved. All of our hosts take pride in their homes and it would be unfair to subject them to circumstances in which their possessions might be abused or the other houseguests disturbed by an unruly child or animal.
- Please note that many hosts have their own resident pets. If you are allergic or don't care to be around animals, inquire before making a reservation.
- In homes where smoking is permitted, do check to see if it is restricted in any of the rooms. Most hosts object to cigars.
- Where listings indicate that social drinking is permitted, it usually refers to your bringing your own beverages. Most hosts will provide ice; many will allow you to chill mixers in the refrigerator, and others offer complimentary wine and snacks. A few B&B inns have licenses to sell liquor. Any drinking should not be excessive.
- If Yes is indicated in the listings for airport/station pickup, it means that the host will meet your plane, bus, or train for a fee.
- Feel free to request brochures and local maps so that you can better plan for your visit.
- Do try to fit in with the host's house rules. You are on vacation; he or she isn't!
- A reservation form is included at the back of this book for your convenience; just tear it out and send it in to the B&B of your choice.

Cancellations

Cancellation policies vary from one B&B to another, so be sure to read the fine print on the reservation form. Many require a 15-day notice to refund the entire deposit, after which they will refund only if the room is rebooked. When a refund is due, most keep a processing fee and return the balance. A few keep the deposit and apply it to a future stay.

While these policies may seem harsh, please keep in mind that B&Bs are not hotels, which commonly overbook and where no-show guests can easily be replaced. Your host may have turned down a prospective guest, and may have bought special breakfast food in anticipation of your visit and should not be penalized. If you feel you've been unfairly treated in a cancellation situation, please do let us know.

B&B Reservation Services

There are many host families who prefer not to be individually listed in a book, and would rather have their houseguests referred by a coordinating agency. The organizations listed in this book are all members of the Tourist House Association. They all share our standards regarding the suitability of the host home as to cordiality, cleanliness, and comfort.

The majority do a marvelous job of matching host and guest according to age, interests, language, and any special requirements. To get the best match, it is practical to give them as much time as possible to find the host home best tailored to your needs.

Many have prepared descriptive pamphlets describing the homes on their rosters, the areas in which the homes are located, and information regarding special things to see and do. *Send a self-addressed, stamped, business-size envelope to receive a descriptive directory by return mail along with a reservation form for you to complete.* When returning the form, you will be asked to select the home or homes listed in the brochure that most appeal to you. (The homes are usually given a code number for reference.) The required deposit should accompany your reservation. Upon receipt, the coordinator will make the reservation and advise you of the name, address, telephone number, and travel instructions for your host.

A few agencies prepare a descriptive directory and *include* the host's name, address, and telephone number so that you can contact the host and make your arrangements directly. They charge anywhere from $2 to $11 for the directory.

Several agencies are *membership* organizations, charging guests an annual fee ranging from $5 to $25 per person. Their descriptive directories are free to members and a few of them maintain toll-free telephone numbers for reservations.

Most reservation services have a specific geographic focus. The coordinators are experts in the areas they represent. They can often make arrangements for car rentals, theater tickets, and touring suggestions, and offer information in planning a trip best suited to your interests.

Most work on a commission basis with the host, and that fee is included in the room rates quoted in each listing. Some make a surcharge for a one-night stay; others require a two- or three-night minimum stay for holiday periods or special events. Some will accept a credit card for the reservation, but the balance due must be paid to the host in cash or traveler's checks.

All of their host homes offer a Continental breakfast, and some may include a full breakfast.

Many reservation services in the larger cities have, in addition to the traditional B&Bs, a selection of apartments, condominiums, and houses *without hosts in residence*. This may be appealing to those travelers anticipating an extended stay in a particular area.

Statewide services are listed first in the section for each state. City or regionally based organizations are listed first under the heading for that area. For a complete description of their services, look them up under the city and state where they're based.

NOTE: When calling, do so during normal business hours (for that time zone), unless otherwise stated. Collect calls are not accepted.

2

How to Start Your Own B&B

What It's Like to Be a Host

Hosts are people who like the idea of accommodating travelers and sharing their home and the special features of their area with them. They are people who have houses too large for their personal needs and like the idea of supplementing their income by having people visit. For many, it's a marvelous way of meeting rising utility and maintenance costs. For young families, it is a way of buying and keeping that otherwise-too-large house, as well as a way of furnishing it, since many of the furnishings may be tax deductible. Another advantage is that many state and local governments have recognized the service that some host families perform. In browsing through this book you will note that some homes are listed on the National Historic Register. Some state governments allow owners of landmark and historical houses a special tax advantage if they are used for any business purpose. Check with the Historical Preservation Society in your state for details.

If you have bedrooms to spare, if you sincerely like having overnight guests, if your home is clean and comfortable, this is an opportunity to consider. It is a unique business because *you* set the time of the visit and the length of stay. (Guest houses are not boarding homes.) You invite the guests at *your* convenience, and the extras, such as meals, are entirely up to you. You can provide a cup of coffee, complete meals, or just a room and shared bath. Remember that your income may be erratic and should not be depended upon to pay for monthly bills. However, it can afford you some luxuries.

Although the majority of hosts are women, many couples are finding pleasure in this joint venture. The general profile of a typical host is a friendly, outgoing, flexible person who is proud of his or her home and hometown. The following information and suggestions represent a guideline to consider in deciding whether becoming a B&B host is really for you.

There are no set rules for the location, type, or style of a B&B. Apartments, condos, farmhouses, town houses, beach houses, vacation cottages, houseboats, mansions, as well as the traditional one-family dwelling are all appropriate. The important thing is for the host to be on the premises. The setting may be urban, rural, or suburban, near public transportation or in the hinterlands. Location is only important if you want to have guests every night. Areas where tourism is popular, such as resort areas or major cities, are often busier than out-of-the-way places. However, if a steady stream of visitors is not that important or even desirable, it doesn't matter where you are. People will contact you if your rates are reasonable and if there is something to see and do in your area, or if it is near a major transportation route.

Setting Rates

Consider carefully four key factors in setting your rates: location, private versus shared bath, type of breakfast, and your home itself.

Location: If you reside in a traditional resort or well-touristed area, near a major university or medical center, or in an urban hub or gateway city, your rates should be at least 40% lower than those of the area's major motels or hotels. If you live in an out-of-the-way location, your rates must be extremely reasonable. If your area has a "season"—snow sports in winter, water sports in summer—offer off-season rates when these attractions are not available. Reading through this book will help you to see what is the going rate in a situation similar to yours.

The Bath: You are entitled to charge more for a room with private bath. If the occupants of two rooms share one bath, the rate should be less. If more than five people must share one bathroom, you may have complaints, unless your rates are truly inexpensive.

The Breakfast: Figure the approximate cost of your ingredients, plus something for your time. Allow about $1 to $2 for a Continental breakfast, $2 to $3 for a full American breakfast, and then *include* it in the rate.

Your Home: Plan on charging a fair and reasonable rate for a typical B&B home, one that is warm and inviting, clean and comfortable. If your home is exceptionally luxurious, with king-size beds, Jacuzzi baths, tennis courts, or hot tubs, you will find guests who are willing to pay a premium. If your home is over 75 years old, well restored, with lots of antiques, you may also be able to charge a higher rate.

The Three Bs—Bed, Breakfast, and Bath

The Bedroom: The ideal situation for a prospective host is the possession of a house too large for current needs. The children may be away at college most of the year or may have left permanently, leaving behind their bedrooms and, in some cases, an extra bath. Refurbishing these rooms does not mean refurnishing; an extraordinary investment need not be contemplated for receiving guests. Take a long, hard look at the room. With a little imagination and a little monetary outlay, could it be changed into a bedroom *you'd* be pleased to spend the night in? Check it out *before* you go any further. Are the beds comfortable? Is the carpet clean? Are the walls attractive? Do the curtains or shades need attention? Are there sturdy hangers in the closet? Would emptying the closet and bureau be an impossible task? Is there a good light to read by? A writing table and comfortable chair? Peek under the bed to see if there are dust balls or old magazines tucked away. While relatives and friends would "understand" if things weren't perfect, a paying guest is entitled to cleanliness and comfort.

Equip the guest bureau or dresser with a good mirror, and provide a comfortable chair and good reading light. The clothes closet should be free from your family's clothing and storage items, and stocked with firm, plastic hangers, a few skirt hangers, and some hooks. Sachets hung on the rod will chase musty odors. Provide room-darkening shades or blinds on the windows. And, if your house is located on a busy street, it is wise to have your guest bedrooms in the rear. Paying guests are entitled to a good night's rest! If your tap water is not tasty, it is thoughtful to supply bottled water.

If the idea of sprucing up the room has you overwhelmed, forget the idea and continue to be a guest rather than a host! If, however, a little "spit and polish," replacement of lumpy mattresses, sagging springs, and freshening the room in general presents no problem, continue!

Mattresses should be firm, covered with a mattress pad, attractive linens, and bedspread. Although seconds are OK, good-quality linens are a wise investment, since cheap sheets tend to pill. Offer a selection of pillows of various firmnesses—a choice of down or fiberfill is the ultimate in consideration! Twin beds are often preferred, since many people do not wish to share a bed. Sofa beds are really not comfortable and should be avoided. Is there a bedside lamp and night table on each side of the bed? Bulbs should be at least 75 watts for comfortable reading. A luggage rack is convenient for guests and keeps the bedspread clean. Provide a varied assortment of books, current magazines in a rack, a local newspaper, and some information on what's doing in your town along with a map. If yours is a shared-bath accommodation, do provide a well-lit mirror and convenient electric outlet for makeup and shaving purposes. It will take the pressure off the bathroom! A fresh thermos of ice water and drinking glasses placed on an attractive dresser tray is always appreciated. Put it in the room while the guest is out to dinner, right next to the dish of hard candy or fruit. A fancy candlestick is a pretty accessory and a useful object in case of a power failure. Dresser drawers should be clean and lined with fresh paper. A sachet, flashlight, and a pad and pencil are thoughtful touches. For safety's sake, prohibit smoking in the bedroom. Besides, the odor of tobacco clings forever. Always spray the bedroom with air freshener a few minutes before the guest arrives. On warm or humid days, turn on the air conditioner as well.

From time to time sleep in each guest room yourself. It's the best test.

The Breakfast: Breakfast time can be the most pleasant part of a guest's stay. It is at the breakfast table with you and the other guests that suggestions are made as to what to see and do, and exchanges of experiences are enjoyed. From a guest's point of view, the only expected offering is what is known as a Continental breakfast, which usually consists of juice, roll, and coffee or tea.

Breakfast fare is entirely up to you. If you are a morning person who whips out of bed at the crack of dawn with special recipes for muffins dancing in your head, muffins to be drenched with your homemade preserves followed by eggs Benedict, an assortment of imported coffees or exotic teas—hop to it! You will play to a most appreciative audience. If, however, morning represents an awful intrusion on sleep, and the idea of talking to anyone before noon is difficult, the least you should do is to prepare the breakfast table the night before with the necessary mugs, plates, and silverware. Fill the electric coffeepot and leave instructions that the first one up should plug it in; you can even hook it up to a timer so that it will brew automatically!

Most of us fall somewhere in between these two extremes. Remember that any breakfast at "home" is preferable to getting dressed, getting into a car, and driving to some coffee shop. Whether you decide upon a Continental breakfast or a full American breakfast, consisting of juice or fruit, cereal or eggs, possibly bacon or sausage, toast, rolls, and coffee or tea, is up to you. It is most important that whatever the fare, it be included in your room rate. It is most awkward, especially after getting to know and like your guests, to present an additional charge for breakfast.

With so many of us watching calories, caffeine, and cholesterol, be prepared to offer unsweetened and/or whole grain breads, oat-bran cereals and muffins, and brewed decaf coffee or tea. It is also thoughtful to inquire about your guests' dietary restrictions and allergies. Whatever you serve, do have your table attractively set.

Some Suggestions

- Don't have a messy kitchen. If you have pets, make sure their food dishes are removed after they've eaten. If you have cats, make sure they don't walk along the countertops, and be certain that litter boxes are cleaned without fail. Sparkling clean surroundings are far more important than the decor.
- Let guests know when breakfast will be served. Check to see if they have any allergies, diet restrictions, or dislikes. Vary the menu if guests are staying more than one night.
- Do offer one nonsweet bread for breakfast.
- Consider leaving a breakfast order sheet in each room with a request that it be returned before guests retire. It might read:

We serve breakfast between 7 AM and 10 AM. Please check your preference and note the time at which you plan to eat.

☐ Coffee ☐ Tea ☐ Decaf ☐ Milk ☐ Toast ☐ Muffins
☐ Sweet Rolls ☐ Orange Juice ☐ Tomato Juice ☐ Fruit Cup

The Bath: This really is the third B in B&B. If you are blessed with an extra bathroom for the exclusive use of a guest, that's super. If guests will have to share the facilities with others, that really presents no problem. If it's being shared with your family, the family must always be "last in line." Be sure that they are aware of the guest's importance; the guest, paying or otherwise, always comes first. No retainers, used Band-Aids, or topless toothpaste tubes are to be carelessly left on the sink. The tub, shower, floor, and toilet bowl are to be squeaky clean. The mirrors and chrome should sparkle, and a supply of toilet tissue, fresh soap, and unfrayed towels goes a long way in reflecting a high standard of cleanliness. Make sure that the grout between tiles is free of mildew and that the shower curtain is unstained; add nonskid tape to the tub. Cracked ceilings should be repaired. Paint should be free of chips, and if your bath is wallpapered, make certain no loose edges mar its beauty.

Although it is your responsibility to check out the bath at least twice a day, most guests realize that in a share-the-bath situation they should leave the room ready for the next person's use. It is a thoughtful reminder for you to leave tub cleanser, a cleaning towel or sponge, and bathroom deodorant handy for this purpose. A wastepaper basket, paper towels, and paper cups should be part of your supplies. Needless to say, your hot water and septic systems should be able to accommodate the number of guests you'll have without being overtaxed. Call the plumber to fix any clogged drains or dripping faucets. Make sure that there are enough towel bars and hooks to accommodate the towels of all guests. Extra bathroom touches:

- Use liquid soap dispensers in lieu of bar soap on the sink.
- Provide a place for guests' personal toilet articles; shelves add convenience and eliminate clutter.
- Give different colored towels to each guest.
- Supply each guest room with its own bath soap in a covered soap dish.
- Provide guests with one-size-fits-all terry robes.

The B&B Business

Money Matters: Before embarking upon any business, it's a good idea to discuss it with an accountant and possibly an attorney. Since you'll be using your home for a business enterprise there are things with which they are familiar that are important for you to know. For instance, you may want to incorporate, so find out what the pros and cons are. Ask about depreciation. Deductible business expenses may include refurbishing, furnishings, supplies, printing costs, postage, etc. An accountant will be able to guide you with a simple system of record keeping. Accurate records will help you analyze income and expense, and show if you are breaking even or operating at a profit or a loss.

Taxes: Contact your state department of taxation requesting specific written information regarding tax collection and payment schedules. Get a sales tax number from your county clerk. If you rent rooms less than 15 days a year, you need not report the B&B income on your federal return. Income after the fourteenth day is taxable, and you can take deductions and depreciation allowances against it. If the revenues from running the B&B are insignificant, you can call it "hobby income" and avoid taxes. However, you can't qualify as a business and may lose other tax advantages.

Record Keeping: Open a B&B checking account and use it to pay expenses and to deposit all income, including sales tax associated with the B&B. Write checks whenever possible for purchases; get dated receipts when you can. Estimate the cost of serving breakfast and multiply it by the number of guests you feed annually; keep track of extra expenses for household supplies and utilities.

The Case for Credit Cards: Many guests prefer to stay now and pay later; business travelers like the easy record keeping for their expense sheets. Even if you don't wish to accept them on a regular basis, credit cards give you the opportunity to take a deposit over the phone when there isn't time to receive one by mail. The cost is negligible, generally 4%.

If you do accept a last-minute reservation without a credit card number to guarantee it, make certain the caller understands that if they don't show up, and you have held the room for them, you will have lost a night's rent. You may also remind the caller that if they aren't there by a mutually agreed upon time, you may rent the room to someone else. Needless to say, it is equally important for you to remain at home to receive the guests or to be on hand for a phone call should they get lost en route to your home.

Insurance: It is important to call your insurance broker. Some homeowner policies have a clause covering "an occasional overnight paying guest." See if you will be protected under your existing coverage and, if not, what the additional premium would be. As a member of the THAA, you may participate in our group liability policy under the auspices of Brown, Schuck, Townshend, and Associates.

Every home should be equipped with smoke detectors and fire extinguishers. All fire hazards should be eliminated; stairways and halls should be well lit and kept free of clutter. If you haven't already done so, immediately post prominently the emergency numbers for the fire department, police, and ambulance service.

Safety Reminders: Equip guest bedrooms and bathrooms with nightlights. Keep a flashlight (in working order!) in each bedroom, in case of power failure. Bathrooms should have nonslip surfaces in the tub and shower, and handholds should be installed in bathtubs. Keep a well-stocked first aid kit handy and know how to use it. Learn the Heimlich Maneuver and CPR (cardiopulmonary resuscitation). Periodically test smoke detectors and fire extinguishers to make certain they are in working order.

Regulations: If you have read this far and are still excited about the concept of running a B&B, there are several steps to take at this point. As of this writing, there don't seem to be any specific laws governing B&Bs. Since guests are generally received on an irregular basis, B&Bs do not come under the same laws governing hotels and motels. And since B&Bs aren't inns where emphasis is on food rather than on lodging, no comparison can really be made in that regard either. As the idea grows, laws and regulations will probably be passed. Refer to the back of *Bed & Breakfast U.S.A.* to write to your state's office of tourism for information. The address and phone number are listed for your convenience. You might even call or write to a few B&Bs in your state and ask the host about his or her experience in this regard. Most hosts will be happy to give you the benefit of their experience, but keep in mind that they are busy people and it would be wise to limit your intrusion upon their time.

If you live in a traditional, residential area and you are the first in your neighborhood to consider operating a B&B, it would be prudent to examine closely the character of houses nearby. Do physicians, attorneys, accountants, or psychologists maintain offices in their residences? Do dressmakers, photographers, cosmeticians, or architects receive clients in their homes? These professions are legally accepted in the most prestigious communities as "customary house occupations." Bed and breakfast has been tested in many communities where the question was actually brought to court. In towns from La Jolla, California, to Croton-on-Hudson, New York, bed and breakfast has been approved and accepted.

Zoning boards are not always aware of the wide acceptance of the B&B concept. Possibly the best evidence that you could present to them is a copy of *Bed & Breakfast U.S.A.*, which indicates that it is an accepted practice throughout the entire country. It illustrates the caliber of the neighborhoods, the beauty of the homes, and the fact that many professionals are also hosts. Reassure the zoning board that you will accept guests only by advance reservation. You will not display any exterior signs to attract attention to your home. You will keep your home and grounds properly maintained, attractive, and in no way detract from the integrity of your neighborhood. You will direct guests to proper parking facilities and do nothing to intrude upon the privacy of your neighbors.

After all, there is little difference between the visit of a family friend and a B&B guest, because that is the spirit and essence of a B&B. Just as a friend would make prior arrangements to be a houseguest, so will a B&B guest make a reservation in advance. Neither would just drop in for an overnight stay. We are happy to share letters from hosts attesting to the high caliber, honesty, and integrity of B&B guests that come as a result of reading about their accommodations in this book. There are over 12,000 B&Bs extending our kind of hospitality throughout the United States, and the number is increasing geometrically every day.

You should also bring along a copy of *Bed & Breakfast U.S.A.* when you go to visit the local chamber of commerce. Most of them are enthusiastic, because additional visitors mean extra business for local restaurants, shops, theaters, and businesses. This is a good time to inquire what it would cost to join the chamber of commerce.

The Name: The naming of your B&B is most important and will take some time and consideration because this is the moment when dreams become reality. It will be used on your brochures, stationery, and bills. (If you decide to incorporate, the corporation needs a name!) It should somehow be descriptive of the atmosphere you wish to convey.

Brochure: Once you have given a name to your house, design a brochure. The best ones include a reservation form and can be mailed to your prospective guests. The brochure should contain the name of your B&B, address, phone number, best time to call, your name, a brief description of your home, its ambience, a brief history of the house if it is old, the number of guest rooms, whether or not baths are shared, the type of breakfast served, rates, required deposit, minimum stay requirement if any, dates when you'll be closed, and your cancellation policy. Although widely used, the phrase "Rates subject to change without notice" should be avoided. Rather, state the specific dates when the rates will be valid. A deposit of one night's stay is acceptable, and the promise of a full refund if cancellation is received at least two weeks prior to arrival is typical. If you have reduced rates for a specific length of stay, for families, for senior citizens, etc., mention it.

The Rate Sheet should be a separate insert so that if rates change, the entire brochure need not be discarded. Mention your smoking policy. If you do allow smoking inside the house, do you reserve any bedrooms for nonsmokers? Don't forget to mention the ages of your children, and describe any pets in residence. If you don't accept a guest's pet, be prepared to supply the name, address, and phone number of a reliable local kennel.

If you can converse in a foreign language, say so, because many visitors from abroad seek out B&Bs; it's a marvelous plus to be able to chat in their native tongue. Include your policy regarding children, pets, or smokers, and whether you offer the convenience of a guest refrigerator or barbecue. It is helpful to include directions from a major route and a simple map for finding your home. It's a good idea to include a line or two about yourself and your interests, and do mention what there is to see and do in the area as well as proximity to any major university. A line drawing of your house is a good investment since the picture can be used not only on the brochure but on your stationery, postcards, and greeting cards as well. If you can't have this taken care of locally, write the Tourist House Association. We have a service that can handle it for you.

Take your ideas to a reliable printer for his professional guidance. Don't forget to keep the receipt for the printing bill since this is a business expense.

Confirmation Letter: Upon receipt of a paid reservation, do send out a letter confirming it. You can design a form letter and have it offset printed by a printer, since the cost of doing so is usually nominal. Include the dates of the stay; number of people expected; the rate, including tax; the cancellation policy; as well as explicit directions by car and, if applicable, by public transportation. A simple map reflecting the exact location of your home in relation to major streets and highways is most useful. It is a good idea to ask your guests to call you if they will be traveling and unavailable by phone for the week prior to their expected arrival. You might even want to include any of the house rules regarding smoking, pets, or whatever.

Successful Hosting

The Advantage of Hosting: The nicest part of being a B&B host is that you aren't required to take guests every day of the year. Should there be times when having guests would not be convenient, you can always say you're full and try to arrange an alternate date. But most important, keep whatever date you reserve. It is an excellent idea at the time reservations are accepted to ask for the name and telephone number of an emergency contact should you have to cancel unexpectedly. However, *never* have a guest come to a locked door. If an emergency arises and you cannot reach your prospective guests in time, do make arrangements for someone to greet them, and make alternate arrangements so that they can be accommodated.

House Rules: While you're in the thinking stage, give some thought to the rules you'd like your guests to adhere to. The last thing you want for you or your family is to feel uncomfortable in your own home. Make a list of House Rules concerning arrival and departure during the guests' stay, and specify when breakfast is served. If you don't want guests coming home too late, say so. Most hosts like to lock up at a certain hour at night, so arrange for an extra key for night owls. If that makes you uncomfortable, have a curfew on your House Rules list. If smoking disturbs you, confine the area where it's permitted.

Some guests bring a bottle of their favorite beverage and enjoy a drink before going out to dinner. Many hosts enjoy a cocktail hour too, and often provide cheese and crackers to share with guests. B&Bs cannot sell drinks to guests since this would require licensing. If you'd rather no drinks be consumed in your home, say so.

Many hosts don't mind accommodating a well-behaved pet. If

you don't mind, or have pets of your own, discuss this with your guests before they pack Fido's suitcase. Your House Rules can even be included in your brochure. That way, both host and guest are aware of each other's likes and dislikes, and no hard feelings are made.

Entertaining: One of the most appealing features of being a guest at a B&B is the opportunity to visit in the evening with the hosts. After a day of sightseeing or business, it is most relaxing and pleasant to sit around the living room and chat. For many hosts, this is the most enjoyable part of having guests. However, if you are accommodating several people on a daily basis, entertaining can be tiring. Don't feel you'll be offending anyone by excusing yourself to attend to your own family or personal needs. The situation can be easily handled by having a room to which you can retreat, and offering your guests the living room, den, or other area for games, books, magazines, and perhaps the use of a television or bridge table. Most guests enjoy just talking to one another since this is the main idea of staying at a B&B.

The Telephone: This is a most important link between you and your prospective guests. As soon as possible, have your telephone number included under your B&B name in the white pages. It is a good idea to be listed in the appropriate section in your telephone directory yellow pages. If your home phone is used for a lot of personal calls, ask the local telephone company about call-waiting service, or think about installing a separate line for your B&B. If you are out a lot, give some thought to using a telephone answering device to explain your absence and time of return, and record the caller's message. There is nothing more frustrating to a prospective guest than to call and get a constant busy signal, or no answer at all. Request that the caller leave his or her name and address so that you can mail a reservation form. This will help eliminate the necessity of having to return long-distance calls. If the caller wants further information, he or she will call again at the time you said you'd be home.

B&B guests don't expect a phone in the guest room. However, there are times when they might want to use your phone for a long-distance call. In your House Rules list, suggest that any such calls be charged to their home telephone. Business travelers often have telephone charge cards for this purpose. In either case, you should keep a telephone record book and timer near your instrument. Ask the caller to enter the city called, telephone number, and length of call. Thus, you will have an accurate record should a charge be inadvertently added to your bill. Or, if you wish, you can add telephone charges to the guest bill. A telephone operator will quote the cost of the per-minute charge throughout the country for this purpose.

Maid Service: If you have several guest rooms and bathrooms, you may find yourself being a chambermaid as part of the business. Naturally, each guest gets fresh linens upon arrival. If a guest stays up to three days, it isn't expected that bed linen be changed every day. What is expected is that the room be freshened and the bath be cleaned and towels replaced every day. If you don't employ a full-time maid you may want to investigate the possibility of hiring a high school student on a part-time basis to give you a hand with the housekeeping. Many guests, noticing the absence of help, will voluntarily lend a hand, although they have the right to expect some degree of service, particularly if they are paying a premium rate.

Keys: A great many hosts are not constantly home during the day. Some do "hosting" on a part-time basis, while involved with regular jobs. There are times when even full-time hosts have to be away during the day. If guests are to have access to the house while you are not on the premises, make extra keys and attach them to an oversize key chain. It is also wise to take a key deposit of $50 simply to assure return of the key. Let me add that in the 16 years of my personal experience, as well as in the opinions of other hosts, B&B guests are the most honest people you can have. No one has ever had even a washcloth stolen, let alone the family treasures. In fact, it isn't unusual for the guest to leave a small gift after a particularly pleasant visit. On the other hand, guests are sometimes forgetful and leave belongings behind. For this reason it is important for you to have their names and addresses so that you can return their possessions. They will expect to reimburse you for the postage.

Registering Guests: You should keep a regular registration ledger for the guest to complete before checking in. The information should include the full name of each guest, home address, phone number, business address and telephone, and auto license number. It's a good idea to include the name and phone number of a friend or relative in case of an emergency. This information will serve you well for other contingencies, such as the guest leaving some important article behind, an unpaid long-distance phone call, or the rare instance of an unpaid bill. You may prefer to have this information on your guest bill, which should be designed as a two-part carbon form. You will then have a record and the guest has a ready receipt. (Receipts are very important to business travelers!)

Settling the Bill: The average stay in a B&B is two nights. A deposit equal to one night's lodging is the norm; when to collect the balance is up to you. Most guests pay upon leaving, but if they leave so early that the settling of the bill at that time is inconvenient, you can request the payment the previous night. You might want to consider the convenience of accepting a major credit card, but contact the sponsoring company first to see what percentage of your gross is expected for this service. If you find yourself entertaining more business visitors than vacationers, it might be something you should offer. Most travelers are aware that cash or traveler's checks are the accepted modes of payment. Accepting a personal check is rarely risky, but again, it's up to you. You might include your preference in your brochure.

Other Meals: B&B means that only breakfast is served. If you enjoy cooking and would like to offer other meals for a fee, make sure that you investigate the applicable health laws. If you have to install a commercial kitchen, the idea might be too expensive for current consideration. However, allowing guests to store fixings for a quick snack or to use your barbecue can be a very attractive feature for families traveling with children or for people watching their budget. If you can offer this convenience, be sure to mention it in your brochure. (And be sure to add a line to your House Rules that the guest is expected to clean up.) Some hosts keep an extra guest refrigerator on hand for this purpose.

It's an excellent idea to keep menus from your local restaurants on hand. Try to have a good sampling, ranging from moderately priced to expensive dining spots, and find out if reservations are required. Your guests will always rely heavily upon your advice and suggestions. After all, when it comes to your town, you're the authority! It's also a nice idea to keep informed of local happenings that might be of interest to your visitors. A special concert at the university or a local fair or church supper can add an extra dimension to their visit. If parents are visiting with young children they might want to have dinner out without them; try to have a list of available baby-sitters. A selection of guidebooks covering your area is also a nice feature.

The Guest Book: These are available in most stationery and department stores, and it is important that you buy one. It should contain designated space for the date, the name of the guest, home address, and a blank area for the guest's comments. They generally sign the guest book before checking out. The guest book is first of all a permanent record of who came and went. It will give you an idea of what times during the year you were busiest and which times were slow. Second, it is an easy way to keep a mailing list for your Christmas cards and future promotional mailings. You will also find that thumbing through it in years to come will recall some very pleasant people who were once strangers but now are friends.

Advertising: Periodically distribute your brochures to the local university, college, and hospital, since out-of-town visitors always need a place to stay. Let your local caterers know of your existence since wedding guests are often from out of town. If you have a major corporation in your area, drop off a brochure at the personnel office. Even visiting or relocating executives and salespeople enjoy B&Bs. Hotels and motels are sometimes overbooked; it wouldn't hurt to leave your brochure with the manager for times when there's no room for their last-minute guests. Local residents sometimes have to put up extra guests, so it's a good idea to take an ad out in your local school or church newspaper. The cost is usually minimal. Repeat this distribution process from time to time so that you can replenish the supply of brochures.

Check the back of this book for the address of your state tourist office. Write to them, requesting inclusion in any brochures listing B&Bs in the state.

The best advertising is being a member of the Tourist House Association since all member B&Bs are fully described in this book, which is available in bookstores, libraries, and B&Bs throughout the United States and Canada. In addition, it is natural for THAA members to recommend one another when guests inquire about similar accommodations in other areas. The most important reason for keeping your B&B clean, comfortable, and cordial is that we are all judged by what a guest experiences in any individual

Tourist House Association home. The best publicity will come from your satisfied guests, who will recommend your B&B to their friends.

Additional Suggestions

Extra Earnings: You might want to consider a few ideas for earning extra money in connection with being a host. If guests consistently praise your muffins and preserves, you might sell attractively wrapped extras as take-home gifts. If you enjoy touring, you can plan and conduct a special outing, off the beaten tourist track, for a modest fee. In major cities, you can do such things as acquiring tickets for theater, concert, or sports events. A supply of *Bed & Breakfast U.S.A.* for sale to guests is both a source of income and gives every THAA member direct exposure to the B&B market. Think about offering the use of your washer and dryer. You may, if you wish, charge a modest fee to cover the service. Guests who have been traveling are thrilled to do their wash or have it done for them "at home" rather than wasting a couple of hours at the laundromat.

Several hosts tell me that a small gift shop is often a natural offshoot of a B&B. Items for sale might include handmade quilts, pillows, potholders, and knitted items. One host has turned his hobby of woodworking into extra income. He makes lovely picture frames, napkin rings, and footstools that many guests buy as souvenirs to take home. If you plan to do this, check with the Small Business Administration to inquire about such things as a resale license and tax collection; a chamber of commerce can advise in this regard.

Transportation: While the majority of B&B guests arrive by car, there are many who rely on public transportation. Some hosts, for a modest fee, are willing to meet arriving guests at airports, train depots, or bus stations. Do be knowledgeable about local transportation schedules in your area, and be prepared to give explicit directions for your visitors' comings and goings. Have phone numbers handy for taxi service, as well as information on car rentals.

Thoughtful Touches: Guests often write to tell us of their experiences at B&Bs as a result of learning about them through this book. These are some of the special touches that made their visit special: fresh flowers in the guest room; even a single flower in a bud vase is pretty. One hostess puts a foil-wrapped piece of candy on the pillow before the guest returns from dinner. A small decanter of wine and glasses, or a few pieces of fresh fruit in a pretty bowl on the dresser are lovely surprises. A small sewing kit in the bureau is handy. Offer guests the use of your iron and ironing board, rather than having them attempt to use the bed or dresser. Writing paper and envelopes in the desk invite the guest to send a quick note to the folks at home. If your house sketch is printed on it, it is marvelous free publicity. A pre-bed cup of tea for adults and cookies and milk for children are always appreciated.

By the way, keep a supply of guest-comment cards in the desk, both to attract compliments as well as to bring to your attention the flaws in your B&B that should be corrected.

Join the Tourist House Association: If you are convinced that you want to be a host, and have thoroughly discussed the pros and cons with your family and advisers, complete and return the membership application found at the back of this book. Our dues are $35 annually. The description of your B&B will be part of the next edition of *Bed & Breakfast U.S.A.*, as well as in the interim supplement between printings. Paid-up members receive a complimentary copy of *Bed & Breakfast U.S.A.* You will also receive the THAA's newsletter; regional seminars and conferences are held occasionally and you might enjoy attending. And, as an association, we will have clout should the time come when B&B becomes a recognized industry.

Affiliating with a B&B Reservation Agency: There are 108 agencies listed in *Bed & Breakfast U.S.A.* If you do not care to advertise your house directly to the public, consider joining one in your area. Membership and reservation fees, as well as the degree of professionalism, vary widely from agency to agency, so do check carefully.

Prediction of Success: Success should not be equated with money alone. If you thoroughly enjoy people, are well organized, enjoy sharing your tidy home without exhausting yourself, then the idea of receiving compensation for the use of an otherwise dormant bedroom will be a big plus. Your visitors will seek relaxing, wholesome surroundings, and unpretentious hosts who open their hearts as well as their homes. Being a B&B host or guest is an exciting, enriching experience.

3

B&B Recipes

The recipes that follow are B&B host originals. They've been chosen because of the raves they've received from satisfied B&B guests. The most important ingredient is the heartful of love that goes into each one.

We always have a good response to our request for favorite breakfast recipes. Although we could not publish them all this time, we will use most of them in future editions.

Hewick B&B Pecan Coffee Cake

¾ c. brown sugar
1 pkg. of vanilla pudding (not instant)
1 tbsp. cinnamon
6 tbsp. margarine

1 c. pecans
1 12-oz. package refrigerated,
    unbaked dinner rolls

Preheat the oven to 350°F. Mix together the sugar, pudding, and cinnamon and set aside. Grease a Bundt pan with some of the margarine then coat it with the pecans. Put the rolls in the pan and sprinkle the dry mix over them. Dot with the remaining margarine and let the cake stand covered overnight. Remove the cover and bake for 30 minutes.

Hewick B&B, Urbana, Virginia

Baked Apples New England

6 baking apples (Cortland or
    MacIntosh)
6 heaping tsp. sugar mixed with 1
    tsp. cinnamon

3 tbsp. butter
2 tbsp. water
½ cup raisins (optional)
2 tbsp. rum (optional)

Preheat the oven to 350°F. Core the apples and make a slit through the skin with a knife all the way around, stopping about a third of the way from the top; this keeps the apples from exploding. Place the apples in glass pie plate. Spoon a heaping teaspoon of the sugar-cinnamon mixture into the center of each apple and top with a dab of butter. Pour water into pie plate. Bake 1 hour, basting after 30 minutes. Add water if necessary. You may add raisins to center of apple or a tablespoon of dark rum to the water for a slightly different flavor.

The Captain Ezra Nye House, Sandwich, Massachusetts

Peach Stratta

6 oz. peach baby food, no water added	¾ tsp. cinnamon
1½ c. fresh peaches, diced	4 eggs
1⅓ c. sugar	7 c. French bread, crusts removed
¼ tsp. nutmeg	and cubed

Preheat the oven to 350°F. Mix the first six ingredients together until well blended. Pour over the bread and stir gently. Pour the mixture into a 1-quart casserole dish that has been sprayed with vegetable cooking spray. Bake for 50 to 60 minutes.

Joyce's Blueberry Muffins

1¾ c. flour	1 egg, slightly beaten
⅓ c. sugar	18 oz. pkg. cream cheese, cut into
1 tbsp. baking powder	½-inch cubes
¾ c. milk	¾ c. fresh or frozen blueberries
⅓ c. oil	1 tbsp. lemon juice
1 tsp. grated lemon peel	3 tbsp. sugar

Preheat the oven to 400°F. Mix the flour, sugar, and baking powder in a large bowl and set aside. Add the milk, oil, and grated lemon peel to the egg. Add the egg mixture to the flour mixture, blending until just moistened. Fold in the cream cheese and blueberries. Spoon the batter into greased or lined muffin tins until two-thirds full. Bake for 20 minutes. Mix together the lemon juice and sugar and brush over the muffins. Makes 12 muffins.

Miller's of Montana B&B Inn, Bozeman, Montana

Eggs Benedict Caledonia

1 pkg. Hollandaise sauce mix
3 tbsp. lemon juice
2 English muffins
2 tbsp. butter or margarine

4 slices Canadian bacon or ham
4 eggs
Garnish of choice

Preheat the oven to 160°F. Prepare Hollandaise sauce according to package directions, replacing 3 tablespoons of water with lemon juice and set aside. Toast or broil muffin halves and spread with the butter. Top with slices of the Canadian bacon or ham and keep warm in the oven. Poach the eggs for 3½ minutes in cups sprayed with vegetable oil. When the whites are set but the yolks are still loose, invert the eggs onto muffins. Cover the eggs with the sauce. Garnish with fresh parsley, kiwi slice, strawberry half, or a favorite garnish of your choice. Makes 2 servings.

Caledonia Farm B&B, Flint Hill, Virginia

Banana Butter

4 large ripe bananas, peeled and sliced
3 tbsp. lemon juice

1 tsp. pumpkin pie spice
1½ c. sugar

Place the bananas and lemon juice in a blender and process until smooth. Transfer to a large saucepan and stir in the pumpkin pie spice and sugar. Bring the mixture to a boil, lower the heat and simmer for 15 minutes, stirring frequently. Pour into sterilized jars and store in tightly covered containers in the refrigerator. Makes 3 cups.

Bannick's Bed & Breakfast, Dimondale, Michigan

Mountain Top Bacon

½ c. flour
¼ c. brown sugar

1 tsp. black pepper
1 lb. bacon, sliced

Preheat the oven to 300°F. Mix the flour, brown sugar, and pepper in a plastic bag. Add bacon slices one at a time and shake to coat. Lay the slices out in a baking pan. Bake for 20 to 25 minutes, or until crisp. Serves 4.

Von-Bryan Inn, Sevierville, Tennessee

Health Cereal

5 c. old-fashioned oats
2 c. wheat germ
½ c. sesame seeds, ground
1 c. shredded coconut (optional)
1 c. almonds or other nuts, chopped
   finely

½ tsp. cinnamon
¼ tsp. ground cloves
½ tsp. salt
1 c. brown sugar, or to taste
1 c. corn oil, or to taste
1 c. raisins

Preheat the oven to 350°F. In a large bowl, mix together all the ingredients except the raisins. Pour the mixture into a shallow pan and bake 30 minutes, stirring occasionally. Remove from the oven and stir in the raisins. Serve warm or at room temperature.

Honeysuckle Hill B&B, Madison, Connecticut

Aunt Dolly's Almost in the Country Quiche

¾ c. all-purpose flour
½ c. whole wheat flour
Pinch of salt
6 tbsp. butter
4 to 5 tbsp. ice water
5 slices bacon
1 large onion, chopped
2 large potatoes, thinly sliced
2 eggs

⅔ c. heavy cream
1 tbsp. each chopped parsley and
   chives
½ tsp. salt
¼ tsp. black pepper
½ sweet red pepper, seeded and
   chopped
¾ c. grated cheddar cheese

Preheat the oven to 375°F. In a large bowl, combine the flours and the pinch of salt and cut in the butter until the mixture turns to fine crumbs. Add enough water to make a firm dough. Knead lightly. On a lightly floured surface, roll out the pastry to a 10-inch circle. Ease the pastry into a 9-inch quiche pan, pressing evenly around the side; trim the edge. Prick all over with a fork; refrigerate for 30 minutes, or until the dough is firm. Line with foil, fill with dried beans and bake until set, 12 to 15 minutes. Remove the foil and beans and return the pastry to the oven for another 5 minutes. In a large frying pan, cook the bacon until crisp; remove it with a slotted spoon, allow it to cool, and crumble it. Add the onion and potatoes to the bacon drippings and cook until browned. Drain and set aside. Beat the eggs and cream together. Stir in the parsley, chives, the ½ teaspoon salt, and the black pepper and set aside. Spoon the potatoes and onion into the pastry shell and sprinkle with the bacon and red pepper. Pour in the egg mixture and sprinkle with the cheese. Bake for 20 to 25 minutes. Serve hot or cold.

Aunt Dolly's Attic B&B, Austin, Texas

Garden Harvest Muffins

4 c. all-purpose flour
2½ c. sugar
4 tsp. baking soda
4 tsp. cinnamon
1 tsp. salt
2 c. grated carrots
2 c. grated zucchini
1 c. raisins

1 c. chopped pecans
1 c. coconut
2 tart apples, peeled and grated
6 large eggs
1 c. vegetable oil
1 c. buttermilk
2 tsp. vanilla

Preheat the oven to 375°F. In a large bowl, sift together the flour, sugar, baking soda, cinnamon, and salt. Stir in the carrots, zucchini, raisins, pecans, coconut, and apples. In another bowl, whisk together the remaining ingredients and add to the flour-vegetable mixture. Stir the batter until just blended. Spoon the batter into well-buttered muffin tins (or use paper liners). Bake on the middle rack for 25 to 30 minutes, or until the muffins are springy to the touch. Let the muffins cool in the tins for 5 minutes, then turn them out onto a rack. Makes about 30 muffins.

Leland House, Durango, Colorado

Sausage en Croute

1 sheet frozen Pepperidge Farm puff
    pastry
1 lb. pork sausage
½ c. chopped onion
½ c. chopped green pepper

6 large mushrooms, sliced
1 large tomato, diced
1 c. total shredded Swiss and
    Cheddar cheese
3 tbsp. chopped parsley

Preheat the oven to 425°F. Thaw the puff pastry about 20 minutes. Meanwhile, brown the sausage in a skillet, breaking it into bits. Add the onion, green pepper, and mushrooms and cook until tender. Remove from the heat and pour off the drippings. Add the tomato, cheese, and parsley. Unfold the pastry sheet and roll it out on a lightly floured board to a 13- × -10-inch rectangle. Transfer to a baking sheet lined with brown paper (a grocery bag works well). Spread the sausage mixture on pastry. Roll up from the long side, jelly-roll fashion, and pinch the edges to seal. Bake for 20 minutes, or until golden brown. Serves 6 to 8 guests.

Grand Avenue Inn, Carthage, Missouri

4

Wheelchair Accessible Listings

Although this chapter is small, within a few years *Bed & Breakfast U.S.A.* hopes to have listings from all fifty states and Canada. The requirements are fairly simple. To be listed in this section, all B&Bs must have easy-access entrances and exits. Doorways must be wide enough to admit a wheelchair—36 inches should be wide enough. Toilets and tubs must have reach bars. If the bathroom has a shower, reach bars and a built-in seat are preferable. Wheelchairs should be able to fit under the breakfast table, 26 inches is high enough. It's also a good idea to check to see what kind of activities are available. Many parks, restaurants, shopping areas, museums, beaches, etc. have wheelchair accessibility. If you or someone you know has a B&B that is wheelchair accessible, please turn to page 745 for further details.

Snug Harbor Inn ✪
1226 WEST 10TH AVENUE, ANCHORAGE, ALASKA 99501

Tel: **(907) 272-6249; fax: (907) 272-7100**
Hosts: **Kenneth and Laurine "Sis" Hill**
Location: **Downtown Anchorage**
No. of Rooms: **1**
No. of Private Baths: **1**
Double/pb: **$75**
Open: **All year**
Reduced Rates: **Families**
Breakfast: **Full**

Other Meals: **Available**
Credit Cards: **VISA**
Pets: **Sometimes**
Children: **Welcome**
Smoking: **Permitted**
Social Drinking: **Permitted**
Minimum Stay: **2 nights**
Airport/Station Pickup: **Yes**
Foreign Languages: **Spanish**

This homey cottage is minutes from the parks, shopping areas, museum, and performing arts center of downtown Anchorage. For visitors with disabilities, there is a ground-floor room with an accessible private bath with grab bars. You'll get energy for expeditions from

Ken's ample breakfasts: the menu ranges from eggs and pancakes to homemade muffins with juice and coffee or tea.

Kern River Inn Bed & Breakfast ✪
P.O. BOX 1725, 119 KERN RIVER DRIVE, KERNVILLE, CALIFORNIA 93238

Tel: (619) 376-6750	Open: **All year**
Best Time to Call: **8 AM–8 PM**	Reduced Rates: **Available**
Hosts: **Jack and Carita Prestwich**	Breakfast: **Full**
Location: **50 mi. NE of Bakersfield**	Credit Cards: **MC, VISA**
No. of Rooms: **1**	Pets: **No**
No. of Private Baths: **1**	Children: **Welcome**
Double/pb: **$79–$89**	Smoking: **No**
Single/pb: **$69–$79**	Social Drinking: **Permitted**

Stay in a charming riverfront B&B in a quaint western town within Sequoia National Forest. Marti and Mike specialize in romantic, relaxing getaways. Their accessible room has a queen bed and a Piute-style, wood-burning fireplace. (Your hosts provide the wood.) Native American pictures and macrame wall hangings accent the room's Southwestern color scheme of beige, mauve, and sage green. The bath has grab bars; the full-size, mirror-doored closet has shelving that can be reached from a wheelchair.

Ferncourt Bed and Breakfast
150 CENTRAL AVENUE, SAN MATEO, FLORIDA

Tel: (904) 329-9755	Open: **All year**
Best Time to Call: **Evenings**	Breakfast: **Full**
Host(s): **Jack and Dee Morgan**	Pets: **No**
Location: **25 mi. W of St. Augustine**	Children: **No**
No. of Rooms: **1**	Smoking: **No**
No. of Private Baths: **1**	Social Drinking: **Permitted**
Double p/b: **$45–$65**	Station Pickup: **Yes**

Ferncourt is a restored 1800s farm home, located in a tiny historic hamlet just a few minutes drive from St. Augustine and Daytona Beach. Guests have use of several rooms and the wraparound veranda. Close by, restaurants serve excellent food. Cookies and tea are offered in the evening. Jack does woodworking and upholstery and many examples of his craft are on display throughout the inn. Dee dabbles in painting and loves antiques and flea markets, but her real passion is food, evidenced by the gourmet breakfast she serves. Discover North Central Florida, then retire to all the charm and hospitality of the Victorian era with your hosts. There is a long concrete wheelchair ramp, and one room is set up for the disabled, with a private bath and handrails installed. For hearing impaired guests, a smoke alarm has been installed.

Amanda's B&B Reservation Service ○

1428 PARK AVENUE, BALTIMORE, MARYLAND 21217

Tel: (410) 225-0001; fax: 728-8957
Best Time to Call: 8:30 AM–5:30 PM
Mon.–Fri.
Coordinator: **Betsy Grater**
States/Regions Covered: **Annapolis,
Baltimore, Delaware, District of
Columbia, Maryland, New Jersey,**
Olney, Pennsylvania, Virginia, West
Virginia
Descriptive Directory of B&Bs: $3
Rates (Double):
Modest: **$60**
Luxury: **$75–$125**
Credit Cards: **AMEX, DISC, MC, VISA**

The roster of this reservation service includes nine sites designed for visitors with disabilities—five in downtown Baltimore, two in Annapolis, one in Falston, and one in Chesapeake.

Bed & Breakfast Associates—Bay Colony, Ltd. ○

P.O. BOX 57166, BABSON PARK, BOSTON, MASSACHUSETTS 02157-0166

Tel: (617) 449-5302; (800) 347-5088;
fax: (617) 449-5958
Best Time to Call: 9:30 AM–12:30 PM;
1:30–5 PM Mon.–Fri.
Coordinators: **Arline Kardasis and
Marilyn Mitchell**
States/Regions Covered:
Massachusetts—Boston (Beacon Hill
and Back Bay)
Descriptive Directory of B&Bs: **Free**
Rates (Single/Double)
Luxury: **$89–$95 $95–$99**
Credit Cards: **AMEX, CB, DC, MC,
VISA**

Arline and Marilyn offer three accommodations for disabled travelers. All have private baths. Some are convenient to major colleges and universities.

Golden Slumber Accommodations

640 REVERE BEACH BOULEVARD, REVERE, MASSACHUSETTS 02151

Tel: (617) 289-1053; (800) 892-3231
Best Time to Call: 8 AM–9 PM
Mon.–Sat.
Coordinator: **Leah A. Schmidt**
States/Regions Covered: **Bourne,
Essex, Falmouth, Harwich Port,
Lexington, Peabody, Plymouth,**
Seacoast Massachusetts, Wakefield,
Wareham
Descriptive Directory of B&Bs: $2
Rates (Single/Double):
Modest: **$45–$105**
Average: **$55–$115**
Credit Cards: **MC, VISA**

Approximately one third of this service's listings can properly accommodate wheelchair users and those who are visually impaired. Please phone in advance for additional information, including special arrangements for transportation to and from your host home.

The Over Look Inn
ROUTE 6, 3085 COUNTY ROAD, P.O. BOX 771, EASTHAM,
MASSACHUSETTS 02642

Tel: **(508) 255-1886, (800) 356-1121**	Breakfast: **Full**
Best Time to Call: **9 AM–9 PM**	Credit Cards: **AMEX, MC, VISA**
Hosts: **The Aitchison family**	Pets: **No**
Location: **90 mi. E of Boston**	Children: **Welcome, over 12**
No. of Rooms: **1**	Smoking: **Permitted**
No. of Private Baths: **1**	Social Drinking: **Permitted**
Double p/b: **$65–$125**	Airport/Station Pickup: **Yes**
Open: **All year**	Foreign Languages: **French**

This suite was constructed in accordance with wheelchair-accessibility
codes: the entry has a ramp and the bathroom has grab bars. The bed
is queen-size. Directly across from the inn is the Cape Cod National
Seashore, where the main beach has a parking lot and a ramp
designated for disabled visitors.

Blue Goose Inn ✪
ROUTE 103B, P.O. BOX 117, MT. SUNAPEE, NEW HAMPSHIRE 03772

Tel: **(603) 763-5519**	Breakfast: **Full**
Best Time to Call: **Before noon**	Credit Cards: **MC, VISA**
Hosts: **Meryl and Ronald Caldwell**	Pets: **No**
Location: **10 mi. from I-89**	Children: **Welcome**
No. of Rooms: **1**	Smoking: **Permitted**
No. of Private Baths: **1**	Social Drinking: **Permitted**
Double/pb: **$50**	Airport/Station Pickup: **Yes**
Open: **All year**	

This cozy nineteenth-century Colonial farmhouse is located on scenic
Lake Sunapee, at the base of Mt. Sunapee. Meryl and Ronald offer
one wheelchair accessible room adorned with handmade quilts and
attractive antiques. Breakfast specialties—such as a maple-flavored
biscuit stuffed with bacon, eggs, and cheese—are served on the
enclosed porch. Each evening, you're invited to join your hosts on
the porch, or by the fireplace in the living room, for wine, fruit,
and cheese.

Jemez River Bed & Breakfast Inn ✪
16445 HIGHWAY 4, JEMEZ SPRINGS NEW MEXICO 87025

Tel: **(505) 820-3262**	Double p/b: **$99–$109**
Best Time to Call: **Evenings**	Open: **All year**
Host(s): **Larry and Roxe Ann Clutter**	Reduced Rates: **10% seniors**
Location: **40 mi. NW of Albuquerque**	Breakfast: **Full**
No. of Rooms: **2**	Other Meals: **Available**
No. of Private Baths: **2**	Credit Cards: **AMEX, MC, VISA**

Pets: **Sometimes**   Smoking: **No**
Children: **Welcome**   Social Drinking: **Permitted**

A new, adobe-style home completed in 1994, Jemez River Bed & Breakfast Inn is nestled on 3½ acres in a valley below the Jemez Mountains Virgin Mesa. At night, the murmuring of the Jemez River— located in the B&B's backyard—will lull you to sleep. As you enjoy a hearty breakfast, you'll feast your eyes on breathtaking mountain views through the grand kitchen windows. Authentic Indian pottery, rugs, paintings, arrowheads and kachina dolls decorate the bedrooms, which have individual access to a spacious garden plaza; there, a spring-fed birdbath draws hummingbirds and other wildlife. Stone-lined trails follow the spring around cottonwood trees, large rocks and crevices to secluded riverside rest spots. Two rooms are completely accessible for wheelchair users.

McGillivray's Log Home and Bed and Breakfast ✪
88680 EVERS ROAD, ELMIRA, OREGON 97437

Tel: **(503) 935-3564**   Open: **All year**
Best Time to Call: **8 AM–8 PM**   Breakfast: **Full**
Host: **Evelyn McGillivray**   Credit Cards: **MC, VISA**
Location: **14 mi. W of Eugene**   Pets: **No**
No. of Rooms: **1**   Children: **Welcome**
No. of Private Baths: **1**   Smoking: **No**
Double/pb: **$60–$70**   Social Drinking: **Permitted**
Single/pb: **$50**   Airport/Station Pickup: **Yes**

Fir trees cover the five-acre property surrounding this massive home built with six types of wood and featuring both a split-log staircase and an entry ramp. One room, decorated in a classic Americana motif, has a king-size bed and doorways wide enough for wheelchairs. In the bathroom, there is a six-inch step in the shower stall, which has two grab bars and an adjustable height stool; another grab bar is placed near the toilet. Evelyn usually prepares buttermilk pancakes on an antique griddle her mother used. She also offers fresh-squeezed juice, farm-grown apples and grapes, fresh bread, eggs, and all the breakfast trimmings. This B&B is located only three miles from a vineyard, while country roads and a reservoir for fishing and boating are nearby.

Bed & Breakfast—The Manor ✪
830 VILLAGE ROAD, P.O. BOX 416, LAMPETER, PENNSYLVANIA 17537

Tel: **(717) 464-9564**   No. of Rooms: **2**
Best Time to Call: **9 AM–9 PM**   No. of Private Baths: **1**
Hosts: **Mary Lou Paolini and Jackie** Double/pb: **$75**
  Curtis   Double/sb: **$65**
Location: **3 mi. SE of Lancaster**   Open: **All year**

Reduced Rates: **Available**
Breakfast: **Full**
Other Meals: **Available**
Credit Cards: **MC, VISA**
Pets: **No**

Children: **Welcome**
Smoking: **No**
Social Drinking: **No**
Airport/Station Pickup: **Yes**

Set on 4½ acres of lush Amish farmland, this cozy farmhouse is just minutes away from Lancaster's historic sites and attractions. Guests delight in Mary Lou's delicious breakfasts, with specialties like eggs mornay, apple cobbler, and homemade breads and jams. This cozy inn features two ground-floor bedrooms decorated with country charm and antique beds. Both rooms are easily accessible to the parking area; no steps involved. Guests may join an Old Order Amish family for dinner. A conference room is available for groups. In summer a swim in the pool or a nap under one of the many shade trees is the perfect way to cap a day of touring.

The Cookie Jar B&B ✪

64 KINGSTOWN ROAD, ROUTE 138, WYOMING, RHODE ISLAND 02898

Tel: **(401) 539-2680; (800) 767-4262**
Best Time to Call: **After 5 PM**
Hosts: **Dick and Madelein Sohl**
Location: **7⁄10 mi. off I-95, exit 3A**
No. of Rooms: **2**
No. of Private Baths: **1**
Max. No. Sharing Bath: **4**
Double/pb: **$65**
Double/sb: **$60**

Single/sb: **$54**
Open: **All year**
Reduced Rates: **Available**
Breakfast: **Full**
Pets: **No**
Children: **Welcome**
Smoking: **No**
Social Drinking: **Permitted**

The heart of this house, the living room, was a blacksmith's shop built in 1732; the original ceiling, hand-hewn beams and granite walls are still in use. Fittingly, Dick and Madelein have furnished their home with a mixture of antique, country, and contemporary pieces. You'll enjoy looking around their property, which includes a barn, flower garden, and lots of fruit trees, berry bushes, and grapevines. Two rooms, each with a sink, are ideal for visitors with disabilities. The bathroom has a wall-mounted grab bar at the toilet and a large shower stall (3 by 4 feet) with a built-in fiberglass seat. Despite the rural setting, it's only a short drive to the University of Rhode Island and cities like Mystic and Providence.

Selby House Bed & Breakfast ✪

226 PRINCESS ANNE STREET, FREDERICKSBURG, VIRGINIA 22401

Tel: **(703) 373-7037**
Hosts: **Jerry and Virginia Selby**
Location: **54 mi. S of Washington, D.C.**

No of Rooms: **4**
No. of Private Baths: **4**
Double/pb: **$70**

Single/pb: **$60**
Open: **All year**
Reduced Rates: **Available**
Breakfast: **Full**
Credit Cards: **MC, VISA**

Pets: **No**
Children: **Welcome**
Smoking: **No**
Social Drinking: **Permitted**
Station Pickup: **Yes**

Selby House has two barrier-free, ground-level rooms. In 1986, Jerry designed and built this annex to fulfill his dream of extending hospitality to physically challenged guests. All doorways are 36 inches wide. The bedrooms have large baths with grab bars and other necessary adaptations. Both guest rooms connect to a large community area as well as the dining room, and their cement patios provide easy access to all inn facilities.

The Iris Inn ✪
191 CHINQUAPIN DRIVE, WAYNESBORO, VIRGINIA 22980

Tel: **(703) 943-1991**
Best Time to Call: **10 AM–8 PM**
Hosts: **Wayne and Iris Karl**
Location: **25 mi. W of Charlottesville**
No. of Rooms: **1**
No. of Private Baths: **1**
Double/pb: **$75–$80**
Single/pb: **$65**
Open: **All year**
Reduced Rates: **Corporate,
Sun.–Thurs.**

Breakfast: **Full**
Credit Cards: **MC, VISA**
Pets: **No**
Children: **Welcome, by arrangement**
Smoking: **No**
Social Drinking: **Permitted**
Minimum Stay: **2 nights weekends**
Airport Pickup: **Yes**

Southern charm and grace in a totally modern facility overlooking the historic Shenandoah Valley from the Blue Ridge Mountains' wooded western slope—that's what awaits you at the Iris Inn. It's ideal for a weekend retreat, a refreshing change for the business traveler, and a tranquil spot for tourists to spend a night or more. The wheelchair-accessible room is comfortably furnished and delightfully decorated with nature and wildlife motifs. The bathroom has a lavatory without a vanity, for easier use. There are grab bars at the toilet and on the sides of the shower, which also has a seat. A pocket door connects the bathroom and bedroom. For your convenience, a ramp leads from the parking lot level to the porch.

A Burrow's Bay B&B
4911 MACBETH DRIVE, ANACORTES, WASHINGTON 98221

Tel: **(206) 293-4792**
Best Time to Call: **8 AM–10 PM**
Hosts: **Beverly and Winfred Stocker**
Location: **92 mi. N of Seattle**
Suite: **$95**
Open: **All year**
Breakfast: **Continental, plus**

Credit Cards: **MC, VISA**
Pets: **Sometimes**
Children: **Welcome**
Smoking: **No**
Social Drinking: **Permitted**
Airport/Station Pickup: **Yes**

Enjoy sweeping views of the San Juan Islands from this lovely contemporary Northwest home. The guest suite consists of a large sitting room with a view and a comfortable bedroom. There are no stairs and all doors are of standard widths. In the bathroom, a towel bar doubles as a grab bar as you enter the tub-shower; a second grab bar is at the front of the tub, in the middle wall area. You will enjoy the privacy and relaxation that comes from having your own deck, fireplace, TV, and entrance. In the morning, select your breakfast from Beverly and Winfred's extensive buffet. Ask your hosts for directions to Washington Park, restaurants, and ferries to nearby islands. They can also help you plan day trips to Victoria, British Columbia, Deception Pass, and Port Townsend.

5

State-by-State Listings

ALABAMA

Ashville •

Birmingham •   • Talladega

Montgomery •

Roses and Lace Country Inn ✪
P.O. BOX 852, FIFTH STREET AT NINTH AVENUE SOUTH, ASHVILLE, ALABAMA 35953

Tel: **(205) 594-4366, 594-4660**
Hosts: **Mark and Shirley Sparks**
Location: **40 mi. NE of Birmingham**
No. of Rooms: **4**
No. of Private Baths: **2**
Max. No. Sharing Bath: **4**
Double/pb: **$65**
Single/pb: **$55**
Double/sb: **$55**
Single/sb: **$45**

Suites: **$75**
Open: **All year**
Reduced Rates: **10% after 4 nights**
Breakfast: **Full**
Credit Cards: **MC, VISA**
Pets: **Sometimes**
Children: **Welcome**
Smoking: **No**
Social Drinking: **Permitted**

A friendly greeting awaits you at this handsome two-story Victorian with a wraparound porch and stained-glass windows. As you cross the threshold, your hosts Mark and Shirley will invite you to relax with a beverage and snack. Their home, lovingly restored over a two-year period by the entire family, contains fine woodwork and many antiques. Ask about other landmark buildings in the area; St. Clair County is an old, historic part of Alabama. For modern pleasures, visit Birmingham's thoroughbred racetrack, or take a day trip to the Huntsville Space and Rocket Center.

Lattice Inn B&B ✪

1414 SOUTH HULL STREET, MONTGOMERY, ALABAMA 36104

Tel: (205) 832-9931	Guest Cottage: $70 per day, $200
Best Time to Call: **Before 10 AM, after**	weekly, $750 monthly, sleeps up to 4
4 PM	Open: **All year**
Host: **Michael Pierce**	Reduced Rates: **10% seniors**
Location: ¾ mi. S of Montgomery	Breakfast: **Full**
No. of Rooms: 4	Pets: **Sometimes**
No. of Private Baths: 4	Children: **No**
Double/pb: $55–$65	Smoking: **No**
Single/pb: $50	Social Drinking: **Permitted**

Located in Montgomery's historic garden district, this turn-of-the-century home (built in 1906) has been restored to create a comfortable retreat for today's traveler. The shady front porch has just enough lattice to provide privacy as you read the morning paper or lounge on the swing. Tall windows accentuate the eleven-foot ceilings and fireplaces of the library, living room, and dining room. The spacious guest rooms have their own fireplaces and distinctive furniture, including a high-postered bed Michael produced for his own use. And thanks to the pool and multilevel decks in the backyard, warm weather visitors can unwind with a dip and a nap in the sun.

Red Bluff Cottage ✪

551 CLAY STREET, MONTGOMERY, ALABAMA
(MAILING ADDRESS: P.O. BOX 1026, MONTGOMERY, ALABAMA 36101)

Tel: (205) 264-0056	Open: **All year**
Best Time to Call: **9 AM–10 PM**	Breakfast: **Full**
Hosts: **Anne and Mark Waldo**	Pets: **No**
No. of Rooms: 4	Children: **Welcome (crib)**
No. of Private Baths: 4	Smoking: **No**
Double/pb: $65	Social Drinking: **Permitted**
Single/pb: $55	Airport/Station Pickup: **Yes**
Suite: $85	

This raised cottage is high above the Alabama River in Montgomery's historic Cottage Hill District, close to the State Capitol, Dexter Avenue King Memorial Baptist Church, the First White House of the Confederacy, the Civil Rights Memorial, and Old Alabama Town. The Alabama Shakespeare Festival Theatre, the Museum of Fine Arts, and the expanded zoo are also nearby. The bedrooms are downstairs. Guests come upstairs to read or relax in the living rooms, to enjoy the front porch view, and to have breakfast in the dining room. Many interesting antiques and a music room, complete with harpsichord, add to the charm of this home.

Historic Oakwood Bed & Breakfast ✪
715 EAST NORTH STREET, TALLADEGA, ALABAMA 35160

Tel: **(205) 362-0662**
Hosts: **Al and Naomi Kline**
Location: **45 mi, E of Birmingham**
No. of Rooms: **3**
No. of Private Baths: **1**
Max. No. Sharing Bath: **4**
Double/pb: **$65**
Single/pb: **$55**
Double/sb: **$55**
Single/sb: **$50**

Suites: **$95**
Open: **All year**
Breakfast: **Full**
Pets: **No**
Children: **Welcome, over 10, infants**
Smoking: **No**
Social Drinking: **Permitted**
Airport/Station Pickup: **Yes, $5–$10 fee**

This antebellum home, built in 1847, is listed on the National Register of Historic Places, and furnished with many heirloom antiques. The house was commissioned by Alexander Bowie, the first mayor of Talladega. Enjoy browsing through the antique stores in the area, visiting the International Motorsports Hall of Fame, or exploring DeSoto Caverns. The public golf course and tennis courts and beautiful Cheaha Mt. State Park are nearby. The hearty breakfast your hosts serve features homemade biscuits and Southern grits. Traveling business person or vacationer, enjoy a retreat into the quiet elegance of a bygone area.

The House of Dunn's ✪
204 SOUTH BRUNDIDGE STREET, TROY, ALABAMA 36081

Tel: **(205) 566-9414**
Best Time to Call: **7:30 AM–5 PM**
Hosts: **Gardner and Ramona Dunn**
Location: **40 mi. S of Montgomery**
No. of Rooms: **4**
No. of Private Baths: **4**
Double/pb: **$50**
Open: **All year**

Reduced Rates: **10% seniors**
Breakfast: **Full**
Credit Cards: **DISC, MC, VISA**
Pets: **No**
Children: **Welcome**
Smoking: **No**
Social Drinking: **Permitted**
Airport/Station Pickup: **Yes**

The House of Dunn's is a great place for that uninterrupted excursion away from the big city. The bed and breakfast is located in Troy, where time seems to tick away more slowly than in larger cities. The house itself, built in the 1800s, is full of beautiful woodwork, gorgeous wallpaper, and the original pine floors. A large front porch contains rocking chairs and a swing for a relaxing afternoon, complete with cake and lemonade. After a night of comfort in the elegant rooms, you are sure to enjoy the homestyle country breakfast that awaits you.

ALASKA

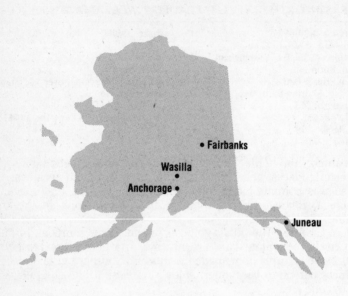

Alaska Bed & Breakfast Association
369 SOUTH FRANKLIN, SUITE 200, JUNEAU, ALASKA 99801

Tel: (907) 586-2959; fax: (907) 463-4453
Best Time to Call: 10 AM–5 PM, weekdays
Coordinators: Betty Lou and Karla Hart
States/Regions Covered: Alaska

Descriptive Directory: $3
Rates (Single/Double):
  Modest: $65–$70
  Average: $60–$70 / $70–$85
  Luxury: $85+ / $95+
Credit Cards: AMEX, MC, VISA

Visit cities, towns, and villages throughout the state: you can choose among historic buildings, modern homes, log cabins, and a few "Alaskana rural" sites. Your hosts include artists, teachers, retirees, homemakers, and government employees. Some B&Bs have amenities like saunas and barbecues, others offer splendid hiking and wildlife viewing. To make it easier to plan your trip, Betty Lou and Karla can arrange railroad, air taxi, ferry, and tour bookings.

Alaska Private Lodgings
P.O. BOX 200047, ANCHORAGE, ALASKA 99520–0047

Tel: (907) 258-1717; fax: (907) 258-6613
Best Time to Call: **9 AM–6 PM**
Coordinator: **Mercy Dennis**
States/Regions Covered: **Anchorage, Denali, Fairbanks, Girdwood, Homer, Hope, Kenai, Palmer, Seward, Talkeetna, Wasilla, Willow**

Descriptive Directory of B&Bs: **$3**
Rates (Single/Double):
  Modest: **$45 / $50**
  Average: **$50 / $75**
  Luxury: **$75 / $125**
Credit Cards: **AMEX, MC, VISA**

Alaskan hosts are this state's warmest resource! Mercy's accommodations range from an original log house of a pioneer's homestead, where the host is in the antique-doll business, to a one-bedroom apartment with a view of Mt. Denali. Many are convenient to the University of Alaska and Alaska Pacific University. There's a $5 surcharge for one-night stays.

The Green Bough ◐
3832 YOUNG STREET, ANCHORAGE, ALASKA 99508

Tel: (907) 562-4636
Best Time to Call: **7 AM–10 AM; 4 PM–8 PM**
Hosts: **Jerry and Phyllis Jost**
Location: **20 min. from airport**
No. of Rooms: **5**
Max. No. Sharing Bath: **4**
Double/pb: **$65–$75**
Single/pb: **$65–$75**
Double/sb: **$50**

Single/sb: **$40–$50**
Suite: **$70**
Open: **All year**
Reduced Rates: **Families**
Breakfast: **Continental, plus**
Pets: **No**
Children: **Welcome**
Smoking: **No**
Social Drinking: **No**

Even on the coldest days, you'll forget about the outside temperature in this comfortable home filled with family furnishings, needlework, and local artifacts. Breakfast features a choice of homemade breads, muffins, and scones served with seasonal fruit and plenty of hot coffee. The Green Bough is located in a quiet residential area close to colleges, shopping, bike trails, and buses. A large yard and deck are available for reading and relaxing. Your hosts have 27 years of experience in this part of the country, and they will gladly help you discover its charms. Special arrangements can be made for storing fishing and camping gear.

Snug Harbor Inn ✪
1226 WEST 10TH AVENUE, ANCHORAGE, ALASKA 99501

Tel: **(907) 272-6249; fax: (907) 272-7100**
Hosts: **Kenneth and Laurine "Sis" Hill**
Location: **Downtown Anchorage**
No. of Rooms: **5**
No. of Private Baths: **5**
Double/pb: **$75**
Single/pb: **$75**
Open: **All year**
Reduced Rates: **Families**

Breakfast: **Full**
Other Meals: **Available**
Credit Cards: **VISA**
Pets: **Sometimes**
Children: **Yes**
Smoking: **Permitted**
Social Drinking: **Permitted**
Minimum Stay: **2 nights**
Airport/Station Pickup: **Yes**
Foreign Languages: **Spanish**

This homey cottage is minutes from bus routes serving downtown Anchorage, with its parks, sports facilities, shopping areas, museum, and performing arts center. Entrance to the Coastal Bike Path—which leads to Earthquake Park—is only three blocks away; your hosts will supply bicycles. You'll get energy for expeditions from Ken's ample breakfasts; the menu ranges from eggs and pancakes to homemade muffins, with juice and coffee or tea.

Alaska's 7 Gables Bed & Breakfast ✪
P.O. BOX 80488, FAIRBANKS, ALASKA 99708

Tel: **(907) 479-0751; fax: (907) 479-2229**
Best Time to Call: **7 AM–10 PM**
Hosts: **Paul and Leicha Welton**
Location: **2 mi. W of Fairbanks**
No. of Rooms: **9**
No. of Private Baths: **7**
Max. No. Sharing Bath: **3**
Double/pb: **$50–$85**
Single/pb: **$50–$75**
Double/sb: **$45–$75**
Single/sb: **$40–$70**
Suites: **$75–$95**

Open: **All year**
Reduced Rates: **30%, Oct.–Apr.**
Breakfast: **Full**
Other Meals: **Available**
Credit Cards: **AMEX, DC, DISC, MC, VISA**
Pets: **Sometimes**
Children: **Welcome**
Smoking: **No**
Social Drinking: **Permitted**
Minimum Stay: **2 nights**
Airport/Station Pickup: **Yes**
Foreign Languages: **Spanish**

The Weltons' large Tudor-style home is central to many city attractions—Riverboat Discovery, Cripple Creek Resort, University Museum, Alaskaland, Gold Dredge #8—and within walking distance of the University of Alaska's Fairbanks campus. Paul designed and built the house, a worthy destination in its own right. You'll enter through a floral solarium, which leads to a foyer with antique stained glass and indoor waterfall. Party planners take note: 7 Gables has a wine cellar and a wedding chapel. Guests can use the laundry facilities, library, Jacuzzi, canoe, and bikes. All rooms have telephones and cable TV; one room is accessible to wheelchair users. Ample breakfasts feature dishes like salmon quiche, crab casserole, and peachy pecan crepes.

The Blue Goose Bed & Breakfast ✪
4466 DARTMOUTH, FAIRBANKS, ALASKA 99709

Tel: (907) 479-6973; within Alaska only (800) 478-6973, Fax: (907) 457-6973	Open: All year
	Reduced Rates: $10 less Oct. 15–Apr. 15
Hosts: Susan and Ken Risse	Breakfast: Full
Location: 5 mi. W of Fairbanks	Credit Cards: MC, VISA, DC, DISC
No. of Rooms: 3	Pets: No
No. of Private Baths: 1	Children: Welcome
Max. No. Sharing Bath: 4	Smoking: No
Double/pb: $75	Social Drinking: Permitted
Double/sb: $55–$65	
Single/sb: $50	

Susan and Ken's trilevel frame house is a modern home with historic accents, thanks to the antique furniture and other old-time treasures. It's convenient, too: city buses stop one block away and the ride to the airport takes all of ten minutes. For diversion, you may want to visit the Riverboat Discovery and the historic Pump House Restaurant. Breakfast is special at the Blue Goose, with blue-ribbon Alaska rhubarb pie baked each morning and served warm. Your hosts may also dish out homemade bread, muffins with Alaska blueberries, or freshly picked low-bush cranberries. The Risses met while working on the pipeline. Ken, a civil engineer, dabbles in woodworking, while Susan is a full-time hostess and mother interested in needlework.

Minnie Street B&B ✪
345 MINNIE STREET, FAIRBANKS, ALASKA 99701

Tel: (907) 456-1802	Open: All year
Host: Marnie and Lambert Hazelaar	Reduced Rates: Winter
Location: In Fairbanks	Breakfast: Full
No. of Rooms: 3	Credit Cards: MC, VISA
No. of Private Baths: 1	Pets: No
Max. No. Sharing Bath: 4	Children: Welcome
Double/pb: $85	Smoking: No
Double/sb: $75	Social Drinking: Permitted
Single/sb: $65	Airport/Station Pickup: Yes
Suites: $100	

This bed and breakfast is located within walking distance of the train depot and only five minutes from downtown, where you will find the post office, banks, gift shops, and restaurants. En route you will cross the beautiful Chena River. The cozy, comfortably decorated guest rooms have queen-size beds. Ample parking is provided with plenty of room for RVs; rental cars are available next door. To save money, grill your dinner on Marnie's barbecue. Her sumptuous breakfasts include homemade breads, omelets, and fruit salad.

Blueberry Lodge B&B ✪
9436 NORTH DOUGLAS HIGHWAY, JUNEAU, ALASKA 99801

Tel: (907) 463-5886	Open: All year
Hosts: Jay and Judy Urquhart	Reduced Rates: Weekly, 10% seniors
Location: 7 mi. N of Juneau	Breakfast: Full
No. of Rooms: 5	Pets: Sometimes
Max. No. Sharing Bath: 4	Children: Welcome
Double/sb: $75	Smoking: No
Single/sb: $70	Social Drinking: Permitted

Relax in a spacious handcrafted log lodge overlooking an inland ocean waterway, a wildlife refuge, and an active eagle nest. The lodge's five bedrooms, three-story living room and library, and overstuffed couches and chairs make it ideal for families to explore the great outdoors. Walk onto tidal estuaries, hike the surrounding beaches and alpine trails, fish for world-class salmon and halibut. Cross-country and downhill skiers can head to Eaglecrest, all of five minutes away. Or just savor a hearty breakfast and catch up on your laundry. Jay, a hard-rock miner, can tell you about working on Admiralty Island, which has more bears than any other place on earth.

ARIZONA

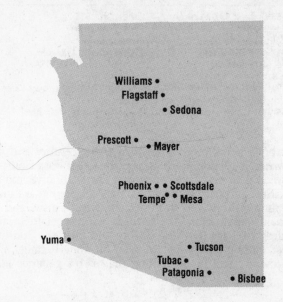

Mi Casa–Su Casa Bed & Breakfast ✪
P.O. BOX 950, TEMPE, ARIZONA 85280-0950

Tel: (602) 990-0682; (800) 456-0682;
  fax: (602) 990-3390
Best Time to Call: 8 AM–8 PM
Coordinator: **Ruth T. Young**
States/Regions Covered:
  Arizona—Ajo, Bisbee, Cave Creek,
Flagstaff, Fountain Hills, Mesa, Page,
Phoenix, Prescott, Scottsdale,
Sedona, Tempe, Tucson, Wickenburg,
Yuma; **Nevada**—Las Vegas; **New
Mexico; Utah**
Rates (Single/Double):
  Modest: **$30–$40**
  Average: **$40–$60**
  Luxury: **$75–$150**
Descriptive Directory: **$9.50**

Ruth's guest houses are located statewide; the cities listed above are
only a partial listing. They are located in cities, suburbs, and rural
settings, all of which are within easy driving range of canyons,
national parks, Indian country, Colorado River gem country, the
Mexican border area, historic mining towns, and water recreation
areas. Send $9.50 for her detailed directory. Arizona State University

and the University of Arizona are convenient to many B&Bs. There is a $5 surcharge for one-night stays.

The Judge Ross House ✪
605 SHATTUCK STREET, BISBEE, ARIZONA 85603

Tel: (602) 432-5597 days; 432-4120 evenings and weekends	Single/sb: $55
	Open: All year
Best Time to Call: Evenings	Breakfast: Full
Hosts: Jim and Bonnie Douglass	Other Meals: Available
Location: 25 mi. SE of Tombstone	Credit Cards: MC, VISA
No. of Rooms: 3	Pets: No
No. of Private Baths: 1	Children: Welcome, over 12
Max. No. Sharing Bath: 4	Smoking: No
Double/pb: $65	Social Drinking: Permitted
Double/sb: $60	Airport/Station Pickup: Yes

A two-story, brick home built at the turn of the century and named for its first owner, a superior court judge, the Judge Ross House has a charmingly old-fashioned look enhanced by decorative moldings, lavish wood trim, and period furniture. Jim and Bonnie are gracious hosts, welcoming visitors with fresh flowers, wine, candy, and magazines. Breakfast varies from day to day, with specialties such as Belgian waffles and eggs Benedict. Bisbee was once the Southwest's largest copper mining area, and the open pit mine remains a major attraction. Browsers will enjoy visiting the town's galleries and antique stores.

Dierker House
423 WEST CHERRY, FLAGSTAFF, ARIZONA 86001

Tel: (602) 774-3249	Breakfast: Full
Host: Dorothea Dierker	Pets: Sometimes
No. of Rooms: 3	Children: Welcome, over 12
Max. No. Sharing Bath: 4	Smoking: No
Double/sb: $45	Social Drinking: Permitted
Open: All year	

This lovely old home in Flagstaff's historic section is located high in the mountains, at an elevation of 7,000 feet. Flagstaff is the hub of wonderful day trips to the Grand Canyon, Native American ruins and reservations, Lake Powell, Monument Valley, and many more sites. The second floor accommodations are extremely comfortable and include many amenities. In the morning, Dorothea serves an excellent and sociable breakfast in the dining room.

Serenity House ✪
P.O. BOX 1254, THIRD STREET AND MAIN, MAYER, ARIZONA 86333

Tel: **(602) 632-4430**
Host: **Sue Ward**
Location: **25 mi. E of Prescott**
No. of Rooms: **2**
Max. No. Sharing Bath: **4**
Double/sb: **$50**
Open: **All year**

Reduced Rates: **$10 less, Oct.–Apr.**
Breakfast: **Continental**
Pets: **No**
Children: **Welcome, over 12**
Smoking: **No**
Social Drinking: **Permitted**
Airport/Station Pickup: **Yes**

This comfortable, country Victorian home is located in an old mining town north of Phoenix and east of Prescott. Built around 1905 by one of the Mayer brothers, who gave this town its name, the home has twelve-foot gabled ceilings, two fireplaces, hardwood floors, original copper and brass door and light fixtures, stained glass, a front porch swing, many large trees, and a pool and hot tub. One guest room has a private entrance to the pool area. There are many antique shops and historical buildings both in Mayer and Prescott. Popular pastimes include gold panning, hiking, rock hounding, and horse racing at Prescott Downs. Special sugar-free diets can easily be accommodated. Locally grown vegetables and fruits are a summer treat.

Casa Del Sol ✪
6951 E. HOBART, MESA, ARIZONA 85207

Tel: **(602) 985-5956**
Hosts: **Ray and Barb Leo**
Location: **20 mi. E of Phoenix**
No. of Rooms: **2**
Max. No. Sharing Bath: **4**
Double/sb: **$50–$55**
Single/sb: **$45**

Open: **All year**
Reduced Rates: **Available**
Breakfast: **Full**
Pets: **Sometimes**
Children: **Welcome**
Smoking: **No**
Social Drinking: **Permitted**

This luxurious Southwestern home sits on an acre of property with desert landscaping, fruit trees, and a solar-heated swimming pool. The guest rooms emphasize comfort with queen-size beds and Southwest decor. The word for breakfast is fresh, from ground coffee and squeezed juice to home-baked breads, muffins and croissants, special omelets, and waffles. Guests are welcome to enjoy the pool, Jacuzzi, fireplace, and VCR. Nearby attractions include beautiful state parks, the Salt River recreation area, Cactus League spring training, great shopping, golf, and restaurants.

The Little House
P.O. BOX 461, 341 SONOITA AVENUE, PATAGONIA, ARIZONA 85624

Tel: **(602) 394-2493**
Hosts: **Don and Doris Wenig**
Location: **60 mi. S of Tucson**
No. of Rooms: **2**
No. of Private Baths: **2**
Double/pb: **$60**
Single/pb: **$50**

Open: **All year**
Breakfast: **Full**
Pets: **No**
Children: **Sometimes**
Smoking: **No**
Social Drinking: **Permitted**

The Wenigs' home is located close to the Mexican border in a small mountain town at an elevation of 4,000 feet. Comfort and privacy are assured in the adobe guest house separated from the main house by a charming courtyard. One of the bedrooms has a queen-size bed; the other has twin beds and is wheelchair accessible. Each bedroom has a fireplace, sitting area, and adjacent patio. Coffee or tea is brought to your room to start the day. Afterward, join Don and Doris for a breakfast of sausage and waffles, eggs from local hens, and home-baked breads. Birdwatching, a visit to a ghost town or silver mine, and shopping in Nogales, Mexico, are pleasant pastimes available.

Arizona Accommodations Reservations
Bed and Breakfast Inn Arizona
GALLERY 3 PLAZA, 3819 NORTH 3RD STREET, PHOENIX, ARIZONA 85012

Tel: **(602) 265-9511;** Reservations
only: **(800) 266-STAY;** Fax: **(602) 263-7762**
Best Time to Call: **10 AM–3 PM**
Coordinator: **Darrell Trapp**
States/Regions Covered: **Ajo, Bisbee, Clifton, Flagstaff, Globe, Lake Havasu City, Lakeside, Oracle, Page, Phoenix, Prescott, Scottsdale, Sedona, Tombstone, Tucson**

Descriptive Directory of B&Bs: **$3**
Rates (Single/Double):
Modest: **$35–$50**
Average: **$51–$75**
Luxury: **$76–$499**
Credit Cards: **AMEX, MC, VISA**
Minimum Stay: **Holidays; 2 nights**

Claiming more mountains than Switzerland and more forests than Minnesota, Arizona boasts spectacular scenery. It is the home of the Grand Canyon, Lake Powell, London Bridge, famous museums, and sporting opportunities. Darrell's choices range from a modestly priced town house with a swimming pool to a historic ranch with a spa, gardens, and a pool that served as the locale for a western film. In business for ten years, this service takes pride in its growing roster of friendly hosts. Seven days' notice is required to cancel reservations.

Maricopa Manor ✪

P.O. BOX 7186, 15 WEST PASADENA AVENUE, PHOENIX,
ARIZONA 85011

Tel: **(602) 274-6302**
Hosts: **Mary Ellen and Paul Kelley**
Location: **5 mi. N of downtown
  Phoenix**
No. of Rooms: **5 suites**
No. of Private Baths: **5**
Suites: **$79–$129**

Open: **All year**
Breakfast: **Continental, plus**
Credit Cards: **No**
Pets: **No**
Children: **Welcome**
Smoking: **No**
Social Drinking: **Permitted**

Inside this Spanish-style manor house built in 1928, you'll find beautiful art, antiques, and warm Southwestern hospitality. The five private suites, spacious public rooms, decks, and gazebo spa create an intimate, Old World atmosphere in an elegant urban setting. Maricopa Manor is in the heart of the Valley of the Sun, convenient to shops, restaurants, museums, churches, and civic and government centers. Advance reservations are required.

Betsy's Bed and Breakfast ✪

1919 ROCK CASTLE DRIVE, PRESCOTT, ARIZONA 86301

Tel: **(602) 445-0123**
Best Time to Call: **Before 9 PM**
Host: **Elizabeth "Betsy" Rominger**
Location: **100 mi. NW of Phoenix**
No. of Rooms: **2**
No. of Private Baths: **2**
Double/pb: **$48–$70**
Single/pb: **$30–$45**

Open: **All year**
Reduced Rates: **15%, over 5 days**
Breakfast: **Full**
Pets: **Sometimes**
Children: **Welcome, over 8**
Smoking: **No**
Social Drinking: **Permitted**

Perched on a rocky hillside, this contemporary redwood house affords visitors a breathtaking view of Prescott, a vibrant town with five museums, three colleges, and myriad antique shops. Betsy, a retired antiques appraiser, will be glad to discuss her own collection; you'll find many distinctive pieces in the guest bedrooms and bathrooms. Breakfast, served at guests' convenience, may include homemade zucchini cakes, cinnamon rolls, and Betsy's own tortilla quiche.

Bed & Breakfast Southwest Reservation Service ✪

6916 EAST MARIPOSA, SCOTTSDALE, ARIZONA 85251

Tel: **(602) 947-9704**
Best Time to Call: **10 AM–5 PM**
Coordinators: **Jo and Jim Cummings**
States/Regions Covered: **Arizona,
  New Mexico, Southern California**

Descriptive Directory of B&Bs: **Free**
Rates (Single/Double):
  Modest: **$40–$60**
  Average: **$50–$65**
  Luxury: **$65–up**

Specializing in unique homestays with private suites and guest houses, this company offers an exciting experience to the traveler coming to the southwest. Hosts, as residents of the area, can give you firsthand information about sports activities, dining opportunities, art exhibits, and answer your questions about the great southwest. The Cummings will be happy to help you plan your vacation with great hosts throughout the southwest. They are currently seeking both unique hosts and enthusiastic guests.

Casa de Mariposa ✪
6916 EAST MARIPOSA, SCOTTSDALE, ARIZONA 85251

Tel: **(602) 947-9704**	Open: **October–April**
Best Time to Call: **10 AM–5 PM**	Breakfast: **Continental**
Hosts: **Jo and Jim Cummings**	Pets: **No**
Location: **15 mi. N of I-10**	Children: **Welcome**
No. of Rooms: **1**	Smoking: **No**
No. of Private Baths: **1**	Social Drinking: **Permitted**
Double p/b: **$80**	Airport/Station Pickup: **Yes**

This very special guest suite has a deluxe king canopy bed, Southwest decor, private entrance, French doors to the patio, kitchenette, and private bath. Located in the original Sunkist orchards, Casa de Mariposa offers golden grapefruit fresh from the tree. This quiet residential neighborhood is in the heart of beautiful Scottsdale, in walking distance of numerous shops, restaurants, theaters, and golf courses. Guests are welcome to soak in the spa, use the hosts' golf clubs or their box seats at the Giants' spring training games.

Valley o' the Sun Bed & Breakfast ✪
P.O. BOX 2214, SCOTTSDALE, ARIZONA 85252

Tel: **(602)941-1281**	Open: **All year**
Best Time to Call: **After 5:30 PM**	Reduced Rates: **Weekly; monthly; seniors**
Host: **Kay Curtis**	
Location: **Tempe**	Breakfast: **Continental, Full**
No. of Rooms: **3**	Pets: **No**
No. of Private Baths: **1**	Children: **Welcome, over 12**
Max. No. Sharing Bath: **4**	Smoking: **Permitted**
Double/pb: **$40**	Social Drinking: **Permitted**
Double/sb: **$35**	Minimum Stay: **2 nights**
Single/sb: **$25**	Airport/Station Pickup: **Yes**

The house is ideally located in the college area of Tempe, but is close enough to Scottsdale to enjoy its fine shops and restaurants. From the patio, you can enjoy a beautiful view of the Papago Buttes and McDowell Mountains. Local attractions include swimming at Big Surf, the Phoenix Zoo, and the Scottsdale Center for the Arts.

Cathedral Rock Lodge ✪
61 LOS AMIGOS LANE, SEDONA, ARIZONA 86336

Tel: (602) 282-7608	Reduced Rates: Available
Host: Carol Shannon and family	Breakfast: Full
Location: 2.7 mi. from Rte. 89A	Credit Cards: DISC, MC, VISA
No. of Rooms: 3	Pets: No
No. of Private Baths: 3	Children: Welcome (crib)
Double/pb: $70–$75	Smoking: No
Suite: $100	Social Drinking: Permitted
Open: All year	

Set in rock terrace gardens surrounded by tall shade trees, this rambling country home boasts spectacular views of the surrounding mountains. The suite has its own deck, built against a giant pine tree. Guest bedrooms feature family treasures and handmade quilts. Each day starts with Carol's hot breads and homemade jams; fresh fruits from local orchards are summertime treats. Lovers of the great outdoors will delight in the natural scenic beauty of the area, and browsers will enjoy the many galleries and shops. In the evening, curl up in front of the fireplace, borrow a book, or select a videotape from your host's collection.

Kennedy House ✪
HC 30, BOX 785K, 2075 UPPER RED ROCK LOOP ROAD, SEDONA, ARIZONA 86336

Tel: (602) 282-1624	Breakfast: Full
Best Time to Call: 10 AM–10 PM	Credit Cards: MC, VISA
Hosts: Tonya and Chuck Kennedy	Pets: No
Location: 116 mi. N of Phoenix	Children: Welcome
No. of Rooms: 2	Smoking: No
No. of Private Baths: 2	Social Drinking: Permitted
Double/pb: $80	Minimum Stay: 2 nights weekends,
Suites: $90	except Dec. and Feb.
Open: Feb.–Dec.; Closed	Airport/Station Pickup: Yes
Thanksgiving and Christmas	
Reduced Rates: $10 less per night, after 3rd day	

This attractively furnished contemporary home lies within walking distance of Red Rock Crossing, the most photographed spot in Arizona. Chuck, a retired wildlife biologist, offers guests a guided nature hike and will cheerfully assist in planning picnics or giving directions to the area's many famous monuments. After a full day of sightseeing, relax with a beverage on the large deck, which overlooks the breathtaking Cathedral Rock.

Moestly Wood Bed & Breakfast ✪
2085 UPPER RED ROCK LOOP ROAD, SEDONA, ARIZONA 86336

Tel: **(602) 204-1461**	Breakfast: **Full**
Best Time to Call: **8 AM–8 PM**	Other Meals: **Available**
Hosts: **Roger and Carolyn Moe**	Credit Cards: **MC, VISA**
Location: **110 mi. N of Phoenix**	Pets: **No**
No. of rooms: **1**	Children: **Welcome**
No. of private baths: **1**	Smoking: **No**
Suite: **$85**	Social Drinking: **Permitted**
Open: **All year**	Minimum Stay: **2 nights on weekends**

This contemporary home is located in the beautiful Arizona red rock country. Just 4 miles out of town you can enjoy spectacular views of Cathedral Rock and the surrounding area, or take a short hike to Red Rock Crossing, one of the state's most photographed sites. Roger and Carolyn enjoy visitors and are happy to help with touring plans, hiking, golfing, or just browsing through Sedona's many shops and galleries. Their large redwood deck is very inviting. Relaxing by the fire is also a comfy, cozy way to spend the evening.

Tubac Country Inn
409 BURRUEL STREET, P.O. BOX 1540, TUBAC, ARIZONA 85646

Tel: **(602) 398-3178**	Reduced Rates: **20% weekly**
Best Time to Call: **Anytime**	Breakfast: **Continental**
Hosts: **Ruth and Jim Goebel**	Pets: **No**
Location: **41 mi. S of Tucson**	Children: **Welcome**
No. of rooms: **3**	Smoking: **No**
Suites: **$75**	Social drinking: **Permitted**
Open: **Closed August**	Airport Pickup: **Yes**

This adorable two-story inn located in the center of Tubac will steal your heart away. Choose a one- or two-bedroom suite, two units have full kitchens for longer stays. Tubac, founded in 1752, is the oldest European settlement in Arizona. Today Tubac is the place where art and history meet. Visit galleries, boutiques, and restaurants all in walking distance of the inn. Within a few minutes you can drive to shopping in Old Mexico, or see missions, museums, and national parks. The area boasts six outstanding golf courses.

Casa Tierra Adobe Bed and Breakfast Inn ✪
11155 WEST CALLE PIMA, TUCSON, ARIZONA 85743

Tel: **(602) 578-3058**	No. of Rooms: **3**
Best Time to Call: **Mornings**	No. of Private Baths: **3**
Hosts: **Karen and Lyle Hymer-**	Double/pb: **$75–$85**
Thompson	Open: **Sept.–May**
Location: **15 mi. W of Tucson**	Reduced Rates: **10% after 7 days**

Breakfast: **Full**
Pets: **No**
Children: **Welcome, over 3**
Smoking: **No**

Social Drinking: **Permitted**
Minimum Stay: **2 nights**
Foreign Languages: **Spanish**

Casa Tierra is located on five acres of beautiful Sonoran desert thirty minutes from downtown Tucson. This secluded desert area has hundreds of saguaro cactus, spectacular mountain views, and brilliant sunsets. Built and designed by owners Lyle and Karen, the all-adobe house features entryways with vaulted brick ceilings, an interior arched courtyard, Mexican furnishings, and a Jacuzzi. Each guest room has a private bath, queen-size bed, microwave, small refrigerator, and private patio and entrance. Nearby attractions include the Desert Museum, the Saguaro National Monument, and Old Tucson. Karen is an artist/photographer; Lyle is a designer/builder who takes tours into Mexico.

Ford's Bed & Breakfast ✪
1202 NORTH AVENIDA MARLENE, TUCSON, ARIZONA 85715

Tel: **(602) 885-1202**
Best Time to Call: **8–10 AM**
Hosts: **Sheila and Tom Ford**
Location: **In Tucson**
No. of Rooms: **2**
No. of Private Baths: **1**
Double/pb: **$50**
Single/pb: **$40**

Suites: **$100; sleeps 4**
Open: **All year**
Breakfast: **Continental**
Pets: **No**
Children: **No**
Smoking: **No**
Social Drinking: **Permitted**
Airport/Station Pickup: **Yes**

A warm welcome awaits you at this air-conditioned ranch-style home in a quiet residential cul-de-sac on Tucson's northeast side. Walk through your private entrance and enjoy a bird's-eye view of the mountains from your own garden patio. Your English-born hostess, a retired nanny and dog breeder, has lived here for 35 years and can direct you to the attractions of the area: Sabino Canyon, Mount Lemmon, Saguaro National Monument, hiking trails, and the like. For easy access, city bus lines run nearby. Guests have use of a microwave, a refrigerator, and the sitting room with a TV.

The Gable House ✪
2324 NORTH MADELYN CIRCLE, TUCSON, ARIZONA 85712

Tel: **(602) 326-4846**
Hosts: **Albert Cummings and Phyllis Fredona**
Location: **6 mi. from I-10, exit Grant Road**
No. of Rooms: **3**
No. of Private Baths: **2**

Max. No. Sharing Bath: **4**
Double/pb: **$85**
Double/sb: **$50–$60**
Open: **All year**
Reduced Rates: **$5 less after 1st night; 10% seniors; 7th day free**
Breakfast: **Continental, plus**

Pets: **No**
Children: **Welcome, over 10**
Smoking: **No**

Social drinking: **Permitted**
Minimum Stay: **2 nights**

This Santa Fe pueblo-style home is named for its most famous resident—Clark Gable—who lived here in the early 1940s, some ten years after the house was built. Centrally located on a one-acre lot in a quiet residential neighborhood, this B&B is within walking distance of shops, restaurants, and a bus stop. It's one mile to Tucson Botanical Gardens and three miles to a large city park with golf, tennis, and other recreational facilities. Albert is a semi-retired real estate broker; Phyllis is a licensed massage therapist. Massage is available on the premises.

Hideaway B&B ✪
4344 EAST POE STREET, TUCSON, ARIZONA 85711

Tel: **(602) 323-8067**
Best Time to Call: **After 5 PM**
Hosts: **Dwight and Ola Parker**
No. of Rooms: **1**
No. of Private Baths: **1**
Guest Cottage: **$40–$52**
Open: **Oct.–June, special arrangements for the rest of year**

Reduced Rates: **Weekly**
Breakfast: **Continental**
Pets: **No**
Children: **No**
Smoking: **No**
Minimum Stay: **3 nights**
Airport/Station Pickup: **Yes**

A cozy bungalow with its own entrance, Hideaway B&B is located in the hosts' backyard in central Tucson, just minutes from two major shopping centers. One mile away, a city park provides lots of diversions, with two golf courses, a driving range, tennis courts, and a zoo. Pima Air Museum, Davis Monthan Air Force Base, the University of Arizona, Colossal Cave, the Old Tucson movie set, and Mt. Lemmon Ski Resort are among the many sights of interest. The air-conditioned accommodations include a private bath, a bedroom, and a sitting room equipped with a TV, VCR, and stereo. Your hosts, a retired art teacher and an engineer/insurance man, enjoy big band music, gardening, and their clown ministry.

Katy's Hacienda ✪
5841 EAST 9TH STREET, TUCSON, ARIZONA 85711

Tel: (602) 745-5695
Host: Katy Gage
Location: 8 mi. from Rte. 10, Grant or
  Kolb exit
No. of Rooms: 2
No. of Private Baths: 1
Max. No. Sharing Bath: 3
Double/pb: $55
Single/pb: $45
Double/sb: $55

Single/sb: $45
Open: All year
Reduced Rates: 10% weekly
Breakfast: Full
Pets: No
Children: Welcome, over 8
Smoking: Permitted
Social Drinking: Permitted
Minimum Stay: 2 nights
Airport/Station Pickup: Yes

An ornamental iron guard protects this adobe brick house filled with charming antiques and glass. Guests can unwind in the backyard and the patio area, or come inside and enjoy the living room and television room. Katy's Hacienda is within walking distance of the bus line, fine restaurants, theaters, and a hospital. The El Con shopping area, the Randolph Golf Course, and the zoo are three miles away.

Mesquite Retreat ✪
3770 NORTH MELPOMENE WAY, TUCSON, ARIZONA 85749

Tel: (602) 749-4884
Best Time to Call: Evenings
Hosts: Jan and Curt Albertson
No. of Rooms: 2
Max. No. Sharing Bath: 4
Double/sb: $50
Single/sb: $45

Open: All year
Breakfast: Full
Pets: No
Children: Welcome, over 12
Smoking: Restricted
Social Drinking: Permitted

At the base of Mt. Lemmon sits this spacious ranch-style house, shaded by mesquite trees in the serene quiet of the desert. Traditional furnishings are accented with antiques and collectibles. All of the sights of Tucson—interesting caves, missions, monuments, and museums—are not far, and fine dining is just 10 minutes away. Save time to enjoy the Albertsons' beautiful pool and spa surrounded by lush vegetation and mountain views. Jan and Curt book only one party at a time; the shared bath would be with the same party only.

Natural Bed and Breakfast ✪
3150 EAST PRESIDIO ROAD, TUCSON, ARIZONA 85716

Tel: (602) 881-4582
Best Time to Call: Mornings
Host: Marc Haberman
No. of Rooms: 2
No. of Private Baths: 1

Max. No. Sharing Bath: 2
Double/pb: $55
Single/pb: $45
Double/sb: $45
Single/sb: $35

Open: **All year**
Reduced Rates: **5% seniors**
Breakfast: **Full**
Other Meals: **Available**

Pets: **Sometimes**
Children: **Welcome**
Smoking: **No**
Social Drinking: **Permitted**

Marc Haberman is a holistic health practitioner, and his B&B is natural in all senses of the word: it's a simply furnished, water-cooled home that provides a nontoxic, nonallergenic environment. The grounds are landscaped with palm and pine trees. Only whole-grain and natural foods are served here and the drinking water is purified. Soothing professional massages are available by request.

Paz Entera Ranch: Bed, Breakfast and Beyond ✪
7501 NORTH WADE STREET, TUCSON, ARIZONA 85754

Tel: **(800) 726-7554**
Best Time to Call: **9 AM–6 PM**
Hosts: **Molli and Glenn Nickell**
Location: **12 mi. N of Tucson**
No. of Rooms: **12**
No. of Private Baths: **12**
Double/pb: **$65–$85**
Single/pb: **$65–$75**
Suites: **$100–$120, sleeps 4**

Open: **All year**
Reduced Rates: **Available**
Breakfast: **Continental**
Credit Cards: **AMEX, MC, VISA**
Pets: **No**
Children: **Welcome, over 10**
Smoking: **No**
Social Drinking: **Permitted**
Foreign Languages: **Spanish**

Paz Entera sits on the slopes of the Tucson Mountains, an ideal setting for artists, photographers, writers, and nature enthusiasts. A Continental breakfast is served in the dining room, or anywhere on the beautifully maintained grounds: patios, gardens, or poolside. Amenities include a deep, well-fed swimming pool and Jacuzzi, shaded hammocks, hiking and walking trails, and quiet spots for reading, napping, or meditating (Paz Entera is Spanish for "inner peace"). Guests may use the massive ranch house, which has hardwood floors and spectacular views of the mountains and desert from every window. The house contains a library, baby grand piano, fireplace, TV, and telephone.

Quail Vista Bed & Breakfast ✪
826 EAST PALISADES DRIVE, TUCSON, ARIZONA 85737

Tel: **(602) 297-5980**
Host: **Barbara Jones**
Location: **10 mi. NW of Tucson**
No. of Rooms: **3**
No. of Private Baths: **2**
Double/pb: **$65–$85**
Open: **All year**

Reduced Rates: **10% weekly**
Breakfast: **Continental**
Pets: **No**
Children: **No**
Smoking: **No**
Social Drinking: **Permitted**
Airport/Station Pickup: **Yes**

Native American artifacts and Mexican tile make this modern, solar-heated adobe an attractive blend of the local cultures. Fiestaware dishes, a player piano, and grandmother's furniture in the guest room evoke memories of an older generation. From a seat on the redwood deck you can watch the gorgeous sunset and stargaze in the evening. The swim-stream hot tub is available for swimming or soaking. Breakfasts include a cereal buffet with several toppings, coffee, tea, juices, and baked goods. Light snacks may be put in the refrigerator. Your hostess, a professional Tucson tour guide, can help you discover the area's highlights, and maps, brochures, and restaurant menus are always on hand.

Redbud House Bed & Breakfast
7002 EAST REDBUD ROAD, TUCSON, ARIZONA 85715

Tel: (602) 721-0218
Hosts: **Ken and Wanda Mayer**
Location: **7 mi. from Rte. 10**
No. of Rooms: 1
No. of Private Baths: 1
Double/pb: $50
Single/pb: $40

Open: **Sept.–May**
Breakfast: **Full**
Pets: **No**
Children: **No**
Smoking: **No**
Social Drinking: **Permitted**

The Mayers' comfortable ranch-style brick home is on a residential street bordered by tall pines and palm trees. There is a view of the Catalina Mountains from the porch. Local attractions are the Saguaro National Monument, the Arizona Sonora Desert Museum, Kitt Peak National Observatory, and Sabino Canyon. You are welcome to use the bicycles, barbecue, and TV, or to just relax on the patio. Several fine restaurants and a recreation complex with Olympic-sized swimming pool are nearby.

The Johnstonian B&B ✪
321 WEST SHERIDAN AVENUE, WILLIAMS, ARIZONA 86046

Tel: (602) 635-2178
Best Time to Call: **Before 8 AM; after 1 PM MST**
Hosts: **Bill and Pidge Johnston**
Location: **55 mi. S. of Grand Canyon National Park**
No. of Rooms: 4
Max. No. Sharing Bath: 4
Double/pb: $65
Single/pb: $60

Double/sb: $50
Single/sb: $45
Suites: $108
Open: **All year**
Breakfast: **Full**
Pets: **No**
Children: **Welcome**
Smoking: **No**
Social Drinking: **Permitted**

As old as the century, this two-story Victorian has been carefully restored and decorated in period style. You'll admire the antique oak furniture and the lovely floral wallpapers. In the winter, guests cluster around the wood-burning stove. Pidge's breakfast specialties include Ukrainian potato cakes, blueberry pancakes, and homemade breads.

Casa de Osgood ✪
11620 IRONWOOD DRIVE, YUMA, ARIZONA 85365

Tel: **(602) 342-0471**	Open: **All year**
Best Time to Call: **Evenings**	Breakfast: **Continental**
Hosts: **Chris and Vickie Osgood**	Pets: **No**
Location: **12 mi. E of Yuma**	Children: **No**
No. of Rooms: **1**	Smoking: **No**
No. of Private Baths: **1**	Social Drinking: **No**
Double/pb: **$65**	Airport Pickup: **Yes**

Casa de Osgood offers wonderful views round the clock. From the dining room, sundeck, or hacienda-style front veranda of this B&B, you can see the Gila Mountains. Feel like a night of stargazing? Arrangements can be made for guests to sleep under the sky in the double bed. If you prefer a roof over your head, you'll appreciate the spacious bedroom with its fireplace and big picture window. Yuma's attractions include museums, community arts groups, and state parks. Fans of waterfront sports can head out for several lakes as well as the Colorado River. Camping, hunting, fishing, and hiking are permitted nearby throughout the Kofa, Chocolate, and Castle Dome mountain ranges.

ARKANSAS

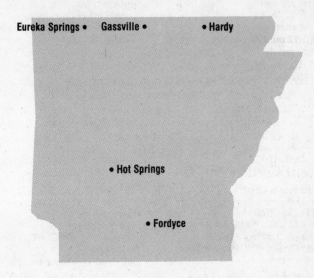

Eureka Springs •   Gassville •   • Hardy

• Hot Springs

• Fordyce

Arkansas and Ozarks Bed & Breakfast ⊘
HC 61, BOX 72, CALICO ROCK, ARKANSAS 72519

Tel: **(501) 297-8211 days, 297-8764
evenings and Sundays**
Coordinator: **Carolyn S. Eck**
Best Time to Call: **9 AM–5 PM**
States/Regions Covered: **Batesville,
Calico Rock, Des Arc, Fayetteville,
Fort Smith, Gassville, Harrison, Hot**
**Springs, Mountain Home, Mountain
View, Norfolk, Ozark, Yellville**
Rates (Single/Double):
Modest: **$30 / $35**
Average: **$35 / $65**
Luxury: **$65 / $85**
Credit Cards: **MC, VISA**

North-central Arkansas boasts an enviable combination of natural
scenic beauty in its forests, rivers, and caves, as well as the homespun
fun of hootenannies, square dancing, and craft shops. Carolyn's
homes include contemporary houses, restored Victorians, Colonials,
and log cabins in the mountains.

Bridgeford House B&B ✪
263 SPRING STREET, EUREKA SPRINGS, ARKANSAS 72632

Tel: (501) 253-7853
Best Time to Call: 10 AM–10 PM
Hosts: Denise and Michael McDonald
No. of Rooms: 4
No. of Private Baths: 4
Double/pb: $75–$95
Open: All year
Reduced Rates: 10% less, Dec.–March

Breakfast: Full
Credit Cards: MC, VISA
Pets: No
Children: Welcome
Smoking: No
Social Drinking: Permitted
Minimum Stay: 2 nights weekends, holidays

A stay at the Bridgeford House is a step into the quiet elegance of yesterday. It is located in the historic district, where Victorian homes line charming streets, and old-fashioned trolleys carry guests to and fro. Denise and Michael will pamper you with coffee or tea in the afternoon or evening. Breakfast is a real eye-opener of fresh fruit, homemade cinnamon rolls, Ozark ham, and delicious egg casseroles.

Crescent Cottage Inn ✪
211 SPRING STREET, EUREKA SPRINGS, ARKANSAS 72632

Tel: (501) 253-6022
Best Time to Call: 9 AM–9 PM
Hosts: Ralph and Phyllis Becker
Location: On Rte. 62B, Historic Loop
No. of Rooms: 4
No. of Private Baths: 4
Double/pb: $75–$115

Open: All year
Breakfast: Full
Credit Cards: DISC, MC, VISA
Pets: No
Children: Welcome, over 13
Smoking: No
Social Drinking: Permitted

Crescent Cottage Inn, built in 1881 for Arkansas' first post-Civil War governor, is listed on the National Register of Historic Places. This celebrated B&B has wonderful views of the mountains. All guest rooms are furnished with antiques; two have double Jacuzzi spas. Ralph and Phyllis serve a full breakfast each morning. Then you'll be ready for the short walk to historic downtown Eureka Springs on a route that leads past lovely springs, shade trees, and a trolley stop.

Harvest House ✪
104 WALL STREET, EUREKA SPRINGS, ARKANSAS 72632

Tel: (501) 253-9363
Best Time to Call: 9 AM–9 PM
Hosts: Bill and Patt Carmichael
No. of Rooms: 4
No. of Private Baths: 4
Double/pb: $75–$85
Open: All year

Breakfast: Full
Credit Cards: MC, VISA
Pets: Sometimes
Children: Welcome, over 12
Smoking: No
Social Drinking: Permitted

Located in the historic district of Eureka Springs, Harvest House is a step off the beaten path, yet close to the bustle of downtown. This turn-of-the-century Victorian house is filled with antiques, collectibles, and family favorites. All guest rooms have private entrances. Breakfast is served in the dining room or, weather permitting, in the screened-in gazebo overlooking pine and oak trees. Bill is a native Arkansan and knows all the hidden treasures of the area. Patt is a shopper with a particular interest in antiques and the local attractions.

Singleton House Bed and Breakfast ☉
11 SINGLETON, EUREKA SPRINGS, ARKANSAS 72632

Tel: **(501) 253-9111; (800) 833-3394**
Best Time to Call: **Anytime**
Host: **Barbara Gavron**
No. of Rooms: **5**
No. of Private Baths: **5**
Double/pb: **$55–$65**
Single/pb: **$55–$65**
Guest Cottage: **$85–$95; open Apr.–Nov.**

Suites: **$75–$95**
Open: **All year**
Reduced Rates: **After 3rd night**
Breakfast: **Full**
Credit Cards: **AMEX, DISC, MC, VISA**
Pets: **No**
Children: **Welcome**
Smoking: **Restricted**
Social Drinking: **Permitted**

You'll find a hidden garden, winding stone paths, and more than fifty birdhouses on the grounds of this Victorian home in Eureka Springs' historic district. For help in identifying your various feathered friends, consult the titles in Singleton House's small nature library. Full breakfasts are served on the balcony overlooking the wildflower garden and lily-filled goldfish pond. After your meal, take a one-block stroll on the historic walking tour footpath to the city's shops, galleries, and cafés. If you prefer, there's an old-fashioned trolley that stops right at Singleton Street. At a second historic district address, your hosts maintain a private guest cottage with a full kitchen, Jacuzzi, and porch with a swing and hammock for two.

Wynne Phillips House ✪
412 WEST FOURTH STREET, FORDYCE, ARKANSAS 71742

Tel: **(501) 352-7202**
Best Time to Call: **Morning**
Hosts: **Colonel and Mrs. James H. Phillips**
Location: **60 mi. S of Little Rock**
No. of Rooms: **4**
No. of Private Baths: **4**
Double/pb: **$55**

Open: **All year**
Breakfast: **Full**
Credit Cards: **MC, VISA**
Pets: **No**
Children: **Yes**
Smoking: **No**
Social Drinking: **Permitted**

A gracious Colonial Revival mansion listed on the National Register of Historic Places, the Wynne Phillips House is filled with antiques and oriental rugs. Mrs. Phillips grew up here, and the bedrooms are furnished with family heirlooms. This is a place where you can enjoy old-fashioned pleasures, such as singing around the piano, or watching the sunset from the wraparound porch. A swimming pool is on the premises; tennis courts are nearby. The generous, Southern-style breakfasts feature fresh fruit, homemade biscuits, eggs, sausage, and grits.

Lithia Springs Bed & Breakfast Lodge ✪
RT. 1, BOX 77-A, GASSVILLE, ARKANSAS 72635

Tel: (501) 435-6100
Best Time to Call: 9 AM–9 PM
Hosts: Paul and Reita Johnson
No. of Rooms: 5
No. of Private Baths: 3
Max. No. Sharing Bath: 4
Double/pb: $50

Double/sb: $45
Open: All year, Dec.–Jan. special
   reservation only
Breakfast: Full
Pets: No
Children: Welcome, over 7
Smoking: No

This 100-year-old former health lodge has been lovingly restored with an additional gift shop featuring many of the hosts' own fine handcrafts. The rooms are furnished with many antiques and period furniture. Breakfast is served in the dining room or on the large screened front porch. Lithia Springs is on 39 acres of meadows and woods. It is near the White and Buffalo Rivers, famous for fishing and canoeing, and between Bull Shoals and Norfork Lakes. It's 10 minutes from Mountain Home and a scenic drive to Blanchard Spring Caverns and Mountain View Folk Center.

Olde Stonehouse Bed & Breakfast Inn ✪
511 MAIN STREET, HARDY, ARKANSAS 72542

Tel: (501) 856-2983
Best Time to Call: 8 AM–10 PM

Hosts: David and Peggy Johnson
No. of Rooms: 6

Diane Phillips '96

No. of Private Baths: **6**
Double p/b: **$55–$65**
Single p/b: **$50–$60**
Suites: **$85**
Open: **All year**
Reduced Rates: **10% seniors**
Breakfast: **Full**
Credit Cards: **DISC, MC, VISA**

Pets: **No**
Children: **Welcome in suites, over 13 in main house**
Smoking: **No**
Social Drinking: **Permitted**
Minimum Stay: **2 nights, holiday weekends and special events**
Station Pickup: **Yes**

Recapture the romance of times past at the Olde Stonehouse. Unwind in lovely air-conditioned rooms decorated with period antiques, quilts, and old lace, plus a ceiling fan and queen-size bed. Curl up in the large rocking chairs on the front porch or take a walk to Old Hardy Town's antique and craft shops. Stroll along the river or join other guests for conversation and games. Awaken to the aroma of freshly brewed coffee and bread baking. After breakfast, canoeing, golfing, shopping, and horseback riding are among the many activities to choose from.

The Gables Inn
318 QUAPAW AVENUE, HOT SPRINGS, ARKANSAS 71901

Tel: **(501) 623-7576; (800) 625-7576**
Best Time to Call: **9 AM–9 PM**
Hosts: **Larry and Shirley Robins**
Location: **50 mi. SW of Little Rock**
No. of Rooms: **4**
No. of Private Baths: **4**
Double/pb: **$50–$70**
Single/pb: **$45–$65**
Open: **All year**

Reduced Rates: **10% seniors**
Breakfast: **Full**
Credit Cards: **AMEX, MC, VISA**
Pets: **No**
Children: **Welcome, over 10**
Smoking: **No**
Social Drinking: **Permitted**
Minimum Stay: **2 nights weekends**

Located three blocks from the historic district and famous Bath House Row, The Gables Inn is a 1905 Victorian, personally restored by the innkeepers. Many special features have been returned to their former beauty, including mantels, light fixtures, and leaded and stained-glass windows. There are wood floors throughout. Upstairs are four guest rooms, all with private baths; furnishings include queen-size beds with handmade quilts and period pieces. Adjacent to the guest rooms is a cozy sitting area where early morning coffee is served, followed by a full breakfast in the turn-of-the-century dining room.

Stillmeadow Farm ✪
111 STILLMEADOW LANE, HOT SPRINGS, ARKANSAS 71913

Tel: **(501) 525-9994**
Hosts: **Gene and Jody Sparling**
Location: **4 mi. S of Hot Springs**
No. of Rooms: **4**
No. of Private Baths: **2**

Max. No. Sharing Bath: **4**
Double/pb: **$60**
Single/pb: **$50**
Suites: **$80**
Open: **All year**

Breakfast: **Full**
Pets: **No**
Children: **Welcome, over 12**

Smoking: **No**
Social Drinking: **Permitted**

Stillmeadow Farm is a reproduction of an 18th-century New England saltbox, set in 75 acres of pine forest with walking trails and an herb garden. The decor is of early country antiques. Your hosts provide homemade snacks and fruit in the guest rooms. For breakfast, freshly baked pastries and breads are served. Hot Springs National Park, Lake Hamilton, the Mid-America Museum, and a racetrack are nearby.

Vintage Comfort B&B Inn ✪
303 QUAPAW AVENUE, HOT SPRINGS, ARKANSAS 71901

Tel: **(501) 623-3258**
Host: **Helen Bartlett**
No. of Rooms: **4**
No. of Private Baths: **4**
Double/pb: **$60–$75**
Single/pb: **$50–$60**
Open: **All year**

Breakfast: **Full**
Credit Cards: **AMEX, MC, VISA**
Pets: **No**
Children: **Welcome, over 6**
Smoking: **No**
Social Drinking: **Permitted**
Airport/Station Pickup: **Yes**

This handsome turn-of-the-century Queen Anne–style home has been faithfully restored, attractively appointed, and air-conditioned. The theme here is comfort and Southern hospitality. Breakfast treats include biscuits and sausage gravy, grits, and regional hot breads. Afterwards, enjoy a short stroll to the famed Bath House Row or a brisk walk to the park, where miles of hiking trails will keep you in shape. Helen will be happy to direct you to the studios and shops of local artists and craftspeople. You are welcome to relax in the old-world sitting room and parlor or on the lovely veranda shaded by magnolia trees.

Williams House Bed & Breakfast Inn ✪
420 QUAPAW AVENUE, HOT SPRINGS, ARKANSAS 71901

Tel: **(501) 624-4275**
Hosts: **Mary and Gary Riley**
Best Time to Call: **Evenings**
Location: **50 mi. SW of Little Rock**
No. of Rooms: **5**
No. of Private Baths: **5**
Double/pb: **$65–$85**
Single/pb: **$60–$75**

Suites: **$75–$85**
Open: **All year**
Breakfast: **Full**
Credit Cards: **AMEX, MC, VISA**
Pets: **No**
Smoking: **No**
Social Drinking: **Permitted**

This Victorian mansion, with its stained-glass and beveled-glass windows, is a nationally registered historical place. The atmosphere is friendly, and the marble fireplace and grand piano invite congeniality. Breakfast menu may include quiche, toast amandine, or exotic egg

dishes. Gary and Mary will spoil you with special iced tea, snacks, and mineral spring water. World health experts recognize the benefits of the hot mineral baths in Hot Springs National Park. The inn is within walking distance of Bath House Row. There's a two-night minimum stay on weekends during March and April.

CALIFORNIA

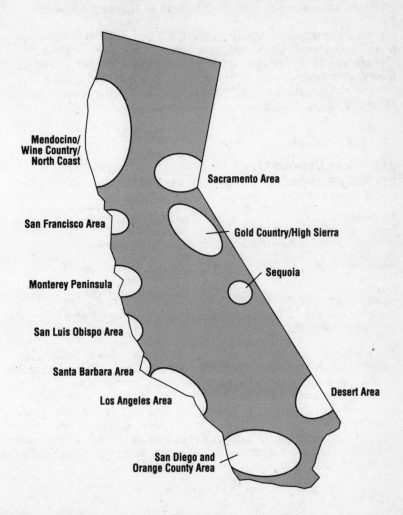

Mendocino/
Wine Country/
North Coast

Sacramento Area

San Francisco Area

Gold Country/High Sierra

Sequoia

Monterey Peninsula

San Luis Obispo Area

Santa Barbara Area

Desert Area

Los Angeles Area

San Diego and
Orange County Area

Bed & Breakfast International ✪
P.O. BOX 282910, SAN FRANCISCO, CALIFORNIA 94128-2910

Tel: (415) 696-1690; (800) 872-4500;
  fax: (415) 696-1699

Best Time to Call: 9 AM–5 PM,
Mon.–Fri.

Coordinator: **Sharene Z. Klein**
States/Regions Covered:
   **California—Berkeley, Los Angeles,
   Palo Alto, San Francisco and the Bay
   Area, Monterey, Napa Valley, Lake
   Tahoe, San Diego, Santa Barbara,
   Yosemite, Las Vegas**

Descriptive Directory: **$7.95**
Rates (Single/Double):
   Modest: **$40–$44 / $44–$58**
   Average: **$54–$72 / $60–78**
   Luxury: **$74 and up / $80 and up**
Credit Cards: **MC, VISA**
Minimum Stay: **2 nights, generally**

The oldest reservation service in the U.S., Bed & Breakfast International lists more than 400 properties throughout California—Victorians, country estates, small inns, separate cottages and apartments, even houseboats. There are over 100 accommodations in San Francisco alone. Itinerary planning is provided for the wine country, Monterey, Yosemite, Tahoe, and southern California.

DESERT AREA

Travellers Repose ✪

P.O. BOX 655, 66920 FIRST STREET, DESERT HOT SPRINGS, CALIFORNIA 92240

Tel: **(619) 329-9584**
Hosts: **Marian and Sam Relkoff**
Location: **12 mi. N of Palm Springs**
No. of Rooms: **3**
No. of Private Baths: **1**
Max. No. Sharing Bath: **4**
Double/pb: **$75**
Double/sb: **$55–$60**
Single/sb: **$50–$54**
Open: **Sept. 1–June 30**

Reduced Rates: **Weekly; 10% families
   on 2nd room**
Breakfast: **Continental**
Pets: **No**
Children: **Welcome, over 12**
Smoking: **No**
Social Drinking: **Permitted**
Airport/Station Pickup: **Yes**
Foreign Languages: **Russian**

Bay windows, gingerbread trim, stained-glass windows, and a white picket fence decorate this charming Victorian home. The warm look of oak predominates in floors, wainscoting, and cabinetry. Guest rooms are decorated with hearts, dolls, and teddy bears everywhere. There's a rose bedroom with antiques and lace, a blue-and-white room with a heart motif, and a green room decorated with pine furniture handcrafted by Sam. A patio, pool, and spa complete the amenities. Golf, tennis, museums, galleries, and posh Palm Springs are nearby. Marian graciously serves tea at 4 PM.

Old Trails Inn

304 BROADWAY, NEEDLES, CALIFORNIA 92363

Tel: **(619) 326-3523**
Best Time to Call: **9 AM–6 PM**
Hosts: **Hank and Edna Wilde**
No. of Rooms: **4**
No. of Private Baths: **4**

Double/pb: **$55**
Single/pb: **$50**
Open: **All year**
Breakfast: **Continental**
Credit Cards: **MC, VISA**

Pets: **Sometimes**
Children: **Yes**
Smoking: **No**

Social Drinking: **Permitted**
Airport/Station Pickup: **Yes**

Old Trails Inn is located in the center of the California-Nevada-Arizona tri-state area, where the many activities include golfing, fishing, swimming, boating, gambling, and ghost town and desert exploring. Rumor has it that a scene in *The Grapes of Wrath* was filmed at this renovated cabin court built in the 1930s. While the exteriors haven't changed much, the individually decorated rooms now boast more luxury and comfort than was the norm in the Depression years. Your hosts are longtime residents—and history, bicycle, and travel buffs. Hank is a retired gas company supervisor and real estate investor, while Edna assists in all family endeavors.

Hotel Nipton ✪
72 NIPTON ROAD, NIPTON, CALIFORNIA 92364

Tel: **(619) 856-2335**
Best Time to Call: **7 AM–6 PM**
Hosts: **Jerry and Roxanne Freeman**
Location: **10 mi. from I-15**
No. of Rooms: **4**
Max. No. Sharing Bath: **4**
Double/sb: **$45**
Open: **All year**
Reduced Rates: **Group**

Breakfast: **Continental**
Other Meals: **Available**
Credit Cards: **MC, VISA**
Pets: **No**
Children: **Welcome**
Smoking: **Permitted**
Social Drinking: **Permitted**
Foreign Languages: **Spanish**

The population of Nipton is 30! The recently restored hotel, with its foot-thick adobe walls, was built in 1904 and is located in the East

Mohave National Scenic Area. Nipton is in the heart of gold-mining territory, 30 minutes from Lake Mohave's Cottonwood Cove. You are welcome to relax on the porch or in the outdoor Jacuzzi. Continental breakfast is served in the lobby at your convenience.

GOLD COUNTRY/HIGH SIERRA

The Matlick House ✪
1313 ROWAN LANE, BISHOP, CALIFORNIA 93514

Tel: **(619) 873-3133**	Reduced Rates: **Corporate discounts**
Best Time to Call: **8 AM–8 PM**	Breakfast: **Full**
Host: **Nanette Robidart**	Pets: **No**
Location: **1 mi. N of Bishop**	Children: **Welcome, over 14**
No. of Rooms: **4**	Smoking: **No**
No. of Private Baths: **4**	Social Drinking: **Permitted**
Suites: **$75–$85**	Airport/Station Pickup: **Yes**
Open: **All year**	

Hikers, backpackers, fishermen, and skiers are drawn to this turn-of-the-century ranch house in Owens Valley, which separates the White Mountains from the Sierra Nevadas. Energetic guests can reserve bicycles and picnic lunches and explore the area on their own. Of course, you may not be hungry for hours after a full breakfast of eggs, bacon, sausage, fresh-squeezed orange juice, sweet bread, homemade biscuits, and coffee or tea. Nanette has deftly combined authentic antiques with modern amenities to assure you a comfortable stay. A gallery showcasing local artists and a fine dinner restaurant are within walking distance.

Country Living Bed and Breakfast ✪
40068 ROAD 88, DINUBA, CALIFORNIA 93618

Tel: **(209) 591-6617**	Open: **Sept.–June**
Best Time to Call: **Before 9 AM**	Breakfast: **Full**
Host: **Barbara Richardson**	Other Meals: **Available**
Location: **30 mi. SE of Fresno**	Pets: **No**
No. of Rooms: **2**	Children: **Welcome**
Max. No. Sharing Bath: **4**	Smoking: **No**
Double/sb: **$45–$55**	Social Drinking: **No**

Once the guest house to the Tagus Ranch Historical site in Tulare, California, this home was moved to its present site in 1959. David and Barbara remodeled the house; inside, you'll see Barbara's own batik works. (Demonstrations and lessons available upon request, for an extra fee.) This area, known as the fruit basket of the world, bursts into bloom in late February and early March. Your map will show you easy access to Sequoia National Park, 40 miles away. Experience the snow and skiing areas in the Sierras, then return to Country Living for a hot shower and cozy bed.

The Heirloom ✪
P.O. BOX 322, 214 SHAKLEY LANE, IONE, CALIFORNIA 95640

Tel: (209) 274-4468
Hosts: Melisande Hubbs and Patricia Cross
Location: 35 mi. E of Sacramento
No. of Rooms: 6
No. of Private Baths: 4
Max. No. Sharing Bath: 2
Double/pb: $75–$92
Single/pb: $65–$82
Double/sb: $60–$75

Single/sb: $55–$70
Open: All year
Reduced Rates: Weekly
Breakfast: Full
Pets: No
Children: Welcome, over 10
Smoking: No
Social Drinking: Permitted
Airport/Station Pickup: Yes

Nestled in the Sierra foothills, yet close to the historic gold mines, wineries, antique shops, and museums, this 1863 mansion, with its lovely balconies and fireplaces, is a classic example of antebellum architecture. It is furnished with a combination of family treasures and period pieces. Patricia and Melisande's hearty breakfast includes such delights as quiche, crêpes, soufflé, and fresh fruits. Afternoon refreshments are always offered.

Chaney House ✪
4725 WEST LAKE BOULEVARD, P.O. BOX 7852, TAHOE CITY, CALIFORNIA 96145

Tel: (916) 525-7333
Hosts: Gary and Lori Chaney
Location: 50 mi. W of Reno, Nevada
No. of Rooms: 4
No. of Private Baths: 2
Max No. Sharing Bath: 4
Double/pb: $95
Double/sb: $95
Suites: $105

Guest Apartment: $110
Open: All year
Breakfast: Full
Pets: No
Children: Welcome, over 12
Smoking: No
Social Drinking: Permitted
Minimum Stay: 2 nights, weekends

Built on the Lake Tahoe shore by Italian stonemasons, Chaney House has an almost medieval quality, with its dramatically arched windows, extra thick walls, and enormous fireplace. The rear of the house faces the waterfront, where the Chaneys' private beach and pier beckon to guests. A water-skiing boat will even be placed at your disposal, by

Chaney House

advance arrangement. Winter visitors can choose from 19 nearby ski areas. All the bedrooms have wood paneling and antique furniture. Breakfasts feature such foods as French toast and quiche.

Cort Cottage ✪
P.O. BOX 245, THREE RIVERS, CALIFORNIA 93271

Tel: **(209) 561-4671**
Best Time to Call: **Before 9 PM**
Hosts: **Gary and Catherine Cort**
Location: **5 mi. W of Sequoia National Park**
Guest Cottage: **$75; sleeps 2**
Open: **All year**

Breakfast: **Continental**
Pets: **No**
Children: **Welcome**
Smoking: **No**
Social Drinking: **Permitted**
Minimum Stay: **2 nights**

Hidden in the Sierra foothill village of Three Rivers, you will find this private guest cottage ten minutes away from the entrance to Sequoia National Park. Built by Gary and Catherine as a house for Grandma, the cottage fits snugly into the hillside and has a panoramic view of mountains and sky. It offers an outdoor hot tub, a fully equipped kitchen, and full bath with step-down tub. Your hosts work as an architect/artist and a part-time nurse, have interests in gardening, crafts, and photography, and own a local art gallery.

LOS ANGELES AREA
El Camino Real Bed & Breakfast ✪
P.O. BOX 5598, SHERMAN OAKS, CALIFORNIA 91403-5598

Tel: (818) 785-8351
Best Time to Call: **Evenings**
Coordinator: **Lisa Reinstein**
States/Regions Covered: **Anaheim,
Beverly Hills, Malibu, Palm Springs,
San Diego, San Fernando Valley; Sun
Valley, ID; Zion, UT**

Rates (Single/Double):
  Modest: **$40–45 / $45–50**
  Average: **$45–$55 / $55–$75**
  Luxury: **N/A $115**
Credit Cards: **No**
Minimum Stay: **2 nights**

This service brings the tradition of California hospitality begun with the Franciscan missions to the present-day traveler. Homes are in beach communities conveniently located to such attractions as Disneyland, Knotts Berry Farm, and the movie studios. Average accommodations are in upper-middle-class homes with swimming pools/spas, except in hilly areas. Lisa offers modest apartments with simple furnishings and a luxurious private guest house on an estate with a hot tub and swimming pool. All hosts are longtime residents of California, familiar with the restaurants, tourist attractions, and the best ways of getting to them.

Fran's Around a Corner Country Cottage ✪
1584 NORTH CYPRESS STREET, LA HABRA HEIGHTS, CALIFORNIA 90631

Tel: (310) 690-6422
Best Time to Call: **After 7 PM,
  weekdays**
Host: **Fran Cooper**
Location: **20 mi. E of Los Angeles**
Guest cottage: **$150, sleeps 4**
Open: **All year**
Reduced Rates: **10% seniors; 10%
  families**

Breakfast: **Continental**
Pets: **No**
Children: **Welcome**
Smoking: **No**
Social Drinking: **Permitted**
Minimum Stay: **2 days**
Airport Pickup: **Yes**

Just around the corner, on a country road, sits this private one-bedroom cottage; its kitchenette is fully equipped, with a refrigerator, microwave, coffeemaker, cooking pans, and eating utensils. The quiet location puts the attractions of Southern California at your feet—Disneyland, Knotts Berry Farm, Movieland Wax Museum, and shopping malls are nearby, and it's a 45-minute drive to the beach.

Casablanca Villa ✪
449 NORTH DETROIT STREET, LOS ANGELES, CALIFORNIA 90036

Tel: **(213) 938-4794**	Breakfast: **Continental**
Host: **Suzanne Moultout**	Pets: **No**
No. of Rooms: **2**	Children: **No**
Max. No. Sharing Bath: **3**	Smoking: **No**
Double/sb: **$60**	Social Drinking: **No**
Single/sb: **$50**	Foreign Languages: **French**
Open: **All year**	

Suzanne Moultout welcomes you to her Spanish-style house located on a quiet, attractive street. Here, guests can enjoy the convenience of being close to West Hollywood, downtown, and Beverly Center, while having a comfortable home base. Your hostess offers an attractive guest room and a shady yard with fruit trees. She will gladly direct you to such nearby sights as Hollywood Hills, CBS Studios, and the beaches. Even if you don't have a car, the area is quite convenient, with a bus stop located within walking distance. This home is not wheelchair accessible.

Marina Bed & Breakfast ✪
P.O. BOX 11828, MARINA DEL REY, CALIFORNIA 90295

Tel: **(310) 821-9862**	Reduced Rates: **Weekly**
Best Time to Call: **5 PM–10 PM**	Breakfast: **Continental**
Hosts: **Peter and Carolyn Griswold**	Pets: **No**
Location: **10 mi. SW of Los Angeles**	Children: **Welcome, over 12**
No. of Rooms: **1**	Smoking: **No**
No. of Private Baths: **1**	Social Drinking: **Permitted**
Suites: **$50–$80**	Minimum Stay: **2 nights**
Open: **All year**	

Peter and Carolyn's two-story house has a spacious studio with a separate entrance, full kitchen, color TV, private bathroom, and two full beds. Have a leisurely breakfast in your room or on the large rooftop yard. Then stroll across the street and admire the thousands of boats and yachts moored in the marina. Nearby, Fisherman's Village offers fine dining, shopping, and harbor cruises. Or you can borrow your hosts' bicycles and strike out for the bike path that runs from Malibu Beach in the north all the way down to San Pedro Harbor, some 35 miles away.

Sea Breeze Bed & Breakfast ✪
122 SOUTH JUANITA, REDONDO BEACH, CALIFORNIA 90277

Tel: **(310) 316-5123**	Location: **19 mi. S of Los Angeles**
Best Time to Call: **6–10 PM**	No. of Rooms: **2**
Hosts: **Norris and Betty Binding**	No. of Private Baths: **2**

Double/pb: **$40–$50**
Single/pb: **$30–$35**
Open: **All year**
Reduced Rates: **10% seniors**
Breakfast: **Continental**

Pets: **No**
Children: **Welcome, over 5**
Smoking: **Permitted**
Social Drinking: **Permitted**
Airport/Station Pickup: **Yes**

The welcome mat is out in front of the lovely stained-glass Colonial doors at Norris and Betty's modest home. A patio-garden is just outside the large guest room, where you may relax after seeing the sights in the area. The Getty Museum and the Pasadena Rose Bowl are within easy reach. Their beach is the start of 22 miles of the Redondo-to-Pacific Palisades bicycle path, and tennis courts are within walking distance. Provisions are available if you prefer to fix breakfast yourself. You are welcome to use the Jacuzzi and TV. UCLA, USC, and Loyola Marymount University are nearby.

The Whites' House ✪
17122 FAYSMITH AVENUE, TORRANCE, CALIFORNIA 90504

Tel: **(310) 324-6164**
Host: **Margaret White**
Location: **5 mi. S of Los Angeles Intl.
  Airport**
No. of Rooms: **2**
No. of Private Baths: **2**
Double/pb: **$30–$35**
Single/pb: **$25**

Open: **All year**
Reduced Rates: **Weekly, monthly**
Breakfast: **Continental**
Pets: **No**
Children: **No**
Smoking: **No**
Social Drinking: **Permitted**

This contemporary home, with its fireplaces, deck, and patio, is located on a quiet street in an unpretentious neighborhood. The airport and lovely beaches are 15 minutes away. Disneyland, Knotts Berry Farm, Universal Studio Tours, and Hollywood are 30 minutes from the door. Use the laundry facilities or kitchen; Margaret wants you to feel perfectly at home.

Coleen's California Casa ✪
11715 SOUTH CIRCLE DRIVE, WHITTIER, CALIFORNIA 90601

Tel: **(310) 699-8427**
Best time to call: **7 AM–7 PM**
Host: **Coleen Davis**
Location: **8 mi. E of Los Angeles**
No. of Rooms: **3**
No. of Private Baths: **3**
Double/pb: **$85**
Single/pb: **$75**
Double/sb: **$75**
Single/sb: **$65**
Suites: **$110, sleeps 5**

Open: **All year**
Reduced Rates: **5% families; weekly**
Breakfast: **Full**
Other Meals: **Available**
Pets: **Sometimes**
Children: **Welcome, over 5**
Smoking: **No**
Social Drinking: **Permitted**
Miniumum Stay: **2 nights**
Airport/Station Pickup: **Yes**
Foreign Languages: **Spanish**

Find your own paradise at this hilltop B&B in a historic Quaker town. Enjoy sunshine and serenity as you sit on the luxuriant patio sampling the full breakfast prepared by your host, a home economist. Dinners are available by prior arrangement. Coleen will be happy to direct you to Disneyland, Knotts Berry Farm, and many other nearby Los Angeles attractions. Tennis courts, jogging and hiking paths, and Whittier College are also close at hand. After sightseeing, refresh yourself with wine and cheese and watch the sunset and the city lights illuminate the sky.

MENDOCINO/WINE COUNTRY/NORTH COAST

The Plantation House ✪
1690 FERRY STREET, ANDERSON, CALIFORNIA 96007

Tel: **(916) 365-2827**
Best Time to Call: **Anytime**
Hosts: **Vi and Bob Webb**
Location: **8 mi. S of Redding**
No. of Rooms: **2**
No. of Private Baths: **2**
Double/pb: **$50**
Suite: **$90**

Open: **All year**
Breakfast: **Full**
Pets: **No**
Children: **No**
Smoking: **No**
Social Drinking: **Permitted**
Airport/Station Pickup: **Yes**

Stay in a sumptuous suite with its own romantic balcony or in one of two elegantly furnished rooms at this antique-filled Queen Anne Victorian. Vi and Bob dress in elaborate Civil War fashions to greet you. Their complimentary hors d'oeuvres, served at your convenience, are so ample that guests have no room for dinner afterward. Schedule breakfast whenever you want it. For this meal, your hosts are decked out in turn-of-century style: bustle dress for Vi, frocked coat, striped morning trousers, and cravat for Bob.

Hillcrest B&B ✪
3225 LAKE COUNTY HIGHWAY, CALISTOGA, CALIFORNIA 94515

Tel: **(707) 942-6334**
Best Time to Call: **After 8 PM**
Host: **Debbie O'Gorman**
Location: **2 mi. N of Calistoga**
No. of Rooms: **3**
No. of Private Baths: **3**
Max. No. Sharing Bath: **4**
Double/pb: **$60–$90**

Double/sb: **$45–$70**
Open: **All year**
Breakfast: **Continental**
Pets: **Sometimes**
Children: **No**
Smoking: **Permitted**
Social Drinking: **Permitted**

Hillcrest has a breathtaking valley view of Mt. St. Helena, in an area famed for its wineries and spas. Without leaving the B&B's 36-acre property, guests can hike, swim, fish, or stay indoors and play the

Steinway grand piano. The house was built by Debbie's great-great-grandfather, and you'll see cherished family heirlooms at every turn. An elegant Continental breakfast of juice, coffee, fresh fruit, and baked goods is served on antique china and silver. For those of you who do not mind paying a higher rate, 3 rooms are available.

Scarlett's Country Inn ✪
3918 SILVERADO TRAIL NORTH, CALISTOGA, CALIFORNIA 94515

Tel: **(707) 942-6669**	Suites: **$115–$150**
Best Time to Call: **9 AM–5 PM**	Guest Cottage: **$305; sleeps 6**
Host: **Scarlett Dwyer**	Open: **All year**
Location: **75 mi. N of San Francisco;**	Breakfast: **Full**
30 mi. from I-80, Napa exit	Pets: **No**
No. of Rooms: **3**	Children: **Welcome**
No. of Private Baths: **3**	Smoking: **No**
Double/pb: **$95**	Social Drinking: **Permitted**
Single/pb: **$80**	Foreign Languages: **Spanish**

This inn is an intimate retreat tucked away in a small canyon in the heart of the famed Napa Valley, just minutes away from wineries and spas. Tranquility, green lawns, and a refreshing swimming pool await you in this peaceful woodland setting. An ample breakfast, featuring freshly squeezed juice, sweet rolls, and freshly ground coffee, is served on the deck, at poolside, or in your own sitting room. All rooms have separate entrances, queen-size beds, and luxurious linens.

Muktip Manor ✪
12540 LAKESHORE DRIVE, CLEARLAKE, CALIFORNIA 95422

Tel: **(707) 994-9571**	Open: **All year**
Hosts: **Jerry and Nadine Schiffman**	Breakfast: **Full**
Location: **101 mi. N of San Francisco**	Pets: **Welcome**
No. of Rooms: **1 suite**	Children: **Sometimes**
No. of Private Baths: **1**	Smoking: **Permitted**
Suite: **$60**	Social Drinking: **Permitted**

Nadine and Jerry traded the often-frenzied San Francisco lifestyle for an uncomplicated existence by the largest lake in the state. They do not offer Victoriana, priceless antiques, or gourmet food. They do provide comfortable accommodations in an unpretentious beach house, a place to relax on the deck, and the use of their private beach and bicycles. They enjoy windsurfing and canoeing, and have been known to give instruction to interested guests. The motto of Muktip Manor is, "If you wish company, we are conversationalists; if you wish privacy, we're invisible."

Inn Oz ✪

13311 LAKESHORE DRIVE, P.O. BOX 1046, CLEARLAKE PARK, CALIFORNIA 95424

Tel: **(707) 995-0853**
Best Time to Call: **Between 8 AM and 6 PM PST**
Hosts: **Pauline and Charley Stephanski**
Location: **100 mi. N of San Francisco**
No. of Rooms: **1**
No. of Private Baths: **1**
Double/pb: **$60**

Open: **All year**
Reduced Rates: **10% seniors**
Breakfast: **Full, Continental**
Pets: **Yes**
Children: **Welcome**
Smoking: **Permitted**
Social Drinking: **Permitted**

On the shores of California's largest freshwater lake, two hours north of San Francisco by automobile (and faster by house in a cyclone), you'll find country so beautiful it could have inspired L. Frank Baum's tales of the land of Oz. Savor unsurpassed sunsets, full moons, and starry heavens over Clear Lake from your bed or on your private patio. Your spacious chamber has a private entrance, a wood-burning fireplace, and a fully equipped kitchenette; the bathroom has a shower and a tub with a portable whirlpool. Pianists are encouraged to tickle the ivories of the upright Steinway. For additional fun, ask your hosts to show you the doll's house Pauline's grandfather built in 1938.

"An Elegant Victorian Mansion" ✪

1406 'C' STREET, EUREKA, CALIFORNIA 95501

Tel: **(707) 444-3144, 442-5594**
Best Time to Call: **11 AM–7 PM PST**
Hosts: **Doug and Lily Vieyra**

No. of Rooms: **3**
No. of Private Baths: **2**
Max. No. Sharing Bath: **4**

Double/pb: **$95–$115**
Double/sb: **$75–$95**
Single/sb: **$65–$85**
Suite: **$95–$135**
Open: **All year**
Reduced Rates: **Available**
Breakfast: **Full**
Credit Cards: **MC, VISA**

Pets: **No**
Children: **Welcome, over 15**
Smoking: **No**
Social Drinking: **Permitted**
Airport/Station Pickup: **Yes**
Foreign Languages: **Dutch, French, German**

Just a few blocks from Eureka's historic Old Town, on a rise overlooking the city and Humboldt Bay, sits "An Elegant Victorian Mansion." Opulent and gracious, it is one of Eureka's most luxurious homes, offering spirited camaraderie and five-star service. A visit here is like a festive vacation with one's best friends. Warm and friendly hosts serve breakfast in the regal splendor of a National Historic Landmark.

Gingerbread Mansion Inn
400 BERDING STREET, FERNDALE, CALIFORNIA 95536

Tel: **(707) 786-4000; (800) 952-4136**
Host: **Ken Torbert**
Location: **15 mi. S of Eureka**
No. of Rooms: **9**
No. of Private Baths: **9**
Double/pb: **$90–$185**
Single/pb: **$75–$170**
Suites: **$120–$185**
Open: **All year**

Reduced Rates: **Available**
Breakfast: **Full**
Credit Cards: **AMEX, MC, VISA**
Pets: **No**
Children: **Welcome, over 10**
Smoking: **No**
Social Drinking: **Permitted**
Minimum Stay: **2 nights Saturday, holidays, and special events**

Painted peach and yellow, surrounded by English gardens, this striking Victorian landmark is one of northern California's most photographed homes. Guests have a choice not only of bedrooms, but of parlors as well: two are stocked with books and games, a third is set up for afternoon tea, and the fourth displays the inn's own 1,000-piece jigsaw in various stages of completion. In your bedroom there are a bathrobe in the dresser and a hand-dipped chocolate by the bedside. Forgot your raingear? Not to worry, umbrellas are available. In good weather, borrow a house bicycle. For breakfast, homemade muffins, fruit, local cheeses, homemade granola, baked egg dishes, and beverages are served in the formal dining room overlooking the garden.

Avalon House ✪
561 STEWART STREET, FORT BRAGG, CALIFORNIA 95437

Tel: **(707) 964-5555; (800) 964-5556**
Best Time to Call: **9 AM–noon**
Host: **Anne Sorrells**
Location: **One block off Hwy. 1, Fir St. exit**

No. of Rooms: **6**
No. of Private Baths: **6**
Double/pb: **$70–$135**
Open: **All year**
Breakfast: **Full**

Credit Cards: **AMEX, DISC, MC, VISA**
Pets: **No**
Children: **Welcome**

Smoking: **No**
Social Drinking: **Permitted**

Located three blocks from the ocean and one block from the Skunk Train depot, this redwood California Craftsman house makes a great home base for visitors to Mendocino County. Anne, a designer who specializes in historic renovations, drew on her own travels to create an appealing B&B. Her furniture is an eclectic mix of antiques and wicker pieces. The more luxurious rooms have fireplaces and whirlpool baths. Breakfasts are ample: a typical meal might consist of hominy grits with eggs, ham, fried apples, and biscuits or perhaps sour cream pancakes.

Campbell Ranch Inn ✪
1475 CANYON ROAD, GEYSERVILLE, CALIFORNIA 95441

Tel: **(707) 857-3476**
Best Time to Call: **10 AM–8 PM**
Hosts: **Mary Jane and Jerry Campbell**
Location: **1.6 mi. from Rte. 101,**
  Canyon Road exit
No. of Rooms: **6**
No. of Private Baths: **6**
Double/pb: **$85–$165**
Guest Cottage: **$165**

Open: **All year**
Breakfast: **Full**
Credit Cards: **MC, VISA**
Pets: **No**
Children: **Welcome, over 10**
Smoking: **No**
Social Drinking: **Permitted**
Minimum Stay: **2 nights weekends**
Airport/Station Pickup: **Yes**

"Spectacular!" and "charming!" are expressions most often used when guests describe their stay at this picture-perfect hilltop home surrounded by 35 acres in the heart of the Sonoma County wine country. The spacious bedrooms, each with a king-size bed, are handsomely furnished; several have balconies where views of mountains and vineyards are a backdrop to the colorful flower gardens. Breakfast, beautifully served, features a selection of fresh fruit, choice of gourmet egg dishes, homemade breads and cakes, and a variety of beverages. You can burn off the calories on the Campbells' tennis court or in their swimming pool, or borrow a bike to tour the wineries. Water sports and fishing are less than four miles away. Jerry will be happy to make your dinner reservations at one of the area's fine restaurants, but leave room for Mary Jane's dessert, always served "at home."

Palisades Paradise B&B ✪
1200 PALISADES AVENUE, REDDING, CALIFORNIA 96003

Tel: **(916) 223-5305; (800) 382-4649**
Best Time to Call: **Evenings**
Host: **Gail Goetz**

Location: **1¼ mi. from Rte. I-5 exit**
  Hilltop Dr.
No. of Rooms: **2**

Max. No. Sharing Bath: **4**
Double/sb: **$65–$75**
Single/sb: **$60–$70**
Open: **All year**
Reduced Rates: **Available**
Breakfast: **Full**

Credit Cards: **AMEX, MC, VISA**
Pets: **No**
Children: **Welcome, over 6**
Smoking: **No**
Social Drinking: **Permitted**

Enjoy breathtakingly beautiful views from the patio and spa deck of this contemporary riverside home near Shasta College and Simpson College. Stay in either the Cozy Retreat or the Sunset Suite, both aptly named. In the morning, Gail serves ample breakfasts, with gourmet coffee, pastries, and her own Palisades fruit puffs.

Vichy Hot Springs
2605 VICHY SPRINGS ROAD, UKIAH, CALIFORNIA 95482

Tel: **(707) 462-9515**
Best Time to Call: **9 AM–9 PM**
Host: **Gilbert Ashoff**
Location: **105 mi. N of San Francisco**
No. of Rooms: **14**
No. of Private Baths: **14**
Double/pb: **$125**
Single/pb: **$85**
Guest Cottage: **$150–$160**

Open: **All year**
Breakfast: **Continental**
Credit Cards: **AMEX, DC, MC, VISA**
Pets: **No**
Children: **Welcome**
Smoking: **No**
Social Drinking: **Permitted**
Airport Pickup: **Yes**
Foreign Languages: **Spanish**

Choose between twelve individually decorated rooms and two self-contained cottages at this B&B spa. Vichy features naturally sparkling, 90-degree mineral baths, a 104-degree pool, and an Olympic-size pool, along with 700 private acres with trails and roads for hiking, jogging, picnicking, and mountain biking. Staff members offer Swedish massage, reflexology, herbal facials, and acupressure. Set amid native oak, madrone, manzanita, bay, fir, pine, and buckeye, this quiet resort will leave you refreshed and invigorated.

MONTEREY PENINSULA
Happy Landing Inn ✪
P.O. BOX 2619, CARMEL, CALIFORNIA 93921

Tel: **(408) 624-7917**
Best Time to Call: **8:30 AM–9 PM**
Hosts: **Robert Ballard and Dick Stewart**
Location: **120 mi. S of San Francisco**
No. of Rooms: **7**
No. of Private Baths: **7**
Double/pb: **$90–155**
Open: **All year**
Breakfast: **Continental**

Credit Cards: **MC, VISA**
Pets: **No**
Children: **Welcome, over 12**
Smoking: **No**
Social Drinking: **Permitted**
Minimum Stay: **2 nights weekends**
Foreign Languages: **Japanese,
    Portuguese, Spanish**

Located on Monte Verde between 5th and 6th, this Hansel and Gretel–style inn is a charming and romantic place to stay. Rooms with cathedral ceilings open onto a beautiful garden with gazebo, pond, and flagstone paths. Lovely antiques and personal touches, including breakfast served in your room, make your stay special.

Babbling Brook Inn ☉
1025 LAUREL STREET, SANTA CRUZ, CALIFORNIA 95060

Tel: **(408) 427-2437; (800) 866-1131**	Reduced Rates: **Available**
Best Time to Call: **7 AM–11 PM**	Breakfast: **Full**
Host: **Helen King**	Credit Cards: **AMEX, DISC, MC, VISA**
Location: **2 blocks from Hwy. 1**	Pets: **No**
No. of Rooms: **12**	Children: **Welcome, over 12**
No. of Private Baths: **12**	Smoking: **No**
Double/pb: **$85–$150**	Foreign Languages: **French, Spanish**
Open: **All year**	

Cascading waterfalls, a brook, historic waterwheel gardens, and redwood trees surround this country inn. The oldest part of the house was built in 1909 on what was once a tannery and flour mill. Over the years, the house was changed by a number of owners, including the counsel to a czar and a woman known as the countess, who added several rooms and a balcony. It is a rustic, rambling retreat decorated in French country furnishings. Most rooms have a cozy fireplace, private deck, and outside entrance. Your host has owned restaurants and hotels in South America and is an expert in making 2 people or 100 feel equally at home. Helen is a gourmet cook, as you will see from her breakfast repertoire of omelets, stratas, and frittatas. This historic inn is walking distance from the ocean, boardwalk, shops, and tennis courts.

Inn Laguna Creek ☉
2727 SMITH GRADE, SANTA CRUZ, CALIFORNIA 95060

Tel: **(408) 425-0692**	Open: **All year**
Best Time to Call: **9 AM–8 PM**	Reduced Rates: **Available**
Hosts: **Jim Holley and Gay Carlson**	Breakfast: **Full**
Location: **8 mi. N of Santa Cruz**	Credit Cards: **AMEX, MC, VISA**
No. of Rooms: **2**	Pets: **No**
Max. No. Sharing Bath: **4**	Children: **Welcome**
Double s/b: **$85**	Smoking: **No**
Suite: **$125**	Social Drinking: **Permitted**

A distinctive modern residence with a curved roof, this B&B nestles in the redwood forests of the Santa Cruz Mountains. The large rooms have queen-size beds, down comforters, a private deck overlooking the creek, and a private entrance. The sitting room boasts a wet bar, stereo, VCR, and games. A sunning deck with a spa, picnic area, and acres of gardens are yours to enjoy. There are lots of things to do, from hiking, biking, surfing, and beachcombing to whale watching, wine tasting, and antiquing. Sightseers will want to add Roaring Camp and Big Trees Railroad, Mystery Spot, Redwood State Park, Lighthouse Point, and Mission Santa Cruz to their itineraries. A country-style breakfast is served with special attention to dietary restrictions. Herbal tea, cookies, fresh fruit, and popcorn are always available.

Jasmine Cottage ✪
731 RIVERSIDE AVENUE, SANTA CRUZ, CALIFORNIA 95060

Tel: **(408) 429-1415**
Host: **Dorothy Allen**
Location: **1 mi. from Rte 17 or 1 exit from Ocean St.**
No. of Rooms: **1**
Max. No. or Private Baths: **1**
Double p/b: **$65**
Single p/b: **$45**
Open: **All year**

Breakfast: **Full**
Credit Cards: **MC, VISA**
Other Meals: **Available**
Pets: **No**
Children: **Welcome**
Smoking: **No**
Social Drinking: **Permitted**
Airport/Station Pickup: **Yes**

Jasmine Cottage offers easy access to many of Santa Cruz's favorite spots—the boardwalk and Pacific Garden Mall are within walking distance. Summertime presents opportunities to attend the Cabrillo Music Festival and Shakespeare Santa Cruz. Your room, which has a private entrance, is furnished in the style of a 1910 Edwardian bungalow, with a king-size or single bed, TV, stereo, and other modern comforts. Upon arrival, you'll find a complimentary tray of wine and cheese in your room. Dorothy's breakfast specialties include vegetable quiche and buckwheat pancakes.

Knighttime Bed and Breakfast ✪
890 CALABASAS ROAD, WATSONVILLE, CALIFORNIA 95076

Tel: **(408) 684-0528**
Best Time to Call: **8–10 AM; 5–7 PM**
Hosts: **Diane Knight and Ray Miller**
Location: **90 mi. S of San Francisco**
No. of Rooms: **1**
No. of Private Baths: **1**
Double p/b: **$60**
Single p/b: **$50**

Open: **All year**
Breakfast: **Full**
Other Meals: **Available**
Pets: **Sometimes**
Children: **Welcome**
Smoking: **No**
Social Drinking: **Permitted**

A wooden home with a pitched roof and wide porches, Knighttime is set on 26 wooded acres just a few minutes drive from the beaches between Santa Cruz and Monterey. Sunlight bathes the interior filled with art, pine cabinetry, and country comforts. Eclectic furnishings include some antiques as well as reproductions and wicker. The main floor has a country French flavor while the upper floor—the private guest area—is strongly influenced by shells and the sea. This spacious guest area comprises a sitting room, large bath, large bedroom, and a second bedroom that can sleep two additional people in the same party.

SACRAMENTO AREA

The Inn at Shallow Creek Farm ✪
4712 ROAD DD, ORLAND, CALIFORNIA 95963

Tel: **(916) 865-4093**	Reduced Rates: **$10 less after 3rd night**
Best Time to Call: **Evenings**	Breakfast: **Continental**
Hosts: **Mary and Kurt Glaeseman**	Pets: **No**
Location: **3 mi. from I-5**	Children: **Sometimes**
No. of Rooms: **4**	Smoking: **No**
No. of Private Baths: **2**	Social Drinking: **Permitted**
Max. No. Sharing Bath: **4**	Airport/Station Pickup: **Yes**
Double/pb.: **$65**	Foreign Languages: **French, German, Spanish**
Double/sb: **$55**	
Guest Cottage: **$75; sleeps 2–4**	
Open: **All year**	

The orchards of Shallow Creek Farm are known for mandarin and navel oranges and sweet grapefruit. Luscious berries, fresh garden produce, and a collection of exotic poultry, including rare silver guinea hens and African geese, are quite extraordinary. The inn, a gracious turn-of-the-century farmhouse, offers airy, spacious rooms furnished with carefully chosen antiques and family heirlooms, combining nostalgia with country comfort. Breakfast features homemade baked goods and jams, and a generous assortment of fresh fruits or juices and hot beverages.

The Feather Bed ✪
542 JACKSON STREET, QUINCY, CALIFORNIA 95971

Tel: **(916) 283-0102**	Open: **All year**
Hosts: **Bob and Jan Janowski**	Reduced Rates: **10% less on 3rd night**
Location: **70 mi. NW of Reno, Nevada**	Breakfast: **Full**
No. of Rooms: **7**	Credit Cards: **AMEX, DC, MC, VISA**
No. of Private Baths: **7**	Pets: **No**
Double/pb: **$70**	Children: **Welcome**
Single/pb: **$65**	Smoking: **No**
Suite: **$85**	Social Drinking: **Permitted**
Separate Cottages: **$100**	Airport/Station Pickup: **Yes**

This charming Queen Anne was built in 1893 and renovated at the turn of the century. The rooms feature vintage wallpaper, antique furnishings, and charming baths; most have clawfoot tubs. Enjoy a glass of cider in the parlor, or a cool iced tea on the front porch. A full three-course breakfast is served on the patio or in the dining room. The inn is convenient to water sports, snowmobiling, hiking, tennis, and skiing. Your hosts offer complimentary bicycles to help you explore beautiful Plumas National Forest and historic downtown Quincy. Restaurants and the county museum are close by.

SAN DIEGO AND ORANGE COUNTY AREA

Coronado Village Inn ✪
1017 PARK PLACE, CORONADO, CALIFORNIA 92118

Tel: **(619) 435-9318**	Open: **All year**
Best Time to Call: **To 10 PM**	Reduced Rates: **Winter weekly**
Hosts: **Brent and Elizabeth Bogh**	**rate—7th night free**
Location: **3 mi. W of San Diego**	Breakfast: **Continental**
No. of Rooms: **14**	Credit Cards: **AMEX, MC, VISA**
No. of Private Baths: **14**	Pets: **No**
Double/pb: **$50–$70**	Children: **Welcome**
Single/pb: **$50–$70**	Smoking: **Yes**
Suites: **$70–$80; sleeps 4**	Social Drinking: **Permitted**

Enjoy the ambience of yesteryear at this small, European-style hotel. Within easy walking distance are tennis courts, golf courses, boating facilities, quaint shops, fine restaurants, and the white sandy beaches of the Pacific Ocean. San Diego and Mexico are just a short drive away, boasting numerous attractions.

The Blue Door ✪
13707 DURANGO DRIVE, DEL MAR, CALIFORNIA 92014

Tel: **(619) 755-3819**	Open: **All year**
Best Time to Call: **Anytime**	Breakfast: **Full**
Hosts: **Bob and Anna Belle Schock**	Pets: **No**
Location: **20 mi. N of San Diego**	Children: **Welcome, over 16**
No. of Rooms: **1 suite**	Smoking: **No**
No. of Private Baths: **1**	Social Drinking: **Permitted**
Suite: **$50**	

Enjoy New England charm in a quiet southern California setting overlooking exclusive Torrey Pines State Reserve. A garden-level two-room suite with wicker accessories and king or twin beds is yours. The sitting room has a couch, a desk, and a color TV. Breakfast is served in the spacious country kitchen or in the dining room warmed by the fire on chilly days. Anna Belle prides herself on creative breakfast menus featuring homemade baked goods. Breakfast special ties include blueberry muffins, Swedish oatmeal pancakes, and Blue Door orange French toast. Your hosts will gladly direct you to the nearby racetrack, beach, zoo, or University of California at San Diego. There is a $10 surcharge for one-night stays.

Gulls Nest ✪

12930 VIA ESPERIA, DEL MAR, CALIFORNIA
(MAILING ADDRESS: P.O. BOX 1056, DEL MAR, CALIFORNIA 92014)

Tel: **(619) 259-4863**
Best Time to Call: **Before 8:30 AM**
Hosts: **Connie and Mike Segel**
Location: **20 mi. N of San Diego**
No. of Rooms: **2**
No. of Private Baths: **2**
Double/pb: **$65**

Suite: **$85**
Open: **All year**
Breakfast: **Full**
Pets: **No**
Children: **Welcome, over 6**
Smoking: **No**
Social Drinking: **Permitted**

Gulls Nest is a contemporary wood home surrounded by pine trees. The house boasts a beautiful view of the ocean and a bird sanctuary from two upper decks. Guest accommodations consist of a comfortable, quiet room with queen-size bed, TV, private bath, and patio. The suite has a king-size bed and a sitting room that can accommodate a third person for $10 more. Breakfast is served outdoors, weather permitting, and features fresh-squeezed juice, eggs, homemade breads, and coffee cake. Great swimming and surfing are three blocks away at Torrey State Beach. Golf, shops, and restaurants are a 5-minute drive, and Tijuana and the international border are 40 minutes away.

Sea Breeze B&B ✪

121 NORTH VULCAN, ENCINITAS, CALIFORNIA 92024

Tel: **(619) 944-0318**
Host: **Kirsten Richter**
Location: **23 mi. N of San Diego**
No. of Rooms: **5**
No. of Private Baths: **5**
Double/pb: **$75–150**
Double/sb: **$90**
Suite: **$150**

Open: **All year**
Reduced Rates: **10% weekly, seniors, families**
Breakfast: **Continental**
Pets: **No**
Children: **Welcome (playpen)**
Smoking: **Permitted**
Social Drinking: **Permitted**

Choose among a separate apartment, three queen bedrooms, and a penthouse with a private spa, whirlpool tub, and shower in this contemporary two-story home filled with custom, one-of-a-kind furnishings. Sunbathe in privacy on the deck overlooking the Pacific, or stroll down to Moonlight Beach for a refreshing ocean dip. It's a short walk to downtown Encinitas, which boasts many fine restaurants. Mt. Palomar Observatory, Sea World, Del Mar Race Track, and the Mexican border are about a half hour away by car. Guests have use of a kitchenette. Continental breakfasts consist of muffins, fresh fruit, yogurt, and coffee, tea, or hot chocolate.

Hidden Village Bed & Breakfast ✪
9582 HALEKULANI DRIVE, GARDEN GROVE, CALIFORNIA 92641

Tel: (714) 636-8312
Best Time to Call: 8 AM–9 PM
Hosts: **Dick and Linda O'Berg**
Location: **3 mi. S of Anaheim**
No. of Rooms: **4**
No. of Private Baths: **2**
Max. No. Sharing Bath: **2**
Double/pb: **$55**
Single/pb: **$45**
Double/sb: **$50**

Single/sb: **$40**
Suites: **$75**
Open: **All year**
Reduced Rates: **$10 less, Sun.–Thurs.**
Breakfast: **Full**
Pets: **Sometimes**
Children: **Welcome (crib)**
Smoking: **No**
Social Drinking: **Permitted**
Airport/Station Pickup: **Yes**

Linda has decorated this large Colonial home with lacy draperies and handmade quilts; she's a professional weaver, and guests are welcome to browse in her studio. When you're done looking at fabrics, Disneyland, the Anaheim Convention Center, and Orange County's lovely beaches are just minutes away. Couch potatoes can watch tapes on the VCR, while the energetic can borrow the O'Bergs' bicycles and go for a spin. In the mornings, you'll savor a full breakfast of fresh fruit, homemade apple muffins, and quiche or omelets.

Country Comfort Bed and Breakfast ✪
5104 EAST VALENCIA DRIVE, ORANGE, CALIFORNIA 92669

Tel: (714) 532-2802 or 532-4010
Best Time to Call: **Evenings**
Hosts: **Geri Lopker and Joanne Angell**
Location: **5 mi. E of Anaheim**
No. of Rooms: **3**
No. of Private Baths: **3**
Double/pb: **$65**
Single/pb: **$55**
Open: **All year**

Reduced Rates: **10% less after 3rd night**
Breakfast: **Full**
Other Meals: **Available**
Pets: **By arrangement**
Children: **Welcome**
Smoking: **No**
Social Drinking: **Permitted**

Located in a quiet residential area, Geri and Joanne have furnished their home with your comfort and pleasure in mind. It is disabled-accessible with adaptive equipment available. Amenities include a swimming pool, cable TV and VCR, an atrium, fireplace, and the use of bicycles, including one built for two. Breakfast often features delicious Scotch eggs, stuffed French toast and hash, along with fruits and assorted beverages. Vegetarian selections are also available. Disneyland and Knotts Berry Farm are less than seven miles away.

Blom House Bed & Breakfast ✪
1372 MINDEN DRIVE, SAN DIEGO, CALIFORNIA 92111

Tel: **(619) 467-0890**
Hosts: **Bette and John Blom**
Location: **In San Diego**
No. of Rooms: **3**
No. of Private Baths: **3**
Double p/b: **$65**
Single p/b: **$45**
Suite: **$80**
Open: **All year**

Reduced Rates: **15% less than daily rate for one week, $10 less per night Sun.–Thurs.; 10% seniors**
Breakfast: **Full**
Pets: **No**
Children: **Welcome (crib/high chair)**
Smoking: **No**
Social Drinking: **Permitted**
Minimum Stay: **2 nights**

Blom House is a charming one-story cottage located on a bluff in a residential neighborhood, less than ten minutes from the beach, downtown, and all local tourist attractions. The 65-foot deck has a spa and offers a view of the lights from the Hotel Circle below. Guest areas have 14-foot ceilings and antique furnishings, as well as cookies and chocolates. You'll find lots of extras in your room, from the color TV, VCR, phone, and refrigerator, to bathrobes, a hair dryer, an iron and ironing board, and complimentary wine and cheese. A four-course breakfast is served each morning. And for dining, Bette and John have two-for-one coupons for a large variety of neighborhood restaurants.

The Cottage ✪
P.O. BOX 3292, SAN DIEGO, CALIFORNIA 92163

Tel: **(619) 299-1564**
Best Time to Call: **9 AM–5 PM**

Hosts: **Robert and Carol Emerick**
Location: **1 mi. from Rte. 5**

No. of Rooms: **2**
No. of Private Baths: **2**
Double/pb: **$49–$80**
Guest Cottage: **$65–$85; sleeps 3**
Open: **All year**
Breakfast: **Continental**

Credit Cards: **AMEX, MC, VISA**
Pets: **No**
Children: **Welcome**
Smoking: **No**
Social Drinking: **Permitted**

Located in the Hillcrest section, where canyons and old houses dot the landscape, this private hideaway offers a cottage with a king-size bed, full bath, and fully equipped kitchen. Decorated with turn-of-the-century furniture, the wood-burning stove and oak pump organ evoke memories of long ago. It's two miles to the zoo, less to Balboa Park, and it is within easy walking distance of restaurants, shops, and theater. The University of California and the University of San Diego are nearby.

Vera's Cozy Corner ✪
2810 ALBATROSS STREET, SAN DIEGO, CALIFORNIA 92103

Tel: **(619) 296-1938**
Best Time to Call: **Before 10 AM; after 5 PM**
Host: **Vera V. Warden**
No. of Rooms: **1**
No. of Private Baths: **1**
Double/pb: **$50**
Single/pb: **$40**

Open: **All year**
Reduced Rates: **Weekly; 10% seniors**
Breakfast: **Continental**
Pets: **No**
Children: **No**
Smoking: **No**
Social Drinking: **Permitted**
Foreign Languages: **French, German**

This crisp white Colonial with black shutters sits on a quiet cul-de-sac overlooking San Diego Bay. Guest quarters consist of a separate cottage with private patio entrance. Vera offers fresh-squeezed juice from her own fruit trees in season as a prelude to breakfast, served in the Wardens' old-world dining room. The house is convenient to local shops and restaurants, and is a mile from the San Diego Zoo.

SAN FRANCISCO AREA
American Family Inn ✪
P.O. BOX 420009, SAN FRANCISCO, CALIFORNIA 94142

Tel: **(415) 479-1913**
Best Time to Call: **9:30 AM–5 PM Mon.–Fri.**
Coordinators: **Susan and Richard Kreibich**
States/Regions Covered: **Carmel, Marin County, Monterey, Napa, San Francisco, Sonoma (wine country)**

Descriptive Directory: **$2**
Rates (Single/Double):
  Modest: **$45–$55**
  Average: **$65**
  Luxury: **$75–$85**
Credit Cards: **AMEX, DC, MC, VISA**
Minimum Stay: **2 nights**

The San Francisco locations are near all of the famous sights, such as Fisherman's Wharf and Chinatown. Many are historic Victorian houses. Some homes offer hot tubs and sun decks; a few are on yachts and houseboats.

Bed & Breakfast International ✪
P. O. BOX 282910, SAN FRANCISCO, CALIFORNIA 94128-2910

Tel: (415) 696-1690; (800) 872-4500; fax: (415) 696-1699
Best Time to Call: 9 AM–5 PM, Mon.–Fri.
Coordinator: Sharene Z. Klein
States/Regions Covered: California–Berkeley, Los Angeles, Palo Alto, San Francisco, and the Bay Area, Monterey, Napa Valley, Lake Tahoe, San Diego, Santa Barbara, Yosemite, Las Vegas
Rates (Single/Double):
Modest: $40–$44 / $44–$58
Average: $54–$72 / $60–$78
Luxury: $74 and up / $80 and up
Credit Cards: MC, VISA
Minimum Stay: 2 nights, generally

The oldest reservation service in the U.S., Bed and Breakfast International lists more than 400 properties throughout California—Victorians, country estates, small inns, separate cottages and apartments, even houseboats. There are over 100 accommodations in San Francisco alone. Itinerary planning is provided for the wine country, Monterey, Yosemite, Tahoe, and southern California.

Burlingame B&B ✪
1021 BALBOA AVENUE, BURLINGAME, CALIFORNIA 94010

Tel: (415) 344-5815
Hosts: Joe and Elnora Fernandez
Location: ½ mi. from Rte. 101
No. of Rooms: 1
No. of Private Baths: 1
Double/pb: $50
Single/pb: $40
Open: All year
Breakfast: Continental
Pets: No
Children: Welcome
Smoking: No
Social Drinking: No
Airport/Station Pickup: Yes
Foreign Languages: Italian, Spanish

Located in a pleasantly quiet neighborhood, with San Francisco only minutes away by good public transportation. The house offers the privacy of upstairs guest quarters with a view of a creek and native flora and fauna. It's all very clean and cheerfully decorated. Joe and Elnora will direct you to restaurants and shops to suit your budget.

Lore's Haus ✪
22051 BETLEN WAY, CASTRO VALLEY, CALIFORNIA 94546

Tel: (510) 881-1533
Host: Lore Bergman
Location: 25 mi. SE of San Francisco
No. of Rooms: 2
No. of Private Baths: 1
Max. No. Sharing Bath: 4

Double/pb: **$60**
Single/pb: **$55**
Double/sb: **$55**
Single/sb: **$50**
Open: **All year**
Breakfast: **Full**
Pets: **No**

Children: **Welcome, over 14**
Smoking: **Permitted**
Social Drinking: **Permitted**
Airport/Station Pickup: **Yes**
Foreign Languages: **French, German**
Minimum Stay: **2 nights**

Lore's Haus is an attractive ranch home on a quiet street, with a large, beautiful garden. Lore was born in Germany and has spent the last 30 years in Castro Valley. She prides herself on offering Americans a true European atmosphere, with a lot of plants, books, comfortable furnishings, and oriental rugs. Breakfast includes French Brie, fresh German black bread, homemade jams, cold cuts, and eggs. If you like, tours of the Bay Area, Napa Valley, or anyplace else are available in German, French, or English. If you'd like to venture out on your own, the city center is 25 minutes away via car or rapid transit. After a day of touring, come back to Lore's and enjoy a glass of wine.

Old Thyme Inn ✪
779 MAIN STREET, HALF MOON BAY, CALIFORNIA 94019

Tel: **(415) 726-1616**
Best Time to Call: **8 AM–10 PM**
Hosts: **Marcia and George Dempsey**
Location: **30 mi. S of San Francisco**
No. of Rooms: **3**
No. of Private Baths: **3**
Double/pb: **$65–$85**
Single/pb: **$60–$85**
Suites: **$145–$210**

Open: **All year**
Breakfast: **Full**
Credit Cards: **MC, VISA**
Pets: **No**
Children: **Welcome, over 12**
Smoking: **No**
Social Drinking: **Permitted**
Minimum Stay: **Holiday weekends**
Foreign Languages: **French**

The Old Thyme Inn is a restored Victorian house located on the Pacific coast just 35 minutes south of San Francisco. Some rooms have fireplaces, some have baths with double-size whirlpool tubs, and all are decorated with antiques. Your hosts invite you to stroll in George's herb garden; if you like, you can have a cutting kit and take samples home for your own use. George's breakfast includes his justly celebrated buttermilk scones. For those of you who don't mind paying a higher rate, 4 rooms are available.

Zaballa House ✪
324 MAIN STREET, HALF MOON BAY, CALIFORNIA 94019

Tel: **(415) 726-9123**
Best Time to Call: **7 AM–8 PM**
Host: **Kerry Pendercast**
Location: **35 mi. S of San Francisco**
No. of Rooms: **9**
No. of Private Baths: **9**

Double/pb: **$65–$165**
Open: **All year**
Reduced Rates: **Mon.–Thurs.**
Breakfast: **Full**
Credit Cards: **AMEX, DISC, MC, VISA**
Pets: **By arrangement**

Children: **Welcome, over 8**   Social Drinking: **Permitted**
Smoking: **No**

Built in 1859 by Estanislao Zaballo, the community's first city planner, this bed-and-breakfast inn is the oldest house in Half Moon Bay. The inn is located on the same block as two of the coast's finest restaurants and enjoys a wonderful garden setting. The local gardens provide the Inn with an abundance of flowers for all the rooms. Kerry is an expert in neighborhood lore—ask her to tell you about the ghost. In the evenings, guests are invited to share complimentary drinks around the fireplace; in the mornings, all-you-can-eat breakfasts are served.

Adella Villa B&B ✪
P.O. BOX 4528, PALO ALTO, CALIFORNIA 94309

Tel: **(415) 321-5195**
Host: **Tricia Young**
Location: **30 mi. S of San Francisco**
No. of Rooms: **5**
No. of Private Baths: **5**
Double/pb: **$95**
Suites: **$110**
Open: **All year**

Breakfast: **Full**
Credit Cards: **AMEX, DC, MC, VISA**
Pets: **No**
Children: **Welcome, over 10**
Smoking: **No**
Social Drinking: **Permitted**
Airport/Station Pickup: **Yes**
Foreign Languages: **German, Spanish**

This gorgeous, restored 1920s Italian villa is located in an exclusive area near Stanford University and Silicon Valley. The B&B, a pink stucco mansion with white trim, stands on an acre of lush park-like grounds with a Japanese koi pond, an aviary, and a swimming pool. The music foyer boasts a Steinway grand piano crafted in the 1930s. Fans of antiques will find much to admire, including a Louis XVI dining room set, a five-foot nineteenth-century Imari vase, and a French marble commode. But there's nothing old-fashioned about the guest room amenities, such as bathrobes, down comforters, cable TV, sherry and wines, and cooked-to-order breakfasts.

Casa Arguello ✪
225 ARGUELLO BOULEVARD, SAN FRANCISCO, CALIFORNIA 94118

Tel: **(415) 752-9482**
Best Time to Call: **10 AM–6 PM**
Hosts: **Emma Baires and Marina McKenzie**
No. of Rooms: **4**
No. of Private Baths: **2**
Max. No. Sharing Bath: **3**
Double/pb: **$70–$77**
Double/sb: **$55**

Open: **All year**
Breakfast: **Continental, plus**
Pets: **No**
Children: **Welcome, over 7**
Smoking: **No**
Social Drinking: **Permitted**
Minimum Stay: **2 nights**
Foreign Languages: **Spanish**

This spacious duplex has an elegant living room, dining room, and cheerful bedrooms that overlook neighboring gardens. Tastefully decorated with modern and antique furnishings, it is convenient to Golden Gate Park, Golden Gate Bridge, Union Square, and fine shops and restaurants. The University of California Medical School is nearby. Excellent public transportation is close by.

Casita Blanca ✪
330 EDGEHILL WAY, SAN FRANCISCO, CALIFORNIA 94127

Tel: (415) 564-9339	Pets: No
Host: Joan Bard	Children: No
No. of Rooms: 1 cottage	Smoking: No
No. of Private Baths: 1	Social Drinking: Permitted
Guest Cottage: $80; sleeps 2	Minimum Stay: 2 nights
Open: All year	Foreign Languages: French, Spanish
Breakfast: Continental	

Casita Blanca is a guest cottage perched high on a hill, not far from Golden Gate Park. In this delightful hideaway, nestled among giant trees, you'll find twin beds, a private bath with a stall shower, and a complete kitchen stocked for your convenience with all the necessary items. If you tire of sightseeing and shopping, then just curl up in front of the little fireplace, have a glass of wine, and listen to the birds singing outside. Joan also offers accommodations in Carmel-by-the-Sea, Lake Tahoe, Sonoma, Palm Desert, and Maui.

Haus Kleebauer ✪
225 CLIPPER STREET, SAN FRANCISCO, CALIFORNIA 94114

Tel: (415) 821-3866	Open: All year
Best Time to Call: Anytime	Breakfast: Full
Hosts: Don Kern and Howard Johnson	Credit Cards: AMEX, MC, VISA
Location: In San Francisco	Pets: Sometimes
No. of Rooms: 1	Children: Welcome
No. of Private Baths: 1	Smoking: No
Double p/b: $65	Social Drinking: Permitted
Single p/b: $65	Minimum Stay: 2 nights, June to Sept.
Suites: $85	

Haus Kleebauer is a storybook-like Victorian home with all the charm of San Francisco. Built in 1892 by Frederick Kleebauer and his sons, the house retains all of its original beauty. Stained and etched glass windows, elaborate exterior trim, and manicured gardens transport you back to an earlier age of refined elegance and charm. Haus Kleebauer is conveniently located in one of San Francisco's premier neighborhoods, Noe Valley. As one of the city's first suburbs, "the Valley" offers a splendid display of original Victorian architecture. Within walking distance you will find many interesting shops, galler-

ies, restaurants, and coffee houses. Just minutes away by streetcar or bus, you will find all the major tourist attractions that have made San Francisco America's favorite city! For our hearing-impaired friends, Don knows sign language.

Rancho San Gregorio ✪
ROUTE 1, BOX 54, SAN GREGORIO, CALIFORNIA 94074

Tel: **(415) 747-0810; fax: (415) 747-0184**
Hosts: **Bud and Lee Raynor**
Location: **35 mi. S of San Francisco**
No. of Rooms: **3**
No. of Private Baths: **3**
Double/pb: **$65–$80**
Suite: **$135**

Open: **All year**
Reduced Rates: **Available**
Breakfast: **Full**
Pets: **No**
Children: **Welcome**
Smoking: **No**
Social Drinking: **Permitted**
Airport/Station Pickup: **Yes**

Graceful arches and bright stucco characterize this Spanish Mission home set on 15 wooded acres. Rooms are decorated with American antiques and family pieces. Your hosts, Bud and Lee, are glad to share a snack and a beverage. A full feast features eggs or pancakes, fresh fruit and breads, and a variety of meats. The atmosphere is relaxing, and guests are welcome to borrow a book from the library, or play the organ. Rancho San Gregorio is close to the beach, horseback riding, and golf. San Francisco, Half Moon Bay, and a variety of state parks and recreational areas are within an hour's drive. For those of you who don't mind paying a higher rate, 2 rooms are available.

Madison Street Inn ✪
1390 MADISON STREET, SANTA CLARA, CALIFORNIA 95050

Tel: (800) 491-5541	Open: **All year**
Hosts: **Theresa and Ralph Wigginton**	Reduced Rates: **15% seniors**
Location: **1½ mi. from Rte. 880**	Breakfast: **Full**
No. of Rooms: **5**	Other Meals: **Available**
No. of Private Baths: **3**	Credit Cards: **AMEX, DC, MC, VISA**
Max. No. Sharing Bath: **4**	Pets: **No**
Double/pb: **$75–$85**	Children: **Welcome**
Double/sb: **$60**	Smoking: **No**
Single/sb: **$60**	Social Drinking: **Permitted**

This restored, vintage Queen Anne is furnished with oriental rugs and museum-quality antiques, including brass beds and tubs-for-two. Landscaped gardens, a swimming pool, and a hot tub grace the grounds, and a sunny meeting room is available for business gatherings. Belgian waffles or eggs Benedict are often on the breakfast menu. Exciting dinners can be arranged, prepared by Ralph, an accomplished cook. It is convenient to Santa Clara University and San Jose State University.

SAN LUIS OBISPO AREA

Megan's Friends B&B Reservation Service
1776 ROYAL WAY, SAN LUIS OBISPO, CALIFORNIA 93405

Tel: (805) 544-4406	Osos, Morro Bay, Paso Robles, San
Best Time to Call: **Noon–4 PM; 6–10 PM; Mon.–Sat.**	Luis Obispo, Solvang, Sunset Palisades
Coordinator: **Joyce Segor**	Rates (Single/Double):
States/Regions Covered: **Arroyo Grande, Baywood Park, Cambria, Los**	Average: **$50–$85 / $55–$85**
	Luxury: **$100–$125**

Joyce has exclusive listings no other reservation agency has. She is sure to accommodate you in a B&B best suited to your interests and purse; these range from a contemporary showplace to a cozy country cottage. A $10 onetime membership fee, for which you receive a detailed list describing the accommodations, is required. Local attractions include the beaches, wineries, farmers market, and Hearst Castle. Transatlantic travelers take note: through her association with an English B&B reservation service, Joyce can provide clients with lodging in the central London area west or north of Hyde Park and Kensington Gardens. Call or write for more information.

Baywood Bed & Breakfast Inn ✪
1370 SECOND STREET, BAYWOOD PARK, CALIFORNIA 93402

Tel: (805) 528-8888
Best Time to Call: 8 AM–8 PM
Hosts: Pat and Alex Benson and
  Barbie Porter
Location: 12 mi. W of San Luis Obispo
No. of Rooms: 15
No. of Private Baths: 15
Double/pb: $80–$140
Suites: $120–$140
Open: All year

Reduced Rates: Available
Breakfast: Full
Other Meals: Available
Credit Cards: MC, VISA
Pets: No
Children: Welcome
Smoking: No
Social Drinking: Permitted
Minimum Stay: 2 days on holiday
  weekends

This waterfront establishment lies on a tiny peninsula that projects into Morro Bay. Outdoor types will find plenty to do here; the options include kayaking, golfing, hiking, bicycling, and picnicking. Several shops and restaurants are right in town, and Montano De Oro State Park, San Luis Obispo, and Hearst Castle are only minutes away. Each Baywood suite has bay views, cozy seating areas, and a wood-burning fireplace. Guests are treated to afternoon wine and cheese, room tours, and breakfast in bed.

Gerarda's Bed & Breakfast ✪
1056 BAY OAKS DRIVE, LOS OSOS, CALIFORNIA 93402

Tel: (805) 534-0834
Host: Gerarda Ondang
Location: 10 mi. from Hwy. 101
No. of Rooms: 3
No. of Private Baths: 1
Max. No. Sharing Bath: 4
Double/pb: $41.34
Single/pb: $26.50
Double/sb: $41.34

Single/sb: $26.50
Open: All year
Breakfast: Full
Pets: Welcome
Children: Welcome
Smoking: No
Social Drinking: Permitted
Airport/Station Pickup: Yes
Foreign Languages: Dutch, Indonesian

When you stay at Gerarda's, you are in for a veritable Dutch treat! Located in a pleasant, quiet neighborhood, the house is surrounded by interesting landscaping and lovely flower beds. This is a simple home comfortably furnished, with charm and warmth. Breakfast features Dutch delicacies such as honeycake, jams, and breads. Hearst Castle, Morro Bay, and San Luis Obispo are within a half hour's drive. Gerarda has thoughtfully placed a TV in each guest bedroom.

SANTA BARBARA AREA

Carpinteria Beach Condo ✪
1825 CRAVENS LANE, CARPINTERIA, CALIFORNIA 93013

Tel: (805) 684-1579	Breakfast: Continental
Best Time to Call: 7 AM–9 PM	Pets: No
Hosts: Bev and Don Schroeder	Children: Welcome
Location: 11 mi. SE of Santa Barbara	Smoking: No
Guest Condo: $60–$75; sleeps 2 to 4	Social Drinking: Permitted
Open: All year	Station Pickup: Yes
Reduced Rates: Available	

You may view majestic mountains from this one-bedroom condo across the street from the beach. If you tire of the ocean, there is also a swimming pool. Play a set of tennis at the local Polo and Racquet Club, visit your hosts' avocado and lemon ranch less than two miles away, or take a ten-minute drive into Santa Barbara. Breakfast is a do-it-yourself affair in the condo's complete minikitchen.

Long's Seaview Bed & Breakfast ✪
317 PIEDMONT ROAD, SANTA BARBARA, CALIFORNIA 93105

Tel: (805) 687-2947	Open: All year
Best Time to Call: Before 6 PM	Breakfast: Full
Host: LaVerne Long	Pets: No
Location: 1½ mi. from Hwy. 101	Children: No
No. of Rooms: 1	Smoking: No
No. of Private Baths: 1	Social Drinking: Permitted
Double/pb: $75–$79	Airport/Station Pickup: Yes
Single/pb: $75	

Overlooking Santa Barbara's prestigious north side, this ranch-style home is in a quiet, residential neighborhood. Breakfast is usually served on the patio, where you can see the ocean, Channel Islands, and citrus orchards. Convenient to the beach, Solvang, and Santa Ynez Valley, the large, airy bedroom is cheerfully furnished with antiques and king-size bed. The breakfast menu varies from Southern dishes to Mexican specialties.

Ocean View House ✪
P.O. BOX 3373, SANTA BARBARA, CALIFORNIA 93130

Tel: (805) 966-6659	Open: All year
Best Time to Call: 8 AM–5 PM	Breakfast: Continental
Hosts: Bill and Carolyn Canfield	Pets: Sometimes
Location: 2 mi. from Hwy. 101	Children: Welcome
No. of Rooms: 2	Smoking: No
No. of Private Baths: 1	Social Drinking: Permitted
Double/pb: $60	Airport/Station Pickup: Yes
Suite: $80 for 4	Minimum Stay: 2 nights

This California ranch house features a guest room furnished with a queen-size bed and antiques. The adjoining paneled den, with double-bed divan and TV, is available together with the guest room as a suite. While you relax on the patio, you can look out at the sailboats on the ocean. It's a short walk to the beach and local shops. There is a $10 surcharge for one-night stays.

SEQUOIA AREA

Kern River Inn Bed & Breakfast ✪
P.O. BOX 1725, 119 KERN RIVER DRIVE, KERNVILLE, CALIFORNIA 93238

Tel: **(619) 376-6750**	Open: **All year**
Best Time to Call: **8 AM–8 PM**	Reduced Rates: **Available**
Hosts: **Jack and Carita Prestwich**	Breakfast: **Full**
Location: **50 mi. NE of Bakersfield**	Credit Cards: **MC, VISA**
No. of Rooms: **6**	Pets: **No**
No. of Private Baths: **6**	Children: **Welcome**
Double/pb: **$79–$89**	Smoking: **No**
Single/pb: **$69–$79**	Social Drinking: **Permitted**

Stay in a charming riverfront B&B in a quaint Western town within Sequoia National Forest. Carita and Jack specialize in romantic, relaxing getaways. Nearby activities include golf, hiking, biking, whitewater rafting, downhill skiing, and year-round fishing in front of the inn. It's an easy stroll to shops, restaurants, and parks, and a short drive to the giant redwood trees. Your hosts love to fish and hike and can direct you to some of their favorite locations.

COLORADO

Fort Collins •

Estes Park •   • Greeley

Brighton

Winter Park   Arvada • Westminster

Glenwood Springs •   Silverthorne   • • Denver

Vail •   • •   • Lakewood

Georgetown Golden

Grand Junction   Snowmass • •   • Breckenridge

•   Aspen • Minturn

• Cedaredge   • Buena Vista   Manitou Springs

• •

• Gunnison   • Nathrop   Colorado Springs

Ouray •

• Silverton

Durango •

On Golden Pond Bed & Breakfast ✪
7831 ELDRIDGE, ARVADA, COLORADO 80005

Tel: **(303) 424-2296**
Best Time to Call: **Anytime**
Hosts: **John and Kathy Kula**
Location: **15 mi. W of Denver**
No. of Rooms: **5**
No. of Private Baths: **5**
Double/pb: **$50–$80**
Single/pb: **$40–$70**
Suites: **$80–$100**
Open: **All year**

Reduced Rates: **10% Mar., Apr., Nov.;**
  midweek; seniors, families
Breakfast: **Full**
Credit Cards: **MC, VISA**
Pets: **Sometimes**
Children: **Welcome**
Smoking: **No**
Social Drinking: **Permitted**
Airport/Station Pickup: **Yes**
Foreign Languages: **German**

A secluded retreat tucked into the Rocky Mountain foothills, this custom-built, two-story brick home has dramatic views of mountains, prairies, and downtown Denver. Birds and other wildlife are drawn to the ten-acre grounds, which have a fishing pond and hiking trails. After a full breakfast, stroll along the garden path, bicycle by the creek, swim laps in the pool, or ride horses into the foothills. Then join John and Kathy for a late afternoon kaffeeklatsch. Conclude the day with a soak in the hot tub.

Cotten House ✪
102 SOUTH FRENCH STREET, P.O. BOX 387, BRECKENRIDGE, COLORADO 80424

Tel: **(303) 453-5509**	Breakfast: **Full**
Hosts: **Peter and Georgette Contos**	Other Meals: **Available**
Location: **85 mi. W of Denver**	Pets: **No**
No. of Rooms: **2**	Children: **Welcome**
No. of Private Baths: **1**	Smoking: **No**
Max. No. Sharing Bath: **4**	Social Drinking: **Permitted**
Double/sb: **$60–$75**	Foreign Languages: **Greek, French**
Open: **All year**	

Get the feel of Breckenridge's mining days in this restored 1886 Victorian listed on the National Historic Register. Peter and Georgette can tell you about their town's past with the help of period photographs mounted on their walls. The common room—equipped with a TV, VCR, books, and games—is a favorite gathering place, but shopping, restaurants, and evening entertainments will lure you to Main Street, two blocks away. Breckenridge's stunning mountain setting is appealing throughout the year. Admire wildflowers in the spring, attend special summer events, see the aspens change color in the fall; higher rates apply in the winter, when you have access to cold weather activities from the free shuttle bus that stops at the B&B's front door. For those of you who don't mind paying a higher rate, 1 room is available.

Country Gardens ✪
1619 EAST 136TH AVENUE, BRIGHTON, COLORADO 80601

Tel: **(303) 451-1724**	Open: **All year**
Best Time to Call: **12–9 PM**	Reduced Rates: **5% Seniors**
Host(s): **Arlie and Donna Munsie**	Breakfast: **Full**
Location: **13 mi. N of Denver**	Credit Cards: **MC, VISA**
No. of Rooms: **4**	Pets: **No**
No. of Private Baths: **4**	Children: **Welcome, over 12**
Double p/b: **$60–$70**	Smoking: **No**
Single p/b: **$50–$60**	Social Drinking: **Permitted**
Suites: **$95**	Airport/Station Pickup: **Yes**

Picture a Victorian home on four acres with lots of natural landscaping and a panoramic mountain view. This B&B is lovingly decorated with family antiques and country furnishings throughout. Enjoy the rock garden with its waterfall, goldfish pond and flowers, as well as other gardens with walking paths and sitting areas. Relax in the outdoor hot tub or lovely Victorian gazebo. Sit or swing on the covered wraparound porch. A typical country breakfast includes cream cheese pecan waffles with fruit toppings, sausage, homemade muffins, and juice. Country Gardens is one block from an 18-hole municipal golf course and walking/riding trails, one hour from many mountain attractions including old mining towns with legalized gambling.

Trout City Inn ○
BOX 431, BUENA VISTA, COLORADO 81211

Tel: **(719) 495-0348**	Open: **June 1–Oct. 1**
Best Time to Call: **After 6 PM**	Breakfast: **Full**
Hosts: **Juel and Irene Kjeldsen**	Other Meals: **Available**
Location: **5 mi. E of Buena Vista on Hwy. 24**	Credit Cards: **MC, VISA**
	Pets: **No**
No. of Rooms: **4**	Children: **Welcome, over 10**
No. of Private Baths: **4**	Smoking: **No**
Double/pb: **$35–$40**	Social Drinking: **Permitted**

Trout City Inn is a historic site on the famous South Park Narrow Gauge Railroad, and is located at the edge of a trout stream. It is an accurate reconstruction of a mountain railroad depot, with authentic private rail cars containing Pullman berths. The depot rooms feature Victorian decor, high ceilings, and four-poster or brass beds. Glass doors open onto a deck with views of the 14,000-foot peaks of the Continental Divide. Hiking, biking, panning for gold, and fly-fishing are within steps of the front door; white-water rafting is minutes away.

Cedars' Edge Llamas Bed and Breakfast ○
2169 HIGHWAY 65, CEDAREDGE, COLORADO 81413

Tel: **(303) 856-6836**	Open: **All year**
Hosts: **Ray and Gail Record**	Breakfast: **Full**
Location: **50 mi. E of Grand Junction**	Pets: **No**
No. of Rooms: **4**	Children: **Welcome**
No. of Private Baths: **4**	Smoking: **No**
Double/pb: **$45–$75**	Social Drinking: **Permitted**
Single/pb: **$35–$65**	Airport/Station Pickup: **Yes**

Nestled on the southern slope of the Grand Mesa, this modern cedar home offers a panoramic view of several mountain ranges, plus the unique opportunity to share life on a llama-breeding ranch. The accommodations are immaculate. Cheerful rooms are tastefully decorated in pastel shades, with exposed beams, hanging plants, and light streaming in from many windows. Sportsmen and sportswomen can fish for trout, hunt deer and elk, or go cross-country and downhill skiing. After a filling breakfast, guests can join Ray and Gail in feeding or grooming well-behaved four-footed friends—a rewarding experience for all.

Timberline Bed & Breakfast ✪
2457 U50 ROAD, CEDAREDGE, COLORADO 81413

Tel: (303) 856-7379	Single/pb: $30
Best Time to Call: Mornings or evenings	Open: All year
	Breakfast: Continental
Hosts: Al and Shirley Richardson	Pets: Yes
Location: 60 mi. E of Grand Junction	Children: Welcome
No. of Rooms: 1	Smoking: No
No. of Private Baths: 1	Social Drinking: Permitted
Double/pb: $40	Airport/Station Pickup: Yes

Set on a hillside at the foot of Grand Mesa, this B&B occupies the ground floor of a country home surrounded by pinyon, oak, and juniper trees. The three-room suite has a queen-size bed, living room, woodburning stove, and a fully equipped kitchen. Guests may while away the hours with fishing, hiking, boating, and cross-country and downhill skiing. Timberline lies within easy driving distance of Powderhorn Ski Resort, Black Canyon of the Gunnison, Colorado National Monument, and Curecanti National Recreation Area.

Holden House—1902 Victorian Bed & Breakfast Inn
1102 WEST PIKES PEAK AVENUE, COLORADO SPRINGS, COLORADO 80904

Tel: (719) 471-3980	Breakfast: Full
Best Time to Call: 9 AM–9 PM	Credit Cards: AMEX, DC, DISC, MC, VISA
Hosts: Sallie and Welling Clark	Pets: No
No. of Rooms: 6	Children: No
No. of Private Baths: 6	Smoking: No
Double/pb: $70	Social Drinking: Permitted
Suites: $95–$105	
Open: All year	

Built by Isabel Holden, this 1902 storybook Victorian and 1906 carriage house are centrally located near historic Old Colorado City. The inn, lovingly restored by the Clarks in 1985, is filled with antiques and family heirlooms. Named for mining towns, guest rooms are furnished with queen beds, period furnishings, and down pillows. The inn also boasts four romantic suites with tubs for two, mountain views, fireplaces, and more! Gourmet breakfasts, served in summer on the veranda, might include carob chip muffins, Sallie's famous Eggs Fiesta, fresh fruit, gourmet coffee, tea, and juice. Complimentary refreshments, homemade cookies, and turndown service are just some of the Holden House's special touches. Sallie and Welling will be happy to help in planning your itinerary around the many activities in the Pikes Peak Region. Friendly cats Mingtoy and Muffin are in residence.

The Painted Lady Bed & Breakfast Inn ✪
1318 WEST COLORADO AVENUE, COLORADO SPRINGS, COLORADO 80904

Tel: (719) 473-3165	Open: All year
Best Time to Call: After 5 PM	Reduced Rates: 10% seniors
Hosts: Valerie and Zan Maslowski	Breakfast: Full
No. of Rooms: 4	Credit Cards: DISC, MC, VISA
No. of Private Baths: 2	Pets: No
Max. No. Sharing Bath: 4	Children: Welcome, Over 10
Double/pb: $65–$95	Smoking: No
Double/sb: $55–$65	Social Drinking: Permitted

This restored 1894 Victorian home is complete with gingerbread trim, wraparound porches, coach lights, and wonderful mountain views. Inside, the guest rooms feature lace curtains and period furnishings. One room includes a clawfooted "tub for two" for that extra bit of pampering. The common rooms are bright and inviting. A hearty breakfast will ready you for a full day of business, sight-seeing in the Pike's Peak area, or for shopping and browsing just blocks away in historic Old Colorado City. The resident cat will be on hand to greet you, provide a homey atmosphere, and of course, beg for a tummy rub!

The Elizabeth Anne B&B ✪
P.O. BOX 1051, CRESTED BUTTE, COLORADO 81224

Tel: (303) 349-0147	Credit Cards: MC, VISA
Hosts: Carl and Judy Jones	Pets: No
Location: 225 mi. SW of Denver	Children: Welcome, over 6 (large room only)
No. of Rooms: 4	Smoking: No
No. of Private Baths: 4	Social Drinking: Permitted
Double/pb: $69–$85	Minimum Stay: 2 days winter weekends
Single/pb: $58–$68	Airport Pickup: Yes
Open: June 10–Oct. 15; Nov. 15–Apr. 15	
Breakfast: Full	

The Elizabeth Anne is in the National Historic District of Crested Butte, an 1880s mining town. This new Victorian home echoes the warmth and charm of Crested Butte's past. The common areas are decorated with Queen Anne furniture, and the bedrooms have a Victorian appeal of their own. Other amenities are a soothing hot tub, guest refrigerator, and bicycle and ski storage. Recreational opportunities abound, with Nordic and Alpine skiing in the winter. Summer offers mountain biking, hiking, fishing, golfing, and horseback riding. Crested Butte also has a myriad of shops and gourmet restaurants. Your hosts, Carl and Judy, who recently retired from engineering and nursing careers, invite you to come and share their mountain experience.

Queen Anne Bed & Breakfast Inn ✪
2147 TREMONT PLACE, DENVER, COLORADO 80205

Tel: (303) 296-6666; (800) 432-INNS
[4667]; FAX 296-2151
Best Time to Call: Until 9 PM
Host: Tom King
No. of Rooms: 14
No. of Private Baths: 14
Double/pb: $75–$155
Open: All year

Breakfast: Full
Credit Cards: AMEX, DC, DISC, MC,
VISA
Pets: No
Children: Welcome, over 12
Smoking: No
Social Drinking: Permitted

Located in the residential Clements Historic District, this three-story house, built in 1879, faces Benedict Fountain Park. Decorated in the Queen Anne style, the luxurious bedrooms offer mountain or city views along with such touches as heirloom antiques, air-conditioning, and writing desks. Fine art, good books, and unobtrusive chamber music provide a lovely backdrop. A generous breakfast is served, including seasonal fruits, assorted breads, juice, granola, and a special blend of coffee. The Central Business District, museums, shopping, and diverse restaurants are within walking distance. You are always welcome to help yourself to fruit, candy, and soft drinks.

Country Sunshine B&B ✪
35130 HIGHWAY 550 NORTH, DURANGO, COLORADO 81301

Tel: **(303) 247-2853; (800) 383-2853**
Best Time to Call: **9 AM–6 PM**
Hosts: **Jim and Jill Anderson**
No. of Rooms: **6**
No. of Private Baths: **6**
Double/pb: **$77**
Single/pb: **$72**

Open: **All year**
Breakfast: **Full**
Credit Cards: **MC, VISA**
Pets: **No**
Children: **Welcome, over 5**
Smoking: **No**
Social Drinking: **Permitted**

From this spacious ranch home nestled below rocky bluffs, there's a spectacular view of the San Juan Mountains. In summer, breakfast of homemade breads, jams, and blackberry pancakes with pure maple syrup is served on the large deck in view of the narrow-gauge train. In cooler weather, it is set family style in front of the dining room's wood stove.

The Leland House Bed & Breakfast Suites
721 EAST SECOND AVENUE, DURANGO, COLORADO 81301

Tel: **(303) 385-1920; (800) 664-1920**
Best Time to Call: **Days**
Host(s): **Kirk Komick**
Location: **350 mi. NW of Denver**
No. of Rooms: **10**
No. of Private Baths: **10**
Double p/b: **$85–$95**
Suites: **$125–$175**
Open: **All year**

Reduced Rates: **Available**
Breakfast: **Full**
Other Meals: **Available**
Credit Cards: **MC, VISA**
Pets: **No**
Children: **Welcome**
Smoking: **No**
Social Drinking: **Permitted**

Originally built in 1927 as an apartment house, the Leland House was restored by the Komicks as a B&B in 1993. All rooms have cable TV and telephone service. Six suites have separate living rooms, bedrooms, and full service kitchens; four studios have kitchenettes. The interior is decorated with rustic antiques, accented by photos, memorabilia, and biographies of historic figures associated with the property. Leland House is steps away from Durango's historic downtown district and the Durango-Silverton Narrow-Gauge Railroad Station. Gourmet breakfasts consist of fresh-baked goods, homemade granola, and may include fruit-filled French toast or a Southwestern breakfast burrito.

Lightner Creek Inn Bed and Breakfast ○
999 C.R. 207, DURANGO, COLORADO 81301

Tel: **(303) 259-1226; FAX (303) 259-0732**
Best Time to Call: **9 AM–9 PM**
Host(s): **Richard and Julie Houston**
Location: **3 mi W of Durango**
No. of Rooms: **6**
No. of Private Baths: **4**

Max. No. Sharing Bath: **4**
Double p/b: **$95**
Double s/b: **$85**
Open: **All year**
Reduced Rates: **20% Nov. 1–Apr. 30**
Breakfast: **Full**
Other Meals: **Available**

Credit Cards: **DISC, MC, VISA**
Pets: **No**
Children: **Welcome 10 and over**
Smoking: **No**

Social Drinking: **Permitted**
Minimum Stay: **2 Nights Holiday Weekends**

Nestled among rugged peaks, shimmering streams, and grazing llamas and horses, Lightner Creek Inn's 20-acre pastoral setting deserves to be discovered. This 1903 French countryside home has been exquisitely renovated, providing a casual but elegantly romantic retreat. The inn combines charming Victorian detail with antique furnishings and cozy fireplaces, gourmet breakfasts, and the warmth and hospitality of Julie and Richard. While only four miles from Durango (home of the Durango-Silverton Narrow Gauge train), and an easy ride to Mesa Verde, Purgatory, Telluride, and Wolf Creek, the inn offers excellent mountain trails, trout fishing, and spectacular vistas, making a stay here truly memorable.

Logwood—The Verheyden Inn ☉
35060 HIGHWAY 550, DURANGO, COLORADO 81301

Tel: **(303) 259-4396; (800) 369-4082**
Best Time to Call: **After 10 AM, before 9 PM**
Hosts: **Debby and Greg Verheyden**
Location: **212 mi. NW of Albuquerque, New Mexico**
No. of Rooms: **5**
No. of Private Baths: **5**
Double/pb: **$75–$85**
Single/pb: **$55–$65**

Open: **All year**
Reduced Rates: **$10 less winter single occupancy**
Breakfast: **Full**
Credit Cards: **MC, VISA**
Pets: **No**
Children: **Welcome, over 7**
Smoking: **No**
Social Drinking: **Permitted**
Minimum Stay: **Holidays**

Debby and Greg and their sons Michael and Alan invite you to come home to Logwood—an appealing rough-hewn cedar log retreat with a wraparound porch. All five rooms have that perfect Western style, complete with home-stitched country quilts. A full breakfast and homemade award-winning desserts are served for your enjoyment.

River House B&B ☉
495 ANIMAS VIEW DRIVE, DURANGO, COLORADO 81301

Tel: **(303) 247-4775; (800) 254-4775**
Hosts: **Crystal Carroll and Kate and Lars Enggren**
No. of Rooms: **7**
No. of Private Baths: **7**
Double/pb: **$60–$85**
Single/pb: **$55–$70**
Open: **All year**
Reduced Rates: **10% Mar. and Oct.**

Breakfast: **Full**
Other Meals: **Available**
Credit Cards: **DISC, MC, VISA**
Pets: **No**
Children: **Welcome**
Smoking: **No**
Social Drinking: **Permitted**
Airport/Station Pickup: **Yes**

Healthful gourmet breakfasts are served in this B&B's spectacular, 900-square-foot atrium featuring eight skylights, a hot tub, a goldfish pond, and a cascading waterfall. From the bedrooms, views of the Animas River Valley often include elk, deer, geese, and eagles. Skiers enjoy the warmth of three fireplaces, while the large-screen TV is alive with nature videos. The house is often reserved for weddings, reunions, and retreats. Massage and hypnotherapy are offered by appointment.

Scrubby Oaks Bed & Breakfast ✪
P.O. BOX 1047, DURANGO, COLORADO 81302

Tel: **(303) 247-2176**	Single/pb: **$60**
Best Time to Call: **Early mornings; evenings**	Double/sb: **$65**
	Single/sb: **$50**
Host: **Mary Ann Craig**	Open: **All year**
Location: **4 mi. from junction 160 and 550**	Breakfast: **Full**
	Pets: **No**
No. of Rooms: **7**	Children: **Welcome**
No. of Private Baths: **3**	Smoking: **No**
Max. No. Sharing Bath: **4**	Social Drinking: **Permitted**
Double/pb: **$75**	

There's a quiet country feeling to this two-story home set on 10 acres overlooking the spectacular Animas Valley and surrounding mountains. Trees and gardens frame the patios where breakfast is apt to be served. All breads and preserves are homemade, and strawberry Belgian waffles are a specialty. On chilly mornings, the kitchen fireplace is the cozy backdrop for your wake-up cup of coffee or cocoa. You are made to feel part of the family and are welcome to play pool, take a sauna, read a book, watch a VCR movie, or simply take in the crisp air.

Eagle Cliff House ✪
BOX 4312, ESTES PARK, COLORADO 80517

Tel: **(303) 586-5425**	Guest Cottage: **$75–$85**
Best Time to Call: **Early morning**	Open: **All year**
Hosts: **Nancy and Mike Conrin**	Breakfast: **Full**
Location: **2½ mi. W of Estes Park**	Pets: **No**
No. of Rooms: **3**	Children: **Welcome**
No. of Private Baths: **2**	Smoking: **No**
Max. No. Sharing Bath: **4**	Social Drinking: **Permitted**
Double/pb: **$69**	Minimum Stay: **2 nights, weekends**
Double/sb: **$48**	Airport/Station Pickup: **Yes**

Nancy and Mike are dedicated hikers who live within walking distance of Rocky Mountain National Park, so don't be surprised if they invite you for an afternoon's exploration of their favorite "backyard" trails.

Saturday evening get-togethers are commonplace, especially in the summer. Recreational opportunities abound throughout the year, from golf, tennis, and horseback riding, to cross-country and downhill skiing. One guest room of this woodsy retreat is decorated with mementoes of Mexico and the American Southwest; the cottage and the second guest room are furnished in Victorian style.

Wanek's Lodge at Estes
P.O. BOX 898, 560 PONDEROSA DRIVE, ESTES PARK, COLORADO 80517

Tel: (303) 586-5851	Suite: **$98–$108**
Best Time to Call: **Evenings**	Open: **All year**
Hosts: **Jim and Pat Wanek**	Breakfast: **Continental, plus**
Location: **71 mi. NW of Denver**	Pets: **No**
No. of Rooms: **2**	Children: **Welcome, over 12**
Max. No. Sharing Bath: **4**	Smoking: **No**
Double/sb: **$54–$59**	Social Drinking: **Permitted**
Single/sb: **$40–$45**	

Jim and Pat invite you to share their modern mountain inn, located on a ponderosa pine-covered hillside just minutes away from Rocky Mountain National Park. The wood beams, stone fireplace, plants, and beautiful scenery provide a comfortable and relaxed atmosphere. Former educators, your hosts are people-oriented, and staying with them is like being with old friends.

Elizabeth Street Guest House ✪
202 EAST ELIZABETH, FORT COLLINS, COLORADO 80524

Tel: (303) 493-BEDS [2337]	Single/sb: **$43–$45**
Best Time to Call: **10 AM–7 PM**	Open: **All year**
Hosts: **John and Sheryl Clark**	Breakfast: **Full**
Location: **65 mi. N of Denver**	Credit Cards: **AMEX, MC, VISA (for**
No. of Rooms: **3**	**deposits only)**
Max. No. Sharing Bath: **4**	Pets: **No**
Double/pb: **$65–$75**	Children: **Welcome, over 8**
Single/pb: **$55–$60**	Smoking: **No**
Double/sb: **$55–$60**	Social Drinking: **Permitted**

This completely renovated and restored 1905 brick American four-square has leaded windows and oak woodwork. Family antiques, plants, old quilts, and handmade touches add to its charm. All of the bedrooms have sinks. It is close to historic Old Town Square, Estes Park, Rocky Mountain National Park, and a block away from Colorado State University. John and Sheryl will spoil you with their special brand of hospitality and homemade treats.

Hardy House ✪
605 BROWNELL STREET, GEORGETOWN, COLORADO 80444

Tel: **(303) 569-3388**
Best Time to Call: **After 10 AM**
Hosts: **Carla and Michael Wagner**
Location: **50 mi. W of Denver**
No. of Rooms: **4**
No. of Private Baths: **4**
Double/pb: **$73–$77**
Single/pb: **$63–$67**

Suite: **$102**
Open: **All year**
Breakfast: **Full**
Other Meals: **Available**
Pets: **No**
Children: **No**
Smoking: **No**
Social Drinking: **Permitted**

Back in the 1870s this bright red Victorian, surrounded by a white picket fence, was the home of a blacksmith. Inside you can relax by the potbelly parlor stove, sleep under feather comforters, and wake up to savory breakfast dishes such as waffle cheese strata and coffee cake. Guest quarters range from a two-bedroom suite to rooms with king-size or twin beds. In the evening, the Wagners serve coffee and tea. Hardy House is located in the heart of the Historic District, half a block from the shops of Main Street. It is also close to hiking, skiing, and is walking distance from the Loop Railroad. Perhaps the best way to explore the town is on a six-speed tandem mountain bike, which your hosts will gladly lend.

The Kaiser House ✪
932 COOPER AVENUE, GLENWOOD SPRINGS, COLORADO 81601

Tel: **(303) 945-8827**
Best Time to Call: **9 AM–5 PM**
Hosts: **Ingrid and Glen Eash**
Location: **160 mi. W of Denver**
No. of Rooms: **7**
No. of Private Baths: **7**
Double/pb: **$58–$82**
Single/pb: **$45–$75**
Open: **All year**
Reduced Rates: **10% for 4 nights or more**

Breakfast: **Full**
Credit Cards: **DISC, MC, VISA**
Pets: **No**
Children: **Welcome, over 8**
Smoking: **No**
Social Drinking: **Permitted**
Minimum Stay: **Weekends and holidays**
Station Pickup: **Yes**

Located in the center of Glenwood Springs, the "Spa of the Rockies," Kaiser House combines turn-of-the-century charm and modern comforts. Each bedroom, decorated in Victorian style, has a private bath. In the winter, before hitting the ski slopes, savor a gourmet breakfast in either the spacious dining room or the sunny breakfast nook. In the summer, enjoy brunch on the private patio. From Kaiser House, it's an easy walk to parks, shopping, fine restaurants, and the hot-springs pool and vapor caves.

The Dove Inn
711 14TH STREET, GOLDEN, COLORADO 80401-1906

Tel: **(303) 278-2209**
Hosts: **Sue and Guy Beals**
Location: **10 mi. W of downtown Denver**
No. of Rooms: **6**
No. of Private Baths: **6**
Double/pb: **$55–$70**
Single/pb: **$48–$63**

Open: **All year**
Reduced Rates: **10% weekly**
Breakfast: **Full**
Credit Cards: **AMEX, DC, MC, VISA**
Pets: **No**
Children: **Welcome (crib)**
Smoking: **No**
Social Drinking: **Permitted**

The Dove Inn is a charming Victorian on grounds beautifully landscaped with decks, walkways, and huge trees. The house has many bay windows, dormers, and angled ceilings; each room is individually decorated with pretty wallpapers and Victorian touches. Breakfast specialties such as cinnamon rolls and fresh fruit compotes are served. This delightful inn is located in the foothills of West Denver in one of the state's most beautiful valleys, yet it is just minutes from downtown Denver, historic Golden, and many other Rocky Mountain attractions. No unmarried couples, please.

The Cider House ✪
1126 GRAND AVENUE, GRAND JUNCTION, COLORADO 81501

Tel: **(303) 242-9087**
Host: **Helen Mills**
Location: **2 mi. from I-70**
No. of Rooms: **3**
No. of Private Baths: **1**
Max. No. Sharing Bath: **4**
Double/pb: **$42**
Single/pb: **$32**
Double/sb: **$38**
Single/sb: **$28**

Open: **All year**
Reduced Rates: **Available**
Breakfast: **Full**
Other Meals: **Available**
Credit Cards: **MC**
Pets: **Sometimes**
Children: **Welcome**
Smoking: **Permitted**
Social Drinking: **Permitted**
Airport/Station Pickup: **Yes**

Nestled in the heart of Grand Junction is this two-story frame house built at the start of the century. It is comfortably decorated with period furnishings, old-fashioned wallpapers, and nostalgic touches. Lace curtains and French doors add to the elegance of the living room. Sumptuous breakfasts of locally grown fruit, homemade breads, jams, special waffles, and beverages are served in the adjoining dining room. Nearby attractions include the Grand Mesa, river rafting, dinosaur digs, and some of the best winter skiing in the country.

Sterling House Bed & Breakfast Inn ✪
818 12TH STREET, GREELEY, COLORADO 80631

Tel: (303) 351-8805	Breakfast: Full
Host: Lillian Peeples	Other Meals: Available
Location: 55 mi. N of Denver	Pets: No
No. of Rooms: 2	Children: Welcome, over 10
No. of Private Baths: 2	Smoking: Restricted
Double/pb: $49	Social Drinking: Permitted
Single/pb: $44	Minimum Stay: 2nd week in May only
Open: All year	Airport Pickup: Yes
Reduced Rates: Weekly	Foreign Languages: German

One of Greeley's pioneers, cattle baron and banker Asa Sterling built this home for his family in 1886. Under its current ownership, the house retains its Victorian charm, thanks to the period decor and furniture. Downtown Greeley and the University of Northern Colorado are within walking distance, and it's an easy drive to Rocky Mountain National Park. Guests rave about Lillian's full breakfasts, with specialties like German apple pancakes and crêpes Benedict. Romantic candlelight dinners can also be arranged.

Mary Lawrence Inn ✪
601 NORTH TAYLOR, GUNNISON, COLORADO 81230

Tel: (303) 641-3343	Open: All year
Best Time to Call: 10 AM–12 noon	Breakfast: Full
Host: Jan Goin	Credit Cards: MC, VISA
Location: 195 mi. W and S of Denver	Pets: No
No. of Rooms: 5	Children: Welcome
No. of Private Baths: 5	Smoking: No
Double/pb: $69	Social Drinking: Permitted
Single/pb: $63	Airport/Station Pickup: Yes
Suites: $85–$135; sleep 2–4	

An Italianate frame house with spacious, antique-filled guest rooms and comfortable common areas, the Mary Lawrence Inn is located in a well-kept neighborhood inside Gunnison's city limits. Surrounded by wilderness and Forest Service land, this B&B is a haven for sportspeople of all types; the Black Canyon of the Gunnison, the Alpine Tunnel, the town of Crested Butte, and many spectacular mountain vistas are all within an hour's drive.

The Gourmet Bed & Breakfast ✪
2020 BRENTWOOD, LAKEWOOD, COLORADO 80215

Tel: (303) 237-8395	Location: 8 mi. W of downtown
Best Time to Call: Late afternoon	Denver
Host(s): Carol and Richard Lillard	No. of Rooms: 2

No. of Private Baths: **2**
Double p/b: **$70**
Single p/b: **$60**
Open: **All year**
Breakfast: **Full**

Pets: **No**
Children: **No**
Smoking: **No**
Social Drinking: **Permitted**

Located on the quiet west side of Denver, 15 minutes from downtown, this large English Tudor-style home is furnished with antiques, notably in the country pantry. Choose between the second floor bedroom with brass double bed, or the main floor with king-size bed. Enjoy a full gourmet breakfast served in the cozy kitchen viewing the greenhouse, or on the outside deck under the huge oak tree. The hostess is very informed on area restaurants and local interests. It's one block to park with pool, tennis courts, and jogging path, 1½ hours to major ski areas.

Two Sisters Inn
TEN OTOE PLACE, MANITOU SPRINGS, COLORADO 80829

Tel: **(719) 685-9684**
Best Time to Call: **Evenings**
Hosts: **Sharon Smith and Wendy Goldstein**
Location: **4 mi. W of Colorado Springs**
No. of Rooms: **5**
No. of Private Baths: **3**
Max. No. Sharing Bath: **4**
Double/pb: **$70**

Double/sb: **$59**
Guest Cottage: **$90**
Open: **All year**
Breakfast: **Full**
Credit Cards: **MC, VISA**
Pets: **No**
Children: **Welcome, over 7**
Smoking: **No**
Social Drinking: **Permitted**

Built in 1919 as a boardinghouse, this rose-colored Victorian bungalow has been lovingly restored with four bedrooms and a honeymoon cottage in the back garden. Family collectibles, antiques, and fresh flowers fill the sunny rooms. Your hosts, former caterers, set out a gourmet breakfast of home-baked muffins, freshly ground coffee, fresh fruit, and a hot entrée. The inn is located at the base of Pikes Peak, in Manitou Springs' historic district. Nearby attractions include the Garden of the Gods, the cog railway, the U.S. Air Force Academy, and the Olympic Training Center.

The Eagle River Inn ✪
145 NORTH MAIN, BOX 100, MINTURN, COLORADO 81645

Tel: **(303) 827-5761; (800) 344-1750**
Best Time to Call: **7 AM–10 PM**
Hosts: **Richard Galloway**
Location: **100 mi. W of Denver**
No. of Rooms: **12**
No. of Private Baths: **12**
Double/pb: **$89–$190**
Single/pb: **$69–$170**
Open: **All year**

Reduced Rates: **April–Nov.**
Breakfast: **Full**
Credit Cards: **AMEX, MC, VISA**
Pets: **No**
Children: **Welcome, over 12**
Smoking: **No**
Social Drinking: **Permitted**
Minimum Stay: **5 nights Dec. 26–Jan. 2**

The inn's adobe facade and decor are fashioned after the historic inns of Santa Fe. The living room is warm and cozy, accented by an authentic beehive fireplace and a view of the river. The guest rooms are furnished in a Southwestern mode, each with a king-size bed. Minutes away are the slopes of Vail and Beaver Creek. You are invited to join your hosts for wine and cheese each afternoon. An outdoor Jacuzzi has been added for guests' enjoyment.

Claveau's Streamside Bed and Breakfast ✪
18820 C.R. 162, NATHROP, COLORADO 81236

Tel: (719) 395-2553	Single/pb: $55
Best Time to Call: Before 8 AM; after 6 PM	Open: All year
	Breakfast: Full
Hosts: Denny and Kathy Claveau	Pets: No
Location: 130 mi. SW of Denver	Children: Call in advance
No. of Rooms: 3	Smoking: No
No. of Private Baths: 3	Social Drinking: Permitted
Double/pb: $59	Minimum Stay: Holiday weekends

Located within San Isabel National Forest, Claveau's Streamside Bed and Breakfast is in the shadow of the Rockies' Collegiate Peaks. Mt. Princeton, Mt. Yale, Mt. Harvard, Mt. Oxford, and other challenging peaks beckon all to climb their glistening summits. Wildlife abounds here; deer, elk, bighorn sheep, and mountain goats are your hosts' neighbors. Winter offers downhill and cross-country skiing. Summer offers fishing, hiking, white-water rafting, horseback riding, or just relaxing by a stream. Kathy and Denny are environmentally active outdoor advocates. They look forward to helping guests plan their daily adventures, which may range from fine dining to visiting natural hot springs.

Ouray 1898 House ✪
322 MAIN STREET, P.O. BOX 641, OURAY, COLORADO 81427

Tel: (303) 325-4871	Open: May 25–Sept. 25
Best Time to Call: Afternoons	Breakfast: Full
Hosts: Kathy and Lee Bates	Credit Cards: MC, VISA
Location: On Hwy. 550	Pets: No
No. of Rooms: 3	Children: Welcome, over 5
No. of Private Baths: 3	Smoking: No
Double/pb: $58–$78	Social Drinking: Permitted

This 90-year-old house has been carefully renovated and combines the elegance of the 19th century with the comfortable amenities of the 20th. Each guest room features a spectacular view of the San Juan Mountains from its private deck. Breakfast is beautifully served on antique china. Jeep trips, horseback riding, hiking, browsing in the many quaint shops, and relaxing in the hot springs are but a few of the local diversions.

The Yellow Rose ✪
P.O. BOX 725—#5 MUNN PARK, OURAY, COLORADO 81427

Tel: (303) 325-4175	Reduced Rates: **Available**
Best Time to Call: **8 AM–5 PM**	Breakfast: **Full**
Hosts: **Ed and Edith Roark**	Credit Cards: **MC, VISA**
No. of Rooms: **2**	Pets: **No**
Max. No. Sharing Bath: **4**	Children: **Welcome**
Double/sb: **$50**	Smoking: **No**
Single/sb: **$45**	Social Drinking: **Permitted**
Open: **May 1–Oct. 1**	

From every window, you'll enjoy magnificent views of the San Juan Mountains; step outside in this quiet neighborhood and you'll hear the continuous whisper of the Uncompahgre River. At night, sit by the TV in the common room and catch a movie on cable. The Roarks offer incomparable Texas hospitality, with afternoon tea and a full breakfast of your choice.

Mountain Vista Bed & Breakfast ✪
P.O. BOX 1398, 358 LAGOON LANE, SILVERTHORNE, COLORADO 80498

Tel: (303) 468-7700	Double/sb: **$40–$75**
Best Time to Call: **Evening**	Single/sb: **$40–$75**
Hosts: **Sandy Ruggaber**	Open: **All year**
Location: **60 mi. W of Denver**	Reduced Rates: **10% seniors**
No. of Rooms: **3**	Breakfast: **Full, Continental**
No. of Private Baths: **1**	Pets: **No**
Max. No. Sharing Bath: **4**	Children: **Welcome, over 6**
Double/pb: **$40–$75**	Smoking: **No**
Single/pb: **$40–$75**	Social Drinking: **Permitted**

Mountain Vista offers something for everyone. Since it's surrounded by fine resorts like Keystone, Arapahoe Basin, Copper Mountain, Breckenridge, and Vail, guests can enjoy downhill skiing at its best. In the summer, try hiking, kayaking, cycling, golf, tennis, rafting, and fishing (an outdoor grill is available for you to cook your catch). Visit the factory outlet stores or go to the many concerts, festivals, and cultural events offered throughout Summit County. After a busy day, relax by the fireplace with your favorite drink, watch TV, read, do a puzzle, or retire to a warm comfortable room. You will awaken in the morning to the smell of a hearty homemade breakfast.

Starry Pines ✪
2262 SNOWMASS CREEK ROAD, SNOWMASS, COLORADO 81654

Tel: (303) 927-4202
Best Time to Call: 7 AM–9 AM,
   4 PM–9 PM
Host: Shelley Burke
Location: 200 mi. W of Denver
No. of Rooms: 2
Max. No. Sharing Bath: 4
Double/sb: $80–$85
Single/sb: $75–$85

Apartment: $85, for two
Open: All year
Reduced Rates: Available
Breakfast: Continental
Children: Welcome, over 6
Smoking: No
Social Drinking: Permitted
Minimum Stay: 2 nights ski season

On 70 private acres with its own trout stream and a panoramic view of the Rockies, Starry Pines offers you year-round activities and hospitality. Enjoy the Aspen summer music festival, ballet, and theater. Try hot air balloon rides landing in the B&B's fields, or biking, hiking, jeeping, and riding in the back country. For quieter moments, there's a secluded picnic site with horseshoes and a hammock by the stream. Fall unveils spectacular aspen foliage. Winter and spring bring world-renowned skiing at four mountains only 25 minutes away, plus snowshoeing and cross-country skiing at Starry Pines's own door. At the end of the day, bathe in the hot tub on the patio, then sit around the living room fireplace or watch a movie on the VCR.

The Victorian Lady ✪
4199 WEST 76TH AVENUE, WESTMINISTER, COLORADO 80030

Tel: (303) 428-9829
Best Time to Call: Anytime
Host: Karen Sanders
Location: 10 mi. NW of Denver
No. of Rooms: 2
Max. No. Sharing Bath: 4
Double s/b: $60
Single s/b: $50

Open: All year
Breakfast: Full
Other Meals: Available
Pets: No
Children: Welcome, over 8
Smoking: No
Social Drinking: No
Airport/Station Pickup: Yes

You'll step back in time upon entering the Victorian Lady, where the rooms are filled with lovely reminders of another day. This B&B is ideally located for sightseers: just minutes from downtown Denver and public transportation, it's also near I-70, highway to some of the world's best skiing. Breakfast, served in the gazebo during the summer, may consist of cheese strata, almond poppyseed cake with warmed lemon sauce, or an old Western favorite, hearty biscuits and gravy. There's tea in the afternoon and, at bedtime, snacks that are sure to bring on pleasant dreams.

Alpen Rose ✪
244 FOREST TRAIL, P.O. BOX 769, WINTER PARK, COLORADO 80482

Tel: (303) 726-5039; (800) 531-1373	Reduced Rates: 10% seniors
Best Time to Call: Mornings; evenings	Breakfast: Full
Hosts: Robin and Rupert Sommeraver	Credit Cards: AMEX, MC, VISA
Location: 62 mi. W of Denver	Pets: Sometimes
No. of Rooms: 3	Children: Welcome, over 10
No. of Private Baths: 3	Smoking: No
Double/pb: $65–$85	Social Drinking: Permitted
Single/pb: $45–$85	Airport/Station Pickup: Yes
Open: All year	Foreign Languages: Austrian, German

Surrounded by aspen and pine trees, this woodsy retreat is much like the chalets Rupert remembers from his days as an Austrian Ski School instructor. If you want to go skiing, the Winter Park slopes are just 2 miles away. Hiking, fishing, mountain biking, rafting, and golfing are the main summer activities in this area. Throughout the year, a memorable breakfast with Austrian specialties awaits you in the morning; after the day's adventures, a crackling fire, hot tea, and cookies beckon you home. For those of you who don't mind paying a higher rate, 2 rooms are available.

Engelmann Pines ✪
P.O. BOX 1305, WINTER PARK, COLORADO 80482

Tel: (303) 726-4632; (800) 992-9512	Open: All year
Hosts: Heinz and Margaret Engel	Breakfast: Full
Location: 67 mi. W of Denver	Credit Cards: AMEX, MC, VISA
No. of Rooms: 6	Pets: No
No. of Private Baths: 2	Children: Welcome
Max. No. Sharing Bath: 4	Smoking: No
Double/pb: $65–$85	Social Drinking: Permitted
Single/pb: $55–$75	Airport/Station Pickup: Yes
Double/sb: $45–$75	Foreign Languages: German
Single/sb: $35–$65	

From its Rocky Mountain perch, this spacious modern lodge offers spectacular views of the Continental Divide. Bathrooms are equipped with Jacuzzis, and there is a complete kitchen for guests' use. A free bus ferries skiers from the front door to some of Colorado's best ski slopes; cross-country ski aficionados will find a trail just across the road. When the snow melts, it's time to go golfing, hiking, fishing, and horseback riding. In the morning, eager sportsmen and -women can fill up on marzipan cake, muesli, and fresh fruit crêpes.

CONNECTICUT

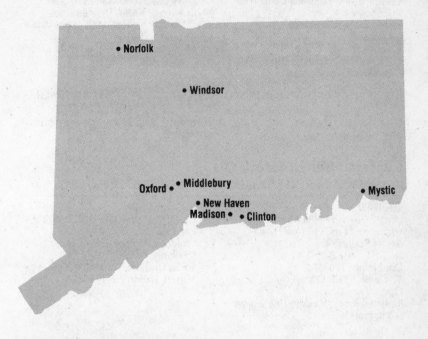

• Norfolk

• Windsor

Oxford • • Middlebury

• New Haven

Madison • • Clinton

• Mystic

Bed and Breakfast, Ltd. ✪
P.O. BOX 216, NEW HAVEN, CONNECTICUT 06513

Tel: (203) 469-3260
Best Time to Call: Sept.–June 5 PM–
  9:30 PM weekdays, weekends
  anytime; July–Aug. anytime
Coordinator: Jack Argenio
States/Regions Covered: Statewide;
  Rhode Island—Providence, Newport

Rates (Single/Double):
  Modest: $45 / $50
  Average: $50 / $60
  Luxury: $60 / $75 and up
Credit Cards: No

Whether you plan to visit one of Connecticut's many fine colleges—including Trinity, Yale, Wesleyan, or the Coast Guard Academy—the Mystic Seaport, picturesque country villages, theater, opera, fine restaurants, it is always pleasant to return to one of Jack's homes-away-from-home with congenial hosts ready to extend warmth and hospitality. They now have 125 listings statewide and offer great variety in host homes and personalized service to guests.

Covered Bridge Bed & Breakfast ✪
P.O. BOX 447A, MAPLE AVENUE, NORFOLK, CONNECTICUT 06058

Tel: **(203) 542-5944; (800) 488-5690**
Best Time to Call: **9 AM–6 PM**
Coordinators: **Hank and Diane Tremblay**
States/Regions Covered:
  Connecticut—Statewide; New York—Amenia, Cherry Plains, Dover Plains; Massachusetts—The Berkshires; Rhode Island

Descriptive Directory: **$3**
Rates (Single/Double):
  Modest: **$60–$80 / $60–$80**
  Average: **$80–$95 / $80–$95**
  Luxury: **$100–$160 / $100–$160**
Credit Cards: **AMEX, MC, VISA**
Minimum Stay: **2 nights holidays, weekends**

If you enjoy historic homes, charming farmhouses, Victorian estates, picture-postcard New England scenery, unsurpassed fall foliage, music festivals, theater, antiquing, auto racing, skiing, white-water rafting, or hiking, call Diane.

Captain Dibbell House ✪
21 COMMERCE STREET, CLINTON, CONNECTICUT 06413

Tel: **(203) 669-1646**
Hosts: **Ellis and Helen Adams**
Location: **21 mi. E of New Haven**
No. of Rooms: **4**
No. of Private Baths: **4**
Double/pb: **$75–$85**
Single/pb: **$65–$75**
Open: **Feb.–Dec.**
Reduced Rates: **Weekly; 10% seniors, 3 or more nights**

Breakfast: **Full**
Credit Cards: **AMEX, DISC, MC, VISA**
Pets: **No**
Children: **Welcome, over 14**
Smoking: **No**
Social Drinking: **Permitted**
Airport/Station Pickup: **Yes**

Ellis and Helen fell in love with this piece of Connecticut shore years ago when they used to come from their home in New York to spend the weekend sailing. They liked it so much, in fact, that they bought this sea captain's home, located just one-half mile from the shore and marinas and a short drive from the town beach, and converted it into a B&B. Clinton is ideally situated for exploring the Connecticut coast; not far away you'll find Hammonassett State Beach, Mystic Seaport and Aquarium, Gillette Castle, the Goodspeed Opera House, the Essex Steam Train, Long Wharf Theater, and Yale. In order to help you enjoy the Connecticut shore they love so much, the Adamses are happy to lend you their bicycles and beach chairs.

Honeysuckle Hill B&B ✪
116 YANKEE PEDDLER PATH, MADISON, CONNECTICUT 06443

Tel: (203) 245-4574	Reduced Rates: Available
Best Time to Call: 5–9 PM	Breakfast: Full
Host: Linda Von Blon	Pets: No
Location: 20 mi. E of New Haven	Children: Welcome, over 6
No. of Rooms: 2	Smoking: No
Max. No. Sharing Bath: 3	Social drinking: Permitted
Double/sb: $85	Minimum Stay: On holiday weekends
Single/sb: $60	Airport/Station Pickup: Yes
Open: May 15–Jan. 15	

Honeysuckle Hill is a large raised ranch located between New Haven and Old Saybrook. This quiet shoreline retreat is close to a variety of activities. The suite, which is good for couples, has a fireplace, queen-size brass bed, sofa, cable TV, and VCR. The smaller room accommodates one guest. A short walk takes you to village boutiques, an art show on the green, and beaches. If you venture farther afield, you can cruise the Connecticut River, tour the Thimble Islands, take in a musical at Goodspeed, or bike to Hammonassett State Park.

Tucker Hill Inn ✪
96 TUCKER HILL ROAD, MIDDLEBURY, CONNECTICUT 06762

Tel: (203) 758-8334; fax: (203) 598-0652	Double/sb: $55–$65
	Open: All year
Best Time to Call: 9 AM–noon; after 4 PM	Reduced Rates: Weekly
	Breakfast: Full
Hosts: Richard and Susan Cebelenski	Credit Cards: MC, VISA
Location: 5 mi. W of Waterbury	Pets: No
No. of Rooms: 4	Children: Welcome
No. of Private Baths: 2	Smoking: No
Max. No. Sharing Bath: 4	Social Drinking: Permitted
Double/pb: $70–$85	

Built in 1920, this large Colonial-style home, just down from the village green, exemplifies warm hospitality and charm. The spacious guest rooms are bright and airy, decorated with fine linens and pretty accessories. Breakfast features such caloric creations as pancakes, waffles, and omelets. Facilities for antiquing, music, theater, golf, tennis, water sports, and cross-country skiing are nearby.

Comolli's House
36 BRUGGEMAN PLACE, MYSTIC, CONNECTICUT 06355

Tel: **(203) 536-8723**	Open: **All year**
Host: **Dorothy M. Comolli**	Breakfast: **Continental**
Location: **1 mi. from I-95, Exit 90**	Pets: **No**
No. of Rooms: **2**	Children: **Welcome, over 12**
No. of Private Baths: **1**	Smoking: **No**
Double/pb: **$85–$95**	Social Drinking: **Permitted**
Single/pb: **$85–$95**	

This immaculate home on a quiet hill overlooking Mystic Seaport is convenient to the sights of Olde Mistick Village and the Aquarium. Dorothy caters to discriminating adults who appreciate a simple, homey atmosphere. The guest rooms are cozy in winter and cool in summer. She is pleased to provide information on sightseeing, sport ing activities, shopping, and restaurants.

Pequot Hotel Bed and Breakfast ⊘
711 COW HILL ROAD, MYSTIC, CONNECTICUT 06355

Tel: **(203) 572-0390**	Reduced Rates: **10% Jan.–Mar.**
Best Time to Call: **8 AM–8 PM**	Breakfast: **Full**
Host: **Nancy Mitchell**	Other Meals: **Available**
Location: **135 mi. NE of New York**	Pets: **Sometimes**
No. of Rooms: **3**	Children: **Welcome, over 10**
No. of Private Baths: **3**	Smoking: **No**
Double/pb: **$85**	Social Drinking: **Permitted**
Suites: **$80**	Airport/Station Pickup: **Yes**
Open: **All year**	

The Pequot Hotel is an authentically restored 1840 stagecoach stop, in the center of the Burnett's Corners Historic District, just 2½ miles from the charming New England seacoast village of Mystic, Connecti-cut. This large, comfortable Greek Revival–style inn is situated on 23 wooded acres convenient to the Mystic Seaport Museum, the Mystic Aquarium, and the new Foxwoods Gambling Casino. At the end of a busy day, guests are free to relax on the large screened porch or in one of the elegant fireplaced parlors. Recommendations and reserva-tions for dinner at one of the area's fine restaurants are provided by the innkeeper, Nancy. In the morning a full country breakfast, includ-ing fresh local fruits and vegetables, is ready when you are. Nancy, a resident for 18 years, has 23 years' experience as an international flight attendant.

Weaver's House ✪
58 GREENWOODS ROAD, NORFOLK, CONNECTICUT 06058

Tel: (203) 542-5108	Open: All year
Hosts: Judy and Arnold Tsukroff	Breakfast: Full
Location: 39 mi. NW of Hartford	Pets: No
No. of Rooms: 4	Children: Welcome
Max. No. Sharing Bath: 4	Smoking: No
Double/sb: $45	Social Drinking: Permitted
Single/sb: $40	Foreign Languages: German

Weaver's House is a turn-of-the-century Victorian facing the Yale Summer School of Music and Art Estate. In the 1930s, it was used as an annex to the Norfolk Inn. The guest rooms are simply decorated with handwoven rag rugs. Your hostess is a talented weaver, who will gladly display her loom for you. There are concerts and art shows in the summer, and two state parks are nearby with blazed hiking trails. Judy offers vegetarian choices at breakfast.

The Old Mill Inn ✪
63 MAPLE STREET, SOMERSVILLE, CONNECTICUT 06072

Tel: (203) 763-1473	Breakfast: Full
Host: Jim and Stephanie D'Amour	Pets: No
Location: 10 mi. S of Springfield, Mass.	Children: No
No. of Rooms: 5	Smoking: Restricted
Max. No. Sharing Bath: 2	Social Drinking: Permitted
Double/sb: $75–$85	Airport/Station Pickup: Yes
Open: All year	

This gracious Greek Revival home, which dates to the 1850s, has a private beach on the Scantic River, so you can loll in a hammock, canoe, or fish to your heart's content. Inside you'll find spacious bedrooms stocked with down comforters, hooded robes, bath sheets, fresh fruit, and purified water. Every evening, hors d'oeuvres are set out in the parlor. Gourmet breakfasts are served either in the dining room, which has hand-painted walls or, at your request, in your own room. For diversion, visit the fun room, with its board games, darts, cable TV, electronic games, and wet bar. A brief drive will take you to golf, the Basketball Hall of Fame, museums, antique shops, and restaurants. Or borrow your hosts' bicycles for a day of touring and end it with a soak in the spa.

The Charles R. Hart House ✪
1046 WINDSOR AVENUE, WINDSOR, CONNECTICUT 06095

Tel: **(203) 688-5555**
Best Time to Call: **8–10 AM, 4–8 PM**
Hosts: **Dorothy and Bob McAllister**
Location: **6 mi. N of Hartford**
No. of Rooms: **3**
No. of Private Baths: **3**
Double/pb: **$75–$85**
Single/pb: **$65–$75**

Open: **All year**
Breakfast: **Full**
Pets: **No**
Children: **Welcome, over 12**
Smoking: **No**
Social Drinking: **Permitted**
Station Pickup: **Yes**

Hartford merchant Charles Hart added luxurious wallcoverings, ceramic tiled fireplaces, and an elegant Palladian window to this farmhouse in 1896, some thirty years after it was built. By the 1940s, the property was serving as a pheasant farm. The current owners have restored it and furnished it with exquisite period pieces. You can hear the past as well as see it, thanks to an antique music box. Local cultural sites span many eras, from the Mark Twain House and Old Newgate Prison to the New England Air Museum at Bradley International Airport. Modern distractions include shopping in Hartford and golf at the challenging Tournament Players Course, home of the Greater Hartford Open.

B&B by the Lake ✪
19 DILLON BEACH ROAD, WINSTED, CONNECTICUT 06098

Tel: **(203) 738-0230 May 15–Oct. 15;**
(914) 232-6864 Oct. 15–May 15
Best Time to Call: **Anytime**

Hosts: **Gayle Holt and Anastasio Rossi**
Location: **25 mi. W of Hartford**
No. of Rooms: **3**

No. of Private Baths: **1**
Max. No. Sharing Bath: **4**
Double/pb: **$85**
Double/sb: **$80**
Open: **May 15–Oct. 15**

Reduced Rates: **5% May; 5% seniors**
Breakfast: **Continental, plus**
Pets: **No**
Smoking: **No**
Social Drinking: **Permitted**

Guests will feel at home in this turn-of-the-century rustic lodge overlooking Litchfield County's West Hill Lake. The wraparound porch affords spectacular views of the encircling woods and Connecticut's cleanest lake, which is well-stocked with fish. Borrow the canoe, snooze on our private beach, or enjoy a country walk. Breakfast can be served on the large, lattice-covered dock. In the evening you can watch TV or a movie, unless you prefer to hear Anastasio play Gershwin or Chopin on the concert grand piano. Guests may also enjoy a door-to-door tour of New York City, since Gayle is a licensed tour guide.

For key to listings, see inside front or back cover.

✪ This star means that rates are guaranteed through December 31, 1995, to any guest making a reservation as a result of reading about the B&B in *Bed & Breakfast U.S.A.*—1995 edition.

Important! To avoid misunderstandings, always ask about cancellation policies when booking.

Please enclose a self-addressed, stamped, business-size envelope when contacting reservation services.

For more details on what you can expect in a B&B, see Chapter 1.

Always mention *Bed & Breakfast U.S.A.* when making reservations!

If no B&B is listed in the area you'll be visiting, use the form on page 743 to order a copy of our "List of New B&Bs."

We want to hear from you! Use the form on page 745.

DELAWARE

Claymont •
• Wilmington
• New Castle

Dagsboro •

Darley Manor Inn B&B ✪
3701 PHILADELPHIA PIKE, CLAYMONT, DELAWARE 19703

Tel: (302) 792-2127; (800) 824-4703
Best Time to Call: 11 AM–10 PM
Host(s): Ray and Judith Hester
Location: 7 mi. N of Wilmington
No. of Rooms: 5
No. of Private Baths: 5
Double p/b: $59–$69
Suites: $69–$89
Open: All year

Reduced Rates: Available
Breakfast: Full
Credit Cards: AMEX, MC, VISA
Pets: No
Children: Welcome, over 12
Smoking: No
Social Drinking: Permitted
Minimum Stay: 2 Nights, Christmas
    and Thanksgiving

This 1790's Historic Register Colonial manor house was home to
Victorian America's most famous illustrator, F.O.C. Darley. His work
accompanied the writing of Hawthorne, Cooper, Irving, Poe, Longfellow, Charles Dickens, and others. Dickens stayed here for two weeks
of rest in 1867. The seventeen rooms, including three parlors, are
decorated in 1850's antiques and reproductions. All rooms have air-

conditioning, TV/VCR, full or wall-canopied queen-size beds, and phones; one suite has a working fireplace. Breakfast is served in the dinning room or on the large porch. The Victorian azalea garden, with small fountains, is great for relaxation. All Brandywine Valley attractions are nearby, including Winterthur, Longwood, Brandywine River Museum, Hagley, and historic Philadelphia. Many good restaurants are within five to ten minutes.

Becky's Country Inn ✪
401 MAIN STREET, DAGSBORO, DELAWARE 19939

Tel: **(302) 732-3953**	Open: **All year**
Best Time to Call: **Evenings**	Reduced Rates: **10% seniors**
Hosts: **Bill and Becky Madden**	Breakfast: **Continental, plus**
Location: **9 mi. W of Bethany Beach**	Pets: **No**
No. of Rooms: **3**	Children: **No**
No. of Private Baths: **3**	Smoking: **No**
Double/pb: **$65–$75**	Social Drinking: **Permitted**
Single/pb: **$55**	

The oldest home in Dagsboro, this Colonial house sits on the main street, just nine miles from the beaches—close enough to enjoy all the beach activities and just far enough away to enjoy country quiet. The library is a great place to be if you need to relax by the fireplace with a good book. In the summer, relax by the pool or on the fifty-foot deck. All the bedrooms are done in a warm country atmosphere. Breakfast is served in the dining room, on the deck, or by the pool. Your hosts can direct you to outlet stores, antiquing spots and fine restaurants.

William Penn Guest House ✪
206 DELAWARE STREET, NEW CASTLE, DELAWARE 19720

Tel: **(302) 328-7736**	Single/sb: **$45**
Best Time to Call: **Anytime**	Open: **All year**
Hosts: **Mr. and Mrs. Richard Burwell**	Breakfast: **Continental**
Location: **2 mi. from I-95**	Pets: **No**
No. of Rooms: **4**	Children: **Welcome, over 3**
Max. No. Sharing Bath: **4**	Smoking: **No**
Double/pb: **$70**	Social Drinking: **Permitted**
Double/sb: **$50**	Foreign Languages: **Italian**

If you're a history buff, perhaps a stay in a 1682 house named for William Penn is what you've been seeking. Located in the heart of New Castle's historic district, the accommodations here are most comfortable. A lovely park for strolling and for the children to play in borders the Delaware shore, just two blocks away. The University of Delaware is 15 minutes from the house.

Bed & Breakfast of Delaware ✪
3650 SILVERSIDE ROAD BOX 177, WILMINGTON, DELAWARE 19810

Tel: (302) 479-9500
Best Time to Call: 9 AM–5 PM Mon.–
  Fri.
Coordinator: **Millie Alford**
States/Regions Covered:
  **Delaware—Bridgeville, Dover,
  Laurel, Lewis, Middletown, Milford,
  New Castle, Newark, Odessa,**

**Wilmington; Pennsylvania—Chadds
Ford, Landenberg, Oxford**
Rates (Single/Double):
  Modest: **$35–$55** / —
  Average: **$45 / $65–$75**
  Luxury: **$80 / $90–$120**
Credit Cards: **MC, VISA**

Whether you are vacationing or traveling on business, Bed & Breakfast of Delaware gives you a choice of quality accommodations with a wide range of facilities. Our lifelong knowledge of Delaware and adjacent areas—a region rich in history, recreation, and corporate activity— allows us to place you where you will feel most welcome according to your lifestyle and budget.

The Boulevard Bed & Breakfast ✪
1909 BAYNARD BOULEVARD, WILMINGTON, DELAWARE 19802

Tel: (302) 656-9700
Hosts: **Charles and Judy Powell**
Location: **½ mi. from I-95, Exit 8**
No. of Rooms: **6**
No. of Private Baths: **4**
Max. No. Sharing Bath: **3**
Double/pb: **$70–$75**
Single/pb: **$65**
Double/sb: **$60**
Single/sb: **$55**

Open: **All year**
Reduced Rates: **Corporate**
Breakfast: **Full**
Credit Cards: **AMEX, MC, VISA**
Pets: **No**
Children: **Welcome**
Smoking: **Permitted**
Social Drinking: **Permitted**
Airport/Station Pickup: **Yes**

This beautifully restored city mansion was built in 1913 and has earned a place on the National Register of Historic Places. Upon entering, you'll be struck by the impressive foyer and magnificent staircase, leading to a landing complete with a window seat and large leaded-glass windows flanked by 15-foot-tall fluted columns. Breakfast is served in the formal dining room or on the screened-in porch. Although Baynard Boulevard is a quiet and peaceful street, it's just a short walk away from the downtown business district. Parks are close by, and it's just a short drive to Hagley, Winterthur, the Delaware Natural History or Art Museum; or head for nearby Chadds Ford, Pennsylvania, and the famous Brandywine River Museum.

DISTRICT OF COLUMBIA

Bed & Breakfast Accommodations, Ltd.
P.O. BOX 12011, WASHINGTON, D.C. 20005

Tel: **(202) 328-3510; fax (202) 332-3885**
Best Time to Call: **10 AM–5 PM Mon.–Fri.; 10 AM–1 PM Sat.**
Coordinators: **Anna Earle and Janet Armbruster**

States/Regions Covered: **Washington, D.C.; Virginia and Maryland suburbs**
Rates: (Single/Double):
    Average: **$40–$150 / $50–$150**
Credit Cards: **AMEX, DC, MC, VISA**
Minimum Stay: **2 nights**

This service has a network of 75 homes, apartments, guest houses, and inns. Most of the accommodations are convenient to public transportation. Several of the homes are historic properties. There is a wide range of accommodations, from budget to luxury.

Bed & Breakfast League/Sweet Dreams and Toast ✪
P.O. BOX 9490, WASHINGTON, D.C. 20016

Tel: **(202) 363-7767**
Best Time to Call: **9 AM–5 PM Mon.-
Thurs., 9 AM–1 PM Fri.**
Coordinators: **Martha Black and
Millie Groobey**
States/Regions Covered: **Washington,
D.C.; Virginia—Arlington**

Rates (Single/Double):
  Modest: **$40–$50 / $50–$60**
  Average: **$50–$70 / $60–$80**
  Luxury: **$75–$115 / $85–$130**
Credit Cards: **AMEX, DC, MC, VISA**
Minimum Stay: **2 nights**

Bed & Breakfast League/Sweet Dreams and Toast reservation services
were merged in 1988. They offer accommodations in privately owned
homes and apartments. Many are in historic districts; all are in good,
safe sections of the city within easy walking distance of an excellent
public transportation system. Gracious hosts will cheerfully direct you
to points of interest, monuments, museums, shops, and restaurants.
The office of this service is closed on federal holidays, Thanksgiving,
and Christmas. A $10 fee is charged for each reservation.

A Capitol Place ✪
134 12TH STREET SE, WASHINGTON, D.C. 20003

Tel: **(202) 543-1020**
Best Time to Call: **Anytime**
Hosts: **Jim and Mary Pellettieri**
Location: **½ mi. E of U.S. Capitol
Building**
No. of Rooms: **1**
No. of Private Baths: **1**
Double p/b: **$85**

Open: **All year**
Breakfast: **Full**
Pets: **No**
Children: **No**
Smoking: **No**
Social Drinking: **Permitted**
Minimum Stay: **2 nights**

Stay in a newly renovated, "English basement" apartment, the entire
lower level of a 100-year-old Victorian rowhouse in the historic district
of Capitol Hill, 12 blocks from the U.S. Capitol. The light sunny
quarters have a private entrance, a bay-fronted living room/dining
room, a den with library bed, cable color TV, desk and telephone, a
bedroom with queen-size bed, a modern bath with tub and shower,
and a fully equipped kitchen. The refrigerator is filled with breakfast
makings—juices, fruits, cheeses, homemade breads and cookies. Located in a well established, friendly neighborhood just off Lincoln
Park, the guest apartment is a 7-minute walk from Eastern Market
Metro and the historic Eastern Market with its cafés and antique
stores. Off-street parking is accessible from the apartment's back door.

Hereford House
604 SOUTH CAROLINA AVENUE, S.E., WASHINGTON, D.C. 20003

Tel: **(202) 543-0102**
Host: **Ann Edwards**
Location: **In D.C.**
No. of Rooms: **4**
Ma. No. Sharing Bath: **4**
Double/sb: **$55–$65**
Single/sb: **$40–$55**
Open: **All year**

Reduced Rates: **10% seniors; $5 less
over 8 nights**
Breakfast: **Full**
Pets: **Sometimes**
Children: **Welcome, over 12**
Smoking: **No**
Social Drinking: **Permitted**

Hereford House is a 1915 brick townhouse with original parquet flooring and wood throughout. It is situated on a tree-lined street on historic Capitol Hill, one block from the subway. The U.S. Capitol, Congressional Library, Smithsonian Institute, and restaurants are all within easy walking distance, making Hereford House the perfect location for visitors to the nation's capital. Bountiful cooked English breakfasts are served by your full-time British hostess. Guests share the company of newly made friends (and resident dog) in the living room.

The Stableford Inn ✪
333 CLEVELAND AVENUE, WASHINGTON, D.C. 20008

Tel: **(202) 333-7159; fax: (202) 333-
4086**
Best Time to Call: **8 AM–8 PM**
Host: **Jean Stableford**
No. of Rooms: **4**
No. of Private Baths: **1**
Max. No. Sharing Bath: **4**
Double/pb: **$85**
Double/sb: **$70**

Single/sb: **$65**
Open: **All year**
Breakfast: **Full**
Pets: **No**
Children: **Welcome, over 5**
Smoking: **Restricted**
Social Drinking: **Permitted**
Minimum Stay: **2 nights**

Enjoy the pleasure of staying in a splendid old Georgian home with high ceilings and a lovely central hall. The spacious living and dining rooms contain artworks, antiques, and treasures from around the world. Outside, relax or smoke in a pretty garden patio or on the balcony or porch. The inn is located in Woodley Park, renowned for its beauty, convenience, and safety; it is home to members of Congress and the media. It is a 15-minute walk to the zoo or the metro stop located near the Sheraton and Shoreham hotels, but your hostess is happy to take guests to the subway in the morning. Washington National Cathedral is across the street. A thirty-minute walk leads the visitor to Georgetown or to Dupont Circle along Embassy Row. Public transportation is available in any direction.

FLORIDA

A & A Bed & Breakfast of Florida, Inc. ✪
P.O. BOX 1316, WINTER PARK, FLORIDA 32790

Tel: **(407) 628-0322**
Best Time to Call: **9 AM–6 PM**
Coordinator: **Brunhilde (Bruni) Fehner**
States/Regions Covered: **Orlando area—Disney World, Epcot; Altamonte Springs, Cape Canaveral (Kennedy Space Center), Maitland, New Smyrna Beach, Sea World,**

Winter Park, Delray Beach, Ft. Myers, St. Augustine
Rates (Single/Double):
  Modest: **$35 / $40**
  Average: **$40 / $55**
  Luxury: **$65 / $125**
Credit Cards: **No**
Minimum Stay: **2 nights**

You should allow several days to really savor all this area has to offer. Bruni's hosts will suggest hints on getting the most out of the major attractions, wonderful un-touristy restaurants, and tips on where to shop for unique gifts to take home. All of her homes have a certain "touch of class" to make you delighted with your visit. Rollins College is close by. There is a surcharge of $10 for one-night stays.

Bed & Breakfast Co.—Tropical Florida ✪
P.O. BOX 262, SOUTH MIAMI, FLORIDA 33243

Tel: (305) 661-3270
Best Time to Call: 9 AM–5 PM Mon.– Fri.
Coordinator: Marcella Schaible
States/Regions Covered: Statewide

Rates (Single/Double):
Modest: $35–$38 / $35–$40
Average: $35–$55 / $40–$60
Luxury: $55–$150 / $60–$170
Credit Cards: AMEX, MC, VISA

Native Floridians, Marcella's hosts live in mansions on historic properties, in homes along the ocean and Gulf of Mexico, in woodland retreats, and on private residential islands. They exude Southern hospitality and want you to come stay in their accommodations that range from a charming cottage to a contemporary condo to unhosted accommodations. The decor may be simple or wildly extravagant. Hosts are ready to direct you to famous attractions or to an undiscovered, special restaurant or shop that only a resident knows about. There is a $5 surcharge for each night stayed less than three.

Bed & Breakfast Scenic Florida ✪
P.O. BOX 3385, TALLAHASSEE, FLORIDA 32315-3385

Tel: (904) 386-8196
Best Time to Call: 9 AM–5 PM Mon.– Fri.
Coordinator: Dianne C. Mahlert
States/Regions Covered: Gainesville, Gulf Beaches, Jacksonville, Orlando, St. Petersburg, Tallahassee

Descriptive Directory of B&Bs: Free
Rates (Single/Double):
Modest: $35–$35
Average: $60–$65
Luxury: $125 / $125
Credit Cards: MC, VISA

Bed & Breakfast Scenic Florida specializes in unique accommodations throughout North and Central Florida and beyond. This service's goal is to attract pleasure and business travelers to beautiful Florida and to help them select the best location to meet their needs and tastes. The people at Bed & Breakfast Scenic Florida inspect all locations and can answer very detailed questions about individual room decor and amenities. They are familiar with the cities and towns and can recommend things to do, where to eat, what to see. The service also provides written confirmation and directions to each accommodation.

Open House Bed & Breakfast Registry—Gold Coast ✪
P.O. BOX 3025, PALM BEACH, FLORIDA 33480

Tel: (407) 842-5190
Best Time to Call: Evenings; weekends

Coordinator: Peggy Maxwell
States/Regions Covered: Boca Raton,

Boynton Beach, Delray Beach,
Jupiter, Lake Worth, Lantana, Palm
Beach, Palm Beach Gardens, Singer
Island, West Palm Beach

Rates (Single/Double):
Average: **$40** / **$45–$55**
Luxury: **$50** / **$60–$110**

Peggy's roster includes classic contemporaries as well as beautifully restored mansions in south Florida's historic districts; there's even an ocean villa. Most of the homes boast swimming pools. All are located in the most desirable residential areas. Guest comment cards rave about our hosts' generous hospitality, extending to guided tours of the many local attractions. Special weekly, monthly, and summer rates. Free brochure.

The 1735 House ✪
584 SOUTH FLETCHER, AMELIA ISLAND, FLORIDA 32034

Tel: **(904) 261-5878; (800) 872-8531**
Best Time to Call: **9 AM–6 PM**
Hosts: **Gary and Emily Grable**
Location: **35 mi. NE of Jacksonville**
No. of Rooms: **5 suites**
No. of Private Baths: **5**
Suite: **$75–$175**
Open: **All year**

Reduced Rates: **Weekly; 5% seniors**
Breakfast: **Continental**
Credit Cards: **DISC, MC, VISA**
Pets: **No**
Children: **Welcome, over 6**
Smoking: **Permitted**
Social Drinking: **Permitted**
Airport/Station Pickup: **Yes, local**

This century-old country inn is situated right on the beach of a beautiful North Florida barrier island; each of the suites has an ocean view. A special treat is the free-standing lighthouse with four levels of living area, including two bedrooms and two baths. The decor throughout is wicker and rattan accented with nautical antiques. Breakfast, complete with freshly baked treats from the Grables' galley, is delivered to your suite along with the morning newspaper. Historic Fernandina Beach, with its lovely restored Victorian homes and shops, is nearby. Gary and Emily can suggest boat charters for those who wish to try their skill at landing a big one.

Historic Parker House ✪
427 WEST HICKORY STREET, ARCADIA, FLORIDA 33821

Tel: **(813) 494-2499, (800) 969-2499**
Best Time to Call: **8 AM to 10 PM**
Hosts: **Bob and Shelly Baumann**
Location: **45 mi. E of Sarasota**
No. of Rooms: **3**
No. of Private Baths: **1**
Max. No. Sharing Bath: **4**
Double/pb: **$75**
Single/pb: **$75**
Double/sb: **$60**

Single/sb: **$60**
Open: **All year**
Reduced Rates: **10%**
Breakfast: **Continental**
Credit Cards: **MC, VISA**
Pets: **No**
Children: **No**
Smoking: **No**
Social Drinking: **Permitted**

Once you step inside the Historic Parker House you become acquainted with a much grander, yet simpler life. The 6000-square-foot home is chock full of antiques, old clocks, and Florida's past. The original section of the home dates to the mid 1890s, a large addition was added in 1914 by the original owners, the Parkers, Florida cattle barons. Located in historic downtown Arcadia, recently named one of the one hundred best small towns in America, the home is close to antique and gift shopping and the Peace River for canoeing. Nearby are all of South Central Florida's attractions.

The Barnacle ✪
ROUTE 1, BOX 780A, LONG BEACH ROAD, BIG PINE KEY, FLORIDA 33043

Tel: (305) 872-3298	Open: All year
Best Time to Call: Before 9 PM	Breakfast: Full
Hosts: Wood and Joan Cornell	Pets: No
Location: Mile marker 33	Children: No
No. of Rooms: 4	Smoking: Permitted
No. of Private Baths: 4	Foreign Languages: French
Double/pb: $75–$100	

This ultimate in privacy is this self-contained cottage—a tropical tree house with stained-glass windows and private terrace. Rooms overlook the ocean or the atrium, with its hot tub and lush plants. One room has a private entrance and opens onto the beach. Every detail in and around their home reflects Wood and Joan's taste, attention to detail, and artistic flair. The structure was built to frame their eclectic collection of statuary, tapestries, and art. Their emphasis is on the sun and sea, with warm hospitality offered in abundance. You can snorkel or fish right off "your own" beach. Bahia Honda State Park and Key West are close by.

Bed & Breakfast-on-the-Ocean "Casa Grande" ✪
P.O. BOX 378, BIG PINE KEY, FLORIDA 33043

Tel: (305) 872-2878	Open: All year
Hosts: Jon and Kathleen Threlkeld	Breakfast: Full
Location: 30 mi. E of Key West	Pets: No
No. of Rooms: 3	Children: No
No. of Private Baths: 3	Smoking: Permitted
Double/pb: $85	Social Drinking: Permitted

This spectacular Spanish-style home, facing the ocean, was custom-designed to suit the natural beauty of the Keys. The large landscaped garden patio, with panoramic beach views, is where you'll enjoy Jon and Kathleen's bountiful breakfast. It is also the site of the hot tub/Jacuzzi for relaxing by day or under a moonlit sky. The large and

airy guest rooms are comfortably cooled by Bahama fans or air-conditioning. Key deer and birds abound. From the private beach, you'll enjoy swimming, fishing, snorkeling, bicycling, and jogging. There's a picnic table, gas grill, hammock, and Windsurfer for guests to use, compliments of the gracious hosts.

Canal Cottage Bed & Breakfast
P.O. BOX 430266, BIG PINE KEY, FLORIDA 33043

Tel: **(305) 872-3881**
Best Time to Call: **Evenings**
Hosts: **Dean and Patti Nickless**
Suites: **$85 for 2**
Open: **All year**
Breakfast: **Continental**

Pets: **No**
Children: **Welcome**
Smoking: **Permitted**
Social Drinking: **Permitted**
Minimum Stay: **2 nights**

Get away and relax! You can be self-sufficient in this unusual wood stilt house. Your accommodations are nestled in the trees and consist of a bedroom with a queen-size bed, a bathroom, a living room with sleeping space for two, and a kitchen stocked for your breakfast, which you can prepare at leisure and enjoy on the porch. Take advantage of local diving, snorkeling, and fishing charters, or bring your own boat to launch at the neighborhood ramp and tie it up at your backyard dock. There are bicycles for those so inclined, and a gas grill to cook your catch. You'll probably see a Key deer, too.

Deer Run ✪
LONG BEACH ROAD, P.O. BOX 431, BIG PINE KEY, FLORIDA 33043

Tel: **(305) 872-2015, 872-2800**
Best Time to Call: **Anytime before 10 PM**

Host(s): **Sue Abbott**
Location: **33 mi. E of Key West**
No. of Rooms: **3**

No. of Private Baths: **3**
Double/pb: **$85–$95**
Single/pb: **$75**
Open: **All year**
Breakfast: **Full**
Pets: **No**

Children: **No**
Smoking: **No**
Social Drinking: **Permitted**
Minimum Stay: **2 nights**
Airport/Station Pickup: **Yes**

Deer Run is a Florida Cracker-style home nestled among lush native trees on the ocean. The house is beautifully designed, with skylights, high ceilings, central air-conditioning, and Bahama fans. The decor boasts many paintings, artifacts, and antiques to compliment wicker and rattan furnishings. Upstairs each room has French doors that open onto a large veranda. Breakfast is served outside overlooking the ocean where you may spot Key deer walking along the beach. Looe Key Coral Reef, Bahia Honda State Park, and Key West are all within easy reach, or you can relax and soak up the rays in the free-form deep spa, where there's room for eight.

Florida Keys House ❖
P.O. BOX 431812, BIG PINE KEY, FLORIDA 33043

Tel: **(800) 833-9857**
Best Time to Call: **8 AM–8 PM**
Hosts: **Capt. Dave and Camille Wiley**
Location: **27 mi. E of Key West**
Suites: **$79–$119**
Open: **All year**
Breakfast: **Continental**

Credit Cards: **MC, VISA**
Pets: **No**
Children: **Welcome**
Smoking: **No**
Social Drinking: **Permitted**
Minimum Stay: **2 nights**
Foreign Languages: **French, Spanish**

Set among an abundance of coconut palm trees, your private guest quarters can accommodate up to four people and consist of one or two bedrooms, a bathroom, living room, and large kitchen stocked with breakfast selections which you may prepare at your convenience. Florida Keys House is canal front with a dock where you can fish, swim, barbecue or just relax in the hammock under the shade trees. Dave and Camille also offer snorkeling and diving trips to beautiful Looe Key Reef. Ask about their specialty, "backcountry flats fishing" for tarpon, bonefish and permit in the Great White Heron Wildlife Refuge.

Vacation in Paradise ❖
ROUTE 1, BOX 641, BIG PINE KEY, FLORIDA 33043

Tel: **(305) 872-9009**
Host: **Joan Thoman**
Location: **30 mi. E of Key West**
Guest Cottage: **$85, for two**
Open: **All year**

Breakfast: **Continental**
Pets: **Sometimes**
Children: **Welcome**
Smoking: **Permitted**
Social Drinking: **Permitted**

True to its name, Vacation in Paradise is located six miles from Bahia Honda State Park (one of the best beaches in the country) and the famed Looe Key Reef. This spacious two-bedroom unit sleeps six and has a large kitchen and living room. Joan offers free dockage twenty feet from your door, a barbeque grill for cooking your dinner, and cable TV. Guests can enjoy fishing, scuba diving, snorkeling and the great nightlife in Key West.

Barrier Island Marine B&B ✪
P.O. BOX 175, 221 SEABREEZE COURT, BOCA GRANDE, FLORIDA 33921

Tel: (813) 964-2626	Single/pb: $65
Best Time to Call: 9 AM–9 PM	Open: All year
Hosts: Johnny and Shirley Johnson	Breakfast: Continental
Location: 50 mi. S. of Sarasota	Pets: No
No. of Rooms: 1	Children: Welcome
No. of Private Baths: 1	Smoking: No
Double/pb: $85	Social Drinking: Permitted

Within walking distance of the beach and state park, this Key West-style stilt home has a private (downstairs) bed, bath, kitchen, and patio area. After a day at the beach, guests are welcome to borrow bikes to ride into the village for lunch or dinner at one of the fine local restaurants. After lunch go for a relaxing walk in the village and enjoy the local shops on this historical island. There are public tennis courts, basketball courts, and beautiful local churches. Fishing and sightseeing trips are also available on local charter boats. Come visit, relax, and enjoy nature on this quiet little island.

Cypress House Bed and Breakfast ✪
8545 C.R. 476B, BUSHNELL, FLORIDA 33513

Tel: (904) 568-0909	Suites: $85; sleeps 4
Best Time to Call: 8 AM–10 PM	Open: All year
Hosts: Jan and Walt Fessler and	Reduced Rates: Seniors, 10%
Thelma Schaum	Breakfast: Continental
Location: 50 mi. N of Tampa	Other Meals: Available
No. of Rooms: 2	Pets: No
Max. No. Sharing Bath: 4	Children: Welcome
Double/sb: $50	Smoking: Restricted
Single/sb: $40	Social Drinking: Permitted

A new log home built in the gracious old Florida style, Cypress House is set on wooded farmland. From the oak rockers on the wide wraparound veranda, you can see oak trees draped with moss. The Webster Flea Market (Mondays only) and Brooksville's Christmas House are nearby, and Disney World and Busch Gardens are an hour away. You won't have to travel far to browse for antiques, fish, hike, or go canoeing. To bolster your energy, your hosts offer a generous breakfast buffet, plus coffee and snacks round-the-clock. Your hosts have five horses and offer one to six hour trail rides.

Sprague House Inn & Restaurant ○

125 CENTRAL AVENUE, CRESCENT CITY, FLORIDA 32012

Tel: **(904) 698-2430**	Breakfast: **Full**
Hosts: **Terry and Vena Moyer**	Other Meals: **Available**
Location: **75 mi. N of Orlando**	Credit Cards: **MC, VISA**
No. of Rooms: **5**	Pets: **No**
No. of Private Baths: **5**	Children: **No**
Double/pb: **$60**	Smoking: **No**
Suite: **$75–$125**	Social Drinking: **Permitted**
Open: **All year**	Airport/Station Pickup: **Yes**

A Steamboat Gothic inn, Sprague House Inn has been welcoming guests since 1905. The comfortably air-conditioned guest rooms are highlighted in antiques. Accents of stained glass and handsome woods are found throughout. The wraparound porches both upstairs and down boast rockers and swings from which you may enjoy the views of the lake. A public boat ramp and dock are a stone's throw away. You are welcome to borrow a cane fishing pole (no license required) or grab your net and try your luck at blue crabs. This one-stoplight town, unspoiled by plastic and neon, claims to be "the bass capital of the world." Terry is the gourmet cook for their on-premises restaurant.

Windsong Garden & Art Gallery ○

5570-4 WOODROSE COURT, FORT MYERS, FLORIDA 33907

Tel: **(813) 936-6378**	Breakfast: **Continental**
Host: **Embe Burdick**	Pets: **No**
No. of Rooms: **2**	Children: **No**
No. of Private Baths: **2**	Smoking: **No**
Double/pb: **$55**	Social Drinking: **Permitted**
Suite: **$55**	Minimum Stay: **2 nights**
Open: **All year**	

This modern clear-shake-and-brick town house has a private courtyard and balcony for your enjoyment. The spacious combination bedroom-and-sitting room is most comfortable. Embe's varied interests include arts, crafts, music, and her household cats. It's close to Sanibel and Captiva islands, Ft. Myers Beach, fine shopping, good restaurants, and the University of Florida. You are welcome to use the pool.

Gaver's Bed & Breakfast ✪

301 EAST SIXTH AVENUE, HAVANA, FLORIDA 32333

Tel: **(904) 539-5611**	Breakfast: **Full**
Hosts: **Shirley and Bruce Gaver**	Pets: **No**
Location: **12 mi. N of Tallahassee**	Children: **Welcome, over 8**
No. of Rooms: **2**	Smoking: **No**
No. of Private Baths: **2**	Social Drinking: **Permitted**
Double/pb: **$65–$75**	Airport/Station Pickup: **Yes**
Open: **All year**	

This B&B, situated on a quiet residential street two blocks from the center of town, is a likely stop for collectors—at last count, Havana had thirty antique shops plus many related businesses. Tallahassee, the state capital and home of Florida State University, is only fifteen minutes away by car. A restored 1907 frame house, Gaver's has a large screened porch, and guests are welcome to watch cable TV in the common area. For breakfast, your hosts will design a menu to suit your preferences.

Harrington House B&B Inn ✪

5626 GULF DRIVE, HOLMES BEACH, FLORIDA 34217

Tel: **(813) 778-5444; (813) 778-6335;**	Breakfast: **Full**
fax: **(813) 778-0527**	Credit Cards: **MC, VISA**
Best Time to Call: **Noon–8 PM**	Pets: **No**
Host: **Jo Davis**	Children: **Welcome, over 12**
Location: **40 mi. SW of Tampa**	Smoking: **No**
No. of Rooms: **12**	Social Drinking: **Permitted**
No. of Private Baths: **12**	Minimum Stay: **2 nights weekends,**
Double/pb: **$79–$85**	**Feb.–Apr.**
Open: **All year**	Airport/Station Pickup: **Yes**

Surrounded by tropical foliage and the gulf's blue waters, this gracious Florida home, built in 1925, has the beach for its backyard. Each of the seven eclectically furnished guest rooms has its own charm and character. Relax by the pool, baste on the beach, take a moonlight stroll, or just let the sound of the surf lull you to sleep. Whatever your pleasure, the warm hospitality will ensure that your stay is a memorable one. For those of you who don't mind paying a higher rate, 10 rooms are available.

Meeks B&B on the Gulf Beaches ✪

19418 GULF BOULEVARD, #407, INDIAN SHORES, FLORIDA 34635

Tel: **(813) 596-5424;** fax: **(813) 593-**	Location: **35 min. from Tampa Airport**
0065	No. of Rooms: **4**
Best Time to Call: **7 AM–10 PM**	No. of Private Baths: **3**
Hosts: **Greta and Bob Meeks**	Double/pb: **$50–$60**

Single/pb: **$45–$55**
Suites: **$75–$85**
Open: **All year**
Breakfast: **Full or Continental**

Pets: **No**
Children: **Welcome**
Smoking: **No**
Social Drinking: **Permitted**

Beach! Pool! Sunsets! Enjoy your stay in this beach condo overlooking the Gulf of Mexico. A beach cottage is sometimes available. Choose your breakfast, then bask in the sun, swim in the gulf, and catch spectacular sunsets from your balcony. Dine at nearby seafood restaurants and visit the local seabird sanctuary, sunken gardens, and the Dali Museum. Other nearby attractions are Busch Gardens in Tampa and sponge diving in Tarpon Springs. This B&B is located between Clearwater and St. Petersburg Beach, only two hours from Walt Disney World. Your hostess is a real estate broker.

Bed & Breakfast of Islamorada ✪
81175 OLD HIGHWAY, ISLAMORADA, FLORIDA 33036

Tel: **(305) 664-9321**
Host: **Dottie Saunders**
Location: **87 mi. S of Miami**
No. of Rooms: **2**
No. of Private Baths: **2**
Double/pb: **$50–$60**
Single/pb: **$45**
Open: **All year**

Reduced Rates: **Available**
Breakfast: **Full**
Credit Cards: **MC, VISA**
Pets: **Sometimes**
Children: **Welcome**
Smoking: **Permitted**
Social Drinking: **Permitted**

Make the most of the Florida Keys while staying in this one-story house. Bicycles and snorkeling gear are at your disposal, and sailing trips on a historic old boat can be arranged. John Pennecamp Coral Reef State Park, 40 minutes away, is a great place for snorkeling and diving, and the whole family can ride in the glass-bottomed boats. Your hostess has had a varied career, from cooking on a freighter to selling real estate; she enjoys waterfront activities, gardening, and photography.

Innisfail ✪
134 TIMBER LANE, JUPITER, FLORIDA 33458

Tel: **(407) 744-5905**
Best Time to Call: **Evenings**
Hosts: **Katherine and Luke Van Noorden**
Location: **20 mi. N of Palm Beach**
No. of Rooms: **1**
No. of Private Baths: **1**
Double/pb: **$51–$60**
Open: **All year**

Reduced Rates: **10% weekly; 10% seniors**
Breakfast: **Continental**
Other Meals: **Available**
Pets: **Welcome**
Children: **Yes**
Smoking: **No**
Social Drinking: **Permitted**
Airport/Station Pickup: **Yes**

A contemporary ranch framed by palm trees, Innisfail—Gaelic for "the abode of peace and harmony"—doubles as a gallery. The Van Noordens are sculptors, and guests are welcome to watch them work in their home studio. While you don't have to be an art lover to visit, it helps to be a pet lover; Katherine and Luke's four-footed family comprises four dogs and two cats. Jupiter has wonderful beaches, but you can get an equally good tan lounging by the Van Noordens' swimming pool. In the morning, a Continental breakfast of coffee or tea, fresh citrus fruit, and muffins or cereal is served.

Hibiscus House ✪
345 WEST ENID DRIVE, KEY BISCAYNE, FLORIDA 33149

Tel: (305) 361-2456	Open: All year
Best Time to Call: 9 AM–5 PM	Reduced Rates: May 1–Dec. 15
Hosts: Bernice and Earl Duffy	Breakfast: Full
Location: 10 mi. SE of Miami	Pets: No
No. of Rooms: 2	Children: No
No. of Private Baths: 2	Smoking: Permitted
Double/pb: $65	Social Drinking: Permitted
Single/pb: $60	Minimum Stay: 2 nights

Welcome to an island paradise only 15 minutes from downtown Miami and 20 minutes from Miami International Airport. Key Biscayne features two lushly landscaped parks, a championship golf course, and miles of white sandy beaches; your hosts offer private beach privileges. Tennis courts and bicycle paths are in plentiful supply. Add to this the famous Miami Seaquarium and easy access to Greater Miami's many attractions and you have all of the ingredients for a very pleasant visit.

Lighthouse Bed & Breakfast ✪
13355 SECOND STREET EAST, MADEIRA BEACH, FLORIDA 33708

Tel: (813) 391-0015	Breakfast: Full or Continental
Hosts: Norm and Maggie Lucore	Credit Cards: MC, VISA
Location: 4 mi. W of St. Petersburg	Pets: Sometimes
No. of Rooms: 5	Children: Welcome
No. of Private Baths: 5	Smoking: Permitted
Double/pb: $45–$85	Social Drinking: Permitted
Open: All year	

This contemporary two-story home is just 300 steps, count them, from the Gulf of Mexico's sandy beaches; to the rear of the house is a classic white lighthouse. Feel free to loll about on the private sun deck, soak in the Jacuzzi, and grill dinner on the gas barbecue. Epcot Center, Busch Gardens, Sea World, and MGM tours are among the local attractions. Breakfast offerings, served either in the lighthouse or outside in the gazebo, range from fruit and pastry in summer to omelets and waffles in winter.

Thurston House
851 LAKE AVENUE, MAITLAND, FLORIDA 32751

Tel: **(407) 539-1911**
Best Time to Call: **9 AM–9 PM**
Hosts: **Carole and Joe Ballard**
Location: **5 mi. N of Orlando**
No. of Rooms: **4**
No. of Private Baths: **4**
Double/pb: **$80–$90**
Single/pb: $80–$90
Open: **All year**

Reduced Rates: **10% seniors**
Breakfast: **Continental, plus**
Credit Cards: **AMEX, DISC, MC, VISA**
Pets: **No**
Children: **Welcome, over 12**
Smoking: **No**
Social Drinking: **Permitted**
Minimum Stay: **Holidays**

Thurston House, though only 5 miles north of downtown Orlando, provides a quiet escape from the world. The 1885 Queen Anne Victorian home has been lovingly restored and boasts beautiful pine woodwork and floors. All rooms are furnished in an eclectic blend of country antiques and reproductions. The setting—five acres overlooking Lake Eulalia—adds to the feeling of tranquility. Guests sit rocking on the wraparound porch with their complimentary afternoon wine and cheese. Within walking distance are antique shops, restaurants, the Maitland Art Center, the Maitland Historical Society Museums, and the Madlyn Baldwin Center for Birds of Prey.

Night Swan Intracoastal Bed & Breakfast ✪
512 SOUTH RIVERSIDE DRIVE, NEW SMYRNA BEACH, FLORIDA 32168

Tel: (904) 423-4940
Best Time to Call: 5–9 PM
Hosts: Martha and Charles
  Nighswonger
Location: 15 mi. S of Daytona Beach
No. of Rooms: 5
No. of Private Baths: 5
Double/pb: $59–$79
Suites: $99; sleeps 4

Open: All year
Reduced Rates: Available
Breakfast: Continental
Credit Cards: AMEX, MC, VISA
Pets: No
Children: Welcome
Smoking: No
Social Drinking: Permitted
Airport/Station Pickup: Yes

Come sit on Night Swan's wraparound porch or by its windows and watch pelicans, dolphins, sailboats, and yachts ply the Atlantic Intracoastal Waterway. Then enjoy the waterfront yourself: surf, swim, fish, drive, or bicycle along the bathing beach two miles to the east. This spacious three-story home in New Smyrna's historic district has a central fireplace and intricate, natural woodwork in every room, and some rooms overlook the Indian River. Continental breakfast is served in the dining room; low cholesterol dishes are a house specialty.

Neva's Bed & Breakfast ✪
520 SOUTHEAST 17TH PLACE, OCALA, FLORIDA 32671

Tel: (904) 732-4607
Best Time to Call: 8 AM
Host: Neva Stanojevich
Location: 40 mi. S of Gainesville
No. of Rooms: 2
Max. No. Sharing Bath: 4
Double/sb: $40

Single/sb: $20
Open: Sept. 1–July 31
Breakfast: Full
Pets: No
Children: No
Smoking: No
Social Drinking: No

This five-bedroom split-level is near shopping malls, churches, and hospitals. Ocala is 80 miles west of Daytona and 80 miles north of Orlando. Attractions closer to home include numerous horse farms and Wild Waters, a six-acre water park just outside Ocala. Within city limits are the Appleton Cultural Center and the Walt Disney World Information/Reservation Center. Your host, a retired schoolteacher, is a church organist who takes great pride in her baking.

PerriHouse Bed & Breakfast Inn
10417 STATE ROAD 535, ORLANDO, FLORIDA 32836

Tel: (407) 876-4830, (800) 780-4830;
  Fax: (407) 876-0241
Best Time to Call: 9 AM–9 PM

Hosts: Nick and Angi Perretti
Location: 3 mi. N of I-4 Exit 27, Lake
  Buena Vista, ON SR 535N

No. of Rooms: 6
No. of Private Baths: 6
Double/pb: $65–$75
Single/pb: $60
Open: All year
Reduced Rates: Seniors, weekly
Breakfast: Continental

Credit Cards: AMEX, DISC, MC, VISA
Pets: No
Children: Welcome (crib)
Smoking: No
Social Drinking: Permitted
Airport/Station Pickup: Yes

PerriHouse is a quiet, private country estate inn secluded on 20 acres of land adjacent to the Walt Disney World Resort complex. Because of its outstanding location, Disney Village and Pleasure Island are only 3 minutes away; EPCOT center is only 5 minutes. It's the perfect vacation setting for families who desire a unique travel experience with a comfortable, convenient home away from home. An upscale Continental breakfast awaits you each morning, and a refreshing pool and heated spa relax you after a full day of activities. Each guest room features its own private bath, entrance, TV, telephone, ceiling fan, and central air/heat. The PerriHouse grounds are being developed and landscaped to create a future bird sanctuary and wildlife preserve. Come bird-watch on the peaceful, tranquil grounds of the PerriHouse estate and wake up to bird songs outside your window. Your hosts, Nick & Angi, instinctively offer their guests a unique blend of cordial hospitality, comfort and friendship!

The Rio Pinar House ✪
532 PINAR DRIVE, ORLANDO, FLORIDA 32825

Tel: (800) 277-4903
Best Time to Call: 7 AM–10 PM
Hosts: Victor and Delores Freudenburg
Location: ½ mi. from E-W Expy.,
   Goldenrod exit
No. of Rooms: 3
No. of Private Baths: 2
Max. No. Sharing Bath: 4
Double/pb: $50
Single/pb: $45

Double/sb: $45
Single/sb: $40
Suites: $80 (family)
Open: All year
Breakfast: Full
Pets: No
Children: Welcome
Smoking: No
Social Drinking: Permitted

Located in the quiet neighborhood near Rio Pinar Golf Course, this home features comfortably furnished rooms, antiques, and filtered air and water. Breakfast includes fresh local fruit and is served on a porch overlooking a garden of flowers and trees. The house is a 30-minute drive from the airport, Disney World, Sea World, and Universal Studios, and six miles from downtown Orlando and its Church Street Station Entertainment Complex.

The Spencer Home ✪
313 SPENCER STREET, ORLANDO, FLORIDA 32839

Tel: (407) 855-5603	Open: All year
Hosts: Neal and Eunice Schattauer	Breakfast: Continental
Location: 2 mi. from I-4	Pets: No
No. of Rooms: 1 suite, 2 bedrooms	Children: Welcome
No. of Private Baths: 1	Smoking: No
Suites: $50–$60; sleeps 2–4	Social Drinking: Permitted
$90–$100; sleeps 4–6	

The guest suite of this comfortable neat, ranch-style house has a private entrance and consists of a bedroom with a double bed, one with a queen-size bed, a living room with a sleeper for two, and a full bathroom. It is completely air-conditioned. You are welcome to freshen your traveling duds in the laundry room and yourselves in the swimming pool. Eunice will start your day with breakfast, and Neal will be pleased to direct you to central Florida's attractions within a half hour from "home."

Bed 'n Breakfast of Greater Daytona Beach ✪
P.O. BOX 1081, ORMOND BEACH, FLORIDA 32175

Tel: (904) 673-2232	Rates (Single/Double):
Coordinator: Rusty Reed	Average: $35–$75
States/Regions Covered: Daytona	Credit Cards: No
Beach, Ormond Beach, Pt. Orange,	Minimum Stay: 3 nights Speed/Bike
Wilbur-by-the-Sea	weeks in Feb. and Mar.

The host homes, each with its own special amenities and charm, are located throughout the greater Daytona area and pride themselves on catering to the needs of each guest. The Space Center and Disney World are within 60 miles. Closer to home, Daytona offers deep-sea fishing, golf, tennis, jai alai, dog racing, theater, and Halifax River cruises. A Daytona International Speedway tour and a drive on "the world's most famous beach" are a must. Yacht enthusiasts will be interested in the new 600-slip Halifax Marina, where they can dock, and then bed-and-breakfast nearby.

Heron Cay ✪
15106 PALMWOOD ROAD, PALM BEACH GARDENS, FLORIDA 33410

Tel: (407) 744-6315	Double/pb: $75–$85
Best Time to Call: 10 AM–10 PM	Double/sb: $75
Hosts: Margie and Randy Salyer	Guest Yacht: $150–$225, sleeps 4–6
Location: 10 mi. N of West Palm Beach	Suites: $125
No. of Rooms: 7	Open: All year
No. of Private Baths: 5	Reduced Rates: Available
Max. No. Sharing Bath: 4	Breakfast: Full or Continental

Pets: **No**   Smoking: **No**
Children: **Welcome**   Social Drinking: **Permitted**

Heron Cay is a Key West–style home on two acres overlooking the intracoastal waterway. The Salyers' private half-acre island protects their dockage—which accommodates boats to 55 feet—and concrete boat ramp. While there are refrigerators in each room, guests also have access to a full kitchen and a laundry room. Other amenities include a Mexican-tiled patio with a swimming pool, a heated spa, and a large barbecue pit. Miles of ocean beaches are five minutes away. Randy and Margie are avid boaters who regularly invite their guests aboard their 48-foot sportfisherman for Palm Beach cruises.

Bed & Breakfast of Tampa Bay ✪
126 OLD OAK CIRCLE, OAK TRAIL, PALM HARBOR, FLORIDA 34683

Tel: **(813) 785-2342**   Double/sb: **$45**
Best Time to Call: **7–9 AM; 6–10 PM**   Single/sb: **$30**
Hosts: **Vivian and David Grimm**   Suite: **$75**
Location: **18 mi. W of Tampa**   Open: **All year**
No. of Rooms: **4**   Breakfast: **Full**
No. of Private Baths: **2**   Pets: **Sometimes**
Max. No. Sharing Bath: **4**   Children: **Welcome**
Double/pb: **$50**   Smoking: **No**
Single/pb: **$40**   Social Drinking: **Permitted**

A premier facility in a premier location: this new Art Deco residence is 1½ miles from the Gulf of Mexico and 25 minutes from Busch Gardens, Dali Museum, and Weeki-Wachee Springs. Shopping, restaurants, churches, and public transportation are within easy walking distance. The Grimms' home has an ivory stucco exterior, with front pillars, a tile roof, and stained-glass doors. Inside, artifacts from their world travels are shown to advantage under 12-foot ceilings. Amenities include a pool and Jacuzzi, a grand piano, and bicycles for local excursions.

Gulf View Inn ○
21722 FRONT BEACH ROAD, PANAMA CITY BEACH, FLORIDA 32413

Tel: **(904) 234-6051**
Hosts: **Raymond and Linda Nance**
Location: **3 mi. W of Panama City**
No. of Rooms: **5**
No. of Private Baths: **5**
Double/pb: **$60**
Single/pb: **$55**

Suites: **$75**
Open: **All year**
Breakfast: **Continental**
Pets: **No**
Children: **Welcome**
Smoking: **Permitted**
Social Drinking: **Permitted**

Gulf View Inn is a two-story beach house painted Cape Cod blue with cream lattice trim. Guest quarters have private entrances, TV, carpeting, and ceiling fans. In the morning, dine on the upstairs sun deck or the porch overlooking the Gulf of Mexico; homemade breads and jellies are specialties of the house. Then it's just 200 feet across the road to the white sand of Panama City Beach. Linda and Raymond's inn is near fishing, sailing, golf, tennis, and restaurants; water parks for the children are within easy reach.

Sunshine Inn ○
508 DECATUR AVENUE, PENSACOLA, FLORIDA 32507

Tel: **(904) 455-6781**
Best Time to Call: **Early mornings**
Hosts: **The Jablonskis**
Location: **8 mi. from I-10; 4 mi. from beach**
No. of Rooms: **2**
No. of Private Baths: **1**
Max. No. Sharing Bath: **4**
Double/sb: **$35**

Suites: **$35 for 2**
Open: **All year**
Breakfast: **Full**
Pets: **No**
Children: **Welcome**
Smoking: **No**
Social Drinking: **Permitted**
Airport/Station Pickup: **Yes**
Foreign Languages: **German**

Sun and swim in the Gulf of Mexico, on the beautiful Emerald Coast of northwest Florida. Your knowledgeable hostess will provide you with all the touring advice you seek. Sunshine Inn is only minutes from the Naval Aviation Museum and the beach. The breakfast specialty is blueberry pancakes. There is a $5 surcharge for one-night stays.

Ruskin House Bed and Breakfast ○
120 DICKMAN DRIVE S.W., RUSKIN, FLORIDA 33570

Tel: **(813) 645-3842**
Best Time to Call: **Anytime**
Host: **Arthur M. Miller, Ph.D.**
Location: **25 mi. S of Tampa; 30 mi. N of Sarasota**
No. of Rooms: **3**

No. of Private Baths: **1**
Max No. Sharing Bath: **4**
Double/pb: **$65**
Double/sb: **$45**
Suites: **$65**
Open: **All year**

Reduced Rates: **7th day free**
Breakfast: **Continental**
Credit Cards: **MC, VISA**
Pets: **No**
Children: **Welcome, over 6**

Smoking: **No**
Social Drinking: **Permitted**
Minimum Stay: **2 nights**
Foreign Languages: **French**

A waterfront home listed on the State Register of Historic Places, this B&B, built in 1910, is graced with verandas and furnished with period antiques. The property abounds in citrus trees, and guests can help themselves to fruit in season. Your host, a poet, editor, and literature professor at New College in Sarasota, is a third-generation inhabitant of Ruskin; his grandfather cofounded the town as a Christian Socialist venture complete with Ruskin College, tuition-free for residents and their families. (The college's only surviving building, just a block from Ruskin House, is enrolled on the National Register of Historic Places.) Ruskin is no longer a utopian community, but the beach and playground are nearby, and it's an easy drive to either Tampa or Sarasota.

Bed and Breakfast Suncoast Accommodations ✪
8690 GULF BOULEVARD, ST. PETE BEACH, FLORIDA 33706

Tel: **(813) 360-1753**
Best Time to Call: **Anytime**
Coordinator: **Mrs. Danie Bernard**
States/Regions Covered: **Aripika, Bradenton, Cortez, Havana, Madeera Beach, New Port Richey, Orlando, Sarasota, St. Pete Beach, Treasure Island**

Rates (Single/Double):
  Modest: **$30 / $50–$60**
  Average: **$40 / $70–$80**
  Luxury: **$50 / $85–$100**
Minimum Stay: **2 nights, 3 on holidays**

Danie's listings range from modest to luxurious, located in town or on the waterfront. Some B&Bs provide laundry services, kitchen privileges, even fishing poles, and bicycles. All are private residences offering comfortable accommodations with hosts who have a genuine interest in sharing their hospitality and knowledge of the area.

Casa de la Paz ✪
22 AVENIDA MENENDEZ, ST. AUGUSTINE, FLORIDA 32084

Tel: **(904) 829-2915**
Best Time to Call: **9 AM–9 PM**
Host: **Jan Maki**
Location: **7 mi. from I-95**
No. of Rooms: **6**
No. of Private Baths: **6**
Double/pb: **$75–$125**
Suites: **$105–$150**

Open: **All year**
Breakfast: **Full**
Credit Cards: **AMEX, DISC, MC, VISA**
Pets: **No**
Children: **No**
Smoking: **No**
Social Drinking: **Permitted**

Overlooking historic Matanzas Bay in the heart of Old St. Augustine is this three-story Mediterranean-style stucco home. The rooms are comfortably furnished in a pleasant blend of the old and new. Amenities in each room include ceiling fans, central air-conditioning and heat, high-quality linens, cable TV, and complimentary sherry or wine. The veranda rooms have private entrances. Guests are welcome to use the private, walled courtyard, well-stocked library, and delightful parlor. It is central to all attractions and convenient to fine restaurants and shops.

Casa de Solana ✪
21 AVILES STREET, ST. AUGUSTINE, FLORIDA 32084

Tel: **(904) 824-3555**
Best Time to Call: **9 AM–6 PM**
Hosts: **Jim McMurry**
No. of Rooms: **4 suites**
No. of Private Baths: **4**
Suites: **$125**
Open: **All year**

Breakfast: **Full**
Credit Cards: **AMEX, DISC, MC, VISA**
Pets: **No**
Children: **No**
Smoking: **No**
Social Drinking: **Permitted**

This is a gorgeous Colonial home built in 1763. It is located in the heart of the historic area, within walking distance of restaurants, museums, and quaint shops. Some of the antique-filled suites have fireplaces, while others have balconies that overlook the lovely garden, or a breathtaking view of Matanzas Bay. Jim and Faye include cable TV, chocolates, a decanter of sherry, and the use of their bicycles.

Castle Garden ✪
15 SHENANDOAH STREET, ST. AUGUSTINE, FLORIDA 32084

Tel: **(904) 829-3839**
Best Time to Call: **9 AM–6 PM**
Hosts: **Bruce and Joyce Kloeckner**
Location: **10 mi. from I-95**
No. of Rooms: **6**
No. of Private Baths: **6**
Double/pb: **$75–$150**
Open: **All year**
Reduced Rates: **20% weekly, $20 less Sun.–Thurs.; 10% seniors**

Breakfast: **Full**
Credit Cards: **AMEX, DISC, MC, VISA**
Pets: **No**
Children: **Welcome**
Smoking: **No**
Social Drinking: **Permitted**
Airport/Station Pickup: **Yes**

The only Moorish-revival dwelling in St. Augustine, Castle Garden dates to the late 1800s; the unusual coquina stone exterior remains virtually untouched since its completion. The completely renovated interior features two magnificent bridal suites, each complete with a sunken bedroom, in-room Jacuzzi, cathedral ceiling, and other wonderful details. Park your car in the B&B's fenced lot and borrow bikes to tour the city, one of the nation's oldest. When you return, rest on the sun porch or stroll the lovely grounds. The Kloeckners give each guest complimentary wine, and pride themselves on preparing mouthwatering country breakfasts "just like Mom used to make."

Kenwood Inn ✪
38 MARINE STREET, ST. AUGUSTINE, FLORIDA 32084

Tel: **(904) 824-2116**
Best Time to Call: **11 AM–10 PM**
Hosts: **Mark, Kerrianne, and Caitlin Constant**
Location: **40 mi. S of Jacksonville**
No. of Rooms: **14**
No. of Private Baths: **14**
Double/pb: **$65–$95**

Single/pb: **$45–$95**
Open: **All year**
Breakfast: **Continental**
Credit Cards: **DISC, MC, VISA**
Pets: **No**
Children: **Welcome, over 8**
Smoking: **No**
Social Drinking: **Permitted**

If you are to discover a Victorian building in Florida, how appropriate that it should be in the historic section of St. Augustine, one of the oldest cities in the U.S. This New England–style inn is a rarity in the South; this one has old-fashioned beds with color-coordinated touches right down to the sheets and linens. Breakfast may be taken in your room, in the courtyard surrounded by trees, or by the swimming pool. Tour trains, waterfront shops, restaurants, and museums are within walking distance. Flagler College is three blocks away.

Old City House Inn & Restaurant ✪
115 CORDOVA STREET, ST. AUGUSTINE, FLORIDA 32084

Tel: (904) 826-0113
Best Time to Call: 8 AM–10 PM
Hosts: Robert and Alice Compton
Location: 6 mi. from I-95, Exit 95
No. of Rooms: 5
No. of Private Baths: 5
Double/pb: $60–$105
Open: All year
Reduced Rates: Weekdays
Breakfast: Full

Other Meals: Available
Credit Cards: AMEX, DC, MC, VISA
Pets: Sometimes
Children: Welcome
Smoking: No
Social Drinking: Permitted
Minimum Stay: 2 nights weekends; 3
 nights some holidays
Airport/Station Pickup: Yes

A majestic example of Colonial-revival architecture, the Old City House Inn & Restaurant, built in 1873, stands in the heart of St. Augustine's historic district. Each of the five cheerfully decorated bedrooms contains a queen-size bed, cable TV, and a private entrance and bath. After a full day of sightseeing, you're invited to join Robert and Alice on the veranda for a complimentary snack and beverage. They will also supply you with bicycles to help you work off the filling gourmet breakfast, which may include quiche, frittatas, pancakes, and waffles.

St. Francis Inn ✪
279 ST. GEORGE STREET, ST. AUGUSTINE, FLORIDA 32084

Tel: (904) 824-6068
Hosts: Stan and Regina Reynolds
Location: 2 mi. from US 1
No. of Rooms: 14
No. of Private Baths: 14
Double/pb: $49–$69
Guest Cottage: $140; sleeps 4–6
Suites: $75–$95

Open: All year
Breakfast: Continental, plus
Credit Cards: MC, VISA
Pets: No
Children: Welcome (crib)
Smoking: No
Social Drinking: Permitted

Built in 1791, the inn is a Spanish Colonial structure with a private courtyard and garden, located in the center of the restored part of town. Balconies are furnished with rocking chairs, and the swimming pool is a great cooling-off spot. The building is made of coquina, a limestone made of broken shells and coral. Due to its trapezoidal shape, there are no square or rectangular rooms. All of St. Augustine's historic and resort activities are within a three-mile radius.

Bayboro House on Old Tampa Bay
1719 BEACH DRIVE SOUTHEAST, ST. PETERSBURG, FLORIDA 33701

Tel: (813) 823-4955
Hosts: Gordon and Antonia Powers
Location: ½ mi. from I-275, Exit 9

No. of Rooms: 4
No. of Private Baths: 4
Double/pb: $75–$85

Open: **All year**	Children: **No**
Breakfast: **Continental**	Smoking: **No**
Credit Cards: **MC, VISA**	Social Drinking: **Permitted**
Pets: **No**	

A unique three-story Queen Anne with airy, high-ceilinged rooms, and a wraparound veranda in view of Tampa Bay, Bayboro House is graced with antique furniture plus tropical plants and flowers. It is the ideal spot for sunning and beachcombing. Visit unusual shops, fine restaurants, the Sunken Gardens, or the Salvador Dali museum. Tampa is 20 minutes away; Walt Disney World and Epcot are 1½ hours away. The Suncoast Dome is five minutes from the door. A self-contained apartment is also available.

Ferncourt Bed and Breakfast

150 CENTRAL AVENUE, SAN MATEO, FLORIDA 32187

Tel: **(904) 329-9755**	Open: **All year**
Best Time to Call: **Anytime**	Breakfast: **Full**
Hosts: **Jack and Dee Morgan**	Pets: **No**
Location: **25 mi. W of St. Augustine**	Children: **No**
No. of Rooms: **1**	Smoking: **No**
No. of Private Baths: **1**	Social Drinking: **Permitted**
Double p/b: **$45–$65**	Station Pickup: **Yes**

Ferncourt is a restored 1800s farm home, located in a tiny historic hamlet just a few minutes drive from St. Augustine and Daytona Beach. Guests have use of several rooms and the wraparound veranda. Close by, restaurants serve excellent food. Cookies and tea are offered in the evening. Jack does woodworking and upholstery and many examples of his craft are on display throughout the inn. Dee dabbles in painting and loves antiques and flea markets, but her real passion is food, evidenced by the gourmet breakfast she serves. Discover North Central Florida, then retire to all the charm and hospitality of the Victorian era with your hosts. They have a long concrete wheelchair ramp and one room set up for the disabled with a private bath and handrails installed. For our hearing-impaired guests there is a smoke alarm installed.

The Dolphin Inn at Seaside ✪
P.O. Box 4732, 107 SAVANNAH STREET, SEASIDE, FLORIDA 32459

Tel: (904) 231-5477; (800) 443-3146	Open: All year
Best Time to Call: Anytime	Breakfast: Continental
Hosts: Richard "Mac" McCullen and Nancy Judkins	Other Meals: Available
	Credit Cards: MC, VISA
Location: 25 mi. W of Panama City	Pets: No
No. of Rooms: 2	Children: Welcome
No. of Private Baths: 2	Smoking: Permitted
Double/pb: $95	Social Drinking: Permitted

Seaside, a unique new community, recaptures the charm and tranquility of turn-of-the-century resort towns with its pastel-hued Victorian houses, white picket fences, brick streets, sugar white beaches, and clear blue waters. The Dolphin Inn is a pink three-story Victorian cottage with stained-glass windows and dolphin-shaped gingerbread trim; inside, a 1909 piano adds to the nostalgia. Guest rooms open onto a veranda with a breathtaking view of the Gulf of Mexico. Mac is a scuba instructor and Nancy also dives, so there is a nautical air to their furnishings, including Nancy's striking shell collection. If you share Mac's passion for old cars, you'll admire his restored 1961 Impala convertible.

Knightswood ✪
P.O. BOX 151, SUMMERLAND KEY, FLORIDA 33042

Tel: (305) 872-2246; (800) 437-5402	Open: All year
Hosts: Chris and Herb Pontin	Breakfast: Full
Location: 26 mi. E of Key West	Pets: No
No. of Rooms: 2	Children: No
No. of Private Baths: 2	Smoking: No
Double/pb: $85	Social Drinking: Permitted
Single/pb: $70	Minimum Stay: 2 nights

Knightswood boasts one of the loveliest water views in the Keys. The guest apartment is self-contained and very private. Snorkeling, fishing, and boating can be enjoyed right from the Pontins' dock. You are welcome to swim in the freshwater pool, relax in the spa, or sunbathe on the white sand beach. Trips to protected Looe Key Coral Reef can be arranged. Fine dining and Key West nightlife are within easy reach.

Fiorito's Bed & Breakfast ✪
421 OLD EAST LAKE ROAD, TARPON SPRINGS, FLORIDA 34689

Tel: **(813) 937-5487**
Best Time to Call: **8 AM–9 PM**
Hosts: **Dick and Marie Fiorito**
Location: **2 mi. E of US 19**
No. of Rooms: **1**
No. of Private Baths: **1**
Double/pb: **$40**
Single/pb: **$35**

Open: **All year**
Breakfast: **Full**
Pets: **No**
Children: **No**
Smoking: **Restricted**
Social Drinking: **Permitted**
Airport/Station Pickup: **Yes**

Just off a quiet road that runs along Lake Tarpon's horse country, this meticulously maintained home on two-and-a-half acres offers respite for the visitor. The guest room and bath are decorated in tones of blue, enhanced with beautiful accessories. Fresh fruit, cheese omelet, homemade bread and jam, and a choice of beverage is the Fioritos' idea of breakfast. It is beautifully served on the tree-shaded, screened terrace. They'll be happy to direct you to the Greek Sponge Docks, deep-sea fishing opportunities, golf courses, beaches, and great restaurants.

Heartsease ✪
272 OLD EAST LAKE ROAD, TARPON SPRINGS, FLORIDA 34689

Tel: **(813) 934-0994**
Best Time to Call: **5 PM–10 PM**
Hosts: **Gerald and Sharon Goulish**
No. of Rooms: **1 cottage**
No. of Private Baths: **1**
Double/pb: **$55**
Single/pb: **$50**
Open: **All year**

Reduced Rates: **Available**
Breakfast: **Continental**
Pets: **No**
Children: **No**
Smoking: **No**
Social Drinking: **Permitted**
Airport Pickup: **Yes**

You'll find plenty of "heartsease," meaning peace of mind and tranquillity, at Gerald and Sharon's guest cottage. Wicker and pine furniture and a green and mauve color scheme create a light, airy feeling. Amenities include a private entrance, a mini-kitchen stocked with a microwave and breakfast fixings, cable TV, private bath, tennis court, and a deck overlooking the in-ground pool. Pluck an orange or a grapefruit from one of the many fruit trees and then settle in the gazebo, an ideal place for observing the bald eagles that nest nearby. Golf courses, Tampa's Old Hyde Park, Harbour Island, and Tarpon Springs' famed sponge docks are all within a short drive.

Inn on the Bayou ☉
P.O. BOX 1545, TARPON SPRINGS, FLORIDA 34688

Tel: **(813) 942-4468**
Host: **Al Stark**
Location: **15–20 mi. NW of Tampa**
No. of Rooms: **3**
No. of Private Baths: **1**
Max. No. Sharing Bath: **2**
Double/pb: **$50**
Single/pb: **$45**
Double/sb: **$50**

Single/sb: **$45**
Open: **All year**
Reduced Rates: **Available**
Breakfast: **Continental**
Pets: **No**
Children: **Welcome, over 7**
Smoking: **No**
Social Drinking: **Permitted**
Airport Pickup: **Yes**

Come stay at this beautiful, contemporary home situated on a quiet bayou. Fish for a big red or watch the blue herons and pelicans nesting in a bird sanctuary behind the B&B. Go for a swim in your hosts' solar-heated pool or soak your cares away in a whirlpool spa. Then take a stroll through the famous sponge docks and do some antiquing in town. The inn is located just minutes from a white sandy beach with breathtaking sunsets. Busch Gardens and Adventure Islands are close by. Private tours with transportation are available.

West Palm Beach Bed & Breakfast ☉
419 32ND STREET, OLD NORTHWOOD HISTORIC DISTRICT, WEST PALM BEACH, FLORIDA 33407-4809

Tel: **(800) 736-4064; (407) 848-4064**
Hosts: **Dennis Keimel and Ron Seitz**
No. of Rooms: **2**
No. of Private Baths: **2**
Double/pb: **$75–$85**
Carriage House: **$115, sleeps 2**
Open: **All year**
Reduced Rates: **$10 less weekly, May–Oct.**

Breakfast: **Continental**
Pets: **No**
Children: **No**
Smoking: **No**
Social Drinking: **Permitted**
Airport/Station Pickup: **Yes**

This enchanting Key West–style cottage is located in the Old Northwood Historic District, one block from the intracoastal waterway. The B&B's colorful Caribbean decor will remind you of the islands. With its own kitchenette, living area, and tropical pool area, the carriage house is perfect for a private weekend getaway.

GEORGIA

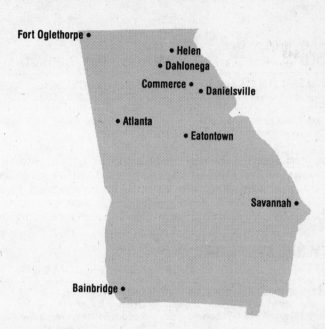

Fort Oglethorpe •

• Helen
• Dahlonega
Commerce •
• Danielsville

• Atlanta

• Eatontown

Savannah •

Bainbridge •

Bed & Breakfast Atlanta ✪
1801 PIEDMONT AVENUE NORTHEAST, SUITE 208, ATLANTA,
GEORGIA 30324

Tel: **(404) 875-0525; (800) 96-PEACH;**
  fax: **(404) 875-9672**
Best Time to Call: **9 AM–5 PM**
  Mon.–Fri.
Coordinator: **Paula Gris**
States/Regions Covered: **Alpharetta,
  Atlanta, Brookhaven, Buckhead,
  Decatur, Dunwoody, Marietta,**

**Roswell, Sandy Springs, Smyrna,
Stone Mountain, Tucker**
Rates (Single/Double):
  Modest: **$40–$48 / $48–$56**
  Average: **$52–$64 / $60–$72**
  Luxury: **$72–$100 / $80–$120**
Credit Cards: **AMEX, MC, VISA**

Visit one of America's most gracious cities, site of the 1996 Olympics,
and experience the hospitality for which Atlanta is famous. Since
1979, Paula has been carefully selecting accommodations for fortunate

travelers, weighing transportation and language needs as well as other personal preferences. There are B&Bs near all major educational, medical, industrial, and convention complexes, such as the Georgia World Congress Center, Emory University, and the Centers for Disease Control. Special rates for long-term relocation and temporary duty assignments can be arranged. There is an $8 surcharge for one-night stays.

Quail Country Bed & Breakfast, Ltd. ✪
1104 OLD MONTICELLO ROAD, THOMASVILLE, GEORGIA 31792

Tel: (912) 226-7218; 226-6882
Coordinators: **Mercer Watt and Kathy Lanigan**
States/Regions Covered: **Thomas County, Thomasville**

Rates (Single/Double):
Average: **$30 / $40**
Luxury: **$40 / $50**
Credit Cards: **No**

Mercer and Kathy have a wide selection of homes, several with swimming pools, in lovely residential areas. There's a lot to see and do, including touring historic restorations and plantations. Enjoy the Pebble Hill Plantation museum, historic Glen Arven Country Club, and the April Rose Festival. There is a $5 surcharge for one-night stays.

The White House B&B ✪
320 WASHINGTON STREET, BAINBRIDGE, GEORGIA 31717

Tel: (912) 248-1703
Hosts: **John and Mary Patterson**
Location: **45 mi. NW of Tallahassee, Florida**
No. of Rooms: **3**
No. of Private Baths: **1**
Max. No. Sharing Bath: **4**
Double/pb: **$45**
Single/pb: **$40**
Double/sb: **$40**

Single/sb: **$35**
Open: **All year**
Reduced Rates: **Over 3 days**
Breakfast: **Continental**
Pets: **No**
Children: **Welcome, over 10**
Smoking: **No**
Social Drinking: **No**
Airport/Station Pickup: **Yes**

This antebellum dogtrot-style home (circa 1840–50) in the historic district of Bainbridge features original hand-hewn columns and rived pine floors. The decor is a blend of family antiques, heirloom fabrics, and needlework. Guests are encouraged to enjoy the swimming pool and gazebo, gallery library, and sitting room. Nearby attractions include historic homes, antique shops, Lake Seminole for fishing and water sports, May Artsfest, and local celebrations. Convenient for business and leisure travelers, we are an easy drive from Plains, Tallahassee, Florida, the Gulf beaches, and Florida theme parks.

The Pittman House ✪
81 HOMER ROAD, COMMERCE, GEORGIA 30529

Tel: **(706) 335-3823**	Single/sb: **$45**
Best Time to Call: **7 AM–9 PM**	Open: **All year**
Hosts: **Tom and Dot Tomberlin**	Breakfast: **Full**
Location: **60 mi. NE of Atlanta**	Credit Cards: **MC, VISA**
No. of Rooms: **4**	Pets: **No**
No. of Private Baths: **3**	Children: **Welcome**
Max. No. Sharing Bath: **4**	Smoking: **No**
Double/pb: **$55**	Social Drinking: **No**
Double/sb: **$50**	

This gracious white Colonial, built in 1890, is decorated throughout with period pieces. If the furniture inspires you, visit Granny's Old Things, an antique shop right next door. Other points of interest include Château Elan Winery, in neighboring Braselton, and the Crawford W. Long Museum—honoring the doctor who discovered the use of ether as an anesthetic—in the town of Jefferson. Swimmers and sailors have their choice of Lake Lanier and Lake Hartwell; Hurricane Shoals is another lovely outdoor recreational area.

The Mountain Top Lodge
ROUTE 7, BOX 150, DAHLONEGA, GEORGIA 30533

Tel: **(706) 864-5257; (800) 526-9754**	Suites: **$115–$125**
Best Time to Call: **10 AM–6 PM**	Open: **All year**
Host: **David Middleton**	Breakfast: **Full**
Location: **70 mi. N of Atlanta**	Pets: **No**
No. of Rooms: **13**	Children: **Welcome, over 12**
No. of Private Baths: **13**	Smoking: **No**
Double/pb: **$65–$85**	Social Drinking: **Permitted**
Single/pb: **$45–$75**	

Flanked by porches and decks, this gambrel-roofed, rustic cedar lodge is a secluded rural retreat on 40 acres, with a 360-degree mountain view. Decorated with art and antiques, the pine furniture and accessories made by mountain craftsmen add to the charm. Dahlonega was the site of America's first gold rush, and nature buffs will appreciate the Chattahoochee National Forest and Amicalola Falls State Park. Rafting, hiking, and horseback riding are all nearby. Don't miss the "Alpine village" of Helen, Georgia, only 30 minutes away. We now offer deluxe rooms with in bath Jacuzzi whirlpool tubs and gas log fireplaces.

Royal Guard Inn
203 SOUTH PARK STREET, DAHLONEGA, GEORGIA 30533

Tel: (706) 864-1713
Best Time to Call: 10 AM–9 PM
Hosts: John and Farris Vanderhoff
Location: 50 mi. N of Atlanta
No. of Rooms: 5
No. of Private Baths: 5
Double/pb: $65–$75
Open: All year

Reduced Rates: 10% seniors,
  Sun.–Thurs.
Breakfast: Full
Credit Cards: MC, VISA
Pets: No
Children: By arrangement
Smoking: No
Social Drinking: Permitted

Located in the northeast Georgia mountains, Dahlonega is where the first major U.S. gold rush occurred in 1828. Dahlonega Gold Museum, Price Memorial Hall—on the site of one of the first U.S. branch mints—and gold-panning areas are all in the heart of the historic downtown. Royal Guard Inn, a half-block from the old town square, is a restored and enlarged old home. John and Farris serve complimentary wine and cheese on the great wraparound porch. Breakfast, served on fine china and silver on crisp white linen, includes a casserole, pastries, or hotcakes from an old family recipe, and fresh fruit and whipped cream.

Honey Bear Hideaway Farm ✪
ROUTE 4, BOX 4106, ROGERS MILL ROAD, DANIELSVILLE, GEORGIA 30633

Tel: (706) 789-2569
Best Time to Call: After 4 PM
Hosts: Ray and Natachia Dodd
Location: 12 mi. N of Athens
No. of Rooms: 4
No. of Private Baths: 3

Double/pb: $50
Single/pb: $45
Open: All year
Breakfast: Full
Other Meals: Available
Credit Cards: MC, VISA

Pets: **Horses**
Children: **Welcome, over 12**
Smoking: **No**

Social Drinking: **Permitted**
Airport/Station Pickup: **Yes**

This 125-year-old farmhouse is nestled among pecan and walnut trees, with a lake nearby. Ray and Natachia are artists who converted the property's two barns into studios. The house is a virtual gallery of antiques and curios; one bedroom is decorated with old-fashioned purses. Visitors will wake up to a Southern, country-style breakfast, with farm-fresh eggs, ham or sausage, and homemade breads and jellies.

The Crockett House ✪
671 MADISON ROAD (U.S. BUSINESS 441), EATONTON, GEORGIA 31024

Tel: **(706) 485-2248**
Hosts: **Christa and Peter Crockett**
Location: **73 mi. E of Atlanta**
No. of Rooms: **6**
No. of Private Baths: **6**
Double/pb: **$65–$75**
Single/pb: **$55–$65**
Open: **All year**

Reduced Rates: **10% Nov.–Feb.;**
 extended stays; seniors; families
Breakfast: **Full**
Pets: **No**
Children: **Welcome**
Smoking: **No**
Social Drinking: **Permitted**
Airport Pickup: **Yes**

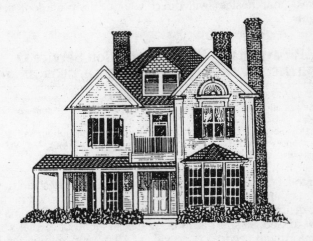

This stately and gracious turn-of-the-century home captures the history and charm of a bygone era. Guests receive a warm welcome and comfortable accommodations year round. The home features seven bedrooms and eleven fireplaces. The large cozy bedrooms are thoughtfully decorated, some with private baths and fireplaces. Separate innkeepers' quarters insure the privacy of guests. Wander throughout the home and enjoy the principal rooms (equipped with telephones and TVs), balcony, wraparound porch, and tranquil setting of the three-acre yard.

Hilltop Haus ✪
P.O. BOX 154, CHATTAHOOCHEE STREET, HELEN, GEORGIA 30545

Tel: (706) 878-2388	Single/sb: $40–$55
Host: **Melissa Dean**	Suite: $65–$125
Best Time to Call: **8 AM–10 PM**	Open: **All year**
Location: **60 mi. from I-85**	Breakfast: **Full**
No. of Rooms: 5	Credit Cards: **MC, VISA**
No. of Private Baths: 3	Pets: **No**
Max. No. Sharing Bath: 3	Children: **Welcome**
Double/pb: $50–$75	Smoking: **Permitted**
Single/pb: $45–$60	Social Drinking: **Permitted**
Double/sb: $45–$70	

This contemporary split-level overlooks the Alpine town of Helen and the Chattahoochee River. It is near the foothills of the Smoky Mountains, six miles from the Appalachian Trail. Rich wood paneling and fireplaces create a homey atmosphere for the traveler. Guests may choose a private room or the efficiency cottage with separate entrance. Each morning a hearty breakfast includes homemade biscuits and preserves. Your hostess will direct you to many outdoor activities and sights.

R.S.V.P. Savannah—B&B Reservation Service ✪
9489 WHITFIELD AVENUE, BOX 49, SAVANNAH, GEORGIA 31406

Tel: (912) 232-7787; (800) 729-7787	Simons Island, Savannah, Tybee
Best Time to Call: **9:30 AM–5:30 PM**	Island; South Carolina—Beaufort,
Mon.–Fri.	Charleston
Coordinator: **Sonja Lazzaro**	Rates (Single/Double): $55–$225
States/Regions Covered:	Credit Cards: **AMEX, MC, VISA**
Georgia—Brunswick, St. Marys, St.	

Accommodations include elegantly restored inns, guest houses, private homes, and even a villa on the water. They're located in the best historic districts as well as along the coast, from South Carolina's Low Country to Georgia's Sea Islands. A special blend of cordial hospitality, comfort, and services is provided. All are air-conditioned in the summer. Facilities for children and the disabled are often available. Please note that while some hosts accept credit cards, most do not.

Joan's on Jones ✪
17 WEST JONES STREET, SAVANNAH, GEORGIA 31401

Tel: **(912) 234-3863**
Hosts: **Joan and Gary Levy**
Location: **140 mi. N of Jacksonville, FL**
Suites: **$85–$95; sleeps 2–4**
Open: **All year**
Reduced Rates: **Weekly**
Breakfast: **Continental**

Pets: **Sometimes**
Children: **Welcome**
Smoking: **No**
Social Drinking: **Permitted**
Minimum Stay: **3 days for St. Patrick's Day week only**

Clip-clopping along the brick streets of the city's historic district, horse-drawn carriages take you back to a more serene and elegant era. This bed and breakfast maintains the old-fashioned mood, with its original heart-pine floors, antique furnishings, and Savannah grey brick walls. (Note the late nineteenth-century documents that slipped behind one of the fireplace mantels.) All the historic places of interest, including the famous squares, are a short walk away. Joan and Gary, former restaurateurs, live upstairs and invite you to tour their home if you're staying at least two nights.

Lion's Head Inn ✪
120 EAST GASTON STREET, SAVANNAH, GEORGIA 31401

Tel: **(912) 232-4580**
Host: **Christy Dell'orco**
Location: **Downtown Savannah**
No. of Rooms: **6**
No. of Private Baths: **6**
Double/pb: **$85–$95**
Single/pb: **$85–$95**
Suites: **$110–$135**
Open: **All year**

Reduced Rates: **Available**
Breakfast: **Continental**
Credit Cards: **AMEX, MC, VISA**
Pets: **No**
Children: **Welcome**
Smoking: **No**
Social Drinking: **Permitted**
Airport/Station Pickup: **Yes**

This elegant nineteenth-century mansion is tastefully adorned with pristine Empire furniture and accessories. A collection of European and American art, Italian marble, and French bronze sculptures and 19th-century lighting beautify each room. The inn is located on Gaston Street, the prime residential street in the historic district. Stroll across the street to picturesque Forsyth Park and enjoy all the historic attractions and amenities within walking distance. The innkeeper, Christy, a retired sales manager, now is a registered Savannah tour guide and antiquarian. She'll help you enjoy gracious living at its best and experience true nineteenth-century grandeur at the Lion's Head Inn.

Four Chimneys ○
2316 WIRE ROAD, THOMSON, GEORGIA 30824

Tel: **(706) 597-0220**
Best Time to Call: **Before 11 AM**
Hosts: **Ralph and Maggie Zieger**
Location: **35 mi. W of Augusta**
No. of Rooms: **4**
No. of Private Baths: **3**
Double/pb: **$50**
Single/pb: **$45**

Open: **All year**
Breakfast: **Continental**
Credit Cards: **MC, VISA**
Pets: **No**
Children: **Welcome, over 12**
Smoking: **Permitted**
Social Drinking: **Permitted**

Escape from the modern world at this early 1800s plantation manor house with a Colonial herb garden and landscaping. Period antique and reproduction furniture complement the original heart pineplank floors, ceilings, and walls. All guest rooms feature four-poster beds and working fireplaces.

HAWAII

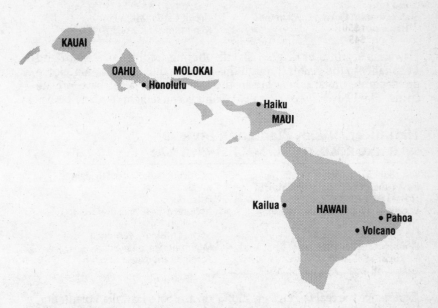

KAUAI

OAHU **MOLOKAI**
• Honolulu

• Haiku
MAUI

Kailua •   **HAWAII**   • Pahoa
                         • Volcano

Babson Reservation Service
3371 KEHA DRIVE, KIHEI, MAUI, HAWAII 96753

Tel: (808) 874-1166; (800) 824-6409
Coordinators: **Ann and Bob Babson**
States/Regions Covered: **All Hawaiian
   Islands**
Descriptive Directory of B&Bs: **No**

Rates (Double):
   Modest: **$60**
   Average: **$80**
   Luxury: **$125**

Ann and Bob can place you in any of 150 guest homes throughout the Hawaii islands, including Molokai and Lanai. Explore beautiful beaches and rain forests and go snorkeling in clear ocean waters. There are plenty of important landmarks, from Iolani Palace—once the home of Hawaii's royal family—to restored missionary villages. Whatever your interests, the Babsons can direct you to convenient locations and knowledgeable hosts.

Bed & Breakfast—Hawaii ✪
P.O. BOX 449, KAPAA, HAWAII 96746

Tel: **(808) 822-7771; (800) 733-1632;**
  fax: **(808) 822-2723**
Best Time to Call: **8:30 AM–4:30 PM**
Coordinators: **Evie Warner (Nancy**
  and Patty)
States/Regions Covered: **All of the**
  Hawaiian Islands

Descriptive Directory: **$10.95**
Rates (Single/Double):
  Modest: **$45 / $55**
  Average: **$65 / $85**
  Luxury: **$85 / $125**
Credit Cards: **MC, VISA**
Minimum Stay: **2 nights**

Hawaii is a group of diverse islands offering traditional warmth and hospitality to the visitor through this membership organization. Some are separate units; others are in the main house. Most have private baths. The University of Hawaii at Oahu is convenient to many B&Bs.

Haikuleana B&B, Plantation Style ✪
555 HAIKU ROAD, HAIKU, MAUI, HAWAII 96708

Tel: **(808) 575-2890**
Best Time to Call: **8 AM–8 PM; HST**
Host: **Frederick J. Fox, Jr.**
Location: **12 mi. E of Kahului**
No. of Rooms: **4**
No. of Private Baths: **4**
Double/pb: **$80–$95**
Single/pb: **$65–$80**
Open: **All year**

Reduced Rates: **After 5th night**
Breakfast: **Full**
Pets: **No**
Children: **Welcome, over 6**
Smoking: **No**
Social Drinking: **Permitted**
Minimum Stay: **2 nights**
Foreign Languages: **Swedish**

Experience the real feelings of "aloha" in an 1850s Hawaiian plantation home. Set in the agricultural district, close to secluded waterfalls and beautiful beaches, Haikuleana is a convenient way station for visitors headed to Hana and Haleakala Crater. Swimming ponds, the world's best windsurfing, and golf courses are all nearby. Fred completely renovated the house; you'll admire its high ceilings, plank floors, porch, and lush Hawaiian gardens. The cool, tropical rooms are furnished with drapes, ticking comforters, wicker, and antiques.

Pilialoha Bed & Breakfast Cottage ✪
2512 KAUPAKALUA ROAD, HAIKU, MAUI, HAWAII 96708

Tel: **(808) 572-1440**
Best Time to Call: **9 AM–9 PM**
Hosts: **Bill and Machiko Heyde**
Location: **10 mi. E of Kahului**
Guest Cottages: **$85**
Open: **All year**
Reduced Rates: **Weekly**

Breakfast: **Continental**
Pets: **No**
Children: **Welcome**
Smoking: **No**
Social Drinking: **Permitted**
Minimum Stay: **2 nights**
Foreign Languages: **Japanese**

Pilialoha, in Hawaiian, means "friendship." Located in lush, cool upcountry Maui on a two-acre property, with half-century-old eucalyptus trees and a cottage garden, Pilialoha is convenient to North Shore beaches, Haleakala National Park, and the road to Hana. This is a separate small house for one group of guests, most comfortable for two people but accommodates up to five. The cottage has a fully equipped kitchen with complimentary assortment of coffee and teas, a cable TV, and private telephone in the living room. Bill enjoys ham radio and welcomes other hams to operate his station. Machiko is an artist and avid gardener.

Bed & Breakfast Manoa ✪
2651 TERRACE DRIVE, HONOLULU, HAWAII 96822

Tel: **(808) 988-6333**	Open: **All year**
Host: **Mary Grace Cade**	Breakfast: **Continental**
Location: **1 mi. N of Honolulu**	Pets: **No**
No. of Rooms: **2**	Children: **Welcome, 1–2½ guest**
No. of Private Baths: **2**	**rooms; no restriction in cottage**
Double/pb: **$65**	Smoking: **No**
Single/pb: **$55**	Social Drinking: **Permitted**
Guest Cottage: **$115–$225, sleeps 7**	Minimum Stay: **3 nights**

Located on a quiet hillside, cooled by gentle breezes and bathed in sunshine and showers, this two-story 1924 home with its separate cottage-apartment embodies the grace and charm of an earlier Hawaii. Every room is filled with light, greenery, and the openness of the outdoors, plus the comfort of deep pile carpeting and excellent beds. From our spacious deck you have spectacular views of Diamond Head, Waikiki, and the Valley. At night, the panorama of nearby Honolulu city lights comes to life. Your hosts are longtime Honolulu residents who work in private practice as counselors and teachers. We take great pleasure in sharing our love of Hawaii with our guests.

Bev & Monty's Bed & Breakfast ✪
4571 UKALI STREET, HONOLULU, OAHU, HAWAII 96818

Tel: **(808) 422-9873**	Open: **All year**
Best Time to Call: **7 AM–9 PM; HST**	Reduced Rates: **Weekly**
Hosts: **Bev and Monty Neese**	Breakfast: **Continental**
Location: **4½ mi. from airport**	Pets: **No**
No. of Rooms: **2**	Children: **Welcome**
Max. No. Sharing Bath: **4**	Smoking: **Permitted**
Double/sb: **$50**	Social Drinking: **Permitted**
Single/sb: **$40**	Airport/Station Pickup: **Yes**

This typical Hawaiian home is convenient to many of Hawaii's most popular attractions. Bev and Monty are just a mile above historic Pearl Harbor, and the Arizona Memorial can be seen from their veranda.

They enjoy sharing a Hawaiian aloha, for a convenient overnight stay or a long vacation where they can share their favorite places with you. This comfortable home is just off the access road leading east to Honolulu and Waikiki, or west to the North Shore beaches, sugar plantations, and pineapple fields. Good hiking country as well as city entertainment and shopping centers are located nearby.

Akamai Bed & Breakfast ✪
172 KUUMELE PLACE, KAILUA, OAHU, HAWAII 96734

Tel: **(808) 261-2227**
Best Time to Call: **8 AM–8 PM**
Host: **Diane Van Ryzin**
No. of Rooms: **2**
No. of Private Baths: **2**
Double/pb: **$60**
Single/pb: **$60**

Open: **All year**
Breakfast: **Full**
Pets: **No**
Children: **Welcome, over 7**
Smoking: **Permitted**
Social Drinking: **Permitted**
Minimum Stay: **3 nights**

Guests at Akamai stay in a separate wing of the house; each room has a private entrance, bath, cable TV, and radio. Honolulu and Waikiki are within a half-hour drive, but you may prefer to lounge by your host's pool or take the eight-minute stroll to the beach. No meals are served here, but your refrigerator is stocked with breakfast foods and the kitchen area is equipped with light cooking appliances, dishes, and flatware. Laundry facilities are also available.

Ali'i Bed & Breakfast ✪
237 AWAKEA ROAD, KAILUA, OAHU, HAWAII 96734

Tel: **(800) 262-9545; (808) 262-9545**
Best Time to Call: **6–7:00 AM**

Host: **Earlene Sasaki**
Location: **10 mi. E of Honolulu**

No. of Rooms: 2
Max. No. Sharing Bath: 4
Double/sb: $45
Single/sb: $40
Guest Apartment: $65–$85, sleeps 2–4
Cottage: $65–$85, sleeps 2-4
Open: All year

Reduced Rates: Extended stays
Breakfast: Continental
Pets: No
Children: Welcome
Smoking: Permitted
Social Drinking: Permitted
Minimum Stay: 3 nights
Foreign Languages: Japanese

On the windward side of Oahu, the white-sand Kailua Beach is a famous swimming and windsurfing retreat. Ali'i's self-sufficient guest units have private entrances, ceiling fans or air conditioners, refrigerators, microwaves, coffeepots, cable TV, and phones for local calls. The cozy cottage has its own little yard with a picnic table. The one-bedroom apartment, furnished with oak and rattan, is wheelchair accessible. The guest rooms offer twins or king beds. The B&B is within walking distance of the beach, bus stop, restaurants, and shopping centers. Ali'i's breakfasts feature Hawaiian fruit and fruit juices, and fresh muffins.

Papaya Paradise ✪
395 AUWINALA ROAD, KAILUA, OAHU, HAWAII 96734

Tel: (808) 261-0316; Fax: (808) 261-0316
Best Time to Call: 7 AM–8 PM; HST
Hosts: Bob and Jeanette Martz
Location: 10 mi. E of Honolulu
No. of Rooms: 2
Double/pb: $65–$70

Open: All year
Breakfast: Continental
Pets: No
Children: Welcome, over 6
Smoking: Permitted
Social Drinking: Permitted
Minimum Stay: 3 nights

The Martz paradise is on the windward side of Oahu, miles from the high-rise hotels, but just 20 miles from the Waikiki/Honolulu airport. Their one-story home is surrounded by a papaya grove and tropical plants and flowers. Each guest room has two beds, a ceiling fan, air-conditioning, cable TV, and its own private entrance. Bob loves to cook, and serves breakfast on the lanai overlooking the pool and Jacuzzi. Kailua Beach, a beautiful white sandy beach four miles long, is within easy walking distance.

Hale Maluhia ✪
76-770 HUALALAI ROAD, KAILUA-KONA, HAWAII 96740

Tel: (808) 329-5773
Best Time to Call: Anytime
Hosts: Ken and Ann Smith
Location: 2 mi. SE of Kailua-Kona
No. of Rooms: 5
No. of Private Baths: 4
Max. No. Sharing Bath: 4

Double/pb: $70–$75
Double/sb: $55
Single/sb: $45
Guest Suites: $235, sleeps 8
Open: All year
Reduced Rates: Available
Breakfast: Continental

Credit Cards: **AMEX, DC, DISC, MC,**
    VISA
Pets: **Sometimes**

Children: **Welcome**
Smoking: **No**
Social Drinking: **Permitted**

From its perch at an elevation of nine hundred feet, this beautiful Hawaiian-designed inn surveys an acre of coffee land in the Holualoa fruit belt. The site is just eight minutes from Kailua-Kona, with easy airport access. All rooms have king- or queen-size beds. Guests are invited to use the spa, pool table, VCR, and beach and snorkeling equipment. Relax in the three common areas or on the two lanais (the Hawaiian term for porch). Fresh bread, local fruit, juice, pastries and one hundred-percent pure Kona coffee are a few of the daily breakfast specialties.

The Orchid Hut ✪
6402 KAAHELE STREET, KAPAA, KAUAI, HAWAII 96746

Tel: **(808) 822-7201; fax: (808) 822-7034; HST**
Hosts: **Norm and Leonora Ross**
Location: **10 mi. E of Lihue Airport**
No. of Rooms: **1**
No. of Private Baths: **1**
Double/pb: **$85**
Open: **All year**
Reduced Rates: **10% weekly**

Breakfast: **Continental**
Pets: **No**
Children: **No**
Smoking: **No**
Social Drinking: **Permitted**
Minimum Stay: **3 nights**
Foreign Languages: **French, Danish,**
    Dutch, Indonesian, Malaysian

Bring your camera and escape to tropical tranquility at a romantic, private hideaway on Kauai, known as "The Garden Island." Norm and Leonora offer the use of their completely equipped three-room contemporary cottage perched high above the Wailua River, encompassing spectacular island and water views. It's a short drive to the beach, shopping, golf, tennis, and fine dining. Local tropical fruit, a variety of cold cereals, tea, and coffee are stocked in your kitchen so you can enjoy breakfast at your own pace and leisure. Guests fly into Lihue Airport, where a car can be rented for the 15-minute drive to the "hut."

Ann & Bob Babson's Vacation Rentals
3371 KEHA DRIVE, KIHEI, MAUI, HAWAII 96753

Tel: **(808) 874-1166; (800) 824-6409**
Hosts: **Ann and Bob Babson**
Location: **15 mi. S of Kahului**
No. of Rooms: **3**
No. of Private Baths: **3**
Double/pb: **$65–$80**
Single/pb: **$65–$80**
Guest Cottage: **$95, for 2—Sleeps 6**

Open: **All year**
Reduced Rates: **Available**
Breakfast: **Continental**
Pets: **No**
Children: **Welcome, over 12**
Smoking: **No**
Social Drinking: **Permitted**
Minimum Stay: **3 nights**

This B&B is located in Maui Meadows, just above beautiful Wailea, with a 180-degree view of the Pacific Ocean looking west. You can see the islands of Lanai and Kahoolawe, and the sunsets are spectacular. The Babsons' spacious home (3,200 square feet) and their two-bedroom, two-bath cottage (700 square feet) are situated on a half-acre of fully landscaped land. The Bougainvillea Suite and Molokini Master Suite include a wonderful Continental breakfast; the Hibiscus Hideaway Apartment and Sunset Cottage have kitchens. All units include telephone for local calls, cable TV, and washer/dryer facilities. Your hosts encourage long-term stays and offer 10% discount for 7-day stays, 20% discount for 30-day stays for direct bookings.

Whale Watch House ✪
726 KUMULANI DRIVE, KIHEI, MAUI, HAWAII 96753

Tel: (808) 879-0570; fax: (808) 874-8102
Best Time to Call: 8 AM–8 PM
Hosts: Patricia and Patrick Lowry
No. of Rooms: 4
No. of Private Baths: 4
Double/pb: $65
Single/pb: $60
Guest Cottage: $85, sleeps 2; $100, sleeps 4; studio, $85

Open: All year
Reduced Rates: 10% less June, July, Sept., Oct.
Breakfast: Continental
Pets: No
Children: No
Smoking: Yes
Social Drinking: Permitted
Minimum Stay: 2 nights

Whale Watch House is located at the very edge of Ulupalakua Ranch on Haleakala, Maui's 10,228-foot dormant volcano. At every turn there are wonderful views of the ocean, the mountains, and the neighboring islands, Lanai and Kahoolawe. Your hosts' lush tropical garden is filled with fruits and flowers, and the swimming pool is large enough for laps. Sunbathe on the large decks around the house, cottage, and pool, or drive down to the beach—you'll be there in five minutes.

Hale Ho'o Maha ✪
P.O. BOX 422, KILAUEA, KAUAI, HAWAII 96754

Tel: (800) 851-0291
Best Time to Call: 7 AM–7 PM
Hosts: Kirby B. Guyer and Toby Searles
Location: 28 mi. N of Lihue Airport
No. of Rooms: 3
No. of Private Baths: 2
Max. No. Sharing Bath: 4
Double/pb: $70
Double/sb: $55–$60

Open: All year
Reduced Rates: 10% after 5th night
Breakfast: Continental
Pets: No
Children: No
Smoking: Permitted
Social Drinking: Permitted
Foreign Languages: Spanish

Escape to a B&B that lives up to its name, which means "house of rest" in Hawaiian. This single-story home is perched on the cliffs along Kauai's north shore. Sandy beaches, rivers, waterfalls, and riding stables are five minutes away. Ask your hosts to direct you to "Queens Bath"—a natural saltwater whirlpool. Guests have full use of the kitchen, gas grill, cable TV, and Boogie boards. When in Rome, do as the Romans: Kirby will teach you to dance the hula and make leis, and Toby will instruct you in scuba diving.

Kula Cottage ✪
206 PUAKEA PLACE, KULA, MAUI, HAWAII 96790

Tel: **(808) 871-6230, 878-2043**	Pets: **No**
Best Time to Call: **8 AM–5 PM**	Children: **Welcome, over 12**
Hosts: **Larry and Cecilia Gilbert**	Smoking: **Permitted**
Location: **16 mi. SE of Kahului**	Social Drinking: **Permitted**
Guest Cottage: **$85, sleeps 2**	Minimum Stay: **2 nights**
Open: **All year**	Foreign Languages: **Spanish**
Breakfast: **Continental**	

Flowers and fruit-bearing trees surround this new, fully-equipped one-bedroom bungalow. There are wonderful views of the ocean and the West Maui Mountains, plus loads of amenities: a wood-burning fireplace, washer and dryer, patio furniture, barbecue, cooler, beach towels, and more. Nearby are restaurants, the beach, a national park, gardens, and a winery. Your hosts can arrange sailing, snorkeling, and helicopter trips for you. The Continental breakfast features home-baked breads, fresh fruit, juice, and coffee or tea.

Kula View Bed and Breakfast ✪
140 HOLOPUNI ROAD (MAILING ADDRESS: P.O. BOX 322), KULA, HAWAII 96790

Tel: **(808) 878-6736**	Open: **All year**
Best Time to Call: **8 AM–6 PM**	Reduced Rates: **10% weekly**
Host: **Susan Kauai**	Breakfast: **Continental**
Location: **16 mi. E of Kahului**	Pets: **No**
No. of Rooms: **1**	Children: **No**
No. of Private Baths: **1**	Smoking: **No**
Double/pb: **$85**	Social Drinking: **Permitted**
Single/pb: **$85**	Minimum Stay: **2 nights**

The fragrances of island fruits and flowers fill the fresh mountain air at this B&B 2,000 feet above sea level, on the slopes of the dormant volcano Haleakala. The upper level guest room has its own private entrance and a spacious deck that faces majestic Haleakala Crater, where the sunrises are nothing short of magical. Breakfast is served at a sun-warmed wicker table overlooking a flower and herb garden. Kula View is surrounded by two acres of lush greenery, yet it is close to Kahului Airport, shopping centers, parks, and beaches.

Aloha Bed and Continental Breakfast ✪
13-3591 LUANA STREET, PAHOA, HAWAII 96778

Tel: **(808) 965-7434**
Best Time to Call: **6 AM–10 PM**
Hosts: **Phyllis and Charles C. Martens**
Location: **21 mi. NW of Hilo**
No. of Rooms: **3**
No. of Private Baths: **3**
Double/pb: **$78**
Single/pb: **$70**
Open: **All year**

Reduced Rates: **15% weekly**
Breakfast: **Continental**
Pets: **No**
Children: **No**
Smoking: **No**
Social Drinking: **Permitted**
Minimum Stay: **2 nights**
Airport pickup: **Yes**
Foreign Languages: **German**

Aloha Bed and Continental Breakfast offers guests a relaxing and comfortable stay. Studios and cottages have private entrances, large picture windows, and sound insulation, for maximum peace and privacy. Each accommodation has air-conditioning, a queen-size bed and a full fridge stocked with a generous variety of breakfast fixings (and an ice maker). For those who like to dine al fresco, there's a patio table and chairs. After savoring your morning meal, take a dip in the pool, then tour the island: this B&B is located near the ocean, active volcano flow, and a myriad of restaurants and shops.

Chalet Kilauea The Inn at Volcano ✪
P.O. BOX 998, VOLCANO, HAWAII 96785

Tel: **(808) 967-7786; (800) 937-7786**
Hosts: **Lisha and Brian Crawford**
Location: **2 mi. NE of Hawaii Volcanoes National Park**
No. of Rooms: **8**
No. of Private Baths: **8**
Double/sb: **$95**
Single/sb: **$95**
Guest Cottage: **$75–$175**

Suite: **$125**
Open: **All year**
Breakfast: **Full**
Pets: **No**
Children: **Welcome**
Smoking: **No**
Social Drinking: **Permitted**
Foreign Languages: **Dutch, French, Portuguese, Spanish**

Chalet Kilauea is moments from Hawaii Volcanoes National Park, at an elevation of 3,800 feet. Guests can examine treasures from around the world in rooms inspired by Pacific, African, and European themes. Relax in the hot tub, enjoy the fireplace, peruse books from the library, and wake up to a gourmet breakfast in the Art Deco dining room.

Hale Kilauea ✪
P.O. BOX 28, VOLCANO, HAWAII 96785

Tel: **(808) 967-7591; (800) 733-3839**
Best Time to Call: **8 AM–10 PM**
Hosts: **Maurice Thomas and Jiranan**
Location: **28 mi. NE of Hilo**
No. of Rooms: **10**
No. of Private Baths: **10**
Double/pb: **$55–$65**
Open: **All year**

Reduced Rates: **10% seniors**
Breakfast: **Continental**
Credit Cards: **AMEX, MC, VISA**
Pets: **Sometimes**
Children: **Welcome**
Smoking: **Permitted**
Social Drinking: **Permitted**

Hale Kilauea is a quiet place near the heart of Volcano Village, just outside Hawaii Volcanoes National Park, the world's only "drive-in volcano." Colorful, exotic native birds live in the towering pines and ohia trees that surround this B&B. After a day of climbing mountains and peering into craters, enjoy an evening of conversation around the living room fireplace. Your host Maurice, a lifelong Volcano resident, has neighbors and friends who know about volcano geology and the history and tradition of old Hawaii.

IDAHO

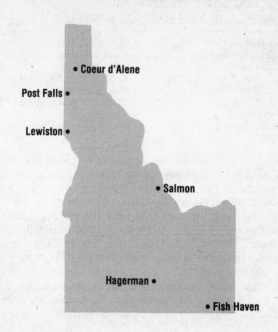

Cricket on the Hearth ☉
1521 LAKESIDE AVENUE, COEUR d'ALENE, IDAHO 83814

Tel: **(208) 664-6926**
Best Time to Call: **4 PM–10 PM**
Hosts: **Al and Karen Hutson**
Location: **30 mi. E of Spokane**
No. of Rooms: **5**
No. of Private Baths: **3**
Max. No. Sharing Bath: **4**
Double/pb: **$70–$80**

Double/sb: **$50–$60**
Open: **All year**
Reduced Rates: **$5 less after 2nd night**
Breakfast: **Full**
Pets: **No**
Children: **Welcome, over 10**
Smoking: **No**
Social Drinking: **Permitted**

Cricket on the Hearth, Coeur d'Alene's first bed-and-breakfast inn, is
a comfortable 1920s cottage with second-story dormer windows and a
large front porch. Guests can unwind in the game room; musicians
should ask Al about the antique pump organ, which has been in his
family since 1916. Lake Coeur d'Alene, just a mile away, is a great
place for boating and fishing. The area's many golf courses will lure

duffers, and the snow-covered slopes will challenge skiers. Morning meals feature fruit, oven-fresh muffins and breads, and main courses like deep-dish French toast with huckleberry sauce.

Bear Lake Bed and Breakfast ✪
500 LOVELAND LANE, FISH HAVEN, IDAHO 83287

Tel: **(208) 945-2688**
Best Time to Call: **Anytime**
Host: **Esther Harrison**
Location: **125 mi. N of Salt Lake City, Utah**
No. of Rooms: **4**
No. of Private Baths: **1**
Max. No. Sharing Bath: **4**
Double/pb: **$75**

Double/sb: **$65**
Open: **All year**
Breakfast: **Full**
Credit Cards: **MC, VISA**
Pets: **Sometimes**
Children: **Welcome, over 12**
Smoking: **No**
Social Drinking: **Permitted**

Make yourselves at home in this spacious secluded log home, hand built and designed by the owners. Sitting on the deck you can absorb the peace and beauty of the turquoise blue lake below. The national forest is half a mile behind the B&B and the colors are a sight to behold in the fall with the yellow aspens and red and orange maples mixed with the green pines. With each guest room decorated in a different decor, you will find total hospitality here, and yummy aromas coming from the kitchen each morning. Take part in all lake activities, including boat rentals. Apart from the waterfront, there is a tour-guided cave, horseback riding, chuck wagon dinners, and mountain biking. Esther subs at local schools and makes items for the B&B gift shop. She has horses and loves the out-of-doors.

The Cary House ✪
17985 U.S. 30 NORTH, HAGERMAN, IDAHO 83332

Tel: **(208) 837-4848**
Best Time to Call: **8 AM–10 PM**
Hosts: **Darrell and Linda Heinemann**
Location: **90 mi. SE of Boise**
No. of Rooms: **4**
No. of Private Baths: **4**
Double/pb: **$55–$75**

Open: **All year**
Breakfast: **Full**
Pets: **No**
Children: **Welcome, over 12**
Smoking: **No**
Social Drinking: **Permitted**

This beautifully restored two-story farmhouse from the late Victorian era is richly furnished with locally obtained antiques. Your hosts, Idaho natives, combine country-style hospitality with gourmet cooking to ensure that your stay is pleasurable. Cary House is located in the lower portion of the Shoshone Gorge of the Snake River, where the abundance of spring water makes for excellent hiking, fishing, and bird-watching. Several splendid golf courses lie within easy driving distance, and day trips can be made to Sun Valley, Craters of the Moon National Monument, and the Sawtooth National Forest.

Shiloh Rose B&B ✪
3414 SELWAY DRIVE, LEWISTON, IDAHO 83501

Tel: (208) 743-2482
Best Time to Call: **Before 10 AM**
Host: **Dorthy Mader**
Location: **100 mi. S of Spokane, Wash.**
Suite: **$75**
Open: **All year**
Reduced Rates: **10% seniors**

Breakfast: **Full**
Credit Cards: **MC, VISA**
Pets: **Sometimes**
Children: **Welcome, over 10**
Smoking: **No**
Social Drinking: **Permitted**
Airport/Station Pickup: **Yes**

Shiloh Rose has one spacious suite. Lovely wallpapers, lace curtains, and fine bed linens give the bedroom a warm, country-Victorian feel. The cozy private sitting room has a wood-burning stove, overflowing bookshelves, and an upright grand piano, as well as a TV and VCR. Breakfasts feature fresh fruit, home-baked muffins, gourmet casseroles, and your choice of coffee or tea. On warm summer evenings, you'll share the backyard with quail and pheasant families. Golf and water sports are available much of the year. The surrounding area is a hunting and fishing paradise and the river levees provide eight miles of hiking and biking trails. But top priority should be given to a day-long jet-boat trip up Hells Canyon, the deepest gorge in the Northwest.

River Cove ✪
P.O. BOX 1862, POST FALLS, IDAHO 83854

Tel: (208) 773-9190
Best Time to Call: **After 5 PM**
Hosts: **Eric and Rosalynd Wurmlinger**
Location: **20 mi. E of Spokane, Washington**
No. of Rooms: **3**
No. of Private Baths: **3**
Suites: **$89**
Open: **All year**

Reduced Rates: **Available**
Breakfast: **Full**
Pets: **Sometimes**
Children: **Welcome, under 5 by arrangement**
Smoking: **No**
Social Drinking: **Permitted**
Airport Pickup: **Yes**

At River Cove, guests enjoy a homey atmosphere with privacy. This new contemporary home is situated on a wooded lot overlooking the beautiful Spokane River. Guests can relax and take in the spectacular view from the patio, or stroll along the many scenic trails by the river. Each morning, breakfast is served in the main dining room or out on the terrace. A complimentary scenic boat cruise or passes to Silverwood Theme Park are included with each two-night stay.

Heritage Inn ✪
510 LENA STREET, SALMON, IDAHO 83467

Tel: **(208) 756-3174**
Best Time to Call: **8 AM–8 PM**
Host: **Audrey Nichols**
Location: **½ mi. from Hwy. 93**
No. of Rooms: **5**
Max. No. Sharing Bath: **3**
Double/sb: **$38–$42**
Single/sb: **$25–$29**

Cottage: **$40**
Open: **All year**
Breakfast: **Continental, plus**
Credit Cards: **MC, VISA**
Pets: **No**
Children: **Welcome**
Smoking: **Restricted**
Social Drinking: **Permitted**

This 100-year-old Victorian farmhouse is set in a valley, surrounded by mountains and pine trees. In the old days, this was a cozy stopover for those traveling by stagecoach. The Heritage has since been lovingly restored and decorated with many antiques. Enjoy a cool drink on the glassed-in sun porch while you enjoy the quiet of this pretty neighborhood. The River of No Return is just half a mile away, and it's just a mile to the city park and swimming pool. Your hostess serves homemade muffins and jams in the sunny dining room or on the porch each morning. She is a native of Salmon and can gladly direct you to restaurants within walking distance, nearby ghost towns, and other places of historic or cultural interest.

ILLINOIS

Galena •   Mundelein •   • Winnetka

Sycamore •   • Chicago

Rock Island •

Navuoo •   • Mossville

Quincy •   • Champaign

Williamsville •

• Arcola

Jerseyville •

• Carlyle   • Mt. Carmel

• Maeystown

Bed & Breakfast/Chicago, Inc. ✪
P.O. BOX 14088, CHICAGO, ILLINOIS 60614-0088

Tel: (312) 951-0085
Coordinator: **Mary Shaw**
States/Regions Covered: **Downtown Chicago, Hyde Park, Near North, North Shore Suburbs**

Rates (Single/Double):
  Modest: **$55 / $65**
  Average: **$65 / $75–$85**
Credit Cards: **AMEX, MC, VISA**

Mary welcomes you to Midwestern hospitality in the "windy city" and its North Shore suburbs. Discover Chicago's outdoor sculpture plazas on foot, shop world-famous Marshall Field's, or observe the skyline from the top of the Sears Tower while staying in one of the over 150 different guest rooms, unhosted furnished apartments, or inns represented by this service. There is a two-night minimum on most accommodations.

B&B Midwest Reservations (formerly B&B Northwest Suburban–Chicago) ○
P.O. BOX 95503, HOFFMAN ESTATES, ILLINOIS 60195-0503

Tel: (800) 34 B AND B [342-2632]
Best Time to Call: 9 AM–5 PM
 Mon.–Fri.
Coordinator: **Martha McDonald-Swan**
States/Regions Covered:
 **Illinois—Cairo, Danforth, Elizabeth,
 Franklin Grove, Galena, Geneva,
 Gurnee, Hinsdale, Morrison,
 Mundelein, Oakbrook, Oak Park,
 Oregon, Wadsworth, West Dundee,**

**Woodstock, Yorkville;
Indiana—Anderson, Franklin,
 Knightstown, Whiteland**
Descriptive Directory of B&Bs: **Free**
Rates (Single/Double):
 Modest: **$45 / $55**
 Average: **$50 / $100**
 Luxury: **$110 / $179**
Credit Cards: **DISC, MC, VISA**

B&B Midwest Reservations (formerly B&B Northwest Suburban–Chicago) has expanded beyond northern Illinois to include southern Illinois and Indiana. Most homes are on historic registers. Hosts enjoy sharing beautiful antiques, handwork, and lots of TLC with their guests. Many also offer numerous special activities and theme weekends, available from suburban locations to country farms.

Curly's Corner ○
RR 2, BOX 590, ARCOLA, ILLINOIS 61910

Tel: (217) 268-3352
Best Time to Call: **Anytime**
Hosts: **Warren and Maxine Arthur**
Location: **35 mi. S of Champaign; 5 mi.
 from I-57**
No. of Rooms: **4**
No. of Private Baths: **2**
Max. No. Sharing Bath: **3**
Double/pb: **$55–$60**

Single/sb: **$40**
Open: **All year**
Breakfast: **Full**
Pets: **No**
Children: **Welcome, over 10**
Smoking: **No**
Social Drinking: **No**
Airport/Station Pickup: **Yes**

This ranch-style farmhouse is located in a quiet Amish community. Your hosts are dedicated to cordial hospitality and will gladly share information about the area or even take you on a tour. They offer comfortable bedrooms with king- or queen-size beds. In the morning, enjoy a wonderful breakfast of homemade biscuits, apple butter, fresh country bacon, and eggs. Curly's Corner is a half mile from beautiful Rockome Gardens.

Country Haus Bed & Breakfast ○
1191 FRANKLIN, CARLYLE, ILLINOIS 62231

Tel: (618) 594-8313; (800) 279-4486
Best Time to Call: **8 AM–10 PM**
Hosts: **Ron and Vickie Cook**

No. of Rooms: **5**
No. of Private Baths: **5**
Double/pb: **$45–$55**

Single/pb: **$40**
Open: **All year**
Reduced Rates: **20% families**
Breakfast: **Full**
Credit Cards: **AMEX, DC, MC, VISA**

Pets: **No**
Children: **Welcome**
Smoking: **No**
Social Drinking: **Permitted**

Country Haus Bed and Breakfast, a cordial establishment that offers simple country comfort, reflects the image of the Carlyle community. It is located one mile from Carlyle Lake, the Midwest's premier sailing lake. We provide clean comfortable lodgings. Firm mattresses, extra pillows, toiletries, robes, and an outdoor hot tub make your stay here a relaxing one. A historic shopping district is only one block away and walking tours of area historic homes are available. A full breakfast is served every morning, where variety is the spice of life. Vickie represents the county's adult literacy program and Ron, the chamber of commerce.

The Golds
2065 COUNTY ROAD, 525 E, CHAMPAIGN, ILLINOIS 61821

Tel: **(217) 586-4345**
Best Time to Call: **Evenings**
Hosts: **Bob and Rita Gold**
Location: **6 mi. W of Champaign**
No. of Rooms: **3**
Max. No. Sharing Bath: **4**
Double/sb: **$45**
Single/sb: **$40**

Open: **All year**
Reduced Rates: **15% weekly**
Breakfast: **Continental**
Pets: **No**
Children: **Welcome**
Smoking: **No**
Social Drinking: **Permitted**
Airport/Station Pickup: **Available**

One of the most beautiful views in Champaign County is yours from the deck of this restored farmhouse. The house is set on six acres surrounded by prime central Illinois farmland. Inside you'll find country antiques, complemented by beautiful wainscoting. An open walnut stairway leads to bedrooms decorated with four-poster beds, handmade quilts, and oriental rugs. Guests can relax by the living room wood stove or enjoy a glass of wine on the deck. Bob and Rita offer garden fruits and cider for breakfast, served with homemade jams, muffins, and coffee cakes. The Golds is two miles from Lake of the Woods, and 20 minutes from the University of Illinois campus. Shopping and restaurants are also within easy reach.

Lake Shore Drive Bed and Breakfast ☉
CHICAGO, ILLINOIS 60614

Tel: (312) 404-5500	Open: All year
Best Time to Call: 9 AM–11 PM, weekdays	Reduced Rates: Available for extended stays
Host: Barbara Marquard	Breakfast: Continental, plus
Location: 2 mi. N of center Chicago	Pets: No
No. of Rooms: 1	Children: No
No. of Private Baths: 1	Smoking: No
Double/pb: $75	Social Drinking: Permitted
Single/pb: $65	Minimum Stay: 2 nights

Barbara welcomes you to her lovely home in the sky, featuring spectacular wraparound views of Lake Michigan, Lincoln Park, and the Chicago skyline. The romantic guest room features cable TV and a dazzling view of the city and the sailboats in Lake Michigan. In good weather, savor a glass of wine and the panoramic views from the rooftop garden. Lake Michigan's beaches, Lincoln Park Zoo, Wrigley Field, jogging and cycling paths, fine dining, jazz and blues clubs, theaters, and great shopping are all within walking distance of this neighborhood. Excellent public transportation provides easy access to downtown, Orchestra Hall, the Art Institute, architectural walking tours, Lake Michigan cruises, Northwestern Memorial Hospital, and McCormick Convention Center. Your gracious and charming hostess can update you on all there is to do and see in Chicago.

Old Town Bed & Breakfast ☉
1451 NORTH NORTH PARK AVENUE, CHICAGO, ILLINOIS 60610

Tel: (312) 440-9268	Breakfast: Continental
Best Time to Call: Anytime	Credit Cards: MC, VISA
Host: Michael Serritella	Pets: No
No. of Rooms: 2	Children: No
Max. No. Sharing Bath: 4	Smoking: No
Double/sb: $65	Social Drinking: Permitted
Open: All year	

This modern town house is furnished with fine art and old family photographs. Each guest room has air-conditioning, a phone, and fully cabled TV. For your convenience there is both on-street and off-street parking. Restaurants, major museums, and public transportation are within walking distance. Enjoy breakfast indoors or, weather permitting, in the private, walled garden. Michael, a former teacher and university administrator, is knowledgeable about the city and surrounding countryside, and is eager to help guests make the most of their trip.

Avery Guest House ✪
606 SOUTH PROSPECT STREET, GALENA, ILLINOIS 61036

Tel: (815) 777-3883	Reduced Rates: 10% seniors; $10 less
Best Time to Call: 9 AM–9 PM	weekdays
Hosts: Flo and Roger Jensen	Breakfast: Continental
Location: 15 mi. E of Dubuque, Iowa	Credit Cards: MC, VISA
No. of Rooms: 4	Pets: No
Max. No. Sharing Bath: 4	Children: Welcome (crib, high chair)
Double/sb: $60	Smoking: No
Single/sb: $50	Social Drinking: Permitted
Open: All year	Airport/Station Pickup: Yes

This spacious, 140-year-old home is located two blocks from historic downtown Galena. Enjoy the view of bluffs and Victorian mansions from an old-fashioned porch swing overlooking the Galena River Valley. Your hosts welcome you to use the piano or bring your own instrument and join them in chamber music. Enjoy delicious homemade muffins and breads along with cheeses and jams each morning. Flo and Roger will gladly direct you to Grant's home, antique shops, and other interesting sights in the historic district.

The Homeridge Bed and Breakfast ✪
1470 NORTH STATE STREET, JERSEYVILLE, ILLINOIS 62052

Tel: (618) 498-3442	Reduced Rates: Corporate rate $10
Best Time to Call: Anytime	less Sun.–Thurs.
Hosts: Sue and Howard Landon	Breakfast: Full
Location: 45 mi. N of St. Louis, Mo.	Credit Cards: MC, VISA
No. of Rooms: 4	Pets: No
No. of Private Baths: 4	Children: Welcome, over 14
Double/pb: $65	Smoking: No
Single/pb: $65	Social Drinking: No
Open: All year	Airport/Station Pickup: Yes

The Homeridge, built in 1867, is a beautiful, warm, 14-room Italianate Victorian private home on eighteen acres in a comfortable country atmosphere. You'll admire the original woodwork, twelve-foot ceilings and crown molding; a hand-carved, curved stairway leads to the third floor with its 12' × 12' cupola or watchtower room. Other details include a 20' × 40' swimming pool and an expansive, pillared front porch. Once the estate of Senator Theodore S. Chapman (1891–1960), this B&B is being reviewed for listing in the National Historic Registry. Homeridge is conveniently located between Springfield, Illinois, and St. Louis, Missouri.

Corner George Inn ✪
CORNER OF MAIN AND MILL, P.O. BOX 103, MAEYSTOWN, ILLINOIS 62256

Tel: **(618) 458-6660; (800) 458-6020**	Breakfast: **Full**
Best Time to Call: **9 AM–9 PM**	Credit Cards: **MC, VISA**
Hosts: **David and Marcia Braswell**	Pets: **No**
No. of Rooms: **5**	Children: **Welcome, over 12**
No. of Private Baths: **5**	Smoking: **No**
Double/pb: **$65–$85**	Social Drinking: **Permitted**
Open: **All year**	Foreign Languages: **German**

A frontier Victorian structure built in 1884—when it was known as the Maeystown Hotel and Saloon—the Corner George Inn has been painstakingly restored. In addition to the five antique-filled guest rooms, there are two sitting rooms, a wine cellar, and an elegant ballroom, where David and Marcia serve breakfast. Maeystown is a quaint 19th-century village; guests can tour it on a bicycle built for two or aboard a horse-drawn carriage. Nearby are St. Louis, Fort de Chartres, Fort Kaskaskia, and the scenic bluff road that hugs the Mississippi.

Old Church House Inn
1416 EAST MOSSVILLE ROAD, MOSSVILLE, ILLINOIS 61552

Tel: **(309) 579-2300**	Double/sb: **$69**
Best Time to Call: **9 AM–9 PM CST**	Single/sb: **$55**
Hosts: **Dean and Holly Ramseyer**	Open: **All year**
Location: **5 minutes N of Peoria**	Breakfast: **Continental, plus**
No. of Rooms: **2**	Credit Cards: **MC, VISA**
No. of Private Baths: **1**	Pets: **No**
Max. No. Sharing Bath: **4**	Children: **Welcome, over 10**
Double/pb: **$85**	Smoking: **No**
Single/pb: **$69 (Mon.–Thurs. only)**	Social Drinking: **No**

Nestled in the scenic Illinois River Valley 5 miles north of Peoria, Old Church House Inn welcomes you to the plush warmth of the Victorian era. Curl up to a crackling fire, take tea in the flower garden, sink deep into the queen-size featherbeds, and enjoy being pampered. Listed on the National Historic American Building Survey, this 1869 church still boasts soaring 18-foot ceilings, tall arched windows, and an "elevated library." Victorian antiques, period furnishings, pedestal sinks, colorful quilts, thick robes, and fine soaps allow guests to relax in luxury. Swiss chocolates, a house specialty, are placed on pillows

during chamber service. Bicycling and cross-country skiing on the Rock Island Trail is just five minutes away, while nearby Peoria features riverboat cruises, cultural attractions, antiquing, and a full range of dining choices to suit your taste!

Living Legacy Homestead Bed and Breakfast ✪
BOX 146A, RR #2, MOUNT CARMEL, ILLINOIS 62863

Tel: **(618) 298-2476**
Best Time to Call: **Noon, evenings**
Host: **Edna Schmidt Anderson**
Location: **50 mi. NW of Evansville, Indiana**
No. of Rooms: **4**
No. of Private Baths: **2**
Max. No. Sharing Bath: **3**
Double/pb: **$70**
Single/pb: **$65**

Double/sb: **$60**
Single/sb: **$55**
Open: **All year**
Reduced Rates: **10% seniors**
Breakfast: **Full**
Other Meals: **Available**
Pets: **No**
Children: **Welcome**
Smoking: **No**
Social Drinking: **No**

Experience country living in this restored turn-of-the-century German homestead, originally an 1870s log house. Music of yesteryear flows from the player piano in the gathering room adjoining the harvest kitchen, featuring a wood-burning cookstove. Wander through the flower, vegetable and herb gardens, the orchard, lane and meadows of this ten-acre nature preserve. Investigate the original farm buildings in the barnyard and pastures. Enjoy a respite under the spreading maple tree, and take in the panoramic scene of rolling farmland and a country church. Browsing in the Attic Treasures Gift Shop in the log room loft, is a pleasant way to walk off the generous country breakfast served downstairs. This log house portion of the structure is the original homestead to which Edna's enterprising German grandparents added the modern 1902 farmhouse and farm buildings. A country quiet night's sleep can be enjoyed in the three guest rooms, which feature antique furnishings of the period and crickets outside your window!

The Poor Farm Bed & Breakfast ✪
POOR FARM ROAD, MOUNT CARMEL, ILLINOIS 62863

Tel: **(800) 646-3276; (618) 262-4663**	Reduced Rates: **Available**
Hosts: **Liz and John Stelzer**	Breakfast: **Full**
Location: **1 mi. N of Mount Carmel**	Other Meals: **Available**
No. of Rooms: **2**	Credit Cards: **AMEX, DISC, MC, VISA**
No. of Private Baths: **2**	Pets: **No**
Double/pb: **$45–$55**	Children: **Welcome**
Single/pb: **$45–$55**	Smoking: **Permitted**
Suites: **$85–$95**	Social Drinking: **Permitted**
Open: **All year**	Airport Pickup: **Yes**

Named for its previous use—as a nineteenth-century shelter for the homeless—this stately, 35-room brick landmark is sure to enchant you with its quiet, country charm. Poor Farm is adjacent to a 25-acre county park and within sight of an 18-hole golf course. Red Hill National Park, Beall Woods Conservation Area and Nature Preserve, a swimming pool, driving range, tennis courts, boating, and fishing are only minutes away. These amenities, plus your hosts' Midwestern hospitality, make this B&B the "inn" place to stay.

Round-Robin Guesthouse ✪
231 EAST MAPLE AVENUE, MUNDELEIN, ILLINOIS 60060

Tel: **(708) 566-7664**	Open: **All year**
Hosts: **George and Laura Loffredo**	Reduced Rates: **10% seniors, families**
Location: **38 mi. NW of Chicago**	Breakfast: **Full**
No. of Rooms: **5**	Credit Cards: **MC, VISA**
No. of Private Baths: **2**	Pets: **No**
Max. No. Sharing Bath: **4**	Children: **Welcome**
Double/pb: **$60**	Smoking: **No**
Double/sb: **$40–$50**	Social Drinking: **Permitted**
Suite: **$110**	

This handsome red Victorian with white trim takes its name from the letters circulated by your hosts' relatives for more than 70 years; to encourage you to write friends and family, George and Laura will provide you with paper, pen, and stamps. The many local diversions ensure that you'll have plenty to write about. Six Flags Great America, the Volo Auto Museum, and the antique village of Long Grove are barely fifteen minutes away by car, and you're never far from golf, swimming, and horseback riding. During the summer, the Chicago Symphony is in residence at nearby Ravinia Park. Or you can enjoy Laura's renditions of classical and ragtime music on the piano. You'll wake up to the aroma of fresh-brewed coffee; coffee cake, muffins, and homemade jam are served between 7:30 and 9:00 AM.

The Ancient Pines Bed & Breakfast ✪
2015 PARLEY STREET, NAUVOO, ILLINOIS 62354

Tel: (217) 453-2767
Best Time to Call: 9 AM–9 PM
Host: Genevieve Simmens
Location: 225 mi. SW of Chicago
No. of Rooms: 3
Max. No. Sharing Bath: 3
Double/sb: $39
Single/sb: $35

Open: All year
Reduced Rates: 15% weekly
Breakfast: Full
Pets: Sometimes
Children: Welcome
Smoking: No
Social Drinking: Permitted

This turn-of-the-century brick home is rich in detail inside and out, from the stained-glass windows and etched-glass front door to the tin ceilings, open staircase, and carved woodwork. Wander through herb and flower gardens, play badminton on the lawn, or listen to music in the library. Local attractions include wineries (Nauvoo holds its own grape festival), Civil War reenactments, historic Mormon homes, and Nauvoo State Park. Whatever your itinerary, you'll wake to the aroma of baking bread, served with eggs and sausage or ham. Special low-cholesterol menus are available upon request.

The Kaufmann House
1641 HAMPSHIRE, QUINCY, ILLINOIS 62301

Tel: (217) 223-2502
Best Time to Call: Noon–9 PM
Hosts: Emery and Bettie Kaufmann
Location: 100 mi. W of Springfield
No. of Rooms: 3
No. of Private Baths: 1
Max. No. Sharing Bath: 4
Double/pb: $65
Single/pb: $60
Double/sb: $50–$55

Single/sb: $40–$45
Reduced Rates: 10% 3 nights or more
Open: All year
Breakfast: Continental, plus
Pets: No
Children: Welcome (crib)
Smoking: No
Social Drinking: No
Airport/Station Pickup: Yes

History buffs will remember Quincy, set right on the Mississippi River, as the scene of the famous Lincoln-Douglas debates, while architecture buffs will be attracted to the town's feast of Victorian styles—Greek Revival, Gothic Revival, Italianate, and Richardsonian. The Kaufmann House was built 100 years ago, and the owners have been careful to maintain its "country" feeling. Guests may enjoy breakfast in the Ancestor's Room, on a stone patio, or at a picnic table under the trees. They are invited to play the piano, watch TV, or enjoy popcorn by the fire. The Kaufmanns describe themselves as "Christians who have a love for God, people, nature, and life."

The Potter House Bed & Breakfast Inn ✪

1906 7 AVENUE, ROCK ISLAND, ILLINOIS 61201

Tel: **(309) 788-1906; (800) 747-0339**
Best Time to Call: **10 AM–9 PM**
Hosts: **Gary and Nancy Pheiffer**
No. of Rooms: **5**
No. of Private Baths: **5**
Double/pb: **$65–$95**
Guest Cottage: **$100, sleeps 4**
Suites: **$75, sleeps 3**
Open: **All year**
Breakfast: **Full**

Credit Cards: **AMEX, DC, DISC, MC, VISA**
Pets: **No**
Children: **Welcome**
Smoking: **No**
Social Drinking: **Permitted**
Minimum Stay: **Special event weekends and peak seasons**
Airport Pickup: **Yes**

Stay in either the main house or the adjacent cottage at this turn-of-the-century property listed on the National Register of Historic Places. Look for the old-fashioned details, from porcelain doorknobs to embossed leather wallcovering and stained- and leaded-glass windows. Even the bathrooms are distinctive: one has its original nickel-plated hardware. You'll notice other historic homes in the neighborhood, which you can tour on foot or aboard a horse-drawn carriage. Gamblers will want to stroll six blocks to the Mississippi, where a riverboat casino is moored. Those who like less risky games can play croquet or shoot baskets on the inn grounds.

Top o' the Morning ✪
1505 19TH AVENUE, ROCK ISLAND, ILLINOIS 61201

Tel: (309) 786-3513
Best Time to Call: **After 5 PM**
Hosts: **Sam and Peggy Doak**
Location: **1½ mi. from Rte. 92, 18th Ave. exit**
No. of Rooms: **3**
No. of Private Baths: **3**

Double/pb: **$50–$75**
Open: **All year**
Breakfast: **Full**
Pets: **No**
Children: **Welcome**
Smoking: **Permitted**
Social Drinking: **Permitted**

Sam and Peggy welcome you to their country estate, set on a bluff overlooking the Mississippi River, near the center of the Quad Cities area. The 18-room mansion is situated at the end of a winding drive on three acres of lawn, orchards, and gardens. The guest rooms, graced with lovely chandeliers and oriental rugs, command a spectacular view of the cities and river. The parlor, with its grand piano and fireplace, is an inviting place to relax. Local attractions are Mississippi River boat rides, harness racing, Rock Island Arsenal, Black Hawk State Park, Augustana College, and St. Ambrose University.

Country Charm Inn ✪
15165 QUIGLEY ROAD, SYCAMORE, ILLINOIS 60178

Tel: (815) 895-5386
Best Time to Call: **Anytime**
Hosts: **Howard and Donna Petersen**

Location: **55 mi. W of Chicago**
No. of Rooms: **3**
No. of Private Baths: **3**

Double/pb: **$35–$75**
Open: **All year**
Reduced Rates: **On a weekly basis**
Breakfast: **Continental, weekdays;
    Full, weekends**
Pets: **No**

Children: **Welcome**
Smoking: **No**
Social Drinking: **No**
Minimum Stay: Only for local
    weekend events

On a tree-topped knoll in rich farming country stands this rambling, turn-of-the-century stucco home. Howard and Donna's comfortable accommodations blend understated elegance with casual warmth and friendliness. Enjoy a full country breakfast on the cozy front porch; house specialties range from egg-cheese dishes and designer pancakes to peach cobblers and pecan roll rings. Then lounge around the sunken fireplace, watch a movie on the large-screen TV with surround sound, borrow a book from the loft library, or roam around the farm. Champ the trick horse sends personal note cards to children telling about his barnyard pals, including llamas and another horse. For those planning to exchange vows, the Peters have built a charming wedding chapel on the property.

Bed and Breakfast at Edie's
233 EAST HARPOLE, P.O. BOX 351, WILLIAMSVILLE, ILLINOIS 62693

Tel: **(217) 566-2538**
Best Time to Call: **After 5 PM,
    weekends**
Host: **Edith L. Senalik**
Location: **10 mi. N of Springfield**
No. of Rooms: **3**
Max. No. Sharing Bath: **4**
Double/sb: **$45**

Single/sb: **$35**
Open: **All year**
Reduced Rates: **Available**
Breakfast: **Continental**
Pets: **No**
Children: **Welcome**
Smoking: **No**
Social Drinking: **Permitted**

Just ten minutes north of the state capital, Springfield, the friendly village of Williamsville offers the peace, quiet, and safety of a small town. Edie's is a 75-year-old mission-style house where guests have use of a formal living room, dining room, and a TV room equipped with cable TV and a video library. Springfield offers the Abraham Lincoln attractions, Springfield Theater Centre, Old State Capitol, Lincoln Land Community College, and Sangamon State University. Historic Petersburg and New Salem, 20 miles to the west, are easily accessible.

Chateau des Fleurs ✪
552 RIDGE ROAD, WINNETKA, ILLINOIS 60093

Tel: **(708) 256-7272**
Best Time to Call: **Mornings**
Host: **Sally Ward**
Location: **15 mi. N of Chicago**

No. of Rooms: **3**
No. of Private Baths: **3**
Double/pb: **$95**
Single/pb: **$90**

Open: **All year**
Reduced Rates: **10% weekly**
Breakfast: **Full**
Pets: **No**

Children: **Welcome, over 11**
Smoking: **No**
Social Drinking: **Permitted**

At Chateau des Fleurs, guests may enjoy the elegance of a French country home and still be only 30 minutes from Chicago's Loop. Antique shops, Lake Michigan, and commuter trains are within walking distance. But there's so much to do at this luxurious B&B, you may not want to leave. Swim in the pool, screen movies on Sally's 50-inch television, tickle the ivories of a Steinway baby grand, or admire the terraced yard and carefully tended gardens. We serve a full breakfast with homemade breads, and turkey and ham.

For key to listings, see inside front or back cover.

✪ This star means that rates are guaranteed through December 31, 1995, to any guest making a reservation as a result of reading about the B&B in *Bed & Breakfast U.S.A.*—1995 edition.

Important! To avoid misunderstandings, always ask about cancellation policies when booking.

Please enclose a self-addressed, stamped, business-size envelope when contacting reservation services.

For more details on what you can expect in a B&B, see Chapter 1.

Always mention *Bed & Breakfast U.S.A.* when making reservations!

If no B&B is listed in the area you'll be visiting, use the form on page 743 to order a copy of our "List of New B&Bs."

We want to hear from you! Use the form on page 745.

INDIANA

Chesterton •

• Peru

• Marion

• Muncie

Middletown •

Rockville •   • Knightstown

• Indianapolis

• Nashville

• Grandview

Evansville •

Gray Goose Inn ✪
350 INDIAN BOUNDARY ROAD, CHESTERTON, INDIANA 46304

Tel: **(800) 521-5127; (219) 926-5781**
Best Time to Call: **9 AM–10 PM**
Hosts: **Tim Wilk and Charles Ramsey**
Location: **60 mi. E of Chicago**
No. of Rooms: **8**
No. of Private Baths: **8**
Double/pb: **$80–$95**
Single/pb: **$80–$95**
Suites: **$110–$135**

Open: **All year**
Reduced Rates: **10% seniors**
Breakfast: **Full**
Credit Cards: **AMEX, DISC, MC, VISA**
Pets: **No**
Children: **Welcome, over 12**
Smoking: **Restricted**
Social Drinking: **Permitted**

Elegant accommodations await you in this English country-style house
overlooking a 30-acre lake. Guest rooms feature four poster beds,
fine linens, and thick, fluffy towels. Some rooms are decorated in
Williamsburg style, some have fireplaces and Jacuzzi. Enjoy a quiet
moment in the common rooms, or relax with a cup of coffee in the
scenic wicker room. Take long walks beside shady oaks, feed the

Canada geese and wild ducks. The Gray Goose is five minutes from Dunes State and National Lakeshore Parks. Swimming, hiking, and fishing sites on Lake Michigan are all within easy reach. Dining and weekend entertainment are within walking distance.

Brigadoon Bed & Breakfast Inn
1201 SOUTH EAST 2ND STREET, EVANSVILLE, INDIANA 47713

Tel: (812) 422-9635
Host: Katelin Forbes
Location: 1 mi. from Hwy. 41
No. of Rooms: 4
No. of Private Baths: 2
Max. No. Sharing Bath: 4
Double/pb: $55
Single/pb: $50
Double/sb: $55
Single/sb: $50

Open: All year
Reduced Rates: Families
Breakfast: Full
Other Meals: Sometimes
Credit Cards: AMEX, DISC, DC
Pets: Sometimes
Children: Welcome (baby-sitter)
Smoking: No
Social Drinking: Permitted
Airport/Station Pickup: Yes

Brigadoon is a white frame Victorian with a gingerbread porch. The inn was built in 1892 and has been thoroughly renovated by the Forbes family. Four fireplaces, original parquet floors, and beautiful stained-glass windows have been lovingly preserved. Modern baths and a country eat-in kitchen have been added. Bedrooms are large and sunny, with accents of lace and ruffles, floral wallpapers, and antique furnishings. Guests are welcome to relax in the parlor or library. Breakfast specialties change daily, and can include a soufflé or quiche served with a lot of homemade breads, jams, and apple butter. This charming Victorian getaway is close to the Historic Preservation area, restaurants, the riverfront, antique shops, the University of Southern Indiana, and the University of Evansville.

The River Belle Bed & Breakfast ✪
P.O. BOX 669, HIGHWAY 66, GRANDVIEW, INDIANA 47615

Tel: (812) 649-2500
Best Time to Call: 8 AM–1 PM
Hosts: Don and Pat Phillips
Location: 33 mi. E of Evansville
No. of Rooms: 6
No. of Private Baths: 2
Max. No. Sharing Bath: 4
Double/pb: $65
Single/pb: $60
Double/sb: $45–$55

Single/sb: $40
Guest Cottage: $60, sleeps 4
Open: All year
Reduced Rates: Weekly
Breakfast: Continental
Credit Cards: MC, VISA
Pets: No
Children: Welcome
Smoking: No
Social Drinking: Permitted

Guests may choose from a selection of accommodations in an 1866 white painted brick steamboat-style house, an 1898 redbrick Italianate house, or an 1860 cottage with full kitchen. These adjacent beauties on the Ohio River have been carefully restored by Pat and Don to serve as their B&B complex. The guest rooms are large and airy, furnished with timeless heirlooms and graced by lace curtains and oriental rugs. You may choose to walk along the riverfront, sit quietly and watch the white squirrels play among the magnolia, pecan, and dogwood trees, or take a side trip to the nearby Lincoln Boyhood National Memorial, Lincoln State Park, the "Young Abe Lincoln" Drama, and Holiday World (the nation's oldest theme amusement park).

The Tranquil Cherub
2164 NORTH CAPITOL AVENUE, INDIANAPOLIS, INDIANA 46202-1251

Tel: (317) 923-9036
Best Time to Call: 8 AM–10 AM; 6 PM–10 PM
Hosts: Thom and Barbara Feit
Location: ½ mi. from I-65 exit 115
No. of Rooms: 3
No. of Private Baths: 1
Max. No. Sharing Bath: 4
Double/pb: $60
Double/sb: $50

Single/sb: $45
Open: All year
Reduced Rates: Weekly
Breakfast: Full
Credit Cards: MC, VISA
Pets: No
Children: Welcome, over 10
Smoking: Restricted
Social Drinking: Permitted
Airport Pickup: Yes

From the central location of this B&B, you are only minutes from downtown. As you enter the foyer, the beautifully crafted oak staircase and pier mirror will draw your eye. Lace curtains, Battenburg lace comforters, wicker furniture, Beardsley prints, and Art Deco furniture decorate the rooms. In the morning, the aroma of freshly brewed coffee—served from an English sideboard in the upstairs hall—will waft to your room. Ease into your day with juice and the paper in the upstairs sitting room. Breakfast is served in the dining room, where beveled glass and a sparkling chandelier accent the oak paneling and fireplace. Weather permitting, you may have your meal on the rear deck overlooking the lily ponds. There is a $5 surcharge for one-night stays.

Old Hoosier House ✪
7601 SOUTH GREENSBORO PIKE, KNIGHTSTOWN, INDIANA 46148

Tel: (317) 345-2969; (800) 775-5315
Hosts: Tom and Jean Lewis
Location: 30 mi. E of Indianapolis
No. of Rooms: 4
No. of Private Baths: 4
Double/pb: $57–$67
Single/pb: $47–$57
Open: All year

Reduced Rates: 10% seniors
Breakfast: Full
Pets: No
Children: Welcome
Smoking: No
Social Drinking: Permitted
Airport/Station Pickup: Yes

The Old Hoosier House takes you back more than 100 years, when the livin' was easier. The rooms are large, with high ceilings, arched windows, antiques, and mementos. A library and patio are available for your pleasure. In the morning you'll wake to the aroma of home-made rolls and coffee. Golfers will enjoy the adjoining golf course, while antique buffs will be glad to know there are hundreds of local dealers in the area. The cities of Anderson and Richmond are close by, and the Indianapolis 500 is within an hour's drive.

Olde Country Club ✪

**8544 SOUTH COUNTY ROAD, 575 WEST,
P.O. BOX 115, KNIGHTSTOWN, INDIANA 46148**

Tel: **(317) 345-5381**	Open: **All year**
Best Time to Call: **Noon–5 PM**	Reduced Rates: **Available**
Hosts: **Dick and Norma Firestone**	Breakfast: **Full**
Location: **35 mi. E of Indianapolis**	Pets: **No**
No. of Rooms: **2**	Children: **No**
No. of Private Baths: **2**	Smoking: **No**
Double/pb: **$60**	Social Drinking: **Permitted**
Single/pb: **$55**	

Dick and Norma, who own one of Knightstown's antique shops, purchased this property in 1961 and expanded it over the years, adding a family room, greenhouse, herb garden, and fish pond. The house once belonged to the Knightstown golf course, and you can practice your chip shots on your hosts' short par three. Rooms are decorated with paisley and floral wallpapers, lace curtains, and, of course, antique furniture. When you're not prowling for antiques of your own—there are lots of shops in town—you can play golf on an eighteen-hole course or ride an old-fashioned train.

Golden Oak Bed & Breakfast

809 WEST FOURTH STREET, MARION, INDIANA 46952

Tel: **(317) 651-9950**	Open: **All year**
Best Time to Call: **9 AM–9 PM**	Breakfast: **Full**
Hosts: **Lois and Dave Lutes**	Credit Cards: **MC, VISA**
Location: **60 mi. N of Indianapolis**	Pets: **No**
No. of Rooms: **4**	Children: **Welcome**
Max. No. Sharing Bath: **3**	Smoking: **No**
Double/sb: **$55**	Social Drinking: **Permitted**
Single/sb: **$50**	

Enjoy the elegance of this beautifully restored two-story home built in the 1890s. Inside, the rooms glow with the rich oak woodwork that inspires this B&B's name. Throughout the house, you'll see hand-crocheted items; similar ones are for sale in your hosts' gift shop. The James Dean Gallery and Historical Museum, the Mississinewa

Battlefield, beaches, golf courses, and antique shops are among the area's attractions. For your dining pleasure, the Hostess House of Marion is within walking distance.

Country Rose B&B ⊘

**5098 NORTH MECHANICSBURG ROAD,
MIDDLETOWN, INDIANA 47356**

Tel: **(317) 779-4501**
Hosts: **Rose and Jack W. Lewis**
Location: **40 mi. NE of Indianapolis**
No. of Rooms: **1**
Max. No. Sharing Bath: **3**
Double/sb: **$55**
Single/sb: **$45**
Suites: **$70–$110**

Open: **All year**
Breakfast: **Full**
Pets: **No**
Children: **Welcome**
Smoking: **No**
Social Drinking: **No**
Minimum Stay: **2 nights Memorial
      Day, NASCAR**

Country Rose is a small-town, garden B&B in historic Raintree County, home of the Indiana Basketball Hall of Fame. Middletown lies 50 minutes from the Indy 500, 30 minutes from Castleton Mall, and 20 minutes from both Ball State and Anderson Universities. You won't drive off on an empty stomach. Rose prepares a full breakfast each morning, featuring specialties like fried mush, fried apples, and country Tennessee biscuits.

Ole Ball Inn ⊘

1000 W. WAYNE STREET, MUNCIE, INDIANA 47303

Tel: **(317) 281-0466**
Best Time to Call: **9 AM–10 PM**
Hosts: **Don, Sharon Green and Larry,
   Kathie Lewis**
Location: **60 mi. SE of Indianapolis**
No. of Rooms: **5**
No. of Private Baths: **5**
Double/pb: **$75**
Suite: **$95**

Open: **All year**
Reduced Rates: **10% seniors**
Breakfast: **Full**
Other Meals: **Available**
Credit Cards: **AMEX, MC, VISA**
Pets: **No**
Children: **Welcome, over 12**
Smoking: **No**
Social Drinking: **Permitted**

Ole Ball Inn offers a Victorian elegance not to be missed. Guest rooms are warm, comfortable, and inviting. Choose from five bedrooms with a four-poster, wrought iron, sleigh or brass bed with pillow-top mattresses, cable TV, and phones. The suite has a fireplace and adjoining patio that lures you to the great outdoors. Floral wallpaper, lace curtains, crystal chandeliers, and thick carpet soothe the weary traveler. Beautiful greens, pinks, and burgundies enhance the decor. Fax and computer facilities are available. The B&B is located 45 minutes from the Indianapolis 500 and a mere two blocks from Ball State University.

Braxtan House Inn B&B ✪
210 NORTH GOSPEL STREET, PAOLI, INDIANA 47454

Tel: **(812) 723-4677**
Best Time to Call: **Anytime**
Hosts: **Duane and Kate Wilhelmi**
Location: **45 mi. S of Bloomington**
No. of Rooms: **6**
No. of Private Baths: **6**
Double/pb: **$55–$75**
Single/pb: **$50–$60**

Open: **All year**
Reduced Rates: **10% Seniors Over 62**
Breakfast: **Full**
Pets: **No**
Children: **Welcome**
Smoking: **No**
Social Drinking: **Permitted**

This Queen Anne Victorian was built in two time periods, first in 1830 and then in 1893. The original cherry, oak, and walnut woodwork is still evident in many of the 21 rooms. The carefully refurbished mansion is decorated with lovely antiques. A full breakfast is served in the dining room, where quiches, pancakes, and a variety of home-baked muffins are on the menu. Paoli Peaks, a ski resort, is 2 miles away, and it's only 15 miles to Patoka, the second largest lake in Indiana. Coffee, tea, and delicious cookies and other snacks are also offered.

Rosewood Mansion ✪
54 NORTH HOOD, PERU, INDIANA 46970

Tel: **(317) 472-7151; fax (317) 472-5575**
Best Time to Call: **8 AM–9 PM**
Hosts: **Lynn and Dave Hausner**
No. of Rooms: **8**
No. of Private Baths: **8**
Double/pb: **$70**
Single/pb: **$60**
Suites: **$85**
Open: **All year**

Reduced Rates: **10% weekly, seniors, families, business travelers (midweek)**
Breakfast: **Full**
Other Meals: **Available by request**
Credit Cards: **AMEX, DISC, MC, VISA**
Pets: **No**
Children: **Welcome**
Smoking: **Restricted**
Social Drinking: **Permitted**
Airport/Station Pickup: **Yes**

Rosewood Mansion is a stately brick Georgian residence constructed in 1862. A winding wooden staircase connects each floor, and stained-glass windows accent each landing. The house is decorated in period style, with floral wallpaper and antique furniture. Because this B&B is located three blocks from downtown Peru, restaurants, shops, public parks, and numerous sports facilities are just minutes away. Guests breakfast on coffee, tea, juice, fresh fruit, freshly baked breads or muffins, and quiche or eggs Benedict. Each room has a TV and phone.

Suit's Us ○
514 NORTH COLLEGE, ROCKVILLE, INDIANA 47872

Tel: (317) 569-5660
Hosts: Bob and Ann McCullough
Location: 50 mi. W of Indianapolis
No. of Rooms: 4
No. of Private Baths: 4
Double/pb: $50–$65
Suite: $125, sleeps 2–6

Open: All year
Breakfast: Continental, plus
Pets: No
Children: Welcome
Smoking: No
Social Drinking: Permitted

This classic plantation-style home, with its widow's walk and generous front porch, dates to the early 1880s. The Strausses, a locally prominent family, bought the house about twenty years later; their overnight guests included Woodrow Wilson, Annie Oakley, James Whitcomb Riley, and John L. Lewis. Today, Ann and Bob extend their hospitality to you. There are books and a color TV in each room, and some even have stereos. Turkey Run Park is ten miles away, while five universities—Indiana State, DePauw, Wabash, St. Mary-of-the-Woods, and Rose-Hulman—are within a thirty-mile radius. Also, Rockville sponsors its own annual event, the Covered Bridge Festival.

IOWA

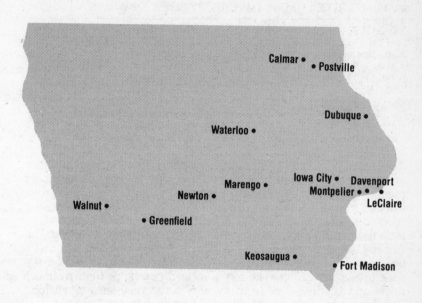

Calmar Guesthouse ✪
103 NORTH STREET, R.R. 1, BOX 206, CALMAR, IOWA 52132

Tel: **(319) 562-3851**
Hosts: **Art and Lucille Kruse**
Location: **10 mi. S of Decorah**
No. of Rooms: **5**
Max. No. Sharing Bath: **5**
Double/sb: **$40–$45**
Open: **All year**

Breakfast: **Full**
Pets: **No**
Children: **Welcome**
Smoking: **No**
Social Drinking: **Permitted**
Airport/Station Pickup: **Yes**

A recent guest reports that "The Calmar Guesthouse is a spacious, lovely, newly remodeled Victorian home located on the edge of town. The atmosphere is enhanced by the friendly, charming manner of Lucille, who made us feel right at home. The rooms were comfortable, private, and pretty. After a peaceful night's sleep, we were served a delicious breakfast of fresh farm eggs with ham and cheeses, croissants with butter and jam, homemade cinnamon rolls, and coffee. I would recommend it to anyone visiting the area." Nearby points of interest include Lake Meyer, the world's smallest church, and Spillville, home of hand-carved Bily Bros. Clocks.

River Oaks Inn ✪
1234 EAST RIVER DRIVE, DAVENPORT, IOWA 52803

Tel: **(319) 326-2629; (800) 352-6016**	Open: **All year**
Best Time to Call: **9 AM–9 PM**	Reduced Rates: **Available**
Hosts: **Bill and Suzanne Pohl; Ron and Mary Jo Pohl**	Breakfast: **Full**
	Credit Cards: **MC, VISA**
Location: **2 mi. from I-80**	Pets: **Sometimes**
No. of Rooms: **5**	Children: **Welcome**
No. of Private Baths: **5**	Smoking: **Restricted**
Double/pb: **$49–$69**	Social Drinking: **Permitted**
Suites: **$89**	Airport/Station Pickup: **Yes**
Carriage House: **$125–$175**	Foreign Languages: **Spanish**

Abner Davison combined Italianate, Victorian, and Prairie architecture when he built his home back in the 1850s. The house is situated on a rolling lot that still shows evidence of the original carriage drive. Choose from a suite with king-size bed, sun porch, and dressing room; the Ambrose Fulton Room, with double bed and garden view; the Mississippi Room, with queen-size bed and window seat; or the Abner Davison Room, which has twin beds or a king-size bed and a bay window. Breakfast is served in the dining room, or out on the deck in warm weather. The inn is located one block from riverboat rides, and is convenient to many area attractions, such as Historic Rock Island Arsenal and the village of East Davenport.

The Richards House
1492 LOCUST STREET, DUBUQUE, IOWA 52001

Tel: **(319) 557-1492**	Open: **All year**
Best Time to Call: **Anytime**	Reduced Rates: **10% Nov.–Apr.; 40% Sun.–Thurs.**
Host: **Michelle Delaney**	
No. of Rooms: **6**	Breakfast: **Full**
No. of Private Baths: **4**	Credit Cards: **AMEX, DC, DISC, MC, VISA**
Max. No. Sharing Bath: **2**	
Double/pb: **$45–$75**	Pets: **Sometimes**
Single/pb: **$45–$75**	Children: **Welcome (crib)**
Double/sb: **$40–$55**	Smoking: **Restricted**
Single/sb: **$40–$55**	Social Drinking: **Permitted**
Suites: **$50–$85**	Airport/Station Pickup: **Yes**

Inside and out, this four-story Victorian is a feast for the eyes, with its gabled roof, stained-glass windows, gingerbread trim, and elaborate woodwork. Rooms are furnished in period style. Guests can continue their journey back in time with a ride on the Fenelon Place Cable Car,

the shortest inclined railway in the country. Then it's time to pay respects to another form of transportation at the Woodward Riverboat Museum. You're welcome to use the kitchen for light snacks; in the morning, Michelle takes over, setting out fresh fruit, waffles, pancakes, sausage, and homemade breads.

Coffey House ✪
1020 AVENUE D, FORT MADISON, IOWA 52627

Tel: **(319) 372-1656**	Open: **All year**
Best Time to Call: **Anytime**	Reduced Rates: Families
Host: **LaVerne Coffey**	Breakfast: **Full**
Location: **200 mi. N of St. Louis,**	Pets: **Yes**
Missouri	Children: **Welcome**
No. of Rooms: **2**	Smoking: **Permitted**
Max. No. Sharing Bath: **4**	Social Drinking: **Permitted**
Double s/b: **$40**	Airport/Station Pickup: **Yes**
Single s/b: **$40**	

A comfortable bed, a hearty breakfast, and a friendly hostess are found in this quiet, homey setting. While the rest of the world is rushing ahead, stop and enjoy the beautiful Mississippi River and its barges and scenic view. Browse in our antique shops and visit Fort Madison's downtown stores—no malls. Enjoy your breakfast on an outdoor patio. La Verne serves freshly baked apple pie for breakfast along with homemade rolls and breads.

Kingsley Inn ✪
707 AVENUE H, FORT MADISON, IOWA 52627

Tel: (319) 372-7074; (800) 441-2327
Best Time to Call: Before 10 PM
Host: Mrs. Myrna Reinhard
Location: On U.S. Highway 61
No. of Rooms: 14
No. of Private Baths: 14
Double/pb: $65–$105
Open: All year
Reduced Rates: Available
Breakfast: Continental, plus

Other Meals: Available
Credit Cards: AMEX, DC, DISC, MC, VISA
Pets: No
Children: Welcome, over 12
Smoking: No
Social Drinking: Permitted
Minimum Stay: Holidays
Station Pickup: Yes

Relax in 1860s Victorian luxury—these spacious rooms are furnished in period antiques with today's modern comforts. Awaken to the aroma of "Kingsley Blend" coffee and enjoy the specialty breakfast in the elegant morning room. Then stroll to the replica 1808 Fort, museum, parks, shops, and antique malls. Historic Nauvoo, Illinois, is 15 minutes away. Treat yourselves to a unique lunch or dinner at Alpha's on the Riverfront, a newly completed restaurant. Amenities include private baths (some whirlpools), CATV, AC, and telephones.

Kountry Klassics ✪
2002 295TH AVENUE, FORT MADISON, IOWA 52627

Tel: (319) 372-5484
Hosts: Sonny and Judy Holmes
Location: 2 mi. N of Fort Madison
No. of Rooms: 3
No. of Private Baths: 2
Max. No. Sharing Bath: 2
Double p/b: $55
Double s/b: $50

Open: All year
Breakfast: Full
Other Meals: Available
Pets: No
Children: Welcome
Smoking: No
Airport/Station Pickup: Yes

If you like a quiet restful sleep in a farm country setting, Kountry Klassics is just the place for you. This B&B is decorated with antiques and lots of linen and lace. You will have your own private entry that is wheelchair accessible. In the morning, you'll be treated to a hearty, hot country breakfast served on Grandma's favorite dishes that conjure memories of the past. Judy's floral designs, displayed throughout the home, create a country-Victorian look that will enhance your peaceful stay.

Mississippi Rose and Thistle Inn ✪
532 AVENUE F, FORT MADISON, IOWA 52627

Tel: (319) 372-7044
Best Time to Call: Anytime
Hosts: Bill and Bonnie Saunders
Location: 20 mi. S of Burlington

No. of Rooms: 4
No. of Private Baths: 4
Double p/b: $70–$105
Single p/b: $65–$105

Open: **All year**
Reduced Rates: **Available**
Breakfast: **Full**
Other Meals: **Available**
Credit Cards: **AMEX, DISC, MC, VISA**

Pets: **No**
Children: **Welcome, over 12**
Smoking: **No**
Social Drinking: **Permitted**
Airport/Station Pickup: **Yes**

A prominent local businessman built this three-story, Italianate Victorian mansion in 1881; more than a hundred years later, the details remain gorgeous, from the brick home's extra-large windows and wraparound porch to the marble fireplaces and hand-carved black walnut staircase. In your room you'll find period antiques, a miniature park bench bookcase and, for a nightcap, a crystal decanter of cream sherry. By prior arrangement, candlelight dinners are served in the private alcove on the first floor. Bill and Bonnie promise that after waking up from a great night's sleep on one of their custom-made beds, you'll be treated to a Victorian culinary excursion featuring egg dishes, fruit, and fresh-baked delicacies.

The Wilson Home ✪
RR 2, BOX 132-1, GREENFIELD, IOWA 50849

Tel: **(515) 743-2031**
Best Time to Call: **5–10 PM**
Hosts: **Wendy and Henry Wilson**
Location: **1 mi. E of Greenfield on Hwy. 92**
No. of Rooms: **2**
No. of Private Baths: **2**

Double/pb: **$65–$85**
Open: **Jan. 15–Oct. 15**
Breakfast: **Full**
Pets: **Sometimes**
Children: **Welcome (crib)**
Smoking: **Permitted**
Social Drinking: **Permitted**

Enjoy the quiet, simple life at The Wilson Home, set in the rolling countryside. The poolhouse encloses a huge indoor pool; a two-level deck filled with plants, wicker and iron furniture, a beverage-stocked kitchenette; and two spacious guestrooms. Breakfasts are served in the sunny dining room of the Wilsons' 1918 farmhouse, which is beautifully decorated with family antiques. Nearby you will find golf, fishing, antiquing, an airplane museum, covered bridges, and John Wayne's birthplace. Pheasant hunting packages available.

Bella Vista Place
2 BELLA VISTA PLACE, IOWA CITY, IOWA 52245

Tel: **(319) 338-4129**	Reduced Rates: **Weekly**
Host: **Daissy Owen**	Breakfast: **Full**
Location: **1 mi. from Highway 80,**	Pets: **No**
Exit 80	Children: **Welcome, over 8**
No. of Rooms: 3	Smoking: **No**
Double/pb: **$65–$75**	Social Drinking: **Permitted**
Single/sb: **$45**	Airport Pickup: **Yes**
Open: **All year**	Foreign Languages: **Spanish**

Daissy has furnished her lovely 1920s home with antiques and artifacts she acquired on her travels in Europe and Latin America. Downtown Iowa City and the University of Iowa are within walking distance of Bella Vista Place; the Hoover Library, the Amana Colonies, and the Amish center of Kalona are all nearby. Full breakfasts feature fruit, orange juice, croissants, jams, eggs, and either coffee or cappuccino.

The Golden Haug ❂
517 EAST WASHINGTON, IOWA CITY, IOWA 52240

Tel: **(319) 338-6452; 354-4284**	Open: **All year**
Best Time to Call: **Anytime**	Reduced Rates: **Available**
Hosts: **Nila Haug and Dennis Nowotny**	Breakfast: **Full**
Location: **2 mi. from I-80, Exit 244**	Pets: **No**
No. of Rooms: 4	Children: **Welcome**
No. of Private Baths: 4	Smoking: **No**
Double/pb: **$65–$85**	Social Drinking: **Permitted**
Single/pb: **$65–$85**	Airport Pickup: **Yes**
Suites: **$65–$90**	

Nila and Dennis's 1920s Arts-and-Crafts house has been restored and updated to provide comfortable accommodations and modern conveniences. Guests can retreat to the comfort of their suites or enjoy the camaraderie of other visitors. With refreshments upon your arrival, evening snacks, and brunch-sized breakfasts, you won't go away hungry. The convenient Iowa City location puts you within walking distance of the University of Iowa, restaurants, stores, and houses of worship.

Mason House Inn of Bentonsport **O**
ROUTE 2, BOX 237, KEOSAUQUA, IOWA 52565

Tel: **(319) 592-3133**
Hosts: **Sheral and William McDermet**
Location: **40 mi. SE of Ottumwa**
No. of Rooms: **9**
No. of Private Baths: **5**
Max. No. Sharing Bath: **3**
Double/pb: **$74**
Single/pb: **$54**
Double/sb: **$49–$59**

Single/sb: **$39–$49**
Open: **All year**
Breakfast: **Full**
Other Meals: **Available**
Credit Cards: **MC, VISA**
Pets: **Sometimes**
Children: **Welcome**
Smoking: **No**
Social Drinking: **Permitted**

Mason House Inn was built next to the Des Moines River by Mormon artisans en route to Salt Lake City. The three-story Georgian house contains 26 rooms. It is the only steamboat inn, built as such, still hosting persons in Iowa. The inn has the only fold-down copper bathtub in the state. Sheral and Bill purchased the inn in 1989 and have done extensive remodeling, allowing for ground-level rooms with private baths. Guests will find a full cookie jar in every room. The entire village is on the National Registry of Historic Places. Iowa's oldest courthouse is six miles to the east. Bill served as a pastor for local congregations for 29 years, and Sheral was a manager for a deli before moving to Bentonsport.

Mississippi Sunrise Bed & Breakfast **O**
18950 GREAT RIVER ROAD, LECLAIRE, IOWA 52753

Tel: **(319) 332-9203**
Hosts: **Ted and Eloise Pfeiff**
Location: **11 mi. E of Davenport**
No. of Rooms: **2**
Max. No. Sharing Bath: **4**
Double/sb: **$45–$50**
Single/sb: **$40–$45**

Open: **Apr.-Oct.**
Reduced Rates: **Weekly**
Breakfast: **Full**
Pets: **No**
Children: **Welcome, over 12**
Smoking: **No**
Social Drinking: **No**

You'll be captivated by the superb panoramic view of the Mississippi River from the dining room, living room, enclosed porch, and large deck of this B&B. This lovely hillside brick home is surrounded by trees, flowers, and birds on one acre of land. It is conveniently located on Highway 67 near Interstate 80. Two bedrooms with a large shared bath, air-conditioning, fireplace, and furnishings designed and built by the hosts provide for your comfort. A full home-cooked breakfast including seasonal fruits and jams from the garden is served. Enjoy the wildlife, the flowers, and the beautiful Mississippi River.

Loy's Bed and Breakfast **○**
RR 1, BOX 82, MARENGO, IOWA 52301

Tel: **(319) 642-7787**
Best Time to Call: **7 AM; noon; 6 PM**
Hosts: **Loy and Robert Walker**
Location: **3 mi. from I-80 exit 216**
No. of Rooms: **3**
No. of Private Baths: **1**
Max. No. Sharing Bath: **4**
Double/pb: **$50–$60**
Single/pb: **$40**

Double/sb: **$50**
Open: **All year**
Breakfast: **Full**
Other Meals: **Available**
Pets: **If caged**
Children: **Welcome**
Smoking: **No**
Social Drinking: **Permitted**

The Walkers invite you to visit their contemporary farmhouse in the heartland of rural Iowa. Enjoy the peaceful surroundings of a large lawn, gardens, and patio. The rooms are furnished in modern and refinished pieces. Guests are welcome to relax in the family room by the fire or to stop by the rec room for a game of shuffleboard or pool, and a treat from the snack bar. If they are not busy with the harvest, your hosts will gladly take you on day trips. Tours may include Plum Grove, Iowa City, Brucemore Mansion, and Herbert Hoover's birthplace. A visit to the nearby lakes is recommended, and a take-along lunch can be arranged. The Amana Colonies is right there and shouldn't be missed.

Varners' Caboose Bed & Breakfast **○**
204 EAST SECOND STREET, P.O. BOX 10, MONTPELIER, IOWA 52759

Tel: **(319) 381-3652**
Best Time to Call: **Afternoons**
Hosts: **Bob and Nancy Varner**
Location: **11 mi. W of Davenport**
No. of Rooms: **1**

No. of Private Baths: **1**
Double/pb: **$55**
Open: **All year**
Breakfast: **Full**
Pets: **Sometimes**

Children: **Welcome**   Social Drinking: **Permitted**
Smoking: **No**   Airport/Station Pickup: **Yes**

Bob and Nancy offer their guests the unique experience of staying in a genuine Rock Island Line caboose. Their home, located close to the Mississippi, was the original Montpelier Depot, and the caboose is a self-contained unit with bath, shower, and kitchen set on its own track behind the house. It sleeps four, with a queen-size bed and two singles in the cupola. The rate is increased to $65 when more than two occupy the caboose. A fully prepared egg casserole, fruit, homemade breads, juice, and coffee or tea are left in the kitchen to be enjoyed at your leisure. Enjoy this quiet town while being a few minutes downstream from the heart of the Quad Cities.

LaCorsette Maison Inn
629 FIRST AVENUE EAST, NEWTON, IOWA 50208

Tel: **(515) 792-6833**   Breakfast: **Full**
Host: **Kay Owen**   Other Meals: **Available**
Location: **25 mi. E of Des Moines**   Pets: **Sometimes**
No. of Rooms: **5**   Children: **By Arrangement**
No. of Private Baths: **5**   Smoking: **No**
Double/pb: **$65–$125**   Social Drinking: **Permitted**
Suites: **$80–$165**   Airport/Station Pickup: **Yes**
Open: **All year**

Bringing a touch of Spanish architecture to the American heartland, this 21-room mansion has all the hallmarks of the Mission style, from its stucco walls and red-tiled roof to its interior oak woodwork. Certain nights of the week, Kay doubles as a chef, preparing elaborate six-course dinners for as many as 57 scheduled guests; the first caller to make reservations selects the entrée, and a house tour precedes the meal. Overnight guests wake up to a full breakfast accented by the herbs and vegetables Kay grows in the backyard. If you want to work off the calories, tennis courts and a pool are in the area.

Old Shepherd House ✪
256 W. TILDEN STREET, BOX 251, POSTVILLE, IOWA 52162

Tel: **(319) 864-3452**	Single/sb: **$30**
Best Time to Call: **10 AM–10 PM**	Open: **All year**
Host: **Rosalyn Krambeer**	Breakfast: **Full**
Location: **25 mi. SE of Decorah**	Pets: **Sometimes**
No. of Rooms: **4**	Children: **Welcome**
No. of Private Baths: **1**	Smoking: **Permitted**
Max. No. Sharing Bath: **2**	Social Drinking: **Permitted**
Double/sb: **$45–$50**	

Postville, a town of 1,500 with four quaint craft shops and a fabulous antiques emporium, is in northeast Iowa in an area known as the state's Little Switzerland. Within a thirty-mile radius you can canoe the Iowa River, or visit sites like the Vesterheim Museum, Effigy Mounds, Villa Louis, Spook Cave, and Bily Brothers clock museum. Shepherd House, built in the early 1880s, is furnished entirely with antique and Victorian pieces. Your hostess is an interior decorator, and she's filled her home with unusual window treatments, restored trunks, and crafts work.

Antique City Inn B&B ✪
400 ANTIQUE CITY DRIVE, P.O. BOX 584, WALNUT, IOWA 51577

Tel: **(712) 784-3722**	Breakfast: **Full**
Host: **Sylvia Reddie**	Other Meals: **Available**
Location: **52 mi. E of Omaha, Nebraska**	Credit Cards: **MC, VISA**
No. of Rooms: **5**	Pets: **No**
No. of Private Baths: **1**	Children: **Welcome, over 12**
Max. No. Sharing Bath: **3**	Smoking: **No**
Double/pb: **$42**	Social Drinking: **Permitted**
Open: **All year**	

This 1911 Victorian residence has been restored to its original state and furnished in period style. You'll admire all the old-fashioned features, such as the wraparound porch, beautiful woodwork, French doors, butler pantry, and dumbwaiter. A block away, in a neighborhood of turn-of-the century brick streets and globed streetlights, you'll find antique shops with more than 200 dealers, plus the restored opera house—home of a country music museum and Iowa's Country Music Hall of Fame. Sylvia's full breakfasts typically consist of juice, fruit, fried potatoes, casseroles, and pecan rolls.

The Daisy Wilton Inn ⊘
418 WALNUT STREET, WATERLOO, IOWA 50703

Tel: (319) 232-0801
Best Time to Call: Afternoons
Hosts: Sue and Al Brase
Location: 100 mi. NE of Des Moines
No. of Rooms: 3
Max. No. Sharing Bath: 4
Double/sb: $55–$65
Single/sb: $50–$60
Open: All year

Reduced Rates: 10% seniors; 10% families
Breakfast: Full
Pets: No
Children: Welcome, over 12
Smoking: No
Social Drinking: Permitted
Airport/Station Pickup: Yes

The Daisy Wilton Inn is a Queen Anne–style Victorian, rich in turn-of-the-century detail. Stained and beveled glass windows adorn the turreted home. Your hosts' cherished antiques and Victorian art nouveau decor complement the interior, which has oak woodwork and a dramatic winding staircase. The parlor, with its bookcase and fireplace, is an inviting room for conversation, music, reading, or games. Stately guest chambers offer luxurious accommodations. Savor the elegant surroundings and pleasant pastimes of the Victorian age.

KANSAS

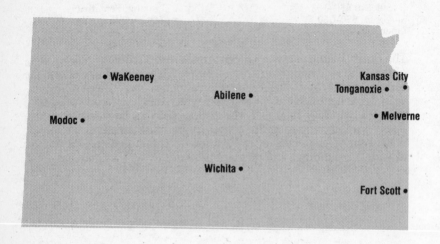

Balfours' House
ROUTE 2, ABILENE, KANSAS 67410

Tel: **(913) 263-4262**
Best Time to Call: **After 5 PM**
Hosts: **Gilbert and Marie Balfour**
Location: **2¼ mi. S of Abilene**
Suites: **$50–$150**
Open: **All year**
Breakfast: **Full**

Credit Cards: **MC, VISA**
Pets: **Sometimes**
Children: **Welcome**
Smoking: **Restricted**
Social Drinking: **Permitted**
Airport/Station Pickup: **Sometimes**

Gilbert and Marie Balfour welcome you to their modern, cottage-style home, set on a hillside. The house is located on just over two acres, and has a spacious yard. Guests have their own private entrance into the family room, which includes a fireplace, piano, and TV. The main attraction of the house is a hexagonal recreation room that has a built-in swimming pool, spa, and dressing area with shower. A separate Southwestern-style bungalow is also available. Your hosts will gladly direct you to the Eisenhower Museum, Greyhound Hall of Fame, and old historic mansions.

Old Glory Guest House ✪

600 NORTH SPRUCE, ABILENE, KANSAS 67410

Tel: **(913) 263-3225**
Best Time to Call: **Anytime**
Hosts: **Sam and Linda Hawes**
Location: **85 mi. W of Topeka**
No. of Rooms: **1**
No. of Private Baths: **1**
Double/pb: **$55**
Single/pb: **$45**
Open: **All year**

Reduced Rates: **Dec.–Feb.**
Breakfast: **Full, Continental**
Credit Cards: **MC, VISA**
Pets: **No**
Children: **Welcome, over 6**
Smoking: **No**
Social Drinking: **Permitted**
Airport/Station pickup: **Yes**

Old glory guest house is a nostalgic 1884 Italianate-style bed & breakfast with a touch of patriotic pride. Located one mile south of Interstate 70 in a quiet residential neighborhood, it is convenient to downtown Abilene, a town of historic mansions, museums and antique/craft shops. Old Glory features tall ceilings, elegant woodwork, pocket doors, and a wraparound side porch. The five-star guestroom, honoring Abilene native Dwight D. Eisenhower, is furnished with a full-size antique bed with matching furniture and modern bath. Eggs Benedict is the breakfast specialty served in the sunny bay-windowed dining room.

Country Quarters ✪

ROUTE 5, BOX 80, FORT SCOTT, KANSAS 66701

Tel: **(316) 223-2889**
Best Time to Call: **After 5 PM**

Host: **Marilyn McQuitty**
Location: **2 mi. S of Fort Scott**

No. of Rooms: **2**
Max. No. Sharing Bath: **4**
Double/sb: **$30**
Open: **All year**
Breakfast: **Full**

Pets: **No**
Children: **Welcome**
Smoking: **Permitted**
Social Drinking: **Permitted**

Marilyn McQuitty welcomes you to a real working farm located outside a charming Victorian town. Her 100-year-old farmhouse is furnished with comfortable family pieces. While you're sitting by the fire, ask to hear the story behind the 100-year-old hearth and hand-carved mantelpiece. Guests are welcome to relax on the porch or visit the ceramic shop located on the premises. There is easy access to the Fort Scott Lake, Gunn Park, and the Fort Scott National Historic Site, an authentically restored military fort dating back to 1892. Downtown you can drive past the magnificent old homes, browse through antiques stores, and visit a one-room schoolhouse.

Krause House ✪
ROUTE 1, BOX 42, MARIENTHAL, KANSAS 67863

Tel: **(316) 379-4627**
Hosts: **Paul and Merilyn Krause**
Location: **13 mi. W of Scott City**
No. of Rooms: **2**
No. of Private Baths: **1**
Max. No. Sharing Bath: **4**
Double/pb: **$40**
Single/pb: **$35**
Double/sb: **$35**

Single/sb: **$30**
Open: **All year**
Reduced Rates: **Families**
Breakfast: **Full**
Pets: **Sometimes**
Children: **Welcome**
Smoking: **No**
Social Drinking: **No**

Experience a working grain farm in the western Kansas countryside. Paul and Merilyn Krause have a remodeled farmhouse surrounded by tall shade trees. Breakfast specialties such as egg casseroles, homemade breads, and cinnamon rolls are served on the glassed-in patio overlooking the flowers and greenery. Krause House is 25 miles from Scott County State Park, where you may fish, boat, hunt for fossils, and see Indian ruins.

Almeda's Bed and Breakfast Inn ✪
220 SOUTH MAIN, TONGANOXIE, KANSAS 66086

Tel: **(913) 845-2295**
Best Time to Call: **Before 9 AM;**
   evenings
Hosts: **Almeda and Richard Tinberg**
Location: **20 mi. W of Kansas City**
No. of Rooms: **6**
No. of Private Baths: **2**
Max. No. Sharing Bath: **4**
Double/pb: **$40**
Single/pb: **$35**

Double/sb: **$30**
Single/sb: **$25**
Suite: **$65**
Open: **All year**
Breakfast: **Continental, plus**
Pets: **No**
Children: **Welcome**
Smoking: **Restricted**
Social Drinking: **Permitted**

This small-town B&B has a tranquil, friendly atmosphere. An inn for decades—during World War I it attained coast-to-coast fame as the Myers Hotel—it was designated a historic landmark in 1983. The rooms are decorated with country flare, accented by antiques from Almeda's collection. Guests may sip a cup of coffee by the stone bar in the room used as a bus stop in the thirties; the movie *Bus Stop* was inspired by this site. A plaque outside the dining room tells the story of the hotel.

Thistle Hill
ROUTE 1, BOX 93, WAKEENEY, KANSAS 67672

Tel: (913) 743-2644
Best Time to Call: 6–8 AM; evenings
Hosts: Dave and Mary Hendricks
Location: 1½ mi. from I-70 exit 120
No. of Rooms: 3
No. of Private Baths: 2
Max. No. Sharing Bath: 4
Double/pb: $55
Single/pb: $45

Double/sb: $55
Single/sb: $45
Open: All year
Breakfast: Full
Pets: No
Children: Welcome
Smoking: Restricted
Social Drinking: Permitted
Airport/Station Pickup: Yes

The entry of this weathered wood country house sets the hospitable tone of this B&B located 325 miles west of Kansas City, or the same distance east of Denver, Colorado. Seasonal wreaths, an Early American bench, antique lanterns, and a big sign saying, "Welcome to Thistle Hill" are the Hendrickses' way of saying they're glad you've come to visit. They're anxious to share with you the pleasures of their rural life, which include cooking, restoring antiques, and working with their team of draft horses. A varied breakfast often includes country fresh eggs, breakfast meats, fresh baked breads, or hotcakes made with whole wheat from their own wheat fields. On chilly mornings it is served near the fireplace. Cedar Bluff Reservoir, for fishing, is 30 miles away; pheasant, waterfowl, and deer roam 10,000 acres of public hunting land nearby.

Vermilion Rose-A Bed and Breakfast Place ✪
1204 NORTH TOPEKA AVENUE,
WICHITA, KANSAS 67214-2843

Tel: (316) 267-7636; fax (316) 267-7642
Best Time to Call: Anytime
Hosts: Marietta Anderson and Ken Kern
Location: 1 mi. N of Downtown Wichita
No. of Rooms: 4
No. of Private Baths: 4
Double/pb: $60–$90

Single/pb: $45–$75
Open: All year
Breakfast: Continental, plus
Other Meals: Available
Credit Cards: MC, VISA
Pets: No
Smoking: No
Social Drinking: Permitted
Airport/Station Pickup: Yes

Vermilion Rose is a new owner-occupied bed and breakfast in a turn-of-the-century home in Wichita's Historic Midtown District. The immediate area had the nickname "lumberman's row," since the proprietors of many early Wichita lumber businesses built their residences here. Guests are invited to enjoy the common room, dining and library areas; for a small additional fee, a fax machine and copier can be at your disposal. Breakfast specialties include fresh fruit, juices, breads, pastries, and seasonal surprises.

For key to listings, see inside front or back cover.

○ This star means that rates are guaranteed through December 31, 1995, to any guest making a reservation as a result of reading about the B&B in *Bed & Breakfast U.S.A.—1995* edition.

Important! To avoid misunderstandings, always ask about cancellation policies when booking.

Please enclose a self-addressed, stamped, business-size envelope when contacting reservation services.

For more details on what you can expect in a B&B, see Chapter 1.

Always mention *Bed & Breakfast U.S.A.* when making reservations!

If no B&B is listed in the area you'll be visiting, use the form on page 743 to order a copy of our "List of New B&Bs."

We want to hear from you! Use the form on page 745.

KENTUCKY

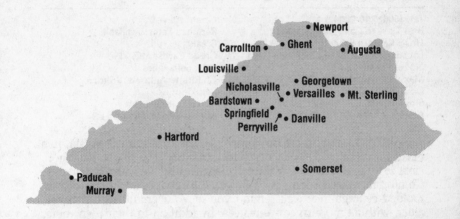

Bluegrass Bed & Breakfast ✪
2964 McCRACKEN PIKE, VERSAILLES, KENTUCKY 40383

Tel: **(606) 873-3208**
Best Time to Call: **9 AM–4 PM**
Coordinator: **Betsy Pratt**
States/Regions Covered: **Berea,
  Danville, Frankfort, Georgetown,
  Lexington, Louisville, Maysville,
  Midway, Paris, Versailles, Winchester**

Rates (Single/Double):
  Modest: **$60**
  Average: **$75**
  Luxury: **$100**

Most of Betsy's B&Bs are in beautiful old houses that grace the country
roads of the area. You may choose among a stone house built in 1796,
a turreted Victorian in downtown Lexington, or a country home
where your bedroom windows look out on thoroughbred horses. Visit
Shakertown, where weavers, smiths, and woodworkers display their
skills in an 1839 restored village. Take a ride on the winding Kentucky
River in a paddlewheel boat. Tour exquisite historic mansions or see

the picturesque homes of such Derby winners as Secretariat and Seattle Slew. And don't miss the 1,000-acre Kentucky Horse Park that includes a theater, museum, track, barns, and hundreds of horses. You may even take a horseback ride, because this place will inspire you.

Augusta White House Inn B&B ✪
307 MAIN STREET, AUGUSTA, KENTUCKY 41002

Tel: **(606) 756-2004**	Open: **All year**
Best Time to Call: **9 AM–11 AM**	Reduced Rates: **Available**
Host: **Rebecca Spencer**	Breakfast: **Full**
Location: **50 mi. SE of Cincinnati, Ohio**	Credit Cards: **MC, VISA**
No. of Rooms: **2**	Pets: **Sometimes**
Max. No. Sharing Bath: **4**	Children: **Welcome, 2 thru 5**
Double/sb: **$79**	Smoking: **No**
Single/sb: **$59**	Social Drinking: **No**
Guest Cottage: **$170, sleeps 4**	Airport/Station Pickup: **Yes**

AWHIBB is located in the downtown section of historic Augusta, in a beautifully restored, two-story brick structure (the Buger Tin Shop, circa 1840) that combines Victorian elegance and Southern hospitality. Comfortably sized rooms with flowered wallpaper and high, crown-molded ceilings may well remind you of your grandparents' home, albeit with all modern conveniences. In addition to their own room, guests have use of the parlor, formal dining and living rooms, and outside garden deck. Breakfast includes fresh-baked bread with an array of gourmet entrees and side dishes to please even the most discriminating palates. Antique shops and excellent restaurants are a short stroll away.

Jailer's Inn ✪
111 WEST STEPHEN FOSTER AVENUE, BARDSTOWN, KENTUCKY 40004

Tel: **(502) 348-5551**	Reduced Rates: **Available**
Best Time to Call: **10 AM–5 PM**	Breakfast: **Continental, Plus**
Hosts: **Challen and Fran McCoy**	Credit Cards: **AMEX, DISC, MC, VISA**
Location: **35 mi. S of Louisville**	Pets: **No**
No. of Rooms: **6**	Children: **Welcome**
No. of Private Baths: **6**	Smoking: **No**
Double/pb: **$55–$85**	Social Drinking: **Permitted**
Open: **Mar.–Dec.**	Station pickup: **Yes**

For the ultimate in unusual experiences, spend the night in "jail" without having committed a crime. Built in 1819, this former jailer's residence originally housed prisoners upstairs, and has been completely remodeled and furnished with fine antiques and oriental rugs. An adjacent building, once used as the women's cell, has been transformed into a charming suite, where bunk beds are suspended from a brick wall and the decor is black-and-white checks instead of stripes. The town is famous for *The Stephen Foster Story*, an outdoor musical production. Take time to visit the Getz Museum of Whiskey History and a Civil War museum, and take a tour of My Old Kentucky Home conducted by guides in antebellum costumes.

Alpine Lodge ○
5310 MORGANTOWN ROAD, BOWLING GREEN, KENTUCKY 42101

Tel: (502) 843-4846
Best Time to Call: 9 AM–9 PM
Hosts: Dr. and Mrs. David Livingston
Location: 60 mi. N of Nashville, Tenn.
No. of Rooms: 5
No. of Private Baths: 3
Max. No. Sharing Bath: 4
Double/pb: $50
Single/pb: $40
Double/sb: $45
Single/sb: $35
Guest Cottage: $150, sleeps 6

Suites: $75
Open: All year
Reduced Rates: Weekly
Breakfast: Full
Other Meals: Available
Pets: Dogs welcome
Children: Welcome
Smoking: Permitted
Social Drinking: Permitted
Airport/Station Pickup: Yes
Foreign Languages: Spanish

The lush bluegrass area of Kentucky is the setting for this spacious Swiss chalet–style home that's situated on four lovely acres and furnished with many antiques. A typical Southern breakfast of eggs, sausage, biscuits and gravy, fried apples, grits, coffee cake, and beverage starts your day. If you can manage to get up from the table, stroll the grounds complete with nature trails and gardens or take a swim in the pool. Afterwards, take in the sights and sounds of Opryland, Mammoth Cave, or the battlefields of historic Bowling Green. In the evening, relax in the living room, where Dr. Livingston, a music professor, may entertain you with selections played on the grand piano.

Bowling Green Bed & Breakfast ○
3313 SAVANNAH DRIVE, BOWLING GREEN, KENTUCKY 42104

Tel: (502) 781-3861
Best Time to Call: Before 10 PM
Hosts: Dr. Norman and Ronna Lee
  Hunter
Location: 3.5 mi. from I-65, exit 22
No. of Rooms: 3
No. of Private Baths: 1
Max. No. Sharing Bath: 4
Double/pb: $55–$65
Single/pb: $45

Double/sb: $55
Single/sb: $45
Open: All year
Reduced Rates: 20% families
Breakfast: Full
Pets: No
Children: Welcome, over 14
Smoking: No
Social Drinking: Permitted
Station Pickup: Yes

Upon entering this lovely home in an attractive, quiet neighborhood, guests receive a warm welcome. Whether you choose the antique walnut twin room or either of the double-bedded rooms, you will find a comfortable, relaxed atmosphere. Enjoy the library and TV in the den, read or chat in the lounge, or take an evening walk to the duck pond and the woods. Breakfast is set out in the dining room, with special dietary needs considered. Afternoon tea is also served. This B&B is located between Mammoth Cave National Park and Nashville, Tennessee. Restaurants, shopping, Western Kentucky University and the historic downtown square are all close by. Your hosts, a retired chemistry professor and a nurse, are involved with foreign exchange and love to travel and meet people.

P. T. Baker House Bed & Breakfast ✪
406 HIGHLAND AVENUE, CARROLLTON, KENTUCKY 41008

Tel: (502) 732-4210 weekends; (800) 74 BAKER [742-1537], outside Kentucky	Guest Cottage: $125, sleeps 6
	Reduced Rates: 10% seniors
	Breakfast: Full
Hosts: Bill and Judy Gants	Credit Cards: MC, VISA
Location: 5 mi. N of I-71 exit 44	Pets: No
No. of Rooms: 3	Children: Welcome, over 10
No. of Private Baths: 3	Smoking: Permitted
Double/pb: $65	Social Drinking: Permitted
Single/pb: $45	Airport/Station Pickup: Yes
Open: All year	

Upon entering this large Victorian home, listed on the National Register of Historic Places, one gets the feeling of having stepped back to the 1800s. The high ceilings, heavy walnut doors, hand-carved cherry staircase, oil lamp chandeliers, and elegant antiques embellish the careful restoration of this ornate house. Upon arrival, you are graciously welcomed with a snack and beverage. A bowl of fresh fruit in your room, a potpourri gift, and breakfast served on antique china and crystal are just some of the special touches. Recreational diversions abound in this area located midway between Cincinnati and Louisville.

Breckinridge House B&B ✪
201 SOUTH BROADWAY, GEORGETOWN, KENTUCKY 40324

Tel: (502) 863-3163	Credit Cards: VISA
Hosts: Annette and Felice Porter	Pets: Sometimes
No. of Rooms: 2 suites	Children: Welcome
Suites: $65–$85	Smoking: Permitted
Open: All year	Social Drinking: Permitted
Breakfast: Full	Airport/Station Pickup: Yes

This charming Georgian home was the residence of John C. Breckinridge, a former vice-president who ran against Abraham Lincoln for the presidency. (After losing the election, Breckinridge became a leading Confederate general.) Each antique-filled suite has a bedroom, sitting room, kitchen, and bath. Breakfast features homemade breads, pecan rolls, fresh fruit, and bacon and eggs.

Jordan Farm Bed & Breakfast ❂
4091 NEWTOWN PIKE, GEORGETOWN, KENTUCKY 40324

Tel: **(502) 863-1944; 868-9002**	Pets: **No**
Best Time to Call: **Anytime**	Children: **Welcome**
Hosts: **Harold and Becky Jordan**	Smoking: **Permitted**
Location: **8 mi. N of Lexington**	Social Drinking: **Permitted**
Suites: **$75, sleeps 4**	Minimum Stay: **2 nights weekends Apr.**
Open: **All year**	**and Oct.**
Breakfast: **Full**	Airport/Station Pickup: **Yes**

Derby fans will want to stay on this 100-acre thoroughbred farm in the middle of Kentucky's legendary horse country. Indeed, the Kentucky Horse Park is only five minutes away. From the guest room's private deck, you can watch the Jordans' horses cavort in the fields. Or drop a line into the fishing pond and try your luck.

Log Cabin Bed and Breakfast ❂
350 NORTH BROADWAY, GEORGETOWN, KENTUCKY 40324

Tel: **(502) 863-3514**	Breakfast: **Continental**
Hosts: **Clay and Janis McKnight**	Pets: **Welcome**
Location: **10 mi. N of Lexington**	Children: **Welcome**
Guest Cottage: **$75 for 2**	Smoking: **Permitted**
Open: **All year**	Social Drinking: **Permitted**

This rustic log cabin was built, circa 1809, with a shake shingle roof and chinked logs. Inside, the living room is dominated by a huge fieldstone fireplace. The master bedroom and bath are on the ground floor and a loft bedroom will sleep additional people with ease. The house has been fully restored and air-conditioned by the McKnights, and is filled with period furnishings. The dining-kitchen wing is equipped with all new appliances and modern amenities. The Log Cabin is located in a quiet neighborhood close to Kentucky Horse Park, Keeneland, and many other historic places. This is the perfect spot to bring the kids and give them a taste of authentic American tradition.

Ghent House B&B ○
411 MAIN STREET, U.S. 42, GHENT, KENTUCKY 41045

Tel: **(502) 347-5807 weekends; (606) 291-0168 weekdays**
Best Time to Call: **After 7 PM; weekends**
Hosts: **Wayne and Diane Young**
Location: **12 mi. N and E of I-71 exit 44**
No. of Rooms: **3**
No. of Private Baths: **3**
Double/pb: **$60**
Single/pb: **$50**

Suites: **$100**
Open: **All year**
Reduced Rates: **Available**
Breakfast: **Full**
Pets: **No**
Children: **Welcome (crib)**
Smoking: **No**
Social Drinking: **Permitted**
Airport/Station Pickup: **Yes**

Ghent House is a gracious antebellum residence, built in the usual style of the day—a central hall with rooms on either side and the kitchen and dining room in the rear. A beautiful fantail window and two English coach lights enhance the front entrance. Guests can look out over the Ohio River and imagine the time when steamboats regularly traveled the waterways. The view includes the lovely homes of the Vevay, Indiana, side of the river.

Ranney Porch Bed & Breakfast ○
3810 HIGHWAY 231 NORTH, HARTFORD, KENTUCKY 42347

Tel: **(502) 298-7972**
Best time to Call: **After 4 PM**
Hosts: **Peggy Jo and Rance Ranney**
Location: **17.7 mi. S of Owensboro**
No. of Rooms: **1**
No. of Private Baths: **1**
Double/pb: **$50**

Single/pb: **$40**
Open: **All year**
Breakfast: **Full**
Pets: **No**
Children: **Welcome**
Smoking: **No**
Social Drinking: **No**

One of the unique features of this country B&B is the fifty-seven-foot porch spanning the length of the building, which is modeled after a Georgia tenant house. The exterior has blue trim, black shutters, and a candy apple red door. Inside, a Story and Clark piano sits on the foyer's red brick floor tiles, which came from the roof of a train depot. In the living room, cherry furniture complements the cherry wood floor. The bedroom's antique quilts and firm mattress assure you a good night's sleep. Numerous special events throughout the year, such as the Bar-be-que Festival, Yellow Banks Dulcimer Festival, and Bluegrass Music Festival, make this a place to visit often.

The Victorian Secret Bed & Breakfast ○
1132 SOUTH FIRST STREET, LOUISVILLE, KENTUCKY 40203

Tel: **(502) 581-1914**
Hosts: **Nan and Steve Roosa**

Location: **1 mi. S of downtown Louisville**

No. of Rooms: **3**
No. of Private Baths: **1**
Max. No. Sharing Bath: **3**
Double/pb: **$68**
Double/sb: **$63**
Open: **All year**

Reduced Rates: **Weekly**
Breakfast: **Continental**
Pets: **No**
Children: **Welcome**
Smoking: **Permitted**
Social Drinking: **Permitted**

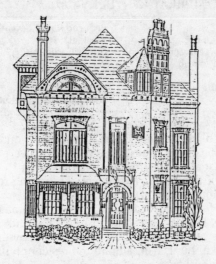

An elegant brick Victorian with lavish woodwork, this B&B has modern amenities like an exercise room with a bench press and a rowing machine, and color TVs in guest rooms. The Louisville area is rich in historic homes. Railbirds and would-be jockeys will want to make pilgrimages to the famous tracks at Churchill Downs (site of the Kentucky Derby) and Louisville Downs (home of harness races).

The Trimble House ✪
321 NORTH MAYSVILLE STREET, MT. STERLING, KENTUCKY 40353

Tel: **(606) 498-6561; 498-7078**
Best Time to Call: **9 AM–10 PM**
Hosts: **Jim and June Hyska**
Location: **29 mi. E of Lexington**
No. of Rooms: **4**
No. of Private Baths: **3**
Max. No. Sharing Bath: **4**
Double/pb: **$60**
Single/pb: **$45**

Double/sb: **$55**
Open: **All year**
Reduced Rates: **10% seniors**
Breakfast: **Full**
Credit Cards: **AMEX, MC, VISA**
Pets: **No**
Children: **Welcome, over 12**
Smoking: **Permitted**
Social Drinking: **Permitted**

An "Old South" plantation-style home located in Mt. Sterling's historic district, the Trimble House (1872) is listed on the Kentucky Historic Register. Visitors can enjoy air-conditioning, comfortable beds, Granny's handmade quilts, and antiques. Pool, exercise room, Jacuzzi, bicycles, and limo available for horse racing events and blue-grass horse farm tours.

Diuguid House Bed & Breakfast ○
603 MAIN STREET, MURRAY, KENTUCKY 42071

Tel: **(502) 753-5470**	Reduced Rates: **Seventh night free**
Best Time to Call: **4–10 PM**	Breakfast: **Full**
Hosts: **Karen and George Chapman**	Credit Cards: **MC, VISA**
Location: **45 mi. S of Paducah**	Pets: **No**
No. of Rooms: **3**	Children: **Welcome**
Max. No. Sharing Bath: **5**	Smoking: **No**
Double/sb: **$40**	Social Drinking: **Permitted**
Open: **All year**	Airport/Station Pickup: **Yes**

Upon walking into this 1890s Queen Anne, listed on the National Register of Historic Places, guests see an impressive sweeping oak staircase and unusual hallway fretwork. In addition to their rooms, visitors have use of the parlor, TV lounge, and dining room. Murray State University houses a local history museum, an art gallery, and the National Boy Scout Museum. The town, a top-rated retirement community, offers lots of theatrical and musical events. For outdoor activities, take the twenty-minute drive to Land Between the Lakes, where you can hike, hunt, fish, admire the resident buffalo herd, or see a working historical farm.

Gateway Bed and Breakfast ○
326 EAST 6TH STREET, NEWPORT, KENTUCKY 41071

Tel: **(606) 581-6447**	Double/sb: **$60**
Best Time to Call: **After 4:30 PM**	Single/sb: **$60**
Hosts: **Ken and Sandy Clift**	Open: **All year**
Location: **1 mi. South of Cincinnati,**	Breakfast: **Full**
Ohio	Credit Cards: **AMEX, MC, VISA**
No. of Rooms: **3**	Pets: **No**
No. of Private Baths: **1**	Children: **Welcome**
Max. No. Sharing Bath: **4**	Smoking: **No**
Double/pb: **$70**	Social Drinking: **Permitted**
Single/pb: **$70**	Airport/Station Pickup: **Yes**

This 1878 townhouse in East Newport's National Historic District won 1992's Great American Homes Award for Bed and Breakfast Restoration from the National Trust for Historic Preservation. Gateway is elegantly decorated in the Victorian period, complete with antique musical devices: a 1910 pump organ, a 1904 Edison Fireside Phonograph, and a 1928 player piano. A full breakfast will be served especially for you in the formal dining room. The inn is conveniently located five minutes from downtown Cincinnati, next door to Palm

Beach Mill Outlet. Fine dining can be found along River Row on the scenic Ohio River.

Sandusky House Bed & Breakfast ✪
1626 DELANEY FERRY ROAD, NICHOLASVILLE, KENTUCKY 40356

Tel: **(606) 223-4730**
Best Time to Call: **8 AM–10 PM**
Hosts: **Jim and Linda Humphrey**
Location: **6 mi. SW of Lexington**
No. of Rooms: **3**
No. of Private Baths: **3**
Double/pb: **$69**
Open: **All year**

Reduced Rates: **Available**
Breakfast: **Full**
Credit Cards: **MC, VISA**
Pets: **No**
Children: **Welcome, over 12**
Smoking: **No**
Social Drinking: **Permitted**
Airport/Station Pickup: **Yes**

The tree-lined drive to the Sandusky House is just a prelude to the handsome Greek Revival residence built about 1850 from bricks fired on the premises. Once the property was a one thousand-acre farm owned by Revolutionary War veteran Jacob Sandusky—he acquired the site in 1780 land grant from Patrick Henry, then the governor of Virginia. Today the B&B sits on a ten-acre estate amid horse farms, yet close to downtown Lexington, Keeneland Race Track, Kentucky Horse Park, and many other attractions.

Ehrhardt's B&B ✪
285 SPRINGWELL LANE, PADUCAH, KENTUCKY 42001

Tel: (502) 554-0644
Best Time to Call: 7–9 AM; 4–6 PM
Hosts: Eileen and Phil Ehrhardt
Location: 1 mi. from I-24
No. of Rooms: 2
Max. No. Sharing Bath: 4
Double/sb: $35
Single/sb: $30
Open: All year

Reduced Rates: 10% seniors
Breakfast: Full
Other Meals: Available
Pets: No
Children: Welcome, over 12
Smoking: Permitted
Social Drinking: Permitted
Airport/Station Pickup: Yes

This brick Colonial ranch home is just a mile off I-24, which is famous for its beautiful scenery. Your hosts hope to make you feel at home in antique-filled bedrooms and a den with a fireplace. Homemade biscuits and jellies, and country ham and gravy are breakfast specialties. Enjoy swimming in the Ehrhardts' pool and boating at nearby Lake Barkley, Ky Lake, and Land Between the Lakes. Paducah features quarterhorse racing from June through November, and the National Quilt Show in April.

1857's B&B ✪
127 MARKET HOUSE SQUARE, PADUCAH, KENTUCKY 42001

Tel: (502) 444-3960; (800) 264-5607
Host: Deborah Bohnert
Location: 155 mi. SE of Nashville, Tenn.
No. of Rooms: 2
Max. No. Sharing Bath: 4
Double/sb: $65
Single/sb: $55
Open: All year

Reduced Rates: Long stays
Breakfast: Continental, plus
Credit Cards: MC, VISA
Pets: Sometimes
Children: Welcome
Smoking: Permitted, game room only
Social Drinking: Permitted
Airport Pickup: Yes

This three-story building, which takes its name from the year of its construction, was placed on the National Historic Register 120 years later. You'll appreciate the home's thoughtful Victorian restoration and its third-floor views of the Ohio River. The Museum of the American Quilt Society, antique and specialty shops, fashionable boutiques, restaurants, and the Market House Cultural Center are all within walking distance.

Elmwood Inn ✪
205 EAST FOURTH STREET, PERRYVILLE, KENTUCKY 40468

Tel: (606) 332-2400
Hosts: Bruce and Shelley Richardson
Location: 35 mi. SW of Lexington

No. of Rooms: 2 suites
Suites: $85
Open: Feb.-Dec.

Breakfast: **Full**
Other Meals: **Available**
Credit Cards: **MC, VISA**
Pets: **No**

Children: **No**
Smoking: **No**
Social Drinking: **Permitted**

Escape the hectic pace of the modern world at this beautifully restored 1842 Greek Revival mansion along a quiet river in the heart of one of Kentucky's most historic small towns. Listed on the National Register of Historic Places—it served as a Civil War field hospital—the inn features guest suites with private sitting rooms, antiques, fireplaces, and a well-stocked library. Join area residents in the dining room for an authentic English afternoon tea Thursday through Saturday. Don't be surprised to find Civil War soldiers or a brass band on the front lawn. Perryville was the site of the only major Civil War battle fought in Kentucky. Perryville Battlefield, Shakertown, Bardstown, and Keeneland are all close by.

Shadwick House ✪
411 SOUTH MAIN STREET, SOMERSET, KENTUCKY 42501

Tel: **(606) 678-4675**
Best Time to Call: **Anytime**
Host: **Ann Epperson**
Location: **84 mi. S of Lexington**
No. of Rooms: **4**
Max. No. Sharing Bath: **4**
Double/sb: **$40**
Single/sb: **$40**

Open: **All year**
Breakfast: **Full**
Credit Cards: **MC, VISA**
Pets: **No**
Children: **Welcome**
Smoking: **No**
Social Drinking: **Permitted**

Shadwick House has been known for its Southern hospitality for more than seventy years—the home was built in 1920 by Nellie Stringer Shadwick, great-grandmother of the present owners. The first floor has been converted into an antique and craft shop. Kentucky ham and biscuits are served for breakfast in the original dining room. This B&B is tucked into the Cumberland Mountain foothills, near Lake Cumberland. Other local attractions are Renfro Valley, Cumberland Falls State Park, Tombstone Junction, and Big South Fork National Park.

Maple Hill Manor B&B ✪
2941 PERRYVILLE ROAD, SPRINGFIELD, KENTUCKY 40069

Tel: **(606) 336-3075**	Reduced Rates: **Available**
Hosts: **Bob and Kay Carroll**	Breakfast: **Full**
No. of Rooms: **7**	Credit Cards: **MC, VISA**
No. of Private Baths: **7**	Pets: **No**
Double/pb: **$60–$85**	Children: **Welcome (crib)**
Single/pb: **$50**	Smoking: **No**
Open: **All year**	Social Drinking: **Permitted**

This hilltop manor house built in 1851 is situated on 14 tranquil acres in the scenic Bluegrass Region of Kentucky. Listed on the National Register of Historic Places, its Italianate design features 13-foot ceilings, 9-foot windows and doors, a profusion of fireplaces, and a solid cherry spiral staircase. The bedrooms are large, airy, and beautifully decorated with carefully chosen antique furnishings. The romantic honeymoon bed chamber has a canopy bed and Jacuzzi bath. In the evening, Bob and Kay graciously offer complimentary beverages and homemade dessert. Within an hour of Lexington and Louisville, you can visit Perryville Battlefield and Shaker Village and take a tour of distilleries. Murder mystery packages and gift certificates available.

Shepherd Place ✪
31 HERITAGE ROAD (U.S. 60), VERSAILLES, KENTUCKY 40383

Tel: **(606) 873-7843**
Hosts: **Marlin and Sylvia Yawn**
Location: **10 mi. W of Lexington**
No. of Rooms: **2**
No. of Private Baths: **2**
Double/pb: **$65–$70**
Single/pb: **$60**
Open: **All year**

Breakfast: **Full**
Credit Cards: **MC, VISA**
Pets: **No**
Children: **Welcome, over 12**
Smoking: **No**
Social Drinking: **Permitted**
Airport/Station Pickup: **Yes**

Marlin and Sylvia encourage you to make yourself comfortable in their pre–Civil War home, built around 1815. Rest in a spacious, beautifully decorated bedroom or relax in the parlor. Enjoy the lovely scenery while sitting on the patio or the porch swing. You might even want to pet the resident ewes, Abigail and Victoria. Brochures, menus, and plenty of ideas will be available to help you plan the rest of your stay.

LOUISIANA

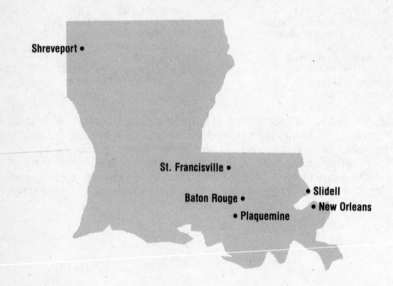

Southern Comfort Bed & Breakfast Reservation Service
P.O. BOX 13294, NEW ORLEANS, LOUISIANA 70118

Tel: **(504) 861-0082**; fax: **(504) 861-3087**
Best Time to Call: **9 AM–1 PM**
Coordinator: **Paula Bandy**
States/Regions Covered:
  Louisiana—statewide;
  Mississippi—statewide;
  Texas—Houston

Rates (Single/Double):
  Modest: **$65–$75**
  Average: **$75–$85**
  Luxury: **$85 / $85–$160**
Credit Cards: **AMEX, MC, VISA**
Minimum Stay: **3–5 nights during special, Mardi Gras, Jazz Festival**

Paula offers you the best of the old and the new South with hosts in urban and rural areas. The above is only a sample list. Special attractions are Civil War and other historic sites; fabulous New Orleans; Acadian (Cajun) country; sports, deep-sea fishing, and racetracks in Louisiana.

Bed & Breakfast, Inc.—New Orleans ✪
1021 MOSS STREET, BOX 52257, NEW ORLEANS, LOUISIANA 70152-2257

Tel: (504) 488-4640; (800) 729-4640;
  fax: (504) 488-4639
Coordinator: Hazell Boyce
States/Regions Covered: New Orleans
Descriptive Directory: Free

Rates (Single/Double):
  Modest: $30–$40 / $40–$50
  Average: $40–$75 / $40–$75
  Luxury: $70–$85 / $70–$85
Credit Cards: No

New Orleans is called The City That Care Forgot. You are certain to be carefree, visiting the French Quarter, taking Mississippi riverboat rides, taking plantation tours, as well as dining in fine restaurants and attending jazz concerts. Hazell's hosts, many with historic properties along the streetcar line and in the French Quarter, will help you get the most out of your stay.

New Orleans Bed & Breakfast and Accommodations ✪
P.O. BOX 8163, NEW ORLEANS, LOUISIANA 70182-8163

Tel: (504) 838-0071, 838-0072; fax:
  (504) 838-0140
Best Time to Call: 8:30 AM–4:30 PM
Coordinator: Sarah-Margaret Brown
States/Regions Covered:
  Louisiana—Covington, Jeanerette,
  Lafayette, Mandeville, Natchitoches,
  New Iberia, New Orleans,
  Shreveport, St. Francisville

Rates (Single/Double):
  Modest: $30–$45 / $40–$45
  Average: $45–$50 / $50–$55
  Luxury: $65–$200
Credit Cards: AMEX, DISC, MC, VISA
  (for deposit only)
Minimum Stay: 5 nights Mardi Gras,
  Jazz Festival; 3 nights Sugar Bowl

Since 1979 Sarah-Margaret has arranged accommodations for visitors in private homes, apartments, and condos. Tell her what you want and she will do her best to please you. Care is given to guests' safety, comfort, and special interests. Discount tickets are available for many attractions.

Beau Séjour ✪
1930 NAPOLEON AVENUE, NEW ORLEANS, LOUISIANA 70115

Tel: (504) 897-3746
Best Time to Call: 10 AM–8 PM
Hosts: Gilles and Kim Gagnon
No. of Rooms: 5
No. of Private Baths: 5
Double/pb: $80
Single/pb: $70
Suites: $100

Open: All year
Breakfast: Continental
Pets: No
Children: Welcome
Smoking: Permitted
Social Drinking: Permitted
Minimum Stay: 2 nights
Foreign Languages: French

Kim and Gil recently restored their 1906 Beau Séjour house to its original character, with beautiful detailing and wood floors. It is decorated in the best New Orleans style, blending country and European antiques with Louisiana and New Orleans touches. Located in one of the most picturesque neighborhoods of New Orleans, surrounded by lush tropical plantings, and on the Mardi Gras parade route, the mansion is convenient to convention and tourist attractions. Kim and Gil are dedicated to New Orleans preservation and enjoy sharing their knowledge of local restaurants, excursions, and the culture of the "Big Easy."

The Chimes Bed & Breakfast

CONSTANTINOPLE AT COLISEUM, BOX 52257, NEW ORLEANS, LOUISIANA 70152-2257

Tel: **(504) 448-4640; (800) 729-4640**
Best Time to Call: **Mon.–Fri. 10 AM–5 PM**
Hosts: **Jill and Charles Abbyad and Susan Smith**
Location: **In New Orleans**
No. of Rooms: **4**
No. of Private Baths: **4**
Double/pb: **$66–$73**

Suites: **$86–$126**
Open: **All year**
Reduced Rates: **Available**
Breakfast: **Continental, plus**
Pets: **Sometimes**
Children: **Welcome**
Social Drinking: **Permitted**
Minimum Stay: **Special events**
Foreign Languages: **French**

These quaint guest quarters sit behind a Victorian uptown home. Stained and leaded glass windows, French doors, cypress staircases, and a brick courtyard enhance the friendly, relaxed atmosphere here. Caring for a property of this magnitude is an ongoing commitment and truly a labor of love. Your hosts, who are coming to the end of a two-year renovation, typify Southern hospitality. Three blocks from St. Charles Avenue, the Chimes Cottages are minutes away from major New Orleans attractions including the French Quarter, convention centers, Audubon Zoological Gardens with the walk-through Louisiana Swamp Exhibit, the Mississippi River, and universities. The historic St. Charles Avenue streetcar makes the famous restaurants, jazz clubs, art galleries, and antique shops accessible without an auto. Your hosts live on the second floor of the main house—their door is always open! They willingly share their vast knowledge of New Orleans, offering suggestions for tours and restaurants. For your convenience, each suite has a telephone, tea/coffeepot, television set, and stereo. Laundry facilities and use of a refrigerator are available.

The Glimmer Inn ☉

1631 SEVENTH STREET, NEW ORLEANS, LOUISIANA 70115

Tel: **(504) 897-1895**
Best Time to Call: **9 AM–9 PM**

Hosts: **Sharon Agiewich and Cathy Andros**

No. of Rooms: **6**
No. of Private Baths: **1**
Max. No. Sharing Bath: **4**
Double/pb: **$85**
Double/sb: **$65**
Single/sb: **$55**

Open: **All year**
Breakfast: **Continental**
Pets: **No**
Children: **Welcome**
Smoking: **Permitted**
Social Drinking: **Permitted**

This restored 1891 Victorian home has wonderful period elements: twelve-foot cove ceilings, cypress woodwork, side and front galleries, a wraparound front porch, and an enclosed brick patio. Public rooms are comfortably furnished for reading, TV viewing and musical enjoyment. The main house's guest rooms are beautifully appointed, with antiques, ceiling fans, and individually controlled air-conditioning and heat. Also offered is a private carriage house with bath, refrigerator, and central air-conditioning and heating. Glimmer Inn is across the street from the historic Garden District, a block from the trolley line and Mardi Gras parade route, and fifteen minutes from the French Quarter. Let Cathy and Sharon know your interests; they pride themselves on meeting guests' travel needs in a relaxed, but attentive atmosphere.

The Levee View ✪
39 HENNESEY COURT, NEW ORLEANS, LOUISIANA 70123

Tel: **(504) 737-5471**
Hosts: **Jack and Clemmie Devereux**
No. of Rooms: **2**
No. of Private Baths: **1**
Max. No. Sharing Bath: **4**
Double/pb: **$40–$50**
Double/sb: **$30–$35**

Open: **All year**
Breakfast: **Continental**
Pets: **No**
Children: **Welcome**
Smoking: **Permitted**
Social Drinking: **Permitted**

The Devereuxs welcome you to their contemporary home, located in a convenient residential suburb of New Orleans. The house is large and attractive, with comfortable family furnishings. Guest quarters are located in a two-story wing with separate entrance, ensuring visitors plenty of privacy and quiet. Breakfast specialties include homemade breads, croissants, and plenty of hot coffee. If you like, you can relax outside on the patio or sip a drink in the gazebo. The levee bordering the Mississippi River is less than 100 feet from the house; many lovely plantation homes are also located nearby. Your hosts will gladly guide you to the best restaurants and shops, and will occasionally baby-sit for the kids while you go out on the town.

Sully Mansion ✪
2631 PRYTANIA STREET, NEW ORLEANS, LOUISIANA 70130

Tel: **(504) 891-0457**
Best Time to Call: **7 AM–10 PM**

Hosts: **Maralee Prigmore**
No. of Rooms: **5**

No. of Private Baths: 5
Double/pb: **$65–$125**
Suites: **$150**
Open: **All year**
Reduced Rates: **June 15–Sept. 1**
Breakfast: **Continental**
Credit Cards: **MC, VISA**

Pets: **Sometimes**
Children: **No**
Smoking: **No**
Social Drinking: **Permitted**
Minimum Stay: **2 nights weekends, 5 nights special events**

A Queen Anne named to honor its architect, Sully Mansion shows his discerning eye in its 12-foot ceilings, 10-foot doors, grand staircase, and stained glass. The house is furnished with a blend of yesterday's antiques and today's comfortable pieces, and most of the bedrooms have fireplaces. Other architectural jewels fill the surrounding historic Garden District; board the St. Charles streetcar for a 15-minute ride to New Orleans's main attractions.

Old Turnerville B&B ✪

23230 NADLER STREET, PLAQUEMINE, LOUISIANA 70764

Tel: **(504) 687-5337**
Best Time to Call: **10 AM–4 PM**
Host: **Brenda Bourgoyne Blanchard**
Location: **20 mi. S of Baton Rouge**
No. of Rooms: **1**
No. of Private Baths: **1**
Double/pb: **$65**
Single/pb: **$60**

Cottage: **$75**
Open: **All year**
Reduced Rates: **10% seniors**
Breakfast: **Continental**
Pets: **No**
Children: **Welcome**
Smoking: **Permitted**
Social Drinking: **Permitted**

Old Turnerville is an 1800s village on the Mississippi in the heart of plantation country. Bed and breakfast accommodations are available at Miss Louise's House, built more than a century ago. The antique-furnished home includes a guest bedroom with private bath, TV, air conditioning, and ceiling fan. Guests can enjoy the swing and rockers on the wide front gallery and stroll along the top of the Mississippi River levee. A separate guest cottage sleeps up to four. Restaurants and historic attractions are close by. Tariff includes guided tour of Miss Louise's House and Marietta's House, an 1800s cottage across the street.

Barrow House B&B ✪

P.O. BOX 1461, 524 ROYAL STREET, ST. FRANCISVILLE, LOUISIANA 70775

Tel: **(504) 635-4791**
Hosts: **Lyle and Shirley Dittloff**
Location: **25 mi. N of Baton Rouge**
No. of Rooms: **8**
No. of Private Baths: **8**
Double/pb: **$75–$90**
Single/pb: **$70**

Suites: **$100–$115**
Open: **All year, except Dec. 21–25**
Breakfast: **Continental**
Pets: **No**
Children: **Welcome**
Smoking: **Permitted**
Social Drinking: **Permitted**

A saltbox erected in 1809, with a Greek Revival wing that was added some four decades later, Barrow House is listed on the National Register of Historic Places. Appropriately enough, Lyle and Shirley have furnished their B&B with 19th-century pieces from the American South. Other notable homes are in the area; the Dittloffs like to send guests on a cassette walking tour of the neighborhood. Afterward, sit on the screened front porch and sip a glass of wine or iced tea. Breakfast options range from a simple Continental meal to a full-course New Orleans spread. Shirley is a fabulous cook, and private candlelight dinners, featuring Cajun and Creole specialties, can also be arranged.

Butler Greenwood ✪

8345 U.S. HIGHWAY 61, ST. FRANCISVILLE, LOUISIANA 70775

Tel: **(504) 635-6312; (800) 749-1928**	Breakfast: **Continental, plus**
Best Time to Call: **Anytime**	Credit Cards: **MC, VISA**
Host: **Anne Butler**	Pets: **Sometimes**
Location: **25 mi. N of Baton Rouge**	Children: **Welcome**
Guest Cottages: **$75, sleeps 2–6**	Smoking: **Permitted**
Open: **All year**	Social Drinking: **Permitted**
Reduced Rates: **Families**	

Butler Greenwood offers four cottages on picturesque plantation grounds. Choose from the 1796 kitchen with exposed beams and skylights, the nineteenth-century cook's cottage with a fireplace and porch swing, the romantic gazebo with antique stained glass windows, or the pond house on its own pond. All four sites have private baths, partial kitchens, and cable TV. Rates include a tour of the main house—listed on the National Register of Historic Places—and the extensive grounds. A tour book is available, describing the area's history and attractions. Continental-plus breakfast is served; other amenities include a pool, nature walks, and ballooning.

2439 Fairfield "A Bed and Breakfast Inn" ○
2439 FAIRFIELD AVENUE, SHREVEPORT, LOUISIANA 71104

Tel: (318) 424-2424	Open: **All year**
Best Time to Call: **7 AM–10 PM**	Reduced Rates: **Available**
Hosts: **Jimmy and Vicki Harris**	Breakfast: **Full**
Location: **½ mi from I-20**	Credit Cards: **AMEX, DC, MC, VISA**
No. of Rooms: **4**	Pets: **No**
No. of Private Baths: **4**	Children: **No**
Double/pb: **$85–$125**	Smoking: **No**
Single/pb: **$85–$125**	Social Drinking: **Permitted**

2439 Fairfield is a meticulously restored three-story Victorian mansion located in the Highland historic district and was featured on the front cover of the 1992 edition of *Bed & Breakfast U.S.A.* This home is surrounded by century-old oaks, rose gardens, and azaleas—you can enjoy the scenic view from your own private balcony complete with porch swings and rocking chairs. The gracious guest rooms are furnished with antiques, Amish quilts, quality linens, feather beds, and down pillows and comforters. Each guest bath has a whirlpool tub. Hearty English breakfasts are served in the morning room. Then it's off to the races at nearby Louisiana Downs. The Strand Theatre, art galleries, and fine restaurants are all within reasonable driving distances.

Salmen-Fritchie House Circa 1895 ○
127 CLEVELAND AVENUE, SLIDELL, LOUISIANA 70458

Tel: (504) 643-1405; (800) 235-4168, for reservations	Open: **All year**
	Reduced Rates: **Available**
Best Time to Call: **8 AM–9 PM**	Breakfast: **Full**
Hosts: **Homer and Sharon Fritchie**	Credit Cards: **AMEX, MC, VISA**
Location: **30 mi. N of New Orleans**	Pets: **No**
No. of Rooms: **5**	Children: **Welcome, over 12**
No. of Private Baths: **5**	Smoking: **No**
Double/pb: **$75–$85**	Social Drinking: **Permitted**
Single/pb: **$75–$85**	Station Pickup: **Yes**
Suites: **$115–$150**	

You'll feel the sense of history as you step inside this magnificent sixteen-room house listed on the National Register of Historic Places. From the front door to the back, the great hall measures twenty feet wide and eighty-five feet long! All the rooms are filled with beautiful antiques, reminiscent of days gone by. Hospitality is a way of life

here. Arrive by 4 PM and you can join your hosts for tea in the parlor and afterward, a tour of the house and grounds. In the morning, you'll receive fresh hot coffee in your room. Then you'll enjoy a full Southern breakfast in the bright, cheery breakfast room.

MAINE

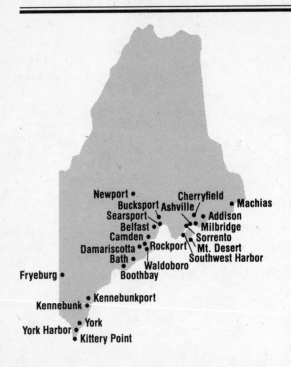

Newport •
Cherryfield •
Bucksport Ashville • Machias
Searsport • • Addison
Belfast • • Milbridge
Camden • • Sorrento
Damariscotta • • Rockport Mt. Desert
Bath • Southwest Harbor
Waldoboro
Fryeburg • Boothbay

Kennebunkport
Kennebunk •

York Harbor • • York
• Kittery Point

Pleasant Bay Bed and Breakfast ☉
BOX 222 WEST SIDE ROAD, ADDISON, MAINE 04606

Tel: (207) 483-4490
Hosts: **Leon and Joan Yeaton**
Location: **42 mi. N of Ellsworth**
No. of Rooms: 3
No. of Private Baths: 1
Max. No. Sharing Bath: 4
Double/pb: **$65**
Single/pb: **$60**
Double/sb: **$55**

Single/sb: **$45**
Open: **All year**
Breakfast: **Full**
Credit Cards: **MC, VISA**
Pets: **No**
Children: **Welcome**
Smoking: **No**
Social Drinking: **Permitted**

The Yeatons' 110-acre llama farm rests on a knoll by the shores of Pleasant Bay and the Pleasant River. Watch shorebirds and seals play in the rising and falling tides. Explore the shoreline in seclusion or meander along rustic trails, accompanied by a gentle llama. Relax before the hearth at sunset. In the morning, you'll wake up to a full down east breakfast made with farm-fresh eggs laid by your hosts' own chickens.

Green Hill Farm ✪
RR 1, BOX 328, ASHVILLE, MAINE 04607

Tel: **(207) 422-3273**
Best Time to Call: **Before 10 AM; after 4 PM**
Hosts: **Ted and Nuna Cass**
Location: **17 mi. E of Ellsworth**
No. of Rooms: **2**
Max. No. Sharing Bath: **4**
Double/sb: **$45**
Single/sb: **$40**

Open: **Late May–late Oct.**
Reduced Rates: **Available**
Breakfast: **Full, Continental**
Pets: **Sometimes**
Children: **Welcome**
Smoking: **Restricted**
Social Drinking: **Permitted**
Foreign Languages: **Spanish**

Stay in an 1820s home in a rural neighborhood, surrounded by fields, a large vegetable garden, and a small apple orchard on the edge of the forest. From its 35 acres, Green Hill Farms looks out over woods to the peaks of Acadia National Park. It's a convenient day trip to Campobello Island, and Bar Harbor is 45 minutes away. Ted and Nuna are experienced travelers who have settled down here to raise sheep, spin, knit, and garden.

Elizabeth's Bed and Breakfast ✪
360 FRONT STREET, BATH, MAINE 04530

Tel: **(207) 443-1146**
Best Time to Call: **Anytime**
Host: **Elizabeth Lindsay**
Location: **40 mi. up the coast from Portland**
No. of Rooms: **5**
Max. No. Sharing Bath: **4**
Double/sb: **$50–$65**

Single/sb: **$45**
Open: **Apr. 15–Jan. 1**
Breakfast: **Continental**
Pets: **No**
Children: **Welcome, over 12**
Smoking: **Permitted**
Social Drinking: **Permitted**

Elizabeth's Bed and Breakfast is a fine old Federalist house, painted a traditional white with green shutters. Each bedroom is furnished in country antiques. Bath is famed as a shipbuilding center, and the Maine Maritime Museum merits a visit. It's also fun to walk around the downtown area, which has been restored to its 19th-century glory. Breakfast includes juice, cereal, muffins, and jam. During the summer, Elizabeth prepares Sunday brunches.

Fairhaven Inn ✪
RR 2, BOX 85, NORTH BATH ROAD, BATH, MAINE 04530

Tel: **(207) 443-4391**
Hosts: **George and Sallie Pollard**

Location: **35 mi. N of Portland**
No. of Rooms: **7**

No. of Private Baths: **5**
Max. No. Sharing Bath: **4**
Double/pb: **$60–$70**
Double/sb: **$50–$60**
Single/sb: **$40–$50**
Open: **All year**

Breakfast: **Full**
Pets: **Yes**
Children: **Yes**
Smoking: **No**
Social Drinking: **Permitted**

An 18th-century Colonial mansion on a hill above the Kennebec River, Fairhaven Inn is furnished with antique and country pieces. Shaded by hemlock, birch, and pine trees, the 27-acre grounds lure cross-country skiers in the winter, and strollers year round. Around the bend, Bath Country Club is open to the public for golfing, and beaches are nearby. Birdwatchers can study migratory waterfowl at Merrymeeting Bay. You'll get stamina for the day's activities from ample breakfasts of juice, fresh fruit, home-baked breads, and main courses such as blintzes, eggs Benedict, and orange honey French toast.

"Glad II" ✪
60 PEARL STREET, BATH, MAINE 04530

Tel: **(207) 443-1191**
Host: **Gladys Lansky**
Location: **⁷⁄₁₀ mi. from US 1**
No. of Rooms: **2**
Max. No. Sharing Bath: **4**
Double/sb: **$50**
Open: **All year**

Breakfast: **Continental**
Credit Cards: **MC, VISA**
Pets: **No**
Children: **Welcome, over 8 (in own room)**
Smoking: **No**
Social Drinking: **Permitted**

This spic-and-span white house, with its crisp green trim, is comfortable and attractively furnished. Gladys delights in pleasing her guests with breakfasts featuring fresh, homemade treats. You are welcome to play the piano, borrow a book from her library, and visit or watch TV in the parlors. It's an easy walk to the Maritime Museum, a short drive to Popham Beach, Reid State Park, Boothbay Harbor, L. L. Bean, and the Brunswick Naval Air Station. Bowdoin College is eight miles away.

Horatio Johnson House ✪
36 CHURCH STREET, BELFAST, MAINE 04915

Tel: **(207) 338-5153**
Hosts: **Helen and Gene Kirby**
Location: **30 mi. S of Bangor**
No. of Rooms: **3**
No. of Private Baths: **3**
Double/pb: **$55**
Single/pb: **$45**

Open: **All year**
Breakfast: **Full**
Pets: **No**
Children: **No**
Smoking: **Permitted**
Social Drinking: **Permitted**

While the rest of the world is rushing ahead, the small seafaring town of Belfast is rediscovering its past. The waterfront and old town buildings are being refurbished to reflect the way things used to be. Your hosts offer good company and comfortable lodging in a 19th-century home five minutes from the ocean. The Kirbys offer a variety of breakfast specialties, such as Belgian waffles and blueberry pancakes. They will glady recommend flea markets, antique shops, and restaurants galore.

Kenniston Hill Inn
ROUTE 27, P.O. BOX 125, BOOTHBAY, MAINE 04537

Tel: (207) 633-2159; (800) 992-2915
Best Time to Call: 10 AM–10 PM
Hosts: Susan and David Straight
Location: 50 mi. N of Portland
No. of Rooms: 10
No. of Private Baths: 10
Double/pb: $65–$95
Open: All year

Breakfast: Full
Other Meals: MAP available
Credit Cards: MC, VISA
Pets: No
Children: Welcome, over 13
Smoking: No
Social Drinking: Permitted

Kenniston Hill Inn is a center-chimney Georgian Colonial dating back to 1786. The house is warm and gracious, with a large front porch and open-hearth fireplace. The bedrooms, four with fireplaces, are tastefully decorated with antiques and fresh flowers. David and Susan offer sumptuous breakfast specialties such as peaches and cream French toast, or maple walnut pancakes with cinnamon butter. The inn is surrounded by large, shady maples and fields of flowers, but is within easy reach of the harbor, shops, restaurants, boat rides, and the beautiful Maine coastline. Fireside dining is offered during the winter months, November–April.

L'ermitage ✪
219 MAIN STREET, BUCKSPORT, MAINE 04416

Tel: (207) 469-3361
Best Time to Call: After 4 PM
Hosts: Ginny and Jim Conklin
Location: 19 mi. E of Bangor; 1 block
  from US 1
No. of Rooms: 3
Max. No. Sharing Bath: 2
Double/sb: $60
Single/sb: $60
Open: All year

Reduced Rates: 20% off-season
Breakfast: Full
Other Meals: Available
Credit Cards: MC, VISA
Pets: By arrangement
Children: By arrangement
Smoking: Permitted
Social Drinking: Permitted
Airport/Station Pickup: Yes

L'ermitage is a 19th-century white Colonial with black shutters, dating back to the 1830s. Your hosts have patterned their inn after those found in Europe. The spacious rooms are furnished in period antiques, oriental carpets, and collectibles. A small gourmet restaurant is on the premises and features an extensive wine list. L'ermitage is on Penobscot Bay, near Ft. Knox.

Blue Harbor House
67 ELM STREET, ROUTE 1, CAMDEN, MAINE 04843

Tel: (207) 236-3196; (800) 248-3196;
   fax: (207) 236-6523
Hosts: **Dennis Hayden and Jody Schmoll**
Location: **85 mi. NE of Portland**
No. of Rooms: **10**
No. of Private Baths: **10**
Double/pb: **$85–$125**

Open: **All year**
Breakfast: **Full**
Credit Cards: **AMEX, DISC, MC, VISA**
Pets: **By arrangement**
Children: **Welcome**
Smoking: **No**
Social Drinking: **Permitted**
Airport/Station Pickup: **Yes**

Camden is one of the prettiest coastal villages in New England. This 1835 Cape Cod house has been completely renovated and captures the essence of a bygone era. Each room is decorated in country antiques, stenciled walls, and handmade quilts. Guests enjoy visiting with each other in the common room, furnished with comfortable chairs and accented by antique stoneware, samplers, and folk art. The spacious dining room, with its views of Mt. Battie, is the setting for the generous breakfast that features homemade breads, delicious egg dishes, and Maine blueberries. It's a few minutes' walk to many fine restaurants, unique shops, and the famous Windjammer fleet.

Camden Maine Stay ✪
22 HIGH STREET, CAMDEN, MAINE 04843

Tel: **(207) 236-9636**
Best Time to Call: **8 AM–9 PM**
Hosts: **Peter and Donny Smith, Diana Robson**

Location: **85 mi. NE of Portland**
No. of Rooms: **8**
Max. No. Sharing Bath: **4**
Double/pb: **$90**

Double/sb: **$75**
Single/sb: **$65**
Suite: **$110 for 2**
Open: **All year**
Reduced Rates: **Off-season**
Breakfast: **Full**

Credit Cards: **MC, VISA**
Pets: **No**
Children: **Welcome, over 10**
Smoking: **No**
Social Drinking: **Permitted**

A comfortable bed, a hearty breakfast, and a friendly innkeeper are found in this treasured old Colonial home. Listed on the National Register of Historic Places and located in Camden's historic district, the inn is a five-minute walk from the harbor, shops, and restaurants. Whether you relax by a crackling log fire, sit on the deck overlooking a wooded glen, or stroll by the brook behind the barn, you will find the Maine Stay to be the perfect base from which to explore midcoast Maine.

The Elms Bed and Breakfast
84 ELM STREET, ROUTE 1, CAMDEN, MAINE 04843

Tel: **(207) 236-6250**
Best Time to Call: **9:30 AM–9:30 PM**
Host: **Joan A. James**
Location: **150 mi. N of Boston, Mass.**
No. of Rooms: **6**
No. of Private Baths: **3**
Max. No. Sharing Bath: **4**
Double/pb: **$85**
Double/sb: **$65**

Suite: **$75**
Open: **All year**
Reduced Rates: **Off-season**
Breakfast: **Full**
Credit Cards: **MC, VISA**
Pets: **No**
Children: **Welcome, over 12**
Smoking: **No**
Social Drinking: **Permitted**

Joan keeps candles burning in the windows to welcome you to her lovingly restored Colonial home, built in 1806. Inside, period-style furnishings will take you back two centuries. Camden offers sailing, hiking, and skiing, and the fall foliage is spectacular. Or just stroll over to the city harbor, with its shops, galleries, and restaurants. Breakfast always consists of home-baked breads and such memorable entrées as French toast stuffed with puréed peaches and sour cream.

Hawthorn Inn
9 HIGH STREET, CAMDEN, MAINE 04843

Tel: **(207) 236-8842; Fax: (207) 236-6181**
Best Time to Call: **9 AM–9 PM**
Hosts: **Pauline and Brad Staub**
Location: **On Rte. 1, 150 mi. N of Boston**
No. of Rooms: **10**
No. of Private Baths: **10**
Double/pb: **$75–$145**

Suites: **$95–$145**
Reduced Rates: **$20 less daily Nov. 1–May 25**
Breakfast: **Full**
Credit Cards: **MC, VISA**
Pets: **No**
Children: **Welcome, over 10**
Smoking: **No**
Social Drinking: **Permitted**

The airy rooms of this Victorian inn are an elegant mixture of the old and the new. Guests are welcome to coffee while relaxing on the deck or getting warm by the fire. Tea is served at 4 PM. All rooms overlook either Mt. Battie or Camden Harbor. A score of sports can be enjoyed in the area, and shops and restaurants are a short walk away. Children are welcome at any age in the suites.

Ricker House ✪
PARK STREET, P.O. BOX 256, CHERRYFIELD, MAINE 04622

Tel: (207) 546-2780	Reduced Rates: Available
Hosts: William and Jean Conway	Breakfast: Full
Location: 32 mi. E of Ellsworth	Pets: No
No. of Rooms: 3	Children: Welcome (crib)
Max. No. Sharing Bath: 4	Smoking: No
Double/sb: $50	Social Drinking: Permitted
Single/sb: $45	Airport/Station Pickup: Yes
Open: All year	

Built in 1803, this comfortable Federal Colonial has grounds that border the Narraguagus River, one of the best salmon rivers in the States. The village is quaint and historic, and it is fun to tour it on foot or by bike. Reasonable restaurants offer great menus, and all feature fabulous local lobster. Your hosts will be pleased to direct you to a fresh water lake and the best places to canoe and mountain climb.

Brannon-Bunker Inn ✪
H.C.R. 64, BOX 045L, DAMARISCOTTA, MAINE 04543

Tel: (207) 563-5941	Single/sb: $50
Best Time to Call: 9 AM–9 PM	Suites: $70–$110
Hosts: Jeanne and Joseph Hovance	Open: All year
No. of Rooms: 7	Breakfast: Continental, plus
No. of Private Baths: 5	Credit Cards: AMEX, MC, VISA
Max. No. Sharing Bath: 2	Pets: No
Double/pb: $65	Children: Welcome
Single/pb: $60	Smoking: No
Double/sb: $55	Social Drinking: Permitted

The Brannon-Bunker Inn is an informal, relaxing inn, ideally situated in rural, coastal Maine. Guests may choose from accommodations in the 1900 converted barn or the carriage house across the stream. Each room is individually decorated in styles ranging from Colonial to Victorian. Hosts Jeanne and Joseph Hovance will help you plan your days over breakfast. Nearby activities include golf, ocean swimming at Pemaquid Beach Park, and fishing on the Damariscotta River.

The Oxford House Inn ✪
105 MAIN STREET, FRYEBURG, MAINE 04037

Tel: **(207) 935-3442**
Best Time to Call: **Anytime**
Hosts: **John and Phyllis Morris**
Location: **50 mi. W of Portland**
No. of Rooms: **5**
No. of Private Baths: **5**
Double/pb: **$75–$95**
Single/pb: **$50**
Open: **All year**

Breakfast: **Full**
Other Meals: **Available**
Credit Cards: **AMEX, DC, DISC, MC, VISA**
Pets: **No**
Children: **Welcome**
Smoking: **No**
Social Drinking: **Permitted**

Located in a Colonial village and surrounded by lakes and mountains, this charming 1913 Edwardian home has served as an inn and restaurant since 1985. Spacious guest rooms are tastefully decorated with old-fashioned flair. A full hearty breakfast is served on the enclosed back porch with panoramic mountain views. Gourmet dinners are served from 6 to 9 PM by reservation. In addition to fine dining, Oxford House offers easy access to many local activities; scenic drives, antiquing, hiking, canoeing, skiing, and tax-free outlet shopping are only minutes away.

The Alewife House
1917 ALEWIVE ROAD, KENNEBUNK, MAINE 04043

Tel: **(207) 985-2118**
Best Time to Call: **8 AM–11 PM**
Hosts: **Maryellen and Tom Foley**
Location: **25 mi. S of Portland**

No. of Rooms: **2**
No. of Private Baths: **2**
Double/pb: **$75–$80**
Open: **All year**

Breakfast: **Continental**
Credit Cards: **MC, VISA**
Pets: **No**

Children: **Welcome, over 12**
Smoking: **No**
Social Drinking: **Permitted**

Step back in time as you enter this 1756 farmhouse, located on six acres of rolling hills and gardens. Inside, the house is decorated with antiques; more are sold in the on-site shop. Awaken to the aroma of hot muffins, fresh fruit, and fresh-perked coffee served on the sunporch each morning. Then explore the area's coastline or the many nearby lakes.

Arundel Meadows Inn
P.O. BOX 1129, KENNEBUNK, MAINE 04043

Tel: **(207) 985-3770**
Best Time to Call: **9 AM–9 PM**
Hosts: **Mark Bachelder and Murray Yaeger**
Location: **2 mi. N of Kennebunk**
No. of Rooms: **7**
No. of Private Baths: **7**
Double/pb: **$75–$95**

Suites: **$95–$110**
Open: **All year**
Breakfast: **Full**
Pets: **Sometimes**
Children: **Welcome, over 11**
Smoking: **No**
Social Drinking: **Permitted**

The Arundel Meadows Inn is situated on three and a half acres next to the Kennebunk River. Murray, a retired professor, and Mark, a professional chef, have always loved this area, and it is a dream come true for them to watch others enjoy it. They renovated this 165-year-old house themselves, and meticulously planned the decor. Several guest rooms have fireplaces and two suites sleep four. Mark's beautifully prepared breakfast specialties are the perfect start for your day. It's just three minutes to the center of town, and about ten to Kennebunk Beach. In the afternoon, come back to the inn for tea and enjoy pâtés, homemade sweets, and beverages.

English Meadows Inn ✪
141 PORT ROAD, KENNEBUNK, MAINE 04043

Tel: **(207) 967-5766**
Best Time to Call: **Mornings**
Host: **Charlie Doane**
Location: **35 mi. S of Portland**
No. of Rooms: **13**
No. of Private Baths: **9**
Max. No. Sharing Bath: **4**
Double/pb: **$85–$95**
Double/sb: **$78**
Guest Cottage: **$120; sleeps 4**
Suites: **$120**

Open: **All year**
Reduced Rates: **25% Nov.–Apr.; 10% May–June**
Breakfast: **Full**
Credit Cards: **MC, VISA**
Pets: **No**
Children: **Welcome, over 10**
Smoking: **No**
Social Drinking: **No**
Airport/Station Pickup: **Yes**

Inside this Victorian farmhouse, period antiques and reproductions transport visitors to a bygone time. But prominently displayed works of local painters and craftspeople demonstrate why Kennebunkport is known as a haven for artists, artisans, and authors. Your host is a native New Englander and retired naval officer; the specialty of the day, in addition to the sumptuous breakfasts, is sharing your experiences with Charlie and his family.

Lake Brook Guest House ✪
57 WESTERN AVENUE, KENNEBUNK, MAINE 04043

Tel: **(207) 967-4069**	Suite: **$90**
Best Time to Call: **9 AM–9 PM**	Open: **All year**
Host: **Carolyn A. McAdams**	Breakfast: **Full**
Location: **25 mi. S of Portland**	Pets: **No**
No. of Rooms: **4**	Children: **Welcome**
No. of Private Baths: **4**	Smoking: **No**
Double/pb: **$75–$90**	Social Drinking: **Permitted**
Single/pb: **$60**	Foreign Languages: **Spanish**

Lake Brook is an appealing turn-of-the-century New England farmhouse. Its wraparound porch is equipped with comfortable rocking chairs, and flower gardens stretch right down to the tidal brook that feeds the property. The shops and restaurants of Dock Square are within easy walking distance, and Kennebunk Beach is a little more than one mile away. Breakfasts include such main dishes as quiche, baked French toast, and Mexican chili eggs and cheese.

Captain Fairfield Inn ✪
CORNER PLEASANT AND GREEN STREETS, P.O. BOX 1308, KENNEBUNKPORT, MAINE 04046

Tel: **(207) 967-4454**	Reduced Rates: **5% seniors**
Best Time to Call: **9 AM–8 PM**	Breakfast: **Full**
Hosts: **Bonnie Dunn and Dennis Tallagnon**	Credit Cards: **AMEX, MC, VISA**
	Pets: **Sometimes**
Location: **24 mi. S of Portland**	Children: **Welcome, over 10**
No. of Rooms: **9**	Smoking: **No**
No. of Private Baths: **9**	Social Drinking: **Permitted**
Double/pb: **$85–$150**	Minimum Stay: **2 nights weekends**
Single/pb: **$65–$125**	Airport/Station Pickup: **Yes**
Open: **All year**	

From this gracious sea captain's mansion in Kennebunkport's historic district, you can walk to the village green and harbor, Dock Square marinas, shops, restaurants, and beaches. Period furnishings and wicker lend tranquility and charm to the bright, beautiful bedrooms; some have fireplaces. Guests may relax in the living room and study, or stroll the tree-shaded grounds. You'll awaken to birdsong, the smell of sea air, and the aroma of gourmet coffee, followed by a wonderful breakfast prepared by chef/owner Dennis.

The Green Heron Inn ✪
P.O. BOX 2578, OCEAN AVENUE, KENNEBUNKPORT, MAINE 04046

Tel: (207) 967-3315	Guest Cottage: $125
Best Time to Call: Noon–6 PM	Reduced Rates: Weekly
Hosts: Charles and Elizabeth Reid	Breakfast: Full
Location: 4½ mi. from US 1	Pets: Sometimes
No. of Rooms: 10	Children: Welcome (crib)
No. of Private Baths: 10	Smoking: Permitted
Double/pb: $64–$94	Social Drinking: Permitted
Single/pb: $52–$78	

This immaculate inn, circa 1908, with its inviting porch and striped awnings, furnished simply and comfortably, is located between the river and the ocean in this Colonial resort village. The full Yankee breakfast is a rib-buster! This is a saltwater fisherman's heaven, close to shops and galleries, with boating, golf, swimming, and tennis all nearby. For those of you who don't mind paying a higher rate, 1 room is available.

Gundalow Inn ✪
6 WATER STREET, KITTERY, MAINE 03904

Tel: (207) 439-4040	Location: 50 mi. N of Boston
Hosts: Cevia and George Rosol	No. of Rooms: 6

No. of Private Baths: **6**	Credit Cards: **MC, VISA**
Double/pb: **$80–$105**	Pets: **No**
Single/pb: **$70–$95**	Children: **Welcome, over 16**
Open: **All year**	Smoking: **No**
Breakfast: **Full**	Social Drinking: **Permitted**

Gundalow Inn is a wonderful brick Victorian overlooking Portsmouth harbor. Guest rooms are comfortably furnished with antiques; most have water views. Savor a hearty home-cooked breakfast by the fireplace or on the patio. Stroll over to Colonial Portsmouth, a town noted for its museums, theaters, restaurants, cafés, gardens, festivals, boat tours, and antique and craft shops. Strawbery Banke and Prescott Park are within walking distance. It's a ten-minute drive to beaches and factory outlets, and the White Mountains are two hours away. Of course, you can always relax with a book on the porch or patio or in the parlor.

Clark Perry House ✪
59 COURT STREET, MACHIAS, MAINE 04654

Tel: **(207) 255-8458**	Open: **All year**
Best Time to Call: **Before 8 PM**	Reduced Rates: **10% less after 3 nights**
Hosts: **Robin and David Rier**	Breakfast: **Full**
Location: **90 mi. E of Bangor**	Pets: **No**
No. of Rooms: **2**	Children: **Welcome**
Max. No. Sharing Bath: **4**	Smoking: **No**
Double/sb: **$55**	Social Drinking: **No**
Single/sb: **$49**	Airport/Station Pickup: **Yes**

Machias—an Indian word meaning "Bad Little Falls"—is a quiet coastal town with its own branch of the University of Maine. This 1868 Victorian was built for its namesake, a leading businessman in the local lumber and shipping industries. Roque Bluffs State Park and Jasper Beach are nearby, and shops, restaurants, churches, and historic places lie within walking distance of the B&B. Guest rooms are decorated with antiques, comforters, and tea kettles, and the sitting room has a piano for your enjoyment. Breakfast may include home-baked breads, muffins, blueberry pancakes, and fresh fruit. Robin, a full-time hostess and mother, is interested in painting, photography, and gardening. She shares that last hobby with David, a parts store owner and airplane pilot.

Moonraker Bed & Breakfast ✪
MAIN STREET, ROUTE 1, MILBRIDGE, MAINE 04658

Tel: **(207) 546-2191**	No. of Rooms: **5**
Best Time to Call: **9 AM–9 PM**	Max. No. Sharing Bath: **4**
Hosts: **Bill and Ingrid Handrahan**	Double/pb: **$50–$55**
Location: **29 mi. N of Ellsworth**	Double/sb: **$45**

Single/sb: **$40**
Open: **All year**
Breakfast: **Full**
Other Meals: **Available**
Credit Cards: **MC, VISA**

Pets: **No**
Children: **Welcome**
Smoking: **No**
Social Drinking: **Permitted**

This Queen Anne mansion offers an in-town location in a rural village setting. Rooms, on the second and third story, have outstanding views and turn-of-the-century mahogany furnishings. Restaurants, light shopping, and an inexpensive movie theater are a short walk from the doorstep. It's a pleasant stroll to the Narraguagus River, where you may see seals sunning themselves. Your hosts serve full breakfasts as well as four o'clock tea, so you'll have energy to explore the area. Ocean view.

Bed & Breakfast Year 'Round—the MacDonalds ❂
P.O. BOX 52, MT. DESERT, MAINE 04660

Tel: **(207) 244-3316**
Best Time to Call: **Anytime**
Hosts: **Stan and Binnie MacDonald**
Location: **45 mi. S of Bangor**
No. of Rooms: **3**
No. of Private Baths: **1**
Max. No. Sharing Bath: **4**
Double/pb: **$75**
Double/sb: **$65**
Open: **All year**

Reduced Rates: **$15 less Oct. 15–June 15**
Breakfast: **Full**
Credit Cards: **MC, VISA**
Pets: **No**
Children: **Welcome, over 6**
Smoking: **No**
Social Drinking: **Permitted**
Minimum Stay: **2 nights**

Built in 1850 in Somesville, Mt. Desert's first permanent settlement, this B&B is listed on the National Register of Historic Places. The beautifully furnished home has views of the water and mountains from almost every window. In addition to having full use of the living and music rooms, guests may lounge on the screened porch, in the garden courtyard, or in the backyard. At this location, you'll have the pleasure of village living apart from summer crowds. There's much to enjoy on foot, notably Somes Harbor, historic Brookside Cemetery, a bookstore, a museum, and a summer theater. Acadia National Park and the Northeast Harbor's larger towns are nearby. You'll be ready to go exploring after breakfasting on fresh fruit, blueberry pancakes or crepes, and homemade breads and muffins. Stan and Binnie enjoy reading and music—Stan plays a mean banjo!

Black Friar Inn ❂
10 SUMMER STREET, BAR HARBOR, MT. DESERT ISLAND, MAINE 04609

Tel: **(207) 288-5091**
Best Time to Call: **12–3 PM; evenings**

Hosts: **Barbara and Jim Kelly**
No. of Rooms: **6**

No. of Private Baths: **6**
Double/pb: **$85–$110**
Single/pb: **$80–$105**
Open: **May–Nov.**
Reduced Rates: **May 1–June 15**
Breakfast: **Full**
Credit Cards: **MC, VISA**

Pets: **No**
Children: **Welcome, over 12**
Smoking: **No**
Social Drinking: **Permitted**
Minimum Stay: **2 nights July 1–
    Columbus Day**
Airport/Station Pickup: **Yes**

This uniquely restored Victorian incorporates beautiful woodwork, mantels, and tin from area churches and homes. Afternoon refreshments are served in the sunroom, which is paneled in cyprus and embossed tin, or by the fireside in the intimate English pub. Full breakfasts include fresh fruit, juice, eggs, Belgian waffles, and home-baked breads, rolls, and muffins, served in the dining area, featured on the back cover of the 1992 edition of *Bed & Breakfast U.S.A.* Guests have a short walk to shops, restaurants, and the waterfront; it's an easy drive to Acadia National Park.

Hearthside B&B ✪
7 HIGH STREET, BAR HARBOR, MT. DESERT ISLAND, MAINE 04609

Tel: **(207) 288-4533**
Hosts: **Susan and Barry Schwartz**
No. of Rooms: **9**
No. of Private Baths: **9**
Double/pb: **$75–$115**
Open: **All year**
Reduced Rates: **Before June 15**

Breakfast: **Full**
Credit Cards: **MC, VISA**
Pets: **No**
Children: **Welcome, over 10**
Smoking: **No**
Social Drinking: **Permitted**

On a quiet street, just a short walk to town, is this gracious home, recently redecorated in the manner of a country cottage. Breakfast is served buffet-style, featuring home-baked muffins and cakes, eggs, pancakes, hot cereal, a fresh fruit bowl, and beverages. You are invited to share the special ambience of a living room with a cozy fireplace and brimming with books. Some rooms have a balcony or a fireplace.

The Kingsleigh Inn ✪
P.O. BOX 1426, 100 MAIN STREET, SOUTHWEST HARBOR, MT. DESERT ISLAND, MAINE 04679

Tel: **(207) 244-5302**
Hosts: **Tom and Nancy Cervelli**
Location: **45 mi. E of Bangor**
No. of Rooms: **8**
No. of Private Baths: **8**
Double/pb: **$85–$95**
Suite: **$155**
Open: **All year**

Reduced Rates: **Available**
Breakfast: **Full**
Credit Cards: **MC, VISA**
Pets: **No**
Children: **Welcome, over 12**
Smoking: **No**
Social Drinking: **Permitted**

Built at the turn of the century, the Kingsleigh Inn is a shingled and pebble-dash Colonial revival. The house overlooks Southwest Harbor, where generations of boatbuilders and fishers have earned their living. All guest rooms are tastefully decorated and many have beautiful harbor views. Afternoon refreshments are served on a wraparound porch overlooking the harbor or, on cooler days, by a crackling fire. For breakfast your hosts serve freshly brewed coffee, teas, juices, homebaked muffins and breads, fresh fruit, and a daily specialty, such as omelets, quiches, blueberry pancakes, or French toast. Tom and Nancy take pleasure in welcoming you to Mt. Desert Island and will gladly direct you to swimming, hiking, fishing expeditions, whale-watching, restaurants, and shopping.

The Lamb's Ear ✪
P.O. BOX 30, CLARK POINT ROAD, SOUTHWEST HARBOR, MT. DESERT ISLAND, MAINE 04679

Tel: **(207) 244-9828**	Open: **May–Nov.**
Hosts: **Elizabeth and George Hoke**	Breakfast: **Full**
Location: **45 mi. E of Bangor**	Credit Cards: **MC, VISA**
No. of Rooms: **6**	Pets: **No**
No. of Private Baths: **6**	Children: **Welcome, over 10**
Double/pb: **$65–$85**	Smoking: **No**
Suite: **$125**	Social Drinking: **Permitted**

A stately home that dates to the mid-19th century, The Lamb's Ear overlooks the waterfront of Southwest Harbor, a quaint fishing village. While swimming, sailing, and fishing are the primary activities here, you'll want to set aside time to explore nearby galleries, museums, and Acadia National Park. After a full breakfast of eggs, Belgian waffles, fresh fruit, and muffins, you'll be ready for the day's adventures.

Lindenwood Inn ○

P.O. BOX 1328, SOUTHWEST HARBOR, MT. DESERT ISLAND, MAINE 04679

Tel: **(207) 244-5335**	Reduced Rates: **Nov. 1–June 1**
Host: **James King**	Breakfast: **Full**
No. of Rooms: **15**	Pets: **No**
No. of Private Baths: **15**	Children: **Welcome, over 12 in Inn,**
Double/pb: **$65–$95**	**any age cottages and apartments**
Suites: **$95–$135**	Smoking: **No**
Cottages and Apartments: **$95–$155**	Social Drinking: **Permitted**
Open: **All year**	

Built at the turn of the century as a sea captain's home, the inn derives its name from the stately linden trees that line the front lawn. Each room is individually decorated and many enjoy harbor views from sun-drenched private balconies. On cool mornings you'll be greeted by glowing fireplaces and a hearty full breakfast. Relax and unwind in one of the inn's elegant sitting rooms or on the large shaded front porch, where you can hear the sounds of the working harbor. Acadia National Park and all the island's activities are only minutes away.

Penury Hall ○

BOX 68, MAIN STREET, SOUTHWEST HARBOR, MT. DESERT ISLAND, MAINE 04679

Tel: **(207) 244-7102**	Breakfast: **Full**
Hosts: **Gretchen and Toby Strong**	Pets: **No**
No. of Rooms: **3**	Children: **Welcome, over 16**
Max. No. Sharing Bath: **3**	Smoking: **No**
Double/sb: **$60**	Social Drinking: **Permitted**
Single/sb: **$50**	Minimum Stay: **2 nights June 1–**
Open: **All year**	**Oct. 30**
Reduced Rates: **Nov. 1–April 30**	Airport/Station Pickup: **Yes**

This gray frame house is on the quiet side of Mt. Desert Island. Built in 1830, it is comfortably furnished with traditional pieces, antiques, and original art. Gretchen and Toby are cosmopolitan and cordial. Their motto is: "Each guest is an honorary member of the family," and you'll soon feel at home. Knowledgeable about the area's highlights, they'll direct you to special shops and restaurants and all of the best things to see and do. Breakfast often features eggs Benedict and blueberry pancakes or cinnamon waffles. You are welcome to use the canoe or sail the 19-foot day sailor. After a day of hiking or skiing, relax in the sauna. There's a $10 surcharge for one-night stays.

Pointy Head Inn ✪

H.C.R. 33 BOX 2A, BASS HARBOR, MT. DESERT ISLAND, MAINE 04653

Tel: **(207) 244-7261**
Best Time to Call: **9:30 AM–3 PM**
Hosts: **Doris and Warren Townsend**
Location: **18 mi. S of Bar Harbor**
No. of Rooms: **6**
No. of Private Baths: **2**
Max. No. Sharing Bath: **4**
Double/pb: **$85**
Double/sb: **$65**

Single/sb: **$45**
Open: **May 15–Oct.**
Breakfast: **Full**
Pets: **No**
Children: **Welcome, over 10**
Smoking: **No**
Social Drinking: **Permitted**
Airport/Station Pickup: **Yes**

In Colonial times a sea captain made his home here, overlooking beautiful Bass Harbor. Today, this sprawling inn is a haven for artists and photographers who appreciate the quiet side of Mount Desert Island. The house is decorated with nautical accents and homey furnishings. One of its special qualities is the beautiful sunsets that can be enjoyed from your room or the comfortable porch. The inn is set in a quaint fishing village bordering Acadia National Park. Swimming, canoeing, nature trails, fishing, and mountain climbing are just a few of the activities that can be enjoyed locally. A variety of restaurants, shops, and galleries are within walking distance.

Lake Sebasticook B&B ✪

P.O. BOX 502, 8 SEBASTICOOK AVENUE, NEWPORT, MAINE 04953

Tel: **(207) 368-5507**
Hosts: **Bob and Trudy Zothner**

Location: **1 mi. off I-95, Exit 39**
No. of Rooms: **3**

B. Ramsey
8-88

Max. No. Sharing Bath: **3**
Double/sb: **$50**
Single/sb: **$37.50**
Open: **May–Oct.**
Breakfast: **Full**

Pets: **No**
Children: **No**
Smoking: **No**
Social Drinking: **No**
Airport/Station Pickup: **Yes**

This gracious white Victorian, with its front wraparound porch and screened-in second-story sun porch, stands so near to Lake Sebasticook that guests can hear the calls of ducks and loons. In summer, the lake is a haven for swimmers and fishermen; in winter, it freezes, providing an outlet for cross-country skiers. Bob and Trudy, who love the outdoors, will direct you to the best locations. Full country breakfasts, with homemade breads and jams, will supply you with the energy to enjoy the great outdoors.

Twin Gables ✪

4 SPEAR STREET AT BEAUCHAMP STREET, ROCKPORT, MAINE 04856

Tel: **(207) 236-4717**
Best Time to Call: **After 10 AM**
Hosts: **Don and Nina Woolston**
Location: **85 mi. NE of Portland**
No. of Rooms: **3**
No. of Private Baths: **2**
Max. No. Sharing Bath: **4**
Double/pb: **$85**
Single/sb: **$65**

Suite/pb: **$120**
Open: **June–mid-Oct.**
Breakfast: **Full**
Pets: **No**
Children: **Welcome, over 8**
Smoking: **No**
Social Drinking: **Permitted**
Minimum Stay: **2 nights**

Located in a quiet residential area between Portland and Bar Harbor, this 17-room 1855 home offers a suite, double room, and twin room, each laden with fresh flowers, books, and candy. Outside, regal arborvitae arch hedges and floral and herb gardens are maintained for your pleasure. It's a one-block walk to Rockport Harbor. Nearby are Belted Galloway cattle, Vesper Hill Chapel, antique shops, art galleries, concerts, boating, sailing, hiking, biking, and golf. Gourmet breakfasts are served on the white wicker sunporch. Don is retired from NASA and Nina from the State Department and legal work.

Brass Lantern Inn ✪

81 WEST MAIN STREET, P.O. BOX 407, SEARSPORT, MAINE 04974

Tel: **(207) 548-0150; (800) 691-0150**
Hosts: **Dan and Lee Anne Lee; Pat Gatto**
Location: **35 mi. SE of Bangor**
No. of Rooms: **4**
No. of Private Baths: **4**
Double/pb: **$65–$70**
Single/pb: **$65**
Open: **All year**

Reduced Rates: **30% Nov. 1–May 30; 10% seniors**
Breakfast: **Full**
Credit Cards: **MC, VISA**
Pets: **No**
Children: **Welcome, over 7**
Smoking: **No**
Social Drinking: **No**

Sea captain James Gilmoure Pendleton built this home for his bride in 1850; later he left the helm to become president of Searsport's first bank. The inn is tastefully decorated with antiques and family heirlooms and features an extensive doll collection. Hearty breakfast fare, such as homemade muffins and pancakes filled with blueberries, is served in the dining room, which has its original ornate tin ceiling. Points of interest include Moosepoint State Park and the Penobscot Marine Museum. The Collectible Train Shop, located on the premises, has antique Lionel trains.

Bass Cove Farm B&B ✪
H.C. 32 BOX 132, ROUTE 185, SORRENTO, MAINE 04677

Tel: **(207) 422-3564**
Hosts: **Mary Ann Solet and Michael Tansey**
Location: **40 mi. SE of Bangor**
No. of Rooms: **3**
No. of Private Baths: **1**
Max. No. Sharing Bath: **4**
Double/sb: **$50**
Single/sb: **$45**
Suite: **$75–$80**

Open: **All year**
Reduced Rates: **10% less Nov.–Apr.; suite, weekly**
Breakfast: **Continental**
Credit Cards: **MC, VISA**
Pets: **Sometimes**
Children: **Welcome, over 12**
Smoking: **No**
Social Drinking: **No**
Minimum Stay: **2 nights for suite**

Sorrento, 30 miles from Bar Harbor and Acadia National Park, is a coastal Maine town with 200 year-round residents and an active summer colony. This circa 1840s farmhouse looks out on Bass Cove. Breakfast features home-baked breads or muffins. Guests are welcome to use the exercise room, relax in the library/parlor/game room, and explore the gardens. Outdoor enthusiasts find many places to hike, bike, mountain climb, swim, boat, or take a drive. Shops and flea markets beckon to those seeking antiques, crafts, or treasures from local attics. Mary Ann does editorial work in her "electronic cottage"; she is a fiber craftsperson and avid gardener. Michael, a former teacher with training in paralegal studies, is building a greenhouse for the farm.

Harbour Woods Mount Desert Island ✪
P.O. BOX 1214, SOUTHWEST HARBOR, MAINE 04679

Tel: **(207) 244-5388**
Best Time to Call: **Anytime**
Hosts: **Margaret Eden and James Paviglionite**
Location: **20 mi. S of Ellsworth**
No. of Rooms: **3**
No. of Private Baths: **3**
Double/pb: **$65–$105**

Guest Cottage: **$85–$105; sleeps 6**
Open: **All year**
Reduced Rates: **Available**
Breakfast: **Full**
Pets: **No**
Children: **Welcome, over 12**
Smoking: **No**
Social Drinking: **Permitted**

Built in the mid-1800s, this rambling farmhouse combines today's comforts with yesterday's charms. Shops, restaurants, and the harbor front are all within walking distance. Each spacious guest room has either a garden or a harbor view, plus a queen-size bed, plush carpet, and a private bath stocked with oversized towels and luxurious soaps. Snack on afternoon refreshments by the hearth in winter, or on the porch in summer; for an extra warm-weather treat, you'll get to see hummingbirds dart around the flowers. Breakfast is guaranteed to please, thanks to entrées like Margaret's herb-baked eggs and her melon salad served with lime-mint dressing. For those of you who don't mind paying a higher rate, 1 room is available.

The Island House ☉
CLARK POINT ROAD, P.O. BOX 1006, SOUTHWEST HARBOR, MAINE 04679

Tel: (207) 244-5180
Best Time to Call: AM
Host: Ann Bradford
Location: 21 mi. S of Ellsworth
No. of Rooms: 4
No. of Private Baths: 2
Max. No. Sharing Bath: 4
Double/pb: $50–$70
Single/pb: $40–$60
Double/sb: $45–$60
Single/sb: $35–$55

Carriage House: $95–$135
Suites: $120, sleeps 4
Open: All year
Reduced Rates: Available
Breakfast: Full
Pets: No
Children: Welcome, over 10
Smoking: No
Social Drinking: Permitted
Minimum Stay: 2 nights in August

Launched in the mid-1800s as Mt. Desert Island's first summer hotel, The Island House retains its old-time charm as a gracious seacoast family home. Furnishings collected from Ann's childhood in Southeast Asia blend beautifully with the spacious, simply decorated rooms. Breakfasts, served in the dining room, may include eggs Florentine, blueberry coffee cake, and a sausage or cheese casserole. Your host knows the island well and will be happy to help you plan your day. Acadia National Park is two miles away and Bar Harbor is 15 miles away.

Broad Bay Inn & Gallery ☉
1014 MAIN STREET, P.O. BOX 607, WALDOBORO, MAINE 04572

Tel: (207) 832-6668
Hosts: Jim and Libby Hopkins
Location: 80 mi. N of Portland
No. of Rooms: 5
Max. No. Sharing Bath: 4
Double/sb: $40–$75
Single/sb: $35–$60
Open: All year

Breakfast: Full
Credit Cards: MC, VISA
Pets: No
Children: Welcome, over 12
Smoking: No
Social Drinking: Permitted
Foreign Languages: French

The inn, set in a charming midcoast village, is a classic Colonial, circa 1830, with light, airy, handsomely decorated rooms. Some guest rooms have canopy beds, and all have Victorian furnishings. There's a large deck on which to sip afternoon tea or sherry, and the Hopkins' garden is lovely enough to be included in local Garden Club tours. This is a convenient base from which to enjoy the quaint fishing villages, the lighthouse, and the Audubon Sanctuary. Guests can swim at Damariscotta Lake, and morning or evening sailboat cruises are easily arranged. A sumptuous breakfast often includes crêpes and herbed cheese omelets. Jim and Libby are theater buffs and retired commercial artists; they have a gallery, which is located in the two-story barn behind the inn. Water color workshops are offered in the summer.

Tide Watch Inn ✪
P.O. BOX 94, PINE STREET, WALDOBORO, MAINE 04572

Tel: **(207) 832-4987**	Single/pb: **$50**
Best Time to Call: **Anytime**	Double/sb: **$50**
Hosts: **Mel and Cathy Hanson**	Single/sb: **$40**
Location: **62 mi. N of Portland; 1⁷⁄₁₆ mi. from Rte. 1**	Open: **All year**
No. of Rooms: **3**	Breakfast: **Full**
No. of Private Baths: **1**	Pets: **No**
Max. No. Sharing Bath: **4**	Children: **Welcome**
Double/pb: **$60**	Smoking: **Permitted**
	Social Drinking: **Permitted**

Built in 1850, this twin Colonial home is located on the shore of the Medomak River. The first five-masted schooners were crafted right by the inn. You are welcome to bring your boat or canoe, or just watch the local fishermen sail with the tide. Cathy's forte is keeping the inn shipshape, and guests comment on the comfortable ambience she's created. Mel's talent as a retired chef is evident in the ambitious and delicious breakfasts that might include asparagus cordon bleu.

Terra Field Bed & Breakfast ✪
BRANN ROAD BOX 1950, WEST LEVANT, MAINE 04456

Tel: **(207) 884-8805**
Hosts: **William and Carol Terra**
Location: **12 mi. NW of Bangor**
No. of Rooms: **3**
Max. No. Sharing Bath: **4**
Double/pb: **$65**
Single/pb: **$55**
Double/sb: **$40–$55**
Single/sb: **$35–$50**
Guest Cottage: **$65 sleeps 2, $10 each additional guest**

Open: **All year**
Reduced Rates: **15% weekly**
Breakfast: **Full**
Pets: **Yes**
Children: **Welcome**
Smoking: **Permitted**
Social Drinking: **Permitted**
Airport/Station Pickup: **Yes**

Talk about happy landings! Terra Field, a 102-acre hay farm near Bangor, has its own sod runway suitable for single-engine and small twin-engine planes. Bill constructed his elegant contemporary home with wood and fieldstone from the premises. You're welcome to wander in the fields, swim or canoe in the large pond, hike along wooded trails, or just take in the sights from the sunny deck. For breakfast, the specialty is eggs Penobscot, made with local fiddlehead ferns.

The Cape Neddick House ✪
1300 ROUTE 1, P.O. BOX 70, CAPE NEDDICK (YORK), MAINE 03902

Tel: **(207) 363-2500**
Hosts: **John and Dianne Goodwin**
Location: **12 mi. N of Portsmouth, New Hampshire**
No. of Rooms: **5**
No. of Private Baths: **5**

Double/pb: **$55–$75**
Single/pb: **$55–$70**
Suites: **$75–$95**
Open: **All year**
Reduced Rates: **Weekly**
Breakfast: **Full**

Pets: **No**   Smoking: **No**
Children: **Welcome, over 5**   Social Drinking: **Permitted**

Replete with family treasures, this inherited 1885 Victorian farmhouse is located in the historic coastal town of York. Relax by a roaring fire in the living room in fall or winter, or cool off on the deck overlooking gardens and woods in spring and summer. Shop till you drop at nearby factory outlets, boutiques, and antique shops, or observe Mother Nature's creations on rural roads, in wildlife sanctuaries, and on the beaches. Sleep in antique-filled bedrooms under handmade quilts. Awake to the scent of cinnamon popovers, strawberry scones, peach almond torte, or ham and apple biscuits—enough to sustain you for another day of exploring the Maine coast.

The Wild Rose of York B&B
78 LONG SANDS ROAD, YORK, MAINE 03909

Tel: **(207) 363-2532**   Open: **All year**
Best Time to Call: **6–10 PM**   Reduced Rates: **Oct. 16–May 31**
Hosts: **Fran and Frank Sullivan**   Breakfast: **Full**
No. of Rooms: **3**   Pets: **No**
No. of Private Baths: **3**   Children: **Welcome**
Double/pb: **$65–$85**   Smoking: **No**
Single/pb: **$50**   Social Drinking: **Permitted**

This handsome house, built in 1814, sits high on a hill within easy range of the ocean breezes. The bedrooms are cozy, with antique beds, patchwork quilts, fireplaces, and Fran's special artistic touches. Breakfast is special and may feature peach pancakes or nut waffles. In summer, an old-fashioned trolley will take you to the beach. Deep-sea fishing, golf, hiking, shops, galleries, and factory outlets are nearby diversions. In winter, sledding, skating, and cross-country skiing are all fun.

Canterbury House ✪
432 YORK STREET, P.O. BOX 881, YORK HARBOR, MAINE 03911

Tel: **(207) 363-3505**   Breakfast: **Full, Continental**
Best Time to Call: **Early mornings**   Other Meals: **Available**
Hosts: **James T. Pappas and Jim S. Hager**   Credit Cards: **MC, VISA**
Location: **50 mi. N of Boston, Mass.** Pets: **No**
No. of Rooms: **7**   Children: **Welcome, over 12**
No. of Private Baths: **2**   Smoking: **Restricted**
Max. No. Sharing Bath: **4**   Social Drinking: **Permitted**
Double/pb: **$75**   Minimum Stay: **2 nights in season**
Double/sb: **$59–$69**   Airport/Station Pickup: **Yes**
Open: **All year**   Foreign Languages: **French, Greek, German**
Reduced Rates: **7th night free**

A lovely white Victorian overlooking unspoiled York Harbor, Canterbury House is within walking distance from the beach and other local attractions. Guests enjoy large hotel amenities while being pampered in a homey atmosphere. A scrumptious breakfast, served on fine Royal Albert china in either the dining room or, weather permitting, the scenic front porch, features hot muffins fresh from your hosts' own bakery.

For key to listings, see inside front or back cover.

○ This star means that rates are guaranteed through December 31, 1995, to any guest making a reservation as a result of reading about the B&B in *Bed & Breakfast U.S.A.*—1995 edition.

Important! To avoid misunderstandings, always ask about cancellation policies when booking.

Please enclose a self-addressed, stamped, business-size envelope when contacting reservation services.

For more details on what you can expect in a B&B, see Chapter 1.

Always mention *Bed & Breakfast U.S.A.* when making reservations!

If no B&B is listed in the area you'll be visiting, use the form on page 743 to order a copy of our "List of New B&Bs."

We want to hear from you! Use the form on page 745.

MARYLAND

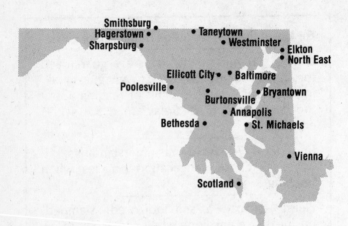

Smithsburg •
Hagerstown •
Sharpsburg •
• Taneytown
• Westminster
• Elkton
• North East
Ellicott City • • Baltimore
Poolesville •
• Bryantown
Burtonsville •
• Annapolis
Bethesda •
• St. Michaels
• Vienna
Scotland •

Bed & Breakfast of Maryland/The Traveller in Maryland, Inc. ✪
P.O. BOX 2277, ANNAPOLIS, MARYLAND 21404-2277

Tel: (410) 269-6232; (800) 736-4667;
fax: (410) 263-4841
Best Time to Call: **9 AM–5 PM**
Coordinator: **Greg Page**
States/Regions Covered: **Annapolis, Baltimore, Central Maryland, Eastern and Southern shore, Western Maryland; London, England, United Kingdom**

Descriptive Directory: $5
Rates (Single/Double):
  Modest: **$55 / $60**
  Average: **$60 / $70**
  Luxury: **$80 / $100**
Credit Cards: **AMEX, MC, VISA**

Maryland is the home of Annapolis, site of the United States Naval Academy; Baltimore, home to the restored Inner Harbor and locale of historic Fort McHenry of "Star-Spangled Banner" fame; and Chesapeake Bay, known for its excellent harbors and fabulous fishing.

Greg's carefully selected hosts are anxious to show off their expertise in helping you discover all of those special places that will make your visit memorable.

The Barn On Howard's Cove ✪
500 WILSON ROAD, ANNAPOLIS, MARYLAND 21401

Tel: **(410) 266-6840**	Open: **All year**
Hosts: **Graham and Libbie Gutsche**	Reduced Rates: **$5 less after 3rd night**
Location: **25 mi. SE of Baltimore**	Breakfast: **Full**
No. of Rooms: **2**	Pets: **No**
Max. No. Sharing Bath: **4**	Children: **Welcome**
Double/sb: **$70**	Smoking: **No**

Located near Annapolis, the Barn of Howard's Cove offers charming accommodations. This converted 1850 horsebarn is decorated in a country style; quilts and antiques abound. Two bedrooms offer private, adjoining one-half-baths and shared bath-shower. Both rooms overlook a beautiful cove off Severn River. Breakfasts may feature omelets, French toast made with homemade cinnamon raisin bread, eggs Benedict, etc. Hosts Libbie and Graham share cooking and welcoming guests. Both are involved in arts, crafts, and gardening; Graham is a physics professor at the Naval Academy. Deep-water docking is available. Sailing schools, historic homes and gardens, bike paths, and crafts and antique shops, as well as Baltimore and Washington, D.C., are within easy access.

Chesapeake Bay Lighthouse B&B ✪
1423 SHARPS POINT ROAD, ANNAPOLIS, MARYLAND 21401

Tel: **(410) 757-0248**	Breakfast: **Continental, plus**
Hosts: **Bill and Janice Costello**	Credit Cards: **MC, VISA**
Location: **30 mi. E. of Washington, DC**	Pets: **No**
No. of Rooms: **3**	Children: **No**
No. of Private Baths: **3**	Smoking: **No**
Double/pb: **$85**	Social Drinking: **Permitted**
Open: **All year**	Minimum Stay: **2 nights**
Reduced Rates: **10% Seniors**	

For the vacation of a lifetime, come to Annapolis, a picturesque colonial town with cobblestone streets, the Naval Academy, the Chesapeake, and blue crab and sailboats galore. Join your hosts on the breezy bay shore in a full-size replica of a typical cottage-style lighthouse. On this three-acre setting you'll enjoy panoramic views from every room: you'll see osprey and blue heron feeding, plus spectacular vistas of the Bay Bridge, Thomas Point Lighthouse, and the entrance to the Annapolis harbor. For closer views, you can borrow binoculars from Bill and Janice. Other amenities include individually controlled air-conditioning units in all guest rooms, and an upstairs common room with a well-stocked refrigerator.

College House Suites ✪
ONE COLLEGE AVENUE, ANNAPOLIS, MARYLAND 21401

Tel: (410) 263-6124	Credit Cards: MC, VISA
Best Time to Call: 10 AM–4 PM	Pets: No
Hosts: Jo Anne and Don Wolfrey	Children: No
Suites: $160	Smoking: No
Open: All year	Social Drinking: Permitted
Breakfast: Continental	Minimum Stay: 2 nights

This brick town house is nestled between the U.S. Naval Academy and St. John's College. The Annapolitan suite has a fireplace, Laura Ashley decor, and a private entrance through the ivy-covered courtyard. The Colonial suite has superb oriental rugs, antiques, and views of the Academy. The hosts pay close attention to details such as fresh flowers, fruit baskets, and chocolates. College House Suites is a short walk to the city dock, Paca House and Gardens, fine restaurants, fascinating shops and boutiques, art and antique galleries, museums, historic buildings, churches, and theater. A "breakfast-out" option is available.

Amanda's B&B Reservation Service ✪
1428 PARK AVENUE, BALTIMORE, MARYLAND 21217

Tel: (410) 225-0001; fax: (410) 728-8957	Jersey, Pennsylvania, Virginia, West Virginia
Best Time to Call: 8:30 AM–5:30 PM Mon.–Fri., Sat. 8:30 AM–Noon	Descriptive Directory: $3 Rates (Double):
Coordinator: Betsy Grater	Modest: $60
States/Regions Covered: Delaware, District of Columbia, Maryland, New	Luxury: $75–$125 Credit Cards: AMEX, DISC, MC, VISA

Amanda's, a reliable source of information for the traveler, ensures that bed and breakfast accommodations meet high standards of comfort, cleanliness, and ambiance. This service seeks to follow the example of the original Amanda—a sailing ship, acclaimed for its cleanliness, that made Baltimore a port of call.

Betsy's Bed and Breakfast ✪
1428 PARK AVENUE, BALTIMORE, MARYLAND 21217

Tel: (410) 383-1274	No. of Private Baths: 3
Best Time to Call: 9:30 AM–10 PM	Double/pb: $75
Hosts: Betsy Grater	Single/pb: $65
No. of Rooms: 3	Open: All year

Breakfast: **Full**	Children: **Welcome**
Credit Cards: **AMEX, MC, VISA**	Smoking: **No**
Pets: **No**	Social Drinking: **Permitted**

A petite estate, this four-story row house is in Bolton Hill, a historic Baltimore neighborhood listed on the National Registry. The interior features 12-foot ceilings with center medallions, a hall floor inlaid with oak and walnut, crown moldings, and carved marble fireplaces. This charming old house is uniquely decorated with a large collection of original brass rubbings, heirloom quilts, and interesting wall groupings. Modern amenities include a hot tub. Betsy's B&B is just a few blocks from a new light-rail stop at "Cultural Station," and steps away from Meyerhoff Symphony Hall, the Lyric Opera House, Antique Row, and the Maryland Institute of Art. The Inner Harbor is seven minutes away by car.

Mulberry House ✪
111 WEST MULBERRY STREET, BALTIMORE, MARYLAND 21201

Tel: **(410) 576-0111**	Breakfast: **Full**
Hosts: **Charlotte and Curt Jeschke**	Pets: **No**
No. of Rooms: **4**	Children: **Welcome, over 16**
Max. No. Sharing Bath: **4**	Smoking: **No**
Double/sb: **$75**	Social Drinking: **Permitted**
Open: **All year**	Foreign Languages: **German**

Mulberry House, in downtown Baltimore, was built circa 1830 as a Federal-period town house. Over the years a fourth floor and a courtyard were added, and a painstaking restoration has now taken place. The owners have added special touches, such as leaded glass in first-floor transoms, fan windows, and needlepoint cushions from 19th-century wallpaper designs. Guests may choose from the Victorian, Far East, Federal, and Pineapple rooms, all professionally decorated. Guests are treated like old friends, and are welcome to relax in the sitting room with its grand piano, sofa, and fireplace. A sumptuous breakfast is served at an 18th-century banquet table each morning. The house is within walking distance of many shops, museums, restaurants, historic sights, and the waterfront area.

The Winslow Home ✪
8217 CARAWAY STREET, CABIN JOHN, BETHESDA, MARYLAND 20818

Tel: **(301) 229-4654**	Double/sb: **$45**
Best Time to Call: **After 5 PM**	Single/sb: **$35**
Hosts: **Jane Winslow**	Open: **All year**
Location: **7 mi. W of Washington, D.C.**	Reduced Rates: **Seniors, families**
No. of rooms: **2**	Breakfast: **Full**
Max. No. Sharing Bath: **4**	Pets: **Welcome**

Children: **Welcome**   Social Drinking: **No**
Smoking: **No**   Airport/Station Pickup: **Yes**

You may enjoy the best of two worlds while staying at Jane's. This comfortable home is located in a lovely residential section of Bethesda, just 20 minutes from downtown Washington, D.C. Imagine touring the capital with some extra pocket money saved on high hotel costs. You are welcome to use the kitchen, laundry facilities, and piano. Georgetown, George Washington, and American universities are close by. There's a $5 surcharge for one-night stays.

Shady Oaks of Serenity ✪
P.O. BOX 842, BRYANTOWN, MARYLAND 20617-0842

Tel: **(800) 597-0924**
Best Time to Call: **After 4 PM till 11 PM**
Hosts: **Kathy and Gene Kazimer**
Location: **35 mi. from Washington, D.C.**
Suites: **$65**

Open: **All year**
Breakfast: **Continental**
Pets: **No**
Children: **Welcome, over 14**
Smoking: **No**
Social Drinking: **Permitted**

Shady Oaks of Serenity is a new Georgia Victorian situated on three acres and surrounded by trees. This secluded home is off the beaten path, yet within a 45-minute drive of the nation's capital and Annapolis, home of the U.S. Naval Academy. Just down the road is Amish country with antiques and unique shops, historic churches, the renowned Dr. Mudd Home, and Gilbert Run Park, a favorite county stop. Also, this retreat may be of interest to those visiting patients at the Charlotte Hall Veterans Home, only minutes away. Decorated with the Amish theme, the suite has a private bath. Visitors are welcome to gather in the sitting room, the front porch or enjoy an evening on the deck. This room has a king-size bed for a peaceful night's rest. Kathy and Gene cordially invite you to be a guest in their home and visit historic Charles County. The morning brings fresh coffee, homemade muffins or breads and a variety of fresh fruits.

The Taylors' B&B ✪
P.O. BOX 238, BURTONSVILLE, MARYLAND 20866-0238

Tel: **(301) 236-4318**
Best Time to Call: **9–11 AM; 7–9 PM**
Hosts: **Ruth and Fred Taylor**
Location: **30 min. from Washington, D.C., and the Inner Harbor**
No. of Rooms: **1**
No. of Private Baths: **1**
Double/pb: **$60**

Open: **All year**
Breakfast: **Continental**
Pets: **No**
Children: **No**
Smoking: **No**
Social Drinking: **Permitted**
Foreign Languages: **French**

This gracious two-story Colonial home offers a breath of fresh country air just 30 minutes from Washington, D.C., and Baltimore's Inner Harbor district. Guests can enjoy the grand piano, the extensive collection of books in the library, and Ruth's paintings. In warm weather, cool drinks are served in the gazebo; in winter, guests gather by the fireplace in the family room. Both of your hosts are retired. Ruth likes to read, sew, paint, and cook; Fred enjoys reading, writing, history, and music. They've traveled extensively and know how to make guests feel welcome. Tennis courts, horseback riding, and nature trails are nearby.

Chevy Chase Bed & Breakfast
6815 CONNECTICUT AVENUE, CHEVY CHASE, MARYLAND 20815

Tel: **(301) 656-5867**
Best Time to Call: **Anytime**
Host: **S. C. Gotbaum**
Location: **1 mi. N of Washington**
No. of rooms: **2**
No. of Private Baths: **2**
Double/pb: **$65**
Single/pb: **$55**

Open: **All year**
Reduced Rates: **Families**
Breakfast: **Continental, plus**
Pets: **No**
Children: **Welcome**
Smoking: **No**
Social Drinking: **Permitted**

Enjoy the convenience of being close to the transportation and sights of Washington, D.C., and Maryland's Montgomery County while staying at a relaxing, turn-of-the century, country-style house. Rooms have beamed ceilings and are filled with rare tapestries, Oriental rugs, baskets, copperware and native crafts from Mexico to the Mideast. The garden room has a cathedral ceiling and private deck. The gabled skylight room has a king-size bed. Your host is a sociologist with a private consulting business. Breakfast items include homemade breads, jams, pancakes, French toast, and a special blend of Louisiana coffee. When you want to take a break from touring, the lovely garden will soothe you.

The Garden Cottage at Sinking Springs Herb Farm ☉
234 BLAIR SHORE ROAD, ELKTON, MARYLAND 21921

Tel: **(410) 398-5566**
Best Time to Call: **9 AM–9 PM**
Hosts: **Ann and Bill Stubbs**
Location: **4½ mi. from Rte. 40**
No. of Rooms: **1**
No. of Private Baths: **1**
Guest Cottage: **$85; sleeps 3**
Open: **All year**
Reduced Rates: **5% seniors**

Breakfast: **Full**
Credit Cards: **MC, VISA**
Other Meals: **Available**
Pets: **Sometimes**
Children: **Welcome**
Smoking: **No**
Social Drinking: **Permitted**
Airport/Station Pickup: **Yes**

Guests frequently comment on the peaceful beauty of this 128-acre historical farm. The garden cottage has a sitting room and fireplace adjoining the bedroom. Breakfast features coffee ground from organically grown beans, herbal teas, homemade buns, fruit, and juice. A full country breakfast prepared with unprocessed food fresh from the farm is available at no extra charge. Lectures on herbs and craft classes are available, and a gift shop is on the premises. Longwood Gardens and the famed Winterthur Museum are close by. Historic Chesapeake City is five minutes away.

Hayland Farm

5000 SHEPPARD LANE, ELLICOTT CITY, MARYLAND 21042

Tel: **(410) 531-5593**
Host: **Dorothy Mobley**
Location: **Bet. Baltimore and D.C.**
No. of Rooms: **3**
No. of Private Baths: **1**
Max. No. Sharing Bath: **4**
Double/pb: **$60**
Single/pb: **$40**

Double/sb: **$40**
Single/sb: **$25**
Open: **All year**
Breakfast: **Full**
Pets: **No**
Children: **No**
Smoking: **No**
Social Drinking: **Permitted**

When you breathe the country-fresh air, it may surprise you that Baltimore and Washington, D.C., are only a short drive away. At Hayland Farm you will find gracious living in a large manor house furnished in a handsome, yet comfortable, style. Dorothy is retired and has traveled extensively. She enjoys sharing conversation with her guests. In warm weather, the 20- by 50-foot swimming pool is a joy.

Beaver Creek House Bed and Breakfast ✪

20432 BEAVER CREEK ROAD, HAGERSTOWN, MARYLAND 21740

Tel: **(301) 797-4764**
Best Time to Call: **Anytime**
Hosts: **Don and Shirley Day**
Location: **4 mi. E of Hagerstown**
No. of Rooms: **5**
No. of Private Baths: **3**
Max. No. Sharing Bath: **4**
Double/pb: **$85**
Single/pb: **$75**
Double/sb: **$85**

Single/sb: **$75**
Open: **All year**
Reduced Rates: **$10 less Mon.–Thurs.**
Breakfast: **Full**
Credit Cards: **AMEX, DISC, MC, VISA**
Pets: **No**
Children: **Welcome, over 10**
Smoking: **No**
Social Drinking: **Permitted**
Airport/Station Pickup: **Yes**

This turn-of-the-century country home enjoys a wonderful view of South Mountain. Start your day with a bountiful country breakfast served on the wraparound screened porch. Then it's off to South Mountain for a hike along the Appalachian Trail. Or perhaps you'd rather bicycle along the scenic country roads. Civil War buffs will want to visit nearby historic parks like Antietam Battlefield and Harpers Ferry, while duffers can choose between two professional courses. Whatever your pleasure, save time to explore the beautifully maintained B&B grounds, with their gardens, fish pond, and patio.

Lewrene Farm B&B ✪
9738 DOWNSVILLE PIKE, HAGERSTOWN, MARYLAND 21740

Tel: (301) 582-1735
Hosts: Lewis and Irene Lehman
Location: 3½ mi. from I-70 and I-81
No. of Rooms: 5
No. of Private Baths: 3
Max. No. Sharing Bath: 4
Double/pb: $75–$90
Double/sb: $50–$65

Suites: $90
Open: All year
Breakfast: Full
Children: Welcome
Smoking: No
Social Drinking: No
Foreign Languages: Spanish

Lewis and Irene will help you discover the peaceful beauty of their 125-acre farm located in a historic area near the Antietam Battlefield. Guests are treated like old friends and are welcome to lounge in front of the fireplace or to play the piano in the Colonial-style living room. You're invited to enjoy snacks and a video in the evening. Harpers Ferry, Fort Frederick, the C&O Canal, and Gettysburg are nearby. Irene sells antiques and collectibles on the premises.

Sunday's Bed & Breakfast ✪
39 BROADWAY, HAGERSTOWN, MARYLAND 21740

Tel: (800) 221-4828
Best Time to Call: Anytime
Host: Bob Ferrino
Location: 70 mi. NW of Washington, D.C.
No. of Rooms: 3
No. of Private Baths: 1
Max. No. Sharing Bath: 3
Double/pb: $85
Single/pb: $65–$75
Double/sb: $65–$75

Single/sb: $55–$65
Open: All year
Reduced Rates: Available
Breakfast: Full
Other Meals: Available
Pets: Sometimes
Children: Welcome
Smoking: No
Social Drinking: Permitted
Airport Pickup: Yes

Built in 1890, this elegant Queen Anne Victorian is located in Hagerstown's historic north end, on a street lined with other grand old homes. Relax in your room or in the many public areas and porches. You may want to visit the area's numerous attractions, such as the National Historical Parks of Antietam, Harpers Ferry, Whitetails Ski Resort, and the C&O Canal. Or choose among the myriad other historic sites, antique shops, fishing areas, golf courses, museums, shopping outlets, and theaters.

The Mill House B&B ✪
102 MILL LANE, NORTH EAST, MARYLAND 21901

Tel: **(410) 287-3532**	Single/sb: **$60–$70**
Best Time to Call: **Before 9 AM; after 4 PM**	Open: **March 1–Dec. 1**
	Breakfast: **Full**
Hosts: **Lucia and Nick Demond**	Credit Cards: **MC, VISA**
Location: **40 mi. NE of Baltimore**	Pets: **No**
No. of Rooms: **2**	Children: **Welcome, over 12**
Max. No. Sharing Bath: **4**	Smoking: **No**
Double/sb: **$65–$75**	Social Drinking: **Permitted**

A genuine mill house that dates to the early 18th century, this B&B is furnished entirely in antiques. You'll see picturesque mill ruins and wildflowers on the grounds, but you won't see the parlor's original Queen Anne paneling; that was purchased by Henry Francis Du Pont and installed in his Winterthur estate bedroom. The Winterthur Museum and the Brandywine River Museum are less than an hour's drive away, as is Baltimore's Inner Harbor. Sightseers will be sustained with a full breakfast, including homemade breads fresh from the oven.

Rocker Inn ✪
17924 ELGIN ROAD, POOLESVILLE, MARYLAND 20837

Tel: **(301) 972-8543**	Single/pb: **$40**
Best Time to Call: **After 5:30 PM**	Open: **All year**
Host: **Nancy Hopkinson**	Breakfast: **Continental**
Location: **25 mi. NW of Washington, D.C.**	Pets: **Sometimes**
	Children: **Welcome**
No. of Rooms: **1**	Smoking: **No**
No. of Private Baths: **1**	Social Drinking: **Permitted**
Double/pb: **$45**	

Built in 1915 as a local telephone house, Rocker Inn takes its name from the rocking chairs and two swings that fill its 48-foot front porch. Inside, the home is decorated in an informal country mode. Walking tours of Poolesville and Frederick, along with a hike on the C&O Canal, are minutes away. For more ambitious excursions, Harpers Ferry, Gettysburg Battlefield, and historic Leesburg are within an hour's drive.

Parsonage Inn ✪
210 NORTH TALBOT STREET, ST. MICHAELS, MARYLAND 21663

Tel: **(800) 394-5519**	Double/pb: **$92–$124**
Hosts: **Peggy and Bill Parsons**	Open: **All year**
Location: **11 mi. off Rte. 50**	Reduced Rates: **10% seniors; $10 less midweek, off-season**
No. of Rooms: **8**	
No. of Private Baths: **8**	Breakfast: **Full**

Credit Cards: **MC, VISA**
Pets: **No**
Children: **Welcome**

Smoking: **Restricted**
Social Drinking: **Permitted**

Built in the 1880s with bricks fired in the St. Michaels brickyard, the Parsonage Inn was completely restored in 1985. This striking Victorian B&B is part of the town's historic district, and it's an easy stroll to shops, restaurants, and the Chesapeake Bay Maritime Museum. More ambitious guests may borrow the inn's 12-speed bicycles and venture farther afield.

St. Michael's Manor B&B ✪
ST. MICHAEL'S MANOR, SCOTLAND, MARYLAND 20687

Tel: **(301) 872-4025**
Hosts: **Joe and Nancy Dick**
Location: **9 mi. S of St. Marys City**
No. of Rooms: **4**
Max. No. Sharing Bath: **4**
Double/sb: **$65**
Single/sb: **$50**

Open: **All year**
Reduced Rates: **Nov. 1–Apr. 1**
Breakfast: **Full**
Pets: **No**
Children: **By arrangement**
Smoking: **Downstairs**
Social Drinking: **Permitted**

St. Michael's Manor was built in 1805 on land patented to Leonard Calvert during the seventeenth century. Today, the white stucco manor home on picturesque Long Neck Creek is included in the state's Pilgrimage Tour. The beautiful handcrafted woodwork has been preserved and is complemented by antiques and handcrafts. Your hosts offer you the use of a canoe, paddleboat, bikes, and swimming pool. Estate wine tasting is also available. The manor house is near Point Lookout State Park, the Chesapeake Bay, and historic St. Marys City.

Jacob Rohrbach Inn
P.O. BOX 607, SHARPSBURG, MARYLAND 21782

Tel: **(301) 432-5079**	Single/pb: **$70**
Best Time to Call: **9 AM–4 PM**	Open: **All year**
Host: **Denise Yeager**	Reduced Rates: **10% seniors**
Location: **70 mi. NW of Washington,**	Breakfast: **Full**
D.C.	Pets: **No**
No. of Rooms: **3**	Children: **Welcome, over 6**
No. of Private Baths: **3**	Smoking: **No**
Double/pb: **$80**	Social Drinking: **Permitted**

This great brick and stone house survived the Battle of Antietam with relatively minor damage only to have its owner murdered by Confederate raiders in 1864. Today, the Jacob Rohrbach Inn looks much as it did during the Civil War, permitting patrons a unique view into the past. Antietam Battlefield surrounds the inn and Harpers Ferry Historical Park is just twenty minutes away. Tour the battlefield, bicycle the C&O Canal, visit quaint country shops, or just curl up with a book in front of a warm fire. White-water rafting, horseback riding, and skiing are nearby; if you'd rather travel by car, a leisurely one-hour trip leads through the Shenandoah Valley to the Skyline Drive.

Blue Bear Bed & Breakfast ✪
13810 FRANK'S RUN ROAD, SMITHSBURG, MARYLAND 21783

Tel: **(800) 381-2292**	Single/pb: **$50–$55**
Best Time to Call: **After 4 PM**	Open: **All year**
Host: **Ellen Panchula**	Breakfast: **Continental**
Location: **6 mi. from I-70, Exit 35**	Pets: **No**
No. of Rooms: **2**	Children: **Welcome, over 12**
No of Private Baths: **2**	Smoking: **No**
Double/pb: **$60–$65**	Social Drinking: **Permitted**

Ellen is a full-time schoolteacher from September through June, so she can entertain guests during the week only in July and August; during the school year it's strictly weekends only. Her home is decorated in an informal country mode, with several antiques complementing the decor. Smithsburg is located in apple and peach country. It is convenient to the Antietam Battlefield in Sharpsburg, and to many fine restaurants in Hagerstown. Homemade breads, coffee cakes, quiche, fresh fruit, and beverages constitute the breakfast menu. Snacks, dessert, and wine and cheese are generously offered in the evenings.

Null's Bed & Breakfast ✪
4910 BAPTIST ROAD, TANEYTOWN, MARYLAND 21787

Tel: **(410) 756-6112**	Double/sb: **$50**
Hosts: **Francis and Betty Null**	Single/sb: **$45**
Location: **8 mi. S of Gettysburg, Penn.**	Open: **All year**
No. of Rooms: **2**	Breakfast: **Full**
No. of Private Baths: **1**	Pets: **No**
Max. No. Sharing Bath: **4**	Children: **Welcome**
Double/pb: **$55**	Smoking: **Permitted**
Single/pb: **$50**	Social Drinking: **Permitted**

Francis Null grew up in this blue farmhouse, which has always been in his family. While it is no longer a working farm, the property's 22 acres invite exploration. Ask your hosts about the furniture; some pieces are genuine antiques, others are artful reproductions Francis created in his woodworking shop. Taneytown is about nine miles from Gettysburg, and Baltimore, Washington, D.C., and Amish country are all accessible by car. Homemade bread and jam accompany Betty's full breakfasts.

The Tavern House ✪
111 WATER STREET, P.O. BOX 98, VIENNA, MARYLAND 21869

Tel: **(410) 376-3347**
Hosts: **Harvey and Elise Altergott**
Location: **15 mi. NW of Salisbury**
No. of Rooms: **4**
Max. No. Sharing Bath: **4**
Double/sb: **$65–$75**
Single/sb: **$60–$70**
Open: **All year**

Breakfast: **Full**
Credit Cards: **MC, VISA**
Pets: **No**
Children: **Welcome, over 12**
Smoking: **Permitted**
Social Drinking: **Permitted**
Foreign Languages: **German, Spanish**

Vienna is a quiet little town on the Nanticoke River, where one can escape the stress of the 20th century. Careful restoration has brought back the simple purity of this Colonial tavern. The stark white "lime, sand, and hair" plaster accents the authentic furnishings. This is a place for those who enjoy looking at the river and marshes, watching an osprey, or taking a leisurely walk. Days begin with fruits of the season and end with complimentary cheese and wine. For the sports minded, there's tennis, boating, and flat roads for bicycling, all within easy reach. This is an excellent base for exploring the Eastern Shore, interesting small towns, and Blackwater National Wildlife Refuge.

Winchester Country Inn ✪
430 SOUTH BISHOP STREET, WESTMINSTER, MARYLAND 21157

Tel: **(410) 876-7373; (800) 887-3950**
Best Time to Call: **9 AM–7 PM**
Hosts: **Estella Williams and Cynthia Rosembloom**
Location: **35 mi. NW of Baltimore**
No. of Rooms: **5**

No. of Private Baths: **3**
Max. No. Sharing Bath: **4**
Double/pb: **$29.95–$65**
Open: **All year**
Reduced Rates: **Sun.–Thurs.**
Breakfast: **Full**

Credit Cards: **MC, VISA**
Pets: **No**
Children: **Welcome, over 6**

Smoking: **No**
Social Drinking: **Permitted**

Built in the 1760s, this inn is one of the oldest inns in Carroll County. It is furnished with period antiques that enhance the interior. It is only a quarter of a mile to the historic Carroll County Farm Museum, which is the site of special events such as the Maryland Wine Festival. It is within walking distance of the Farmers Market, where produce, flowers, and crafts may be bought. Breakfast includes farm-fresh eggs and country sausage or ham.

For key to listings, see inside front or back cover.

○ This star means that rates are guaranteed through December 31, 1995, to any guest making a reservation as a result of reading about the B&B in *Bed & Breakfast U.S.A.*—1995 edition.

Important! To avoid misunderstandings, always ask about cancellation policies when booking.

Please enclose a self-addressed, stamped, business-size envelope when contacting reservation services.

For more details on what you can expect in a B&B, see Chapter 1.

Always mention *Bed & Breakfast U.S.A.* when making reservations!

If no B&B is listed in the area you'll be visiting, use the form on page 743 to order a copy of our "List of New B&Bs."

We want to hear from you! Use the form on page 745.

MASSACHUSETTS

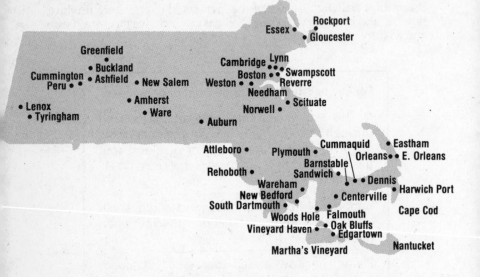

Bed & Breakfast Marblehead & North Shore ✪
P.O. BOX 35, NEWTONVILLE, MASSACHUSETTS 02160

Tel: (617) 964-1606; (800) 832-2632 in
the U.S. outside Massachusetts and
Canada; fax: (617) 332-8572
Best Time to Call: 8:30 AM–9 PM
Mon.–Fri., 9 AM–noon Sat., 7 PM–9
PM Sun.
Coordinator: **Sheryl Felleman**
States/Regions Covered:
**Massachusetts—Beverly, Danvers,
Gloucester, Hamilton, Manchester,**
Marblehead, Middleton,
Newburyport, Peabody, Plum Island,
Rockport, Salem, Swampscott,
Topsfield; Maine; New Hampshire;
Vermont
Rates (Single/Double):
Modest: $45–$55 / $55–$65
Average: $55–$70 / $65–$80
Luxury: $70–$100 / $85–$175
Credit Cards: **AMEX, MC, VISA**

Come home to the history and culture of New England! Stay in one of
the beautiful B&B homes, small inns, or furnished apartments in
historic oceanside towns on Massachusetts' North Shore. This area is
known for its rich past, beautiful beaches and harbors, recreational
activities, wonderful restaurants, and friendly New England hospital-

ity. Easy access by public transportation to Boston. Selected B&Bs in fall foliage and ski areas elsewhere in New England. Daily, weekly, or monthly rates.

Bed & Breakfast in Minuteman Country
P.O. BOX 1344, CAMBRIDGE, MASSACHUSETTS 02140

Tel: (617) 576-1492; (800) 888-0178
Best Time to Call: 10 AM–5 PM
 Mon.–Fri, 10 AM–3 PM Sat.
Coordinators: Tally and Pamela
 Carruthers
States/Regions Covered: Boston,
 Cambridge, Lexington, and
 surrounding areas

Rates (Single/Double):
 Average: $50 / $80
 Luxury: $70 / $110
Credit Cards: AMEX, MC, VISA
Minimum Stay: 2 nights

Tally and Pamela can place you in host homes convenient to historic Lexington and Concord, downtown Boston, or in Cambridge. Many are close to Harvard and MIT, Lahey Clinic, historic Wright Tavern, Emerson's home, Walden Pond, and the Charles River. Unusual restaurants, specialty shops, and cultural happenings abound. Just tell your host about your interests and you will be assured of excellent advice. There's a $10 surcharge for one-night stays.

Bed & Breakfast/Inns of New England ✪
128 SOUTH HOOPE POLE ROAD, GUILFORD, CONNECTICUT 06437

Tel: (800) 582-0853
Best Time to Call: 9 AM–8 PM
Coordinator: Ernie Taddei
States/Regions Covered:
 Connecticut, Maine, Massachusetts,
 New Hampshire, Rhode Island,
 Vermont

Descriptive Directory: $2
Rates (Single/Double):
 Modest: $45–$50
 Average: $55–$65
 Luxury: $80–$85
Credit Cards: MC, VISA

Stay anywhere in New England, near historic sites, natural attractions, and schools and colleges. Vacation on the seacoast, in the Berkshires, or even on a 125-acre maple sugar farm. This reservation service has something for everyone; the more than 100 guest homes range from an 18th-century Colonial to a stately Georgian mansion.

BOSTON AREA

Bed & Breakfast Associates—Bay Colony, Ltd. ✪
P.O. BOX 57166, BABSON PARK, BOSTON, MASSACHUSETTS 02157-0166

Tel: (617) 449-5302; (800) 347-5088;
 fax: (617) 449-5958

Best Time to Call: 9:30 AM–12:30 PM;
 1:30–5 PM Mon.–Fri.

Coordinators: **Arline Kardasis and
Marilyn Mitchell**
States/Regions Covered: **Boston,
Brookline, Cambridge, Cape Cod,
Concord, Framingham, Gloucester,
Newton, North Shore, South Shore**
Descriptive Directory: **Free**

Rates (Single/Double):
Modest: **$45–$50 / $55–$60**
Average: **$55–$65 / $65–$75**
Luxury: **$70–$100 / $80–$125**
Credit Cards: **AMEX, CB, DC, MC,
VISA**
Minimum Stay: **2 nights**

A wide variety of 150 host homes, inns, and apartments is available in
the city, in the country, and at the shore. They range from historic
brownstones to contemporary condominiums. Many are convenient
to the major colleges and universities.

Bed & Breakfast Greater Boston & Cape Cod
A Division of Bed & Breakfast Marblehead & North
Shore ✪
P.O. BOX 35, NEWTONVILLE, MASSACHUSETTS 02160

Tel: **(617) 964-1606; (800) 832-2632
(outside Massachusetts) in U.S.A. and
Canada; fax: (617) 332-8572**
Best Time to Call: **8:30 AM–9 PM
Mon.–Fri., 9 AM–noon Sat., 7 PM–9
PM Sun.**
Coordinator: **Suzanne Ross**
States/Regions Covered: **Boston,**

**Brookline, Cambridge, Chestnut Hill,
Concord, Newton, Cape Cod**
Rates (Single/Double):
Modest: **$45–$55 / $55–$65**
Average: **$55–$70 / $65–$80**
Luxury: **$70–$100 / $85–$165**
Credit Cards: **AMEX, MC, VISA**

Explore the city and the many tourist attractions this region offers,
then escape to the beautiful beaches of Cape Cod. Whether you
choose an antique Victorian, restored inn, classic Colonial, charming
ocean-view apartment, cozy carriage house, or contemporary condo,
you will experience the finest New England hospitality. Many accommodations close to area colleges and universities and public transportation.

Greater Boston Hospitality ✪
P.O. BOX 1142, BROOKLINE, MASSACHUSETTS 02146

Tel: **(617) 277-5430**
Coordinator: **Kelly Simpson**
States/Regions Covered: **Boston,
Brookline, Cambridge, Gloucester,
Lexington, Marblehead, Needham,
Newton, Wellesley, Winchester**

Descriptive Directory: **Free**
Rates (Single/Double):
Modest: **$35 / $45**
Average: **$45 / $55**
Luxury: **$55 / $100**
Credit Cards: **MC, VISA**

Kelly's accommodations are convenient to many of the 75 colleges and
universities in the greater Boston area. They're in inns, condos, or
self-serve apartments. Many include parking, most are near public
transportation. What a boon it is for people applying to school, and to

parents visiting undergrads, to have a home-away-from-home nearby. There's a $10 surcharge for one-night stays.

Host Homes of Boston ✪
P.O. BOX 117, WABAN BRANCH, BOSTON, MASSACHUSETTS 02168

Tel: (617) 244-1308; fax: (617) 244-5156
Best Time to Call: 9 AM–noon; 1:30–4:30 PM weekdays
Coordinator: Marcia Whittington
States/Regions Covered: Boston, Brookline, Cambridge, Cohasset, Hamilton, Lincoln, Milton, Needham, Newton, Quincy, Southborough, Sudbury, Wellesley, Westwood, Weymouth
Descriptive Directory: Free
Rates (Single/Double):
  Modest: $52–$61 / $57–$61
  Average: $52–$75 / $61–$87
  Luxury: $75–$108 / $85–$125
Credit Cards: AMEX, MC, VISA
Minimum Stay: 2 nights

Since 1982, Marcia has culled a variety of select private homes in excellent areas near major hotels and institutions, historic sites, and good public transportation. Hosts offer free parking (except downtown), hearty breakfasts, and a cordial welcome to their city of colleges, universities, museums, and cultural life. To fax your reservation request, please use the form in the directory.

The Missing Bell ✪
16 SACRAMENTO STREET, CAMBRIDGE, MASSACHUSETTS 02138

Tel: (617) 876-0987
Best Time to Call: 9 AM–10 PM
Hosts: Kristin Quinlan and J. P. Massar
Location: 1 mi. N of Boston
No. of Rooms: 2
Double p/b: $75–85
Open: Feb.–Dec.
Reduced Rates: Available
Breakfast: Continental plus
Credit Cards: MC, VISA
Pets: No
Children: Welcome, 10 or older
Smoking: No
Social Drinking: Permitted
Minimum Stay: 2 nights

Built by a family of cabinetmakers in 1883, this Queen Anne Victorian is rich in ornate woodwork. Original period details include fireplaces, intricate spindlework, a crystal chandelier, and stained glass windows. Your room and bath are freshly renovated and furnished with beautiful antiques, lace curtains, and down comforters. Come down to a homemade breakfast in the extraordinary dining room. Specialties include baked apple souffle pancakes, pears poached in raspberry sauce, sour cream Belgian waffles, and creamy nutmeg muffins. Harvard Square is just a 10 minute walk away and from there a short subway ride leads to Boston's major attractions.

George Fuller House ✪
148 MAIN STREET, ESSEX, MASSACHUSETTS 01929

Tel: (508) 768-7766	Reduced Rates: 10% less Nov. 1–May 31
Best Time to Call: 10 AM–10 PM	
Hosts: Cindy and Bob Cameron	Breakfast: Full
Location: 3 mi. off Rte. 128, Exit 15	Credit Cards: AMEX, DISC, MC, VISA
No. of Rooms: 7	Pets: No
No. of Private Baths: 7	Children: Welcome, over 6
Double/pb: $75–$90	Smoking: No
Suites: $115	Social Drinking: Permitted
Open: All year	Airport/Station Pickup: Yes

This handsome Federalist home retains much of its 19th-century paneling and woodwork; four of the guest rooms have working fireplaces. The Camerons have decorated the house with antique beds, handmade quilts, braided rugs, and caned Boston rockers. Three hundred years ago, Essex was a shipbuilding center. Among landlubbers, Essex's main claim to fame is its antique shops. Whether you venture out on sea or on land, you'll be fortified by Cindy's versions of breakfast classics, such as her French toast drizzled with brandied lemon butter.

Williams Guest House ✪
136 BASS AVENUE, GLOUCESTER, MASSACHUSETTS 01930

Tel: (508) 283-4931	Guest Cottage: $450 weekly for 2
Best Time to Call: 8 AM–8 PM	Open: May 1–Nov. 1
Host: Betty Williams	Reduced Rates: Off-season, before June 17 and after Labor Day
Location: 30 mi. N of Boston	
No. of Rooms: 7	Breakfast: Continental
No. of Private Baths: 5	Pets: No
Max. No. Sharing Bath: 4	Children: Welcome, in cottage
Double/pb: $60	Smoking: Permitted
Double/sb: $50	Social Drinking: Permitted

Located five miles from Rockport, and one and a half miles from Rocky Neck, Gloucester is a quaint fishing village on the North Shore. Betty's Colonial Revival house borders the finest beach, Good Harbor. The guest rooms are furnished with comfort in mind. Betty will be happy to suggest many interesting things to do, such as boat tours, sport fishing, whale-watching trips, sightseeing cruises around Cape Ann, the Hammond Castle Museum, and the shops and galleries of the artist colony.

Diamond District Bed and Breakfast ✪
142 OCEAN STREET, LYNN, MASSACHUSETTS 01902-2007

Tel: **(617) 599-4470; (800) 666-3076**
Hosts: **Sandra and Jerry Caron**
Location: **11 mi. NE of Boston**
No. of Rooms: **6**
No. of Private Baths: **6**
Double/pb: **$85**
Suite: **$125, sleeps 2–4**
Open: **All year**

Reduced Rates: **Available**
Breakfast: **Full**
Credit Cards: **AMEX, DC, MC, VISA**
Pets: **Sometimes**
Children: **Welcome**
Smoking: **No**
Airport/Station Pickup: **Yes**

This 22-room Georgian clapboard mansion was built in 1911 by P. J. Harney, a local shoe manufacturer. Features include a gracious foyer and a staircase winding its way up three floors; a spacious living room with Mexican mahogany, marble fireplace, and French doors leading to a large 36×14 veranda that overlooks the gardens and ocean, and a banquet-size dining room. The 44-page architect's specifications permitted only the best of materials to be used. Antiques and oriental rugs fill the house. Furnishings include an 1895 Rosewood Kanabe concert grand piano and custom Chippendale dining room table and chairs signed by Joseph Gerty, a 1940s Boston custom furniture maker. Bedrooms offer a custom 1870s Victorian bed and twin beds by Charak, another Boston custom furniture maker. Each room boasts the elegance of yesteryear.

The Thistle
31 FAIRFIELD STREET, NEEDHAM, MASSACHUSETTS 02192

Tel: **(617) 444-5724**
Best Time to Call: **Anytime**
Hosts: **Leo and Susan Rainville**
Location: **10 mi. SW of Boston**
No. of Rooms: **2**
No. of Private Baths: **1**
Max. No. Sharing Bath: **4**

Double/pb: **$60**
Single/pb: **$50**
Double/sb: **$55**
Single/sb: **$45**
Open: **All year**
Reduced Rates: **Seniors 10%**
Breakfast: **Continental**

Pets: **No**
Children: **No**
Smoking: **No**

Social Drinking: **Permitted**
Station Pickup: **Yes**

Relax in this peaceful setting on a tree-lined street just a few blocks off Route 128 and Interstate 95. The Thistle offers easy access to colleges, business districts, restaurants, and golf courses, not to mention the many historic tourist sites in Boston, Lexington, Concord, Quincy, and Plymouth. Ask your hosts to suggest activities; Leo enjoys woodworking and deep-sea fishing, while Susan likes sightseeing, walking, and swimming.

1810 House Bed & Breakfast ✪
147 OLD OAKEN BUCKET ROAD, NORWELL, MASSACHUSETTS 02061

Tel: **(617) 659-1810**
Best Time to Call: **8 AM–noon**
Hosts: **Susanne and Harold Tuttle**
Location: **20 mi. S of Boston**
No. of Rooms: **3**
No. of Private Baths: **1**
Max. No. Sharing Bath: **4**
Double/pb: **$65–$70**
Double/sb: **$60–$65**

Open: **All year**
Reduced Rates: **25% families taking 2 rooms**
Breakfast: **Full**
Pets: **No**
Children: **Welcome, over 6**
Smoking: **No**
Social Drinking: **No**

The 1810 House is located in Norwell, a beautiful historic town halfway between Boston and Plymouth. The antique half-Cape boasts wide pine floors, stenciled walls, beamed ceilings, three working fireplaces, plus oriental rugs and lovely antiques. Harold is a woodworker who did extensive restoration in the house, while Susanne is a seamstress who created the custom window treatments. A tour of the area in their 1915 Model T depot hack adds to the feeling of a bygone era and is part of the fun of staying at the 1810 House.

Golden Slumber Accommodations
640 REVERE BEACH BOULEVARD, REVERE, MASSACHUSETTS 02151

Tel: **(617) 289-1053; (800) 892-3231**
Best Time to Call: **8 AM–9 PM Mon.–Sat.**
Coordinator: **Leah A. Schmidt**
States/Regions Covered:
Massachusetts Seacoast: Bourne, Essex, Falmouth, Harwick Port, Lexington, Peabody, Plymouth, Wakefield, Wareham

Descriptive Directory of B&Bs: **Free**
Rates (Single/Double):
Modest: **$45–$55**
Average: **$55–$75**
Luxury: **$75–$115**
Credit Cards: **MC, VISA**

Golden Slumber Accommodations features an array of exquisite homes, small gracious inns, and courteous hosts representing the finest in affordable, personalized lodging in the favored New England tradition. This service provides superior accommodations along the Massachusetts seacoast, including the north and south shores, Cape Cod and greater Boston. All facilities are inspected annually. Children are welcome and wheelchair access is available at many locations.

Mooringstone for Nonsmokers ✪

12 NORWOOD AVENUE, ROCKPORT, MASSACHUSETTS 01966-1715

Tel: **(508) 546-2479**	Reduced Rates: **Available**
Best Time to Call: **9 AM–9 PM**	Breakfast: **Continental**
Hosts: **David and Mary Knowlton**	Credit Cards: **AMEX, MC, VISA**
Location: **35 mi. N of Boston**	Pets: **No**
No. of Rooms: **3**	Children: **No**
No. of Private Baths: **3**	Smoking: **No**
Double/pb: **$76.57–$84**	Social Drinking: **Permitted**
Single/pb: **$76.57–$84**	Minimum Stay: **2 nights**
Open: **May 15–Oct. 15**	Airport/Station Pickup: **Yes**

David and Mary expanded their home in 1987 to establish this contemporary, smoke-free B&B. Each of the quiet, comfortable, ground-floor rooms has cable TV, a refrigerator, a microwave oven, and room-controlled air-conditioning and heat, while bed sizes range from twin to king. There's parking for all guests. A great base for day trips to Boston, Salem, and Newburyport, Rockport is a notable destination in its own right: Walt Disney Productions named the harbor—a great site for whale watching—one of the ten "most scenic places in the country." And Mary promises that once you eat one of her muffins, you'll come back for more.

The Allen House ✪

18 ALLEN PLACE, SCITUATE, MASSACHUSETTS 02066

Tel: **(617) 545-8221**	Double/sb: **$69–$99**
Best Time to Call: **Mornings; evenings**	Open: **All year**
Hosts: **Christine and Iain Gilmour**	Breakfast: **Full**
Location: **32 mi. SE of Boston**	Pets: **No**
No. of Rooms: **6**	Children: **Welcome, over 16**
Max. No. Sharing Bath: **4**	Smoking: **No**
No. of Private Baths: **4**	Social Drinking: **Permitted**
Double/pb: **$79–$125**	Airport/Station Pickup: **Yes**

With views of the village center, this white gabled Victorian overlooks the yacht harbor, where Scituate's commercial fishermen unload lobster and cod. When the Gilmours came to the United States in 1976, they brought along the lovely furniture of their native Great Britain. English antiques fill the house. They also imported British rituals:

high tea is a frequent celebration. For breakfast, Christine, a professional caterer, offers standards such as waffles, pancakes, and homemade breads as well as gourmet treats. Allen House is distinguished by good music and good food. Iain, an accomplished musician, cheerfully shares the large library of classical music.

Marshall House ✪
11 EASTERN AVENUE, SWAMPSCOTT, MASSACHUSETTS 01907

Tel: **(617) 595-6544**	Breakfast: **Continental**
Hosts: **Pat and Al Marshall**	Credit Cards: **AMEX, MC, VISA**
Location: **10 mi. N of Boston**	Pets: **No**
No. of Rooms: **3**	Children: **Welcome, over 6**
Max. No. Sharing Bath: **4**	Smoking: **No**
Double/sb: **$60–$70**	Social Drinking: **Permitted**
Single/sb: **$50–$60**	Minimum stay: **2 nights, weekends**
Open: **All year**	Airport/Station Pickup: **Yes**
Reduced Rates: **10% seniors**	

Marshall House, built circa 1900, is located just a short walk from the beaches of the North Shore. The many porches of this spacious home offer salty breezes and an ocean view. Inside, the rooms are decorated with country furnishings, some cherished antiques, and accents of wood and stained glass. The bedrooms have modern amenities such as color televisions and refrigerators. Guests are welcome to relax in the common room and warm up beside the wood stove. This B&B is located ten miles from Logan International Airport. Pat and Al will gladly direct you to nearby restaurants, historic seacoast villages, and popular bicycle touring routes.

Oak Shores ✪
64 FULLER AVENUE, SWAMPSCOTT, MASSACHUSETTS 01907

Tel: **(617) 599-7677**	Single/sb: **$50**
Best Time to Call: **Evenings**	Open: **Apr. 1–Dec. 1**
Host: **Marjorie McClung**	Breakfast: **Continental**
Location: **13 mi, N of Boston**	Pets: **No**
No. of Rooms: **2**	Children: **Welcome, over 9**
Max. No. Sharing Bath: **4**	Smoking: **No**
Double/sb: **$60**	Social Drinking: **Permitted**

This 60-year-old Dutch Colonial is located on Boston's lovely North Shore. Enjoy rooms filled with fine restored furniture, and sleep in the comfort of old brass and iron beds. Relax in the private, shady garden, on the deck, or take a two-block stroll to the beach. Swampscott was the summer White House of Calvin Coolidge. It is a convenient place to begin tours of nearby Marblehead, birthplace of the United States Navy, and Salem, famous for its witch trials. Marjorie is glad to help with travel plans, and has an ample supply of maps and brochures.

Webb-Bigelow House
863 BOSTON POST ROAD, WESTON, MASSACHUSETTS 02193

Tel: **(617) 899-2444**	Double/sb: **$80**
Hosts: **Mr. and Mrs. Robert C. Webb**	Open: **Jan.–Mar., weekends only**
Location: **4 mi. from Rte. 90, Exit 15**	Breakfast: **Full**
No. of Rooms: **3**	Pets: **No**
No. of Private Baths: **2**	Children: **Welcome, over 10**
Max. No. Sharing Bath: **1**	Smoking: **No**
Double/pb: **$85**	Social Drinking: **Permitted**
Single/pb: **$80**	Minimum Stay: **2 nights Sept.–Oct.**

Experience old New England in this historic 1827 house built by Alphaeus Bigelow Jr. The Webbs added to its charm, surrounding it with lawns and flowers. Today it sits on three acres in Weston's National Registered Historic District and remains one of the finest preserved residences on the Post Road. Explore a wooded trail, relax by the pool, admire the fall foliage, or just read by a cozy fire (each guest room has a fireplace and a sitting area). Hearty breakfasts, featuring fruit from the Webbs' orchards, are served in the formal dining room or on the pool deck. This B&B is twenty minutes from Radcliffe, Harvard, Wellesley, MIT, Boston University, and Boston College. Area attractions include Longfellow's Wayside Inn, Faneuil Hall Market Place, Plymouth, Salem, and Concord.

CAPE COD/MARTHA'S VINEYARD

Bed & Breakfast Cape Cod ○
P.O. BOX 341, WEST HYANNISPORT, MASSACHUSETTS 02672-0341

Tel: **(508) 775-2772; fax: (508) 775-2884**	Descriptive Directory: **Free**
Best Time to Call: **8:30 AM–7:30 PM**	Rates (Single/Double):
Coordinator: **Clark Diehl**	Modest: **$38 / $50**
States/Regions Covered: **Cape Cod, Martha's Vineyard, Nantucket; Boston Area—Cape Ann, Gloucester, Cohasset, Marshfield, Scituate**	Average: **$55 / $65**
	Luxury: **$85 / $185**
	Credit Cards: **AMEX, DISC, MC, VISA**
	Minimum Stay: **2 nights in season**

It's a little over an hour's drive from Boston to the charm, history, and relaxation of Cape Cod and the islands. Choose from more than ninety of Clark's inspected and approved restored sea captains' houses, host homes, or small inns. Enjoy the warm-water beaches on Nantucket Sound and golf, biking, and other recreational activities. Don't miss the discount shopping. Your hosts can direct you to things to do, including whale watches and antiques. Seafood restaurants and pleasant evening entertainment at a theater are at your disposal. There is a $5 surcharge for one-night stays. Write, call, or fax for the free descriptive directory.

House Guests—Cape Cod and the Islands ❂
BOX 1881, ORLEANS, MASSACHUSETTS 02653

Tel: **(508) 896-7053; (800) 666-HOST**
Best Time to Call: **9 AM–9 PM**
Coordinator: **Richard Griffin**
States/Regions Covered: **Cape Cod,
 Martha's Vineyard, Nantucket**
Descriptive Directory: **Free**

Rates (Single/Double):
 Modest: **$40 / $48–$58**
 Average: **$50–$60 / $59–$75**
 Luxury: **$60–$150 / $76–$187**
Credit Cards: **AMEX, DISC, MC, VISA**
Minimum Stay: **2 nights Memorial Day
 weekend through Columbus Day**

Richard's accommodations range from a simple single bedroom with shared bath to historic homes furnished with antiques. Some are on the ocean; others are in wooded country areas. There are even a few self-contained guest cottages on private estates. A $15 peak season (May 1–Oct. 31) booking fee entitles clients of Richard's service to an unlimited number of lodging reservations. During off-season, the fee is $10.

Orleans Bed & Breakfast Associates ❂
P.O. BOX 1312, ORLEANS, MASSACHUSETTS 02653

Tel: **(508) 255-3824; (800) 541-6226**
Best Time to Call: **8 AM–8 PM**
Coordinator: **Mary Chapman**
States/Regions Covered: **Cape
 Cod—Brewster, Chatham, Harwich,
 Orleans, Truro, Wellfleet**
Descriptive Directory: **Free**

Rates (Single/Double):
 Modest: **— / $60**
 Average: **— / $80**
 Luxury: **— / $180**
Credit Cards: **DISC, MC, VISA**
Minimum Stay: **2 nights**

Mary offers a variety of accommodations with a diversity of styles, and guests may choose from historic to contemporary houses, all compatible with the atmosphere of the Cape. The fine reputation this service enjoys is largely due to the attitude of the host to the guest. Under Mary's direction, hosts meet regularly to share experiences, role-play B&B situations, and tour member homes. Each host is aware that a guest's experience reflects on the association as a whole. We applaud the professionalism of this organization! A $10 booking fee is charged per reservation.

Bacon Barn Inn
P.O. BOX 621, 3400 MAIN STREET, BARNSTABLE, MASSACHUSETTS 02630

Tel: **(508) 362-5518**
Best Time to Call: **8 AM–8 PM**

Hosts: **Mary and Robert Guiffreda**
Location: **3 mi. off Rte. 6, Exit 6**

No. of Rooms: **3**
No. of Private Baths: **3**
Double/pb: **$85–$95**
Single/pb: **$65–$75**
Open: **All year**
Reduced Rates: **Lower rates Nov. 15–May 15**

Breakfast: **Full**
Pets: **No**
Children: **Welcome, over 14**
Smoking: **No**
Social Drinking: **Permitted**
Minimum Stay: **2 nights during peak season**

You can still see the original posts and beams in this beautifully restored barn, which dates to the 1820s. For more examples of early-19th-century architecture (and fine 20th-century dining), stroll over to Barnstable Village. Snacks and afternoon tea are served at Bacon Barn Inn, and there is a refrigerator for guests' use. Full breakfasts feature juice, coffee, muffins, and French toast or pancakes.

Copper Beech Inn on Cape Cod ✪
497 MAIN STREET, CENTERVILLE, MASSACHUSETTS 02632-2913

Tel: **(508) 771-5488**
Best Time to Call: **8:30 AM–5:30 PM**
Host: **Joyce Diehl**
Location: **4 mi. W of Hyannis**
No. of Rooms: **3**
No. of Private Baths: **3**
Double/pb: **$80–$90**
Open: **All year**

Breakfast: **Full**
Credit Cards: **AMEX, MC, VISA**
Pets: **No**
Children: **Welcome, over 11**
Smoking: **Permitted**
Social Drinking: **Permitted**
Airport/Station Pickup: **Yes**

Home of the largest European beech tree in Cape Cod, the inn, listed on the National Register of Historic Places, is set in the heart of town amid private estates and vintage homes. It features traditional furnishings, formal parlors, and well-kept grounds with sunning areas. Golf, tennis, fishing, sailing, and swimming are available nearby; Craigville Beach is less than a mile away. The Hyannis ferry to Nantucket and Martha's Vineyard is four miles away. All rooms have air-conditioning.

The Acworth Inn ✪
4352 MAIN STREET, P.O. BOX 256, CUMMAQUID, MASSACHUSETTS 02637

Tel: (800) 362-6363; (508) 362-3330
Best Time to Call: Anytime
Hosts: Reg and Beverly Walter
Location: 5 mi. N of Hyannis
No. of Rooms: 4
No. of Private Baths: 4
Double p/b: $55–$85
Single p/b: $55–$85
Open: All year

Reduced Rates: 30% Oct.–May
Credit Cards: AMEX, MC, VISA
Pets: No
Children: Welcome, over 12
Smoking: No
Social Drinking: Permitted
Minimum Stay: 2 nights holidays
Airport/Station Pickup: Yes

Acworth Inn sits quietly alongside the Old Kings Highway that winds through the historic, unspoiled north side of Cape Cod. Located near the town of Barnstable, Acworth Inn offers guests an opportunity to experience the gracious lifestyle of a bygone era. The Inn, circa 1860, is especially noted for the many hand-painted furnishings that decorate each of the bright, airy guest rooms—the work of innkeeper Reg Walter. From its central location, day trips to Martha's Vineyard, Nantucket and all points on the Cape are easily accomplished.

Isaiah Hall B&B Inn
152 WHIG STREET, DENNIS, MASSACHUSETTS 02638

Tel: (508) 385-9928; (800) 736-0160
Best Time to Call: 8 AM–10 PM
Host: Marie Brophy
Location: 7 mi. E of Hyannis
No. of Rooms: 11
No. of Private Baths: 10
Max. No. Sharing Bath: 4
Double/pb: $74–$102
Single/pb: $64–$92
Double/sb: $57

Single/sb: $52
Open: Apr. 1–mid-Oct.
Breakfast: Continental, plus
Credit Cards: AMEX, MC, VISA
Pets: No
Children: Welcome, over 7
Smoking: Permitted (9 nonsmoking
  rooms)
Social Drinking: Permitted

This Cape Cod farmhouse built in 1857 offers casual country living on the quiet, historic northside. The house is decorated in true New England style with quilts, antiques, and oriental rugs. Four rooms have balconies and one has a fireplace. Within walking distance are the beach, good restaurants, the Cape Playhouse, and countless antique and craft shops. It is also close to freshwater swimming, bike paths, and golf.

The Over Look Inn ✪
ROUTE 6, 3085 COUNTY ROAD, P.O. BOX 771, EASTHAM,
MASSACHUSETTS 02642

Tel: (508) 255-1886; (800) 356-1121 (in Mass.)	Breakfast: Full
	Credit Cards: AMEX, MC, VISA
Best Time to Call: 9 AM–9 PM	Pets: No
Hosts: Ian and Nan Aitchison	Children: Welcome, over 12
Location: 90 mi. E of Boston	Smoking: Permitted
No. of Rooms: 10	Social Drinking: Permitted
No. of Private Baths: 10	Airport/Station Pickup: Yes
Double/pb: $65–$125	Foreign Languages: French
Open: All year	

From its site opposite the entrance to the Cape Cod National Seashore, Over Look Inn offers immediate access to more than 30 miles of unspoiled beaches. The Aitchisons are happy to arrange such activities as bike tours, hikes, clambakes, and deep-sea fishing expeditions. The inn itself is a grand Queen Anne–style mansion with wraparound porches and landscaped gardens; inside, period furniture complements the rich mahogany woodwork. On the walls you'll see paintings by the innkeepers' younger son. In the evenings guests are welcome to browse in the library or enjoy a game of billiards in the Hemingway room. Breakfasts feature Scottish dishes like kedgeree. Wheelchair-accessible suite includes entry ramp and bathroom with grab bars and queen-size bed.

The Penny House Inn ✪
P.O. BOX 238, ROUTE 6, EASTHAM, MASSACHUSETTS 02651

Tel: (508) 255-6632; (800) 554-1751	Reduced Rates: 10% Sept. 15–June 24
Hosts: Bill and Margaret Keith	Breakfast: Full
No. of Rooms: 10	Credit Cards: AMEX, DISC, MC, VISA
No. of Private Baths: 10	Pets: No
Suites: $85–$125	Children: Welcome, over 8
Double/pb: $80–$110	Smoking: Permitted
Open: All year	Social Drinking: Permitted

This mid-eighteenth century sea captain's house is centrally located in the Nauset Light Beach area of the National Seashore in North Eastham. The bow-roofed building was converted to a country inn in the early 1980s when it was carefully restored and refurbished. Set on two acres of lawn and trees, the inn is surrounded by miles of bicycle paths and nature trails. The Inn offers a variety of accommodations and each room is uniquely furnished with antiques, collectibles, and wicker furniture. All rooms have extra pillows, designer comforters and sheets, and oversized bath towels. A full country breakfast is served each morning.

The Parsonage Inn
202 MAIN STREET, P.O. BOX 1501, EAST ORLEANS,
MASSACHUSETTS 02643

Tel: (508) 255-8217	Open: **All year**
Best Time to Call: **10 AM–6 PM**	Reduced Rates: **Oct.–May**
Hosts: **Ian and Elizabeth Browne**	Breakfast: **Continental**
Location: **90 mi. SE of Boston**	Credit Cards: **MC, VISA**
No. of Rooms: 8	Pets: **No**
No. of Private Baths: 8	Children: **Welcome, over 6**
Double/pb: **$75–$90**	Smoking: **No**
Suites: **$95–$100**	Social Drinking: **Permitted**

This quiet, romantic inn is housed in a charming 18th-century parsonage just one-and-a-half miles from the sparkling waters at Nauset Beach. Bike trails, lakes, galleries, fine stores, and restaurants are all nearby. Delicious Continental breakfasts are served in the morning; in the evening, your hosts set out complimentary hors d'oeuvres in the parlor. And fresh floral arrangements add a special touch to the comfortable, tastefully decorated rooms.

The Arbor ✪
222 UPPER MAIN STREET, P.O. BOX 1228, EDGARTOWN, MARTHA'S
VINEYARD, MASSACHUSETTS 02539

Tel: (508) 627-8137	Reduced Rates: **May 1–June 14; Sept. 16–Oct. 30**
Best Time to Call: **8 AM–8 PM**	Minimum stay: **3 nights in season**
Host: **Peggy Hall**	Breakfast: **Continental**
Location: **7 mi. SE of Woods Hole Ferry**	Credit Cards: **MC, VISA**
No. of Rooms: 10	Pets: **No**
No. of Private Baths: 8	Children: **Welcome, over 12**
Max. No. Sharing Bath: 4	Smoking: **Permitted**
Double/pb: **$100–$135**	Social Drinking: **Permitted**
Double/sb: **$90–$95**	
Open: **May 1–Oct. 31**	

This turn-of-the-century guest house offers island visitors a unique experience in comfort and charm. The house is a short distance from downtown, and at the same time provides the feeling of being away from it all. Relax in a hammock, enjoy tea on the porch, and retire to a cozy room filled with the smell of fresh flowers. Peggy provides setups and mixers at cocktail time, and will gladly direct you to unspoiled beaches, walking trails, sailing, fishing, and the delights of Martha's Vineyard.

Captain Tom Lawrence House—1861
75 LOCUST STREET, FALMOUTH, MASSACHUSETTS 02540

Tel: (508) 540-1445; (800) 266-8139	Location: **67 mi. S of Boston**
Best Time to Call: **8 AM–noon**	No. of Rooms: 6
Host: **Barbara Sabo**	No. of Private Baths: 6

Double/pb: **$85–$104**
Open: **All year**
Reduced Rates: **Off-season**
Breakfast: **Full**
Credit Cards: **MC, VISA**

Pets: **No**
Children: **Welcome, over 11**
Smoking: **No**
Social Drinking: **Permitted**
Foreign Languages: **German**

Captain Lawrence was a successful whaler in the 1800s. When he retired from the sea, he built himself a town residence on Locust Street. Today, the house remains much as he left it, including the original hardwood floors, circular stairwell, high ceilings, and antique furnishings. In the morning, Barbara serves a hearty breakfast of fruit and creative entrées. Her Black Forest bread and Belgian waffles are truly special. She grinds her own flour from organically grown grain. She will gladly help you get around town—it's half a mile to the beach, a short walk to downtown Falmouth, and four miles to Woods Hole Seaport.

Hewins House Bed & Breakfast ✪
20 HEWINS STREET, FALMOUTH, MASSACHUSETTS 02540

Tel: **(508) 457-4363**
Best Time to Call: **9 AM–5 PM**
Host: **Virginia Price**
Location: **In Falmouth Village of Cape Cod**
No. of Rooms: **2**
No. of Private Baths: **2**
Double/pb: **$80**
Single/pb: **$65**
Suites: **$140**

Open: **All year**
Reduced Rates: **10% after 4 nights or off-season**
Breakfast: **Continental**
Pets: **No**
Children: **Welcome**
Smoking: **No**
Social Drinking: **Permitted**
Minimum Stay: **2 nights**
Station Pickup: **Yes**

Elegant accommodations, 19th-century charm, and warm hospitality await you at this gracious old Federal home on the historic Village Green. Queen-size beds, cotton sheets, feather pillows, and firm mattresses assure a good night's sleep. A two-room suite with adjoining bath is perfect for couples traveling together or families. Feel free to play the Steinway or relax with a book in the living room. Breakfast is served in the elegant Federal dining room. Enjoy the attractions of Falmouth or use Hewins House as a base from which to explore the Cape as well as the surrounding area.

Palmer House Inn ✪
81 PALMER AVENUE, FALMOUTH, MASSACHUSETTS 02540

Tel: **(508) 548-1230; (800) 472-2632; fax: (508) 540-1878**
Best Time to Call: **10 AM–10 PM**
Hosts: **Ken and Joanne Baker**
Location: **1 block from Rte. 28**

No. of Rooms: **8**
No. of Private Baths: **9**
Double/pb: **$85–$150**
Single/pb: **$75–$140**
Open: **All year**

Reduced Rates: **Off-season**
Breakfast: **Full**
Credit Cards: **AMEX, DC, DISC, MC, VISA**

Pets: **No**
Children: **Welcome, over 10**
Smoking: **No**
Social Drinking: **Permitted**

SG '90

Warmth and charm are evident in this turn-of-the-century Victorian home, with its stained-glass windows, soft warm wood, antiques, and collectibles. Centrally located within the Historic District, it is convenient to recreational diversions, miles of sandy beaches, ferries, and Woods Hole. Guests rave about breakfast entrées such as pain perdue with orange cream and Vermont maple syrup, Belgian waffles with honey butter, or Finnish pancakes and strawberry soup served in the dining room on fine linen, china, and crystal. Return from your afternoon activities and enjoy a glass of lemonade in a rocker on the front porch. Spend your after-dinner hours relaxing before the fire place or sampling theater offerings close by.

Village Green Inn ✪
40 WEST MAIN STREET, FALMOUTH, MASSACHUSETTS 02540

Tel: **(508) 548-5621**
Hosts: **Linda and Don Long**
Location: **15 mi. S of Bourne Bridge**
No. of Rooms: **5**
No. of Private Baths: **5**
Double/pb: **$85–$100**
Suites: **$100–$120**
Open: **All year**

Reduced Rates: **15% Nov. 1–Memorial Day**
Breakfast: **Full**
Pets: **No**
Children: **No**
Smoking: **No**
Social Drinking: **Permitted**
Airport/Station Pickup: **Yes**

This lovely Victorian is located on Falmouth's Village Green. Feel free to relax on the outdoor porch or in the parlor. Breakfast is a treat that includes hot, spiced fruit, eggs Mornay, homemade breads and muffins, and freshly ground coffee. Linda and Don look forward to pampering you with such delights as sherry, cordials, lemonade, fresh flowers, and sinfully delicious chocolates.

The Coach House ✪
74 SISSON ROAD, HARWICH PORT, MASSACHUSETTS 02646

Tel: **(508) 432-9452**	Open: **May–Oct.**
Hosts: **Sara and Cal Ayer**	Breakfast: **Continental**
Location: **1 mi. from Rtes. 39 and 124**	Credit Cards: **MC, VISA**
No. of Rooms: **2**	Pets: **No**
No. of Private Baths: **2**	Children: **No**
Double/pb: **$65–$70**	Smoking: **Permitted**
Single/pb: **$65**	Social Drinking: **Permitted**

Built in 1909, The Coach House was the original barn of one of Cape Cod's old estates. In the mid-1950s, the barn was fully converted into a lovely Cape Cod home. The rooms are quiet and elegant, and guests may choose from king- and queen-size beds. A breakfast of fresh fruit compote, home-baked muffins, coffee cake, or croissants is served in the dining room each morning. Enjoy three picturesque harbors, beautiful beaches, sailing, windsurfing, golf, and tennis. A 21-mile hard-surface bike trail will take you through the scenic woods and cranberry bogs to the National Seashore. Your hosts will gladly recommend shops, museums, fine restaurants, and summer theater.

Dunscroft by-the-Sea (Inn & Cottage) ✪
24 PILGRIM ROAD, HARWICH PORT, MASSACHUSETTS 02646

Tel: **(508) 432-0810**	Open: **All year**
Best Time to Call: **9 AM–10 PM**	Breakfast: **Full**
Hosts: **Alyce and Wally Cunningham**	Credit Cards: **AMEX, MC, VISA**
Location: **80 mi. SE of Boston**	Pets: **No**
No. of Rooms: **9**	Children: **Welcome, over 12**
No. of Private Baths: **9**	Smoking: **Restricted**
Double/pb: **$75–$125**	Social Drinking: **Permitted**
Guest Cottage: **$125–$155**	

Its cedar shingles weathered a traditional waterfront grey, this Colonial inn offers everything you'd expect from a Cape Cod B&B: flower gardens, spacious grounds, an enclosed sun porch, a piano in the living room, and a private mile-long beach. Harwich Port's shops, galleries, and restaurants are within easy walking distance. You'll awaken to the aroma of freshly ground coffee as Alyce prepares a full, generous breakfast.

Cynthia & Steven's ✪

36 SEVENTH STREET, NEW BEDFORD, MASSACHUSETTS 02740

Tel: **(508) 997-6433**
Best Time to Call: **After 7 PM**
Hosts: **Cynthia Poyant & Steven Saint-Aubin**
Location: **55 mi. S of Boston**
No. of Rooms: **4**
No. of Private Baths: **3**
Max. No. Sharing Bath: **4**
Double/pb: **$50–$60**
Single/pb: **$30–$40**

Double/sb: **$50**
Single/sb: **$30**
Open: **All year**
Reduced Rates: **10% family, seniors**
Breakfast: **Continental**
Pets: **Sometimes**
Children: **Welcome**
Smoking: **Permitted**
Social Drinking: **Permitted**
Airport/Station Pickup: **Yes**

Located in the historic district, this 1800s Victorian home is within walking distance of downtown. Some of the local attractions include the Whaling Museum, art museum, Rotch Jones Duff Museum, and beaches. Cape Cod and Newport, RI, are only 30 minutes away. The home has undergone thoughtful restoration, reflected in the tasteful decor throughout. Family photographs, books, and curio pieces are displayed in the sitting and dining rooms. Your hosts enjoy active exercise and sports. Cynthia is a social worker and Steven is an anesthetist. They welcome you to relax with them.

The Beach Rose ✪

COLUMBIAN AVENUE, BOX 2352, OAK BLUFFS, MASSACHUSETTS 02557

Tel: **(508) 693-6135**
Best Time to Call: **9 AM–9 PM**
Hosts: **Gloria and Russ Everett**
Location: **70 mi. SE of Boston**
No. of Rooms: **3**
Max. No. Sharing Bath: **4**
Double/sb: **$60–$85**
Single/sb: **$60**
Open: **May–Oct.**

Reduced Rates: **Off-season**
Breakfast: **Continental, plus**
Pets: **Sometimes**
Children: **Welcome**
Smoking: **No**
Social Drinking: **Permitted**
Minimum Stay: **2 nights holiday weekends**

The Beach Rose is named for the colorful island plant, *Rosa rugosa*, whose pink flowers and bright red rose hips punctuate the island dunes. This charming home, nestled in an oak and pine woodland on Martha's Vineyard, is decorated in country antique style. Greet the morning with a breakfast of fresh fruit, a delicious entreé du jour, homemade muffins and jams, and freshly brewed beverages. Your hosts provide warm hospitality and personal attention. Guests will want to see the gingerbread cottages of the Methodist camp-meeting grounds, the Gay Head cliffs, and the historic whaling homes of Edgartown. The Vineyard has a myriad of sightseeing and other activities to offer visitors: biking, sailing, nature trails, fishing, pictur-esque beaches, and much more.

Academy Place Bed & Breakfast ☉

8 ACADEMY PLACE, P.O. BOX 1407, ORLEANS, MASSACHUSETTS 02653

Tel: (508) 255-3181	Reduced Rates: Available
Hosts: Sandy and Charles Terrell	Breakfast: Continental
Location: 25 mi. E of Hyannis	Credit Cards: MC, VISA
No. of Rooms: 5	Pets: No
No. of Private Baths: 3	Children: Welcome, over 6
Max. No. Sharing Bath: 4	Minimum stay: 2 nights weekends
Double/pb: $75–$85	from July 1 through Labor Day
Double/sb: $65	Smoking: No
Open: Memorial Day–Columbus Day	Station Pickup: Yes

A quaint Cape Cod home on the village green with comfortable beds awaits you. This 1752 house with many antique charms and period antiques is on the edge of Orleans' shopping district. Many fine retail stores and restaurants are a short walk away. For swimming, sunbathing, and fishing, the Atlantic Ocean and Cape Cod Bay beaches are within 2½ miles. The Cape Cod National Seashore is 10 minutes by car or can be reached by a paved bike path, which is ¼ mile from the house. A Continental breakfast of homemade hot tasty muffins and breads with chilled juices and fresh fruits, freshly brewed coffee, teas or hot chocolate is served daily.

Morgan's Way Bed and Breakfast ☉

NINE MORGAN'S WAY, ORLEANS, CAPE COD, MASSACHUSETTS 02653

Tel: (508) 255-0831	Open: All year
Best Time to Call: 11:30 AM–9 PM	Reduced Rates: Available
Hosts: Page McMahan and Will Joy	Breakfast: Full
Location: 90 mi. SE of Boston	Pets: No
No. of Rooms: 1	Children: Welcome, over 12
No. of Private Baths: 1	Smoking: No
Double/pb: $85	Social Drinking: Permitted
Single/pb: $80–$85	Minimum Stay: 2 nights; 1 week for
Guest Cottage: $650 weekly; sleeps 3	cottage

This dramatic contemporary home, overlooking five acres of gardens and wooded land, offers guests a peaceful, romantic getaway. Soaring cathedral ceilings, oak beams, arched windows with panoramic views, oriental carpets, and porcelains give a feeling of luxury throughout. Specially appointed bedrooms have queen-size beds; those desiring extra privacy may prefer to stay in the poolside guest cottage. For those of you who do not mind paying a higher rate, other rooms are available. Relax on the massive, flower-filled deck or lounge by the large heated pool after a refreshing swim. Page's memorable breakfasts include creative fruit courses, delicious entrees, and homemade breads; she always has low-fat and low-cholesterol alternatives on hand. Morgan's Way is located just one mile from Orleans center and two miles from Nauset Beach; golf courses, lakes, bike trails, galleries, shops, and restaurants are all nearby. Page, an avid gardener, has a background in health administration, and Will is a civil engineer; they love sharing their property and Cape Cod, and will treat you as their special house guest. For those of you who do not mind a higher rate, 1 room is available.

Avalon ✪

32 GROVE STREET, SANDWICH, MASSACHUSETTS 02563

Tel: **(508) 833-1449**	Suites: **$65**
Best Time to Call: **Evenings**	Open: **All year**
Host: **Karen A. Zappula**	Reduced Rates: **15% weekly**
Location: **60 mi. S of Boston**	Breakfast: **Continental**
No. of Rooms: **3**	Pets: **Sometimes**
Max. No. Sharing Bath: **4**	Children: **Welcome, over 8**
Double/sb: **$55**	Smoking: **No**
Single/sb: **$35**	Social Drinking: **No**

Avalon is located in a tranquil setting on Shawme Pond. This contemporary home has a casual, airy atmosphere thanks to its many large windows. A breakfast of memorable homemade muffins, breads, jams, fresh fruit plates, or French toast drizzled with pure Vermont maple syrup is served in the dining room overlooking the pond, or on the back deck. This B&B is within walking distance of Heritage Plantation, the glass and doll museums, crafts and art shops, and fine dining. Beach chairs and bikes are available and there is canoe access to the pond.

Barclay Inn ✪

40 GROVE STREET, SANDWICH, MASSACHUSETTS 02563

Tel: **(508) 888-5738**	Single/sb: **$45**
Best Time to Call: **8 AM–8 PM**	Guest Cottage: **$425 weekly**
Hosts: **Patricia and Gerald Barclay**	Open: **All year**
Location: **50 mi. S of Boston**	Breakfast: **Continental**
No. of Rooms: **2**	Pets: **No**
No. of Private Baths: **1**	Children: **No**
Max. No. Sharing Bath: **4**	Smoking: **No**
Double/pb: **$75**	Social Drinking: **Permitted**
Single/pb: **$60**	Minimum Stay: **1 week for cottage**
Double/sb: **$55**	Airport/Station Pickup: **Yes**

Located near the center of Sandwich, Cape Cod's oldest town, this bed-and-breakfast makes an ideal home base whether you plan to hunt for antiques or just work on a tan. Local museums house everything from hand-blown glass to military artifacts, and the beach is only a few minutes away. Barclay Inn has two guest rooms; those desiring extra privacy may prefer to stay at the Kelman House, a one-bedroom cottage overlooking Peter's Pond. Whichever you choose, you'll savor Continental breakfasts that include glazed orange rolls, coffee cake, and raspberry cream cheese.

The Captain Ezra Nye House ✪
152 MAIN STREET, SANDWICH, MASSACHUSETTS 02563

Tel: (800) 388-2278; fax: (508) 888-2940
Best Time to Call: 9 AM–9 PM
Hosts: Elaine and Harry Dickson
Location: 60 mi. SE of Boston
No. of Rooms: 7
No. of Private Baths: 5
Max. No. Sharing Bath: 4
Double/pb: $70–$90
Single/pb: $70–$90
Double/sb: $55–$70
Single/sb: $55–$70
Suites: $85–$90

Open: All year
Reduced Rates: 10% over 6 days; lower rates winter
Breakfast: Full
Credit Cards: AMEX, DISC, MC, VISA
Pets: No
Children: Welcome, over 6
Smoking: No
Minimum Stay: 2 nights in season, weekends, and all holidays
Airport/Station Pickup: Yes
Foreign Languages: Spanish

The Captain Ezra Nye House is a stately 1829 Federal home built by a seafarer noted for his record-breaking North Atlantic crossings and daring ocean rescues. The house sits in the heart of Sandwich, the oldest town on Cape Cod, and is within walking distance of museums, shops, and fine restaurants. Guests rooms are tastefully decorated in soft pastel tones, antiques, and an eclectic art collection. Hearty homemade breakfasts are served in the dining room. A cozy den with fireplace and parlor with piano complete the common areas.

Dillingham House ✪
71 MAIN STREET, SANDWICH, MASSACHUSETTS 02563

Tel: (508) 833-0065
Best Time to Call: 6–8 PM
Host: Kathleen Kenney
Location: 60 mi. S of Boston
No. of Rooms: 3
No. of Private Baths: 3
Double/pb: $75
Open: All year

Reduced Rates: $20 less Nov.–Mar.; $10 less Apr., May, Oct.
Breakfast: Continental
Pets: Sometimes
Children: Welcome
Smoking: Permitted
Social Drinking: Permitted
Minimum Stay: 2 nights off-season

Dillingham House is named for its first owner, who helped to found Sandwich, Cape Cod's oldest town. The house has many of the hallmarks of 17th-century construction, such as wide pine floors, exposed beams and rafters, and cozy brick hearths. Kathy is a Cape native and loves to discuss local lore. Your hosts charter sailing trips and lend bicycles to landlubbers. A Continental breakfast of juice, fresh fruit, muffins, and coffee or tea will fortify you for your excursions, whether they occur on land or on sea.

Hawthorn Hill ✪
P.O. BOX 777, SANDWICH, MASSACHUSETTS 02563

Tel: **(508) 888-3333**	Breakfast: **Full**
Best Time to Call: **Mornings**	Pets: **Sometimes**
Host: **Maxime Caron**	Children: **Sometimes**
Location: **60 mi. S of Boston**	Smoking: **Permitted**
No. of Rooms: **2**	Social Drinking: **Permitted**
No. of Private Baths: **2**	Airport/Station Pickup: **Yes**
Double/pb: **$65–$70**	Foreign Languages: **German**
Open: **May–Nov.**	

This rambling English country house, off Grove Street, is set on a hill surrounded by trees, with both the conveniences of an in-town location and the pleasantness of a country setting. The property has a spring-fed pond for boating and swimming, and there is plenty of space for long walks through the woods. Inside, your host welcomes you to large, sunny rooms, comfortably furnished. Hawthorn Hill is close to beaches, fishing, museums, and shops, and is adjacent to the Heritage Plantation. Maxime will gladly help plan sightseeing in this historic town or day trips to many nearby points of interest.

The Summer House ✪
158 MAIN STREET, SANDWICH, MASSACHUSETTS 02563

Tel: **(508) 888-4991**	Open: **All year**
Best Time to Call: **9 AM–10 PM**	Reduced Rates: **10% seniors; Nov. 1–**
Hosts: **David and Kay Merrell**	**May 31, $10 less per room**
Location: **60 mi. SE of Boston**	Breakfast: **Full**
No. of Rooms: **5**	Credit Cards: **AMEX, DISC, MC, VISA**
No. of Private Baths: **1**	Pets: **No**
Max. No. Sharing Bath: **4**	Children: **Welcome, over 6**
Double/pb: **$65–$75**	Smoking: **No**
Single/pb: **$55–$65**	Social Drinking: **Permitted**
Double/sb: **$55–$65**	Station Pickup: **Yes**
Single/sb: **$45–$55**	

An elegant 1835 Greek Revival inn in the heart of historical Sandwich Village, the Summer House has been featured in *Country Living* magazine. The large, sunny rooms of this bed and breakfast are decorated with fireplaces, antiques, hand-stitched quilts, and flowers, and the grounds boast lovely English-style gardens. Restaurants, museums, shops, a pond and gristmill, and the boardwalk to the beach are all within strolling distance. Bountiful full breakfasts are served at tables for two, while afternoon tea is served in the garden.

Nancy's Auberge ○
102 MAIN STREET, P.O. BOX 4433, VINEYARD HAVEN, MARTHA'S VINEYARD, MASSACHUSETTS 02568

Tel: **(508) 693-4434**
Best Time to Call: **Evenings**
Host: **Nancy Hurd**
Location: **7 mi. SE of Woods Hole Ferry**
No. of Rooms: **3**
No. of Private Baths: **1**
Max. No. Sharing Bath: **4**
Double/pb: **$98**
Double/sb: **$78–$88**
Open: **All year**

Reduced Rates: **Available**
Breakfast: **Continental**
Credit Cards: **MC, VISA**
Pets: **No**
Children: **Welcome**
Smoking: **No**
Social Drinking: **Permitted**
Minimum Stay: **Summer season; holiday weekends**

Nancy's Auberge is a 150-year-old island home with a harbor view, convenient location and three fireplaces. Comfortable and inviting whatever the season, the antique-filled B&B offers as much privacy as you seek. One guest remarked, "It's so picturesque. It's like living on a postcard." Since it's just a block and a half from the ferry, a car is not necessary. However, off-street parking is available. Within a few blocks are some of the island's finest restaurants, the Vineyard Playhouse, the Katherine Cornell Theatre, artisans' shops, windsurfing, sailing, and tennis. Nearby are excellent golf courses, horseback riding, and world-famous beaches. The town beach is a block away. Nancy's passions are travel, music, sports, and cooking.

Mulberry Bed and Breakfast ○
257 HIGH STREET, WAREHAM, MASSACHUSETTS 02571

Tel: **(508) 295-0684**
Best Time to Call: **Before 9 AM, after 4 PM**
Host: **Frances Murphy**
Location: **52 mi. S of Boston**
No. of Rooms: **3**
Max. No. Sharing Bath: **4**
Double/sb: **$45–$55**

Open: **All year**
Reduced Rates: **15% weekly**
Breakfast: **Continental, plus**
Pets: **No**
Children: **Welcome, over 10**
Smoking: **No**
Social Drinking: **Permitted**
Airport/Station Pickup: **Yes**

Frances Murphy welcomes you to her vintage Cape Cod home, built in 1847. The house is one and a half stories and is painted white with red shutters. It is named for the mulberry tree in the yard that attracts many birds and provides shade from the summer sun. Frances has created a home-away-from-home atmosphere, where guests can relax in a small living room with a piano, or join her in a larger living-dining area with fireplace. Spend the night in an Early American–style bedroom and have breakfast on the spacious private deck. Home-baked breads and muffins, casseroles, and fresh fruit are served with jams and jellies made from Frances's fruit trees. In the afternoon, snacks and cool drinks are served. Mulberry Bed and Breakfast is located in the historic part of town, ten minutes from the beach.

The Marlborough ○
320 WOODS HOLE ROAD, FALMOUTH, WOODS HOLE, MASSACHUSETTS 02543

Tel: (508) 548-6218
Best Time to Call: 10 AM–9 PM
Host: Diana Smith
Location: 2½ mi. from Rte. 28
No. of Rooms: 5
No. of Private Baths: 5
Double/pb: $85–$105
Single/pb: $80–$100

Open: All year
Breakfast: Full
Credit Cards: MC, VISA
Pets: No
Children: Welcome, over 2
Smoking: No
Social Drinking: Permitted

This faithful reproduction of a full Cape house is beautifully decorated with antiques, collectibles, fabric wall coverings, and matching bed linens. It is situated on a shaded half-acre with a paddle tennis court, swimming pool, and hammock. It's 1 mile to a private beach. Ferries to Martha's Vineyard are a mile away. Diana serves a full gourmet breakfast year round.

CENTRAL/WESTERN/SOUTHERN MASSACHUSETTS

American Country Collection—Massachusetts
4 GREENWOOD LANE, DELMAR, NEW YORK 12054

Tel: (518) 439-7001
Best Time to Call: 10 AM–5 PM
  Mon.–Fri.
Coordinator: Arthur Copeland
States/Regions Covered: Amherst,
  Egremont, Great Barrington, Lenox,
  Northampton, Peru, Sheffield,
  Williamstown, Worthington, West
  Stockbridge

Descriptive Directory: $6
Rates (Single/Double):
  Modest: $55
  Average: $75
  Luxury: $110 / $125
Credit Cards: AMEX, MC, VISA

The American Country Collection offers comfortable lodging in private homes and inns throughout western Massachusetts. The hosts pride themselves on the charm and cleanliness of their establishments, and the personal attention and hospitality given to each traveler. Locations range from Victorian and Early American homes to elegant mansions and full-service country inns. From the quiet Berkshire hills to the heritage of Pioneer Valley, the accommodations appeal to both businesspeople and vacationers. In addition, this service handles reservations for eastern New York and all of Vermont, northern New Hampshire, and the island of St. Thomas in the Caribbean.

Allen House Inn ✪
599 MAIN STREET, AMHERST, MASSACHUSETTS 01002

Tel: **(413) 253-5000**	Breakfast: **Full**
Hosts: **Alan and Ann Zieminski**	Pets: **No**
Location: **5 mi. from Rte. 91, Exit 19**	Children: **Welcome**
No. of Rooms: **5**	Smoking: **No**
No. of Private Baths: **5**	Social Drinking: **Permitted**
Double/pb: **$55–$95**	Minimum Stay: **College and fall**
Single/pb: **$45–$85**	**foliage weekends**
Open: **All year**	

This 1886 Queen Anne Stick-style Victorian features period antiques, decor, and art wall coverings by designers from the Aesthetic movement, which emphasized art in interior decoration; Charles Eastlake, Walter Crane, and William Morris are represented. Allen House is located on three scenic acres in the heart of Amherst, within walking distance of Emily Dickinson House, Amherst College, the University of Massachusetts, and innumerable galleries, museums, theaters, shops, and restaurants. Free busing is available throughout the five-college area. A full formal breakfast is served.

Emma C's B&B ✪
18 FRENCH FARM ROAD, ATTLEBORO, MASSACHUSETTS 02703

Tel: **(508) 226-6365; fax: (508) 226-4763**	Double/sb: **$55–$65**
	Single/sb: **$45–$55**
Best Time to Call: **9 AM–9 PM**	Open: **All year**
Hosts: **Caroline and Jim Logie**	Breakfast: **Full**
Location: **10 mi. N of Providence, R.I.**	Pets: **Sometimes**
No. of Rooms: **3**	Children: **Welcome (crib)**
No. of Private Baths: **1**	Smoking: **No**
Max. No. Sharing Bath: **4**	Social Drinking: **Permitted**
Double/pb: **$60–$70**	Airport/Station Pickup: **Yes**
Single/pb: **$50–$60**	

Folk art, decorative stencils, antique four-poster beds, and handmade quilts make this country Colonial home a warm and friendly place. Your hosts enjoy discussing their world travels with guests. Caroline's well-balanced breakfasts include her own granola, home-baked muffins, fresh fruit, and freshly ground coffee. It's only 45 minutes to Boston or Cape Cod. Emma C's is only minutes to both Wheaton College in Norton and Brown University in Providence.

Captain Samuel Eddy House ✪
609 OXFORD STREET SOUTH, AUBURN, MASSACHUSETTS 01501

Tel: (508) 832-7282	Open: All year
Best time to call: 10 AM–9 PM	Reduced rates: Available
Hosts: Diedre and Mike Meddaugh	Breakfast: Full
Location: 3 mi. S of Worcester	Credit Cards: VISA
No. of rooms: 5	Pets: No
No. of private baths: 5	Children: Welcome, over 5
Double p/b: $65	Smoking: No
Single p/b: $55	Social drinking: Permitted
Suites: $90 sleeps 4	

The Captain Samuel Eddy House, circa 1765, has been operating as a bed & breakfast since 1988, but is now under new management. The Meddaughs, formerly of the Arnold Taft House in Mendon, MA, have further restored the center chimney colonial home. It is handsomely decorated with period antiques and reproduction pieces. There are two fireplaced common rooms, one for quiet relaxation, the other has a television. Breakfast and afternoon tea are served in the keeping room with its huge fireplace, and the sun room overlooks the gardens, woods, and Eddy Pond. The B&B is less than one mile from the Mass Turnpike and covenient to Worcester area colleges, the U. Mass Medical Center, Sturbridge, and the Brimfield Antique Shows.

1797 House ✪
1797 UPPER STREET, BUCKLAND, MASSACHUSETTS 01338

Tel: (413) 625-2975	Single/pb: $58
Best Time to Call: 5 PM–9 PM	Open: Jan. 2–Oct. 31
Host: Janet Turley	Breakfast: Full
Location: 13 mi. from Rte. 91, Exit 26	Pets: No
No. of Rooms: 3	Children: No
No. of Private Baths: 3	Smoking: No
Double/pb: $65–$80	Social Drinking: Permitted

This white, center-hall Colonial, circa 1797, has a lovely screened-in porch for summer enjoyment and four fireplaces and down quilts for cozy winter pleasure. Prestigious Deerfield Academy, Old Deerfield, Sturbridge Village, and the historic sights of Pioneer Valley are all close by. The University of Massachusetts, Smith, Amherst, and Williams are convenient to Janet's home. Sensational breakfast treats include stuffed croissants, French toast, and special casseroles, along with fresh fruit and breakfast meats.

Windfields Farm ✪
154 WINDSOR BUSH ROAD, CUMMINGTON, MASSACHUSETTS 01026

Tel: **(413) 684-3786**	Open: **May 1–Mar. 1**
Best Time to Call: **Before 9 PM**	Breakfast: **Full**
Hosts: **Carolyn and Arnold Westwood**	Pets: **No**
Location: **20 mi. E of Pittsfield**	Children: **Welcome, over 12**
No. of Rooms: **2**	Smoking: **No**
Max. No. Sharing Bath: **4**	Social Drinking: **Permitted**
Double/sb: **$60**	Minimum Stay: **2 nights most**
Single/sb: **$45**	**weekends**

Since 1983, the Westwoods have been welcoming guests to their secluded nineteenth-century homestead in the rolling Berkshire countryside. The hundred-acre estate includes organic gardens, flower beds, wild blueberry fields, and a brook and a pond. Hiking and skiing trails, a state forest, and the Audubon Wildlife Sanctuary are within walking distance. Arnold, a retired Unitarian minister, built his own sugarhouse and greenhouse and doubles as publisher of a local monthly newspaper. Carolyn is an award-winning gardener. Both are active in community affairs and conservation, and, during the late winter mud season, they make maple syrup from their property's 500 taps.

Hitchcock House ✪
15 CONGRESS STREET, GREENFIELD, MASSACHUSETTS 01301

Tel: **(413) 774-7452**	No. of Rooms: **5**
Hosts: **Elizabeth and Peter Gott**	No. of Private Baths: **2**
Location: **30 mi. N of Springfield**	Max. No. Sharing Bath: **4**

Double/pb: **$70–$85**
Single/pb: **$60**
Double/sb: **$60–$75**
Single/sb: **$40**
Suites: **$110–$130; sleeps 4–5**
Open: **All year**

Reduced Rates: **Available**
Breakfast: **Full**
Pets: **By arrangement**
Children: **Welcome, over 6**
Smoking: **Restricted**
Social Drinking: **Permitted**

This 1881 Victorian gem is minutes away from tennis courts, a variety of golf courses, hiking trails, fabulous fall foliage, cross-country and downhill skiing, historic Old Deerfield, museums, and nine well-known schools and colleges. The town center and many places of worship are within easy walking distance. Wake up to a sumptuous breakfast or take the special no-meal rate. Rooms are decorated with period furniture, country quilts, and other accessories. Hitchcock House has fireplaces, porches, patios, gardens, horseshoe pitching, croquet courts, and an abundance of genial hospitality.

Garden Gables Inn ☉
141 MAIN STREET, LENOX, MASSACHUSETTS 01240

Tel: **(413) 637-0193**
Hosts: **Lynn and Mario Mekinda**
Location: **10 mi. off Mass Pike, Exit 2**
No. of Rooms: **12**
No. of Private Baths: **12**
Double/pb: **$65–$190**
Single/pb: **$60–$170**
Open: **All year**
Reduced Rates: **10% weekly;**
 midweek, off-season

Breakfast: **Full**
Credit Cards: **AMEX, DISC, MC, VISA**
Pets: **No**
Children: **Welcome, over 12**
Smoking: **Restricted**
Social Drinking: **Permitted**
Minimum Stay: **3 nights weekends July,**
 Aug., holidays

Built in 1790 and expanded a little more than a century later, this white clapboard house has dark green shutters and, true to its name, a gambrel roof with three gables. Inside, the antique furniture and floral wallpapers are reminiscent of an earlier era, but there is nothing old-fashioned about the inviting 72-foot swimming pool in the backyard. The Berkshires in summertime are rich in cultural activities, with music at Tanglewood, dance at Jacob's Pillow, and the Williamstown Theatre Festival. Winter visitors can choose between the area's downhill ski slopes and cross-country trails; spring through fall, Lenox's stables cater to the horsey set. Plan your day over a buffet-style breakfast of fresh fruit and berries, homemade bran and blueberry muffins, cereals, crumb cakes, and low-fat yogurts.

Bullard Farm Bed & Breakfast ☉
89 ELM STREET, NORTH NEW SALEM, MASSACHUSETTS 01364

Tel: **(508) 544-6959**
Host: **Janet Kraft**

Location: **75 mi. W of Boston**
No. of Rooms: **4**

Max. No. Sharing Bath: **4**
Double/sb: **$70**
Single/sb: **$60**
Suite: **$90, sleeps 4**
Open: **All year**
Reduced Rates: **Available**
Breakfast: **Full**

Credit Cards: **MC, VISA**
Pets: **Sometimes**
Children: **Welcome, over 3**
Smoking: **No**
Social Drinking: **Permitted**
Airport/Station Pickup: **Yes**

Just half an hour from Amherst and historic Deerfield, you'll find this 200-year-old restored Colonial home with all the trimmings, like six working fireplaces, exposed beams, and treasured family antiques. Allow plenty of time for surveying the 300-acre property, with its rhododendron gardens, cultivated blueberries, hiking and cross-country ski trails, old swimming hole, and 18th-century mill sites. The renovated barn with an upper level dance floor serves as a conference center offering occasional nature programs, jazz concerts, and other events. Sleigh rides and hayrides are available upon request.

Chalet d'Alicia ✪
EAST WINDSOR ROAD, PERU, MASSACHUSETTS 01235

Tel: **(413) 655-8292**
Hosts: **Alice and Richard Halvorsen**
Location: **15 mi. E of Pittsfield**
No. of Rooms: **3**
Max. No. Sharing Bath: **4**
Double/sb: **$55**

Open: **All year**
Breakfast: **Full**
Pets: **Sometimes**
Children: **Welcome**
Smoking: **Permitted**
Social Drinking: **Permitted**

Chalet d'Alicia is set high in the Berkshire Mountains overlooking the majestic countryside. This Swiss chalet–style home offers a private, casual atmosphere. The large front deck is a perfect spot for reading, sunning, or chatting. Alice and Richard are proud to make everyone feel at home. For breakfast they serve homemade muffins, and jams made from local wild berries. The property has a pond and plenty of places for cross-country skiing. Tanglewood, Jacob's Pillow, and the Williamstown Theatre Festival are all within easy reach.

Perryville Inn ✪
157 PERRYVILLE ROAD, REHOBOTH, MASSACHUSETTS 02769

Tel: **(508) 252-9239**
Best Time to Call: **8 AM–8 PM**
Hosts: **Tom and Betsy Charnecki**
Location: **8 mi. E of Providence, R.I.**
No. of Rooms: **5**
No. of Private Baths: **3**
Max. No. Sharing Bath: **4**
Double/pb: **$55–$85**

Double/sb: **$50**
Open: **All year**
Breakfast: **Continental**
Credit Cards: **AMEX, MC, VISA**
Pets: **No**
Children: **Welcome**
Smoking: **Restricted**
Social Drinking: **Permitted**

This 19th-century restored Victorian, listed on the National Register of Historic Places, is located on four and a half acres, featuring a quiet brook, stone walls, and shaded paths. You are welcome to use your hosts' bikes for local touring. There's a public golf course across the road. It's a short drive to antique shops, museums, and fine seafood restaurants. Don't miss a traditional New England clambake. All rooms are furnished with antiques and accented with colorful, hand-made quilts. Brown University, Wheaton College, and the Rhode Island School of Design are within a 10-mile radius of the inn.

Salt Marsh Farm ✪

322 SMITH NECK ROAD, SOUTH DARTMOUTH, MASSACHUSETTS 02748

Tel: **(508) 992-0980**
Hosts: **Larry and Sally Brownell**
Location: **5 mi. SW of New Bedford**
No. of Rooms: **2**
No. of Private Baths: **2**
Double/pb: **$65–$85**
Single/pb: **$65–$85**
Open: **All year**
Reduced Rates: **Available**
Breakfast: **Full**

Credit Cards: **MC, VISA**
Pets: **No**
Children: **Welcome, over 5**
Smoking: **No**
Social Drinking: **Permitted**
Minimum Stay: **2 nights summer weekends, holidays**
Airport/Station Pickup: **Yes, fee charged**

Surrounded by old stone walls, this Colonial farmhouse, built in c. 1730, is part of a 90-acre nature preserve with a variety of wildlife. The hay fields, pine groves, freshwater pond, and wetlands afford a peaceful setting for a leisurely stroll. With its original wide-board floors, low ceilings, working fireplaces, and treasured family heirlooms, the house suggests a journey through time. Sally's scrumptious breakfast features her own organically grown fruits, prize-winning muffins, and farm-fresh eggs taken right from the nest.

The Golden Goose ✪
MAIN ROAD, BOX 336, TYRINGHAM, MASSACHUSETTS 01264

Tel: **(413) 243-3008**
Best Time to Call: **8 AM–8 PM**
Hosts: **Lilja and Joseph Rizzo**
Location: **4 mi. from Mass. Tpk., Exit 2-Lee**
No. of Rooms: **7**
Max. No. Sharing Bath: **4**
Double/pb: **$85–$100**
Single/pb: **$80–$100**
Double/sb: **$75–$80**
Single/sb: **$70–$75**

Suites: **$115–$125**
Open: **All year**
Reduced Rates: **Available**
Breakfast: **Continental, plus**
Pets: **No**
Children: **Welcome, in suite**
Smoking: **No**
Social Drinking: **Permitted**
Minimum Stay: **2–3 nights weekends during Tanglewood season; 2 nights weekends during fall foliage**

The inn lies between Stockbridge and Lenox in the Berkshires. Antique beds with firm new mattresses, and washstands, are in each bedroom. Lilja and Joseph serve hors d'oeuvres and drinks by the fireside in the two common rooms. In warm weather, you may play croquet, volleyball, badminton, hike the Appalachian Trail, or fish for trout in the brook across the street and barbecue it at "home." In summer, the cultural attractions of Tanglewood and Jacob's Pillow are nearby. Skiing is popular in winter. A $5 surcharge is added for one-night stays. For those of you who don't mind paying a higher rate, 3 rooms are available.

The Wildwood Inn ✪
121 CHURCH STREET, WARE, MASSACHUSETTS 01082

Tel: **(413) 967-7798**
Best Time to Call: **After 4 PM**
Hosts: **Fraidell Fenster and Richard Watson**
Location: **70 mi. W of Boston**
No. of Rooms: **7**
Max. No. Sharing Bath: **4**
Double/sb: **$40–$85**

Open: **All year**
Reduced Rates: **10%, weekly**
Breakfast: **Full**
Pets: **No**
Children: **Welcome, over 6**
Smoking: **No**
Social Drinking: **Permitted**

Everything about this old-fashioned country home, with its rambling two acres, is designed to help you unwind. There's a swing on the porch, a hammock under the firs, a blazing fire in the winter, a Norman Rockwell–esque brook-fed swimming hole in the summer. Your host Fraidell has furnished her guest rooms with heirloom quilts and American primitive antiques, all of which work to spell welcome.

Homemade bread and Wildwood's own peach butter and "country yummies" are included with breakfast. Sturbridge Village, Old Deerfield, and Amherst offer recreational activities that are all close by. You can stroll to the tennis court or borrow the canoe, or visit in the parlor for stimulating conversation. Fraidell does her best to spoil you.

NANTUCKET

Lynda Watts Bed & Breakfast ✪
30 VESTAL STREET, BOX 478, NANTUCKET, MASSACHUSETTS 02554

Tel: **(508) 228-3828**	Breakfast: **Continental**
Hosts: **Lynda and David Watts**	Pets: **No**
No. of Rooms: **2**	Children: **Welcome**
Max. No. Sharing Bath: **4**	Smoking: **Permitted**
Double/sb: **$65**	Social Drinking: **Permitted**
Open: **All year**	Minimum Stay: **2 nights**
Reduced Rates: **20% Jan. 1–Apr. 15**	

Lynda and David's 15-year-old saltbox house is located on a quiet street in a residential neighborhood, only a seven-minute walk to town. It is simply furnished and guest rooms are equipped with TVs. Weather permitting, breakfast is served on the sunny patio.

Seven Sea Street Inn ✪
7 SEA STREET, NANTUCKET, MASSACHUSETTS 02554

Tel: **(508) 228-3577**
Hosts: **Matthew and Mary Parker**
No. of Rooms: **8**
No. of Private Baths: **8**
Double/pb: **$85–$165**
Open: **All year**
Reduced Rates: **Oct.–June**
Breakfast: **Continental**

Credit Cards: **MC, VISA**
Pets: **No**
Children: **Welcome, over 7**
Smoking: **No**
Social Drinking: **Permitted**
Minimum Stay: **2 nights weekends May–Oct.**
Foreign Languages: **French**

This romantic red-oak post-and-beam country inn is located on a quiet side street in the town's historic district. Each bedroom is decorated with Colonial-style furniture, fishnet canopy beds, handmade quilts, and braided rugs covering wide-plank pine floors. A small refrigerator and cable TV will please those who like to snack and view in private. Don't miss the spectacular sunset from the widow's walk overlooking the harbor and do take some time to relax in the Jacuzzi whirlpool. After a good night's sleep, you may have breakfast served to you in bed.

Location: **35 mi. SW of Traverse City**
No. of Rooms: **4**
No. of Private Baths: **4**
Double/pb: **$69**
Single/pb: **$59**
Open: **All year**
Breakfast: **Continental**

Credit Cards: **MC, VISA**
Pets: **Sometimes**
Children: **Welcome, over 10**
Smoking: **No**
Social Drinking: **Permitted**
Minimum Stay: **2 nights on weekends June–Aug.**

Whether you sip lemonade on the screened porch in summer or enjoy a hot toddy by the fire in winter, the Windermere Inn on beautiful Crystal Lake makes comfort its top priority. Situated in scenic Benzie County, the inn has Sleeping Bear National Lakeshore to its north, Crystal Mountain ski resort to its south, Interlochen Arts Academy to its east, Lake Michigan and its beaches to its west, and golf courses all around. Anne and Cameron can help make your stay as eventful or relaxing as you wish. Your day begins with native fruits and muffins in summer, breakfast casseroles and breads in winter.

Celibeth House

ROUTE 1, BOX 58A, M-77 BLANEY PARK ROAD, BLANEY PARK, MICHIGAN 49836

Tel: **(906) 283-3409**
Host: **Elsa Strom**
Location: **60 mi. W of Mackinac Bridge**
No. of Rooms: **7**
No. of Private Baths: **7**
Double/pb: **$40–$50**
Single/pb: **$35–$45**

Open: **May 1–Dec. 1**
Reduced Rates: **10% after 2nd night**
Breakfast: **Continental**
Credit Cards: **MC, VISA**
Pets: **No**
Children: **Welcome**
Smoking: **No**
Social Drinking: **Permitted**

This lovely house, built in 1895, is situated on 85 acres overlooking a small lake. Many of the scenic attractions of Michigan's Upper Peninsula lie within an hour's drive. Guests may enjoy a cozy living room, a quiet reading room, a comfortably furnished porch, an outdoor deck, and lots of nature trails. Elsa is a retired personal manager who enjoys reading, gardening, traveling, and collecting antiques.

Dewey Lake Manor Bed & Breakfast ✪

11811 LAIRD ROAD, BROOKLYN, MICHIGAN 49230

Tel: **(517) 467-7122**
Best Time to Call: **Before 11 PM**
Hosts: **Joe, Barb, Barry and Tandy Phillips**
Location: **45 mi. SW of Ann Arbor**
No. of Rooms: **4**
No. of Private Baths: **4**
Double/pb: **$55–$65**
Single/pb: **$50–$60**
Open: **All year**

Reduced Rates: **Available**
Breakfast: **Continental, plus**
Other Meals: **Available, picnic baskets**
Credit Cards: **MC, VISA**
Pets: **No**
Children: **Welcome**
Smoking: **No**
Social Drinking: **Permitted**
Minimum Stay: **3 nights on race weekends**

This 1870s Italianate home sits on the shore of Dewey Lake in the Irish Hills of southern Michigan. Four spacious, airy rooms are furnished with antiques and old-fashioned wallpapers. Guests may linger over a Continental-plus breakfast in the formal dining room or on the porch overlooking the lake. Picnics, bonfires, volleyball, or croquet may be enjoyed on the large lawn. Nearby is the Stagecoach Stop Dinner Theater, as well as golf courses, quaint towns, and many antique shops. Come experience the country with the Phillips family.

The Calumet House ☯
1159 CALUMET AVENUE, P.O. BOX 126, CALUMET, MICHIGAN 49913

Tel: (906) 337-1936	Open: All year
Hosts: George and Rose Chivses	Breakfast: Full
Location: 10 mi. N of Hancock-Houghton	Pets: No
	Children: No
No. of Rooms: 2	Smoking: No
Max. No. Sharing Bath: 4	Social Drinking: Permitted
Double/sb: $30	Airport/Station Pickup: Yes
Single/sb: $25	Foreign Languages: Finnish

The Calumet House is set in a historic old mining town, known for its clean air and scenic vistas. Built in 1895, the house boasts its original woodwork and is filled with local antique furnishings. In the morning, you're in for a treat with Rose's home cooking. Breakfast specialties include English scones, pancakes, local berries in season, and home-made jam. Calumet House is within walking distance of the village, with its opera house, museum, and antique shops. Your hosts will also direct you to local hunting and fishing, as well as to places that any botanist would call paradise. It's 10 miles north of Michigan Technological University and Suomi College.

Michigamme Lake Lodge ☯
BOX 97, CHAMPION, MICHIGAN 49814

Tel: (800) 358-0058	Reduced Rates: Available
Hosts: Frank and Linda Stabile	Breakfast: Continental
Location: 30 mi. W of US 41	Credit Cards: MC, VISA
No. of Rooms: 6	Pets: No
No. of Private Baths: 3	Children: Welcome
Max. No. Sharing Bath: 2	Smoking: No
Double/pb: $59–$85	Social Drinking: Permitted
Open: All year	

Built in 1934, listed on the State and National Historical Register, this two-and-a-half-story lodge is a fine representative of the "great camps" that punctuated Michigan's Upper Peninsula. Guests can relax by a crackling fire in the massive stone fireplace gracing the large central hall. Lake Michigamme provides opportunities for canoeing,

No. of Private Baths: **4**
Double/pb: **$63**
Single/pb: **$58**
Open: **All year**
Reduced Rates: **10% Jan., Feb.;**
  weekly; 10% seniors

Credit Cards: **MC, VISA**
Breakfast: **Full**
Pets: **No**
Smoking: **No**
Social Drinking: **Permitted**

Built in 1860, Shadowlawn Manor has been restored and refurbished with your comfort in mind. Art and Al have been collecting furniture, silverware, crystal, and antique accessories for years, and they have used it all to great advantage at Shadowlawn. They will be happy to direct you to the lake, beach, golf course, or Hillsdale College's arboretum. You are welcome to relax on the screened-in porch, where, in springtime, the lilacs perfume the air.

Dutch Colonial Inn
560 CENTRAL AVENUE, HOLLAND, MICHIGAN 49423

Tel: **(616) 396-3664**
Best Time to Call: **Anytime**
Hosts: **Bob and Pat Elenbaas and**
  Diana Klungel
Location: **30 mi. W of Grand Rapids**
No. of Rooms: **5**
No. of Private Baths: **5**
Double/pb: **$70–$90**

Suites: **$100–$110**
Open: **All year**
Breakfast: **Full**
Pets: **No**
Children: **Welcome, over 10**
Smoking: **No**
Social Drinking: **No**
Airport/Station Pickup: **Yes**

Bob and Pat Elenbaas invite you to experience Dutch hospitality in their spacious Colonial inn. The house is set in a quiet, residential section, with a large yard and lovely sun porch. Rooms are furnished with traditional family antiques, some dating back to the 1830s. Choose from a bedroom with lovely candlewicking on the drapes, comforters, and pillow shams; a suite with Victorian furnishings and its own sitting area; or the Jenny Lind Room, with its antique beds and dusty rose accents. Breakfast specialties such as quiche, home-made rolls, and muffins are served in the formal dining room. The Elenbaases are centrally located in a beautiful city, famous for its tulip festival, original Dutch windmill, and miles of sandy beaches on Lake Michigan.

Seven Oaks Farm ✪
7891 HOLLISTER ROAD, LAINGSBURG, MICHIGAN 48848

Tel: **(517) 651-5598**
Best Time to Call: **Evening**
Host: **Mary C. Pino**
Location: **15 mi. NE of East Lansing**
No. of Rooms: **1**
No. of Private Baths: **1**
Double/pb: **$50**
Single/pb: **$35**

Open: **All year**
Breakfast: **Continental**
Pets: **Yes**
Children: **Welcome**
Smoking: **Permitted**
Social Drinking: **Permitted**
Airport/Station Pickup: **Yes**

This beautiful country home with antique furnishings, built in 1847, is located on 100 acres of peaceful woods and farmland pleasant for walking. Golf, auctions, antique stores, an elegant restaurant and Sleepyhollow State Park (for swimming and cross-country skiing) are only two miles away. An outlet and other shopping malls, as well as music, theater and sports at Michigan State University, are just fifteen minutes away. The State Capital is twenty-five minutes away. Your hostess, an attorney, raises sheep and has two children. Children and pets are welcome. Come enjoy country comfort and refreshments.

Centennial ☉
5774 MAIN STREET, P.O. BOX 54, LEXINGTON, MICHIGAN 48450

Tel: **(810) 359-8762**	Reduced Rates: **Available**
Best Time to Call: **After 2:30 PM**	Breakfast: **Full (weekends),**
Hosts: **Daniel and Dilla Miller**	**Continental (midweek)**
Location: **20 mi. N of Port Huron**	Pets: **No**
No. of Rooms: **4**	Children: **Welcome, over 10**
No. of Private Baths: **4**	Smoking: **No**
Double/pb: **$65**	Social Drinking: **Permitted**
Single/pb: **$55**	Minimum Stay: **2 nights holiday**
Open: **All year**	**weekends**

Centennial is a warm, inviting home furnished in traditional styles. Sit on the side porch listening to the singing birds and bubbling, splashing fountain, or stroll among the well-maintained lawns and gardens. Daniel and Dilla take the greatest pleasure in making your stay special. After a great night's sleep in the comfortable bedrooms, you'll wake up to fresh-brewed coffee and a homemade breakfast. The fresh fruit comes to the table from your hosts' garden and trees.

Governor's Inn ☉
LEXINGTON, MICHIGAN 48450

Tel: **(810) 359-5770**	Open: **Memorial through Labor Day**
Hosts: **Jane and Bob MacDonald**	**weekends**
Location: **20 mi. N of Port Huron**	Breakfast: **Continental**
No. of Rooms: **3**	Pets: **No**
No. of Private Baths: **3**	Children: **Welcome, over 12**
Double/pb: **$50**	Smoking: **Permitted**
Single/pb: **$50**	Social Drinking: **Permitted**

A handsome residence built in 1859, it is located near the shore of Lake Huron. It has been refurbished to its original "summer home" style. Wicker furniture, rag rugs, iron beds, and green plants accent the light, airy decor. You can stroll to the nearby beach, browse through interesting shops, fish from the breakwater, or play golf or tennis. Jane and Bob, both educators, look forward to sharing their quaint village surroundings with you.

Pine Manor Bed & Breakfast ✪
1436 TENTH STREET, MARTIN, MICHIGAN 49070

Tel: **(616) 672-9164**	Single/pb: **$45**
Host: **Patricia L. Peden**	Open: **All year**
Location: **2 mi. from route US 131,**	Breakfast: **Continental**
Exit 55	Pets: **No**
No. of Rooms: **2**	Children: **Welcome, over 10**
No. of Private Baths: **2**	Smoking: **No**
Double/pb: **$55**	Social Drinking: **Permitted**

This century-old farmhouse, lovingly restored over the last 20 years, sits back from the main road amid landscaped lawns and old pines. Breakfast is served in the bright, wrought-iron breakfast room or in the formal dining room. Accommodations are private, with an upstairs sitting room offering a TV, VCR, books, and games. Patricia, who is retired, enjoys cooking, entertaining, and gardening, and will happily direct you to antique shops, golf and skiing facilities, and local restaurants.

Benson House B&B ✪
618 EAST LAKE STREET, PETOSKEY, MICHIGAN 49770

Tel: **(616) 347-1338**	Reduced Rates: **Available**
Best Time to Call: **After 10 AM**	Breakfast: **Full**
Hosts: **Rod and Carol Benson**	Credit Cards: **MC, VISA**
No. of Rooms: **3**	Pets: **No**
No. of Private Baths: **3**	Children: **Welcome, over 6**
Double/pb: **$78–$85**	Smoking: **No**
Single/pb: **$78–$85**	Social Drinking: **Permitted**
Open: **All year**	Airport/Station Pickup: **Yes**

From the beautiful veranda of Benson House, you can admire Lake Michigan's Little Traverse Bay, just as guests did in 1878 when this Victorian inn first opened its doors. Petoskey is in the heart of Michigan's Little New England; the town's Gaslight District offers excellent shopping and dining. Mackinac Island is just a short drive away, as are numerous beaches, lakes, and other points of interest. The area's scenic roads wind through forests, valleys, and upland meadows. Five major ski resorts provide the Midwest's best downhill and cross-country skiing. For those of you who don't mind paying a higher rate, 1 other room is available.

Raymond House Inn ✪
111 SOUTH RIDGE STREET, M-25, PORT SANILAC, MICHIGAN 48469

Tel: **(810) 622-8800; (800) 622-7229**	No. of Rooms: **7**
Hosts: **The Denisons**	No. of Private Baths: **7**
Location: **30 mi. N of Port Huron**	Double/pb: **$55–$70**

Open: **Apr. 1–Dec. 31**
Reduced Rates: **10% seniors**
Breakfast: **Full**
Pets: **No**

Children: **Welcome, over 12**
Smoking: **No**
Social Drinking: **Permitted**

Shirley will put you right at ease in her antique-filled inn with the conveniences of today and the ambience of 1895. Each bedroom is furnished with period furniture, brightly colored spreads, and lace curtains. There's an old-fashioned parlor and a dining room where you are served breakfast. Sport fishermen and sailboat enthusiasts will enjoy this area; cultural activities, quilting bees, and the annual summer festival are longtime traditions here. There is a antique and gift shop in the inn.

Paint Creek B&B ✪
971 DUTTON ROAD, ROCHESTER HILLS, MICHIGAN 48306

Tel: **(313) 651-6785**
Hosts: **Loren and Rea Siffring**
Location: **35 mi. N of Detroit**
No. of Rooms: **3**
Max. No. Sharing Bath: **3**
Double/sb: **$40–$45**
Single/sb: **$35–$40**

Open: **All year**
Reduced rates: **Available**
Breakfast: **Full**
Pets: **Sometimes**
Children: **Welcome**
Smoking: **No**
Social Drinking: **Permitted**

Located on 3½ woodsy acres, this B&B brings guests close to nature. During the day, sit in the family room and watch the birds and squirrels; at night, check out the raccoons and opossums that gather on the feeding platform. For those who want to experience the great outdoors, there's hiking, biking, and cross-country skiing on the trail adjoining the property, plus four recreational parks less than fifteen minutes away. Sightseers will want to visit the Stoney Creek historic district, Oakland University, Pontiac Silverdome, the Palace (home of the Detroit Pistons), and Pine Knob Ski Hill and its outdoor concert facility.

Sherwood Forest Bed & Breakfast ✪
938 CENTER STREET, P.O. BOX 315, SAUGATUCK, MICHIGAN 49453

Tel: **(800) 838-1246**
Best Time to Call: **9 AM–10 PM**
Hosts: **Keith and Sue Charak**
Location: **40 mi. SW of Grand Rapids**
No. of Rooms: **5**
No. of Private Baths: **5**
Double p/b: **$60–$140**
Open: **All year**
Breakfast: **Continental**

Other Meals: **Available**
Credit Cards: **MC, VISA**
Pets: **No**
Children: **Welcome, over 12**
Smoking: **No**
Social Drinking: **Permitted**
Minimum Stay: **2 nights, weekends;
     May 1–Oct. 31**
Airport/Station Pickup: **Yes**

Woods surround this beautiful, 1890s Victorian home with a large wraparound porch. All guest rooms are furnished with antiques; one has a Jacuzzi and another has a fireplace. Outside is a heated swimming pool and deck, along with a separate cottage that sleeps seven. Lake Michigan and a public beach are half a block away. The area's wide white sandy beaches are the perfect place for strolling, swimming, or watching spectacular sunsets. Saugatuck's attractions include chamber music, art galleries, summer theater, charming gift shops, golf, charter boats, sailing, cross-country skiing, and fine dining.

Rummel's Tree Haven ○
41 NORTH BECK STREET, M-25, SEBEWAING, MICHIGAN 48759

Tel: (517) 883-2450
Best Time to Call: **Afternoons; evenings**
Hosts: **Carl and Erma Rummel**
Location: **28 mi. NE of Bay City**
No. of Rooms: **2**
Double/pb: **$40**
Single/pb: **$30**

Open: **All year**
Breakfast: **Full**
Pets: **Sometimes**
Children: **Welcome (crib)**
Smoking: **Permitted**
Social Drinking: **Permitted**
Airport/Station Pickup: **Yes**

A tree grows right through the porch and roof of this charming old home that was built by the Beck family in 1878. Guests can relax in large, airy rooms furnished with twin beds and comfortable family pieces. City dwellers are sure to enjoy the small-town friendliness and the quiet of the countryside. Saginaw Bay offers fine fishing, hunting, boating, birdwatching, or just plain relaxing. Carl and Erma offer color TV, videocassettes, and the use of the barbecue and refrigerator. They love having company and will do all they can to make you feel welcome and relaxed.

Csatlos' Csarda ✪
P.O. BOX 523, STEPHENSON, MICHIGAN 49887

Tel: **(906) 753-4638**	Open: **All year**
Host: **Barb Upton**	Breakfast: **Continental**
Location: **70 mi. N of Green Bay,**	Pets: **No**
Wisconsin	Children: **No**
No. of Rooms: **2**	Smoking: **No**
Max. No. Sharing Bath: **4**	Social Drinking: **Permitted**
Double/sb: **$28**	Airport/Station Pickup: **Yes**
Single/sb: **$22**	Foreign Languages: **Hungarian**

Barb offers a touch of things Hungarian to those who wish to sample the charm of a very small town. Two blocks east of the front door and you're downtown; two blocks west and you're in a farmer's field! Lakes and beaches are nearby for summer swimming and boating or winter fishing. Cross-country ski trails are plentiful. It is a perfect spot to stop for the night for those travelers going to Chicago, Milwaukee, Mackinac Island, or Canada.

Linden Lea, A B&B on Long Lake
279 SOUTH LONG LAKE ROAD, TRAVERSE CITY, MICHIGAN 49684

Tel: **(616) 943-9182**	Breakfast: **Full**
Hosts: **Jim and Vicky McDonnell**	Pets: **No**
Location: **9 mi. W of Traverse City**	Children: **Welcome**
No. of Rooms: **2**	Smoking: **No**
Max. No. Sharing Bath: **4**	Social Drinking: **Permitted**
Double/sb: **$70**	Minimum Stay: **Holiday weekends**
Open: **All year**	Airport/Station Pickup: **Yes**
Reduced Rates: **$5 less Nov.–April**	

Linden Lea is an extensively remodeled and expanded 1900 lakeside cottage set on a private sandy beach surrounded by woods. The bedrooms are comfortably furnished in country style, accented with antiques. You are certain to enjoy the window seats and the panoramic views of Long Lake. The area offers the Interlochen Center for the Arts National Music Camp, a PGA golf course, and local wineries. Breakfast features local specialties, such as smoked bacon, maple syrup, and berries that make the home-baked muffins so delicious.

Peninsula Manor ✪
8880 PENINSULA DRIVE, TRAVERSE CITY, MICHIGAN 49686

Tel: **(616) 929-1321**	Max. No. Sharing Bath: **4**
Hosts: **Karen and Will Williamson**	Double/pb: **$85**
Location: **3 mi. N of Traverse City**	Double/sb: **$70**
No. of Rooms: **3**	Open: **All year**
No. of Private Baths: **1**	Reduced Rates: **10% seniors**

Breakfast: **Full**
Pets: **No**
Children: **Sometimes**
Smoking: **No**

Social Drinking: **Permitted**
Minimum Stay: **Holiday weekends**
Airport Pickup: **Yes**

Peninsula Manor, located on Old Mission Peninsula, is a contemporary home with spacious rooms and beachfront property on Grand Traverse Bay. The area is home to the National Cherry Festival and the Interlochen National Music Camp and Center for the Arts. Excellent golf, tennis, skiing, water sports, and hiking and biking areas are available. Relax on a deck and enjoy the bay view or gather in the family room to watch TV, play games, or socialize. Homemade jam, muffins, and coffee cake accompany the nutritious breakfast.

Bed & Breakfast Reservations of Michigan ✪
4655 CHAREST, WATERFORD, MICHIGAN 48327

Tel: **(810) 682-2665**
Best Time to Call: **6–10 PM**
Coordinators: **Tom and Denise Erhart**
States/Region Covered: **Bayview,**
   Detroit, Eaton Rapids, Fennville,
   Fruitport, Ludington, Marquette, St.
   Clair, St. Ignace, Traverse City

Rates (Single/Double):
   Modest: **$40 / $50**
   Average: **$60 / $75**
   Luxury: **$80 /$80–$220**
Credit Cards: **MC, VISA**

Tom and Denise represent more than fifty B&B homes and inns throughout the entire state. Choices include a large country inn in a charming nineteenth-century fairy tale village, a recently erected Victorian mansion overlooking International Waterway, and a Bavarian-style country home with authentic German decor and a delightful German host.

MINNESOTA

- Stacy
- Minneapolis/St. Paul
- Norwood
- Dundas
- Lake City
- Round Lake
- Sherburn
- Spring Valley

Martin Oaks B&B ✪
107 FIRST STREET, DUNDAS, MINNESOTA 55019

Tel: (507) 645-4644
Best Time to Call: **Before noon or after 6 PM**
Hosts: **Marie and Frank Gery**
Location: **35 mi. S of Minneapolis and St. Paul**
No. of Rooms: **2**
Max. No. Sharing Bath: **4**
Double/sb: **$69**
Single/sb: **$55**
Open: **All year**

Breakfast: **Full**
Other Meals: **Available**
Credit Cards: **MC, VISA**
Pets: **No**
Children: **Sometimes**
Smoking: **No**
Social Drinking: **Permitted**
Minimum Stay: **2 nights during college events**
Airport/Station Pickup: **Yes**

Built in 1869 by the treasurer of the thriving Archibald Mill just across the Cannon River, Martin Oaks is listed on the National Register of Historic Places. The architecture combines elements of Italianate and Greek Revival styles. Some rooms have their original pine floors, and all are furnished with comfortable antiques. Local activities abound, with options like golf, tennis, skiing, biking, hiking, canoeing, antiquing, and bookstore browsing. St. Olaf and Carleton colleges are minutes away. After serving you fresh fruit, egg dishes, and home-baked goodies, your hostess, a storyteller, will probably end breakfast by regaling you with an episode or two of local history.

The Prairie House on Round Lake ✪
RR 1, BOX 105, ROUND LAKE, MINNESOTA 56167

Tel: (507) 945-8934	Single/sb: $45
Hosts: **Ralph and Virginia Schenck**	Open: **All year**
No. of Rooms: **4**	Breakfast: **Full**
No. of Private Baths: **1**	Pets: **Welcome**
Max. No. Sharing Bath: **4**	Children: **Welcome**
Double/pb: **$55**	Smoking: **No**
Single/pb: **$55**	Social Drinking: **Permitted**
Double/sb: **$45**	Airport/Station Pickup: **Yes**

Built in 1879 by a prominent Chicago businessman, this farmhouse is a retreat from the bustle of city life. It's a working horse farm: American paint horses roam the pasture, and three barns house both young stock in training and show horses that are exhibited all over the world. A cupola rising from the central stairway is circled by four dormer bedrooms on the second floor. Antique furniture accented with equine touches reflects the spirit of the farm. Fishing, hiking, swimming, boating, and tennis are at the doorstep.

The Garden Gate ✪
925 GOODRICH AVENUE, ST. PAUL, MINNESOTA 55105

Tel: **(612) 227-8430; (800) 967-2703**	Open: **All year**
Hosts: **Mary and Miles Conway**	Breakfast: **Continental**
Location: **1 mi. from I-94 exit**	Credit Cards: **No**
Lexington Parkway	Pets: **Sometimes**
No. of Rooms: **3**	Children: **Welcome**
Max. No. Sharing Bath: **3**	Smoking: **No**
Double/sb: **$60**	Social Drinking: **Permitted**
Single/sb: **$50**	Airport/Station Pickup: **Yes**

A garden of delights awaits you at this Victorian duplex in the heart of St. Paul's Victoria Crossing neighborhood, within easy reach of downtown, the airport, the capitol, and the Mall of America. The Gladiola, Rose, and Delphinium rooms are as beautiful as their name-sakes. A typical breakfast may include fresh fruit, baked pastries, cereal, and yogurt. To pamper the body as well as the palate, guests may arrange to have a therapeutic massage.

Four Columns Inn ☉
RT. 2, BOX 75, SHERBURN, MINNESOTA 56171

Tel: (507) 764-8861
Best Time to Call: **Anytime**
Hosts: **Norman and Pennie Kittleson**
Location: **150 mi. W of Minneapolis**
No. of Rooms: **4**
No. of Private Baths: **3**
Max. No. Private Baths: **3**
Max. No. Sharing Bath: **4**
Double p/b: **$60–$70**
Single p/b: **$60–$70**

Doulbe s/b: **$50**
Single s/b: **$50**
Open: **All year**
Reduced Rates: **10% families**
Breakfast: **Full**
Pets: **No**
Children: **Sometimes**
Smoking: **No**
Social Drinking: **Permitted**
Airport/Station Pickup: **Yes**

Built as a guest house in 1884, this former stagecoach stop now welcomes the modern-day traveler. Lovingly remodeled by the Kittlesons during the last forty-five years, this Victorian mansion offers four rooms—including the very popular Bridal Suite. Throughout, the house is filled with antiques and musical instruments, including a player piano and a 1950s jukebox. A walnut-paneled den, two working fireplaces, circular stairway, and a library complete your home-away-from-home. A full breakfast served with warm hospitality rounds out your stay in the country. Four Columns is located in south central Minnesota, just two miles from I-90.

Chase's Bed & Breakfast
508 NORTH HURON, SPRING VALLEY, MINNESOTA 55975

Tel: (507) 346-2850
Hosts: **Bob and Jeannine Chase**
Location: **26 mi. S of Rochester**
No. of Rooms: **5**
No. of Private Baths: **5**
Double/pb: **$75**
Single/pb: **$60**
Open: **Feb.–Dec.**

Reduced Rates: **15% weekly**
Breakfast: **Full**
Credit Cards: **DISC, MC, VISA**
Pets: **No**
Children: **Sometimes**
Smoking: **No**
Social Drinking: **Permitted**
Airport/Station Pickup: **Yes**

William H. Strong built this Second Empire–style home in 1879 for $8,000. At the time, it was considered to be the most handsome home in the county. Over the years, the house has been an office, motel, and rest home, and is now listed on the National Register of Historic Places. Guests will find elegant rooms furnished in period antiques, many of which are for sale. Bob and Jeannine serve a hearty breakfast and offer snacks and setups in the evening. Nearby activities include swimming, tennis, golf, trout fishing, and hiking. Chase's is 18 miles from the airport, and 28 miles from the Mayo Clinic. The Amish area is nearby.

Kings Oakdale Park Guest House ✪
6933 232 AVENUE NORTHEAST, STACY, MINNESOTA 55079

Tel: **(612) 462-5598**
Hosts: **Donna and Charles Solem**
Location: **38 mi. N of St. Paul**
No. of Rooms: **3**
No. of Private Baths: **2**
Double/pb: **$32**
Single/pb: **$26**
Double/sb: **$30**
Single/sb: **$25**

Suites: **$35**
Open: **All year**
Breakfast: **Continental**
Pets: **Sometimes**
Children: **No**
Smoking: **Permitted**
Social Drinking: **Permitted**
Foreign Languages: **French**

This comfortable home is situated on four landscaped acres on the banks of Typo Creek. The picnic tables, volleyball net, and horseshoe game are sure signs of a hospitable country place. It is a serene retreat for people on business trips to the Twin Cities. The Wisconsin border and the scenic St. Croix River, where boat trips are offered, are minutes from the house. Charles and Donna will direct you to the most reasonable restaurants in town. For late snacks, refrigerators in the bedrooms are provided.

MISSISSIPPI

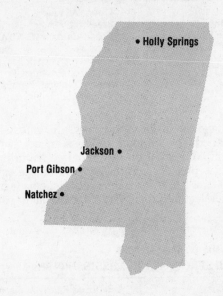

• Holly Springs

Jackson •

Port Gibson •

Natchez •

Lincoln, Ltd. Bed & Breakfast—Mississippi Reservation Service

P.O. BOX 3479, 2303 23RD AVENUE, MERIDIAN, MISSISSIPPI 39303

Tel: **(601) 482-5483; resv. only: (800) 633-MISS [6477]; fax: (601) 693-7447**
Best Time to Call: **9 AM–5 PM**
Coordinator: **Barbara Lincoln Hall**
States/Regions Covered: **Statewide**

Descriptive Directory: **$3.50**
Rates (Single/Double):
 Average: **$55–$65 / $65–$75**
 Luxury: **$85–$125 / $95–$165**
Credit Cards: **AMEX, MC, VISA**

For the traveling businessperson or for the vacationer, a stay with one of Barbara's hosts offers a personal taste of the finest Southern hospitality. All rooms have private baths. Mississippi abounds with historic-house tours, called "pilgrimages," in March and April, and Natchez and Vicksburg have similar pilgrimages in autumn. In May, Meridian is host to the Jimmie Rodgers Festival. Accommodations range from a cozy, historic log cabin to an elegant antebellum mansion.

Hamilton Place
105 EAST MASON AVENUE, HOLLY SPRINGS, MISSISSIPPI 38635

Tel: (601) 252-4368
Best Time to Call: After 4:30 PM
Hosts: Linda and Jack Stubbs
Location: 35 mi. SE of Memphis, Tenn.
No. of Rooms: 3
No. of Private Baths: 3
Double/pb: $75
Single/pb: $65
Guest Cottage: $75

Open: All year
Breakfast: Full
Credit Cards: MC, VISA
Pets: No
Children: Welcome
Smoking: Permitted
Social Drinking: Permitted
Airport/Station Pickup: Yes

On the National Register of Historic Places, this antebellum home, circa 1838, is furnished with heirloom antiques. In fact, Linda and Jack have a delightful antique shop on the premises featuring furniture, china, and cut glass. Breakfast can be enjoyed on the veranda or in the garden gazebo. You'll love the taste of the homemade biscuits with strawberry or honey-lemon butter. You are welcome to use the sauna or swimming pool.

Eastport Inn Bed & Breakfast ✪
100 SOUTH PEARL STREET, IUKA, MISSISSIPPI 38852

Tel: (601) 423-2511
Best Time to Call: 8 AM–5 PM
Host: Betty Watson
No. of Rooms: 7
No. of Private Baths: 7
Double/pb: $50
Single/pb: $40
Suites: $50
Open: All year

Reduced Rates: Available
Breakfast: Continental
Other Meals: Available
Credit Cards: AMEX, DC, DISC, MC, VISA
Pets: No
Children: Welcome
Smoking: No
Social Drinking: Permitted

This gracious home was built in 1864 and is decorated in period style, with four-poster beds and floral bedspreads. For swimming and boating, Pickwick Lake is six miles away; Shiloh National Park, Tishomingo State Park, Coleman State Park, and the Natchez Trace Drive are also nearby.

Oak Square Plantation ✪
1207 CHURCH STREET, PORT GIBSON, MISSISSIPPI 39150

Tel: (601) 437-4350; (800) 729-0240
Best Time to Call: Anytime
Hosts: Mr. and Mrs. William D. Lum

Location: On Hwy. 61 between Natchez and Vicksburg
No. of Rooms: 12

No. of Private Baths: **12**
Double/pb: **$85–$95**
Single/pb: **$70–$75**
Open: **All year**
Breakfast: **Full**

Credit Cards: **AMEX, DISC, MC, VISA**
Pets: **No**
Children: **Welcome**
Smoking: **No**
Social Drinking: **Permitted**

Port Gibson is the town that Union General Ulysses S. Grant said was "too beautiful to burn." Oak Square is the largest and most palatial antebellum mansion, circa 1850, in Port Gibson, and is listed on the National Register of Historic Places. The guest rooms are all furnished with family heirlooms, and most have canopied beds. Guests will enjoy the courtyard, gazebo, and beautiful grounds. A chairlift for upstairs rooms is available. You will enjoy the delightful Southern breakfast and tour of the mansion. Your hosts offer complimentary wine, tea, or coffee, and will enlighten you on the many historic attractions in the area.

For key to listings, see inside front or back cover.

⊙ This star means that rates are guaranteed through December 31, 1995, to any guest making a reservation as a result of reading about the B&B in *Bed & Breakfast U.S.A.*—1995 edition.

Important! To avoid misunderstandings, always ask about cancellation policies when booking.

Please enclose a self-addressed, stamped, business-size envelope when contacting reservation services.

For more details on what you can expect in a B&B, see Chapter 1.

Always mention *Bed & Breakfast U.S.A.* when making reservations!

If no B&B is listed in the area you'll be visiting, use the form on page 743 to order a copy of our "List of New B&Bs."

We want to hear from you! Use the form on page 745.

MISSOURI

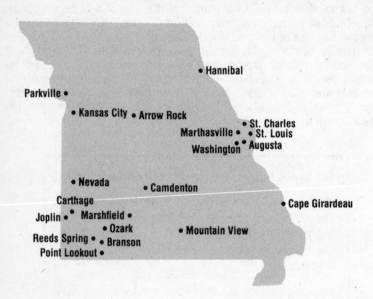

Bed & Breakfast Kansas City—Missouri & Kansas
P.O. BOX 14781, LENEXA, KANSAS 66285

Tel: (913) 888-3636
Coordinator: Edwina Monroe
States/Regions Covered:
  Kansas—Lenexa, Overland Park,
  Wichita; Missouri—Grandview,
  Independence, Kansas City, Lee's
Summit, Parkville, St. Joseph,
Springfield, Warrensburg, Weston
Rates (Single/Double):
  Average: $35 / $40–$50
  Luxury: $60 / $65–$130
Credit Cards: No

You will enjoy visiting such places as the Truman Library and home, Crown Center, Country Club Plaza, Arrowhead Stadium, Royals Stadium, Kemper Arena, the Missouri Repertory Theatre, and the American Heartland Theater, Nelson Art Gallery, New Theatre Restaurant, Toy & Miniature Museum.

Borgman's Bed & Breakfast ○
ARROW ROCK, MISSOURI 65320

Tel: **(816) 837-3350**
Best Time to Call: **7–9 AM**
Hosts: **Helen and Kathy Borgman**
Location: **100 mi. E of Kansas City**
No. of Rooms: **4**
Max. No. Sharing Bath: **4**
Double/sb: **$45–$50**
Single/sb: **$40**

Open: **All year**
Reduced Rates: **10% 3 nights**
Breakfast: **Continental**
Other Meals: **Dinner (winter only)**
Pets: **Sometimes**
Children: **Welcome**
Smoking: **No**
Social Drinking: **Permitted**

This 1860 home is spacious and comfortable, and it is furnished with cherished family pieces. Helen is a seamstress, artisan, and baker. Wait till you taste her fresh breads! Daughter Kathy is a town tour guide, so you will get firsthand information on this National Historic Landmark town at the beginning of the Santa Fe Trail. A fine repertory theater, the Lyceum, is open in summer. Craft shops, antique stalls, and the old country store are fun places to browse in. Good restaurants are within walking distance.

Lindenhof ✪

P.O. BOX 52, WALNUT AND JACKSON STREET, AUGUSTA, MISSOURI 63332

Tel: **(314) 228-4617**
Best Time to Call: **7 AM–10 PM**
Host: **Mary L. Peters**
Location: **25 mi. SW of St. Louis**
No. of Rooms: **5**
No. of Private Baths: **3**
Max. No. Sharing Bath: **4**
Double/pb: **$65**
Single/pb: **$60**
Double/sb: **$55**

Single/sb: **$50**
Open: **All year**
Reduced Rates: **Available**
Breakfast: **Full**
Credit Cards: **MC, VISA**
Pets: **Sometimes**
Children: **Welcome**
Smoking: **No**
Social Drinking: **Permitted**
Airport/Station Pickup: **Yes**

Located in historic Augusta, Lindenhof is a country Victorian home decorated with antiques and comfortable furniture. In addition to the bedrooms, there is a parlor-dining room for guests to enjoy. Within easy walking distance are several wineries; cyclists only have to ride five blocks to get on the Katy Bike Trail, which runs next to town. For big city pleasures, St. Louis is an hour away.

Ozark Mountain Country B&B Service

BOX 295, BRANSON, MISSOURI 65616

Tel: **(417) 334-4720; (800) 695-1546**
Best Time to Call: **10 AM–4 PM; 7–10 PM**
Coordinator: **Kay Cameron**

States/Regions Covered:
Missouri—Branson, Camdenton, Hollister, Joplin, Kimberling City, Marionville, Shell Knob, Springfield;

Arkansas—Eureka Springs;
Oklahoma—Tulsa
Rates (Single/Double):
Modest: **$35–$45**

Average: **$50–$65**
Luxury: **$70–$95**
Credit Cards: **AMEX, MC, VISA (5% Surcharge)**

After receiving a stamped, self-addressed legal envelope, Kay will send you a complimentary copy of her descriptive listings of more than one hundred carefully selected small inns, private cottages, and luxurious suites. She will also include coupons. Discounts are available for groups, honeymooners, and stays of more than three nights.

The Brass Swan ✪
H.C.R. 5, BOX 2368-2, BRANSON, MISSOURI 65616

Tel: **(417) 334-6873; (800) 280-6873**
Best Time to Call: **9 AM–9 PM**
Hosts: **Dick and Gigi House**
Location: **35 mi. S of Springfield**
No. of Rooms: **4**
No. of Private Baths: **4**
Double/pb: **$70–$80**
Single/pb: **$65–$75**

Open: **All year**
Breakfast: **Full**
Credit Cards: **DISC, MC, VISA**
Pets: **No**
Children: **Call ahead**
Smoking: **Restricted**
Social Drinking: **Permitted**

This elegant contemporary home has all the modern conveniences that will make your stay in Branson a wonderful, memorable experience. The Brass Swan is located in a quiet wooded area with a view of beautiful Lake Taneycomo, but it is only 1½ easy-to-travel miles to the Grand Palace and other attractions on 76 Country Blvd. The spacious guest rooms have sitting areas and private baths; some have private entrances and hot tubs. Use the game room, treadmill, hot tub, microwave, and refrigerator and wet bar, which are stocked with complimentary snacks and beverages. A family-style breakfast is served daily.

Country Gardens B&B ✪
1825 LAKESHORE DRIVE, BRANSON, MISSOURI 65616

Tel: **(417) 334-8564; (800) 727-0723**
Hosts: **Bob and Pat Cameron**
Location: **3 mi. E of downtown Branson**
No. of Rooms: **3**
No. of Private Baths: **3**
Double/pb: **$80**
Single/pb: **$75**
Guest Cottage: **$80**

Suites: **$95**
Open: **All year**
Breakfast: **Full**
Credit Cards: **DISC, MC, VISA**
Pets: **No**
Children: **Welcome, over 12**
Smoking: **Restricted**
Airport/Station Pickup: **Yes**

A parklike setting of gardens and a waterfall surround this wood-frame-and-rock home, located on beautiful Lake Taneycomo. The

Camerons have a variety of accommodations with private entrances. The Rose Suite consists of three rooms and features a large bathroom with spa. The Bittersweet Room is decorated with antiques and has a private deck overlooking the water. Dogwood has a single whirlpool tub and kitchen for those who like to prepare light meals. Breakfast specialties such as waffles with strawberries, and hot biscuits with eggs are served in the garden room overlooking the garden. Bob and Pat invite you to swim in the pool and enjoy a picnic under the trees. They say the best trout fishing around is right on the lake, and they have boats and fishing docks for anglers. Music lovers will be glad to know that there are 22 different country music shows in the area.

Josie's, the Peaceful Getaway ✪
H.C.R. 1, BOX 1104, BRANSON, MISSOURI 65616

Tel: (417) 338-2978; (800) 289-4125	Open: All year
Best Time to Call: 7 AM–10 PM	Reduced Rates: Available
Hosts: Bill and JoAnne Coats	Breakfast: Full
Location: 50 mi. S of Springfield, Missouri	Credit Cards: MC, VISA
	Pets: No
No. of Rooms: 3	Children: Welcome, over 5
No. of Private Baths: 3	Smoking: No
Double/pb: $55–$75	Social Drinking: Permitted
Single/pb: $50–$70	Minimum Stay: 2 nights, Oct.–May
Suite: $95	

In addition to its spectacular waterfront setting on Table Rock Lake, Josie's features a contemporary design, brown cedar siding, an outdoor Jacuzzi and a veranda with a panoramic view. Inside there are woodburning fireplaces, cathedral ceilings, antiques, and stained glass, thoughtfully accented by lace and candlelight. One room is a suite with a double whirlpool bath. Nearby attractions include Silver Dollar City, Branson's own music shows and a marina. JoAnne, a full-time hostess, and Bill, a civil engineer, can tell you all about the local sights.

Schroll's Lakefront B&B ✪
418 NORTH SYCAMORE STREET, BRANSON, MISSOURI 65616

Tel: (417) 335-6759	Open: All year
Best Time to Call: 9 AM–9 PM	Reduced Rates: Available
Hosts: Jeffrey Schroll and family	Breakfast: Full
Location: 35 mi. S of Springfield	Credit Cards: DISC, MC, VISA
No. of Rooms: 4	Pets: No
No. of Private Baths: 4	Children: Welcome
Double/pb: $75	Smoking: No
Single/pb: $60	Social Drinking: Permitted
Suites: $75 sleeps 2	

A new rustic cedar home located in downtown Branson awaits your arrival. It's an easy walk to shops and restaurants or to Lake Taneycomo, locally known for its trout. Outstanding country and popular music concerts and Silver Dollar City bring visitors back again and again. Each suite has its own entrance and decor; some have whirlpool tubs, cable TV, a telephone, and refrigerators, and two rooms have complete kitchens. Unwind completely with a bath in the outdoor hot tub. You'll begin the day with an Ozark breakfast in a room overlooking the lake.

Ramblewood Bed and Breakfast ✪
402 PANORAMIC DRIVE, CAMDENTON, MISSOURI 65020

Tel: **(314) 346-3410**	Single/sb: **$45**
Best Time to Call: **After 5 PM**	Open: **All year**
Host: **Mary Massey**	Breakfast: **Full**
Location: **90 mi. S of Columbia**	Pets: **No**
No. of Rooms: **2**	Children: **No**
Max. No. Sharing Bath: **4**	Smoking: **No**
Double/sb: **$50**	Social Drinking: **Permitted**

Ramblewood is a Pilgrim-red home with white trim. Set on a quiet, wooded lot, it has the feel of an English country cottage. Spend the night in an attractive, comfortable room and awaken to breakfast served on a sunny deck. Ham-and-cheese omelets and homemade breads are specialties of the house. The inn is minutes from Lake of the Ozarks, HaHa Tonka State Park and Castle, and antique shops, malls, and restaurants to suit any taste. After a busy day, enjoy a cool drink on the porch.

Bellevue Bed & Breakfast ✪
312 BELLEVUE, CAPE GIRARDEAU, MISSOURI 63701

Tel: **(800) 768-6822; (314) 335–3302**	Breakfast: **Full**
Hosts: **Fred and Jackie Hoelscher**	Credit Cards: **MC, VISA**
Location: **100 mi. S of St. Louis**	Pets: **No**
No. of Rooms: **2**	Children: **Welcome**
No. of Private Baths: **2**	Smoking: **No**
Double/pb: **$55**	Social Drinking: **Permitted**
Single/pb: **$45**	Airport/Station Pickup: **Yes**
Open: **All year**	

Built in 1891, this Second Empire Victorian home has been faithfully returned to its turn-of-the-century elegance. The original ceiling stencils have been restored in the dining room and parlor. Both bedrooms, furnished in antiques, have queen-size beds. A full breakfast served in the formal dining room features fresh breads and seasonal fruits. Guests may enjoy a leisurely stroll to the nearby riverfront and shopping at the many nearby antique and specialty shops. Fred is a retired salesman who will make you feel at home and tell you all you want to know about the area.

Grand Avenue Inn ✪
1615 GRAND AVENUE, CARTHAGE, MISSOURI 64836

Tel: **(417) 358-7265**
Best Time to Call: **8 AM–5 PM**
Hosts: **Betty Nisich and Paula Hunt**
Location: **10 mi. E of Joplin**
No. of Rooms: **4**
No. of Private Baths: **1**
Max. No. Sharing Bath: **4**
Double/pb: **$65–$85**
Double/sb: **$55–$65**
Suites: **$95–$115**

Open: **All year**
Reduced Rates: **Available**
Breakfast: **Full**
Credit Cards: **MC, VISA**
Pets: **No**
Children: **Welcome, over 5**
Smoking: **No**
Social Drinking: **Permitted**
Airport/Station Pickup: **Yes**

Built in 1893, the Grand Avenue Inn is a breathtaking mansion of the Victorian era, with four stained glass windows, handsome woodwork, and a winding oak staircase. Guests will rest in elegantly furnished rooms and wake to breakfast served in the formal dining room or on the veranda. Afternoons can be spent lounging by the pool. Complimentary beverages and a cheese tray are available between 4 and 6 PM. For your comfort, there is central heating and air-conditioning throughout the house.

Garth Woodside Mansion
NEW LONDON GRAVEL ROAD, RR1, HANNIBAL, MISSOURI 63401

Tel: **(314) 221-2789; (800) 896-1397**
Best Time to Call: **10 AM–7 PM**

Hosts: **Irv and Diane Feinberg**
Location: **99 mi. N of St. Louis**

No. of Rooms: **8**
No. of Private Baths: **8**
Double/pb: **$65–$110**
Open: **All year**
Breakfast: **Full**

Credit Cards: **MC, VISA**
Pets: **No**
Children: **Welcome, over 12**
Smoking: **No**
Social Drinking: **Permitted**

This Second Empire Victorian, built in 1871, has a three-story flying staircase, 14-foot ceilings, and eight handcarved marble fireplaces. Many of the room furnishings date back to the original owners. Stroll the 39 country acres, then sit down for a leisurely afternoon beverage. Breakfast, served in the formal dining room, features peach French toast, fluted quiche cups, and eggs picante. This location is ideal for touring Mark Twain country or for a romantic getaway. What's more, your hosts will pamper you with wonderful extras like nightshirts and turndown service.

Visages ✪
327 NORTH JACKSON, JOPLIN, MISSOURI 64801

Tel: **(417) 624-1397**
Best Time to Call: **8 AM–10 PM**
Hosts: **Bill and Marge Meeker**
Location: **3 mi. W of Rte. 71**
No. of Rooms: **3**
No. of Private Baths: **1**
Max. No. Sharing Bath: **4**
Double/pb: **$60**
Single/pb: **$55**

Double/sb: **$40–50**
Single/sb: **$35–45**
Open: **All year**
Breakfast: **Full**
Credit Cards: **AMEX**
Pets: **Sometimes**
Children: **Welcome (crib)**
Smoking: **No**
Social Drinking: **Permitted**

Visages takes its name from the twenty sculptured faces imbedded in the masonry walls surrounding the house, a distinctive chocolate-brown Colonial that dates to 1898. The Meekers bought the house as an abandoned wreck in 1977 and spent the next ten years refurbishing it; not surprisingly, Bill lists woodworking as one of his hobbies. They serve a full Ozark Mountain country breakfast.

Pridewell ✪
600 WEST 50TH STREET, KANSAS CITY, MISSOURI 64112

Tel: **(816) 931-1642**
Best Time to Call: **4–9 PM**
Hosts: **Edwin and Louann White**
No. of Rooms: **2**
No. of Private Baths: **1**
Double/pb: **$70**
Single/pb: **$65**

Open: **All year**
Breakfast: **Full**
Pets: **No**
Children: **Welcome**
Smoking: **No**
Social Drinking: **Permitted**

This fine Tudor residence is situated in a wooded residential area on the battlefield of the Civil War's Battle of Westport. The Nelson Art Gallery, the University of Missouri at Kansas City, and the Missouri

Repertory Theatre are close by. It is adjacent to the Country Club Plaza shopping district, which includes several four-star restaurants, tennis courts, and a park.

The Dickey House Bed & Breakfast Inn ○
331 SOUTH CLAY STREET, MARSHFIELD, MISSOURI 65706

Tel: **(417) 468-3000**	Breakfast: **Full**
Hosts: **William and Dorothy Buesgen**	Credit Cards: **MC, VISA**
Location: **22 mi. NE of Springfield**	Pets: **No**
No. of Rooms: **6**	Children: **Welcome, over 12**
No. of Private Baths: **6**	Smoking: **Permitted**
Double/pb: **$45–$95**	Social Drinking: **Permitted**
Single/pb: **$40–$90**	Airport Pickup: **Yes**
Open: **All year**	Foreign Languages: **German**
Reduced Rates: **Available**	

As you approach this lovely Colonial Revival mansion, named for the prominent lawyer who built it in 1908, the Ionic columns, widow's walk, and front entrance with beveled glass will transport you to a bygone era. Each bedroom is furnished with antiques and reproductions. Outside, oak trees and benches punctuate the lawns and gardens. An Amish settlement, the Buena Vista Exotic Animal Park, Laura Ingalls Wilder Museum, and Bass Pro Shop are among the nearby points of interest. Branson and Silver Dollar City are one hour to the south. To revive you after the day's activities, your hosts offer complimentary beverages and snacks.

Gramma's House
1105 HIGHWAY D, MARTHASVILLE, MISSOURI 63357

Tel: **(314) 433-2675**	Single/sb: **$50**
Best Time to Call: **8 AM–5 PM**	Guest Cottage: **$90**
Hosts: **Judy and Jim Jones**	Open: **All year**
Location: **50 mi. W of St. Louis**	Breakfast: **Full**
No. of Rooms: **4**	Credit Cards: **MC, VISA**
No. of Private Baths: **2**	Pets: **Sometimes**
Max. No. Sharing Bath: **4**	Children: **Welcome**
Double/pb: **$75**	Smoking: **No**
Single/pb: **$50**	Social Drinking: **Permitted**
Double/sb: **$65**	

At this romantic 150-year-old farmhouse, morning starts with a full, hearty breakfast like Gramma used to make. You can relax and maybe hear the bobwhite's call, reminding you of special times you spent at your own grandparents' home. Accommodations range from bedrooms to a snug cottage—formerly a smokehouse—with its own fireplace and sleeping loft. There are antique shops in Marthasville and Washington, and wineries in Augusta, Dutzow, and Hermann.

Close by is the Missouri River hiking and biking trail. The historic Daniel Boone home and burial site are also in the area.

Red Horse Inn ✪
217 SOUTH MAIN STREET, NEVADA, MISSOURI 64772

Tel: **(417) 667-7796; (800) 245-3685**	Single/sb: **$40**
Best Time to Call: **12–5 PM**	Open: **All year**
Hosts: **Victor and Sharon McCullough**	Reduced Rates: **10% seniors**
Location: **95 mi. S of Kansas City**	Breakfast: **Full**
No. of Rooms: **5**	Credit Cards: **MC, VISA**
No. of Private Baths: **1**	Pets: **Sometimes**
Max. No. Sharing Bath: **4**	Children: **Welcome**
Double/pb: **$45**	Smoking: **No**
Single/pb: **$40**	Social Drinking: **Permitted**
Double/sb: **$45**	

Come stay with us on your way to Branson, the Lakes area or traveling through Missouri. Experience the friendly hospitality of our air-conditioned turn-of-the-century home furnished in antiques. Guests can walk to the town square for a movie or shopping, or just relax on the front porch or deck. Nevada has golfing, parks, a museum, auto racing or summer baseball for your entertainment, tree-shaded streets invite strollers. Home of Cottey College, a women's two-year college founded in 1884. Full breakfast is served daily. Come as a guest and leave as a friend.

Bed & Breakfast at Merrywoods ✪
493 BLUFF DRIVE, OZARK, MISSOURI 65721

Tel: **(417) 581-5676**	Suites: **$125, sleeps 2–4**
Best Time to Call: **7–9 AM; or after 7 PM**	Open: **All year**
	Reduced Rates: **Available**
Hosts: **Gail and David Beard**	Breakfast: **Continental**
Location: **10 mi. S of Springfield**	Credit Cards: **MC, VISA**
No. of Rooms: **3**	Pets: **No**
No. of Private Baths: **3**	Children: **No**
Double/pb: **$55–$85**	Smoking: **No**
Single/pb: **$55**	Social Drinking: **No**

Merrywoods is located high on the Finley River bluff just north of Ozark. Branson, the country entertainment mecca, is 24 miles away; Bass Pro Shop and Wilson Creek Civil War Battlefield are also nearby. Constructed in 1980, this B&B offers three spacious suites and can accommodate wheelchairs. Amenities include decks, balconies, fireplaces, air-conditioning and, for high-tech users, a fax and a modem.

Down-to-Earth Lifestyles
ROUTE 22, PARKVILLE, MISSOURI 64152

Tel: **(816) 891-1018**
Hosts: **Lola and Bill Coons**
Location: **15 mi. N of downtown Kansas City**
No. of Rooms: **4**
No. of Private Baths: **4**
Double/pb: **$75**
Single/pb: **$65**
Open: **All year**

Reduced Rates: **Families**
Breakfast: **Full**
Other Meals: **Available**
Pets: **No**
Children: **Welcome**
Smoking: **Permitted**
Social Drinking: **Permitted**
Airport/Station Pickup: **Yes**

This spacious new earth-integrated home, with its picture windows and skylights, emphasizes close contact with nature. It's located on an 85-acre ranch, where there are horses and cows, a fishing pond, and lots of space for mind and soul. The furnishings complement the country setting, and the heated indoor pool, exercise room, and jogging and walking trails will keep you in shape. Lola and Bill will be pleased to suggest nearby places of interest if you can bear to tear yourself away from this restorative haven.

Cameron's Crag ✪
P.O. BOX 526, POINT LOOKOUT, MISSOURI 65726

Tel: **(417) 335-8134; (800) 933-8529**
Host: **Glen Cameron**
Location: **3 mi. S of Branson**
No. of Rooms: **3**
No. of Private Baths: **3**
Double/pb: **$75–$95**
Single/pb: **$70–90**
Suites: **$95; sleeps 2**
Open: **All year**

Reduced Rates: **$10 less Jan.–Mar., after 1st night**
Breakfast: **Full**
Other Meals: **Available**
Pets: **No**
Children: **Welcome, infants, over 6**
Smoking: **No**
Social Drinking: **Permitted**
Airport Pickup: **Yes**

Enjoy your choice of three delightful accommodations in this striking contemporary home perched high on a bluff overlooking Lake Taneycomo. All three suites have private entrances—one has a king-size bed, refrigerator; the other has a queen-size bed, and a deck with a spa. You'll savor one of your hosts' hearty breakfasts before you explore area attractions like Silver Dollar City, Table Rock State Park, and Mutton Hollow Craft Village.

Journey's End Bed & Breakfast ✪
H.C.R. 6, BOX 4632, REEDS SPRING, MISSOURI 65737

Tel: **(417) 338-2685**
Best Time to Call: **7 AM–10 AM, 7 PM–10 PM**

Host: **Liz Bass**
Location: **5 mi W of Branson**
No. of Rooms: **1**

No. of Private Baths: **1**
Guest Cottage: **$60–$80; sleeps 2–4**
Open: **May 1–Oct. 31**
Reduced Rates: **10% after 3rd night**
Breakfast: **Continental**

Pets: **No**
Children: **Infants only**
Smoking: **No**
Social Drinking: **Permitted**

Built in the 1920s to house visitors to Marvel Cave—the nation's third-largest commercial cavern—this yellow-and-white clapboard cottage has been recently renovated. The main room contains sleeping, sitting, and dining areas, plus a telephone and a TV. The large bath boasts an old-fashioned pedestal tub, separate shower, and dressing table, while the kitchenette has a refrigerator and microwave. Continental breakfast is brought to the cabin on a tray at a prearranged time; weather permitting, you can dine al fresco on the patio. Because it's surrounded by the Tri-Lakes area of the Ozarks, Journey's End offers both privacy and ready access to country music shows, water sports, crafts and antique shops, factory outlets, and, of course, Silver Dollar City, the 1880s mining-town theme park built around Marvel Cave.

Doelling Haus ✪
4817 TOWNE SOUTH, ST. LOUIS, MISSOURI 63128

Tel: **(314) 894-6796**
Best Time to Call: **8 AM–10 PM**
Hosts: **David and Carol Doelling**
Location: **7 mi. S of St. Louis**
No. of Rooms: **2**
No. of Private Baths: **1**
Double/pb: **$60**

Single/sb: **$35**
Open: **All year**
Breakfast: **Full**
Pets: **Sometimes**
Children: **Welcome**
Smoking: **No**
Social Drinking: **Permitted**

Warmly furnished with European and American antiques and collectibles, Doelling Haus re-creates old-world hospitality. Carol, who lived in Germany, will direct you to wonderful places for antiquing; David will gladly show off his old baseball cards. Enjoy the peaceful patio and swings, or walk around the friendly neighborhood. Many points of interest are nearby, such as the Arch, historic Kimmswick, recreational areas, malls, and fine restaurants. But before you head out, you'll fortify yourself with a full breakfast featuring German, French, and American specialties, fresh-ground coffee, and homemade breads and cakes.

Lafayette House ✪
2156 LAFAYETTE AVENUE, ST. LOUIS, MISSOURI 63104

Tel: **(314) 772-4429**
Hosts: **Sarah and Jack Milligan**
No. of Rooms: **5**
No. of Private Baths: **2**

Max. No. Sharing Bath: **4**
Double/pb: **$60**
Double/sb: **$50**
Suite: **$75**

Open: **All year**
Breakfast: **Full**
Pets: **Sometimes**
Children: **Welcome (crib)**

Smoking: **Permitted**
Social Drinking: **Permitted**
Minimum Stay: **2 nights in suite**
Airport/Station Pickup: **Yes**

This 1876 Queen Anne mansion is located in the historic district overlooking Lafayette Park. The house is furnished comfortably with some antiques and traditional furniture. The suite on the third floor, accommodating six, has a private bath and kitchen. Your hosts serve a special egg dish and homemade breads each morning, and offer wine, cheese, and crackers later. They will gladly take you on tour or can direct you to the Botanical Gardens, Convention Center, and other nearby attractions.

Soulard Inn ✪
1014 LAMI, ST. LOUIS, MISSOURI 63104

Tel: **(314) 773-3002**
Host: **Ray Ellerbeck**
Suites: **$55–$85**
Open: **All year**
Reduced Rates: **Available**

Breakfast: **Full**
Pets: **Sometimes**
Children: **No**
Smoking: **No**
Social Drinking: **Permitted**

One of the oldest buildings in St. Louis, this recently renovated inn is a showplace in the Soulard neighborhood, which takes its name from a French naval officer who disembarked here in 1796. Guests are only moments from the finest blues and jazz clubs, superb restaurants, and other entertainment. Your hosts promise to give you the highest level of service and one of the best breakfasts you've ever eaten.

The Winter House ○
3522 ARSENAL STREET, ST. LOUIS, MISSOURI 63118

Tel: (314) 664-4399
Hosts: Kendall and Sarah Winter
Location: 1 mi. S of I-44; 1 mi. W of I-55
No. of Rooms: 3
No. of Private Baths: 3
Double/pb: $65
Single/pb: $60
Suites: $80 for 2

Open: All year
Reduced Rates: After 2nd night
Breakfast: Continental, plus
Credit Cards: AMEX, DC, MC, VISA
Pets: No
Children: Welcome
Smoking: No
Social Drinking: Permitted

This ten-room Victorian, built in 1897, features a first-floor bedroom with a pressed-tin ceiling, and a second-floor suite with a balcony and decorative fireplace. Breakfast, served in the dining room on crystal and antique Wedgwood, always includes fresh-squeezed orange juice. Fruit, candy, and fresh flowers are provided in bedrooms; tea and live piano are available by reservation. Nearby attractions include the Missouri Botanical Garden, which adjoins Tower Grove Park, a Victorian walking park on the National Register of Historic Places. The Arch, Busch Baseball Stadium, the zoo, the symphony, and Union Station are all within four miles, and fine dining is in walking distance.

The Schwegmann House B&B Inn ○
438 WEST FRONT STREET, WASHINGTON, MISSOURI 63090

Tel: (800) 949-ABNB
Hosts: Cathy and Bill Nagel
Location: 50 mi. W of St. Louis
No. of Rooms: 10
No. of Private Baths: 8
Max. No. Sharing Bath: 4
Double/pb: $75
Single/pb: $65
Double/sb: $60

Single/sb: $50
Open: All year
Breakfast: Full
Credit Cards: MC, VISA
Pets: No
Children: Welcome, weekdays
Smoking: No
Social Drinking: Permitted

A three-story 1861 Georgian brick house included on the National Register of Historic Places, it is located on the Missouri River. It is tastefully furnished with antiques; handmade quilts complement the decor of each guest room. It is close to Daniel Boone's home, Meramec Caverns, Missouri's Rhineland wineries, antique shops, and fine restaurants. Relax in the graceful parlor by the fireside or stroll the gardens that overlook the river. The innkeeper serves a bountiful breakfast, including fresh-ground coffee, breads and breakfast specialties, local sausages and grape juice from Missouri's vineyards.

Washington House B&B Inn ✪
3 LAFAYETTE STREET, WASHINGTON, MISSOURI 63090

Tel: **(314) 239-2417**
Hosts: **Kathy and Chuck Davis**
Location: **50 mi. W of St. Louis**
No. of Rooms: **3**
No. of Private Baths: **3**
Double/pb: **$65–$75**
Single/pb: **$55**

Open: **All year**
Breakfast: **Full**
Pets: **No**
Children: **Welcome**
Smoking: **No**
Social Drinking: **Permitted**

Facing the Missouri River, this two-story brick Federal-style building was built as an inn during the late 1830s. In the heart of the historic district, avid preservationists Kathy and Chuck have painstakingly restored it, using period antiques and decorations of the era. The rooms are air-conditioned and have canopy beds. This is wine country, and many nearby wineries offer tours and tasting.

MONTANA

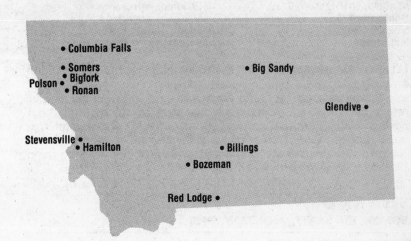

- Columbia Falls
- Somers
- Bigfork
Polson • • Ronan
• Big Sandy
Glendive •
Stevensville •
• Hamilton
• Billings
• Bozeman
Red Lodge •

Bed and Breakfast Western Adventure
P.O. BOX 20972, BILLINGS, MONTANA 59104

Tel: **(406) 259-7993**
Best Time to Call: **10 AM**
Coordinator: **Paula Deigert**
States/Regions Covered: **Idaho;
   Montana; South Dakota—Black
   Hills; Wyoming**

Rates (Single/Double):
   Modest: **$35–$49**
   Average: **$50–$64**
   Luxury: **$65–$195**
Credit Cards: **MC, VISA**

These areas—famous for their national parks, fishing streams, ski resorts, and spectacular scenery—are perfect for outdoor enthusiasts. Enjoy the wonders of Glacier Park in Montana, Yellowstone Park in Wyoming, and Mt. Rushmore in South Dakota. Then explore the fascinating past of the Old West with rodeos, Native American pow-wows, and other attractions that celebrate the history and the natural resources of the four states.

O'Duach'Ain Country Inn
675 FERNDALE DRIVE, BIGFORK, MONTANA 59911

Tel: **(406) 837-6851; (800) 837-7460**	Open: **All year**
Best Time to Call: **Anytime**	Breakfast: **Full**
Hosts: **Margot and Tom Doohan**	Other Meals: **Available**
Location: **17 mi. S of Kalispell**	Credit Cards: **AMEX, DISC, MC, VISA**
No. of Rooms: **5**	Pets: **Sometimes**
Max. No. Sharing Bath: **3**	Children: **Welcome**
Double/sb: **$75**	Smoking: **Restricted**
Single/sb: **$65**	Social Drinking: **Permitted**
Suites: **$95**	Airport/Station Pickup: **Yes**

O'Duach'Ain is a gracious three-level log home set on five beautiful acres. Inside, you'll find a casual atmosphere of open wood logs, stone fireplaces, antiques, and artwork. Guests are welcome to relax on the deck and take in the spectacular view. In the morning, your hosts provide a gourmet breakfast, featuring freshly prepared international dishes. Margot and Tom will direct you to nearby Glacier National Park, Swan Lake, Big Mountain ski area, and Flatland Lake. Walking trails abound.

Sky View ✪
BOX 408, BIG SANDY, MONTANA 59520

Tel: **(406) 378-2549; 386-2464**	Reduced Rates: **Families**
Best Time to Call: **Anytime**	Breakfast: **Continental**
Hosts: **Ron and Gay Pearson and family**	Other Meals: **Available**
Location: **75 mi. N of Great Falls**	Pets: **Sometimes**
No. of Rooms: **3**	Children: **Welcome**
Double/pb: **$50**	Smoking: **Permitted**
Single/pb: **$40**	Social Drinking: **Permitted**
Guest Cottage: **$40–$60**	Airport/Station Pickup: **Yes**
Open: **May 1–Dec. 1**	

Sky View is a working ranch located in an area known for its wild and rugged ambience, sparse population, and spectacular scenery. It's in the heart of Lewis and Clark country, just off a major highway to Glacier National Park. The Pearson family enjoys people of all ages and looks forward to sharing its lifestyle with guests, keeping you informed of local rodeos, Indian powwows, river float trips, tours, and hunting and fishing opportunities. Children enjoy their playground, and baby-sitters are available. A public swimming pool and tennis courts are nearby.

The Josephine Bed & Breakfast ✪
514 NORTH 29TH STREET, BILLINGS, MONTANA 59101

Tel: **(406) 248-5898**	Open: **All year**
Best Time to Call: **4–6 PM**	Reduced Rates: **Medical and extended**
Hosts: **Doug and Becky Taylor**	**stays**
No. of Rooms: **5**	Breakfast: **Full**
No. of Private Baths: **1**	Credit Cards: **MC, VISA**
Max. No. Sharing Bath: **4**	Pets: **No**
Double/pb: **$68**	Children: **Welcome, over 12**
Single/pb: **$58**	Smoking: **No**
Double/sb: **$58**	Social Drinking: **Permitted**
Single/sb: **$48**	Airport Pickup: **Yes**

This lovely, historic home is comfortably elegant. The porch, with its swing and quaint seating, offers the ideal place for breakfast or relaxing. Charming picket fences, shade trees, and flowers take you back in time. Each room is individually decorated with antiques, collectibles, and old photographs. Doug, a Billings native, enjoys cooking and travel, Becky enjoys crafts and antiques, and both are knowledgeable about the area. The B&B is within walking distance of downtown's museums, galleries, theaters, and shopping. It's only minutes to the airport, horse-racing rodeos, golf courses, and historic attractions. Skiing and Little Big Horn (Custer) Battlefield are an hour away; Yellowstone National Park is a beautiful 3-hour drive via scenic Beartooth Pass.

Kirk Hill Bed & Breakfast ✪
7960 SOUTH 19TH ROAD, BOZEMAN, MONTANA 59715

Tel: **(406) 586-3929**	Open: **All year**
Best Time to Call: **6 PM–9 PM**	Breakfast: **Continental**
Hosts: **Charlie and Pat Kirk**	Credit Cards: **MC, VISA**
Location: **6 mi. S of Bozeman**	Pets: **No**
No. of Rooms: **3**	Children: **Welcome, over 12**
Max. No. Sharing Bath: **4**	Smoking: **No**
Double/sb: **$55–$65**	Social Drinking: **Permitted**
Single/sb: **$50–$60**	

Kirk Hill Bed & Breakfast is a 1905 farmhouse tucked among the mountains surrounding Gallatin Valley. Charlie and Pat raise Irish setters, horses, llamas, sheep, ducks, and cashmere goats; pictures of these animals decorate guests' bedrooms. You might see less domesticated species on the Kirk Hill Nature Trail, on forty acres adjacent to the B&B property. For more outdoor adventures, your hosts can arrange horseback tours, rafting trips, and guides for hunting and fishing. For winter sports, Bridger and Big Sky Skiing Areas are within an hour's drive. In Bozeman, one big attraction is the Museum of the Rockies, known for its dinosaur collection and planetarium. The city is also the home of Montana State University, with an enrollment of about ten thousand students.

Millers of Montana Bed & Breakfast Inn ✪
1002 ZACHARIA LANE, BOZEMAN, MONTANA 59715

Tel: (406) 763-4102	Single/sb: $45
Hosts: Doug and Joyce Miller	Open: All year
Location: 12 mi. SW of Bozeman	Reduced Rates: 7th day free
No. of Rooms: 4	Breakfast: Full
No. of Private Baths: 2	Pets: Sometimes
Max. No. Sharing Bath: 4	Children: Welcome
Double/pb: $60–$70	Smoking: No
Double/sb: $50	Social Drinking: Permitted

This Cape Cod–style house is on a secluded 20-acre ranch, with breathtaking views of the Spanish Peaks and the Bridger Mountains. Quiet and comfortable, the B&B is furnished with country pieces and antiques. Yellowstone National Park is one hour away, and it's only 30 minutes to the Madison, Jefferson, and Yellowstone Rivers. For blue ribbon trout fishing, walk over to the Gallatin River. Bozeman itself, home of Montana State University and the Museum of the Rockies, is worth visiting. Doug is in construction, and ranching, softball, and fishing are his hobbies. Joyce, a full-time hostess who retired from a culinary career, is interested in cooking, sewing, and crafts.

Torch and Toes B&B
309 SOUTH THIRD AVENUE, BOZEMAN, MONTANA 59715

Tel: (406) 586-7285; (800) 446-2138	Reduced Rates: Government
Best Time to Call: 8 AM–noon	employees
Hosts: Ronald and Judy Hess	Breakfast: Full
Location: 100 mi. SE of Helena	Pets: No
No. of Rooms: 4	Children: Welcome
No. of Private Baths: 4	Smoking: No
Double/pb: $65–$70	Social Drinking: Permitted
Single/pb: $55	Airport/Station Pickup: Yes
Open: All year	

Set back from the street, this Colonial Revival house is centrally located in the Bon Ton Historic District. Lace curtains, leaded glass windows, and period pieces remind one that this is a house with a past. Ron is a professor of architecture at nearby Montana State University; Judy is a weaver interested in historic preservation. Their home is furnished in a charming blend of nostalgic antiques, humorous collectibles, and fine furnishings. Breakfast always includes a special egg dish, fresh fruit, and muffins. Afterward, relax on the redwood deck in summer, or by a cozy fire in winter. Nearby attractions include blue-ribbon trout streams, hiking, skiing, and the Museum of the Rockies. Yellowstone National Park is one and a half hours away.

Voss Inn ✪
319 SOUTH WILLSON, BOZEMAN, MONTANA 59715

Tel: (406) 587-0982	Open: **All year**
Best Time to Call: **9:30 AM–9:30 PM**	Breakfast: **Full**
Hosts: **Bruce and Frankee Muller**	Credit Cards: **MC, VISA**
Location: **3 mi. from I-90**	Pets: **No**
No. of Rooms: **6**	Children: **Sometimes**
No. of Private Baths: **6**	Smoking: **No**
Double/pb: **$75–$80**	Social Drinking: **Permitted**
Single/pb: **$65–$75**	

This handsome 100-year-old brick mansion, flanked by Victorian gingerbread porches, is set like a gem on a tree-lined street in historic Bozeman. The bedrooms are elegantly wallpapered and furnished with brass and iron beds, ornate lighting, oriental throw rugs over polished hardwood floors—a perfect spot for a first or second honeymoon. The parlor has a good selection of books, as well as a chess set for your pleasure. It's north of Yellowstone, on the way to Glacier, with trout fishing, mountain lakes, and skiing within easy reach. Don't miss the Museum of the Rockies on the Montana State University campus ten blocks away.

Bad Rock Country Bed & Breakfast ✪
480 BAD ROCK DRIVE, COLUMBIA FALLS, MONTANA 59912

Tel: **(406) 892-2829; (800) 422-3666**	Breakfast: **Full**
Hosts: **Jon and Sue Alper**	Other Meals: **Available**
Location: **15 mi. from Glacier Park**	Credit Cards: **AMEX, CB, DC, DISC,**
No. of Rooms: **2**	**MC, VISA**
No. of Private Baths: **2**	Pets: **No**
Double/pb: **$90–$95**	Children: **Welcome, over 10**
Suites: **$110–$125**	Smoking: **No**
Open: **All year**	

Experience country living in this ranch-style farmhouse on 30 acres in Flathead Valley. Guest rooms feature antique furniture and queen-size beds. Three living rooms provide a place to relax, read, sit by the fireplace and look at nearby Columbia Mountain, or watch satellite television. Explore the surrounding woods and pastures: hiking in the summer, cross-country skiing in the winter. Soak in the secluded hot tub in a time reserved exclusively for you, and gaze at the lights of the Big Mountain ski runs. Geese fly overhead at sunset; coyotes howl at night. Sundance eggs, Montana potato pie, huckleberry muffins, and buffalo steaks are some of the specialties offered at a full breakfast. The summer offers opportunities for fishing, hiking, white-water rafting, canoeing, jet skiing, horseback riding, and swimming. In the winter there is skiing from late November through mid-April at nearby Big Mountain. You can also try snowmobiling and dog sledding. Museums, galleries, casinos, and antique stores are found in the nearby towns of Kalispell, Whitefish, Bigfork, and Columbia Falls. For those who don't mind paying a higher rate, a third room is available.

The Hostetler House Bed & Breakfast ✪
113 NORTH DOUGLAS STREET, GLENDIVE, MONTANA 59330

Tel: **(406) 365-4505**	Reduced Rates: **Weekly**
Best Time to Call: **Anytime**	Breakfast: **Full**
Hosts: **Craig and Dea Hostetler**	Pets: **No**
No. of Rooms: **2**	Children: **No**
Max. No. Sharing Bath: **4**	Smoking: **No**
Double/sb: **$45**	Social Drinking: **Permitted**
Single/sb: **$35**	Airport/Station Pickup: **Yes**
Open: **All year**	

Located one block from the Yellowstone River and two blocks from downtown shopping and restaurants, the Hostetler House is a charming 1912 historic home with two comfortable guest rooms done in casual country decor. Nearby are parks, a swimming pool, tennis courts, antique shops, churches, a golf course, a museum, Dawson Community College, fishing, hunting, and hiking. Guests may relax in the hot tub, sitting room, enclosed sun porch, or on the deck. Wake up to the smell of freshly ground gourmet coffee, tea, and homemade bread. A full breakfast is served on Grandma's china in the dining room, sun porch, or on the deck. Dea is an interior decorator who grew up on a nearby wheat farm, and Craig is a mechanical engineer, pilot, and avid outdoorsman.

The Bavarian Farmhouse B&B ✪
163 BOWMAN ROAD, HAMILTON, MONTANA 59840

Tel: **(406) 363-4063**	Single/sb: **$35**
Best Time to Call: **Anytime**	Open: **All Year**
Hosts: **Peter and Ahn Reuthlinger**	Reduced Rates: **Available**
Location: **44 mi. S of Missoula**	Breakfast: **Full**
No. of Rooms: **5**	Pets: **Sometimes**
No. of Private Baths: **4**	Children: **Welcome**
Max. No. Sharing Bath: **3**	Smoking: **No**
Double/pb: **$50**	Social Drinking: **Permitted**
Single/pb: **$40**	Foreign Languages: **German**
Double/sb: **$45**	

Wilkommen to this 1880s farmhouse on open ranchland just outside the Bitterroot Range of the Rocky Mountains. Peter and Ahn are artists and world travelers interested in horses and the human potential movement. They extensively remodeled this home, drawing upon Peter's Bavarian background to create a European-style B&B. With advance notice, your hosts will arrange raft trips, trail rides, and hunting and fishing expeditions. Whatever your plans, you'll begin the day with an ample German farm breakfast of juice, cereal, eggs, cheese, cold cuts, breads, jam, and coffee and tea.

Deer Crossing ○
396 HAYES CREEK ROAD, HAMILTON, MONTANA 59840

Tel: (406) 363-2232; (800) 763-2232
Best Time to Call: 8 AM
Host: Mary Lynch
Location: 45 mi. S of Missoula
No. of Rooms: 5
No. of Private Baths: 3
Max. No. Sharing Bath: 4
Double/pb: $75–$95
Double/sb: $60
Bunk House: $50, sleeps 2–4
Suites: $65–$95

Open: All year
Reduced Rates: 5% seniors
Breakfast: Full
Other Meals: Available
Credit Cards: MC, VISA
Pets: No
Children: Welcome
Smoking: No
Social Drinking: Permitted
Airport/Station Pickup: Yes

Here is your invitation to experience Western hospitality at its finest. Deer Crossing is situated along the Lewis and Clark Trail on 24 acres of tall pines and pasture overlooking the Bitterroot Valley. Sit back and relax, or get involved in the ranch's daily activities. There are historic sites to visit, while athletic types can go swimming, rafting, fishing, skiing, hiking, and hunting. Accommodations include a large guest room, a suite with a spacious tub and a window overlooking the fields, and a bunkhouse that gives guests the feel of the Old West.

Angel Point Guest Suites ○
829 ANGEL POINT ROAD, BOX 768, LAKESIDE, MONTANA 59922

Tel: (406) 844-2204
Best Time to Call: Mornings
Hosts: Linda and Wayne Muhlestein
Location: 12 mi. S of Kalispell
Suites: $110–$120
Open: All year
Breakfast: Full

Credit Cards: MC, VISA
Pets: No
Children: Welcome, over 12
Smoking: No
Social Drinking: Permitted
Minimum Stay: 2 nights

This secluded, luxurious getaway was constructed and designed with couples in mind. Exclusively located on Angel Point peninsula on Flathead Lake, the inn has a private beach, dock, lake platforms, gazebo, firepit, and huge bench-swings nestled amidst giant fir trees. Each suite includes original artwork, a grand balcony with log railings, immense windows with panoramic views, a complete kitchen, and a sitting area with fine furniture. While the property is so spectacular most guests don't want to leave, some of the local attractions are Glacier National Park, Big Mountain winter sports, Jewel Basin Hiking Area, scenic golf courses, and white-water rafting. But first, you'll tuck in a wonderful western breakfast.

Hawthorne House ✪
304 THIRD AVENUE, EAST, POLSON, MONTANA, 59860

Tel: (406) 883-2723
Best Time to Call: **After 5 PM, weekends**
Hosts: **Gerry and Karen Lenz**
Location: **70 mi. N of Missoula**
No. of Rooms: **6**
Max. No. Sharing Bath: **4**
Double/sb: **$50**

Single/sb: **$45**
Open: **All year**
Breakfast: **Full**
Pets: **No**
Children: **Welcome, over 12**
Smoking: **No**
Social Drinking: **No**

In the small western Montana town of Polson, at the foot of Flathead Lake, you'll find Hawthorne House, an English Tudor home on a quiet shady street. In summer, cheerful window boxes welcome the weary traveler. The house is furnished with antiques from Karen's grandparents. There are plate collections, Indian artifacts, and glassware. The kitchen has some interesting collections. Breakfast is always special, with something baked fresh each morning. Nearby attractions include Glacier National Park, the National Bison Range, Kerr Dam, and great scenic beauty. Golf abounds. There are always activities on the lake and river.

Hidden Pines Bed & Breakfast ✪

792 LOST QUARTZ ROAD, POLSON, MONTANA 59860

Tel: **(406) 849-5612**
Best Time to Call: **10 AM–10 PM**
Hosts: **Earl and Emy Atchley**
Location: **10 mi. NW of Polson Mt.**
No. of Rooms: **4**
Max. No. Sharing Bath: **4**
Double/pb: **$60**

Double/sb: **$45**
Open: **All year**
Breakfast: **Full**
Pets: **No**
Children: **Welcome**
Smoking: **No**
Airport/Station Pickup: **Yes**

Stress and tension melt away in the quiet surroundings of Hidden Pines Bed & Breakfast. Relax on the deck of this rustic retreat and watch squirrels and deer graze right in front of you. Bring your canoe and bathing suit for fun in Flathead Lake; pack binoculars for viewing Wild Horse Island. Cross-country skis are useful when the snow flies, and hiking shoes will come in handy year-round. At the end of the day, unwind in the living room and tune in to your favorite TV show or screen a movie on the VCR. Depending on your appetite, Emy will serve you a full country breakfast or lighter Continental fare.

Swan Hill ✪

460 KINGS POINT ROAD, POLSON, MONTANA 59860

Tel: **(406) 883-5292**
Best Time to Call: **Evenings**
Hosts: **Larry and Sharon Whitten**
Location: **60 mi. N of Missoula**
No. of Rooms: **4**
No. of Private Baths: **2**
Max. No. Sharing Bath: **4**
Double p/b: **$85**

Double s/b: **$75**
Open: **All year**
Breakfast: **Full**
Credit Cards: **MC, VISA**
Pets: **Sometimes**
Children: **Welcome, over 12**
Smoking: **No**
Social Drinking: **Permitted**

A spacious redwood home on ten acres, Swan Hill overlooks the majestic Mission Mountains and Flathead Lake. Year-round, guests can go swimming, whatever the weather—the 7,000-square-foot home contains an indoor pool, as well as a sauna. Of scenic interest nearby are Glacier National Park and the Bison Range, while Jewel Basin has excellent hiking. Golfers have a good choice of courses and there are plenty of fishing spots. Visits to Western art galleries, antique shops, summer theater, and fine restaurants will fill your days. This B&B is wheelchair accessible.

Willows Inn ✪

224 SOUTH PLATT AVENUE, RED LODGE, MONTANA 59068

Tel: **(406) 446-3913**
Best Time to Call: **Mornings, afternoons**

Hosts: **Elven, Kerry, and Carolyn Boggio**
Location: **60 mi. SW of Billings**

No. of Rooms: **5**
No. of Private Baths: **3**
Max. No. Sharing Bath: **4**
Double/pb: **$55–$65**
Double/sb: **$55**
Single/sb: **$50**
Guest Cottages: **$65 for 2**
Open: **All year**
Reduced Rates: **10% after 4th night;
10% seniors**

Breakfast: **Continental**
Credit Cards: **DISC, MC, VISA**
Pets: **No**
Children: **Welcome**
Smoking: **No**
Social Drinking: **Permitted**
Minimum Stay: **2 nights in cottage**

Tucked beneath the majestic Beartooth Mountains in the northern Rockies, the historic town of Red Lodge provides an ideal setting for this charming three-story Queen Anne. Flanked by giant evergreens and colorful flower beds, the inn is reminiscent of a bygone age, complete with white picket fence, gingerbread trim, and front porch swing. Overstuffed sofas and wicker pieces complement the warm and cheerful decor. Delicious homebaked pastries are Elven's specialty—she uses her own Finnish recipes for these mouthwatering treats. Championship rodeos, excellent cross-country and downhill skiing, opportunities to hike, golf, and fish abound in this special area, still unspoiled by commercial progress. Yellowstone National Park is only 65 miles away.

The Timbers Bed and Breakfast
1184 TIMBERLANE ROAD, RONAN, MONTANA 59864

Tel: **(406) 676-4373; (800) 775-4373**
Best Time to Call: **10 AM**
Hosts: **Doris and Leonard McCravey**
Location: **65 mi. N of Missoula**
No. of Rooms: **2**
No. of Private Baths: **1**
Max. No. Sharing Bath: **4**
Suites: **$95–$115; sleeps 2**

Open: **Jan. 3–Nov. 21**
Breakfast: **Full, Continental**
Credit Cards: **MC, VISA**
Pets: **No**
Children: **Welcome, over 12**
Smoking: **No**
Social Drinking: **Permitted**

The Timbers is situated at the base of the Rocky Mountain Mission Range on 21 secluded acres, midway between Glacier National Park and Missoula, Montana. The house has a wraparound deck, and is glassed in to provide a magnificent view of the Missions. Cathedral ceilings, hand-hewn beams, a barnwood dining area, and furnishings that Doris and Leonard collected give their home a sophisticated yet warm country feel. Leonard can tell you about his 27 years on the professional rodeo circuit while you enjoy one of Doris's wonderful country breakfasts. Nearby attractions include Flathead Lake, National Bison Range, Glacier National Park, golf, and water sports, fishing, horseback riding, skiing, white-water rafting, art galleries, local rodeos, and powwows.

Osprey Inn Bed & Breakfast
5557 HIGHWAY 93 SOUTH, SOMERS, MONTANA 59932

Tel: (406) 857-2042; (800) 258-2042
Best Time to Call: 8 AM–9 PM
Hosts: Sharon and Wayne Finney
Location: 8 mi. S of Kalispell
No. of Rooms: 5
No. of Private Baths: 4
Double/pb: $85
Single/pb: $80
Suite: $160

Guest Cottage: $85
Open: All year
Breakfast: Full
Credit Cards: AMEX, MC, VISA
Pets: No
Children: Welcome, over 9
Smoking: No
Social Drinking: Permitted
Airport/Station Pickup: Yes

Yes, you can see osprey—as well as geese, loons, and grebes—from the deck of this rustic lakeshore retreat. In the summer, guests are welcome to bring along a boat or canoe; in the winter, pack your skis. Cameras and binoculars come in handy throughout the year. You'll start the day with fresh seasonal fruit, home-baked cinnamon rolls, and pancakes with homemade fruit syrups.

Country Caboose ✪
852 WILLOUGHBY ROAD, STEVENSVILLE, MONTANA 59870

Tel: (406) 777-3145
Host: Lisa Thompson
Location: 35 mi. S of Missoula
No. of Rooms: 1
No. of Private Baths: 1
Double/pb: $50
Single/pb: $50

Open: May–Sept.
Breakfast: Full
Pets: No
Children: Welcome
Smoking: No
Social Drinking: Permitted

If you enjoy romantic train rides, why not spend the night in an authentic caboose? This one dates back to 1923, is made of wood, and is painted red, of course. It is set on real rails in the middle of the countryside. The caboose sleeps two and offers a spectacular view of the Bitterroot Mountains, right from your pillow. In the morning, breakfast is served at a table for two. Specialties include huckleberry pancakes, quiche, and strawberries in season. Local activities include touring St. Mary's Mission, hiking the mountain trails, fishing, and hunting.

NEBRASKA

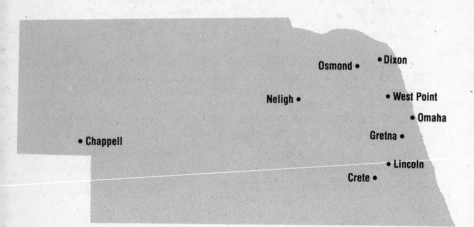

Osmond •   • Dixon

Neligh •   • West Point

  • Omaha

• Chappell   Gretna •

  • Lincoln

Crete •

Bed & Breakfast of the Midwest ✪
230 SOUTH MAPLE, WEST POINT, NEBRASKA 68788

Tel: **(402) 372-5904; (800) 392-3625**
Best Time to Call: **9 AM–5 PM**
Coordinator: **Karen Wesche**
States/Regions Covered: **Iowa, Kansas, Minnesota, Nebraska, North Dakota, South Dakota**

Descriptive Directory of B&Bs: **$3**
Rates (Single/Double):
  Modest: **$25–$55**
  Average: **$45–$75**
  Luxury: **$55–$225**
Credit Cards: **No**

This reservation service maintains high standards of service, comfort, and cleanliness at its sites, which are inspected. There are more than fifty participating B&Bs, all of them known for their down-home country hospitality. Bed & Breakfast of the Midwest prides itself on having a variety of guest homes that display what Midwest living is all about.

The Cottonwood Inn ○
802 SECOND STREET, CHAPPELL, NEBRASKA 69129

Tel: (308) 874-3250
Best Time to Call: 8 AM–9 PM
Hosts: Barb and Bruce Freeman
Location: 130 mi. E of Cheyenne
No. of Rooms: 6
Max. No. Sharing Bath: 4
Double/sb: $40
Single/sb: $35
Open: All year

Reduced Rates: 10% seniors
Breakfast: Full
Other Meals: Available
Credit Cards: MC, VISA
Pets: Sometimes
Children: Welcome (crib)
Smoking: No
Social Drinking: Permitted

Built as a rooming house in 1917, the Cottonwood Inn still has its original floors, light fixtures, and dumbwaiter. The balconies and the large front porch are perfect places to enjoy a summer evening. In cooler months, you can sit around the living room fireplace. Signs of the Old West abound in Chappell—the Oregon and Mormon trails, the Pony Express, and the first transcontinental railroad and highway all went through this town, which boasts a restored period home and an art museum. Other amenities include the public golf course, tennis courts, and swimming pool.

The Parson's House ○
638 FOREST AVENUE, CRETE, NEBRASKA 68333

Tel: (402) 826-2634
Hosts: Harold and Sandy Richardson
Location: 25 mi. SW of Lincoln
No. of Rooms: 2
Max. No. Sharing Bath: 4
Double/sb: $35
Single/sb: $30

Open: All year
Breakfast: Full
Pets: No
Children: No
Smoking: No
Social Drinking: No
Airport/Station Pickup: Yes

Enjoy warm hospitality in this newly refinished, turn-of-the-century home tastefully decorated with antiques. Doane College lies one block away; the beautiful campus is just the place for a leisurely afternoon stroll. It's just a short drive to Lincoln, the state's capital and home of the University of Nebraska. Harold, a Baptist minister with the local U.C.C. church, runs a remodeling business while Sandy runs the bed and breakfast. After a day's activity, they invite you to relax in their modern whirlpool tub and make their home yours for the duration of your stay.

The Georges ○
ROUTE 1, BOX 50, DIXON, NEBRASKA 68732

Tel: (402) 584-2625
Best Time to Call: 6:30 AM–7 PM

Hosts: Carolyn and Marie George
Location: 35 mi. W of Sioux City, Iowa

No. of Rooms: **3**
Max. No. Sharing Bath: **4**
Double/sb: **$40**
Single/sb: **$35**
Open: **All year**
Breakfast: **Full**
Other Meals: **Available**

Pets: **Sometimes**
Children: **Welcome**
Smoking: **No**
Social Drinking: **Permitted**
Airport/Station Pickup: **Yes**
Foreign Languages: **Swedish**

The Georges have a large, remodeled farmhouse with a spacious backyard. They offer the opportunity to see a farming operation at firsthand, right down to the roosters crowing and the birds singing in the morning. They prepare a hearty country breakfast featuring homemade jellies and jams. The Georges are close to Wayne State College and Ponca State Park.

Bundy's Bed and Breakfast ✪
16906 SOUTH 255, GRETNA, NEBRASKA 68028

Tel: **(402) 332-3616**
Best Time to Call: **7 AM–9 PM**
Hosts: **Bob and Dee Bundy**
Location: **30 mi. S of Omaha**
No. of Rooms: **4**
Max. No. Sharing Bath: **4**
Double/sb: **$35**

Single/sb: **$20**
Open: **All year**
Breakfast: **Full**
Pets: **Sometimes**
Children: **No**
Smoking: **No**
Social Drinking: **No**

The Bundys have a pretty farmhouse painted white with black trim. Here you can enjoy country living just 30 minutes from downtown Lincoln and Omaha. The rooms are decorated with antiques, attractive wallpapers, and collectibles. In the morning, wake up to farm-fresh eggs and homemade breads. The house is just a short walk from a swimming lake, and is three miles from a ski lodge.

The Rogers House ✪
2145 B STREET, LINCOLN, NEBRASKA 68502

Tel: **(402) 476-6961**
Best Time to Call: **10 AM–9 PM**
Host: **Nora Houtsma**
No. of Rooms: **8**
No. of Private Baths: **8**
Double/pb: **$45–$63**
Single/pb: **$40–$54**

Open: **All year**
Breakfast: **Full**
Credit Cards: **AMEX, MC, VISA**
Pets: **No**
Children: **Welcome, over 10**
Smoking: **Permitted**
Social Drinking: **Permitted**

This Jacobean Revival–style brick mansion was built in 1914 and is a local historic landmark. There are three sun porches, attractively furnished with wicker and plants, and the air-conditioned house is decorated with lovely antiques. Nora will direct you to the diverse cultural attractions available at the nearby University of Nebraska, the surrounding historic district, and antique shops. Don't miss a visit to the Children's Zoo and the beautiful Sunken Gardens. Breakfast is hearty and delicious. A professional staff of five is eager to serve you.

The Offutt House
140 NORTH 39TH STREET, OMAHA, NEBRASKA 68131

Tel: (402) 553-0951
Host: Jeannie K. Swoboda
Location: 1 mi. from I-80
No. of Rooms: 9
No. of Private Baths: 7
Max. No. Sharing Bath: 4
Double/pb: $65-$85
Single/pb: $55-$75
Double/sb: $55

Single/sb: $45
Suites: $70-$100
Open: All year
Reduced Rates: After 5th night
Breakfast: Continental
Pets: Sometimes
Children: Welcome
Smoking: Restricted
Social Drinking: Permitted

This comfortable mansion, circa 1894, is part of the city's Historic Gold Coast, a section of handsome homes built by Omaha's wealthiest residents. Offering peace and quiet, the rooms are air-conditioned, spacious, and furnished with antiques; some have fireplaces. Jeannie will direct you to nearby attractions such as the Joslyn Museum or the Old Market area, which abounds with many beautiful shops and fine restaurants. She graciously offers coffee or wine in late afternoon.

Willow Way Bed & Breakfast ☉
ROUTE 2, BOX A20, OSMOND, NEBRASKA 68765

Tel: (402) 748-3593
Best Time to Call: After 6 PM
Hosts: Norman and Jacquie Lorenz
Location: 130 mi. NW of Omaha
No. of Rooms: 4
No. of Private Baths: 2
Max. No. Sharing Bath: 4
Double/pb: $45
Single/pb: $35

Double/sb: $45
Single/sb: $35
Open: All year
Breakfast: Full
Pets: Yes
Children: Welcome
Smoking: No
Social Drinking: Permitted

Your hosts are retired dairy farmers who run an antiques store and an interior decorating business in addition to this B&B. They make baskets using the local red willow, hence the name Willow Way. Jacquie and Norman built their guest house in 1988 out of lumber from several barns and houses in the area. Osmond is a town of about 800 midway between O'Neal, Nebraska, and Sioux City, Iowa. Ashfall Fossil Beds State Historical Park is thirty miles to the west.. Whether you want to inspect fossils or just relax, your hosts promise to give you old-fashioned small-town hospitality.

NEVADA

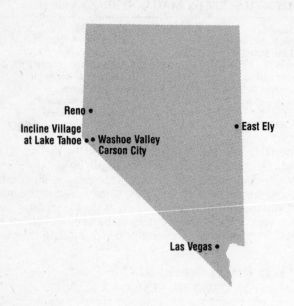

Reno •

Incline Village
at Lake Tahoe • • Washoe Valley
Carson City

• East Ely

Las Vegas •

Steptoe Valley Inn ✪
P.O. BOX 151110, 220 EAST 11TH STREET, EAST ELY, NEVADA 89315-1110

Tel: **(702) 289-8687 June–Sept.;**
  (702) 435-1196 (Oct.–May)
Hosts: **Jane and Norman Lindley**
Location: **70 mi. W of Great Basin
  National Park**
No. of Rooms: **5**
No. of Private Baths: **5**
Double/pb: **$77.78**
Single/pb: **$66.70**

Open: **June–Sept.**
Breakfast: **Full**
Credit Cards: **AMEX, MC, VISA**
Pets: **No**
Children: **By arrangement**
Smoking: **No**
Social Drinking: **Permitted**
Foreign Languages: **Spanish**

This inn opened in July 1991 after major reconstruction. Located near
the Nevada Northern Railway Museum, it was originally Ely City
Grocery of 1907. The five second-floor rooms have country decor and
private balconies, and the elegant Victorian dining room and library
are downstairs. The large yard has mature trees, gazebo, and rose

garden. Norman is an airline captain and ex-rancher and Jane is a retired stewardess and local tour guide. Their guests can enjoy cool nights, scenic countryside, the "Ghost Train of Old Ely," the Great Basin National Park, and Cave Lake State Park or just relax on the veranda!

Las Vegas B&B ✪

CONTACT: BED AND BREAKFAST INTERNATIONAL, P.O. BOX 282910, SAN FRANCISCO, CALIFORNIA 94128-2910

Tel: (415) 696-1690; (800) 872-4500	Double/sb: $50
Best Time to Call: 9 AM–4 PM	Single/sb: $45
Host: Sharene Z. Klein	Open: All year
No. of Rooms: 4	Breakfast: Full
No. of Private Baths: 2	Pets: No
Max. No. Sharing Bath: 3	Children: Swimmers only
Double/pb: $65	Smoking: Permitted
Single/pb: $52	Social Drinking: Permitted

Located a few minutes from the fabled "Strip" of hotels, casinos, and restaurants is this two-story contemporary home. The quiet, residential neighborhood is a welcome respite from the 24-hour hoopla available nearby. You are welcome to use your host's swimming pool.

Deer Run Ranch Bed and Breakfast ✪

5440 EASTLAKE BOULEVARD, WASHOE VALLEY, CARSON CITY, NEVADA 89704

Tel: (702) 882-3643	Reduced Rates: $10 less Mon.–Thurs.
Best Time to Call: 6 AM–9 AM, 6 PM–9 PM	Breakfast: Full
	Credit Cards: AMEX, MC, VISA
Hosts: David and Muffy Vhay	Pets: No
Location: 8 mi. N of Carson City	Children: Welcome, over 12
No. of Rooms: 2	Smoking: No
No. of Private Baths: 2	Social Drinking: Permitted
Double/pb: $85	Minimum Stay: 2 nights, holidays and special events weekends
Open: All year	

Deer Run Ranch, a working alfalfa farm, overlooks Washoe Lake and the Sierra Nevada Mountains. Navajo rugs, old photographs, and paintings by well-known local artists grace the comfortable guest areas, lending western ambience to this house designed and built by your host, who is an architect. Your hosts also have a pottery studio, woodshop, and large garden on the premises. Things to do in the area include skiing, biking, hiking, and hang gliding; Washoe Lake State Park is next door. For fine dining, casino hopping, and entertainment, Lake Tahoe, Reno, Virginia City, and Carson City are only minutes away.

NEW HAMPSHIRE

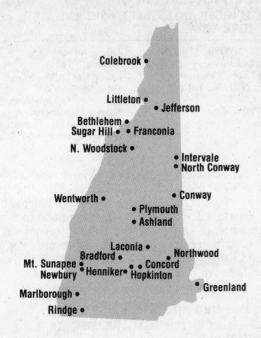

New Hampshire Bed & Breakfast ✪
128 SOUTH HOOP POLE ROAD, GUILFORD, CONNECTICUT 06437

Tel: **(800) 582-0853**
Best Time to Call: **9 AM–8 PM**
Coordinator: **Ernie Taddei**
States/Regions Covered:
   **Connecticut—Statewide, Maine,
   Massachusetts, New Hampshire,
   Rhode Island, Vermont**

Descriptive Directory: **$2**
Rates (Single/Double):
   Modest: **$35–$50 / $40–$50**
   Average: **$35–$50 / $50–$65**
   Luxury: **$60–$85 / $65–$90**
Credit Cards: **MC, VISA**

Here is New Hampshire travel planning made easy. Just one call puts
you in touch with more than 75 locations convenient to the state's
breathtaking scenery, four-season recreation, tax-free shopping outlets, and other exciting attractions. Hosts are close to all schools and

colleges. Experience 18th-century Colonial inns, spacious lakefront homes, large working farms, and ocean and mountainside residences—all with gracious owner hospitality.

Glynn House Victorian Inn ✪
P.O. BOX 719, 43 HIGHLAND STREET, ASHLAND, NEW HAMPSHIRE 03217

Tel: **(603) 968-3775; (800) 637-9599**	Open: **All year**
Best Time to Call: **Anytime**	Breakfast: **Full**
Hosts: **Karol and Betsy Paterman**	Credit Cards: **MC, VISA**
Location: **60 mi. N of Manchester**	Pets: **No**
No. of Rooms: **6**	Children: **Welcome, over 5**
No. of Private Baths: **4**	Smoking: **Restricted**
Double/sb: **$75**	Social Drinking: **Permitted**
Double/pb: **$85**	Foreign Languages: **Polish, Russian**
Single/pb: **$75**	

Built in 1896, this gracious Queen Anne Victorian is shadowed by the majestic White Mountains and nestled among the Squam Lakes—where the movie *On Golden Pond* was filmed. The elegant interior is enhanced by ornate oak woodwork and fine antique furnishings. For a romantic experience, a hearty breakfast is served on a setting of embroidered tapestry and fine china. Afterward, enjoy boating, swimming, and fishing, or hike the scenic mountain trails. In winter, ski Waterville, Loon, or Tenney Mountain, all close by.

Candlelite Inn Bed and Breakfast ✪
R.R.1 BOX 408, OLD CENTER ROAD, BRADFORD, NEW HAMPSHIRE 03221

Tel: **(603) 938-5571**	Hosts: **Les and Marilyn Gordon**
Best Time to Call: **Evenings**	Location: **20 mi. W of Concord**

CANDLELITE INN

No. of Rooms: **6**
No. of Private Baths: **6**
Double/pb: **$65–$75**
Single/pb: **$55–$65**
Open: **All year**
Reduced Rates: **Available**

Breakfast: **Full**
Credit Cards: **DISC, MC, VISA**
Pets: **No**
Children: **Welcome**
Smoking: **No**
Social Drinking: **Permitted**

Candlelite is an 1897 Victorian inn nestled on three acres in the Lake Sunapee region. True to this B&B's name, your hosts serve a candlelit breakfast in the lovely dining room or in the sun room overlooking the pond. On a lazy summer day sip lemonade on the gazebo porch; on a chilly winter evening drink hot chocolate by a warm, cozy fire in the parlor. The inn is just minutes from three ski areas, shopping, antiquing, and restaurants. Les enjoys woodworking and tole painting, while Marilyn pursues cross stitching, quilting, and crafts.

Monadnock B&B ✪
1 MONADNOCK STREET, COLEBROOK, NEW HAMPSHIRE 03576

Tel: **(603) 237-8216**
Best Time to Call: **8 AM–9 PM**
Hosts: **Barbara and Wendell Woodard**
Location: **1 block from the junction of Rtes. 3 and 26**
No. of Rooms: **7**
Max. No. Sharing Bath: **4**
Double/sb: **$40**
Single/sb: **$30**

Open: **All year**
Reduced Rates: **15% weekly**
Breakfast: **Full**
Pets: **Sometimes**
Children: **Welcome (crib)**
Smoking: **Permitted**
Social Drinking: **Permitted**
Airport/Station Pickup: **Yes**

When Wendell was in the Air Force, the Woodards lived all over the world, and their house is decorated with pieces collected in Europe and Asia. Now they have settled in New Hampshire's North Country, within walking distance of Vermont and only a 15-minute drive from Canada. Wendell cheerfully directs skiers, hunters, fishermen, and golfers to all his favorite haunts. But first, Barbara will ply guests with a hearty breakfast, featuring specialties such as sausage quiche, pancakes, and omelets, accompanied by endless supplies of coffee and tea.

The Foothills Farm ✪
P.O. BOX 1368, CONWAY, NEW HAMPSHIRE 03818

Tel: **(207) 935-3799**
Best Time to Call: **Early evenings**
Hosts: **Kevin Early and Theresa Rovere**
Location: **40 mi. W of Portland**
No. of Rooms: **4**
Max. No. Sharing Bath: **2**
Double/sb: **$42–$48**
Single/sb: **$32**
Open: **All year**
Reduced Rates: **Available; 10% seniors**

Breakfast: **Full**
Credit Cards: **AMEX, MC, VISA**
Pets: **Sometimes**
Children: **Welcome**
Smoking: **No**
Social Drinking: **Permitted**
Minimum Stay: **2 nights weekends, during fall foliage, and holidays**
Airport/Station Pickup: **Yes**

This restored 1850s clapboard farmhouse is located on a quiet back road in the foothills of the White Mountains. The house is surrounded by flowers, a vegetable garden, and asparagus fields. The well-groomed grounds also include a trout stream and plenty of room to bike or cross-country ski. Bedrooms are furnished in period antiques, and one has a fireplace. Guests are welcome to relax in the den, where they'll find books and a crackling fire. In warmer weather, the screened-in porch overlooking the fields and gardens is a favorite spot. Breakfast specialties such as eggs Benedict with home fries, and blueberry pancakes with sausage are served in a country kitchen, which has an antique stove and pine paneling. Kevin and Theresa have bicycles to lend and are glad to direct you to the sights of this scenic region. Scores of restaurants, factory outlets, and canoeing, hiking, and ski areas are also nearby.

Mountain Valley Manner ✪
P.O. BOX 1649, 148 WASHINGTON STREET, WESTSIDE ROAD, CONWAY, NEW HAMPSHIRE 03818

Tel: **(603) 447-3988**
Best Time to Call: **8 AM–9 PM**
Hosts: **Bob, Lynn, and Amy Lein**
Location: **125 mi. N of Boston, Mass.**
No. of Rooms: **4**
No. of Private Baths: **2**
Max. No. Sharing Bath: **4**
Double/pb: **$55–$78**
Single/pb: **$45–$68**
Double/sb: **$45–$78**
Single/sb: **$35**

Suites: **$58–$88**
Open: **All year**
Reduced Rates: **10%, after 3 days; 20%, after 4 days**
Breakfast: **Full**
Credit Cards: **DISC, MC, VISA**
Pets: **No**
Children: **Welcome**
Smoking: **No**
Social Drinking: **Permitted**
Station Pickup: **Yes**

This friendly restored country Victorian at the Kancamagus Highway is in sight of two romantic covered Kissing Bridges and Mt. Washington. Elegant, individually decorated, air-conditioned guest rooms are furnished with numerous antiques. Full country breakfast, afternoon tea/beverages, and hot chocolate before bed are all included. Refresh yourself in the pool, swim in the pristine Saco River across the street, stroll through Lynn's Victorian gardens, or mosey over to the shopping outlets. Just minutes to five ski areas, miniature and PGA golf, water slides, hiking, and the health club.

Blanche's B&B ✪
EASTON VALLEY ROAD, FRANCONIA, NEW HAMPSHIRE 03580

Tel: **(603) 823-7061**
Best Time to Call: **Before 9 PM**
Hosts: **Brenda Shannon and John Vail**
Location: **5 mi. SW of Franconia**
No. of Rooms: **5**

No. of Private Baths: **2**
Max. No. Sharing Bath: **4**
Double/pb: **$80–$85**
Double/sb: **$60–$65**
Single/sb: **$35–$50**

Open: **All year**
Reduced Rates: **Weekly, groups**
Breakfast: **Full**
Credit Cards: **AMEX, MC, VISA**
Other Meals: **Available to groups**
Pets: **No**
Children: **Welcome**

Smoking: **No**
Social Drinking: **Permitted**
Minimum Stay: **2 nights holiday weekends, Christmas vacation week, fall foliage season**
Airport/Station Pickup: **Yes**

Set in a meadow near the Appalachian Trail, this steep-gabled, Victorian farmhouse, circa 1887, is decorated with family pieces and auction finds. Brenda and John provide cotton linens on comfortable beds, a hearty breakfast, and good advice about the nearby hiking and cross-country ski trails. Franconia Notch and Cannon Mountain are a 10-minute drive. Your hosts will be happy to suggest the best spots for antiques, crafts, bird-watching, or help you discover the simple pleasures.of life in the White Mountains.

Bungay Jar Bed & Breakfast

EASTON VALLEY ROAD, P.O. BOX 15, FRANCONIA, NEW HAMPSHIRE 03580

Tel: **(603) 823-7775**
Hosts: **Kate Kerivan and Lee Strimbeck**
Location: **6 mi. from Rte. I-93, Exit 38**
No. of Rooms: **6**
No. of Private Baths: **4**
Max. No. Sharing Bath: **4**
Double/pb: **$80–$120**
Double/sb: **$60–$75**
Single/sb: **$50**
Open: **All year**

Breakfast: **Full**
Other Meals: **Available for groups**
Credit Cards: **AMEX, DISC, MC, VISA**
Pets: **No**
Children: **Welcome, over 6**
Smoking: **No**
Social Drinking: **Permitted**
Minimum Stay: **2 nights foliage season, holiday weekends**

Built in 1969 from an 18th-century barn, this post-and-beam house is nestled among twelve acres of woodland bounded by a river, forest, and spectacular mountain views. In winter, guests are greeted by a crackling fire and the aroma of mulled cider in the two-story living room reminiscent of a hayloft. Antique country furnishings (many for sale) enhance the decor. Apple pancakes served with local maple syrup are a specialty, as are homemade breads, preserves, fruit compotes, granola, and imaginative egg dishes. Refreshments of cider and cheese are served each afternoon. Your hosts are avid hikers and skiers, so you are sure to benefit from their expert knowledge.

Ayres Homestead Bed & Breakfast ✪
47 PARK AVENUE, GREENLAND, NEW HAMPSHIRE 03840

Tel: **(603) 436-5992**	Single/sb: **$45**
Hosts: **David and Priscilla Engel**	Suites: **$95**
Location: **3 mi. W of Portsmouth**	Open: **All year**
No. of Rooms: **3**	Breakfast: **Full**
No. of Private Baths: **1**	Pets: **Sometimes**
Max. No. Sharing Bath: **4**	Children: **Welcome**
Double/pb: **$55**	Smoking: **No**
Single/pb: **$50**	Social Drinking: **Permitted**
Double/sb: **$50**	

The Thomas Ayres House, begun in 1737 as a two-room post-and-beam structure, has been enlarged and remodeled many times in its 250-year history. Priscilla and Dave will tell you of the famous people, including Paul Revere, George Washington, and John Adams, who passed by its doors. Set on six acres on the historic village green, its nine rooms have wainscoting, exposed beams, and wide board floors; seven have fireplaces. The bedrooms are made cozy with antiques, braided rugs, afghans, and rockers. Breakfast is served in the dining room on an antique table set in front of a brick fireplace with artfully displayed pewterware and ironware.

Henniker House ✪
BOX 191, 2 RAMSDELL ROAD, HENNIKER, NEW HAMPSHIRE 03242

Tel: **(603) 428-3198**	Single/sb: **$55**
Best Time to Call: **Anytime**	Open: **All year**
Host: **Bertina Williams**	Reduced Rates: **10% after 7th night**
Location: **14 mi. W of Concord**	Breakfast: **Full**
No. of Rooms: **4**	Other Meals: **Available**
No. of Private Baths: **3**	Credit Cards: **MC, VISA**
Max. No. Sharing Bath: **3**	Pets: **No**
Double/pb: **$65**	Children: **Welcome**
Single/pb: **$60**	Smoking: **No**
Double/sb: **$60**	Social Drinking: **Permitted**

Bertina's very special 19th-century Victorian offers old-world charm with modern amenities. A Jacuzzi and seasonal pool open onto a 50-foot deck that overlooks the Contoocook River. Henniker is the site of New England College and the Fibre Studio of Arts and Crafts. Activities abound, from music festivals and theater to hiking, fishing, and skiing. Best of all is waking to the aroma of Bertina's homemade breakfast served in the bright, airy solarium, with its scenic river view.

Windyledge Bed and Breakfast ✪
1264 HATFIELD ROAD, HOPKINTON, NEW HAMPSHIRE 03229

Tel: **(603) 746-4054**	Single/sb: **$45**
Best Time to Call: **Anytime**	Open: **All year**
Hosts: **Dick and Susan Vogt**	Reduced Rates: **15% after 7th night**
Location: **11 mi. W of Concord**	Breakfast: **Full**
No. of Rooms: **3**	Credit Cards: **MC, VISA**
No. of Private Baths: **1**	Pets: **No**
Max. No. Sharing Bath: **4**	Children: **Welcome**
Double/pb: **$75**	Smoking: **No**
Single/pb: **$65**	Social Drinking: **Permitted**
Double/sb: **$55**	Airport/Station Pickup: **Yes**

This elegant hilltop Colonial is surrounded by nine acres of fields and woods, bordered by picturesque hills and the White Mountains beyond. Dick's delicious apricot glaze French toast or honey-and-spice blueberry pancakes are served at your pleasure on the airy sun porch or outside deck or in the country dining room. Nearby are lakes, a golf course, skiing, craft shops, and numerous restaurants. After a full day's activities, return "home" to an invigorating dip in the pool or to a movie from Dick's vast videocassette collection.

view of the mountains, and a crystal clear lake—the third largest in the state. The house has a cathedral ceiling and oak beams, floors, and trim; the sunny, open rooms are decorated with comfortable furniture and antiques, for homeyness. In warm weather, breakfast is served on the large covered deck off the kitchen. Guests are encouraged to walk down to the Gouins' private dock, where they'll find a canoe and rowboat, and chairs for lounging. For hikers, the White Mountains are 20 minutes away.

The Beal House Inn ✪
247 WEST MAIN STREET, LITTLETON, NEW HAMPSHIRE 03561

Tel: **(603) 444-2661**
Best Time to Call: **8 AM–10 PM**
Hosts: **Catherine and Jean-Marie (John) Fisher-Motheu**
Location: **90 mi. N of Concord in the White Mountains**
No. of Rooms: **13**
No. of Private Baths: **9**
Max. No. Sharing Bath: **4**
Double/pb: **$50–$80**
Single/pb: **$50**
Double/sb: **$55–$60**
Single/sb: **$45**

Suites: **$85**
Open: **All year except Nov.**
Reduced Rates: **15% groups and extended stays**
Breakfast: **Continental**
Other Meals: **Available**
Credit Cards: **MC, VISA**
Pets: **No**
Children: **Welcome**
Smoking: **No**
Social Drinking: **Permitted**
Station Pickup: **Yes**
Foreign Languages: **French**

Experience the White Mountains in this 1833 landmark! An inn since 1938, Beal House has charming guest rooms cozy with antiques, canopy beds, down comforters, and special touches. With native artwork and antiques for sale, the inn is a living shop as well. Breakfast gatherings by candlelight feature true Belgian waffles prepared by your Belgian-born host. Dinner in the jazzy little dining room consists of robust European fare. Beal House is located three hours from both Montreal and Boston, close to skiing, hiking, fishing, golf, historic sites, and other attractions.

Peep-Willow Farm ✪
51 BIXBY STREET, MARLBOROUGH, NEW HAMPSHIRE 03455

Tel: **(603) 876-3807**
Best Time to Call: **Before 8 AM; after 8 PM**
Host: **Noel Aderer**
Location: **7 mi. E of Keene**
No. of Rooms: **3**
Max. No. Sharing Bath: **4**
Double/sb: **$50**

Single/sb: **$30**
Open: **All year**
Breakfast: **Full**
Pets: **No**
Children: **Welcome**
Smoking: **No**
Social Drinking: **Permitted**
Airport/Station Pickup: **Yes**

Noel Aderer has a new Colonial farmhouse on a working thorough-bred horse farm. She raises and trains horses for competition, and while there is plenty of room for petting and admiring, guests are not permitted to ride. Peep-Willow is named after horses number one and two, respectively. It is a charming place, with lots of wood accents and antiques. Breakfast specialties include French toast, with local maple syrup, and bacon and eggs. Guests are welcome to watch farm chores, visit the horses, and enjoy a cup of coffee with Noel, who has done everything from working on a kibbutz to training polo ponies for a maharajah.

Blue Goose Inn
ROUTE 103B, P.O. BOX 117, MT. SUNAPEE, NEW HAMPSHIRE 03772

Tel: **(603) 763-5519**	Single/sb: **$41.50**
Best Time to Call: **Before noon**	Open: **All year**
Hosts: **Meryl and Ronald Caldwell**	Breakfast: **Full**
Location: **10 mi. From I-89**	Credit Cards: **MC, VISA**
No. of Rooms: **5**	Pets: **No**
No. of Private Baths: **4**	Children: **Welcome**
Max. No. Sharing Bath: **3**	Smoking: **No**
Double/pb: **$55**	Social Drinking: **Permitted**
Single/pb: **$45**	Airport/Station Pickup: **Yes**
Double/sb: **$50**	

This well-restored, early 19th-century Colonial farmhouse is located on 3½ acres along Lake Sunapee, at the base of Mt. Sunapee. The cozy, comfortable guest rooms are furnished in a quaint, country style. Make yourself at home in any of the common areas. The living room has a fireplace, TV, VCR, and book and video library; the card and game room has plenty of diversions; there's refrigerator space in the kitchen, and the porch, weather permitting, is ideal for breakfast and snacks. Kids will have fun in the summer playhouse. The Mt. Sunapee area is a mini-resort for vacationers of all ages, offering boating, swimming, hiking, downhill and cross-country skiing, snow-mobiling, crafts fairs, antiquing, and much more.

The 1806 House ✪
RT 103 TRAFFIC CIRCLE, NEWBURY, NEW HAMPSHIRE 03255
(MAILING ADDRESS: P.O. BOX 54, MT. SUNAPEE,
NEW HAMPSHIRE 03772)

Tel: **(603) 763-4969**	Double/pb: **$85**
Best Time to Call: **8 AM–10 PM**	Open: **All year**
Hosts: **Gene and Lane Bellman**	Reduced Rates: **10% seniors**
Location: **100 mi. NNW of Boston**	Breakfast: **Full, Continental**
No. of Rooms: **5**	Credit Cards: **MC, VISA**
No. of Private Baths: **4**	Pets: **No**

Children: **Welcome, over 6**
Smoking: **No**
Social Drinking: **Permitted**

Minimum Stay: **2 nights**
Airport/Station Pickup: **Yes**

Nestled in the unspoiled New Hampshire countryside at the base of Mt. Sunapee, the 1806 House provides sophisticated country lodging. Recently restored to its original condition, the home has beamed ceilings, wide plank floors, and a charming living room complete with candlelight, cozy couches and wing chairs, and a wood-burning stove. A grand piano and classical music offer just the right ingredients for a romantic getaway. Every room has been tastefully decorated with period furnishings including brass beds adorned with fine linens, down comforters, and soft, plush pillows. A special gourmet breakfast is served in a charming country dining room on the finest china and silver. No breakfast would be complete without candlelight and a Pavarotti aria. Now explore the area.

Every season brings an array of activities—from skiing and hiking to boating and swimming at the beach just steps away across the road.

The Buttonwood Inn ✪

P.O. BOX 1817, MT. SURPRISE ROAD, NORTH CONWAY, NEW HAMPSHIRE 03860

Tel: **(603) 356-2625; (800) 258-2625**
Hosts: **Claudia and Peter Needham**
Location: **1½ mi. from Rte. 16**
No. of Rooms: **9**
No. of Private Baths: **3**
Max. No. Sharing Bath: **4**
Double/pb: **$76–$100**
Single/pb: **$53–$80**
Double/sb: **$52–$90**
Single/sb: **$45–$80**
Open: **All year**

Reduced Rates: **Available; families**
Breakfast: **Full**
Other Meals: **Available Jan. and Feb.**
Credit Cards: **AMEX, DC, MC, VISA**
Pets: **No**
Children: **Welcome, over 3**
Smoking: **Restricted**
Social Drinking: **Permitted**
Minimum Stay: **2 nights weekends Jan. and Feb.; 3 nights holiday weekends**

Enjoy our 1820s cape in its secluded spot on Mt. Surprise. Only two miles from North Conway. Nine uniquely appointed guest rooms, fireplaced common rooms, gardens, pool, cross-country skiing from our doorstep. Full breakfast. Dinners served in winter. Perfect spot for romantic getaways, families, groups, reunions, or weddings.

The Center Chimney—1787 ✪

RIVER ROAD, P.O. BOX 1220, NORTH CONWAY, NEW HAMPSHIRE 03860

Tel: **(603) 356-6788**
Best Time to Call: **Anytime**
Host: **Farley Ames Whitley**
Location: **120 mi. N of Boston**

No. of Rooms: **4**
Max. No. Sharing Bath: **4**
Double/sb: **$44–$55**
Single/sb: **$38**

Open: **All year**
Reduced Rates: **$5 day after midweek stay**
Breakfast: **Continental**
Pets: **No**

Children: **Welcome**
Smoking: **Permitted**
Social Drinking: **Permitted**
Minimum Stay: **2 nights holiday weekends**

Featured on calendars and postcards for its distinctive construction, this B&B is one of the oldest center chimney capes in North Conway, a quaint New England village near the Saco River. From canoeing to rock climbing, there's recreation here throughout the year. Farley's cozy living room has a fireplace, piano, and cable TV. Continental breakfast is served buffet-style in the kitchen.

The Victorian Harvest Inn ✪

28 LOCUST LANE, BOX 1763, NORTH CONWAY, NEW HAMPSHIRE 03860

Tel: **(603) 356-3548; (800) 642-0749**
Best Time to Call: **10 AM–8 PM**
Hosts: **Linda and Robert Dahlberg**
Location: **140 mi. N of Boston, Ma.**
No. of Rooms: **6**
No. of Private Baths: **4**
Max. No. Sharing Bath: **4**
Double/pb: **$65–$85**
Single/pb: **$55–$75**
Double/sb: **$55–$65**
Single/sb: **$45**
Suite: **$120–$130**

Open: **All year**
Reduced rates: **Available**
Breakfast: **Full**
Credit Cards: **AMEX, DISC, MC, VISA**
Pets: **No**
Children: **Welcome, over 6**
Smoking: **No**
Social Drinking: **Permitted**
Minimum Stay: **2 days, foliage and holidays**
Airport/Station Pickup: **Yes**

With its lush landscaped grounds and views of both the Moat and the nearby Presidential Ranges, this multi-gabled 1853 Victorian is the perfect getaway. Start your day with a country breakfast which could consist of Belgian waffles, French toast, or Bob's apple cake. Guests can listen to music, read, play the piano, or relax by the pool. All rooms have air-conditioning and are decorated with antiques and homemade quilts. On each bed, you will find a teddy bear to adopt for the length of your stay.

Wilderness Inn ✪

ROUTES 3 AND 112, RFD 1, BOX 69, NORTH WOODSTOCK, NEW HAMPSHIRE 03262

Tel: **(603) 745-3890**
Best Time to Call: **7 AM–10 PM**
Hosts: **Michael and Rosanna Yarnell**
Location: **120 mi. N of Boston**
No. of Rooms: **8**
No. of Private Baths: **6**
Max. No. Sharing Bath: **4**

Double/pb: **$50–$80**
Single/pb: **$45–$70**
Double/sb: **$40–$65**
Single/sb: **$35–$55**
Suites: **$60–$90**
Open: **All year**
Reduced Rates: **Midweek; off-season**

Breakfast: **Full**
Credit Cards: **AMEX, MC, VISA**
Pets: **No**
Children: **Welcome**
Smoking: **Permitted**

Social Drinking: **Permitted**
Airport/Station Pickup: **Yes**
Foreign Languages: **French, Italian, Bengali, Amharic**

Escape from it all at this mountainside retreat where, depending on the season, you can ski, swim, ride a bike, and hike to your heart's content. Restaurants, craft shops, and a golf course are all nearby. Fresh fruit, café au lait, and cranberry-walnut pancakes will lure you out of bed in the morning, but if you prefer, the Yarnells will bring a Continental breakfast to your room.

Meadow Farm
JENNESS POND ROAD, NORTHWOOD, NEW HAMPSHIRE 03261

Tel: **(603) 942-8619**
Hosts: **Douglas and Janet Briggs**
Location: **18 mi. E of Concord**
No. of Rooms: **3**
Max. No. Sharing Bath: **4**
Double/sb: **$60**
Single/sb: **$45**
Open: **All year**

Reduced Rates: **Families**
Breakfast: **Full**
Credit Cards: **AMEX**
Pets: **Sometimes**
Children: **Welcome**
Smoking: **No**
Social Drinking: **Permitted**

Meadow Farm is set on 50 acres of quiet woods and horse pastures. The house is an authentic New England Colonial dating back to 1770, with wide-pine floors, beamed ceilings, and old fireplaces. In the morning, a country breakfast of homemade breads, seasonal fruit, and local syrup is served in the keeping room. Guests are invited to relax on the private beach on an adjacent lake. The property also has plenty of wooded trails for long walks or cross-country skiing. Meadow Farm is an ideal location for those en route to Concord, the seacoast, or the mountains.

Grassy Pond House
RINDGE, NEW HAMPSHIRE 03461

Tel: **(603) 899-5166, 899-5167**
Best Time to Call: **Mornings**
Hosts: **Carmen Linares and Robert Multer**
Location: **60 mi. NW of Boston**
No. of Rooms: **3**
No. of Private Baths: **2**
Max. No. Sharing Bath: **4**
Double/pb: **$65**

Double/sb: **$55**
Single/sb: **$45**
Open: **All year**
Breakfast: **Full**
Pets: **No**
Children: **Welcome, over 14**
Smoking: **No**
Social Drinking: **Permitted**

This secluded 19th-century farmhouse is set among 150 acres of woods and fields. The house has been restored, enlarged, and decorated in period pieces. Guest quarters, overlooking the gardens and lake, feature a private entrance and a living room with fireplace. Breakfast specialties include pancakes with local maple syrup, fresh eggs and bacon, and plenty of good Colombian coffee. This setting, high in the Monadnock region, is perfect for hiking, skiing, boating, fishing, and swimming.

The Tokfarm ✪
BOX 1124, R.R. 2, RINDGE, NEW HAMPSHIRE 03461

Tel: **(603) 899-6646**	Open: **Apr. 1–Nov. 29**
Best Time to Call: **Early mornings;**	Breakfast: **Continental**
evenings	Pets: **No**
Host: **Mrs. W. B. Nottingham**	Children: **No**
Location: **50 mi. NW of Boston**	Smoking: **No**
No. of Rooms: **5**	Social Drinking: **Permitted**
Max. No. Sharing Bath: **4**	Airport/Station Pickup: **Yes**
Double/sb: **$35–$45**	Foreign Languages: **Dutch, French,**
Single/sb: **$22**	**German**

This 150-year-old farmhouse has a spectacular view of three states from its 1,400-foot hilltop. Mt. Monadnock, the second most climbed peak in the world (Mt. Fuji is first), is practically in its backyard! Mrs. Nottingham raises Christmas trees and is a world traveler. She'll recommend things to keep you busy. Don't miss the lovely Cathedral of the Pines. Franklin Pierce College is nearby.

The Hilltop Inn ✪
SUGAR HILL, NEW HAMPSHIRE 03585

Tel: **(603) 823-5695**	Open: **All year**
Hosts: **Mike and Meri Hern**	Breakfast: **Full**
Location: **2½ mi. W of Franconia**	Pets: **Welcome**
No. of Rooms: **6**	Children: **Welcome, over 4**
No. of Private Baths: **6**	Smoking: **Restricted**
Double/pb: **$60–$85**	Social Drinking: **Permitted**
Single/pb: **$50–$75**	Airport/Station Pickup: **Yes**
Suites: **$85–$110**	

The Hilltop Inn is a sprawling, 19th-century Victorian located in a small, friendly village. Inside, you'll find a warm, cozy atmosphere, comfortable furnishings, and lots of antiques. The kitchen is the heart of the house in more ways than one. In the morning, homemade muffins are served fresh from the old-fashioned Garland stove. In the evening, the sunsets from the deck are breathtaking. Your hosts are professional caterers and are pleased to cater to you. Fine dining Wed.–Sat. 6–8 PM in the Victorian candlelit dining room. Local attractions include Franconia Notch, White Mountain National Forest, North Conway, great skiing, and spectacular foliage.

Hilltop Acres ✪
**EAST SIDE AND BUFFALO ROAD, WENTWORTH,
NEW HAMPSHIRE 03282**

Tel: **(603) 764-5896**	Reduced Rates: **Available**
Host: **Marie A. Kauk**	Breakfast: **Continental, plus**
Location: **60 mi. NW of Concord**	Credit Cards: **MC, VISA**
No. of Rooms: **4**	Pets: **Sometimes**
No. of Private Baths: **4**	Children: **Welcome**
Double/pb: **$65**	Smoking: **No**
Single/pb: **$65**	Social Drinking: **Permitted**
Guest Cottage: **$80–$160**	Airport/Station Pickup: **Yes**
Open: **May 1–Nov. 1**	Foreign Languages: **German**

Hilltop Acres, a peaceful country retreat located in a quaint New England village, is a pleasant, scenic drive from major tourist attractions (e.g., Old Man of the Mountains) in both the lakes and mountain regions. Rooms are comfortable, affording peaceful scenes of the surrounding landscape. Cozy housekeeping cottages are available May through November. A large pine-panelled recreation room with cable TV, piano, fireplace, and games awaits your pleasure, and a spacious well-tended lawn area is suitable for relaxation and outdoor games. There are paintings and antique furniture throughout, as well as an extensive library. Your hostess enjoys travel, painting, and music, and freelances as a legal word processor.

NEW JERSEY

Amanda's Bed & Breakfast Reservation Service ✪
21 SOUTH WOODLAND AVENUE, EAST BRUNSWICK, NEW JERSEY
08816

Tel: (908) 249-4944; fax: (908) 246-1961
Best Time to Call: **Mornings**
Coordinator: **Orie Barr**
States/Regions Covered: **New Jersey—Alloway, Avon-by-the-Sea, Belmar, Cape May, Clinton, Frenchtown, Lambertville, North Wildwood, Ocean City, Pemberton, Stewartsville, White House Station, Woodbine; Pennsylvania—Emmaus, Milford, Chalfont**
Rates: (Single/Double):
Modest: **$50 / $65**
Average: **$80**
Luxury: **$165**
Credit Cards: **MC, VISA**

Amanda's, a reliable source of information for the traveler, ensures that bed and breakfast accommodations meet high standards of comfort, cleanliness, and ambiance. This service seeks to follow the example of the original Amanda—a sailing ship, acclaimed for its cleanliness, that made Baltimore a port of call.

Bed & Breakfast of Princeton—A Reservation Service
P.O. BOX 571, PRINCETON, NEW JERSEY 08542

Tel: **(609) 924-3189; fax: (609) 921-6271**
Coordinator: **John W. Hurley**
States/Regions Covered: **Princeton**

Rates (Single/Double):
  Average: **$40–$55 / $50–$65**
Credit Cards: **No**

Princeton is a lovely town; houses are well set back on carefully tended lawns, screened by towering trees. Some of John's hosts live within walking distance of Princeton University. Nassau Hall, circa 1756, is its oldest building; its chapel is the largest of any at an American university. Nearby corporate parks include national companies, such as RCA, Squibb, and the David Sarnoff Research Center. Restaurants feature every imaginable cuisine, and charming shops offer a wide variety of wares. Personal checks are accepted for deposit or total payment in advance; cash or traveler's checks are required for any balance due.

Down The Shore B&B ◐
201 SEVENTH AVENUE, BELMAR, NEW JERSEY 07719

Tel: **(908) 681-9023**
Best Time to Call: **Before noon**
Hosts: **Annette and Al Bergins**
Location: **1 block from ocean**
No. of rooms: **2**
No. of private baths: **2**
Double p/b: **$65–$75**
Single p/b: **$65–$75**
Open: **All year**

Reduced Rates: **2 day specials, off season**
Breakfast: **Full**
Pets: **No**
Smoking: **No**
Social Drinking: **No**
Minimum Stay: **2 nights in season**
Station Pickup: **Yes**

Down the Shore's name couldn't be more appropriate—this B&B is located one block from the boardwalk and the beach. When you want to get out of the sun, rest up in your comfortable, air-conditioned room, read, play games on the shaded porch, or watch TV in the parlor. Racing fans can choose between the thoroughbreds at Monmouth Park and the trotters at Freehold Raceway, while the culturally inclined can catch world-class entertainment at the Garden State Arts Center. A complete breakfast is served each morning, including fresh fruit, juices, baked casseroles, and homemade granola.

The Abbey Bed and Breakfast ◐
34 GURNEY STREET AND COLUMBIA AVENUE, CAPE MAY, NEW JERSEY 08204

Tel: **(609) 884-4506**
Best Time to Call: **8 AM–5:30 PM**
Hosts: **Jay and Marianne Schatz**

Location: **38 mi. S of Atlantic City**
No. of Rooms: **14**
No. of Private Baths: **14**

Double/pb: **$100–$190**
Single/pb: **$90–$180**
Suites: **$115–$180**
Open: **Apr.–mid-Dec.**
Reduced Rates: **Available**
Breakfast: **Full**

Credit Cards: **DISC, MC, VISA**
Pets: **No**
Children: **Welcome, over 12**
Smoking: **No**
Social Drinking: **Permitted**
Station Pickup: **Yes**

The Abbey consists of two nationally registered buildings, decorated in period style. The main house, built in 1869 by Philadelphia coal baron John McCreary, is a 22-room Gothic revival villa with a 65-foot tower and arched and ruby glass windows. The adjacent Second Empire cottage was built in 1873 for John's son, George. While the furnishings are formal, the attitude is not: guests share their experiences with each other at the family-style breakfast and at late afternoon tea. The beach is a block away, and beach chairs and tags are provided in season. During the summer, croquet games occur on the regulation-size lawn court to the applause of onlookers. Parking is provided either on site or at a lot nearby.

Albert G. Stevens Inn ✪
127 MYRTLE AVENUE, CAPE MAY, NEW JERSEY 08204

Tel: **(609) 884-4717; (800) 890-CATS**
Hosts: **Diane and Curt Diveing Rangen**
Location: **40 mi. S of Atlantic City**
No. of Rooms: **9**
No. of Private Baths: **9**
Double/pb: **$65–$115**
Single/pb: **$65–$85**
Suites: **$160**

Open: **Feb.–Dec.**
Breakfast: **Full**
Credit Cards: **DISC, MC, VISA**
Pets: **No**
Children: **No**
Smoking: **No**
Social Drinking: **Permitted**

Built in 1898, this Queen Anne Victorian boasts an unusual floating staircase and a wraparound veranda where summertime guests can enjoy their two-course breakfasts. Inside, the house is decorated with Victorian treasures, crystal, and porcelain. Cape May's better beaches and the Washington Street Mall are a ten-minute walk away. For a superb end to your day, soak in the 350-gallon hot tub, or relax in the sunroom; herbal tea and refreshments are always available. Stroll through the unusual Cat's garden and experience a feline fantasy.

Barnard-Good House ✪
238 PERRY STREET, CAPE MAY, NEW JERSEY 08204

Tel: **(609) 884-5381**
Best Time to Call: **9 AM–9 PM**
Hosts: **Nan and Tom Hawkins**
No. of Rooms: **1**
No. of Private Baths: **1**
Double/pb: **$85**
Suites: **$115**
Open: **Apr.–Nov.**

Breakfast: **Full**
Pets: **No**
Children: **Welcome, over 14**
Smoking: **No**
Social Drinking: **Permitted**
Minimum Stay: **2 nights spring and fall; 3 nights summer**

trails, and picnic areas. The guest suite occupies the south wing of the house and consists of a small parlor with fireplace and an adjoining bedroom and private bath. In the morning, a help-yourself buffet of hot drinks, homemade breads, muffins, and fresh fruits awaits you. The Jeremiah J. Yereance House is just five minutes from the Meadowlands Sports Complex.

Bed & Breakfast Adventures ✪
SUITE 132, 2310 CENTRAL AVENUE, NORTH WILDWOOD, NEW JERSEY 08260

Tel: (609) 522-4000; (800) 992-2632
Best Time to Call: 9 AM–5 PM
Coordinator: Diane DiFilippo
States/Regions Covered: All New Jersey and Eastern Pennsylvania: New Jersey: Cape May, Flemington, Morristown, Ocean Grove/Spring Lake, Princeton, Trenton; Pennsylvania: Allentown/Bethlehem, Lancaster, Reading/Berks Cty.

Descriptive Directory of B&Bs: $5
Rates (Single/Double):
  Modest: 40–$55
  Average: $60–$75
  Luxury: $115–$295
Credit Cards: AMEX, DISC, MC, VISA
Minimum Stay: Sometimes

Diane provides an economical alternative to hotels with her efficient and friendly reservation service. Thanks to its wide range of accommodations—all personally inspected for cleanliness, comfort and graciousness—Bed & Breakfast Adventures can meet any request, whether it be a one-night stopover or the relocation of corporate personnel.

Candlelight Inn ✪
2310 CENTRAL AVENUE, NORTH WILDWOOD, NEW JERSEY 08260

Tel: (609) 522-6200
Best Time to Call: 8 AM–11 PM
Hosts: Paul and Diane DiFilippo
Location: 7 mi. N of Cape May
No. of Rooms: 8
No. of Private Baths: 8
Double/pb: $80–$235
Open: Feb.–Dec.
Reduced Rates: 10% seniors; weekly

Breakfast: Full
Credit Cards: AMEX, DISC, MC, VISA
Pets: No
Children: No
Smoking: No
Social Drinking: Permitted
Airport/Station Pickup: Yes
Foreign Languages: French
Minimum Stay: 3 nights July and Aug.

Leaming Rice, Sr., built this Queen Anne Victorian at the turn of the century. The house remained in the family until Diane and Paul restored it and created a bed and breakfast. Large oak doors with beveled glass invite you into the main vestibule, which has a fireplace nook. A wide variety of original gas lighting fixtures may be found throughout the house. Guest rooms have fresh flowers and are furnished with period pieces and antiques. Breakfast is served in the dining room with a built-in oak breakfront, and chestnut pocket doors. A hot tub and sun deck are special spots for relaxing. In the afternoon, enjoy tea and cookies on the wide veranda. This elegant inn is convenient to the beaches, boardwalk, and historic Cape May.

BarnaGate Bed & Breakfast ✪
637 WESLEY AVENUE, OCEAN CITY, NEW JERSEY 08226

Tel: **(609) 391-9366**
Hosts: **The Barna family**
Location: **10 mi. S of Atlantic City**
No. of Rooms: **5**
No. of Private Baths: **2**
Max. No. Sharing Bath: **4**
Double/pb: **$65–$75**
Double/sb: **$65–$70**
Open: **All year**

Breakfast: **Continental**
Credit Cards: **MC, VISA**
Pets: **No**
Children: **Welcome, over 10**
Smoking: **No**
Social Drinking: **Permitted**
Minimum Stay: **Summer holiday weekends**
Airport/Station Pickup: **Yes**

This 1895 seashore Victorian, painted a soft peach with mauve and burgundy trim, is only three and a half blocks from the ocean. The attractively furnished bedrooms have paddle fans, antique furnishings, pretty quilts, and wicker accessories. You'll enjoy the homey atmosphere and the sensitive hospitality; if you want privacy, it is respected, if you want company, it is offered. Antique shops, great restaurants, the quaint charm of Cape May, and the excitement of Atlantic City are close by.

Horseback riding, skiing, hiking, and golf are available nearby. Judy and Jerris will gladly direct you to the Sandia Ski Area, Albuquerque's Old Town, Sante Fe, the Indian Cultural Center, and other points of interest. Prize-winning coffee cake, muffins, and more are breakfast delights. Cheese and wine or coffee, tea, and cookies are served in the evening.

The Corner House ✪

9121 JAMES PLACE NORTHEAST, ALBUQUERQUE, NEW MEXICO 87111

Tel: (505) 298-5800
Host: Jean Thompson
Location: 4 mi. N of I-40
No. of Rooms: 3
No. of Private Baths: 1
Max. No. Sharing Bath: 3
Double/pb: $50–$65
Double/sb: $40–$50
Single/sb: $30–$35

Open: All year
Reduced Rates: 10% families, seniors
Breakfast: Full
Other Meals: Available
Pets: Sometimes
Children: Welcome (crib)
Smoking: No
Social Drinking: Permitted

Jean welcomes you to her handsome Southwestern-style home, decorated in a delightful mix of antiques and collectibles. Breakfast specialties include Jean's homemade muffins. The Corner House is located in a quiet residential neighborhood within view of the magnificent Sandia Mountains. It is convenient to Old Town Albuquerque, Santa Fe, many Indian pueblos, and the launch site for the International Balloon Fiesta.

Rio Grande House ✪

3100 RIO GRANDE BOULEVARD NORTHWEST, ALBUQUERQUE, NEW MEXICO 87107

Tel: (505) 345-0120
Best Time to Call: Anytime
Hosts: Richard Gray and James Hughes

Location: 4 mi. N of Rte. I-40, Exit Rio
  Grande Blvd.
No. of Rooms: 5

No. of Private Baths: **5**
Double/pb: **$55–$85**
Single/pb: **$45–$55**
Open: **All year**
Breakfast: **Full**

Pets: **Sometimes**
Children: **Welcome**
Smoking: **Permitted**
Social Drinking: **Permitted**

This landmark white adobe residence is close to historic Old Town, major museums, Rio Grande Nature Center, and the International Balloon Fiesta launch site. Southwestern charm is reflected through the beamed ceilings, brick floors, and kiva fireplaces. Museum-quality antiques and collectibles from East Africa, Nepal, Yemen, and Pakistan are used to decorate each room. Jim, a college professor, writer, and actor, will be happy to relate their history.

Hacienda Vargas ✪

1431 EL CAMINO REAL, P.O. BOX 307, ALGODONES, NEW MEXICO 87001

Tel: **(505) 867-9115**
Best Time to Call: **8:30 AM–5 PM**
Hosts: **Paul and Julie DeVargas**
Location: **20 mi. S of Santa Fe**
No. of Rooms: **4**
No. of Private Baths: **4**
Double/pb: **$69–$79**
Suites: **$89–$109**
Open: **All year**
Reduced Rates: **Available**

Breakfast: **Full**
Other Meals: **Available**
Credit Cards: **MC, VISA**
Pets: **No**
Children: **Welcome, over 12**
Smoking: **No**
Social Drinking: **Permitted**
Minimum Stay: **Balloon Fiesta,**
      Christmas, Indian Market
Foreign Languages: **Spanish, German**

Hacienda Vargas is a romantic hideway in a historic old adobe hacienda, completely restored and elegantly decorated with antiques. The beautiful rooms have fireplaces and private entrances, one room has a Jacuzzi tub. Use the hot tub and the barbecue area in the gardens and admire the majestic view of the New Mexico Mesas and Sandia Mountain. Golf, fishing, snow skiing, horseback riding, and hiking are nearby. This B&B is conveniently located a few minutes south of Santa Fe and north of Albuquerque. Romance packages are available. Paul and Julie are ex-bankers who love history and have traveled extensively.

Catherine Kelly's Bed & Breakfast ✪

311 SMOKEY BEAR BOULEVARD, P.O. BOX 444, CAPITAN, NEW MEXICO 88316

Tel: **(505) 354-2335**
Best Time to Call: **11 AM–7 PM**
Host: **Amanda Tudor**
Location: **150 mi. SE of Albuquerque**
Suites: **$100–$125**
Open: **All year**
Reduced Rates: **10% seniors**

Breakfast: **Continental**
Credit Cards: **MC, VISA**
Pets: **Sometimes**
Children: **Welcome**
Smoking: **No**
Social Drinking: **No**

Dedicated to the memory of Glasgow-born Catherine Kelly Grantham, this B&B offers family accommodations with traditional Scottish comfort. Scottish memorabilia abounds in the common areas. Awaken to the smell of freshly baked bread, hot tea, freshly brewed coffee, and a generous buffet breakfast. Choose Catherine's suite, which has a king-size bed and a child's room with a twin, or Mr. G's two-story suite, which has bedrooms, a sitting area, and kitchenette. The area's numerous attractions include Ski Apache, Lincoln National Forest, Captain Bonito Lake, and old Lincoln Town—Billy the Kid's stomping grounds.

La Posada de Chimayó ○
P.O. BOX 463, CHIMAYÓ, NEW MEXICO 87522

Tel: (505) 351-4605	Reduced Rates: Weekly in winter
Host: Sue Farrington	Breakfast: Full
Location: 30 mi. N of Santa Fe	Credit Cards: MC, VISA (for deposits)
No. of Rooms: 4	Pets: Sometimes
No. of Private Baths: 4	Children: Welcome, over 12
Double/pb: $85	Smoking: No
Single/pb: $75	Social Drinking: Permitted
Open: All year	Foreign Languages: Spanish

Chimayó is known for its historic old church and its tradition of fine Spanish weaving. This is a typical adobe home with brick floors and *viga* ceilings. The suite is composed of a small bedroom and sitting room, and is made cozy with Mexican rugs, handwoven fabrics, comfortable furnishings, and traditional corner fireplaces. Sue's breakfasts are not for the fainthearted, and often feature stuffed French toast or chiles rellenos. Wine or sun tea are graciously offered after you return from exploring Bandelier National Monument Park, the Indian pueblos, cliff dwellings, and the "high road" to Taos.

Sagebrush Circle Bed & Breakfast
23 SAGEBRUSH CIRCLE, CORRALES, NEW MEXICO 87048

Tel: (505) 898-5393	Reduced Rates: Available
Best Time to Call: 8:30 AM–9 PM	Breakfast: Continental
Hosts: Barbara and Victor Ferkiss	Other Meals: Available
Location: 10 mi. NW of Old Town Albuquerque	Pets: No
	Children: Welcome, 12 and older
No. of Rooms: 2	Smoking: No
No. of Private Baths: 2	Social Drinking: Permitted
Double/pb: $62–$70	Minimum Stay: 2 nights
Single/pb: $55–$62	Airport/Station Pickup: Yes
Open: All year	

Sagebrush Circle is a dramatic pueblo-style home nestled in the hills of Corrales, a Spanish village settled in the sixteenth century. All rooms have magnificent views of the Sandia Mountains. During cooler mornings, freshly brewed coffee and homemade breads and muffins are served in the great room, which has a 16-foot beamed ceiling. In warmer weather, guests can eat outdoors. As you dine, you may hear the neighing of horses or see brilliantly colored balloons rise in the turquoise sky—they float over the house during Balloon Fiesta in October. Two friendly dogs share living quarters with Barbara and Victor, who are delighted to give advice and information about the area.

La Casita Guesthouse ✪
P.O. BOX 103, DIXON, NEW MEXICO 87527

Tel: **(505) 579-4297**
Hosts: **Sara Pene and Celeste Miller**
Location: **25 mi. S of Taos**
Guest Cottage: **$60–$100, sleeps 2–4**
Open: **All year**
Breakfast: **Continental**

Pets: **No**
Children: **Welcome**
Smoking: **No**
Social Drinking: **Permitted**
Foreign Languages: **Spanish**

The rural mountain village of Dixon is home to many artists and craftspeople. La Casita is a traditional New Mexico adobe with *vigas*, *latillas*, and Mexican tile floors. Guests enjoy use of the living room, fully equipped kitchen, two bedrooms, one bath, and a lovely patio. It is a perfect spot for relaxing and is just minutes from the Rio Grande, river rafting, hiking, and cross-country skiing. Indian pueblos, ancient Anasazi ruins, museums, art galleries, horseback-riding ranches, and alpine skiing are within an hour's drive. Sara and Celeste are weavers.

Silver River Adobe Inn ✪
P.O. BOX 3411, FARMINGTON, NEW MEXICO 87499

Tel: (505) 325-8219
Best Time to Call: **Anytime**
Hosts: **Diana Ohlson and David Beers**
Location: **180 mi. NW of Albuquerque**
No. of Rooms: **1**
No. of Private Baths: **1**
Suite: **$55–$85**
Open: **All year**

Breakfast: **Continental**
Credit Cards: **MC, VISA**
Pets: **No**
Children: **Welcome, over 12**
Smoking: **No**
Social Drinking: **Permitted**
Airport/Station Pickup: **Yes**

Silver River Adobe Inn is a newly constructed, traditional New Mexican home with massive timber beams and exposed adobe. From its cliffside perch, it overlooks the fork of the San Juan and La Plata rivers. Indian reservations, Aztec ruins, and ski slopes are all within striking distance of this B&B.

Dancing Bear B&B ✪
314 SAN DIEGO LOOP (MAILING ADDRESS: P.O. 128), JEMEZ SPRINGS, NEW MEXICO 87025

Tel: (505) 829-3336
Best Time to Call: **8 AM–8 PM**
Host: **Carol A. Breen**
Location: **60 mi. N of Albuquerque**
No. of Rooms: **3**
No. of Private Baths: **3**
Suites: **$55–$110**
Open: **All year**

Breakfast: **Full**
Other Meals: **Available**
Credit Cards: **MC, VISA**
Pets: **No**
Children: **No**
Smoking: **No**
Social Drinking: **Permitted**

You are sure to find serenity at this river retreat at the base of a dramatic sandstone mesa, a bit off the beaten path from Santa Fe. During your stay you will have the opportunity to visit the owner's on-site pottery studio. (Workshops and lessons can be arranged.) Local artisans' handcrafted pieces are exhibited throughout the house, and some are for sale. As you get ready for bed, you can anticipate having breakfast by candlelight or by the riverside. The resident chef is sure to whip up homemade muffins and other culinary delights; special dietary needs are never a problem.

Jemez River B&B Inn ✪
16445 HIGHWAY 4, JEMEZ SPRINGS, NEW MEXICO 87025

Tel: (505) 829-3262
Best Time to Call: **Evenings**
Hosts: **Larry and Roxe Ann Clutter**
Location: **40 mi. NW of Albuquerque**
No. of Rooms: **6**
No. of Private Baths: **6**
Double/pb: **$99–$109**
Open: **All year**

Reduced Rates: **10% seniors**
Breakfast: **Full**
Other Meals: **Available**
Credit Cards: **AMEX, MC, VISA**
Pets: **Sometimes**
Children: **Welcome**
Smoking: **No**
Social Drinking: **Permitted**

The Jemez River Bed & Breakfast Inn is a new, adobe-style, American Indian decorated home built during the winter of 1993–94. It is nestled on three and a half acres in a valley directly beneath the towering Jemez Mountains Virgin Mesa and is surrounded by mighty cottonwood trees, rolling hills and arroyos. Breathtaking views of the morning, sun-drenched Mesa, its splendid colors, and the immense tent rocks overlooking the Inn can be seen from grand, picturesque windows that surround a sizable breakfast table, assuring everyone an enchanting image while enjoying a hearty breakfast. The endless murmur of the Jemez River, located in its own backyard, can be heard from your room and its soothing song will lull you into a deep sleep. The Inn has six air-conditioned rooms, each with private bath, and most important, sound-proofing between the rooms for the privacy the customers deserve. Each room is individually named and decorated with Southwestern Indian tribes' and pueblos' authentic artifacts, pottery, rugs, paintings, arrowheads, kachina dolls and much more. The rooms surround a large outdoor garden plaza filled with birds, hundreds of hummingbirds, and other wildlife, with an underground spring supplying an oversized, continuous-flowing bird bath that cascades into a small stream that incrementally makes its way to the river just behind the Inn. Each room has individual access to and from the plaza, as well as the many stone-lined trails that follow the overflowing spring through vast cottonwood trees, large rocks and crevices that lead to several secluded and relaxing spots along the Jemez River. Come and experience for yourself the restful atmosphere of the Jemez River B&B Inn.

Casa del Rey Bed & Breakfast
305 ROVER, LOS ALAMOS, NEW MEXICO 87544

Tel: **(505) 672-9401**	Open: **All year**
Best Time to Call: **After 5 PM**	Reduced Rates: **Weekly; families**
Host: **Virginia L. King**	Breakfast: **Continental, plus**
No. of Rooms: **2**	Pets: **No**
Max. No. Sharing Bath: **4**	Children: **Welcome, over 5**
Double/sb: **$45**	Smoking: **No**
Single/sb: **$35**	Social Drinking: **Permitted**

This adobe contemporary home is located in the quiet residential area of White Rock, and is situated in the Jemez Mountains with a view of Santa Fe across the valley. The surroundings are rich in Spanish and Indian history. Pueblos, museums, Bandelier National Monument, skiing, hiking trails, tennis, and golf are all within easy reach. Virginia is rightfully proud of her beautifully kept house, with its pretty flower gardens. In summer, her breakfast of granola, home-baked rolls and muffins, along with fruits and beverages, is served on the sun porch, where you can enjoy the lovely scenery.

The Red Violet Inn ☉
344 NORTH SECOND STREET, RATON, NEW MEXICO 87740

Tel: (505) 445-9778; (800) 624-9778
Best Time to Call: 9 AM–8 PM
Hosts: John and Ruth Hanrahan
Location: 1 mi. from I-25, Exit 455
No. of Rooms: 4
No. of Private Baths: 2
Max. No. Sharing Bath: 4
Double/pb: $60–$65
Double/sb: $55
Single/sb: $45–$50

Open: Mar. 1–Jan. 30
Reduced Rates: 10% Oct. 15–Mar.
Breakfast: Full
Other Meals: Available
Pets: No
Children: Welcome, over 12
Smoking: No
Social Drinking: Permitted
Airport/Station Pickup: Yes

Follow the Santa Fe Trail and step back into the past at this appealing 1902 redbrick Victorian home three blocks from Raton's historic downtown. Guests have use of the parlor, dining room, porches, and enclosed flower-filled yard. Repeat visitors arrange to be on hand for the classical music and social hour, from 5:30 to 6:30 PM. Late arrivals are welcomed with a glass of sherry. Upon request, tea or coffee is delivered to your room when you wake up. Full breakfast is served in the formal dining room, accompanied by friendly conversation. A theater and a gallery are within a few blocks, and hiking and fishing facilities are six miles away. Other area attractions include a golf course, several antique shops and a museum; Capulin Volcano National Monument is only 30 minutes away.

Casa Rinconada del Rio ☉
BOX 10A, TAOS HIGHWAY 68, RINCONADA, NEW MEXICO 87531

Tel: (505) 579-4466
Host: JoAnne Gladin-de la Fuente
Location: 20 mi. S of Taos; 45 mi. N. of
    Santa Fe
Guest Houses: $55–$130
Open: All year

Breakfast: Continental
Pets: Sometimes
Children: Welcome
Smoking: Yes
Social Drinking: Permitted
Foreign Languages: Greek

Casa Rinconada is nestled in the canyon of Sangre de Cristo Mountains, the spectacular backdrop for this historic northern village. Thirty-foot *vigas* adorned with skulls and lights border the entry to the guest houses—two traditional tin-roofed adobes which are artfully decorated for your comfort and pleasure. The backyard is an orchard where guests are invited to enjoy seasonal fruit and stroll along the banks of the legendary Rio Grande. Indian pueblos, opera, galleries, rafting, historic churches and more are all within a short drive.

Bed & Breakfast of New Mexico ○
P.O. BOX 2805, SANTA FE, NEW MEXICO 87504

Tel: (505) 982-3332
Best Time to Call: 9 AM–5 PM
Coordinator: Rob Bennett
States/Regions Covered: Statewide
Descriptive Directory: Free

Rates (Single/Double):
　Average: $75 / $90
　Luxury: $95 / $200
Credit Cards: AMEX, DISC, MC, VISA

Do come and enjoy the Santa Fe Opera in summer, the vibrant colors of the aspens in autumn, or skiing in winter. Don't miss the Indian pueblos and ancient cliff dwellings, the national forest areas, art colonies, museums, and Taos.

American Artists Gallery-House ○
FRONTIER ROAD, P.O. BOX 584, TAOS, NEW MEXICO 87571

Tel: (505) 758-4446; (800) 532-2041
Best Time to Call: Anytime
Hosts: Elliot and Judie Framan
Location: 3 blocks from Main St.
No. of Rooms: 7
No. of Private Baths: 7
Double/pb: $68–$95
Guest Cottage: $68

Open: All year
Breakfast: Full
Pets: No
Children: Welcome
Smoking: No
Social Drinking: Permitted
Airport/Station Pickup: Yes

This charming hacienda is filled with artwork, and has a splendid view of Taos Mountain. Your hosts will gladly advise on shops and boutiques. Their home is close to Rio Grande Gorge State Park, 900-year-old Taos Pueblo, and places to go fishing, skiing, and rafting. Fireplaces, the outdoor hot tub, gardens, and a sculpture courtyard will delight you.

Harrison's B&B ○
P.O. BOX 242, TAOS, NEW MEXICO 87571

Tel: (505) 758-2630
Hosts: Jean and Bob Harrison
Location: 1½ mi. from Rte. 64
No. of Rooms: 2
No. of Private Baths: 2
Double/pb: $40–$50
Single/pb: $30–$40

Open: All year
Reduced Rates: 10% after 4th night
Breakfast: Full
Pets: No
Children: Welcome (crib)
Smoking: No
Social Drinking: Permitted

The Harrisons have lived in this large adobe just outside of Taos for 25 years. The house overlooks town from the foot of the western mesa and, framed by trees and bushes, boasts lovely mountain views. Inside, original works of art enhance the Southwestern decor. The Harrisons are just over two miles from the Taos plaza, and are conveniently located near many outdoor pursuits, including skiing, hiking, fishing, and river rafting.

NEW YORK

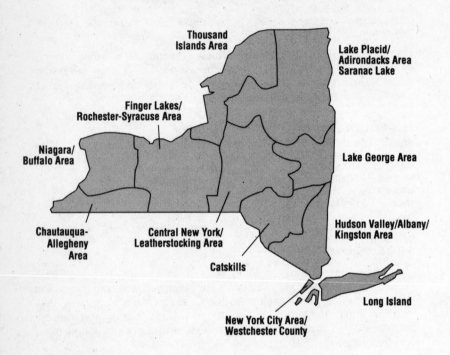

CATSKILLS

Maplewood ✪
PARK ROAD, P.O. BOX 40, CHICHESTER, NEW YORK 12416

Tel: **(914) 688-5433**
Best Time to Call: **After 7 PM**
Hosts: **Nancy and Albert Parsons**
Location: **25 mi. NW of Kingston**
No. of Rooms: **4**
Max. No. Sharing Bath: **4**
Double/sb: **$55–$65**

Single/sb: **$40**
Open: **All year**
Breakfast: **Full**
Pets: **No**
Children: **Welcome**
Smoking: **No**
Social Drinking: **Permitted**

A Colonial manor on a quiet country lane, and nestled among stately maples, this is a charming B&B. Each spacious bedroom has a view of the Catskills. In summer, you can swim in the in-ground pool, or play badminton, croquet, or horseshoes. In winter, ski Belleayre, Hunter, and Cortina, all only 12 miles away. In any season, enjoy the art galleries, boutiques, great restaurants, and theater at Woodstock, 20 minutes away. After a great day outdoors, come home to a glass of wine and good conversation. After a good night's sleep, you'll enjoy freshly squeezed orange juice, homemade breads and pastries, and freshly ground coffee.

River Run ✪
MAIN STREET, FLEISCHMANNS, NEW YORK 12430

Tel: (212) 254-4884
Best Time to Call: 11 AM–11 PM
Hosts: Larry Miller and Jeanne Palmer
Location: 2½ hrs from NYC; 35 mins.
 W of Woodstock
No. of Rooms: 10
No. of Private Baths: 6
Max. No. Sharing Bath: 2
Double/pb: $40–$85
Single/pb: $36–$72
Double/sb: $40–$65

Single/sb: $25–$58
Open: All year
Reduced Rates: Groups; longer stays
Breakfast: Full
Credit Cards: MC, VISA
Pets: Welcome
Children: Welcome
Smoking: Restricted
Social Drinking: Permitted
Minimum Stay: 2 nights peak seasons;
 3 nights holiday weekends

In 1887, at the confluence of the Bushkill and Little Red Kill trout streams, Addison Scott built a classic Victorian summer "cottage." Today, as River Run, this exquisite village landmark invites guests to enjoy the pleasures of every season. Tennis, swimming, theater, restaurants, a museum, antiques, and a weekly country auction are all within walking distance, while Belleayre/Highmount skiing (downhill & cross-country), magnificent Forest Preserve hiking trails, fishing, golf, river float trips, and horseback riding are just minutes away. Rejuvenate on the delightful front porch or in the book-filled parlor, complete with piano and fireplace. Step into the oak-floored dining room, bathed in the colors of the inn's signature stained-glass windows, and enjoy hearty, homemade breakfasts and refreshments. The bus from New York City stops right at the front door!

The Eggery Inn
COUNTY ROAD 16, TANNERSVILLE, NEW YORK 12485

Tel: (518) 589-5363
Best Time to Call: 10 AM–8 PM
Hosts: Julie and Abe Abramczyk
No. of Rooms: 15
No. of Private Baths: 13
Max. No. Sharing Bath: 4
Double/pb: $75–$95
Double/sb: $85–$90
Open: All year
Reduced Rates: Off-season

Breakfast: Full
Credit Cards: AMEX, MC, VISA
Pets: No
Children: Welcome
Smoking: Restricted
Social Drinking: Permitted; full liquor
 license
Minimum Stay: 2 nights weekends; 3
 nights holiday weekends

This Dutch Colonial farmhouse, built circa 1900, is nestled in the northern Catskills at an elevation of 2,200 feet. Guest rooms, decorated in a country motif, have carpeting, color TV, and comforters or spreads. Queen-size and two-bed accommodations are available, and six first-floor rooms are accessible to guests in wheelchairs. The public room's oak balustrade, Franklin stove, player piano, Mission Oak furniture, and panoramic views invite guests to relax. Breakfast selections include omelets, fruit-filled hotcakes, and heart-smart entrees. The inn is ideal for small groups and can be theme-catered by prior arrangement. Hiking trails, scenic waterfalls, the famous Woodstock colony, and the alpine ski areas of Hunter and Windham mountains are nearby.

Sunrise Inn ✪
RD 1, BOX 232B, WALTON, NEW YORK 13856

Tel: **(607) 865-7254**	Guest Cottage: **$60 for 2**
Best Time to Call: **9 AM–11 PM**	Open: **All year**
Hosts: **James and Adele Toth**	Reduced Rates: **10% seniors**
Location: **135 mi. NW of New York City; 5 mi. from Rte. 17**	Breakfast: **Continental**
	Pets: **No**
No. of Rooms: **2**	Children: **Welcome (crib)**
Max. No. Sharing Bath: **4**	Smoking: **No**
Double/sb: **$45**	Social Drinking: **Permitted**
Single/sb: **$35**	

Relax and enjoy the sound of the bubbling brook that borders the landscape of this 19th-century farmhouse. You'll awaken to the aroma of Irish soda bread and other homemade goodies, which you are invited to enjoy in the dining area or, weather permitting, on the wraparound porch. Afterward, browse through the antique shop adjoining the inn. Area activities include fishing, canoeing, golfing, skiing, country fairs, and fine dining. End the day in quiet and homey comfort around the parlor wood stove.

CENTRAL NEW YORK/LEATHERSTOCKING AREA

Bed and Breakfast Leatherstocking ✪
P.O. BOX 53, HERKIMER, NEW YORK 13350

Tel: **(800) 941-BEDS**	Descriptive Directory: **$3**
Best Time to Call: **9 AM–9 PM**	Rates: (Single/Double):
Coordinator: **Joe Martuscello**	Modest: **$25–$45**
States/Regions Covered: **Adirondack Foothills, Central New York, Colgate University, Cooperstown, Hamilton College, Mohawk Valley, Syracuse, Utica**	Average: **$40–$50**
	Luxury: **$50–$75 +**
	Credit Cards: **MC, VISA**
	Minimum Stay: **Sometimes**

Leatherstocking Country is an 11-county region of New York that extends from the Catskills across the Mohawk Valley to the central Adirondacks. It's a region to be visited in all seasons for all reasons, and its residents warmly welcome visitors. Recreational sports and activities, outlet shopping, antiques, fairs, and fine dining are waiting for you, and your B&B host will tell you where to find the best of everything. Send $3 for a descriptive directory.

Pickle Hill Bed and Breakfast ✪
795 CHENANGO STREET, BINGHAMTON, NEW YORK 13901

Tel: **(607) 723-0259**	Open: **All year**
Best Time to Call: **Anytime**	Reduced Rates: **On long stays**
Hosts: **Leslie and Tom Rossi**	Breakfast: **Full**
Location: **185 mi. NW of New York City**	Credit Cards: **No**
	Pets: **No**
No. of Rooms: **2**	Children: **Welcome**
Max. No. Sharing Bath: **4**	Smoking: **Yes, area available**
Double/sb: **$50**	Social Drinking: **Permitted**
Single/sb: **$40**	Airport/Station Pickup: **Yes**

Make yourself comfortable at Pickle Hill, built more than 100 years ago. Read, listen to music, and play board games in the lounge, then rally around the living room piano for a songfest, or join your hosts in the family room for conversation. Sports lovers can play bocci, basketball, or badminton on the side lawn; baseball fields, tennis courts, golf courses, bike paths, and cross-country ski trails are all nearby. Mark Twain's Elmira home, the Farmer's Museum, and the Baseball Hall of Fame in Cooperstown are all within driving distance. Closer to home, Binghamton's Performing Arts Center supplies top-notch entertainment, and the Tri-Cities Opera Company features some of the nation's most promising young singers.

Chalet Waldheim ✪
R.D. 1, BOX 51-G-2, BURLINGTON FLATS, NEW YORK 13315

Tel: **(607) 965-8803**	Breakfast: **Continental, plus**
Hosts: **Franzi and Heinz Kuhne**	Pets: **No**
Location: **12 mi. W of Cooperstown**	Children: **No**
No. of Rooms: **2**	Smoking: **No**
Max. No. Sharing Bath: **4**	Social Drinking: **Permitted**
Double/sb: **$75**	Minimum Stay: **Holiday weekends, special events**
Suites: **$95; sleeps 2–4**	
Open: **All year**	Station Pickup: **Yes**
Reduced Rates: **15% seniors; 20% over 5 days**	Foreign Languages: **German**

Share the quiet seclusion of an adult retreat in this very special hilltop setting amid 75 acres of forest and field. This finely crafted chalet, modeled in age-old Black Forest style, was built by its occupants in 1990. Located in Leatherstocking Country, the Chalet is perfect for all that the village of Cooperstown offers: lakes, museums, opera. This B&B's European country atmosphere permits you to relax totally amidst the warmth of classic antique furnishings and abundant art work. Breakfast is a bountiful Continental buffet which includes freshly baked breads and house specialties.

Halcyon Place Bed & Breakfast ○

197 WASHINGTON STREET, P.O. BOX 244, CHEMUNG, NEW YORK 14825

Tel: **(607) 529-3544**	Open: **All year**
Best Time to Call: **After 4 PM**	Reduced Rates: **10% weekly**
Hosts: **Yvonne and Douglas Sloan**	Breakfast: **Full**
Location: **12 mi. E of Elmira**	Pets: **No**
No. of Rooms: 3	Children: **Welcome, over 12**
No. of Private Baths: 1	Smoking: **No**
Max. No. Sharing Bath: 4	Social Drinking: **Permitted**
Double/pb: **$60**	Station Pickup: **Yes**
Double/sb: **$50**	

Yvonne and Douglas named their B&B after the bird who calmed the turbulent seas in Greek myths. Halcyon Place will have a similar effect on you. Furnished with period antiques, this 1825 Greek Revival retains many of its original features: six-over-six windows of hand-blown glass, wide plank floors, and paneled doors. You won't lack for activities here, thanks to local wineries, Corning Glass Works, Watkins Glen State Park and Race Track, Mark Twain Country Trolley Tours (your hosts will provide free tickets), antique shops, golf courses, and Finger Lakes water sports. Breakfast is served in front of the fire in the winter and on the screened porch in the summer. Some of your hosts' specialties include rum sticky buns, herb omelets, waffles, and raspberry muffins.

Creekside Bed & Breakfast ○

RD 1, BOX 206, COOPERSTOWN, NEW YORK 13326

Tel: **(607) 547-8203**	Reduced Rates: **10% after 5th night**
Best Time to Call: **Anytime**	Breakfast: **Full**
Hosts: **Fred and Gwen Ermlich**	Credit Cards: **AMEX, MC, VISA**
Location: **2 mi. S of Cooperstown**	Pets: **No**
No. of Rooms: 4	Children: **Welcome (crib)**
No. of Private Baths: 4	Smoking: **No**
Double/pb: **$70–$85**	Social Drinking: **Permitted**
Guest Cottage: **$99; sleeps 2**	Minimum Stay: **2 nights seasonal**
Suites: **$89–$125**	**weekends; 3 nights holiday weekends**
Open: **All year**	Foreign Languages: **French, German**

This nationally renowned B&B offers beautiful furnishings in an elegant atmosphere. All rooms have private baths, queen-size beds, color TV, and HBO. The Bridal Suite, Penthouse Suite, and Honeymoon Cottage are ideal for newlyweds and other romantics. You can amble through the flower gardens and lawns, and fish or take a dip in the creek. Gwen and Fred, who perform with the Glimmerglass Opera, serve a full breakfast catering to guests who are looking for something special.

Litco Farms Bed and Breakfast ✪
P.O. BOX 1048, COOPERSTOWN, NEW YORK 13326

Tel: **(607) 547-2501**	Reduced Rates: **Dec.–Mar.**
Hosts: **Margaret and Jim Wolff**	Breakfast: **Full**
Location: **2 mi. NW of Cooperstown**	Pets: **No**
No. of Rooms: **4**	Children: **Welcome**
Max. No. Sharing Bath: **4**	Smoking: **No**
Double/sb: **$59–$79**	Social Drinking: **Permitted**
Suites: **$99**	Airport/Station Pickup: **Yes**
Open: **All year**	

Seventy acres of unspoiled meadows and woodlands are yours to explore at Litco Farms. The day begins with fresh-baked breads, fresh eggs, milk, and local bacon, served in the dining room–library. Borrow a canoe to fish on Canadarago Lake, which is stocked with freshwater salmon. There are other places to paddle, including Glimmerglass, the lake made famous by James Fenimore Cooper. After spending a day at the Baseball Hall of Fame, guests may relax and unwind around the large in-ground pool. Heartworks, a charming quilt crafts shop, is on the premises.

Whisperin Pines Chalet ✪
RD 3, BOX 248, COOPERSTOWN, NEW YORK 13326

Tel: **(607) 547-5640**	Breakfast: **Full**
Best Time to Call: **Anytime**	Pets: **No**
Hosts: **Joyce and Gus Doucas**	Children: **Welcome**
No. of Private Baths: **4**	Smoking: **Permitted**
Max. No. Sharing Bath: **4**	Social Drinking: **Permitted**
Double/sb: **$55–$65**	Airport/Station Pickup: **Yes**
Suites: **$100 for 2**	Foreign Languages: **French, Greek**
Open: **All year**	

Guests may choose from a variety of accommodations, including some with canopy beds, fireplaces, private balconies—even a bubble bath for two. The country setting offers a private walking trail, waterfalls, and a brook from which the lucky can catch a trout for breakfast. The chalet is equipped with a wheelchair ramp. A delicious country breakfast is served in the cozy dining room featuring country-fresh eggs, milk, and butter; homemade sausage and bacon; and Vermont maple syrup.

The White Pillars Inn ✪
82 SECOND STREET, DEPOSIT, NEW YORK 13754

Tel: **(607) 467-4191**	Open: **All year**
Best Time to Call: **8–10 AM; 5–10 PM**	Reduced Rates: **10% AARP members**
Host: **Najla Aswad**	Breakfast: **Full**
Location: **25 mi. SE of Binghamton**	Other Meals: **Dinner (reservations**
No. of Rooms: **5**	**required)**
No. of Private Baths: **3**	Credit Cards: **AMEX, DC, DISC, MC,**
Max. No. Sharing Bath: **4**	**VISA**
Double/pb: **$65–$85**	Pets: **No**
Single/pb: **$55**	Children: **Welcome**
Double/sb: **$55**	Smoking: **No**
Single/sb: **$45**	Social Drinking: **Permitted**
Suites: **$85–$110 (sleeps 4)**	Airport/Station Pickup: **Yes**

Here's the perfect place to do nothing but eat. With selections like Grand Marnier pecan cream cheese stuffed French toast, fluffy omelets filled with sun-dried tomatoes and fresh mozzarella, New York City bagels, home-baked muffins and coffee cakes, and robust, steaming coffee, five-course gourmet breakfasts are the highlight of your stay. The large guest rooms of this handsome Greek Revival mansion (circa 1820) are magnificently furnished with musuem-quality antiques, inviting beds with fluffy comforters and pillows, concealed televisions and telephones, well-stocked refrigerators, and plenty of reading light. And Najla's cookies are always available in her trademark bottomless cookie jar.

Sunrise Farm ✪
RD 3, BOX 95, NEW BERLIN, NEW YORK 13411-9614

Tel: **(607) 847-9380**	Reduced Rates: **Families; weekly**
Hosts: **Janet and Fred Schmelzer**	Breakfast: **Full**
Location: **20 mi. from I-88**	Other Meals: **Available**
No. of Rooms: **1**	Pets: **No**
No. of Private Baths: **1**	Children: **Welcome**
Double/pb: **$50**	Smoking: **No**
Single/pb: **$35**	Social Drinking: **Permitted**
Open: **All year**	

Scottish Highland cattle are raised on this 70-acre certified organic farm about 20 miles from both Cooperstown and Oneonta. A restful night is assured in the large, comfortable second-floor guest room where, on clear nights, the stars can be seen through the skylight. Breakfast features home-baked goods, homemade preserves, and honey from the farm's hives. In winter, a wood stove keeps the house cozy. Several state parks lie a short distance away, and the local diversions include swimming, hiking, golf, horseback riding, cross-country skiing, ice skating, boating, and antiquing. Hunters welcome.

Country Spread Bed & Breakfast ✪
P.O. BOX 1863, 23 PROSPECT STREET, RICHFIELD SPRINGS, NEW YORK 13439

Tel: (315) 858-1870	Single/sb: $40
Best Time to Call: 7 AM–8 AM; 4 PM–9 PM	Suites: $80
	Open: All year
Hosts: Karen and Bruce Watson	Breakfast: Full
Location: 20 mi. SE of Utica on Rte. 28	Credit Cards: MC, VISA
	Pets: No
No. of Rooms: 2	Children: Welcome (crib)
Max. No. Sharing Bath: 4	Smoking: No
Double/pb: $60	Social Drinking: Permitted
Single/pb: $45	Minimum Stay: Sometimes
Double/sb: $50	Airport/Station Pickup: Yes

Longtime area residents Karen and Bruce have restored their 1893 cozy home into a wonderful retreat, tastefully decorated in country style. Your day will start with warm muffins, homemade preserves, pancakes with pure maple syrup, fresh eggs, granola, and chilled juice. Relax on the deck with the newspaper, and then visit some of the area's attractions, including Cooperstown, museums, summer theater, opera, fine dining, antique and specialty shops, and small-town happenings. Nearby Canadarago and Otsego lakes offer excellent boating, fishing, and swimming.

Jonathan House ✪
39 EAST MAIN STREET, P.O. BOX 9, RICHFIELD SPRINGS, NEW YORK 13439

Tel: (315) 858-2870	Single/sb: $55
Hosts: Jonathan and Peter Parker	Suites: $75
Location: 14 mi. N of Cooperstown	Open: All year
No. of Rooms: 4	Breakfast: Full
No. of Private Baths: 2	Credit Cards: AMEX, MC, VISA
Max. No. Sharing Bath: 4	Pets: No
Double/pb: $65	Children: Welcome
Single/pb: $65	Smoking: No
Double/sb: $55	Social Drinking: Permitted

The Parker brothers enjoy cooking and entertaining, so, when they were both widowed, their friends suggested that they open a B&B. Their 1883 house, a hybrid of the Eastlake and Stick styles, has three full floors and a tower room on a fourth level—a total of 17 rooms. The house is elegantly decorated with antiques (some that belonged to the brothers' great-grandparents and grandparents), fine paintings, and oriental rugs. Breakfast is served in the dining room—with bone china, damask linen, and English silver.

CHAUTAUQUA/ALLEGHENY AREA

Plumbush, A Victorian Bed & Breakfast ✪
P.O. BOX 864, CHAUTAUQUA, NEW YORK 14722

Tel: **(716) 789-5309**
Best Time to Call: **Weekdays**
Hosts: **George and Sandy Green**
Location: **90 mi. SW of Buffalo**
No. of Rooms: 5
No. of Private Baths: 5
Double/pb: **$75–$85**
Single/pb: **$65–75**
Open: **All year**

Breakfast: **Full**
Credit Cards: **DISC, MC, VISA**
Pets: **No**
Children: **Welcome, over 12**
Smoking: **No**
Social Drinking: **Permitted**
Minimum Stay: **Peak seasons, weekends**

Immerse yourself in a bygone era. The intrinsic beauty of this 1865 Italianate villa is situated on 125 acres of meadow and woods. Painted in a monochromatic scheme of pink to mauve to burgundy, a tower offers a commanding view of the countryside. Eleven-foot-high ceilings, arched windows, and ceiling fans assure guests an airy, restful night's sleep. Savory baked treats, fruit, fresh coffee, a variety of teas, and homemade granola start the day. Activities run the gamut from water sports and a musical treat to a visit to the famed Chautauqua Institute, just a mile away.

Spindletop on Chautauqua Lake ✪
POLO DRIVE OFF EAST AVENUE, GREENHURST, NEW YORK 14742

Tel: **(716) 484-2070**
Hosts: **Lee and Don Spindler**
Location: **4 mi. W of Jamestown**

No. of Rooms: **4**
No. of Private Baths: **4**
Double/pb: **$60–$75**

Open: **All year**
Reduced Rates: **Available**
Breakfast: **Continental, plus**
Credit Cards: **AMEX, DISC, MC, VISA**

Pets: **No**
Children: **Welcome (swimmers only)**
Smoking: **Restricted**
Social Drinking: **Permitted**

Casually elegant and elegantly casual, oriental carpets and fine furnishings create a lovely background to this air-conditioned home, where all guest rooms overlook Chautauqua Lake. You can relax around the secluded swimming pool, tie your boat at the Spindlers' dock, or enjoy such distractions as Amish quilt shops, antique stores, wineries, art galleries, or seasonal sports opportunities. The famed Chautauqua Institute is nearby.

Scio House
RD 1, BOX 280F, SCIO, NEW YORK 14880

Tel: **(716) 593-1737**
Host: **Mary Ellen Fitzgibbons**
Location: **90 mi. S of Buffalo**
No. of Rooms: **4**
Max. No. Sharing Bath: **4**
Double/pb: **$55**
Single/pb: **$40**
Double/sb: **$45**
Single/sb: **$35**

Suites: **$45–$55**
Open: **All year**
Breakfast: **Full or Continental**
Credit Cards: **AMEX**
Pets: **No**
Children: **Welcome**
Smoking: **Permitted**
Social Drinking: **Permitted**
Airport/Station Pickup: **Yes**

Gracious Victorian atmosphere and old-fashioned hospitality await you at Scio House. Built by a local banker circa 1870, the house retains its original woodwork, pocket doors, and high ceilings. The wraparound porch with its wicker furniture invites you to sit and relax. Stroll the garden or just enjoy the privacy of your room. Have your choice of full or Continental breakfast, served in the formal dining room with heirloom linen, china, and silver.

FINGER LAKES/ROCHESTER AREA

Adventures Bed & Breakfast Reservation Service ✪
P.O. BOX 567, GENESEE, NEW YORK 14454

Tel: **(716) 243-5540; (800) 724-1932**
Best Time to Call: **9 AM–5 PM**
Coordinator: **Andrea B. Barnhoorn**
States/Regions Covered: **Finger Lakes, Genesee Valley Area, Rochester**

Rates (Single/Double):
  Modest: **$45 / $60**
  Average: **$65 / $80**
  Luxury: **$85 / $150**

Adventures is more than a reservation service representing B&B's in the Finger Lakes and Genesee Valley Region. Adventures can plan an exciting visit for you whether it's cross-country skiing or fishing, a biking excursion or a business meeting, a retreat or a wedding. Travel through country roads, hills, and velvet green vineyards. Stroll the path of history in a working Colonial village, take a hot-air balloon ride over Letchworth State Park, bicycle along the Erie Canal tow paths. Spend a day antiquing, or hike along the Sea Way Trail. Visit the museums, planetarium, and theaters Rochester has to offer. Enjoy the fun-filled festivals throughout the Finger Lakes and Rochester area. All accommodations are within a few hours of Niagara Falls, Corning, Syracuse, and Toronto by car.

Elaine's Reservation Service for Bed & Breakfasts
4987 KINGSTON ROAD, ELBRIDGE, NEW YORK 13060

Tel: **(315) 689-2082**
Best Time to Call: **After 9:30 AM**
Coordinator: **Elaine Samuels**
States/Regions Covered: **Auburn, Baldwinsville, Cayuga Lake, Finger Lakes, Oneida Lake, Rome, Saranac Lake, Syracuse and suburbs, Waterloo**

Rates (Single/Double):
  Modest: **$35 / $45**
  Average: **$45 / $55**
  Luxury: **$60 / $150**
Credit Cards: **No**

Elaine has many host homes in the vicinity of Syracuse University, theaters, ski areas, the Finger Lakes, lovely old villages, excellent discount shopping centers, and exclusive boutiques. Syracuse is her hometown, and if you tell her your interests, she is certain to find you the perfect home-away-from-home.

Addison Rose Bed & Breakfast ✪
37 MAPLE STREET, ADDISON, NEW YORK 14801

Tel: **(607) 359-4650**
Hosts: **Bill and Mary Ann Peters**
No. of Rooms: **3**
No. of Private Baths: **3**
Double/pb: **$65–$75**
Single/pb: **$65–$75**

Open: **All year**
Breakfast: **Full**
Pets: **No**
Children: **No**
Smoking: **No**
Social Drinking: **Permitted**

Warmth, friendliness, and hospitality characterize this bed and breakfast, which combines elegance and country charm. Built in 1892, this magnificent Queen Anne home has been painstakingly restored by the Peters family and furnished with period antiques to recapture the ambience of the Victorian age. Guest rooms, named for the original owners and other local personalities, suggest a bygone era. The city of Corning, museums, and Finger Lake wineries are just minutes away.

Pandora's Getaway ✪
83 OSWEGO STREET, BALDWINSVILLE, NEW YORK 13027

Tel: **(315) 635-9571**
Best Time to Call: **Anytime**
Host: **Sandy Wheeler**
Location: **3 mi. from Route 90 Exit 90**
No. of Rooms: **4**
No. of Private Baths: **2**
Max. No. Sharing Bath: **2**
Double/pb: **$80**
Single/pb: **$70**
Double/sb: **$55**

Single/sb: **$50**
Open: **All year**
Reduced Rates: **Available**
Breakfast: **Full**
Credit Cards: **MC, VISA**
Pets: **No**
Children: **Welcome (crib)**
Smoking: **Restricted**
Social Drinking: **Permitted**
Airport Pickup: **Yes**

Standing on an imposing hill with lawns sloping to the street, Pandora's Getaway, an 1845 Greek Revival home, is a local landmark listed on the National Register of Historic Places. The stately trees sheltering the house add to its grandeur. Let Sandy and Harold show you upstate hospitality at its best. Guests are welcome to enjoy the entire B&B, including the front porch with rockers and the large living room with a fireplace. Rooms are furnished with interesting antiques, collectibles, and crafts, some of them for sale. Breakfast, served in the formal dining room with pieces drawn from Sandy's collection of colorful Depression glass, features specialties like quiche, homemade breads, and fresh fruit.

Roberts-Cameron House ✪
68 NORTH STREET, CALEDONIA, NEW YORK 14423

Tel: **(716) 538-6316**
Best Time to Call: **Evenings**
Hosts: **Elizabeth and Robert Wilcox**
Location: **12 mi. SW of Rochester**
No. of Rooms: **2**
Max. No. Sharing Bath: **4**
Double/sb: **$50**
Single/sb: **$40**

Open: **All year**
Reduced Rates: **20% families**
Breakfast: **Full**
Pets: **Sometimes**
Children: **Welcome**
Smoking: **Permitted (downstairs)**
Social Drinking: **Permitted**
Airport/Station Pickup: **Yes**

A clapboard farmhouse built in 1886 by William Roberts, a descendant of an early Scottish settler, this B&B is furnished with family antiques and collectibles from western New York. If you want to acquire some antiques of your own, the surrounding countryside is prime browsing territory, and Elizabeth runs her own antique and crafts shop. Just five minutes from the front door, the Genesee Country Museum lets visitors spend a day strolling through a recreated 19th-century hamlet; costumed villagers and craftspeople go about their daily chores May through October. Your hosts serve a generous country breakfast featuring New York maple syrup.

Edgewater Hollow B&B ✪
4880 WEST LAKE ROAD, CAZENOVIA, NEW YORK 13035

Tel: **(315) 655-8407**	Open: **All year**
Host: **Eleanor Karl Rooney**	Reduced Rates: **Families**
Location: **15 mi. E of Syracuse**	Breakfast: **Continental**
No. of Rooms: **4**	Pets: **No**
No. of Private Baths: **4**	Children: **Welcome, over 8**
Double/pb: **$80**	Smoking: **Permitted**
Single/pb: **$50**	Social Drinking: **Permitted**
Suites: **$100**	

Aptly named, Edgewater Hollow, located on the western shore of Cazenovia Lake, has a quiet, relaxing atmosphere. Guests can enjoy sunbathing, swimming, fishing, windsurfing, canoeing, cross-country and downhill skiing, golfing, tennis, or even a boat tour of the lake—the last option courtesy of your host. If you need a break from sports, pay a visit to Finger Lakes wineries, the old Erie Canal, Burnet Park Zoo, the Baseball Hall of Fame, Madison-Bouckville Antique Show, and the city of Syracuse. Down quilts and, in season, fresh wildflower bouquets picked on the premises, add to the warmth of the bedrooms. Breakfast is served on the patio in the summer and by a warm fire in the winter.

1865 White Birch Bed & Breakfast
69 EAST FIRST STREET, CORNING, NEW YORK 14830

Tel: **(607) 962-6355**	Single/sb: **$55**
Hosts: **Kathy and Joe Donahue**	Open: **All year**
Location: **Off Rte. 17**	Breakfast: **Full**
No. of Rooms: **4**	Credit Cards: **AMEX, MC, VISA**
No. of Private Baths: **2**	Pets: **No**
Max. No. Sharing Bath: **4**	Children: **Welcome**
Double/pb: **$75**	Smoking: **No**
Single/pb: **$60**	Social Drinking: **Permitted**
Double/sb: **$65**	Airport/Station Pickup: **Yes**

The red-carpet treatment awaits you at this spacious 1865 Victorian home that has been restored to show off the beautifully crafted winding staircase and hardwood floors. Guests are welcome to choose a game or enjoy television by the fire in the common room. After a good night's sleep in a comfortable queen-size bed, you'll wake to the smell of homemade breads, muffins, and plenty of hot coffee. The White Birch is located in a residential area just two blocks from restored downtown Corning, and near such attractions as the Corning Glass Center, Rockwell Museum, and many fine wineries.

Fox Ridge Farm B&B ✪
4786 FOSTER ROAD, ELBRIDGE, NEW YORK 13060

Tel: **(315) 673-4881**
Best Time to Call: **8 AM–9 PM**
Hosts: **Marge and Bob Sykes**
Location: **17 mi. SW of Syracuse**
No. of Rooms: **3**
No. of Private Baths: **1**
Max. No. Sharing Bath: **3**
Double/pb: **$65**
Single/pb: **$50**
Double/sb: **$55**

Single/sb: **$40**
Open: **All year**
Reduced Rates: **Available**
Breakfast: **Full**
Pets: **No**
Children: **Welcome, over 6**
Smoking: **No**
Social Drinking: **Permitted**
Airport Pickup: **Yes**

Fox Ridge Farm B&B is located on a quiet rural road surrounded by woods. Hiking trails wander through the 120 acres of woodlands, stately pines, and sparkling streams—a paradise for birders. These same trails are also used for cross-country skiing or snowshoeing in the winter. Stroll around the expansive lawns and flower gardens or kick off your shoes in the spacious family room, which has wood paneling, hardwood floors, a wood-burning stove, a TV, stereo, and reading library. Each guest room is individually decorated with floral wallpaper, handmade quilts, hardwood floors, or carpeting and in some cases, four-poster beds. One room, overlooking the flower garden, has both double and single beds. Hearty breakfasts are served in the large country kitchen, with its stone fireplace.

Woods Edge ✪
151 BLUHM ROAD, FAIRPORT, NEW YORK 14450

Tel: **(716) 223-8877**
Best Time to Call: **8 AM–6 PM**
Hosts: **Betty and Bill Kinsman**
Location: **8 mi. SE of Rochester**
No. of Rooms: **3**
No. of Private Baths: **3**
Double/pb: **$70–$75**
Single/pb: **$55**
Guest cabin: **$90–$95**

Open: **All year**
Reduced Rates: **Long stays; families**
Breakfast: **Full**
Pets: **No**
Children: **Welcome (crib, high chair)**
Smoking: **No**
Social Drinking: **Permitted**
Airport Pickup: **Yes**

Woods Edge is nestled among fragrant pines in a secluded location only 20 minutes from downtown Rochester. The hideaway cabin is a romantically decorated private lodge: a large living room with a fireplace and cathedral ceiling, a bedroom with a queen-size bed, full kitchen, and private bath. The main house has two additional bedrooms, one with king-size or twin beds, the other with a queen-size bed; each has a private bath. Both rooms are decorated with white walls, barn beams, and early country pine furnishings. Full breakfasts are served on the screened porch if weather permits. Cabin guests may have the refrigerator stocked or join everyone else in the main house for their morning meal.

Sandy Creek Manor House ✪
1960 REDMAN ROAD, HAMLIN, NEW YORK 14464

Tel: (716) 964-7528	Open: All year
Best Time to Call: Anytime	Reduced Rates: Weekly; fisherman's
Hosts: Shirley Hollink and James	discounts
Krempasky	Breakfast: Full
Location: 20 mi. W of Rochester	Credit Cards: DISC, MC, VISA
No. of Rooms: 3	Pets: Sometimes
Max. No. Sharing Bath: 4	Children: Welcome, over 12
Double/sb: $70	Smoking: No
Single/sb: $60	Social Drinking: Permitted

Six wooded acres and perennial gardens surround this 1910 English Tudor merely a stroll away from Sandy Creek. Natural woodwork, stained-glass windows, feather pillows, and Amish quilts summon up thoughts of a bygone era, while an antique player piano adds to the nostalgic mood. Full breakfasts include fresh fruit and homemade breads. Hamlin Beach is only 5 minutes away; you can reach Rochester in 30 minutes and Niagara Falls in less than an hour and a half.

Blushing Rose B&B ✪
11 WILLIAM STREET, HAMMONDSPORT, NEW YORK 14840

Tel: (607) 569-3402; (800) 982-8818	Reduced Rates: 10% seniors, travel
Best Time to Call: Anytime	agents
Hosts: Ellen and Bucky Laufersweiler	Breakfast: Full
Location: 20 mi. W of Corning	Pets: No
No. of Rooms: 4	Smoking: No
No. of Private Baths: 4	Social Drinking: Permitted
Double/pb: $65–$85	Minimum Stay: 2 nights holiday
Single/pb: $55	weekends
Open: All year	

Blushing Rose is like something right out of a country magazine, thanks to the quilts, wall hangings, wreaths, and candles that decorate this B&B. Hammondsport is located at the southern end of the Finger

Lakes region, and it's a short walk to Keuka Lake. Watkins Glen, Corning, and the famous Finger Lakes wineries are all a short drive away. You'll look forward to breakfast: baked French toast, lemon poppy-seed waffles, and strawberry bread are among the house specialties.

Hoosick Bed and Breakfast ✪

ROUTE 7 TROY-BENNINGTON ROAD, P.O. BOX 145, HOOSICK, NEW YORK 12089

Tel: (518) 686-5875	Reduced Rates: 5% families
Hosts: Maria and John Recco	Breakfast: Full
Location: 8 mi. W of Bennington, Vt.	Pets: Yes
No. of Rooms: 3	Children: Welcome
Max. No. Sharing Bath: 4	Smoking: No
Double/sb: $45	Social Drinking: Permitted
Single/sb: $35	Foreign Languages: Greek, Spanish
Open: All year	

This recently restored 1840 Greek Revival farmhouse is located fifteen miles from Williamstown, Massachusetts, forty miles from Saratoga Springs, a half hour from the ski slopes of Vermont and the Berkshires, and minutes from local antique centers. Right on site there are barnyard animals to feed and an open field for relaxing, walking, or cross-country skiing. Breakfast specialties might include fresh-baked Texas-size muffins, blueberry pancakes, eggs, coffee, and juice, which you can enjoy privately or with your hosts. Maria and John also offer guests evening tea and the use of a full kitchen.

Hanshaw House ✪

15 SAPSUCKER WOODS ROAD, ITHACA, NEW YORK 14850

Tel: (607) 257-1437	10–15% Dec. 1–Apr. 1; corporate/
Best Time to Call: Before 10 PM	educational rate $60–$65 for a single
Host: Helen Scoones	Breakfast: Full
No. of Rooms: 4	Credit Cards: AMEX, MC, VISA
No. of Private Baths: 4	Pets: No
Double/pb: $65–$98	Children: Welcome
Single/pb: $60–$90	Smoking: No
Suites: $70–$135; sleeps 3	Social Drinking: Permitted
Open: All year	Airport/Station Pickup: Yes
Reduced Rates: 10–15% weekly;	

Not far from downtown Ithaca, this woodframe farmhouse seems light-years away. Built in the 1830s, it has all the comforting country touches, from its white picket fence and dark blue shutters, to the down-filled quilts and pillows in the bedrooms. Bird-lovers should stroll down the road to Cornell's Laboratory of Ornithology and

Sapsucker Woods, a bird sanctuary. Breakfasts include fresh fruit, juice, homemade muffins, and a hot entrée such as pancakes or waffles.

Peregrine House
140 COLLEGE AVENUE, ITHACA, NEW YORK 14850

Tel: (607) 272-0919
Best Time to Call: 8 AM–12 noon
Hosts: Nancy Falconer and Susan Vance
No. of Rooms: 8
No. of Private Baths: 9
Double/pb: $69–$109
Open: All year

Reduced Rates: Nov. 20–Apr. 1; weekly
Breakfast: Full
Credit Cards: MC, VISA
Pets: No
Children: Welcome, over 8
Smoking: Restricted
Social Drinking: Permitted

This three-story brick home, with mansard roof, dates back to 1874. Its faux-marble fireplaces and carved-wood ceilings have been beautifully preserved and are accented with Victorian oak furnishings. Pick a good book in the library and relax in a wing chair, or watch some television in your air-conditioned bedroom. Mexican, Italian, Greek, and Indian food can all be enjoyed within a short walk from here. Peregrine House is two blocks from the Cornell campus and only a few blocks from the Ithaca Commons. Cayuga Lake's wonderful boating and swimming, the wine country, biking, hiking, and cross-country skiing are all close by.

A Fonda House Bed and Breakfast
1612 ROCHESTER STREET, LIMA, NEW YORK 14485

Tel: (716) 581-1040; (800) 662-7126
Best Time to Call: 7 AM–7 PM
Host: Millie Fonda

Location: 15 mi. S of Rochester
No. of Rooms: 3
No. of Private Baths: 1

Max. No. Sharing Bath: **4**
Double/pb: **$65**
Double/sb: **$55**
Open: **All year**
Breakfast: **Full**

Pets: **No**
Children: **By arrangement**
Smoking: **No**
Airport/Station Pickup: **Yes**

Receive a warm welcome at the Fondas' National Register Listed home built in Italianate style, circa 1853. Stroll down the tree-lined drive and step back into a slower time. Allow yourself to be pampered in this Victorian setting. Enjoy an evening in front of the fireplace on a cold winter night or catch a summer breeze on one of the many porches shaded by trees planted a century ago. Bike or walk the short distance to the 200-year-old village of Lima, known for its many antique shops and eating places. Breakfast on homemade goodies. It's an easy day trip to Toronto, Niagara Falls, Corning, and Fingerlake Wineries.

Allan's Hill Bed and Breakfast
2446 SAND HILL ROAD, MT. MORRIS, NEW YORK 14510

Tel: **(716) 658-4591**
Best Time to Call: **After 5 PM**
Hosts: **George and Joyce Swanson**
Location: **35 mi. S of Rochester**
No. of Rooms: **3**
Max. No. Sharing Bath: **4**
Double/sb: **$75**
Single/sb: **$70**

Open: **All year**
Breakfast: **Full**
Pets: **No**
Children: **Welcome**
Smoking: **No**
Social Drinking: **Permitted**
Airport/Station Pickup: **Yes**

Sixteen acres of land surround this restored 1830 country home, giving guests the chance to stroll through stately walnut groves, sit by the pond, picnic, and go bird-watching and cross-country skiing. Nearby Letchworth State Park offers a spectacular, 17-mile drive along the gorge of the Genesee River. The area's wineries will lure you with tours and tastings, and Rochester, with its museums, shops, concerts, and theaters, is within easy driving distance.

The Wagener Estate Bed & Breakfast ✪
351 ELM STREET (ROUTE 54-A), PENN YAN, NEW YORK 14527

Tel: **(315) 536-4591**
Hosts: **Norm and Evie Worth**
Location: **20 mi. from NYS Thruway,
    Exit 42, Geneva**
No. of Rooms: **4**
No. of Private Baths: **2**
Max. No. Sharing Bath: **3**
Double/pb: **$70**
Single/pb: **$60**

Double/sb: **$60**
Single/sb: **$50**
Open: **All year**
Breakfast: **Full**
Credit Cards: **AMEX, MC, VISA**
Pets: **No**
Children: **Welcome, over 5**
Smoking: **No**
Social Drinking: **Permitted**

The Worths raised their family in this 16-room historic house, furnished with antiques and country charm, located at the edge of the village on four scenic acres with shaded lawns, apple trees, and gentle breezes. The pillared veranda is a perfect spot for quiet reflection, conversation, and refreshments. Once the home of Abraham Wagener, the founder of Penn Yan, this B&B is perfectly situated for visits to wine country, the Corning Glass Museum, Watkins Glen, and beautiful Keuka Lake. The Worths are retired now and "have always loved to travel." They continue, "Now we feel we are still traveling, because people from other states and countries bring the world to our door."

Dartmouth House
215 DARTMOUTH STREET, ROCHESTER, NEW YORK 14607

Tel: (716) 271-7872, 473-0778; (800) 724-6298
Best Time to Call: **Anytime**
Hosts: **Ellie and Bill Klein**
Location: **⅒ mi. from I-490, Exit 18**
No. of Rooms: 3
No. of Private Baths: 3
Double/pb: **$65–$95**
Single/pb: **$60–$90**
Open: **All year**

Breakfast: **Full**
Credit Cards: **AMEX, MC, VISA**
Pets: **No**
Children: **Welcome, over 10**
Smoking: **No**
Social Drinking: **Permitted**
Minimum Stay: **2–4 nights some weekends**
Airport/Station Pickup: **Yes**

This 1905 stucco English Tudor is located in the prestigious, quiet, architecturally fascinating Park Avenue neighborhood. A massive fireplace, family antiques, oriental rugs, padded window seats, box-beamed ceilings, leaded-glass windows, and the great oak kitchen create an elegant atmosphere where visitors find friendliness and warmth in abundance. One guest said, "In this Edwardian gem the king himself would feel at home and even commoners are treated royally!" Bill is a retired Kodak engineer now teaching at R.I.T., and Ellie, a former educator, delights in pampering guests with outstanding breakfasts, served by candlelight, that might include eggs Chardonnay or oatmeal-blueberry pancakes. Guests enjoy being able to walk to the George Eastman Mansion and International Museum of Photography, the Rochester Museum and Science Center, the Planetarium, boutiques, restaurants, and antique shops.

Lake View Farm Bed & Breakfast ☉
4761 ROUTE 364, RUSHVILLE, NEW YORK 14544

Tel: (716) 554-6973
Hosts: **Betty and Howard Freese**
Location: **15 mi. from NYS Thruway, Exit 44**
No. of Rooms: 2

Max. No. Sharing Bath: **4**
Double/sb: **$55**
Single/sb: **$40**
Reduced Rates: **10% after 2nd night; weekly**

Breakfast: **Full**	Children: **Welcome, over 8**
Credit Cards: **AMEX**	Smoking: **No**
Pets: **No**	Social Drinking: **Permitted**

Several rooms have a view of Canandaigua Lake, a Seneca Indian word meaning The Chosen Place. The simple architecture and bright and airy atmosphere create a pleasant background for family antiques and pictures. Stroll the grounds, rest in a hammock, or enjoy the pond and sunsets. Take the time to explore the 170 acres; in winter, cross-country ski. In summer, restaurants and a public beach are two minutes away.

HUDSON VALLEY/ALBANY/KINGSTON AREA

American Country Collection
4 GREENWOOD LANE, DELMAR, NEW YORK 12054

Tel: **(518) 439-7001**	Utica, Cooperstown, Hudson Valley,
Best Time to Call: **10 AM–5 PM**	Lakes George and Champlain
Mon.–Fri.	Rates (Single/Double):
Coordinator: **Arthur Copeland**	Modest: **$35–$50 / $35–$55**
States/Regions Covered: **Adirondacks,**	Average: **$50–$60 / $55–$85**
Albany, Binghamton, Catskill	Luxury: **$60–$95 / $85–$135**
Mountains, Schenectady, Troy	Credit Cards: **AMEX, MC, VISA**
(Capital District), Saratoga, Syracuse,	Descriptive Directory: **$6**

The American Country Collection offers comfortable lodging in private homes and small inns. Accommodations range from a 1798 farmhouse, where guests are treated to a pancake breakfast with homemade maple syrup, to a stately Georgian home with canopy beds, fireplaces, and oriental rugs. Each host offers distinctive touches, such as fresh flowers in the room or breakfast in bed. Many homes have lakefront property, swimming pools, tennis courts or Jacuzzis. All are in areas of scenic and cultural interest, convenient to such attractions as the Baseball Hall of Fame, Empire State Plaza, Saratoga Racetrack, Lake George and ski areas. In addition, this service handles reservations for western Massachusetts, northern New Hampshire, Vermont, and St. Thomas.

Ananas Hus Bed and Breakfast ✪
ROUTE 3, P.O. BOX 301, AVERILL PARK, NEW YORK 12018

Tel: **(518) 766-5035**	Breakfast: **Full**
Best Time to Call: **7–9 AM, after 6 PM**	Pets: **No**
Hosts: **Thelma and Clyde Tomlinson**	Children: **Welcome, over 12**
Location: **6 mi. from Rte. 22**	Smoking: **No**
No. of Rooms: **3**	Social Drinking: **Permitted**
Max. No. Sharing Bath: **4**	Foreign Languages: **Norwegian**
Double/sb: **$60**	Minimum Stay: **2 nights holiday**
Single/sb: **$50**	**weekends**
Open: **All year**	

The welcome mat is out at this hillside ranch home on 30 acres, with a panoramic view of the Hudson River Valley. It is informally furnished in the Early American style, accented with mementos from your hosts' international travels and Thelma's lovely needlework. Thelma is a former schoolteacher; Clyde was in the food business. They are serious amateur photographers who compete internationally. It is 15 minutes to Jiminy Peak and Brodie Mountain ski areas; 30 minutes to Tanglewood, Williamstown Theatre Festival, and Clark Art Institute in Massachusetts.

The Gregory House Inn ✪
P.O. BOX 401, ROUTE 43, AVERILL PARK, NEW YORK 12018

Tel: **(518) 674-3774; (800) 497-2977**	Reduced Rates: **Weekly**
Best Time to Call: **5 PM**	Breakfast: **Continental**
Hosts: **Melissa and Christopher Miller**	Other Meals: **Available**
Location: **10 mi. E of Albany**	Credit Cards: **AMEX, DC, MC, VISA**
No. of Rooms: **12**	Pets: **No**
No. of Private Baths: **12**	Children: **Welcome, over 6**
Double/pb: **$75–$80**	Smoking: **No**
Single/pb: **$65–$70**	Social Drinking: **Permitted**
Open: **All year**	

The Gregory House is a clapboard Colonial dating back to 1830. Recently, the building was expanded to include beautifully appointed guest rooms and a common room, all in keeping with a relaxed, country style. The house is surrounded by the Catskill, Adirondack, Berkshire, and Green mountains, affording year-round beauty and recreation. The inn is also near the Saratoga Performing Arts Center, Tanglewood, Hancock Shaker Village, and Saratoga Springs. Your hosts invite you to explore their beautifully landscaped property and to join them for fine dining in the restaurant. Christopher is a graduate of the Culinary Institute of America and specializes in international cuisine.

Battenkill Bed & Breakfast Barn ✪
ROUTE 313, RD 1, BOX 143, CAMBRIDGE, NEW YORK 12816-9717

Tel: **(518) 677-8868; (800) 676-8768**	Breakfast: **Full**
Hosts: **Veronica and Walt Piekarz**	Other Meals: **Available**
Location: **30 mi. E of Saratoga**	Credit Cards: **AMEX, DISC, MC, VISA**
No. of Rooms: **2**	Pets: **No**
Max. No. Sharing Bath: **4**	Children: **Welcome**
Double/sb: **$60**	Smoking: **Permitted**
Single/sb: **$45**	Social Drinking: **Permitted**
Open: **All year**	

Relax and enjoy yourself at this post-and-beam home nestled in the Annaquassicoke Valley. Veronica delights in creative cooking while

Walt, a jazz musician, is always ready to talk shop. Winter activities here include snowshoeing and cross-country skiing, with longer trails nearby. The rest of the year, guests can go fishing, canoeing, kayaking, tubing, and biking; the B&B's property borders the Battenkill River, and equipment may be rented from your hosts.

Point of View
RR 2, BOX 766 H, RIDGE ROAD, CAMPBELL HALL, NEW YORK 10916

Tel: (914) 294-6259; (800) 294-6259
Hosts: Bill and Elaine Frankle
Location: 60 mi. NW of New York City
No. of Rooms: 2
No. of Private Baths: 2
Double/pb: $65
Single/pb: $55
Open: All year
Breakfast: Full

Credit Cards: MC, VISA
Pets: Sometimes
Children: Welcome
Smoking: No
Social Drinking: Permitted
Minimum Stay: 2 nights holiday weekends
Airport/Station Pickup: Yes
Foreign Languages: French

Point of View offers back-home comfort, spacious, modern rooms, and country atmosphere. Guest rooms have a separate entrance, queen-size beds, phone with free local dialing, cable TV, and spectacular views of farms and distant mountains. Breakfast, served in your private sitting room, features fresh-brewed coffee, orange juice, and all the trimmings. From its central Orange County location, this B&B is close to West Point Military Academy, Sugar Loaf Village of Craftsman, Hall of Fame of the Trotter, Woodbury Commons Factory Outlets, Sterling Forest, Brotherhood Winery, Storm King Art Center, and Museum Village. Within easy driving distance are Vernon Valley, Hunter Mountain, and Bellayre ski areas. Hiking and cross-country skiing are nearby at Minnewaska State Park and Mohonk Mountain House. Elaine, a counselor and certified hypnotherapist, and Bill, a pastor, know Orange County intimately—they have lived in the area for more than twenty-five years.

Alexander Hamilton House ✪
49 VAN WYCK STREET, CROTON-ON-HUDSON, NEW YORK 10520

Tel: (914) 271-6737
Best Time to Call: 8 AM–6 PM
Host: Barbara Notarius
Location: 30 mi. NW of New York City
No. of Rooms: 6
No. of Private Baths: 6
Double/pb: $95–$105
Single/pb: $50–$75
Suites: $130–$150
Open: All year

Breakfast: Full
Credit Cards: AMEX, DISC, MC, VISA
Pets: No
Children: Welcome
Smoking: No
Social Drinking: Permitted
Minimum Stay: 2 nights weekends
Airport/Station Pickup: Yes
Foreign Languages: French

No, Hamilton didn't live here; this beautiful Victorian home was built some eight decades after his death, and one suite is named for the victor in the duel between Hamilton and Aaron Burr. The property, with its 35-foot in-ground swimming pool, small apple orchard, and spectacular Hudson River views, would please even the most patrician lodgers. West Point, Van Cortlandt Manor, Boscobel, and Storm King Art Center are all nearby, and New York City is within striking distance. After sightseeing, relax in the large living room complete with fireplace, piano, and numerous antiques. Baby equipment is available for guests with small children.

The Milton Bull House ○

1065 ROUTE 302, PINE BUSH, NEW YORK 12566

Tel: **(914) 361-4770**	Open: **All year**
Best Time to Call: **9 AM–9 PM**	Reduced Rates: **Weekly**
Hosts: **Ellen and Graham Jamison**	Breakfast: **Full**
Location: **75 mi. NW of New York City**	Pets: **No**
No. of Rooms: **2**	Children: **Welcome**
No. of Private Baths: **1**	Smoking: **No**
Max. No. Sharing Bath: **4**	Social Drinking: **Permitted**
Double/sb: **$59**	Airport/Station Pickup: **Yes**
Single/sb: **$48.26**	Foreign Languages: **French**

The Milton Bull House is a traditional bed and breakfast. The historic house has nine large rooms furnished with antiques. Part of the house dates to 1816 and is Federal in style. The two guest rooms share a full bath. The house is located in a lovely area of the Hudson Valley—in the foothills of the Shawangunk Mountain Ridge—which provides wonderful scenery as well as opportunities for hiking and rockclimbing. Shopping malls, such as Woodbury Common, antique marts and wineries are nearby. Although the area is rural, the Bull House is very close to Route 17, the NYS Thruway and I-84. There are sixty acres of open farmland, lawns, gardens, orchards and an in-ground swimming pool. Rates include an old-fashioned farm breakfast with homebaking.

Maggie Towne's B&B ○

PHILLIPS ROAD, PITTSTOWN, NEW YORK (MAILING ADDRESS: BOX 82, RD 2, VALLEY FALLS, NEW YORK 12185)

Tel: **(518) 663-8369; 686-7331**	Open: **All year**
Host: **Maggie Towne**	Breakfast: **Full**
Location: **14 mi. E of Troy**	Pets: **Sometimes**
No. of Rooms: **3**	Children: **Welcome (crib)**
Max. No. Sharing Bath: **4**	Smoking: **No**
Double/sb: **$45**	Social Drinking: **Permitted**
Single/sb: **$35**	

This lovely old Colonial is located amid beautiful lawns and trees. Enjoy a cup of tea or glass of wine before the huge fireplace in the family room. Use the music room or curl up with a book on the screened-in porch. Mornings, your host serves home-baked goodies. She will gladly prepare a lunch for you to take on tour or enjoy at the house. It's 20 miles to historic Bennington, Vermont, and 30 to Saratoga.

The Marshall House
115 COURT STREET, PLATTSBURGH, NEW YORK 12901

Tel: (518) 566-8691	Double/sb: $55–$70
Best Time to Call: 7–9 PM	Single/sb: $45–$60
Hosts: **Harriette Walker and Donna Corodimas**	Open: **All year**
	Reduced Rates: **Available**
Location: **25 mi. E of Burlington, Vermont**	Breakfast: **Full**
	Credit Cards: **MC, VISA**
No. of Rooms: 4	Pets: **No**
No. of Private Baths: 2	Children: **Welcome, over 5**
Max. No. Sharing Bath: 4	Smoking: **No**
Double/pb: $70–$80	Social Drinking: **Permitted**
Single/pb: $60–$70	Minimum Stay: **2 days on weekends**

This fine Queen Anne Victorian boasts a turret, wrap-around veranda, slate roof, painted-lady exterior, and a location in Plattsburgh's historic district, a few blocks between the college and Lake Champlain. Listed on the National Register of Historic Places, Marshall House combines authentic period features—lavish, ornate woodwork and stained glass—with warm hospitality and the down-home comfort of good food generously served. The Adirondacks, Lake Placid, Montreal, and Vermont are all within a short driving distance.

Sharon Fern's Bed & Breakfast ✪
8 ETHIER DRIVE, TROY, NEW YORK 12180

Tel: (518) 279-1966	Open: **All year**
Best Time to Call: **Mornings**	Reduced Rates: **10% seniors**
Hosts: **Bill and Sharon Ernst**	Breakfast: **Full**
Location: **10 mi. from NYS Thruway**	Pets: **No**
No. of Rooms: 2	Children: **Welcome (crib)**
Max. No. Sharing Bath: 3	Smoking: **No**
Double/sb: $50	Social Drinking: **Permitted**
Single/sb: $45	

Bill and Sharon's tri-level contemporary home rests on a quiet street in the country just 20 minutes outside of Albany, New York's capital. Enjoy spacious accommodations plus many extras, including an in-ground pool, a recreation room with a Ping-Pong table, and a beautiful backyard, where badminton and croquet will test your mettle. Skiers and hikers will find mountains in nearly every direction—the Adirondacks, Catskills, and Green Mountains are all a half hour away.

LAKE GEORGE AREA

Hilltop Cottage ✪
P.O. BOX 186, 6883 LAKESHORE DRIVE, BOLTON LANDING, NEW YORK 12814

Tel: **(518) 644-2492**
Best Time to Call: **Anytime**
Hosts: **Anita and Charlie Richards**
Location: **8 mi. from I-87**
No. of Rooms: **4**
No. of Private Baths: **2**
Max. No. Sharing Bath: **4**
Double/pb: **$60**
Double/sb: **$50**

Guest cabin: **$70**
Open: **All year**
Breakfast: **Full**
Credit Cards: **MC, VISA**
Children: **Welcome, over 4**
Smoking: **Restricted**
Social Drinking: **Permitted**
Foreign Languages: **German**

Hilltop Cottage is a clean, comfortable, renovated caretaker cottage in the beautiful Lake George–Eastern Adirondack region. You can walk to the beach, marinas, shops, and restaurants. Guests will enjoy the hearty breakfasts, homey atmosphere, helpful hosts, wood-burning stove, and fall foliage. A guest cabin is also available.

Crislip's Bed & Breakfast ✪
693 RIDGE ROAD, QUEENSBURY, NEW YORK 12804-9717

Tel: **(518) 793-6869**
Hosts: **Ned and Joyce Crislip**
Location: **20 mi. N of Saratoga Springs**
No. of Rooms: **4**
No. of Private Baths: **3**
Max. No. Sharing Bath: **3**
Double/pb: **$55–$75**
Single/pb: **$45–$65**
Single/sb: **$35**
Open: **All year**

Reduced Rates: **Over 3 nights**
Breakfast: **Full**
Credit Cards: **AMEX, MC, VISA**
Pets: **Sometimes**
Children: **Welcome**
Smoking: **No**
Social Drinking: **Permitted**
Minimum Stay: **Major holiday weekends**
Airport/Station Pickup: **Yes**

Located between Saratoga Springs and Lake George, this Quaker-built Federal home provides spacious accommodations complete with period antiques, four-poster beds, and down comforters. The country breakfast menu features buttermilk pancakes, scrambled eggs, and sausages. Ned Crislip, a music teacher, and his wife, Joyce, invite you to enjoy the grounds surrounding their dwelling, which include nearly two acres of lawn and gardens, old stone walls, and mountain views of Vermont.

The Inn on Bacon Hill ✪
P.O. BOX 1462, SARATOGA SPRINGS, NEW YORK 12866

Tel: **(518) 695-3693**
Best Time to Call: **7–10 AM**
Host: **Andrea Collins-Breslin**
Location: **8 mi. E of Saratoga Springs**
No. of Rooms: **4**
No. of Private Baths: **2**
Max. No. Sharing Bath: **4**
Double/pb: **$75–$125**
Double/sb: **$65–$115**
Suites: **$85–$135; sleeps 2**

Open: **All year**
Reduced Rates: **Available**
Breakfast: **Full**
Credit Cards: **MC, VISA**
Pets: **No**
Children: **Welcome, over 13**
Smoking: **No**
Social Drinking: **Permitted**
Minimum Stay: **Weekends during racing season—2 days**

Experience the peace and quiet of elegant country living and the fun and excitement of nearby city life. Relax in this large, beautifully restored 1862 home, with its four air-conditioned bedrooms, original marble fireplaces and wallcoverings, high ceilings, and finely crafted moldings and woodwork that take you back to Victorian times. A hearty country breakfast is served daily, with early morning coffee or afternoon beverages to be enjoyed in the screened-in gazebo surrounded by soothing rural settings and the distant hills of Vermont. Albany, Lake George, and Vermont are all within a 45-minute drive. Like many others, innkeeper Andrea Collins-Breslin left the corporate world to pursue a career in hospitality with no regrets!

Six Sisters Bed and Breakfast ✪
149 UNION AVENUE, SARATOGA SPRINGS, NEW YORK 12866

Tel: (518) 583-1173; fax: (518) 587-2470
Hosts: **Kate Benton and Steve Ramirez**
Location: **30 mi. N of Albany**
No. of Rooms: **4**
No. of Private Baths: **4**
Double/pb: **$65–$85**
Single/pb: **$60–$80**
Suites: **$75–$130**
Open: **All year**
Reduced Rates: **10%–15%**

Sun.–Thurs. Nov.–Mar.; **10% seniors; corporate, extended stays**
Breakfast: **Full**
Pets: **No**
Children: **Welcome, over 10**
Smoking: **No**
Social Drinking: **Permitted**
Minimum Stay: **Special weekends, racing season**
Station Pickup: **Yes**

Some people visit this town for its naturally carbonated mineral waters, other people for its racetracks. Bathers and railbirds will both be delighted by Kate and Steve's 1890 Victorian, named for the former's sisters. All rooms have air conditioning and either king- or queen-size beds (except for the second floor parlor suite, which has two double beds). After sampling one of Steve's mouth-watering breakfasts, guests are encouraged to take a mug of coffee, tea, or cider out to the veranda overlooking Saratoga's streets and racecourse. Then it's an easy walk to boutiques, antique shops, restaurants, and the National Museum of Racing.

LAKE PLACID/ADIRONDACKS AREA
Crown Point Bed & Breakfast ✪
ROUTE 9 N, MAIN STREET, CROWN POINT, NEW YORK 12928

Tel: (518) 597-3651
Hosts: **Hugh and Sandy Johnson**
Location: **7 mi. N of Ticonderoga**
No. of Rooms: **5**
No. of Private Baths: **5**
Double/pb: **$50–$65**
Single/pb: **$50–$65**
Suites: **$95; sleeps 4**
Open: **All year**
Reduced Rates: **10% seniors**

Breakfast: **Continental, plus**
Credit Cards: **MC, VISA**
Pets: **Sometimes**
Children: **Welcome**
Smoking: **No**
Social Drinking: **Permitted**
Minimum Stay: **2 nights on holiday weekends**
Foreign Languages: **Spanish**

Return to an era of stately Victorian elegance. Sleep in a hundred-year-old manor house graciously furnished with period antiques. The 18-room house, built in 1886 by Richard Wyman, a local banker, took three years to complete. It was designed by Witherbee and Sherman and constructed by Italian craftsmen. Six different kinds of paneled woodwork (oak, cherry, mahogany, pine, chestnut, and walnut), pocket doors, and four fireplaces grace the house. Enjoy a summer evening on one of the three porches, view the sunrise over the Green

Mountains of Vermont, or experience the double rainbows of the Adirondack region.

Gatehouse Herbs Bed & Breakfast ✪
98 VAN BUREN STREET, DOLGEVILLE, NEW YORK 13329

Tel: (315) 429-8366	Open: June thru Oct. 12th
Best Time to Call: 5 PM–9 PM	Reduced Rates: 10% if longer than
Hosts: Carol and Kermit (Kerry) Gates	15 days
Location: 30 mi. E of Utica	Breakfast: Full
No. of Rooms: 3	Pets: Sometimes
No. of Private Baths: 3	Children: Welcome
Double/pb: $75	Smoking: No
Single/pb: $65	Social Drinking: Permitted
Suites: $85	

Nestled in the Adirondack foothills and overlooking a lily pond in the charming village of Dolgeville, Gatehouse Herbs Bed & Breakfast is an exquisite example of Victorian architecture. Its twelve-acre grounds include English gardens, wooded walks, and a bubbling brook. There are three guest rooms, decorated with family antiques. Fresh fruit and cold spring water are complimentary in each room. Enjoy bountiful breakfasts in the dining room or on the breakfast porch. Specialties include multigrain pancakes with fresh local maple syrup, omelets, blueberry muffins, or scones. Saratoga Springs, Cooperstown, and the oldest Russian Orthodox Monastery in the U.S. are within an hour's drive. Hiking, biking, and canoeing in the Adirondack Park are just minutes away.

The Book & Blanket Bed & Breakfast ✪
ROUTE 9N (P.O. BOX 164), JAY, NEW YORK 12941

Tel: (518) 946-8323	Double/sb: $45–$50
Best Time to Call: Anytime	Single/sb: $35–$40
Hosts: Kathy, Fred, and Daisy the	Open: All year
Basset Hound	Breakfast: Full
Location: 17 mi. E of Lake Placid	Pets: Sometimes
No. of Rooms: 3	Children: Welcome
No. of Private Baths: 1	Smoking: Restricted
Max. No. Sharing Bath: 4	Social Drinking: Permitted
Double/pb: $65	Station Pickup: Yes
Single/pb: $65	

This 125-year-old Greek revival residence is situated on the east branch of the Ausable River in Jay, N.Y.—an Adirondack hamlet complete with covered bridge and village green. Filled with antiques and books for borrowing and browsing, this house boasts three guest bedrooms honoring Jane Austen, F. Scott Fitzgerald, and Jack London. In winter, guests can relax before a fire; in summer the porch swing is just the thing. Whiteface Ski Mountain is seven miles away, and Lake

Placid a mere 17. Ausable Chasm, Fort Ticonderoga, and ferries to Vermont are easy day trips. The owners enjoy baking, juggling, and their adorable basset hound.

Brook's Sunshine Cottage ✪
6 MAPLE STREET, LAKE PLACID, NEW YORK 12946

Tel: **(518) 523-3661; fax: (518) 523-2331**	Open: **All year**
Best Time to Call: **9 AM–8 PM**	Reduced Rates: **Available**
Hosts: **Bernadine and Joseph Brooks**	Breakfast: **Full**
Location: **150 mi. N of Albany**	Credit Cards: **MC, VISA**
No. of Rooms: **4**	Pets: **No**
Max. No. Sharing Bath: **4**	Children: **Welcome, over 10**
Double/pb: **$75**	Smoking: **No**
Double/sb: **$55–$60**	Social Drinking: **Permitted**
Single/sb: **$40**	Minimum Stay: **2 nights winter and summer, weekends**
Suites: **$75–$99; sleeps 4**	Airport/Station Pickup: **Yes**

This century-old B&B is located one block from Main Street in the center of the Olympic Village. Skating, tobogganing, downhill and cross-country skiing, boating, biking, visiting Olympic venues, and hiking the forty-six majestic Adirondack peaks are just some of the activities to pursue during your stay. Brook's Sunshine Cottage offers guests four bedrooms, two fireplaces, TV, VCR, off-street parking, and a bountiful breakfast buffet. Also available are two suites, each equipped with a full kitchen, TV, and living room.

Highland House Inn ✪
3 HIGHLAND PLACE, LAKE PLACID, NEW YORK 12946

Tel: **(518) 523-2377**	Open: **All year**
Best Time to Call: **Mornings**	Reduced Rates: **Apr.–May, Nov.**
Hosts: **Teddy and Cathy Blazer**	Breakfast: **Full**
Location: **25 mi. from Rte. 87, Exit 30**	Pets: **No**
No. of Rooms: **7**	Children: **Welcome**
No. of Private Baths: **7**	Smoking: **Restricted**
Double/pb: **$65–$75**	Social Drinking: **Permitted**
Single/pb: **$55–$65**	Airport/Station Pickup: **Yes**

The Highland House Inn is located in a lovely residential section, just above Main Street in the village of Lake Placid. The decor is Adirondack—wallpapers are of rich green, rose, and ivory backgrounds, and birch tree furnishings abound. The dining area runs the length of the house, bordered by glass on three sides; it's full of flowering plants year-round. Breakfasts are served to order, including blueberry pancakes, French toast, eggs, sausages, cereals, etc. A huge deck spans the length of the Inn, wrapping around two clumps of birch trees and supporting a wonderful 7-person hot tub spa. The bedrooms are on the second and third floors. Most have a double and single bed in the room. A remote control color television is in each room along with other necessary amenities for a comfortable stay.

Fogarty's Bed and Breakfast ✪
37 RIVERSIDE DRIVE, SARANAC LAKE, NEW YORK 12983

Tel: **(518) 891-3755; (800) 525-3755**	Open: **All year**
Best Time to Call: **After 3 PM**	Breakfast: **Full**
Hosts: **Jack and Emily Fogarty**	Pets: **No**
Location: **150 mi. N of Albany**	Children: **Welcome**
No. of Rooms: **5**	Smoking: **Permitted**
Max. No. Sharing Bath: **3**	Social Drinking: **Permitted**
Double/sb: **$45**	Airport Pickup: **Yes**
Single/sb: **$30**	

High on a hill overlooking Lake Flower and Mts. Baker, McKenzie, and Pisgah—but only three minutes from the center of town—you'll find Fogarty's. The B&B porches, wide doors, and call buttons attest to its past as a cure cottage. The living and dining rooms are decorated with handsome woodwork, and the bathrooms have the original 1910 fixtures. Swimmers and boaters can use Fogarty's dock, and cross-country skiers will find trails within a mile. More ambitious athletes should take a brief drive to Lake Placid's Olympic courses or the slopes of Whiteface and Big Tupper. Emily and Jack are Adirondack natives, so feel free to ask them for suggestions.

Moose River House Bed and Breakfast ✪
12 BIRCH STREET, THENDARA, NEW YORK 13472

Tel: **(315) 369-3104**	Open: **All year**
Best Time to Call: **8 AM–8 PM**	Reduced Rates: **10% seniors, families;** after 3rd night
Hosts: **Kate and Bill Labbate**	Breakfast: **Full**
Location: **48 mi. N of Utica**	Pets: **No**
No. of Rooms: **4**	Children: **Welcome, over 12**
No. of Private Baths: **2**	Smoking: **No**
Max. No. Sharing Bath: **4**	Social Drinking: **Permitted**
Double/pb: **$85**	
Double/sb: **$65**	

Back in the 19th century, Moose River House was accessible only by the *Fawn*, a tiny side-wheeler that steamed upstream from Minnehaha, where New York's only wooden train rails terminated. Today there are several routes to this northern Adirondack inn. However you get there, you won't want to leave. From cross-country and downhill skiing in the winter to hiking, horseback riding, and waterfront sports in the summer, the recreational options are vast. And the adjacent town of Old Forge has a wealth of shops and restaurants, in addition to the Enchanted Forest amusement park.

LONG ISLAND

Country Life B&B ✪
237 CATHEDRAL AVENUE, HEMPSTEAD, NEW YORK 11550

Tel: (516) 292-9219
Best Time to Call: 6–9 PM
Hosts: Wendy and Richard Duvall
Location: 20 mi. E of New York City,
on the Garden City line
No. of Rooms: 4
No. of Private Baths: 4
Double/pb: $60–$85

Suite: $95–$150; sleeps 4–5
Open: All year
Breakfast: Full
Pets: No
Children: Welcome (crib)
Smoking: No
Social Drinking: Permitted
Foreign Languages: German, Spanish

Guests feel right at home in this charming Dutch Colonial, with four-poster beds and antique reproductions. Soda and cheese are served on arrival, and breakfast features puff pancakes and French toast. Guests enjoy the garden or visiting nearby sights. Kennedy International Airport and La Guardia Airport are less than 40 minutes away; Adelphi and Hofstra universities and the Nassau Coliseum are one mile away.

Mainstay Bed & Breakfast ✪
579 HILL STREET, SOUTHAMPTON, NEW YORK 11968

Tel: (516) 283-4375
Best Time to Call: AM
Host: Elizabeth Main
Location: 80 mi. E of New York City
No. of Rooms: 8
No. of Private Baths: 3
Max. No. Sharing Bath: 4
Double/pb: $50–$165
Double/sb: $50–$120
Suite: $150–$215

Open: All year
Reduced Rates: Available
Breakfast: Continental
Credit Cards: MC, VISA
Pets: No
Children: Welcome
Smoking: No
Social Drinking: No
Minimum Stay: 2 nights weekends
June–Labor Day

This charmingly restored Colonial guest house was built in the 1870s. Once a country store, Mainstay now accommodates those looking for a cozy retreat where they can enjoy white sandy beaches, nature walks, sports, biking, and dining. Rooms are beautifully decorated with antique iron and brass beds. The large master suite has a fireplace, TV, and claw-footed tub. (If you fall in love with the furniture, you may be able to buy it—many of the antique and European country pieces are available for purchase.) Breakfast, typically including homemade muffins, cereals, fruit, juice, and coffee, is served in the dining room. The B&B is within walking distance of antique shops, other stores, galleries, and museums.

1880 Seafield House ✪
2 SEAFIELD LANE, WESTHAMPTON BEACH, NEW YORK 11978

Tel: (800) 346-3290
Best Time to Call: 9 AM–5 PM
Host: Elsie Collins
Location: 90 mi. E of New York City
No. of Rooms: 3 suites
No. of Private Baths: 3
Suites: $175

Open: All year
Reduced Rates: $95, Oct. 15–May 15
Breakfast: Full
Pets: No
Children: No
Smoking: No
Social Drinking: Permitted

This 100-year-old home in posh Westhampton is five blocks from the beach, and boasts its own pool and tennis court. Victorian lounges, a caned rocker, piano, hurricane lamps, Shaker benches, Chinese porcelain all combine to create the casual, country inn atmosphere. When the sea air chills Westhampton Beach, the parlor fire keeps the house toasty warm. The aromas of freshly brewing coffee and Mrs. Collins' breads and rolls baking in the oven are likely to wake you in time for breakfast. You'll leave this hideaway relaxed, carrying one of Mrs. Collins' homemade goodies.

NEW YORK CITY AREA/WESTCHESTER COUNTY

Abode Bed & Breakfast, Ltd. ✪
P.O. BOX 20022, NEW YORK, NEW YORK 10028

Tel: (212) 472-2000
Best Time to Call: Mon.–Fri., 9 AM–
    5 PM; Sat., 10 AM–2 PM
Coordinator: Shelli Leifer

States/Regions Covered: Manhattan
Rates (Single/Double): $75–$125
Credit Cards: AMEX
Minimum Stay: 2 nights

Shelli is a friendly, savvy New Yorker with sensitive insight as to which guest would be most comfortable with what host. Her roster grows steadily with accommodations in safe neighborhoods that are "East Side, West Side, and all around the town." Unhosted brownstones boasting a country-inn ambience and unhosted luxury apartments are especially attractive for couples traveling together. Prices range from $99 for a studio to $300 for 3 bedrooms. Reduced rates are available for extended stays. Theaters, museums, galleries, restaurants, and shopping are within easy reach of all accommodations.

Bed & Breakfast (& Books)
35 WEST 92ND STREET, NEW YORK, NEW YORK 10025

Tel: (212) 865-8740
Best Time to Call: 10 AM–5 PM
    Mon.–Fri.
Coordinator: Judith Goldberg
States/Regions Covered: Manhattan

Rates (Single/Double):
    Average: $60–$75 / $80–$90
Credit Cards: AMEX
Minimum Stay: 2 nights

Accommodations are conveniently located in residential areas near transportation and within walking distance of many cultural attractions. Hosts are photographers, psychologists, lawyers, dancers, teachers, and artists. They are pleased to share their knowledge of fine shops, reasonable restaurants, galleries, theater, and bookstores. There's a $20 surcharge for one-night stays. Unhosted apartments are $90 to $150 for two.

Bed & Breakfast Network of New York
134 WEST 32ND STREET, SUITE 602, NEW YORK, NEW YORK 10001

Tel: (212) 645-8134; (800) 900-8134
Best Time to Call: 8 AM–noon;
  2–6 PM
Coordinator: Mr. Leslie Goldberg
States/Regions Covered: New York
  City

Rates (Single/Double):
  Modest: $50 / $70
  Average: $80 / $90
Credit Cards: No

Accommodations appropriate to your purpose and purse are available, from the chic East Side to the arty West Side; from SoHo to Greenwich Village. They range from a historic brownstone, where the host is an artist, to a terraced apartment near Lincoln Center. Leslie's hosts are enthusiastic about the Big Apple and happy to share their insider information with you. Unhosted apartments range from $80 to $300 in price.

Stella Marina Enterprise ✪
58-29 74TH STREET, ELMHURST, NEW YORK 11373

Tel: (212) 475-6092; (800) 219-9251;
  fax: (718) 478-2113
Best Time to Call: 9 AM–5 PM
Coordinator: Vincenzo D'Aleo
States/Regions Covered: All fifty
  states, Italy

Rates (Single/Double)
  Modest: $60 / $85
  Average: $70 / $95
  Luxury: $80 / $95–$110
Minimum Stay: Two nights

At a bed and breakfast, you get the warmth of a friendly atmosphere—at considerable savings. Stella Marina Enterprise offers bed and breakfast accommodations in numerous locations in New York City and worldwide. In addition, this company can provide the full range of travel services, including flight reservations and cruise bookings. Unhosted furnished apartments are also available.

Urban Ventures ✪
P.O. BOX 426, NEW YORK, NEW YORK 10024

Tel: (212) 594-5650; fax: 947-9320
Best Time to Call: Mon.–Fri., 9 AM–5
  PM
Coordinator: Mary McAulay

States/Regions Covered: New
  York—Manhattan; New Jersey
Rates (Single/Double):
  Modest: $50 / $60

Average: **$60–$70 / $75–$80**
Luxury: **$75–$80 / $90–$120**
Credit Cards: **AMEX, CB, DISC, MC,
VISA**

Minimum Stay: **2 nights B&Bs; 3 nights
unhosted apartments**

Great values are offered by this registry. Mary has bedrooms and complete apartments located throughout New York City, including landmarked historic districts. She'll be happy to help with theater tickets, restaurant information, current museum exhibits, and special tours. Unhosted apartments range from $70 to $140 for two.

The Villa ✪
90 ROCKLEDGE ROAD, BRONXVILLE, NEW YORK 10708

Tel: **(914) 337-7050; messages: (914)
337-5595; fax: (914) 337-5661**
Host: **Helen Zuckermann**
Location: **6 mi. N of New York City**
No. of Rooms: **2**
No. of Private Baths: **2**
Double/pb: **$80**
Single/pb: **$70**
Suites: **$110**
Open: **All year**

Reduced Rates: **Available**
Breakfast: **Continental**
Other Meals: **Available**
Pets: **No**
Children: **Welcome**
Smoking: **Permitted**
Social Drinking: **Permitted**
Airport/Station Pickup: **Yes**
Foreign Languages: **French, German,
Italian, Spanish**

A spacious country residence, The Villa was formerly owned by Columbia University—when Dwight Eisenhower was the university's president, he spent weekends here. You'll want to do the same, thanks to the quiet, convenient setting, the large terraces and gardens, and extras like a hot tub and a home office equipped with a personal computer, typewriter, copier, and fax machine (secretarial services can also be arranged). Continental breakfast is set out in a small, sunny dining room, and snacks and beverages are available at other times of the day.

Kroghs Nest ✪
4 HILLCREST ROAD, HARTSDALE, NEW YORK 10530

Tel: **(914) 946-3479**
Best Time to Call: **7 AM–10 PM**
Hosts: **Claudia and James P. Krogh**
Location: **21 mi. N of New York City
Grand Central Station**
No. of Rooms: **3**
No. of Private Baths: **2**
Max. No. Sharing Bath: **4**
Double/pb: **$60**
Single/pb: **$55**
Double/sb: **$50**

Single/sb: **$45**
Open: **All year**
Reduced Rates: **15% weekly; students**
Breakfast: **Full**
Credit Cards: **AMEX**
Pets: **No**
Children: **Welcome (crib & highchair)**
Smoking: **No**
Social Drinking: **Permitted**
Airport/Station Pickup: **Yes**

Built in 1896, this Center Hall Victorian sits on a hillside acre, enclosed by greenery and beautiful flowers. You'll admire the authentic Colonial decor: breakfast is served on a large antique table surrounded by pine cupboards and porcelain ornaments. The upstairs bedrooms are air-conditioned; two rooms have color TVs. Washing machines and dryers are available for guests' use. The location couldn't be more convenient, since New York City's stores, historic sites, museums, restaurants, and theaters are easily accessible. Educational institutions within 10 miles include Sarah Lawrence College, Pace Westchester University, the State University of New York at Purchase, and New York Medical College.

NIAGARA/BUFFALO AREA

International Bed & Breakfast Club, Inc.
504 AMHERST STREET, BUFFALO, NEW YORK 14207

Tel: **(800) 723-4262**
Best Time to Call: **9 AM–9 PM,**
  everyday
Coordinator: **Georgia Brannan**
States/Regions Covered: **Florida,**
  Massachusetts, New York,
  Pennsylvania, South Carolina;
  Canada: Ontario

Descriptive Directory of B&Bs: **$10**
Rates (Single/Double):
  Modest: **$40**
  Average: **$65 / $85**
Credit Cards: **AMEX, DISC, MC, VISA**

The International Bed and Breakfast Club opens your world to home-spun hospitality, with locations in metropolitan areas, historic districts, exclusive suburbs, getaway resorts, and quiet countryside settings. All B&Bs are guaranteed for comfort, cleanliness, and hospitality, and reservations come complete with maps and directions to each destination. Customized area lists and trip planning services are available.

The Eastwood House ✪
45 SOUTH MAIN STREET, ROUTE 39, CASTILE, NEW YORK 14427

Tel: **(716) 493-2335**
Best Time to Call: **Before 8:30 AM;**
  after 6 PM
Host: **Joan Ballinger**
Location: **63 mi. SE of Buffalo on**
  Rte. 39
No. of Rooms: **2**
Max. No. Sharing Bath: **4**

Double/sb: **$30**
Single/sb: **$25**
Open: **All year**
Breakfast: **Continental**
Pets: **Sometimes**
Children: **Welcome, over 5**
Smoking: **No**
Social Drinking: **Permitted**

This comfortable older home in a rural area is close to the Genesee Country Museum, Letchworth State Park, which is called the Grand Canyon of the East, Geneseo and Houghton colleges, and Silver Lake, known for fishing and boating. Delicious hot muffins, fresh fruits, and a choice of beverages are typical breakfast fare. Joan will be happy to direct you to local wineries and the Corning Glass factory and museum.

The Teepee ✪
14396 FOUR MILE LEVEL ROAD, GOWANDA, NEW YORK 14070-9796

Tel: (716) 532-2168
Hosts: **Max and Phyllis Lay**
Location: **30 mi. S of Buffalo**
No. of Rooms: **3**
Max. No. Sharing Bath: **3**
Double/sb: **$45**
Single/sb: **$35**

Open: **All year**
Breakfast: **Full**
Pets: **Sometimes**
Children: **Welcome (crib)**
Smoking: **Permitted**
Social Drinking: **Permitted**
Airport/Station Pickup: **Yes**

Max and Phyllis Lay are Seneca Indians living on the Cattaraugus Indian Reservation. Their airy four-bedroom home is clean, modern, and decorated with family Indian articles, many of them crafted by hand. The reservation offers country living and the opportunity of seeing firsthand the customs of a Native American community. A fall festival with arts, crafts, and exhibition dancing is held in September. Canoeing, fishing, rafting, cross-country and downhill skiing, and a sport called snowsnake are among the local activities. Your hosts will gladly arrange tours of the Amish community, and hot-air balloon rides over the beautiful rolling hills.

The Cameo Inn ✪
4710 LOWER RIVER ROAD, LEWISTON, NEW YORK 14092

Tel: (716) 754-2075
Best Time to Call: **9 AM–9 PM**
Hosts: **Gregory and Carolyn Fisher**
Location: **5 mi. N of Niagara Falls**
No. of Rooms: **4**
No. of Private Baths: **2**
Max. No. Sharing Bath: **4**
Double/pb: **$80**
Single/pb: **$75**
Double/sb: **$65** .
Single/sb: **$60**
Suites: **$115**

Open: **All year**
Reduced Rates: **10% Jan.–Apr.;**
5 nights or more
Breakfast: **Full**
Credit Cards: **MC, VISA**
Pets: **No**
Children: **Welcome**
Smoking: **No**
Social Drinking: **Permitted**
Minimum Stay: **2 nights holiday**
weekends

Gregory and Carolyn's authentically furnished Queen Anne Victorian home commands a majestic view of the lower Niagara River. Located just 25 miles north of Buffalo and 5 miles north of Niagara Falls, The Cameo is conveniently situated for sightseeing, antiquing, fishing and boating, golfing, bicycling, or shopping at local factory outlets and malls. History buffs will want to travel 5 miles north to Old Fort

Niagara, which dates from the American Revolution; the bridge to Canada is minutes away. A full country breakfast is served in the dining room each morning.

Manchester House
653 MAIN STREET, NIAGARA FALLS, NEW YORK 14301

Tel: **(716) 285-5717**	Reduced Rates: **Available**
Best Time to Call: **9 AM–6 PM**	Breakfast: **Full**
Hosts: **Lis and Carl Slenk**	Credit Cards: **MC, VISA**
No. of Rooms: **4**	Pets: **No**
Max. No. Sharing Bath: **4**	Children: **Welcome**
Double/sb: **$70**	Smoking: **No**
Single/sb: **$50**	Social Drinking: **Permitted**
Open: **All year**	Foreign Languages: **German**

Before it was incorporated, Niagara Falls was known as Manchester—hence the name for this tastefully renovated B&B, which was a doctor's office for more than sixty years. Lis and Carl collected ideas and furniture for their home during the ten years they spent in England and Germany. Manchester House is conveniently located near the falls, with easy access to Canada. (Spacious off-street parking is provided.) The bright, cheerful guest rooms offer a choice of queen-size or single beds. Breakfast features home-baked specialties.

THOUSAND ISLANDS AREA

Battle Island Inn ✪
BOX 176, RD 1, FULTON, NEW YORK 13069

Tel: **(315) 593-3699**	Open: **All year**
Hosts: **Joyce and Richard Rice**	Breakfast: **Full**
Location: **30 mi. N of Syracuse**	Pets: **No**
No. of Rooms: **6**	Children: **Welcome**
No. of Private Baths: **6**	Smoking: **No**
Double/pb: **$60–$80**	Social Drinking: **Permitted**
Single/pb: **$50–$65**	

The Rice family welcomes you to their pre–Civil War estate, which they restored themselves with lots of love and hard work. The inn is across the street from a golf course and is surrounded by fields and orchards. The rooms feature Victorian antiques and marble fireplaces. Guest bedrooms are spacious and elegant with imposing high-backed beds. Joyce is a full-time host, who will tempt your palate with homemade rolls, biscuits, and crêpes. Richard is a systems analyst who oversees the challenges of an 1840s house. Whether you're enjoying the privacy of your room or socializing in the formal front parlor, you are sure to appreciate the friendly family atmosphere.

NORTH CAROLINA

Germanton
Mt. Airy • Winston-Salem • Weldon
Sparta • • Greensboro • Tarboro
Boone • Banner • Durham
Spruce Pine • Elk Raleigh • • Wilson Kill Devil Hills
Burnsville •
• Washington
Clyde • Asheville • Taylorsville
Waynesville • • Hendersonville • Salisbury
Franklin • • Pisgah Forest Statesville New Bern
Murphy • Highlands • • Tryon • Charlotte Morehead City • • Beaufort
Saluda • Swansboro
• Wilmington

Abbington Green Bed and Breakfast Inn
46 CUMBERLAND CIRCLE, ASHEVILLE, NORTH CAROLINA 28801

Tel: **(704) 251-2454**
Best Time to Call: **9 AM–9 PM**
Hosts: **Valerie, Gabrielle and Julie Larrea**
Location: **¾ mi from I-240 Exit 4C**
No. of Rooms: **6**
No. of Private Baths: **6**
Double/pb: **$85–$110**
Suites: **$120**

Open: **All year**
Breakfast: **Full**
Credit Cards: **AMEX, MC, VISA**
Pets: **No**
Children: **Welcome, over 10**
Smoking: **No**
Social Drinking: **Permitted**
Minimum Stay: **2 nights weekends**

Enjoy elegance with a romantic English flavor. This sunlit 1908 Colonial Revival home in the Montford Historic District is a delight to behold inside and out. Stylishly appointed guest rooms are named after parks and gardens around London; each has a canopy-draped queen-size bed, antiques, fine rugs, and air-conditioning. Three guest rooms have fireplaces. Play piano or chess, daydream, or relax with a

Tug Hill Lodge ☉
8091 SALISBURY STREET, BOX 204, SANDY CREEK, NEW Y

Tel: **(315) 387-5326**
Best Time to Call: **After 3 PM**
Host: **Margaret Clerkin**
Location: **40 mi. N of Syracuse**
No. of Rooms: **5**
Max. No. Sharing Bath: **3**
Double/sb: **$60**

Single/sb: **$30**
Open: **All year**
Breakfast: **Full**
Pets: **Sometimes**
Children: **Sometimes**
Smoking: **No**
Social Drinking: **Permitted**

Margaret's large Italianate Victorian home, with cupola, was buil
1872. The interior is comfortable, with a two-story sun room and de
Down quilts on the double or queen-size beds ensure a cozy night
sleep. A full English breakfast is the house specialty, but if you prefe
vegetarian food or are on a special diet, give Margaret fair notice and
she'll accommodate you. Ski, fish, hunt, go to a local concert or
theater, shop, or simply curl up with a good book and rest.

good book beside the parlor or living room fireplaces. Start each morning with a homemade breakfast featuring crepes or quiche. Abbington Green is located minutes from Biltmore House, Blue Ridge Parkway, University of North Carolina, and fine restaurants and shops.

Acorn Cottage ✪
25 SAINT DUNSTANS CIRCLE, ASHEVILLE, NORTH CAROLINA 28803

Tel: **(704) 253-0609**
Best Time to Call: **10 AM–9 PM**
Host: **Connie Stahl**
Location: **1¼ mi. from Route I40, exit 50/50B**
No. of Rooms: **4**
No. of Private Baths: **4**
Double/pb: **$75–$85**
Single/pb: **$70–$80**

Open: **All year**
Breakfast: **Full**
Credit Cards: **MC, VISA**
Pets: **No**
Children: **Welcome**
Smoking: **No**
Social Drinking: **Permitted**
Minimum Stay: **2 nights weekends, March 15–Dec. 31**

An English country cottage in the woodsy heart of Asheville, Acorn is built of local granite; the interior boasts maple floors and a granite fireplace. The guest rooms feature queen-size beds, fine linens, air-conditioning, TV, and baths stocked with special soaps. A delicious full breakfast is served each morning with fresh fruit, varied entrees, juice, coffee, tea, and an assortment of breads, muffins, and coffee-cakes. Then you're ready for the quarter-mile trip to the Biltmore Estate.

Applewood Manor
62 CUMBERLAND CIRCLE, ASHEVILLE, NORTH CAROLINA 28801

Tel: **(704) 254-2244**
Best Time to Call: **11 AM–9 PM**
Hosts: **Susan Poole and Maryanne Young**
Location: **¾ mi. from Rte. 240, Exit 4C**
No. of Rooms: **4**
No. of Private Baths: **4**
Double/pb: **$85–$95**
Single/pb: **$80–$90**
Guest Cottage: **$115**

Suite: **$105**
Open: **All year**
Reduced Rates: **10% Jan.–Feb.; 10% seniors (Sept. only)**
Breakfast: **Full**
Credit Cards: **DISC, MC, VISA**
Pets: **No**
Children: **Welcome, over 12**
Smoking: **No**
Social Drinking: **Permitted**
Minimum Stay: **2 nights weekends**

Built in 1908, this Colonial Revival home boasts wide porches with rockers and a swing, and two manicured acres perfect for a game of badminton or croquet. Fine lace curtains, antique furnishings, heart-pine floors covered with oriental rugs, and bright and airy rooms, most with fireplaces and balconies, are found throughout. Breakfast always includes something special, such as orange-pecan waffles or apple and brie omelets. It's only a mile away from fine restaurants, antique and crafts shops, an art museum, theater, and the Thomas Wolfe Memorial.

Cairn Brae ✪
217 PATTON MOUNTAIN ROAD, ASHEVILLE, NORTH CAROLINA 28804

Tel: **(704) 252-9219**	Breakfast: **Full**
Hosts: **Milli and Ed Adams**	Credit Cards: **MC, VISA**
No. of Rooms: **3**	Pets: **No**
No. of Private Baths: **3**	Children: **Welcome, over 10**
Double/pb: **$85**	Smoking: **No**
Suites: **$100–$130**	Social Drinking: **Permitted**
Open: **Apr. 1–Nov. 30**	Airport/Station Pickup: **Yes**

Cairn Brae is a secluded mountain retreat on wooded acreage, just minutes from downtown Asheville. Enjoy the beautiful mountain views and walking trails, or relax by the fireplace in the cozy guest living room. Afternoon refreshments are served on the terrace, and a full homemade breakfast is offered in the morning.

Carolina Bed & Breakfast ✪
177 CUMBERLAND AVENUE, ASHEVILLE, NORTH CAROLINA 28801

Tel: **(704) 254-3608**	Open: **All year**
Best Time to Call: **7 AM–9 PM**	Breakfast: **Full**
Hosts: **Sam and Karin Fain**	Credit Cards: **MC, VISA**
Location: **½ mi. from route 240, Exit 4C**	Pets: **No**
	Children: **Welcome, over 12**
No. of Rooms: **5**	Smoking: **No**
No. of Private Baths: **5**	Social Drinking: **Permitted**
Double/pb: **$80–$90**	Minimum Stay: **2 nights holidays, in season weekends**
Single/pb: **$65–$75**	
Guest Cottage: **$110**	

This turn-of-the-century Colonial Revival home has been painstakingly restored; feel free to relax on the front and back porches, or just take in the view from the second-floor guest rooms, with their distinctive, twelve-over-one panes. In springtime, the grounds bloom with dogwoods and rhododendrons. On cooler days, you can curl up in front of one of the house's seven fireplaces. Your hosts serve a different full breakfast each day; the usual fare includes eggs or quiche and fresh bread and muffins.

The Colby House
230 PEARSON DRIVE, ASHEVILLE, NORTH CAROLINA 28801

Tel: **(704) 253-5644; (800) 982-2118**
Hosts: **Everett and Ann Colby**
No. of Rooms: **4**
No. of Private Baths: **4**
Double/pb: **$80–$110**
Open: **All year**

Breakfast: **Full**
Credit Cards: **MC, VISA**
Pets: **No**
Children: **Welcome, over 12**
Smoking: **Restricted**
Social Drinking: **Permitted**

This elegant Dutch-Tudor house in the Montford Historic District is a special place, thanks to its porch, beautiful gardens, and inviting fireplaces. Each guest room has its own individual decor and queen-size beds. Refreshments are available at all times, and wine and cheese are served in the evening. Breakfasts vary daily, but are always served on fine china, with heirloom crystal and silver. Southern hospitality abounds in your hosts' personal attention to every guest's needs.

Corner Oak Manor ✪
53 ST. DUNSTANS ROAD, ASHEVILLE, NORTH CAROLINA 28803

Tel: **(704) 253-3525**
Best Time to Call: **9 AM–9 PM**
Hosts: **Karen and Andy Spradley**
Location: **1¼ mi. from Rte. 40, Exit 50**
No. of Rooms: **4**
No. of Private Baths: **4**
Double/pb: **$85**
Single/pb: **$65**
Cottage: **$100**

Open: **All year**
Breakfast: **Full**
Credit Cards: **AMEX, DISC, MC, VISA**
Pets: **No**
Children: **Welcome, over 12 in house, under 12 in cottage**
Smoking: **No**
Social Drinking: **Permitted**

Surrounded by maple, oak, and evergreen trees, this lovely English Tudor home is located minutes away from the famed Biltmore Estate and Gardens. The rooms have queen-size beds beautifully covered in fine linen. The window treatments and coordinated wall coverings could easily grace the pages of a decorating magazine. Handmade wreaths, weavings, and stitchery complement the furnishings. Breakfast specialties include orange French toast, blueberry-ricotta pancakes, or four-cheese-herb quiche. A living room fireplace, baby grand piano, outdoor deck, and Jacuzzi are among the gracious amenities.

Flint Street Inns
100 & 116 FLINT STREET, ASHEVILLE, NORTH CAROLINA 28801

Tel: **(704) 253-6723**
Hosts: **Rick, Lynne, and Marion Vogel**
Location: **¼ mi. from Rte. 240**
No. of Rooms: **8**
No. of Private Baths: **8**

Double/pb: **$80**
Single/pb: **$65**
Open: **All year**
Breakfast: **Full**
Credit Cards: **AMEX, DISC, MC, VISA**

Pets: **No**   Smoking: **Permitted**
Children: **No**   Social Drinking: **Permitted**

These turn-of-the-century homes on an acre with century-old trees are listed on the National Register of Historic Places. Stained glass, pine floors, and a claw-footed bathtub are part of the Victorian decor. The inns are air-conditioned for summer comfort; some have fireplaces for winter coziness. Guests are served wine, coffee, and soft drinks. The Blue Ridge Parkway is close by.

The Banner Elk Inn Bed & Breakfast ⊘
ROUTE 3, BOX 1134, HIGHWAY 194 NORTH, BANNER ELK, NORTH CAROLINA 28604

Tel: **(704) 898-6223**
Best Time to Call: **9 AM–10 PM**
Host: **Beverly Lait**
Location: **17 mi. W of Boone**
No. of Rooms: **4**
No. of Private Baths: **2**
Max. No. Sharing Bath: **4**
Double/pb: **$60–$95**
Single/pb: **$60–$85**
Suites: **$90–$140; sleeps 4**
Double/sb: **$60–$75**
Single/sb: **$50–$65**

Open: **All year**
Reduced Rates: **Available**
Breakfast: **Full**
Credit Cards: **MC, VISA**
Pets: **Yes**
Children: **Welcome**
Smoking: **No**
Social Drinking: **Permitted**
Minimum Stay: **Mid-July; first 2 weeks of Oct.; ski season Dec. 25–Mar. 30; 2 nights weekends**
Foreign Languages: **Spanish, German**

Your host, Beverly, spent years with the Foreign Service, and original tapestries, artwork, and antiques from around the world fill her stunningly renovated historic home. The inn is located halfway between the Sugar Resort and Beech Mountain ski slopes, near such major tourist attractions as Grandfather Mountain and Natural Habitat, Linville Falls, Valle Crucis, and the Blue Ridge Parkway. You'll have energy to visit all these places after Beverly's full breakfasts of homemade breads, eggs, fruit, juice, and coffee or tea.

Delamar Inn ✪
217 TURNER STREET, BEAUFORT, NORTH CAROLINA 28516

Tel: **(919) 728-4300**	Open: **All year**
Best Time to Call: **Anytime**	Breakfast: **Continental, plus**
Hosts: **Tom and Mabel Steepy**	Credit Cards: **MC, VISA**
Location: **140 mi. SE of Raleigh**	Pets: **No**
No. of Rooms: **3**	Children: **Welcome, over 10**
No. of Private Baths: **3**	Smoking: **Restricted**
Double/pb: **$85**	Social Drinking: **Permitted**
Single/pb: **$85**	Airport/Station Pickup: **Yes**

The Delamar Inn, built in 1866, is located in historic Beaufort, North Carolina's third oldest town. The inn offers three guest rooms furnished with antiques, each room with a private bath. After a delightful breakfast, stroll down to the historic restoration grounds, maritime museum, or the open-air bus, or browse in the waterfront specialty shops. Tom and Mabel, your hosts, can offer directions to local beaches for shell collecting, sunbathing, or fishing. Try a short ride to Fort Macon, Tryon Palace, or the ferry to the Outer Banks. A selection of the '91 and '92 historic homes tour, the Delamar Inn welcomes you.

Grandma Jean's Bed and Breakfast ✪
254 MEADOWVIEW DRIVE, BOONE, NORTH CAROLINA 28607

Tel: **(704) 262-3670**	Pets: **No**
Best Time to Call: **Anytime**	Children: **Welcome, under 2 and**
Host: **Dr. Jean Probinsky**	**over 6**
No. of Rooms: **3**	Smoking: **Permitted**
Max. No. Sharing Bath: **4**	Social Drinking: **Permitted**
Double/sb: **$50–$60**	Airport/Station Pickup: **Yes**
Single/sb: **$40**	Minimum Stay: **2 nights**
Open: **Apr. 1–Nov. 1**	Foreign Languages: **Spanish**
Breakfast: **Continental**	

Wicker furniture and lots of rocking chairs make this a cozy country home. Boone offers easy access to the Blue Ridge Parkway, and Appalachian State University—the summer residence of the North Carolina Symphony—is just one mile away. Grandma Jean prides herself on her Southern hospitality. Her Continental breakfast includes coffee, tea, seasonal fruit, and croissants with homemade preserves.

Estes Mountain Retreat ✪
ROUTE 1, BOX 1316A (OFF BAKER'S CREEK ROAD), BURNSVILLE,
NORTH CAROLINA 28714

Tel: **(704) 682-7264**
Best Time to Call: **After 7 PM**
Hosts: **Bruce and Maryallen Estes**
Location: **37 mi. NE of Asheville**
No. of Rooms: **2**
No. of Private Baths: **1**
Max. No. Sharing Bath: **4**
Double/pb: **$60**
Double/sb: **$55**

Open: **All year**
Reduced Rates: **15% weekly; 10%
seniors**
Breakfast: **Full**
Pets: **No**
Children: **Welcome, over 3**
Smoking: **No**
Social Drinking: **Permitted**
Foreign Languages: **French**

Breathtaking mountain views await you at this three-level cedar log
home with a rock chimney, fireplace, and porches. Because Burnsville
is in Pisgah National Forest, you won't have to travel far to go rafting,
fishing, hiking, and rock and gem hunting, and there's golfing next
door at Mountain Air Country Club. Mt. Mitchell, Linville Caverns,
outdoor theater, the Biltmore Mansion, and the Carl Sandburg Home
are all within an hour's drive.

Hamrick Inn ✪
7787 HIGHWAY 80 SOUTH, BURNSVILLE, NORTH CAROLINA 28714

Tel: **(704) 675-5251**
Best Time to Call: **Mornings**
Hosts: **Neal and June Jerome**
Location: **55 mi. NE of Asheville; 16
mi. from I-40, Exit 72**
No. of Rooms: **4**
No. of Private Baths: **4**
Double/pb: **$50–$60**

Single/pb: **$45–$55**
Open: **Apr. 2–Oct. 31**
Reduced Rates: **Weekly**
Breakfast: **Full**
Pets: **No**
Children: **Welcome**
Smoking: **Permitted**
Social Drinking: **Permitted**

This charming three-story Colonial-style stone inn is nestled at the
foot of Mt. Mitchell, the highest mountain east of the Mississippi
River. Much of the lovely furniture was built by Neal and June. The
den has a fine selection of books as well as a TV set for your
enjoyment. There is a private porch off each bedroom, where you may
take in the view and the cool mountain breezes. Golfing, hiking,
fishing, rock hounding, craft shopping, and fall foliage wandering
are local activities. Pisgah National Park, Linville Caverns, Crabtree
Meadows, and the Parkway Playhouse are area diversions.

The Elizabeth ✪
2145 EAST 5TH STREET, CHARLOTTE, NORTH CAROLINA 28204

Tel: **(704) 358-1368**
Best Time to Call: **Evenings**

Host: **Joan Mastny**
Location: **3 mi. from Rte. I-77, Exit 10B**

No. of Rooms: **2**
No. of Private Baths: **2**
Double/pb: **$58**
Single/pb: **$55**
Guest Cottage: $70–$78
Open: **All year**

Breakfast: **Continental**
Credit Cards: **MC, VISA**
Pets: **No**
Children: **Welcome, over 12**
Smoking: **No**
Social Drinking: **Permitted**

This 1927 Prairie Style house is located in Elizabeth, Charlotte's second oldest suburb. Wander the old tree-lined streets and discover lovely historic homes. Antique shops, a variety of restaurants, and the Mint Museum of Art are all within walking distance. Guest quarters consist of the Garden Room, featuring Laura Ashley wallpapers and linens, and the Guest Cottage, a decorator's dream in blue and white. Each has a courtyard entrance, private bath, antique brass and iron double bed, central air-conditioning, television, and private telephone. Amenities include complimentary coffee, tea, juice, and hot chocolate. A hearty Continental breakfast-in-a-basket is brought to your room.

The Homeplace
5901 SARDIS ROAD, CHARLOTTE, NORTH CAROLINA 28270

Tel: **(704) 365-1936**
Hosts: **Peggy and Frank Dearien**
Location: **10 mi. from I-77; I-85**
No. of Rooms: **4**
No. of Private Baths: **2**
Max. No. Sharing Bath: **4**
Double/pb: **$78**
Single/pb: **$78**
Double/sb: **$68**

Single/sb: **$68**
Open: **All year**
Breakfast: **Full**
Credit Cards: **AMEX, MC, VISA**
Pets: **No**
Children: **Welcome, over 10**
Smoking: **No**
Social Drinking: **No**

The warm and friendly atmosphere hasn't changed since 1902. The minute you arrive at this country Victorian and walk up to the wraparound porch with its rockers, you'll feel you've "come home." The handcrafted staircase, 10-foot beaded ceilings, and heart pine floors add to the interior's beauty. It's convenient to malls, furniture and textile outlets, and treasure-filled antique shops.

Still Waters ✪
6221 AMOS SMITH ROAD, CHARLOTTE, NORTH CAROLINA 28214

Tel: **(704) 399-6299**
Best Time to Call: **Evenings**
Hosts: **Janet and Rob Dyer**

Location: **3 mi. W of Charlotte**
No. of Rooms: **3**
No. of Private Baths: **3**

Double/pb: **$65–$85**
Open: **All year**
Reduced Rates: **Available**
Breakfast: **Full**
Credit Cards: **MC, VISA**
Pets: **No**

Children: **Welcome**
Smoking: **No**
Social Drinking: **Permitted**
Minimum Stay: **2 nights weekends only May 1–Nov. 15**

Relax on the river just outside Charlotte city limits—only minutes away from downtown, the airport, or the interstates, but a world away from the bustle of everyday life. Visit this lakefront log home on two wooded acres. Enjoy the deck, garden, dock, and boat ramp, or play on the sport court. Guests stay in either of two large rooms or in a suite. Full breakfasts always feature homemade sourdough rolls and fresh-ground coffee.

Windsong: A Mountain Inn ⊙
120 FERGUSON RIDGE, CLYDE, NORTH CAROLINA 28721

Tel: **(704) 627-6111**
Best Time to Call: **8 AM–9 PM**
Hosts: **Donna and Gale Livengood**
Location: **36 mi. W of Asheville**
No. of Rooms: **5**
No. of Private Baths: **5**
Double/pb: **$85**
Single/pb: **$81–$85**
Open: **Feb.–Dec.**

Reduced Rates: **10%, singles and weekly bookings**
Breakfast: **Full**
Credit Cards: **MC, VISA**
Pets: **No**
Children: **Welcome, over 8**
Smoking: **No**
Social Drinking: **Permitted**

From its mountainside perch near Waynesville, this immense contemporary log home affords spectacular views of the surrounding countryside. Inside, the house is bright and airy, thanks to the large windows and skylights and the high exposed-beam ceilings. Each oversized room boasts its own patio, fireplace, and deep tubs for two. There are a tennis court and in-ground pool, plus a billiard table and an extensive video library with in-room VCRs. You'll love their llama herd with group pack trips going into the national forests. Nearby attractions include horseback riding, white-water rafting, Cherokee Indian Reservation, Great Smoky Mountain National Park, Biltmore House, and the Appalachian Trail. You'll relish home-baked breakfast goods. Typical entrées are buckwheat banana pancakes and egg-sausage strata with mushrooms.

The Blooming Garden Inn ⊙
513 HOLLOWAY STREET, DURHAM, NORTH CAROLINA 27701

Tel: **(919) 687-0801**
Best Time to Call: **Evenings**
Hosts: **Frank and Dolly Pokrass**
Location: **Downtown Durham**

No. of Rooms: **5**
No. of Private Baths: **5**
Double/pb: **$85–$95**
Suites: **$135–$150**

Open: **All year**
Reduced Rates: **Available**
Breakfast: **Full**
Credit Cards: **AMEX, DC, DISC, MC, VISA**

Pets: **No**
Children: **Welcome**
Smoking: **No**
Social Drinking: **Permitted**

If you appreciate flowers—and who doesn't?—you'll love staying at this restored 1892 Victorian with glorious gardens at every turn. The house is handsome, too, with its gabled roof, beveled and stained-glass windows, and wraparound porch supported by Tuscan columns. What's more, you're right in the center of Durham's historic Holloway District, just moments from shops, galleries, theaters, Duke University, and the University of North Carolina. For the ultimate in pampering, luxury suites with Jacuzzis are available.

Buttonwood Inn ✪
190 GEORGIA ROAD, FRANKLIN, NORTH CAROLINA 28734

Tel: **(704) 369-8985**
Best Time to Call: **After 5 PM**
Host: **Liz Oehser**
Location: **75 mi. SW of Asheville**
No. of Rooms: **4**
No. of Private Baths: **2**
Max. No. Sharing Bath: **4**
Double/pb: **$60–$75**
Single/pb: **$50**

Double/sb: **$55**
Single/sb: **$45**
Suites: **$95**
Open: **Apr. 15–Nov. 15**
Breakfast: **Full**
Pets: **No**
Children: **Welcome, over 10**
Smoking: **Permitted**
Social Drinking: **Permitted**

The Buttonwood is a small country inn surrounded by towering pines, a spacious lawn, and mountain views. The original residence was a small cottage built in the late 1920s adjacent to the greens of the Franklin golf course. Years later, a new wing was added with rustic, charming rooms. Guests may choose from comfortable bedrooms decorated with antiques, cozy quilts, and handcrafts, many of which are offered for sale. Breakfast selections include sausage-apple ring, eggs Benedict, or cheese frittata, with coffee cake and plenty of hot coffee or tea. Golfers will be glad to be so close to the beautiful fairways and Bermuda grass greens right next door. Nearby there are also crafts shops, hiking trails, the Blue Ridge Parkway, gem mines, and plenty of places to swim and ride.

Heritage Inn ✪
101 HERITAGE HOLLOW, FRANKLIN, NORTH CAROLINA 28734

Tel: **(704) 524-4150**	Reduced Rates: **10% less Nov.–Mar.**
Best Time to Call: **9 AM-9 PM**	Breakfast: **Full**
Host: **Sally Wade**	Pets: **No**
Location: **135 mi. NE Atlanta, Georgia**	Children: **Welcome, over 12**
No. of Rooms: **4**	Smoking: **No**
No. of Private Baths: **4**	Social Drinking: **Permitted**
Double/pb: **$55–$65**	Minimum Stay: **2 nights, holiday and**
Single/pb: **$48**	**October weekends**
Open: **All year**	Airport Pickup: **Yes**

Rocking on the veranda over a cascading waterfall is one of the favorite pastimes at this tin-roofed, in-town country inn. Nestled in the Smoky Mountains tall pines, it is close to gem mining, whitewater rafting, hiking trails, and country auctions, within walking distance of museums, mountain crafts and antique shops. On the premises is a gallery of tribal art and artifacts that Sally collected in her world travels. Each immaculate, tastefully furnished room has its own entrance and porch for added privacy. Kitchenettes are available. A full breakfast and evening dessert are served. Complimentary beverages are offered throughout the day and evening at the lovely, creekside gazebo.

MeadowHaven Bed & Breakfast ✪
NC HIGHWAY 8, P.O. BOX 222, GERMANTON, NORTH CAROLINA 27019

Tel: **(910) 593-3996**	Cabins: **$125–$175**
Best Time to Call: **9 AM-9 PM**	Open: **All year**
Hosts: **Samuel and Darlene Fain**	Breakfast: **Full, Continental, plus**
Location: **16 mi. N of Winston-Salem**	Pets: **No**
No. of Rooms: **3**	Children: **No**
No. of Private Baths: **3**	Smoking: **No**
Double/pb: **$60–$90**	

| Social drinking: **Permitted, in guest rooms** | Minimum Stay: **2 nights, holidays all accommodations, 2 nights, weekends cabins** |

MeadowHaven is a chalet-style retreat on 25 acres, with stunning mountain views from the B&B's large deck. Immerse yourself in the hot tub or the heated indoor pool, grab some snacks from the pantry, and test your skills in the game room, at the fishing pond, or on the archery ranges. For honeymooners, the Lovebirds' Retreat, with its whirlpool tub and steam shower, is ideal. You won't have to travel far for horseback riding, canoeing, and golf; other local attractions include a winery, an art gallery, and Sauratown Mountain. Darlene, a former controller for the Marriott Corporation, runs her family's construction business, and Sam is a retail manager interested in greenhouse gardening, magic, and birds.

Belle Meade Inn ✪

804 BALSAM ROAD, HAZELWOOD, NORTH CAROLINA 28738 (MAILING ADDRESS: P.O. BOX 1319, WAYNESVILLE, NORTH CAROLINA 28786)

Tel: **(704) 456-3234**	Reduced Rates: **10% AARP; weekly**
Hosts: **Gloria and Al DiNofa**	Breakfast: **Full**
Location: **27 mi. W of Asheville**	Credit Cards: **DISC, MC, VISA**
No. of Rooms: **4**	Pets: **No**
No. of Private Baths: **4**	Children: **Welcome, over 6**
Double/pb: **$55–$60**	Smoking: **No**
Single/pb: **$50–$55**	Social Drinking: **Permitted**
Open: **All year**	

Nestled in the mountains, and within easy reach of the Great Smoky National Park, this elegant home is a frame dwelling built in the craftsman style popular in the early 1900s. The warm richness of the chestnut woodwork in the formal rooms and the large stone fireplace in the living room complement the appealing blend of antique and traditional furnishings. The friendly attention to guests' needs is exemplified in such thoughtful touches as "early bird" coffee brought to your door, complimentary refreshments on the veranda, and fresh flowers and mints in your room. Nearby attractions include Biltmore House, Catalooche Ski Slope, mountain art and crafts festivals, and white-water rafting and tubing.

The Waverly Inn ✪

783 NORTH MAIN STREET, HENDERSONVILLE, NORTH CAROLINA 28792

Tel: **(800) 537-8195; (704) 693-9193**	Location: **20 mi. S of Asheville**
Best Time to Call: **9:30 AM–10 PM**	No. of Rooms: **14**
Hosts: **John and Diane Sheiry**	No. of Private Baths: **14**

Double/pb: **$89–$109**
Single/pb: **$79**
Open: **All year**
Reduced Rates: **Off-season**
Breakfast: **Full**

Credit Cards: **AMEX, DISC, MC, VISA**
Pets: **No**
Children: **Welcome**
Smoking: **Permitted**
Social Drinking: **Permitted**

Built as a boardinghouse in 1898, the Waverly is distinguished by its handsome Eastlake staircase—a factor that earned the inn a listing on the National Register of Historic Places. Furnishings like four-poster canopy beds and claw-footed tubs combine Victorian stateliness and Colonial Revival charm. You'll walk away sated from all-you-can-eat breakfasts of pancakes and French toast. Noteworthy local sites include the Biltmore Estate, the Carl Sandburg house, the Blue Ridge Parkway, and the Flat Rock Playhouse.

Colonial Pines Inn ✪
ROUTE 1, BOX 22B, HICKORY STREET, HIGHLANDS, NORTH CAROLINA 28741

Tel: **(704) 526-2060**
Best Time to Call: **Afternoons**
Hosts: **Chris and Donna Alley**
Location: **80 mi. SW of Asheville**
No. of Rooms: **7**
No. of Private Baths: **7**
Double/pb: **$85**
Single/pb: **$75**
Suites: **$95**

Guest Cottage: **$85–$200; sleeps 4**
Open: **All year**
Reduced Rates: **Available**
Breakfast: **Full**
Credit Cards: **MC, VISA**
Pets: **No**
Children: **Welcome, in cottage only**
Smoking: **No**
Social Drinking: **Permitted**

Located in a charming, uncommercial mountain resort town, this white Colonial is flanked by tall columns and is surrounded by two acres. The scenic view may be enjoyed from comfortable rocking chairs on the wide veranda. Donna, a former interior decorator, has furnished the inn with antiques, art, and interesting accessories. Chris is a classical guitarist, woodworker, and great cook. The hearty breakfast includes a variety of homemade breads.

The Guest House ✪
RT. 2, BOX 64914 (HWY E 64), HIGHLANDS, NORTH CAROLINA 28741

Tel: **(704) 526-4536**
Best Time to Call: **9 AM–9 PM**
Host: **Juanita Hernandez**
Location: **100 mi. NE of Atlanta**
No. of Rooms: **4**
No. of Private Baths: **4**
Double/pb: **$68–$85**
Single/pb: **$60–$70**
Open: **All year**
Reduced Rates: **Available**

Breakfast: **Full**
Credit Cards: **MC, VISA**
Pets: **No**
Children: **Welcome**
Smoking: **No**
Social Drinking: **Permitted**
Minimum Stay: **Weekends July–Sept., holidays, and October**
Foreign Languages: **Spanish, German**

A charming Alpine-style mountain chalet nestled among stately trees, this B&B is more ample than its compact looks suggest. Inside you'll admire the plush, cream-colored carpeting, chestnut paneling, light wallcoverings, teakwood furniture, and native stone fireplace. Deep contemporary seats invite guests to slip off their shoes and relax. Partake of the spectacular view from the open deck, with its sun umbrella and rocking chairs. After a restful night in your tastefully decorated room—accented with Juanita's artistic touches—you'll wake up to one of her superb breakfasts.

Ye Olde Stone House
ROUTE 2, BOX 7, HIGHLANDS, NORTH CAROLINA 28741

Tel: **(704) 526-5911**
Best Time to Call: **Afternoons; evenings**
Hosts: **Jim and Rene Ramsdell**
Location: **80 mi. SW of Asheville**
No. of Rooms: **4**
No. of Private Baths: **4**
Double/pb: **$65–$75**
Single/pb: **$60–$65**
Chalet: **$95–$115, sleeps 4**
Open: **All year**

Reduced Rates: **10% Sun.–Thurs.; weekly**
Breakfast: **Full**
Credit Cards: **MC, VISA**
Pets: **No**
Children: **Welcome**
Smoking: **No**
Social Drinking: **Permitted**
Minimum Stay: **2 nights holiday weekends**

Built of stones taken from a local river by mule and wagon, the house is less than a mile from the center of town, where you will find a nature center, museum, galleries, tennis courts, swimming pool, and shops offering antiques or mountain crafts. The rooms are bright, cheerful, and comfortably furnished. The sun room and porch are perfect spots to catch up on that book you've wanted to read. On cool evenings, the Ramsdells invite you to gather round the fireplace for snacks and conversation.

Ye Olde Cherokee Inn Bed & Breakfast ◎
500 NORTH VIRGINIA DARE TRAIL, KILL DEVIL HILLS, NORTH CAROLINA 27948

Tel: **(919) 441-6127; (800) 554-2764**
Best Time to Call: **Evenings**
Hosts: **Bob and Kaye Combs**
Location: **75 mi. S of Norfolk**
No. of Rooms: **6**
No. of Private Baths: **6**
Double/pb: **$55–$85**
Open: **Apr. 1–Oct. 30**
Reduced Rates: **$5 less per night, seniors**

Breakfast: **Continental**
Credit Cards: **AMEX, MC, VISA**
Pets: **No**
Children: **No**
Smoking: **No**
Social Drinking: **Permitted**
Minimum Stay: **3 nights July–Aug.; 4 nights holidays**

feet from the Atlantic Ocean you'll find this beach house
paround porches, soft cypress interiors, and white ruffled
Cherokee Inn is near the historic Roanoke Island settlement,
itteras, and the Wright Brothers Memorial at Kitty Hawk. Of
you may just want to spend the day at the beach. In the
, curl up with a book or watch TV. You'll start the next day
iffee and pastries.

ehead Manor Bed & Breakfast ❂
ORTH TENTH STREET, MOREHEAD CITY,
TH CAROLINA 28557

(919) 726-9233
sts: **Bob and Brenda Thorne**
cation: **160 mi. SE of Raleigh**
o. of Rooms: **8**
No. of Private Baths: **3**
Max. No. Sharing Bath: **4**
Double/pb: **$69**
Single/pb: **$65**
Double/sb: **$59**
Single/sb: **$55**
Open: **Memorial weekend thru Labor Day**

Reduced Rates: **$10 less Sun.–Thurs.**
Breakfast: **Full**
Credit Cards: **MC, VISA**
Pets: **No**
Children: **Welcome, over 5**
Smoking: **No**
Social Drinking: **Permitted**
Minimum Stay: **Holidays, 2 nights**
Airport Pickup: **Yes**

Venture out and explore the treasures of this pleasant coastal community. Cape Lookout National Seashore, wild ponies, historic Beaufort, and miles of sandy beach await you. Within walking distance are the restaurants, shops, and charter boats of the waterfront district. The inn offers a casual, laid-back atmosphere reminiscent of grandma's house. Old and new blend gracefully together in this refreshing summer place. With three porches and a courtyard laced with shrubs and flowers, there's room to socialize or just sit and rock your cares away. Bob and Brenda invite you to join them on the crystal coast.

The Merritt House Bed & Breakfast ❂
618 NORTH MAIN STREET, MT. AIRY, NORTH CAROLINA 27030

Tel: **(910) 786-2174**
Best Time to Call: **9 AM–9 PM**
Hosts: **Rich and Pat Margels**
Location: **30 mi. N of Winston-Salem**
No. of Rooms: **4**
No. of Private Baths: **2**
Max. No. Sharing Bath: **4**
Double/pb: **$75**
Single/pb: **$65**
Double/sb: **$55**

Single/sb: **$40**
Open: **All year**
Reduced Rates: **10%, seniors**
Breakfast: **Full**
Credit Cards: **MC, VISA**
Pets: **No**
Children: **Welcome**
Smoking: **No**
Social Drinking: **Permitted**
Airport/Station Pickup: **Yes**

Southern hospitality awaits you at Merritt House, a brick Victorian home built in 1901, with accommodations reminiscent of that gracious, slow-paced era. Upon arrival, you are greeted with refreshments served in your room, the common room or, in nice weather, on the wraparound porch. Throughout your stay you will receive as much personal attention—or quiet solitude—as you desire. Rich and Pat can arrange dinner or theater reservations for you and direct you to the local attractions. Breakfast specialties include gourmet selections that are as nutritious as they are delicious. Located in the Blue Ridge Mountains foothills, this B&B is 30 miles from Winston-Salem, 20 minutes from Pilot Mountain State Park, and 15 miles from the Blue Ridge Parkway.

Huntington Hall Bed and Breakfast ✪
500 VALLEY RIVER AVENUE, MURPHY, NORTH CAROLINA 28906

Tel: **(704) 837-9567; (800) 824-6189;** fax: **(704) 837-2527**	Reduced Rates: **15% Dec.–Feb., based on availability**
Best Time to Call: **8 AM–9 PM**	Breakfast: **Full**
Hosts: **Bob and Kate DeLong**	Credit Cards: **AMEX, DC, DISC, MC, VISA**
Location: **100 mi. N. of Atlanta, Georgia**	Pets: **No**
No. of Rooms: **5**	Children: **Welcome**
No. of Private Baths: **5**	Smoking: **No**
Double/pb: **$65**	Social Drinking: **Permitted**
Single/pb: **$49**	Airport/Station Pickup: **Yes**
Open: **All year**	

Two huge maple trees shade this pleasant clapboard home, circa 1881; tall columns accent the front porch, and English ivy and Virginia creeper climb the low stone wall surrounding the property. Each spacious bedroom blends the old-world charm of tall windows, wooden floors, and Victorian decor with such modern amenities as cable TV and private baths. Wonderful breakfasts served on the sun porch precede the day's explorations of the historical district in nearby Brasstown, or of the Valley River Valley—original home of the Cherokee Indians and site of their "Trail of Tears." Both Bob and Kate are outdoor enthusiasts, eager to help guests plan white-water rafting trips on the Nanathala and Ocoee rivers and hikes in Great Smoky Mountain National Park.

The Aerie ✪
509 POLLOCK STREET, NEW BERN, NORTH CAROLINA 28560

Tel: **(919) 636-5553; (800) 849-5553**	Double/pb: **$79–$85**
Hosts: **Gina and David Hawkins**	Single/pb: **$54–$64**
Location: **120 mi. E of Raleigh**	Open: **All year**
No. of Rooms: **7**	Breakfast: **Full**
No. of Private Baths: **7**	Credit Cards: **AMEX, MC, VISA**

Pets: **No**
Children: **Welcome**
Smoking: **Permitted**

Social Drinking: **Permitted**
Airport/Station Pickup: **Yes**

Just one block from Tryon Palace, the Aerie has the closest accommodations to all of New Bern's historic attractions. This Victorian inn was a private residence for almost a century. Today it is furnished with fine antiques and reproductions. Each of the seven individually decorated rooms has a modern bath, telephone, and cable TV. Complimentary wine, beer, soft drinks, and light refreshments are offered throughout your stay, and a generous country breakfast awaits you each morning in the dining room.

Harmony House Inn
215 POLLOCK STREET, NEW BERN, NORTH CAROLINA 28560

Tel: **(919) 636-3810**
Best Time to Call: **9 AM–6 PM**
Hosts: **A. E. and Diane Hansen**
Location: **110 mi. SE of Raleigh**
No. of Rooms: **9**
No. of Private Baths: **9**
Double/pb: **$85**
Single/pb: **$55**

Open: **All year**
Breakfast: **Full**
Credit Cards: **AMEX, MC, VISA**
Pets: **No**
Children: **Welcome**
Smoking: **No**
Social Drinking: **Permitted**

Built in 1850, the inn is located in the historic district just four blocks from Tryon Palace and one block from the confluence of the Trent and Neuse rivers. About 7,000 square feet in area, the house is graced with spacious hallways and an aura of elegance. The air-conditioned guest accommodations are furnished with antiques and fine reproductions. You are welcome to help yourself to soft drinks and ice from the well-stocked guest refrigerator. Relax in the parlor, on the front porch with its rockers and swings, or in the pretty backyard.

New Berne House Bed and Breakfast Inn ●
709 BROAD STREET, NEW BERN, NORTH CAROLINA 28560

Tel: **(919) 636-2250; (800) 842-7688**
Hosts: **Marcia Drum and Howard Bronson**
Location: **1 mi. from Hwy. 70**
No. of Rooms: **7**
No. of Private Baths: **7**
Double/pb: **$80**
Single/pb: **$60**
Open: **All year**

Reduced Rates: **AAA, AARP**
Breakfast: **Full**
Credit Cards: **AMEX, MC, VISA**
Pets: **No**
Children: **Welcome, over 12**
Smoking: **No**
Social Drinking: **Permitted**
Airport/Station Pickup: **Yes**

Located in the heart of New Bern's historic district, this brick Colonial is furnished in the style of an English country manor with a mixture of antiques, traditional pieces, and attic treasures. Guests are pampered with afternoon tea or coffee served in the parlor. A sweeping stairway leads upstairs to romantic bedchambers, one with a brass bed reportedly rescued in 1897 from a burning brothel. Breakfast specialties such as praline and cream waffles, honey-glazed ham, and homemade breads and muffins are served in the dining room. New Berne House is within walking distance of Tryon Palace, North Carolina's Colonial capitol, and the governor's mansion. Ask about the exciting Mystery Weekends.

Key Falls Inn ✪
151 EVERETT ROAD, PISGAH FOREST, NORTH CAROLINA 28768

Tel: (704) 884-7559	Suites: $85
Best Time to Call: 9 AM–10 PM	Open: All year
Hosts: Clark and Patricia Grosvenor, and Janet Fogleman	Breakfast: Full
	Credit Cards: AMEX, DC, MC, VISA
No. of Rooms: 4	Pets: No
No. of Private Baths: 4	Children: Welcome, over 3
Double/pb: $55–$70	Smoking: No
Single/pb: $47.50–$62.50	Social Drinking: Permitted

Visitors to this B&B will be able to make the most of western North Carolina's natural and cultural attractions. Key Falls Inn is situated on a 28-acre estate with its own tennis court, pond, and outdoor barbecue. For quieter moments, sit on one of the porches and enjoy the mountain views. Music lovers will want to get tickets to the acclaimed Brevard Festival, an annual summer event. Complimentary tea is served in the afternoon.

Rowan Oak House ✪
208 SOUTH FULTON STREET, SALISBURY, NORTH CAROLINA 28144

Tel: (704) 633-2086; (800) 786-0437	Reduced Rates: 10% seniors
Hosts: Bill and Ruth Ann Coffey	Breakfast: Full
Location: 1 mi. from I-85	Pets: No
No. of Rooms: 3	Children: Welcome, over 12
No. of Private Baths: 1	Smoking: Restricted
Double/pb: $65–$85	Social Drinking: Permitted
Single/pb: $55–$85	Airport/Station Pickup: Yes
Open: All year	Foreign Languages: Spanish

Milton Brown built the Rowan Oak House for his bride, Fannie, in 1902. Set in the heart of the West Square historic district, this Queen Anne features a cupola, wraparound porch, and carved oak door. Step through the dark wood entry to see the intricate woodwork and stained glass. The original fixtures are well preserved and complemented by period furnishings and reproductions. Ruth Ann and Bill invite you to choose from four lavishly appointed guest rooms, including the master bedroom, which features a double Jacuzzi and a fireplace in the bathroom. Breakfast is served downstairs in the formal dining room, beneath the painting of Queen Louise of Prussia. In the afternoon, tea or a glass of cheesewine can be enjoyed in the garden, on the porch, or in the sitting room amid the curios and Victorian knickknacks. Your hosts can guide you to Salisbury's antebellum architecture and an abundance of nearby lakes, parks, and golf courses. For those of you who don't mind paying a higher rate, 1 room is available.

The Oaks
P.O. BOX 1008, SALUDA, NORTH CAROLINA 28773

Tel: **(704) 749-9613**	Open: **All year**
Best Time to Call: **Anytime**	Breakfast: **Full**
Hosts: **Ceri and Peggy Dando**	Credit Cards: **MC, VISA**
Location: **12 mi. S of Hendersonville**	Pets: **No**
No. of Rooms: **4**	Children: **No**
No. of Private Baths: **4**	Smoking: **No**
Double/pb: **$55–$64**	Social Drinking: **Permitted**
Guest Cottage: **$85–$125**	

The Saluda mountain breezes benefit this turreted Victorian, built in 1894. Your hosts provide a low-key, welcoming atmosphere. Bedrooms are decorated in period style, with interesting antique "bits and bobs." Your tariff includes a generous breakfast for two. The surrounding porch offers a place for you to relax and mull over plans before you amble down to Main Street's many antique and crafts shops. Carl Sandburg's home and Flat Rock Playhouse are nearby.

Turby Villa B&B ✪
STAR ROUTE 1, BOX 48, SPARTA, NORTH CAROLINA 28675

Tel: **(910) 372-8490**	Open: **All year**
Host: **Mrs. Maybelline Turbiville**	Breakfast: **Full**
No. of Rooms: **3**	Pets: **No**
No. of Private Baths: **3**	Children: **Welcome**
Double/pb: **$50**	Smoking: **Permitted**
Single/pb: **$35**	Social Drinking: **Permitted**

At an altitude of 3,000 feet, this contemporary two-story brick home is the centerpiece of a 20-acre farm. The house is surrounded by an acre of trees and manicured lawns, and the lovely views are of the scenic Blue Ridge Mountains. Breakfast is served either on the enclosed porch with its white wicker furnishings or in the more formal dining room with its Early American–style furnishings. Mrs. Turbiville takes justifiable pride in her attractive, well-maintained B&B.

The Richmond Inn ◉

101 PINE AVENUE, SPRUCE PINE, NORTH CAROLINA 28777

Tel: (704) 765-6993	Single/pb: $45–$65
Best Time to Call: Anytime	Open: All year
Hosts: Lenore Boucher and Bill Ansley	Breakfast: Full
Location: 4 mi. from Blue Ridge Pkwy.,	Credit Cards: MC, VISA
Exit 331	Pets: No
No. of Rooms: 7	Children: Welcome
No. of Private Baths: 7	Smoking: No
Double/pb: $55–$75	Social Drinking: Permitted

Surrounded by towering pines, this white wooden house trimmed with black window shutters has a stone terrace and rock walls. It is furnished in a comfortable blend of antiques and family treasures. Most mornings, Lenore fixes a Southern repast with bacon, eggs, and grits. Spruce Pine is the mineral capital of the world, and panning for gemstones such as garnets and amethysts is a popular pastime. Hiking the Appalachian Trail, playing golf, or working out at your hosts' community spa will keep you in shape. Internationally known artists schedule shows throughout the year.

Cedar Hill Farm B&B

778 ELMWOOD ROAD, STATESVILLE, NORTH CAROLINA 28677

Tel: (704) 873-4332; (800) 484-8457	Guest Cottage: $75
Ext. 1254	Open: All year
Best Time to Call: Before 2 PM; after	Breakfast: Full
5 PM	Credit Cards: MC, VISA
Hosts: Brenda and Jim Vernon	Pets: Sometimes
Location: 45 mi. N of Charlotte	Children: Welcome
No. of Rooms: 2	Smoking: No
No. of Private Baths: 2	Social Drinking: Permitted
Double/pb: $60–$70	

A three-story Federal farmhouse furnished with antique and country pieces, Cedar Hill is surrounded by 32 acres of rolling green, the better to feed the Vernons' sheep. Brenda and Jim sell fleece coverlets and crafts from their own hand-spun wool; they also make furniture and cure turkey and ham in a smokehouse on site. Stay in the farmhouse or in a private cottage. Either way you'll have an air-conditioned room with a telephone and cable TV. The country breakfasts will leave you full, thanks to servings of ham, sausage, fruit, potatoes, and buttermilk biscuits with homemade preserves. You can work off calories swimming in your hosts' pool or playing badminton, but you might want to relax in a porch rocker or hammock first. The cottage now has a working fireplace.

Madelyn's Bed & Breakfast

514 CARROLL STREET, STATESVILLE, NORTH CAROLINA 28677

Tel: **(704) 872-3973**
Best Time to Call: **9 AM–5 PM**
Hosts: **John and Madelyn Hill**
Location: **45 mi. N of Charlotte**
No. of Rooms: **3**
No. of Private Baths: **3**
Double/pb: **$55–$65**
Open: **All year**

Reduced Rates: **10% seniors**
Breakfast: **Full**
Credit Cards: **MC, VISA**
Pets: **No**
Children: **Welcome, over 10**
Smoking: **No**
Social Drinking: **Permitted**
Airport/Station Pickup: **Yes**

Madelyn's B&B is nestled in a quiet neighborhood near downtown, historic districts, and a two-mile par course; outlet shopping is nearby. For more fun, Statesville hosts two annual events—the Carolina Dogwood Festival in the spring and the National Balloon Rally in the fall. Madelyn and John try to make each guest feel special. When you arrive, you'll find fresh fruit, candies, and homemade cookies in your room. A sumptuous breakfast is served where you want it: in the formal dining room, before a cozy fire in the breakfast room, on the sun porch, or even in bed. Your hosts are glad to cater to visitors' special dietary needs.

Scott's Keep ✪

**308 WALNUT STREET, P.O. BOX 1425, SWANSBORO,
NORTH CAROLINA 28584**

Tel: **(910) 326-1257; (800) 348-1257**
Best Time to Call: **Anytime**
Hosts: **Frank and Norma Scott**
Location: **150 mi. SE of Raleigh**
No. of Rooms: **3**
Max. No. Sharing Bath: **4**
Double/pb: **$55**
Double/sb: **$45**

Open: **All year**
Reduced Rates: **15% weekly**
Breakfast: **Full**
Credit Cards: **MC, VISA**
Pets: **No**
Children: **Welcome, over 6**
Smoking: **No**
Social Drinking: **Permitted**

This simple contemporary is located on a quiet street two blocks from the waterfront. Your hosts want you to feel right at home in the bright, spacious living room and comfortable guest rooms. The larger bedroom is decorated with wicker and features an antique trunk, queen-size bed, and colorful quilts. The smaller bedroom is furnished in classic maple with twin beds and grandmother's quilts. For breakfast, Norma serves blueberry or apple spice muffins with fruit and homemade jellies. This historic seaside village is filled with inviting shops and waterside seafood restaurants. Your hosts will point the way to beautiful beaches, waterskiing, sailing, and windsurfing.

Little Warren ✪
304 EAST PARK AVENUE, TARBORO, NORTH CAROLINA 27886

Tel: **(919) 823-1314**
Hosts: **Patsy and Tom Miller**
Location: **Easy access from I-95**
No. of Rooms: **3**
No. of Private Baths: **3**
Double/pb: **$65**
Single/pb: **$58**
Open: **All year**
Reduced Rates: **Corporate, upon request**

Breakfast: **Full**
Credit Cards: **AMEX, DISC, MC, VISA**
Pets: **No**
Children: **Welcome, over 6**
Smoking: **Permitted**
Social Drinking: **Permitted**
Airport/Station Pickup: **Yes**
Foreign Languages: **Spanish**

Little Warren is actually a large and gracious family home built in 1913. It is located along the Albemarle Trail in Tarboro's historic district. The deeply set, wraparound porch overlooks one of the last originally chartered town commons still in existence. Inside, you'll find rooms of beautiful antiques from England and America. In the morning, choose from a full English, Southern, or expanded Continental breakfast. Antiques are available at the Passers-Buy shop owned by the hosts.

Barkley House Bed & Breakfast ✪
ROUTE 6, BOX 12, TAYLORSVILLE, NORTH CAROLINA 28681

Tel: **(704) 632-9060**
Best Time to Call: **Mornings**
Host: **Phyllis Barkley**
Location: **60 mi. NW of Charlotte**
No. of Rooms: **3**
No. of Private Baths: **3**
Double/pb: **$49**
Single/pb: **$38**

Open: **All year**
Breakfast: **Full**
Credit Cards: **MC**
Pets: **Sometimes**
Children: **Welcome**
Smoking: **Permitted**
Social Drinking: **Permitted**
Airport/Station Pickup: **Yes**

After staying in European B&Bs, Phyllis opened the first one in Taylorsville, a small town surrounded by mountains. Barkley House is a white Colonial with yellow shutters and a gracious front porch with four columns. The furnishings are homey, combining antiques and pieces from the '50s. Haystack eggs and fruity banana splits are two of Phyllis's breakfast specialties; she'll be happy to cater to guests on restricted diets.

Mill Farm Inn ✪

P.O. BOX 1251, TRYON, NORTH CAROLINA 28782

Tel: (704) 859-6992; (800) 545-6992	Open: All year
Best Time to Call: Mornings	Reduced Rates: 10% seniors
Hosts: Chip and Penny Kessler	Breakfast: Continental
Location: 45 mi. SE of Asheville	Pets: No
No. of Rooms: 9	Children: Welcome
No. of Private Baths: 9	Smoking: No
Double/pb: $55	Social Drinking: Permitted
Single/pb: $45	Foreign Languages: French
Suites: $65–$100	

The Pacolet River flows past the edge of this three-and-one-half-acre property in the foothills of the Blue Ridge Mountains. Sitting porches and the living room with fireplace are fine spots to relax. A hearty breakfast of fresh fruit, cereal, English muffins, preserves, and coffee is served. Crafts shops, galleries, and antiquing will keep you busy.

Acadian House Bed & Breakfast ✪

129 VAN NORDEN STREET, WASHINGTON, NORTH CAROLINA 27889

Tel: (919) 975-3967	Single/pb: $50
Best Time to Call: Mornings and	Suites: $75
evenings	Open: All year
Hosts: Johanna and Leonard Huber	Breakfast: Full
Location: 105 mi. E of Raleigh	Credit Cards: MC, VISA
No. of Rooms: 3	Pets: No
No. of Private Baths: 3	Children: Welcome, over 12
Max. No. Sharing Bath: 4	Smoking: No
Double/pb: $50–$55	Social Drinking: Permitted

Acadian House Bed & Breakfast, a 1900 home located in Colonial Washington, features a unique herringbone-patterned brick porch. It is decorated throughout with antiques and local crafts. A Victorian staircase leads to guest rooms and the library, where books and games are provided. Johanna and Leonard, transplanted New Orleanians, serve a full breakfast featuring southern Louisiana Acadian specialties such as beignets and café au lait along with traditional breakfast foods. Acadian House is one block from the scenic Pamlico River;

museums and antique shops are nearby. The business traveler will find a writing table and telephone available. Fax and copying facilities are also nearby.

Pamlico House ☉
400 EAST MAIN STREET, WASHINGTON, NORTH CAROLINA 27889

Tel: **(919) 946-7184**
Best Time to Call: **9 AM–8 PM**
Hosts: **Lawrence and Jeanne Hervey**
Location: **20 mi. E of Greenville**
No. of Rooms: **4**
No. of Private Baths: **4**
Double/pb: **$65–$75**
Single/pb: **$55–$65**

Open: **All year**
Breakfast: **Full**
Credit Cards: **AMEX, DISC, MC, VISA**
Pets: **No**
Children: **Welcome, over 6**
Smoking: **No**
Social Drinking: **Permitted**
Airport/Station Pickup: **Yes**

Located in the center of a small, historic town, this stately Colonial Revival home's large rooms are a perfect foil for the carefully chosen antique furnishings. Guests are drawn to the classic Victorian parlor or to the spacious wraparound porch for relaxing conversation. Take a self-guided walking tour of the historic district or a stroll along the quaint waterfront. Recreational pleasures abound. Nature enthusiasts enjoy the wildlife and exotic plants in nearby Goose Creek State Park. Should you get homesick for your favorite pet, Lawrence and Jeanne will share theirs.

Weldon Place Inn ☉
500 WASHINGON AVENUE, WELDON, NORTH CAROLINA 27890

Tel: **(919) 536-4582; (800) 831-4470**
Best Time to Call: **Anytime**

Hosts: **Angel and Andy Whitby**
Location: **2 mi. E of Roanoke Rapids**

No. of Rooms: **4**
No. of Private Baths: **3**
Max. No. Sharing Bath: **3**
Double/pb: **$60–$65**
Single/pb: **$55–$60**
Double/sb: **$55**
Single/sb: **$50**
Open: **All year**

Reduced Rates: **Available**
Breakfast: **Full**
Credit Cards: **MC, VISA**
Pets: **No**
Children: **No**
Smoking: **Permitted**
Social Drinking: **No**

If you love antiques and country elegance, step back in time as you cross the threshold of Weldon Place Inn. Sleep in a canopy bed, wake to singing sparrows, and savor a gourmet breakfast. Then explore this historic neighborhood: the inn, built in 1913, stands amid homes that date to the mid 1800s, and nearby, there is a canal system aqueduct that is two decades older. Breakfast specialties like sausage-and-cheese-stuffed French toast and strawberry bread will help to fuel your excursions.

Anderson Guest House ○

520 ORANGE STREET, WILMINGTON, NORTH CAROLINA 28401

Tel: **(910) 343-8128**
Best Time to Call: **8 AM–5 PM**
Hosts: **Landon and Connie Anderson**
No. of Rooms: **2**
No. of Private Baths: **2**
Double/pb: **$65**
Single/pb: **$50**

Open: **All year**
Breakfast: **Full**
Pets: **Sometimes**
Children: **Welcome**
Smoking: **No**
Social Drinking: **Permitted**
Airport/Station Pickup: **Yes**

This 19th-century town house has a private guest house overlooking a garden. The bedrooms have ceiling fans, fireplaces, and air-conditioning. Enjoy cool drinks upon arrival and a liqueur before bed. Breakfast specialties are eggs Mornay, blueberry cobbler, and crêpes. Your host can point out the sights of this historic town and direct you to the beaches.

Catherine's Inn on Orange ○

410 ORANGE STREET, WILMINGTON, NORTH CAROLINA 28401

Tel: **(910) 251-0863; (800) 476-0723**
Best Time to Call: **8 AM–10 PM**
Hosts: **Catherine and Walter Ackiss**
Location: **In Wilmington historical district**
No. of Rooms: **3**
No. of Private Baths: **3**
Double/pb: **$65–$70**
Single/pb: **$55**

Open: **All year**
Reduced Rates: **Available**
Breakfast: **Full**
Credit Cards: **MC, VISA**
Pets: **No**
Children: **Welcome, by arrangement**
Smoking: **Restricted**
Social Drinking: **Permitted**
Airport/Station Pickup: **Yes**

An Italianate residence built by a merchant and Civil War veteran in 1875, this B&B has blue clapboard, white trim, and a white picket fence. All bedrooms have fireplaces. The grounds include a spacious garden and water garden. Guests are within walking distance of museums, historic buildings, and antique shops; beaches and golf courses are minutes away by car. Morning coffee is served in the library, followed by breakfast in the dining room.

Miss Betty's Bed & Breakfast Inn ✪
600 WEST NASH STREET, WILSON, NORTH CAROLINA 27893-3045

Tel: **(919) 243-4447; (800) 258-2058** **(for reservations only)**	Suites: **$70–$75**
Best Time to Call: **8 AM–10 PM**	Open: **All year**
Hosts: **Betty and Fred Spitz**	Breakfast: **Full**
Location: **50 mi. E of Raleigh**	Credit Cards: **AMEX, CB, DC, DISC, MC, VISA**
No. of Rooms: **10**	Pets: **No**
No. of Private Baths: **10**	Children: **No**
Double/pb: **$60–$70**	Smoking: **Restricted**
Single/pb: **$50–$65**	Social Drinking: **Permitted**

One of the best places to stay in the South, Miss Betty's is located in the downtown historic section of Wilson. The B&B comprises three beautifully restored homes—the Davis-Whitehead-Harris House (circa 1858), the adjacent Riley House, and Rosebud (circa 1943)—that recapture bygone elegance and style. Guests can browse for antiques in any of the numerous shops that have given Wilson the title of "Antique Capital of North Carolina." The town is also renowned for its tasty barbecue, gorgeous golf courses, and numerous tennis courts.

Lady Anne's Victorian Bed & Breakfast ✪
612 SUMMIT STREET, WINSTON-SALEM, NORTH CAROLINA 27101

Tel: **(910) 724-1074**	Open: **All year**
Best Time to Call: **8 AM–9 PM**	Reduced Rates: **$10 less suites, Sun.–Thurs.**
Host: **Shelley Kirley**	Breakfast: **Full**
Location: **100 mi. W of Raleigh**	Pets: **No**
No. of Rooms: **4**	Children: **Welcome, over 12, infants under 7 months**
No. of Private Baths: **4**	
Double/pb: **$55–$85**	Smoking: **Permitted**
Single/pb: **$40**	Social Drinking: **Permitted**
Suites: **$85–$95; sleeps 4**	

Warm Southern hospitality surrounds you in this elegant 1890 Victorian. An aura of romance touches each suite or room, all individually decorated with period antiques and treasures and modern luxuries. Some rooms have two-person whirlpool, cable TV, stereo, telephone, and refrigerator. An evening dessert and tea tray served in the privacy of your room helps you relax; a delicious full breakfast is served on fine china and lace in the morning. Lady Anne's is ideally situated near downtown attractions, performances, restaurants, shops, and

Old Salem historic village. The hostess, previously a recreational therapist, now enjoys innkeeping and antique collecting.

Mickle House ✪
927 WEST FIFTH STREET, WINSTON-SALEM, NORTH CAROLINA 27101

Tel: **(910) 722-9045**
Best Time to Call: **9 AM–10 PM**
Host: **Barbara Garrison**
Location: **1 mi. from Rte. 40, Broad St. exit**
No. of Rooms: **2**
No. of Private Baths: **1**
Max. No. Sharing Bath: **3**
Double/pb: **$70**

Single/pb: **$65**
Open: **All year**
Breakfast: **Full**
Credit Cards: **MC, VISA**
Pets: **No**
Children: **No**
Smoking: **No**
Social Drinking: **Permitted**

Step back in time to visit a quaint Victorian cottage painted a soft yellow, with dark green shutters and gingerbread trim. The fully restored home, located in the National Historic District of West End, is furnished with lovely antiques, such as the canopy and poster beds in the guest rooms. Dessert is served in the afternoon or evening, and a full breakfast, with fresh fruit and freshly baked breads and muffins, awaits you in the morning. Old Salem, the Medical Center, and the Convention Center are five minutes away; fine restaurants, parks, shops, and the library are within walking distance.

Wachovia B&B, Inc. ✪
513 WACHOVIA STREET, WINSTON-SALEM, NORTH CAROLINA 27101

Tel: **(910) 777-0332**
Best Time to Call: **9 AM–5 PM**
Host: **Susan Bunting**
Location: **½ mi. S of Winston-Salem**
No. of Rooms: **5**
No. of Private Baths: **2**
Max. No. Sharing Bath: **4**
Double/pb: **$65**
Single/pb: **$55**

Double/sb: **$55**
Single/sb: **$45**
Open: **All year**
Breakfast: **Full**
Pets: **No**
Children: **Welcome (crib)**
Smoking: **No**
Social Drinking: **Permitted**

This white and rose Victorian cottage, with its appealing wraparound porch, is just outside the Old Salem historic district, and antique shops, excellent restaurants, and a scenic strollway are within a one-block radius. Noted institutions like North Carolina School of the Arts and Wake Forest University are only a few miles away. This is a good area for cycling, and guests may borrow the house bicycles. Susan's experience as a pastry chef for a local restaurant is apparent in her full breakfasts. Also offered are complimentary wine and cheese.

NORTH DAKOTA

- Stanley

Carrington •

- Scranton

Historic Jacobson Mansion ✪
RR 2, BOX 15A, SCRANTON, NORTH DAKOTA 58653

Tel: **(701) 275-8291**
Best Time to Call: **Evenings**
Hosts: **Melvin and Charlene Pierce**
Location: **15 mi. N of Scranton**
No. of Rooms: **2**
Max. No. Sharing Bath: **4**
Double/sb: **$50**
Single/sb: **$40**
Open: **All year**

Reduced Rates: **10% after 2nd night;
  10% seniors**
Breakfast: **Full**
Other Meals: **Available**
Pets: **Yes**
Children: **Welcome**
Smoking: **No**
Social Drinking: **Permitted**

This three-story Queen Anne Victorian mansion was built in 1895 by a gentleman farmer and merchant. In 1988 it was rescued from the wrecking ball and moved 450 miles to its present location on a working farm and ranch. Melvin and Charlene have painstakingly restored their home to its former elegance, filling it with antiques and modern conveniences. They invite you and your family to experience their rural activities, from raising cattle and sheep to seeding and farming their lush pastures.

The Triple T Ranch ⊙
RR 1, BOX 93, STANLEY, NORTH DAKOTA 58784

Tel: **(701) 628-2418**	Open: **All year**
Best Time to Call: **Anytime**	Reduced Rates: **Available**
Hosts: **Joyce and Fred Evans**	Breakfast: **Full**
Location: **60 mi. W of Minot**	Pets: **Sometimes**
No. of Rooms: **2**	Children: **Welcome (crib)**
Max. No. Sharing Bath: **4**	Smoking: **No**
Double/sb: **$30**	Social Drinking: **No**
Single/sb: **$25**	

You're warmly invited to come to Joyce and Fred's rustic ranch home, where you're welcome to take a seat in front of the stone fireplace, put your feet up, and relax. There's a lovely view of the hills and the valley, and their herd of cattle is an impressive sight. Lake Sakakawea, for seasonal recreation such as fishing and swimming, is 11 miles away. Indian powwows, area rodeos, and hunting for Indian artifacts are fun. The State Fair is held every July.

OHIO

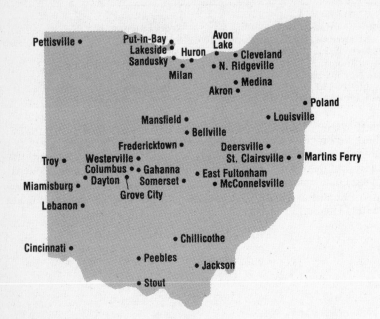

Pettisville •

Put-in-Bay •
Lakeside •
Sandusky •
Huron
Milan •

Avon
Lake •
• Cleveland
• N. Ridgeville
• Medina

Akron •

• Poland

Mansfield •
• Louisville

• Bellville

Fredericktown •

Deersville •

Troy •
Westerville •
Columbus • • Gahanna
Miamisburg •
• Dayton ‌ Somerset •
Grove City

St. Clairsville • • Martins Ferry

• East Fultonham
• McConnelsville

Lebanon •

• Chillicothe

Cincinnati •

• Peebles

• Jackson

• Stout

Helen's Hospitality House
1096 PALMETTO, AKRON, OHIO 44306

Tel: **(216) 724-7151; 724-3034**
Best Time to Call: **8 AM–11 PM**
Host: **Helen Claytor**
Location: **1 mi. from I-77 S, Exit 123B**
No. of Rooms: **2**
No. of Private Baths: **1**
Max. No. Sharing Bath: **4**
Double/pb: **$40**
Single/pb: **$35**
Double/sb: **$35**

Single/sb: **$30**
Open: **All year**
Reduced Rates: **Weekly**
Breakfast: **Full**
Pets: **No**
Children: **Welcome, over 10**
Smoking: **No**
Social Drinking: **Permitted**
Airport/Station Pickup: **Yes**

Located in a quiet neighborhood on a dead-end street, Helen's centrally air-conditioned house is a bit of country in the city. It is a renovated old farmhouse furnished with antiques and reproductions. On warm days, breakfast is served on the screened, glass-enclosed porch. Quaker Square, Akron University, the Firestone PGA, and

Portage Lakes are just a few of the local attractions. Helen is a retired teacher who enjoys being a B&B hostess.

Portage House O
601 COPLEY ROAD, STATE ROUTE 162, AKRON, OHIO 44320

Tel: **(216) 535-1952**	Single/sb: **$34**
Best Time to Call: **8 AM–11 PM**	Open: **Feb. 1–Nov. 30**
Host: **Jeanne Pinnick**	Reduced Rates: **$3 less after 1st night**
Location: **2 mi. from I-77**	Breakfast: **Full**
No. of Rooms: **5**	Pets: **Restricted**
No. of Private Baths: **1**	Children: **Welcome (crib)**
Max. No. Sharing Bath: **4**	Smoking: **No**
Double/pb: **$50**	Social Drinking: **Permitted**
Double/sb: **$40**	Foreign Languages: **French, Spanish**

Steeped in history, this gracious Tudor home, nestled in a parklike setting, dates back to 1917. A stone wall down the street served as the western boundary of the United States in 1785. Jeanne and her late husband Harry, a physics professor at the nearby University of Akron, opened their B&B in 1982. Jeanne manages the B&B and has the coffeepot on with refreshments available for arriving guests. If bread is being baked, you'll be offered some hot out of the oven.

Williams House O
249 VINEWOOD, AVON LAKE, OHIO 44012

Tel: **(216) 933-5089**	Open: **Closed Christmas**
Best Time to Call: **9 AM–9 PM**	Reduced Rates: **20% seniors**
Host: **Margaret Williams**	Breakfast: **Full**
Location: **20 mi. W of Cleveland**	Pets: **No**
No. of Rooms: **1**	Children: **No**
No. of Private Baths: **1**	Smoking: **No**
Double/pb: **$40**	Social Drinking: **Permitted**
Single/pb: **$25**	Airport/Station Pickup: **Yes**

Located a mile from the Lake Erie public beach, Margaret lives in a quiet residential neighborhood. The house is comfortably decorated in a harmonious blend of styles. She serves beverages and snacks upon your arrival, and will help you plan a pleasant visit. Breakfast is a dandy, from juice to cereal to eggs to bacon to coffee or tea.

The Frederick Fitting House O
72 FITTING AVENUE, BELLVILLE, OHIO 44813

Tel: **(419) 886-2863**	No. of Private Baths: **3**
Hosts: **Ramon and Suzanne Wilson**	Double/pb: **$58–$72**
Location: **50 mi. N of Columbus**	Single/pb: **$48–$62**
No. of Rooms: **3**	Open: **All year**

Breakfast: **Full**	Smoking: **No**
Other Meals: **Available**	Social Drinking: **Permitted**
Pets: **No**	Airport/Station Pickup: **Yes**
Children: **Welcome, over 8**	

Named for the prominent Bellville citizen who built it in 1863, the Frederick Fitting House is a restored Italianate home with a hand-stenciled dining room and a garden gazebo. Ramon and Suzanne are avid music buffs; you are welcome to play selections from their jazz and classical collection as you lounge by the sitting-room fire. Nearby, Mohican and Malabar Farm State Parks offer a variety of activities, from cross-country skiing to canoeing. Kingwood Garden, Amish country, and Kenyon, Wooster, and Ashland colleges are a short drive away.

The Old McDill-Anderson Place ✪
3656 POLK HOLLOW ROAD, CHILLICOTHE, OHIO 45601

Tel: **(614) 774-1770**	Single/sb: **$45**
Hosts: **Ruth, Del, and Anne Meyer**	Open: **All year**
Location: **45 mi. S of Columbus**	Reduced Rates: **20% weekly; 10%**
No. of Rooms: **4**	**after 3rd night**
No. of Private Baths: **3**	Breakfast: **Full**
Max. No. Sharing Bath: **4**	Pets: **No**
Double/pb: **$65**	Children: **Sometimes**
Single/pb: **$50**	Smoking: **No**
Double/sb: **$55**	Social Drinking: **No**

This two-story 1864 brick Italianate residence was homesteaded in 1798. Your hosts pursue a variety of interests, including woodworking and historic preservation. They cater to their guests' needs by combining some of the bedrooms to make suites—a boon to families. Some rooms have working fireplaces or wood stoves, down comforters and feather beds, especially nice on chilly nights. Breakfast and snacks feature seasonal food and "from scratch" preparation served in the dining room or screened-in porch. In cooler months you can prepare your own meal under the tutelage of their professional open-hearth cook, using historic recipes and authentic utensils. (An added fee will apply.) You will enjoy the abundant and varied early architecture, scenery, museums, and nationally acclaimed outdoor drama.

Prospect Hill Bed and Breakfast ✪
408 BOAL STREET, CINCINNATI, OHIO 45210

Tel: **(513) 421-4408**	No. of Private Baths: **1**
Best Time to Call: **Anytime**	Max. No. Sharing Bath: **4**
Hosts: **Gary Hackney and Tony Jenkins**	Double/pb: **$85**
Location: **Downtown**	Single/pb: **$85**
No. of Rooms: **3**	Double/sb: **$79**

Single/sb: **$79**
Open: **All year**
Reduced Rates: **10% weekly**
Breakfast: **Full**
Credit Cards: **MC, VISA**

Pets: **No**
Children: **Welcome, over 10**
Smoking: **No**
Social Drinking: **Permitted**

This restored Italianate Victorian town house was built in 1867 on Prospect Hill, Cincinnati's first suburb, now a national historic district. The original woodwork, doors, hardware, and light fixtures remain intact—your hosts are interested in historic preservation. All the rooms have spectacular views, fireplaces, and period antique furniture. It's only a fifteen-minute walk from here to Fountain Square or the Ohio River. Mt. Adams, the University of Cincinnati, Playhouse in the Park, the Music Hall, Eden Park, the William Howard Taft Historic Site, and most area museums and hospitals are within a mile.

Private Lodgings, Inc. ✪
P.O. BOX 18590, CLEVELAND, OHIO 44118

Tel: **(216) 321-3213**
Best Time to Call: **Weekdays 9 AM–noon; 3–5 PM**
Coordinator: **Jean Stanley**
States/Regions Covered: **Cleveland**

Rates (Single/Double):
  Modest: **$32 / $40**
  Average: **$45 / $60**
  Luxury: **$65 / $90**
Credit Cards: **No**

This is a city with world-renowned cultural and biomedical resources, as well as major corporations and recreational areas. Special attention is given to the needs of relocating and visiting professionals, outpatients, and relatives of hospital inpatients, as well as vacationers. Every effort is made to accommodate persons with physical handicaps. Discounted rates are provided for extended stays. Case Western Reserve, John Carroll, and Cleveland State universities are convenient to the B&Bs. A $5 surcharge is made for one-night stays. Office is closed on Wednesday and Saturday.

Harrison House ✪
313 WEST 5TH AVENUE, COLUMBUS, OHIO 43201

Tel: **(614) 421-2202; (800) 827-4203**
Best Time to Call: **Anytime**
Hosts: **Maryanne and Dick Olson**
No. of Rooms: **4**
No. of Private Baths: **4**
Double/pb: **$84**
Single/pb: **$74**
Open: **All year**

Breakfast: **Full**
Credit Cards: **MC, VISA**
Pets: **No**
Children: **Welcome**
Smoking: **No**
Social Drinking: **Permitted**
Airport Pickup: **Yes**

At Harrison House, original cut-glass windows, magnificent woodwork, elegant lace curtains, and picturesque landscaping encourage you to escape back to the past. This Queen Anne Victorian, built in 1890, is listed on the National Register of Historic Places. The B&B is located within walking distance of Battelle Institute and Ohio State University, while downtown Columbus, City Center, and the airport are only minutes away. Breakfast specialties include cinnamon grapefruit, lemon puff crêpes, and Swedish pancakes.

Candlewick Bed & Breakfast ✪
4991 BATH ROAD, DAYTON, OHIO 45424

Tel: **(513) 233-9297**	Open: **All year**
Hosts: **George and Nancy Thompson**	Breakfast: **Continental**
Location: **10 mi. NE of Dayton**	Pets: **No**
No. of Rooms: **2**	Children: **No**
Max. No. Sharing Bath: **4**	Smoking: **No**
Double/sb: **$50–$55**	Social Drinking: **No**
Single/sb: **$40**	Airport Pickup: **Yes**

This tranquil Dutch Colonial home sits atop a hill on five rolling acres. George, a retired engineer, and Nancy, a retired teacher, invite you to spend a quiet, restful night in comfortable rooms containing a charming blend of antiques and Colonial and country furnishings. Continental breakfast includes fresh fruit and juice, choice homemade pastries, and freshly brewed coffee. Weather permitting, enjoy breakfast on the screened porch overlooking a large pond often visited by wild ducks and geese. Convenient to Wright-Patterson Air Force Base and Museum and two major universities, Candlewick is a peaceful retreat, perfect for either business or pleasure.

Prices' Steamboat House B&B ✪
6 JOSIE STREET, DAYTON, OHIO 45403

Tel: **(513) 223-2444**	Open: **All year**
Best Time to Call: **4–12 PM**	Reduced Rates: **10% after 5th night**
Hosts: **Ron and Ruth Price**	Breakfast: **Full**
Location: **On edge of downtown Dayton**	Pets: **No**
	Children: **Welcome, over 12**
No. of Rooms: **3**	Smoking: **No**
No. of Private Baths: **3**	Social Drinking: **Permitted**
Double/pb: **$69**	Airport/Station Pickup: **Yes**
Single/pb: **$59**	

Built in 1852, this grand 22-room mansion is listed on the National Register of Historic Places. The house is furnished with period antiques and oriental rugs. Guests can play the piano, browse in the library, or survey Dayton's skyline from rocking chairs on the first- and second-floor porches. Tours, by reservation only, cover the entire residence, ending in a formal tea. The Dayton Art Institute, the U.S. Air Force Museum, and two universities are a few minutes away.

Full breakfasts feature home-baked sourdough bread or sour cream coffee cake.

Mulberry Lane ✪
224 WEST MAIN STREET, P.O. BOX 61, DEERSVILLE, OHIO 44693

Tel: **(614) 922-0425**
Best Time to Call: **9 AM–5 PM**
Hosts: **Dick and Ferrel Zeimer**
Location: **90 mi. S of Cleveland**
No. of Rooms: **2**
Max. No. Sharing Bath: **4**
Double/sb: **$55**

Single/sb: **$50**
Open: **All year**
Breakfast: **Full**
Pets: **No**
Children: **No**
Smoking: **No**
Social Drinking: **Permitted**

Built in 1830, restored in 1989, and tastefully furnished with antiques and period pieces, Mulberry Lane is a great getaway place. Peaceful little Deersville lies between two large lakes where guests can go fishing and boating. Country auctions, antique shops, glass factories, the birthplaces of Clark Gable and General George Armstrong Custer, early Moravian settlements, and Amish country are all within reach. If you don't feel like touring, you're welcome to relax on the porch swing with a good book. Freshly baked muffins are always served at Dick and Ferrel's breakfasts in their country kitchen.

Hill View Acres ✪
7320 OLD TOWN ROAD, EAST FULTONHAM, OHIO 43735

Tel: **(614) 849-2728**
Hosts: **Jim and Dawn Graham**
Location: **10 mi. SW of Zanesville**
No. of Rooms: **2**
Max. No. Sharing Bath: **4**
Double/sb: **$42.60**
Single/sb: **$37.30**
Open: **All year**

Breakfast: **Full weekends; Continental,
  plus weekdays**
Other Meals: **Available**
Credit Cards: **MC, VISA**
Pets: **No**
Children: **Welcome**
Smoking: **Permitted**
Social Drinking: **Permitted**

Hill View is a comfortable, large white house situated on 21 acres with a fishing pond. Homemade breads and delicious gourmet specialties are breakfast fare. You are welcome to relax on the deck, play the piano, or watch TV. Antique shops, potteries, the famous Y Bridge, and the *Lorena* stern-wheeler are some of the area's attractions. An on-premises pool and year-round spa add to your summer enjoyment.

Heartland Country Resort ✪
2994 TOWNSHIP ROAD 190, FREDERICKTOWN, OHIO 43019

Tel: **(809) 230-7030**
Best Time to Call: **Evenings**

Host: **Dorene Henschen**
Location: **40 mi. NE of Columbus**

No. of Rooms: 4
No. of Private Baths: 2
Max. No. Sharing Bath: 4
Double/pb: $85
Single/pb: $75
Double/sb: $55
Single/sb: $45
Open: All year

Reduced Rates: 10% seniors
Breakfast: Continental, plus
Other meals: Available
Credit Cards: MC, VISA
Children: Welcome
Smoking: No
Social Drinking: Permitted

At the Heartland Country Resort you can rent a horse, bring your own, or just watch others. The bed and breakfast is an inviting, restored 1878 farmhouse with a deck and screened porch. You will experience serenity in this 154-acre country setting with hills, streams, woods, wildlife, pastures, fields, and barns, which you can explore on foot or horseback. During every season, you can enjoy a petting zoo of farm animals and numerous recreation opportunities, both on and near the resort.

Shamrock B&B ✪
5657 SUNBURY ROAD, GAHANNA, OHIO 43230

Tel: (614) 337-9849
Best Time to Call: 8 AM–10 PM
Host: Tom McLaughlin
Location: ½ mi. from I-270 exit 161
No. of Rooms: 2
No. of Private Baths: 2
Double/pb: $55
Single/pb: $45
Open: All year

Reduced Rates: 5% seniors; 10% over 4 days
Breakfast: Full
Other meals: Available
Pets: Sometimes
Children: Welcome, over 10
Smoking: No
Social drinking: Permitted
Airport Pickup: Yes

Shamrock B&B is situated on one and a quarter acres of woods in the northeastern Columbus area. A host of attractions lie nearby: shopping malls, cinemas, Hoover Dam, Inniswoods Botanical Gardens, Busch Brewery, Ohio Historical Village, Short North Gallery Hop, German Village, the symphony, and Ohio State University. Tom is a retired schoolteacher who loves gardening and travel, and his brick home is filled with eighteenth-century antiques and original art. Guest areas are on the first floor, so this B&B is wheelchair accessible.

The Maxwell House ✪
590 HIBBS ROAD, GROVE CITY, OHIO 43137

Tel: (614) 871-9030
Best Time to Call: Anytime
Host(s): Dene and Abe Maxwell
Location: 10 mi. S of Columbus
No. of Rooms: 2
Max. No. Sharing Bath: 4
Double/sb: $60
Single/sb: $50

Open: All year
Breakfast: Full
Pets: No
Children: Welcome, over 8
Smoking: No
Social drinking: Permitted
Airport/Station Pickup: Yes

Listed on the National Register of Historic Places, this nine-room 1845 farmhouse has been restored and furnished in period style. Dene and Abe provide a warm and gracious family atmosphere in a country setting just five minutes from the interstate. Golf, harness and thoroughbred racing, gardens, canoeing, and hiking lie within the immediate vicinity. Columbus, just 15 minutes away, is home to Ohio State University sports, the Ohio Historical Society Museum, the old-fashioned homes of Ohio Village, and fine shopping and dining.

Crager House ✪
402 WEST SOUTH STREET (STATE ROUTE 138 WEST), HILLSBORO, OHIO 45133

Tel: **(513) 393-9999; (800) 432-7199**	Reduced rates: **Available**
Best Time to Call: **After 5 pm**	Breakfast: **Full**
Hosts: **Don and Lynn Crager**	Other Meals: **Available**
Location: **60 mi. SW of Columbus**	Pets: **No**
No. of Rooms: **2**	Children: **Welcome**
Max. No. Sharing Bath: **4**	Smoking: **No**
Double/sb: **$55**	Social Drinking: **Permitted**
Single/sb: **$50**	Airport Pickup: **Yes**
Open: **All year**	

A two-story Colonial brick that dates to the mid-nineteenth century, Crager House is decorated with antiques and charm. Follow the beautiful walnut stairwell upstairs to the purple bedroom, where you'll find a walnut spindle bed built in the late 1800s, and the green room, with its elegant brass bed of slightly later vintage. Spend evenings in your own living room with a fireplace, games, and TV. You'll wake up to a homemade breakfast served in the dining room, lit by one of the home's original pewter chandeliers. Hillsboro is within easy striking distance of Dayton, Cincinnati, and Columbus; closer to home are 7 Caves Park, for spelunking, and Rocky Fork and Paint Creek State Parks, for fishing, boating, and camping. Those who prefer the sport of antiquing will want to visit Old Pants Factory Antique Mall.

Captain Montague's Guest House ✪
229 CENTER STREET, HURON, OHIO 44839

Tel: **(419) 433-4756**	Reduced Rates: **Oct. 1–May 14**
Best Time to Call: **9:30 AM–10 PM**	Breakfast: **Continental, plus**
Hosts: **Judy and Mike Tann**	Pets: **No**
Location: **54 mi. W of Cleveland**	Children: **No**
No. of Rooms: **6**	Smoking: **No**
No. of Private Baths: **6**	Social Drinking: **Permitted**
Double/pb: **$68–$85**	Minimum Stay: **2 nights weekends**
Open: **April 1–Dec. 15**	**Memorial Day–Labor Day**

Just two blocks from the beach at Lake Erie, Judy and Mike have turned their 1876 Southern Colonial into a lavishly appointed accommodation for travelers. The beautiful grounds boast a lattice enclosed garden with a fountain, a gazebo furnished with wicker, and an inground swimming pool. The interior has been comfortably furnished and decorated with Victorian accents. A vintage player piano sets the tone for relaxation while you visit in front of the living room fireplace. Take a walk on the mile-long pier, dine at a nearby restaurant, browse in local shops, or enjoy a play at Ohio's oldest summer theater.

The Maples ✪
14701 STATE ROUTE 93, JACKSON, OHIO 45640

Tel: (614) 286-6067
Best Time to Call: After 4 PM
Hosts: Tony and Maria DeCastro
Location: 75 mi. SE of Columbus
No. of Rooms: 3
No. of Private Baths: 1
Max. No. Sharing Bath: 4
Double/pb: $55
Single/pb: $50
Double/sb: $45

Single/sb: $40
Open: All year
Reduced Rates: 10% seniors, long stays
Breakfast: Full
Credit Cards: AMEX, DISC, MC, VISA
Pets: No
Children: Welcome
Smoking: No
Social Drinking: No

This turn-of-the-century farmhouse is situated on two acres and surrounded by maple trees. The house boasts five fireplaces, massive oak pocket doors, and leaded glass windows. Guest rooms are comfortably furnished with antiques and handmade quilts, and whole-house air-conditioning provides year-round comfort. A hearty breakfast of freshly baked breads and appetizing main dishes is served in the dining room, but guests may prefer to dine on wicker tables on the screened porch or on the stone table in the rose garden. Enjoy the gracious hospitality and friendly atmosphere at The Maples.

Idlewyld Bed & Breakfast ✪
350 WALNUT STREET, LAKESIDE, OHIO 43440 (MAILING ADDRESS: 13458 PARKWAY, LAKEWOOD, OHIO 44107)

Tel: (419) 798-4198; (216) 228-8168
Hosts: Dan and Joan Barris
Location: 70 mi. W of Cleveland
No. of Rooms: 14
No. of Private Baths: 5
Max. No. Sharing Bath: 3
Double/pb: $45–$50
Double/sb: $40– $45

Open: Mid-May–Oct.
Reduced Rates: Available
Breakfast: Continental, plus
Pets: No
Children: Welcome
Smoking: No
Social Drinking: No

A stay at Idlewyld is like visiting an era when life was uncomplicated by high tech. Nestled in a quaint Victorian community on the shore of

Lake Erie, the house is newly decorated in a country antique style. Many rooms feature stenciling. Guests gather in the large dining room for a Continental buffet breakfast, which includes an uncommon assortment of fresh fruit and homemade breads and muffins. Afterward, you can relax on one of the two spacious porches or participate in a myriad of family-oriented activities offered in the Lakeside community.

Hexagon House ✪
419 CINCINNATI AVENUE, LEBANON, OHIO 45036

Tel: **(513) 932-9655**	Single/pb: **$50**
Best Time to Call: **Anytime**	Double/sb: **$55**
Host: **Lois Duncan Hart**	Single/sb: **$45**
Location: **30 mi. N of Cincinnati**	Open: **All year**
No. of Rooms: **2**	Breakfast: **Full**
No. of Private Baths: **1**	Pets: **No**
Max. No. Sharing Bath: **4**	Children: **Welcome, over 12**
Double/pb: **$60**	Smoking: **No**

Built in the mid-1850s on a large, well-landscaped lot, Hexagon House is listed on the National Register of Historic Places due to its unique six-sided exterior, its interesting interior floor plan and history. Rooms are spacious, comfortable, and tastefully decorated. A full breakfast is served on a flexible schedule. The objective of your full-time hostess is to provide each guest with a pleasantly memorable experience. Hexagon House is easy to reach from interstates and covenient to local attractions.

White Tor ✪
1620 OREGONIA ROAD, LEBANON, OHIO 45036

Tel: **(513) 932-5892**	Open: **All year**
Best Time to Call: **Before 9 AM; after 6 PM**	Breakfast: **Full**
	Pets: **No**
Hosts: **Eric and Margaret Johnson**	Children: **No**
Location: **25 mi. N of Cincinnati**	Smoking: **No**
No. of Rooms: **1 suite**	Social Drinking: **Permitted**
No. of Private Baths: **1**	Foreign Languages: **French**
Suite: **$70**	

Just a half hour's drive from both Cincinnati and Dayton, this handsome farmhouse, built in 1862, crowns a hilltop on seven wooded acres. Margaret's full English breakfast will give you stamina for a day of antique shopping or viewing artful stitchery at local quilt shows. Area attractions range from Kings Island and the Beach Waterpark to the Honey and Sauerkraut festivals. Or, simply relax on the porch in view of the pretty Miami Valley, with a good book and cold drink.

The Mainstay ☉
1320 EAST MAIN STREET, LOUISVILLE, OHIO 44641

Tel: (216) 875-1021	Open: All year
Hosts: Mary and Joe Shurilla	Reduced Rates: 15% weekly
Location: 7 mi. E of Canton	Breakfast: Full
No. of Rooms: 3	Pets: No
No. of Private Baths: 3	Children: Welcome, over 3
Double/pb: $50	Smoking: No
Single/pb: $40	Social Drinking: Permitted
Suite: $50; sleeps 3	Airport/Station Pickup: Yes

Enjoy a step backward in time at this century-old Queen Anne Victorian with its richly carved oak woodwork, spacious rooms, original tin ceilings, and numerous antiques. Louisville was the home of Charles Juilliard, founder of the famous New York City music school that bears his name; his house, listed on the National Register of Historic Places, may be toured by arrangement. If you prefer halftime shows to string quartets, you'll probably want to visit the Pro Football Hall of Fame in nearby Canton. Mary and Joe, both educators, greet newly arrived guests with fruit, cheese, and a sparkling beverage. In the morning, have your choice of full or Continental breakfast, with specialties like quiche and home-baked bread.

The Bed & Breakfast at Willow Pond ☉
3360 SR 545 OLIVESBURG ROAD, MANSFIELD, OHIO 44903

Tel: (419) 522-4644; (800) 772-7809	Double/sb: $55
Best Time to Call: 8 AM–8 PM	Open: All year
Hosts: Bud and Marianna Henderson	Breakfast: Full
Location: 5.3 mi. N of Mansfield	Pets: Sometimes
No. of Rooms: 4	Children: Welcome, over 8
No. of Private Baths: 2	Smoking: No
Max. No. Sharing Bath: 4	Social Drinking: Permitted
Double/pb: $65	Minimum Stay: During special events

This beautifully restored, three-story Federal-Adam-style farmhouse, built in 1866, overlooks the big valley of historic Weller Township, a stop on the underground railway to Canada. You'll find plenty to do here, thanks to attractions like Richland Carrousel Park, Kingwood Center Gardens, Ashland University, the mid-Ohio sports car course, and a flourishing Amish community. Willow Pond's rooms, furnished with antiques, include guest quarters, a formal parlor, a farm kitchen, a gathering room with its original cooking fireplace, and a screened porch. There is also a picnic house and a pond with a duck in residence. Breakfasts feature homemade quick breads, fresh fruit, juice, cereal, and a hot entree.

Mulberry Inn ✪
53 NORTH FOURTH STREET, MARTINS FERRY, OHIO 43935

Tel: **(614) 633-6058**
Hosts: **Charles and Shirley Probst**
Location: **5 mi. W of Wheeling, W. Va.**
No. of Rooms: **4**
Max. No. Sharing Bath: **4**
Double/sb: **$45**
Single/sb: **$35**
Open: **All year**

Reduced Rates: **Jan.–Feb.; 10% after 2nd night; 5% seniors**
Breakfast: **Full**
Credit Cards: **DISC, MC, VISA**
Pets: **No**
Children: **Welcome, over 10**
Smoking: **Restricted**
Social Drinking: **Permitted**

Built in 1868, this frame Victorian is on a tree-lined street within walking distance of a Civil War cemetery and the Sedgwick Museum. (Martins Ferry is the oldest settlement in Ohio.) Beautiful woodwork, antiques, and mantels grace the large rooms, and air-conditioning cools the house in summer. A retired medical secretary, Shirley devotes her time to making her guests feel comfortable and welcome, tempting them with her unusual French toast recipe. Dog races, recreational activities, the Fostoria Glass Outlet, the Jamboree-in-the-Hills, Ohio University, and Bethany College are less than 10 miles away.

The Outback Inn ✪
171 EAST UNION AVENUE, McCONNELLSVILLE, OHIO 43756

Tel: **(614) 962-2158**
Best Time to Call: **5 PM**
Hosts: **Emily Matusek and Chuck Borsari**
No. of Rooms: **3**
No. of Private Baths: **3**
Double/pb: **$55–$65**

Open: **All year**
Breakfast: **Continental, full**
Credit Cards: **AMEX**
Pets: **Sometimes**
Children: **No**
Smoking: **No**
Social Drinking: **Permitted**

The Outback Inn is a restored 1880s home located in a tiny historic village midway between Zanesville and Marietta. In addition to the three bedrooms, guests have use of the living room, dining room, kitchen, front porch, and private fenced-in backyard. Emily is a schoolteacher and weaver, her husband a stained-glass artist; their inn displays his own work as well as pieces by contemporary local artists. You'll discover excellent restaurants within three blocks. Animal lovers will want to travel the eight miles to the New Wildlife Preserve, where rare and vanishing species are bred.

The Livery Building ✪
254 EAST SMITH ROAD, MEDINA, OHIO 44256

Tel: **(216) 722-1332**
Best Time to Call: **Evenings**

Hosts: **Lee and Candace Hutton**
Location: **30 mi. S of Cleveland**

No. of Rooms: **3**	Breakfast: **Full**
Max. No. Sharing Bath: **3**	Children: **Welcome, over 6**
Double/sb: **$45**	Smoking: **No**
Single/sb: **$40**	Social Drinking: **Permitted**
Suites: **$65**	Airport Pickup: **Yes**
Open: **All year**	

The Livery Building is a three-story, turn-of-the-century home furnished with antiques, in keeping with the spirit of Medina's restored Victorian square. Breakfasts feature foods from organic and local small farms, including produce from the Huttons' forty-acre fields ten miles outside of town. Lee is an attorney and Candace is a freelance writer; their home business reflects their shared interest in the preservation of small towns and farms. They are happy to help guests with special events and antiques packages. Easy day trips lead to Cleveland's zoo and museums, Cedar Point, Geauga Lake, Sea World, Hale Farm, and regional wineries.

English Manor ✪
505 EAST LINDEN AVENUE, MIAMISBURG, OHIO 45342

Tel: **(513) 866-2288; (800) 676-9456**	Hosts: **Marilyn and Jack Didrichsen**
Best Time to Call: **9 AM–11 PM**	Location: **9 mi. SW of Dayton**

No. of Rooms: **4**	Breakfast: **Full**
No. of Private Baths: **3**	Other Meals: **Available**
Max. No. Sharing Bath: **2**	Credit Cards: **AMEX, DC, DISC, MC,**
Double/pb: **$80**	**VISA**
Single/pb: **$75**	Pets: **No**
Double/sb: **$70**	Children: **Welcome**
Single/sb: **$65**	Smoking: **No**
Open: **All year**	Social Drinking: **Permitted**
Reduced Rates: **10% after 3 nights**	Airport Pickup: **Yes**

Marilyn, a retired real estate investor, and Jack, a retired executive, welcome you to their antique-filled 1920s home in historic Miamisburg. Read by the fireplace, lounge in the hammock, sip lemonade on the wicker porch. Then wander past charming neighborhood homes, or head toward the Great Miami River walking and bike trail. Antique shops, ancient Indian mounds, golf courses, tennis courts, and fine restaurants are all nearby. To start your day, a sumptuous breakfast is served on antique china, silver, and linens.

Gastier Farm Bed & Breakfast ☉
1902 STRECKER ROAD, MILAN, OHIO 44846

Tel: **(419) 499-2985**	Open: **All year**
Best Time to Call: **After 5 PM**	Breakfast: **Continental**
Hosts: **Ted and Donna Gastier**	Credit Cards: **MC, VISA**
Location: **60 mi. W of Cleveland**	Pets: **No**
No. of Rooms: **3**	Children: **Welcome**
Max. No. Sharing Bath: **3**	Smoking: **No**
Double/sb: **$50**	Social Drinking: **No**
Single/sb: **$35**	Aiport/Station Pickup: **Yes**

Ted and Donna's working farm has been a family tradition for more than one hundred years, providing the local community with grain, fresh produce, cattle, and a variety of house plants. Now the farmhouse has become a bed and breakfast. The rooms have all been decorated in a homey country atmosphere. Nearby attractions include Edison Birthplace, Milan Museum, Lake Erie, Cedar Point Amusement Park, and antique shops.

St. George House ☉
33941 LORAIN ROAD, NORTH RIDGEVILLE, OHIO 44039

Tel: **(216) 327-9354**	Max. No. Sharing Bath: **4**
Best Time to Call: **Early mornings;**	Double/pb: **$50**
evenings until 9 PM	Single/pb: **$45**
Hosts: **Helen Bernardine and Muriel**	Double/sb: **$40**
Dodd	Single/sb: **$35**
Location: **30 mi. W of Cleveland**	Open: **All year**
No. of Rooms: **4**	Reduced Rates: **Weekly**
No. of Private Baths: **1**	Breakfast: **Continental**

Pets: **Sometimes**	Social Drinking: **Permitted**
Children: **Welcome, over 12**	Airport/Station Pickup: **Yes**
Smoking: **Permitted**	Minimum stay: **2 nights**

This Colonial gray house, with its bright red shutters, is decorated with furnishings artfully restored by Helen and Muriel. The surrounding property includes barns, a bird sanctuary, and a pond that is home to a variety of wild ducks and frogs. The game room is the evening gathering place and your hosts will gladly join in the fun. Within 35 miles are Case Western Reserve and John Carroll universities, and the famed Cleveland Clinic. Oberlin College is ten miles away. Closer by are the clean beaches of Lake Erie, a zoo, and a variety of theaters.

The Bayberry Inn ✪
25675 STATE ROUTE 41 NORTH, PEEBLES, OHIO 45660

Tel: **(513) 587-2221**	Open: **All year**
Host: **Ruth Shepherd**	Breakfast: **Full, Continental**
Location: **75 mi. E of Cincinnati**	Pets: **No**
No. of Rooms: **3**	Children: **Welcome**
Max. No. Sharing Bath: **4**	Smoking: **No**
Double/sb: **$55**	Social Drinking: **No**
Single/sb: **$45**	

If you expect to find warm hospitality, cozy accommodations with comfortable appointments, and a front porch on which to relax after a hearty old-fashioned breakfast, you won't be disappointed in Ruth's Victorian farmhouse. It's located in Adams County, the hub for those with geological, historical, recreational, and agricultural interests. You are certain to enjoy visiting Serpent Mound, museums, natural wildlife areas, and herb gardens.

Tudor Country Inn ✪
BOX 113, PETTISVILLE, OHIO 43553

Tel: **(419) 445-2531**	Single/sb: **$45**
Best Time to Call: **8:30 AM–9 PM**	Open: **All year**
Hosts: **LeAnna and Dale Gautsche**	Breakfast: **Full**
Location: **30 mi. W of Toledo; 5 mi.**	Pets: **No**
from Ohio Tpke.	Children: **Welcome**
No. of Rooms: **2**	Smoking: **No**
Max. No. Sharing Bath: **4**	Social Drinking: **No**
Double/sb: **$50**	

LeAnna and Dale were restaurant owners until they opened this English Tudor inn. It is set on the edge of a small village, surrounded by farmland in the heart of the Mennonite community. Besides soaking in the hot tub, you may lounge in the great room, where snacks are served in the evenings and a fire burns in winter. Breakfast often includes "Belly Stickers," a creamy-bottom tart, and homemade raised donuts. Local attractions include a farm and crafts village, a country store, and an ice-cream parlor and restaurant, all in the Pennsylvania Dutch style.

Inn at the Green ✪
500 SOUTH MAIN STREET, POLAND, OHIO 44514

Tel: **(216) 757-4688**	Open: **All year**
Best Time to Call: **After 12 PM**	Breakfast: **Continental**
Hosts: **Ginny and Steve Meloy**	Other Meals: **No**
Location: **7 mi. SE of Youngstown**	Credit Cards: **MC, VISA**
No. of Rooms: **4**	Pets: **No**
No. of Private Baths: **4**	Children: **Welcome, over 10**
Double/pb: **$60**	Smoking: **Permitted**
Single/pb: **$55**	Social Drinking: **Permitted**

The Inn at the Green is an 1876 Victorian town house located on the south end of the village green. The rooms have the grandeur of bygone days, with original moldings, 12-foot-high ceilings, and original poplar floors. There are five Italian marble fireplaces and extensive public rooms furnished with gracious antiques. Guests are welcome to relax in the parlor, sitting room, and library. Sleeping quarters are air-conditioned, and are furnished with poster beds, Sealy Posturepedic mattresses, and antiques. Coffee, croissants, muffins, and French jam are served in the greeting room in winter and on the wicker-furnished porch during moderate weather. Enjoy a glass of sherry on the porch overlooking the garden before dinner. Your hosts will gladly direct you to gourmet dining as well as cross-country ski trails, golf, tennis, and the Butler Institute, home of one of the nation's finest American art collections.

The Vineyard ✪
BOX 283, PUT-IN-BAY, OHIO 43456

Tel: **(419) 285-6181**	Open: **All year**
Hosts: **Barbi and Mark Barnhill**	Reduced Rates: **Dec.–Mar.**
Location: **An island 35 mi. E of Toledo**	Breakfast: **Full**
No. of Rooms: **3**	Pets: **Sometimes**
No. of Private Baths: **1**	Children: **No**
Max. No. Sharing Bath: **4**	Smoking: **No**
Double/pb: **$95**	Social Drinking: **Permitted**
Double/sb: **$75**	Minimum Stay: **2 nights in season**
Single/sb: **$75**	Airport/Station Pickup: **Yes**

This 130-year-old wood frame house is set on 20 acres of island seclusion. Your hosts grow Catawba grapes for the local winery, which is part of the region's famous wine industry. Guests are greeted and shown to newly renovated bedrooms furnished with family antiques.

You are invited to sun and swim on a private beach after a day of touring. Local attractions include a picturesque harbor, a monument offering a view of Lake Erie's islands, and a unique Victorian village featuring excellent restaurants. Complimentary bikes are available.

My Father's House Bed and Breakfast ✪
173 SOUTH MARIETTA STREET, ST. CLAIRSVILLE, OHIO 43950

Tel: **(614) 695-5440**	Reduced Rates: **10% after 4 nights**
Best time to Call: **9 AM–9 PM**	Breakfast: **Continental**
Hosts: **Mark and Polly Loy**	Credit Cards: **MC, VISA**
Location: **9 mi. W of Wheeling, W.Va.**	Pets: **No**
No. of Rooms: **3**	Children: **Welcome**
No. of Private Baths: **3**	Smoking: **No**
Double/pb: **$45–$55**	Social Drinking: **No**
Single/pb: **$40–$55**	Station Pickup: **Yes**
Open: **All year**	

This stately Federal home was built in 1810 by Benjamin Ruggles, one of Ohio's first U.S. senators. Today, antique and modern furnishings combine to create a quaint yet comfortable overnight experience. The living room features a romantic open fireplace, while the parlor affords guests the opportunity to watch television. There are many opportunities for shopping and sightseeing in the area. Historic Wheeling, West Virginia, just 15 minutes away, features a variety of attractions, including the spectacular Festival of Lights (November–February).

The Red Gables B&B ✪
421 WAYNE STREET, SANDUSKY, OHIO 44870

Tel: **(419) 625-1189**	Reduced Rates: **Oct. 1–May 1 all**
Best Time to Call: **9 AM–10 PM**	**rooms are $50**
Host: **Jo Ellen Cuthbertson**	Breakfast: **Continental, plus**
Location: **60 mi. W of Cleveland**	Credit Cards: **MC, VISA**
No. of Rooms: **4**	Pets: **No**
No. of Private Baths: **2**	Children: **By arrangement**
Max. No. Sharing Bath: **4**	Smoking: **No**
Double/pb: **$70–$75**	Social Drinking: **Permitted**
Double/sb: **$60–$65**	Station Pickup: **Yes**
Open: **Feb.–Dec.**	

A lovely old Tudor Revival home finished in 1907, The Red Gables is located in the historic Old Plat District. Guests are welcomed into the great room, which features a massive fireplace and large bay window where breakfast is served. The home's many interesting architectural details include lots of oak woodwork. The Red Gables is decorated in a very eclectic style, from Oriental artifacts in the great room to flowered chintz in the bedrooms. The innkeeper, a semi-retired costume maker, has filled the rooms with handmade slipcovers, curtains, and comforters. Guest rooms are light and airy, with easy access to a wicker-filled sitting room, a refrigerator, and coffeemaker or teakettle. Guests have said, "It's like going to Grandma's house!"

Wagner's 1844 Inn ✪
230 EAST WASHINGTON STREET, SANDUSKY, OHIO 44870

Tel: (419) 626-1726	Reduced Rates: Oct.–Apr.
Hosts: Walt and Barb Wagner	Breakfast: Continental
Location: 8 mi. from Ohio Tpke., Exit 7	Credit Cards: DISC, MC, VISA
No. of Rooms: 3	Pets: Sometimes
No. of Private Baths: 3	Children: No
Double/pb: $$60–$80	Smoking: No
Single/pb: $50–$75	Social Drinking: Permitted
Open: All year	Airport/Station Pickup: Yes

This elegantly restored Italianate home, built in 1844, is listed on the National Register of Historic Places. The warm interior features old-fashioned amenities like a billiard room, an antique piano, and a wood-burning fireplace. The screened porch and enclosed courtyard provide tranquil settings for conversation with your hosts Walt, an attorney, and Barb, a registered nurse. Within easy walking distance are parks, tennis courts, antique shops, art galleries, and ferries to Cedar Point Amusement Park and the Lake Erie Islands.

Somer Tea B&B ✪
200 SOUTH COLUMBUS STREET, BOX 308, SOMERSET, OHIO 43783

Tel: (614) 743-2909	Open: All year
Hosts: Richard and Mary Lou Murray	Breakfast: Full
Location: 40 mi. SE of Columbus	Pets: Welcome
No. of Rooms: 2	Children: Welcome
Max. No. Sharing Bath: 4	Smoking: Permitted
Double/sb: $45	Social Drinking: Permitted
Single/sb: $35	

Somerset was the boyhood home of the Civil War general Phil Sheridan. Two of his nieces lived in the Somer Tea, a stately brick residence listed on the National Register of Historic Places. And yes, tea is always available here; guests are encouraged to sit with a cup on the porch swing. Ask Mary Lou to show you her collection of more than 300 teapots. If you'd like to do some collecting yourself, she'll direct you to the region's numerous antique shops and crafts stores. Full country breakfasts, with an egg casserole, a fruit dish, home fries, and raisin bran muffins, are served in the elegant dining room.

100 Mile House Bed & Breakfast ○
U.S. 52, BOX 4866D, STOUT, OHIO 45684

Tel: **(614) 858-2984; (800) 645-2051**	Double/sb: **$55**
Best Time to Call: **Anytime before 10 PM**	Open: **All year**
	Breakfast: **Full**
Hosts: **Jim and Barb Larter**	Other Meals: **Available**
Location: **15 mi. W of Portsmouth**	Pets: **No**
No. of Rooms: **4**	Children: **Welcome**
No. of Private Baths: **2**	Smoking: **No**
Max. No. Sharing Bath: **4**	Social Drinking: **Permitted**
Double/pb: **$65**	Station Pickup: **Yes**

Perhaps the most noted of estates in southern Ohio, this majestic mansion has all anyone could ask for. Beautiful and breathtaking views of the Ohio River, the lush mature landscape, and the birds singing while you sit under your favorite tree give you the feeling of total relaxation. The 11 acres offer plenty of room for a nice walk or you can bask in the sun and enjoy the junior Olympic-size pool. The riverfront stretches for over 600 feet for a gorgeous view. Your hosts offer an evening snack as well as a full breakfast. For sports enthusiasts, 100 Mile House is close to Shawnee State Forest golf course and marina.

Allen Villa B&B
434 SOUTH MARKET STREET, TROY, OHIO 45373

Tel: **(513) 335-1181**	Open: **All year**
Best Time to Call: **9 AM–9 PM**	Breakfast: **Full**
Hosts: **Robert and June Smith**	Credit Cards: **AMEX, MC, VISA**
Location: **20 mi. N of Dayton**	Pets: **No**
No. of Rooms: **4**	Children: **Welcome, over 12**
No. of Private Baths: **4**	Smoking: **Restricted**
Double/pb: **$69–$74**	Social Drinking: **Permitted**
Single/pb: **$49–$54**	Airport/Station Pickup: **Yes**

After painstakingly restoring this Victorian mansion, built in 1874, the Smiths furnished it with the antiques they collect as a hobby. The wooden Venetian blinds, walnut trim, and decorative stencils are all original to the house. This is a good neighborhood for strolling. Other local attractions include a public golf course, Stillwater Vineyards, and Brukner Nature Center. Full breakfasts feature such specialties as vegetable omelets and French toast. You are welcome to use the snack bar with its refrigerator, ice maker, and microwave.

Priscilla's Bed & Breakfast ✪
5 SOUTH WEST STREET (COLUMBUS), WESTERVILLE, OHIO 43081

Tel: **(614) 882-3910**
Best Time to Call: **10 AM–5 PM**
Host: **Priscilla H. Curtiss**
Location: **2 mi. N of Columbus**
No. of Rooms: **3**
No. of Private Baths: **1**
Max. No. Sharing Bath: **4**
Double/pb: **$60**

Double/sb: **$45–$55**
Single/sb: **$40**
Open: **All year**
Breakfast: **Continental**
Pets: **No**
Children: **Welcome**
Social Drinking: **Permitted**
Airport/Station Pickup: **Yes**

Located in a historic area adjacent to Otterbein campus, this 1854 home, surrounded by a white picket fence, abounds with antiques and collectibles. Guests are welcome to borrow bicycles, use the patio, enjoy concerts in the adjoining park, walk to the Benjamin Hanby Museum or the quaint shops, or just stay "home" and relax. Priscilla is an authority on miniatures and dollhouse construction. Everyone enjoys browsing through her on-premises shop.

OKLAHOMA

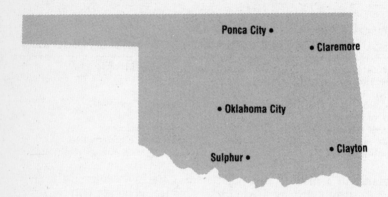

Country Inn
ROUTE 3, BOX 1925, CLAREMORE, OKLAHOMA 74017

Tel: **(918) 342-1894**
Best Time to Call: **8 AM–8 PM**
Hosts: **Leland and Kay Jenkins**
Location: **25 mi. NE of Tulsa**
No. of Rooms: **3**
No. of Private Baths: **3**
Double/pb: **$52**
Single/pb: **$35**

Suite: **$62**
Open: **All year**
Reduced Rates: **10% seniors**
Breakfast: **Full**
Children: **No**
Smoking: **No**
Social Drinking: **Permitted**

Leland and Kay look forward to making you feel right at home in the charming barn-style guest quarters, separate from the main house. They invite you to enjoy the swimming pool, improve your suntan, or just sit back in the shade and enjoy a cool drink. The Will Rogers

Memorial, the J. M. Davis Gun Museum, the 29,500-acre Oologah Lake, and Oral Roberts University are close by. Horse racing buffs will enjoy pari-mutuel betting at Will Rogers Downs during August and September.

Clayton Country Inn ✪
ROUTE 1, BOX 8, HIGHWAY 271, CLAYTON, OKLAHOMA 74536

Tel: **(918) 569-4165, 627-1956**
Best Time to Call: **8 AM–9 PM**
Hosts: **Betty Lundgren, Eula and Al Taylor**
Location: **140 mi. SE of Tulsa**
No. of Rooms: **11**
No. of Private Baths: **11**
Double/pb: **$39**
Single/pb: **$33**

Guest Cottage: **$42; sleeps 5**
Open: **All year**
Breakfast: **Continental**
Other Meals: **Available**
Credit Cards: **MC, VISA**
Pets: **No**
Children: **Welcome**
Smoking: **Permitted**
Social Drinking: **Permitted**

Perched on a hill amid 140 acres and surrounded by the Kiamichi Mountains is this 50-year-old, two-story, stone and wood inn. It's furnished in a simple, traditional style with a beamed ceiling and fireplace. The on-premises restaurant is noted for its fine cooking. Bass fishing at Lake Sardis is two miles away, and an 18,000-acre game preserve is just across the highway. Feel free to bring your horse and enjoy trail rides under the vast Western skies.

Country House ✪
10101 OAKVIEW ROAD, OKLAHOMA CITY, OKLAHOMA 73165

Tel: **(405) 794-4008**	Single/pb: **$45**
Best Time to Call: **8 AM–10 PM**	Open: **All year**
Hosts: **Dee and Nancy Ann Curnutt**	Breakfast: **Full**
Location: **10 mi. SE of center of Oklahoma City**	Pets: **Sometimes**
	Children: **Welcome**
No. of Rooms: **2**	Smoking: **Restricted**
No. of Private Baths: **2**	Social Drinking: **Permitted**
Double/pb: **$50–$85**	

At Country House you will find genuine, old-fashioned hospitality in a warm romantic setting. The house rests on five beautiful acres; the interior is tastefully furnished with 19th-century antiques and country collectibles. Nancy offers in-room color TV on request, as well as a scrumptious breakfast served on the balcony if you wish. For fishing, water sports, and horseback riding go to nearby Lake Draper, where Captain Dee, Nancy's husband, runs a charter boat service. Ask about the large red heart-shaped whirlpool suite.

The Grandison ✪
1841 NORTHWEST FIFTEENTH STREET, OKLAHOMA CITY, OKLAHOMA 73106

Tel: **(405) 521-0011**	Breakfast: **Continental, plus**
Hosts: **Claudia and Bob Wright**	Other Meals: **Available**
Location: **2 mi. off I-44, Tenth St. exit**	Credit Cards: **AMEX, DISC, MC, VISA**
No. of Rooms: **5**	Pets: **Sometimes**
No. of Private Baths: **5**	Children: **Welcome, over 12**
Double/pb: **$45–$85**	Smoking: **Permitted**
Suites: **$90–$125**	Social Drinking: **Permitted**
Open: **All year**	Airport/Station Pickup: **Yes**

Named for its first owner and resident, Grandison Crawford, this turn-of-the-century brick Colonial was expanded in 1919, and again in the 1930s. It is furnished with antiques from many eras, so each bedroom has a distinctive look. The closest attractions—Civic Center Music Hall, the Convention Center, and Oklahoma City's fairgrounds—are just five minutes away. Breakfast consists of a meat or egg dish, fresh fruit, home-baked pastries, and beverage. For snacking, you'll find fruit, nuts, cookies, and mints in your bedroom.

Davarnathey Inn ✪
1001 WEST GRAND, PONCA CITY, OKLAHOMA 74601

Tel: **(405) 765-9922**	No. of Rooms: **3**
Hosts: **David and Shirley Zimmerman**	No. of Private Baths: **3**
Location: **80 mi. S of Witchita, Kans.**	Double/pb: **$65**

Single/pb: **$55**
Open: **All year**
Breakfast: **Full**
Credit Cards: **MC, VISA**
Pets: **No**

Children: **Welcome**
Smoking: **No**
Social Drinking: **Permitted**
Airport/Station Pickup: **Yes**

Built in 1906 by an Oklahoma oilman, Davarnathey Inn has its original fretwork stairway, ornate mirrored mantel, and stained-glass windows. Period furnishings and floral wallpapers sustain the Victorian mood. Guests are encouraged to browse in the library; the musically inclined have both a piano and an organ to play. Other amenities include a hot tub. Snacks are served, but after a full breakfast of fresh baked Scandinavian breads, fruit crêpes, soufflés, and quiche, it may be a while before you're hungry again.

Artesian Bed and Breakfast ✪
1022 WEST 12TH STREET, SULPHUR, OKLAHOMA 73086

Tel: **(405) 622-5254**
Hosts: **Karen and Tom Byrd**
Location: **71 mi. S of Oklahoma City**
No. of Rooms: **2**
No. of Private Baths: **2**
Double/pb: **$60**
Single/pb: **$50**
Suites: **$70**

Open: **All year**
Reduced Rates: **15% Dec.–Mar.**
Breakfast: **Full**
Pets: **No**
Children: **Welcome, over 10**
Smoking: **No**
Social Drinking: **No**

A quiet, homey atmosphere prevails at this 1904 Sears, Roebuck Victorian, where the L-shaped front porch is furnished with swing and willow chairs. Inside, you'll admire the wooden staircase, the tiled parlor fireplace, and the bay windows overlooking the backyard. There's natural beauty at every turn. For hiking, swimming, or just picnicking, Chickasaw Recreation Area is only half a mile away. For fishing, boating, and water skiing, take the ten-mile drive to Arbuckle Lake. Your hosts, a retired veterinarian and a homemaker, can help you make the most of your stay.

OREGON

Seaside •

Newberg • • Oregon City • Welches
Woodburn •
• Stayton

Junction City •
Elmira • • Eugene • Leaburg
• North Bend • Bend

Coos Bay •

Port Oxford •

Grants Pass •

• Ashland

Northwest Bed and Breakfast Travel Unlimited
610 SW BROADWAY, SUITE 606, PORTLAND, OREGON 97205

Tel: (503) 243-7616
Coordinator: LaVonne Miller
States/Regions Covered: California,
  Oregon, Washington;
  Canada—British Columbia

Rates (Single/Double):
  Modest: $35–$55 / $45–$65
  Average: $50–$65 / $65–$85
  Luxury: $65–$100 / $85–$165+
Credit Cards: AMEX, MC, VISA
Descriptive Directory: $7.95

Northwest Bed and Breakfast is a network established in 1979 of
hundreds of host homes and inns throughout the Pacific Northwest.
Send $7.95 for a directory of the lodgings, which include city, subur-
ban, and rural sites in coastal, mountain, and desert regions. There is
a $10 surcharge for one-night stays.

Mt. Ashland Inn ✪

550 MT. ASHLAND ROAD, P.O. BOX 944, ASHLAND, OREGON 97520

Tel: **(503) 482-8707**
Best Time to Call: **11 AM–7 PM**
Hosts: **Elaine and Jerry Shanafelt**
Location: **6 mi. from I-5, Exit 6**
No. of Rooms: **5**
No. of Private Baths: **5**
Double/pb: **$80–$130**
Single/pb: **$75–$125**

Open: **All year**
Breakfast: **Full**
Other Meals: **Dinner available**
   Nov.–Apr. only by arrangement
Pets: **No**
Children: **Welcome, over 10**
Smoking: **No**
Social Drinking: **Permitted**

Nestled among tall evergreens, this beautifully handcrafted log structure is situated on a mountain ridge with views of the Cascade Mountains, including majestic Mt. Shasta. Inside, handcarvings, oriental rugs, homemade quilts, antiques, and finely crafted furniture provide an atmosphere of comfort and elegance. Breakfasts are hearty to satisfy the appetites of skiers and hikers who take advantage of nearby trails. For quiet relaxation, you are welcome to enjoy the sunny deck or curl up with a book by the large stone fireplace.

Royal Carter House ✪

514 SISKIYOU BOULEVARD, ASHLAND, OREGON 97520

Tel: **(503) 482-5623**
Best Time to Call: **Mornings**

Hosts: **Alyce and Roy Levy**
No. of Rooms: **4**

No. of Private Baths: **4**
Double/pb: **$64–$84**
Suites: **$84**
Open: **All year**
Breakfast: **Full**

Pets: **No**
Children: **Welcome, over 7**
Smoking: **No**
Social Drinking: **Permitted**
Airport/Station Pickup: **Yes**

This beautiful 1909 Craftsman home is listed on the National Register of Historic Places. Located four blocks from Ashland's famous Shakespeare Theatre, it is surrounded by lovely old trees in a parklike setting. It is suitably modernized but retains the original room structure. Alyce has added decorator touches of vintage hats and old periodicals to the antique furnishings. The Levys have traveled extensively abroad and will share stories of their experiences with you. Southern Oregon State College is six blocks away.

The Woods House Bed & Breakfast Inn ✪
333 NORTH MAIN STREET, ASHLAND, OREGON 97520

Tel: **(503) 488-1598; (800) 435-8260**
Best Time to Call: **10 AM–10 PM**
Hosts: **Françoise and Lester Roddy**
Location: **½ mi. N of Ashland**
No. of Rooms: **6**
No. of Private Baths: **6**
Double/pb: **$65–$110**
Single/pb: **$65–$105**
Open: **All year**
Reduced Rates: **Available**

Breakfast: **Full**
Credit Cards: **MC, VISA**
Pets: **No**
Children: **Welcome, over 12**
Smoking: **No**
Social Drinking: **Permitted**
Minimum Stay: **2 days June–Oct.;
    weekends Nov.–May**
Station Pickup: **Yes**

The Woods House is located in Ashland's historic district four blocks from the Shakespearean theater, shops, restaurants, and 100-acre Lithia Park. The inn, a 1908 Craftsman home renovated in 1984, has six sunny and spacious guest rooms. Simple furnishings, comprising warm woods, antique furniture and linens, watercolors, oriental carpets and leather books, combine with high-quality amenities to create a sophisticated comfortable atmosphere. The terraced English gardens provide many areas for guests to relax and socialize. Françoise previously worked in human resources and event planning and is skilled in calligraphy, cooking, and needlecrafts. Lester has spent the past 25 years in business management and consulting. Their aim is to make each guest feel like a special friend, not just a paying customer. They strive to anticipate guests' needs and cheerfully accommodate the unexpected, always maintaining the highest standards of cleanliness, cordiality, and fine food.

Farewell Bend Bed & Breakfast
29 NW GREELEY, BEND, OREGON 97701

Tel: **(503) 382-4374**
Best Time to Call: **Anytime**
Host: **Lorene Bateman**

Location: **160 mi. SE of Portland**
No. of Rooms: **2**
No. of Private Baths: **2**

Double/pb: **$65**
Open: **All year**
Reduced Rates: **10% weekly**
Breakfast: **Full**
Credit Cards: **AMEX**

Pets: **No**
Children: **Welcome, over 12**
Smoking: **No**
Social Drinking: **Permitted**
Airport/Station Pickup: **Yes**

Farewell Bend is a recently renovated 1920s Dutch Colonial just minutes from shops, restaurants, and Drake Park—where the town music festival takes place every June and hungry ducks and geese demand bread crumbs year-round. It's only 17 miles to Mt. Bachelor for skiing, and white-water rafting on the Deschutes is a special warm-weather treat. Afterward, settle in the living room with sherry or tea, read a book, or watch a movie on the VCR. All bedrooms have king-size beds, down comforters, and hand-stitched quilts, and bathrooms are supplied with terry robes. Full breakfasts are served in the sunny dining room.

The Old Tower House B&B ✪
476 NEWMARK AVENUE, COOS BAY, OREGON 97420

Tel: **(503) 888-6058**
Best Time to Call: **10 AM**
Hosts: **Don and Julia Spangler**
Location: **5 mi. W of Coos Bay**
No. of Rooms: **3**
Max. No. Sharing Bath: **3**
Double/sb: **$60–$65**
Single/sb: **$55**

Open: **All year**
Breakfast: **Full**
Pets: **No**
Children: **Welcome, over 12**
Smoking: **No**
Social Drinking: **No**
Airport Pickup: **Yes**

At the Old Tower House, Gothic Victorian architecture and antique furnishings bring you back to an earlier era. Choose among the King Room, with its king-size bed; the Rose Room, with its 150-year-old barley twist bed; or the Blue Room, with its antique twin beds. Savor a full breakfast—served on crisp white damask linens and vintage china—in the dining room or on the back porch. Then relax with a book or listen to the stereo in the spacious parlor. If you want to catch your next meal, go fishing and crabbing on the bay, a few yards away. Or hop into your car for a scenic drive along the breathtaking Oregon coast.

McGillivray's Log Home and Bed and Breakfast ✪
88680 EVERS ROAD, ELMIRA, OREGON 97437

Tel: **(503) 935-3564**
Best Time to Call: **8 AM–8 PM**
Host: **Evelyn McGillivray**
Location: **14 mi. W of Eugene**
No. of Rooms: **2**
No. of Private Baths: **2**

Double/pb: **$50–$70**
Single/pb: **$40–$60**
Open: **All year**
Breakfast: **Full**
Credit Cards: **MC, VISA**
Pets: **No**

Children: **Welcome**	Social Drinking: **Permitted**
Smoking: **No**	Airport/Station Pickup: **Yes**

This massive home is situated on five acres covered with pines and firs. The air-conditioned structure is designed with six types of wood, and features a split-log staircase. Guests may choose from a spacious, wheelchair-accessible bedroom, or an upstairs room that can accommodate a family. All are beautifully decorated in a classic Americana motif. Evelyn usually prepares buttermilk pancakes using an antique griddle her mother used to use. She also offers fresh-squeezed juice from farm-grown apples and grapes, fresh bread, eggs, and all the trimmings. It's just three miles to a local vineyard; country roads for bicycling and a reservoir for fishing and boating are close by.

Getty's Emerald Garden B&B ✪
640 AUDEL, EUGENE, OREGON 97404

Tel: **(503) 688-6344**	Breakfast: **Full**
Best Time to Call: **Anytime**	Credit Cards: **AMEX, MC, VISA**
Hosts: **Bob and Jackie Getty**	Pets: **No**
Location: **3 mi. N of Eugene**	Children: **Welcome**
No. of Rooms: **1 suite**	Smoking: **No**
Suite: **$50–$55**	Social Drinking: **Permitted**
Open: **All year**	Airport/Station Pickup: **Yes**
Reduced Rates: **10% weekly**	

Bob and Jackie have lived in Eugene for more than thirty years and can help you plan a wonderful vacation. Their contemporary home has vaulted ceilings, large windows, and a cozy living room with a fireplace. Full breakfasts feature specialties from your hosts' garden. Guests have use of the family room and its piano, TV, and VCR; less sedentary types will want to borrow bicycles and head out for the area's scenic trails. For more activity, visit the local park, which has a heated swimming pool, sauna, hot tubs, jogging trails, and playground. Hult Center for the Performing Arts, Lane County Fairgrounds, the University of Oregon, golf courses, Valley River Shopping Center, and City Center are all within a ten-minute drive.

The House in the Woods ✪
814 LORANE HIGHWAY, EUGENE, OREGON 97405

Tel: **(503) 343-3234**	Single/pb: **$42**
Best Time to Call: **Mornings; evenings**	Double/sb: **$55**
Hosts: **Eunice and George Kjaer**	Single/sb: **$40**
Location: **3 mi. from I-5**	Open: **All year**
No. of Rooms: **2**	Reduced Rates: **Available**
No. of Private Baths: **1**	Breakfast: **Full**
Max. No. Sharing Bath: **2**	Pets: **No**
Double/pb: **$65**	

Children: **Welcome, under 1 and over 14**
Smoking: **No**

Social Drinking: **Permitted**
Airport/Station Pickup: **Yes**
Foreign Languages: **German**

This turn-of-the-century home is situated in a wooded glen surrounded by fir trees, rhododendrons, and azaleas. Inside, you'll find oriental rugs on the original hardwood floors, a cozy fireplace, antiques, and a square grand piano. Guest rooms always have fresh flowers. Breakfast is served in the formal dining room or beside the warmth of the Franklin stove. Specialties of the house include breads, fruit soups, and a variety of egg dishes. The neighborhood is full of wildlife and bicycle and jogging trails, yet is close to shops, art galleries, museums, wineries, and restaurants.

Maryellen's Guest House ✪
1583 FIRCREST, EUGENE, OREGON 97403

Tel: **(503) 342-7375**
Best Time to Call: **9 AM–9 PM**
Hosts: **Maryellen and Bob Larson**
Location: **1 mi. off I-5, Exit 191**
No. of Rooms: **2**
No. of Private Baths: **2**
Double/pb: **$72**
Single/pb: **$62**
Open: **All year**

Reduced Rates: **10% weekly**
Breakfast: **Full**
Other Meals: **Available**
Credit Cards: **MC, VISA**
Pets: **No**
Children: **Welcome, over 12**
Smoking: **No**
Social Drinking: **Permitted**
Airport/Station Pickup: **Yes**

Maryellen's Guest House is one and a half blocks from beautiful Hendricks Park, and just a few minutes away from the University of Oregon campus. In Maryellen's own backyard you'll find a swimming pool and a hot tub. You can also luxuriate in the master suite bathroom, with its double shower and deep Roman tub. In the morning, enjoy Continental breakfast in your room, or come to the dining room for fresh fruit followed by your choice of eggs, cereal, waffles, and muffins. When weather permits, meals can be served on the deck overlooking the pool.

The Oval Door (formerly The Lyon & The Lambe Inn) ✪
988 LAWRENCE STREET, EUGENE, OREGON 97401

Tel: **(503) 683-3160; fax (503) 485-5339**
Hosts: **Judith McLane and Dianne Feist**
No. of Rooms: **4**
No. of Private Baths: **4**
Double p/b: **$65–$83**
Single p/b: **$60–$78**
Open: **All year**

Breakfast: **Full**
Credit Cards: **MC, VISA**
Pets: **No**
Children: **By arrangement**
Smoking: **No**
Social Drinking: **Permitted**
Minimum Stay: **2 nights during conventions, Universary functions**

This inviting 1920s-style home was built as a B&B in 1990. From its location in the heart of downtown Eugene, it's an easy walk to fine restaurants and the Holt Performing Arts Center. The University of Oregon campus is also nearby. Scrumptious breakfasts include a seasonal fruit dish, homemade breads, and a special entree, such as zucchini filbert waffles. You'll also find extra touches like terry robes, Perrier water, Frango Mints, and the Tub Room with its whirlpool bath for two, music, candles, and bubbles.

Pookie's Bed 'n' Breakfast on College Hill ✪
2013 CHARNELTON STREET, EUGENE, OREGON 97405

Tel: **(503) 343-0383; (800) 558-0383**	Single/sb: **$55**
Hosts: **Pookie and Doug Walling**	Open: **All year**
Location: **110 mi. S of Portland**	Reduced Rates: **20% families**
No. of Rooms: **2**	Breakfast: **Full**
No. of Private Baths: **1**	Pets: **No**
Max. No. Sharing Bath: **4**	Children: **Welcome, over 6**
Double/pb: **$80**	Smoking: **No**
Single/pb: **$70**	Social Drinking: **Permitted**
Double/sb: **$65**	

Although it has been remodeled on the outside, this Craftsman-style house, built in 1918, retains much of its original interior charm. One room has antique mahogany furniture and a queen-size bed; the other has oak furnishings and either a single or twin beds. Pookie's is in a quiet older neighborhood just south of downtown, where you'll find great shopping, excellent dining, and access to the Hult Performing Arts Center. The University of Oregon campus is all of a mile away. Early morning coffee is served in the small sitting room upstairs. A full breakfast, with specialties like quiche and orange custard baked French toast, follows.

Endicott Gardens ✪
95768 JERRY'S FLAT ROAD, GOLD BEACH, OREGON 97444

Tel: **(503) 247-6513**	Open: **All year**
Best Time to Call: **10 AM–Noon**	Breakfast: **Continental, plus**
Hosts: **Stewart and Mary Endicott**	Pets: **Sometimes**
No. of Rooms: **4**	Children: **Welcome**
No. of Private Baths: **4**	Smoking: **Permitted**
Double/pb: **$55**	Social Drinking: **Permitted**
Single/pb: **$45**	Airport/Station Pickup: **Yes**

This classic contemporary B&B is across the road from Rogue River, famous for fishing and riverboat trips to white water. The guest rooms are located in a private wing of the house with decks overlooking the forest, mountains, and beautiful grounds. Homegrown strawberries, blueberries, apples, and plums are often featured in delicious breakfast treats served on the deck or in the dining room. In cool weather, the living room with its cozy fireplace is a favorite gathering spot. Mary and Stewart will be happy to share their collection of restaurant menus from nearby eating establishments with you.

Falcon's Crest Inn ❂

87287 GOVERNMENT CAMP LOOP HIGHWAY, P.O. BOX 185, GOVERNMENT CAMP, OREGON 97028

Tel: **(503) 272-3403; (800) 624-7384**	Breakfast: **Full**
Hosts: **BJ and Melody Johnson**	Other Meals: **Available**
Location: **54 mi. E of Portland**	Credit Cards: **AMEX, DISC, MC, VISA**
No. of Rooms: **5**	Pets: **No**
No. of Private Baths: **5**	Children: **Welcome, over 6**
Double/pb: **$85–$99.50**	Smoking: **No**
Suites: **$110–$169; sleeps 2**	Social Drinking: **Permitted**
Open: **All year**	Airport/Station Pickup: **Yes**
Reduced Rates: **Nov.–Mar.; with ski package**	

Falcon's Crest Inn is nestled among the firs on the 4,000-foot level of Mount Hood. The two-story glass front of this elegant, intimate B&B provides a spectacular view of Ski Bowl, a year-round recreational area. Duffers can head to the 27-hole championship course just 12 miles from the front door, and those who love water sports can occupy themselves with fishing, swimming, and white-water rafting. The bedrooms, which are decorated with family heirlooms and keepsakes, have forest or mountain views. In the morning, fresh muffins and a beverage are delivered to your door. Then you'll breakfast on hearty fare like buttermilk pancakes, waffles, or French toast.

Ahlf House Bed & Breakfast ❂

762 N.W. 6TH STREET, GRANTS PASS, OREGON 97526

Tel: **(503) 474-1374; (800) 863-1374**	Open: **All year**
Hosts: **Ken and Cathy Neuschafer**	Breakfast: **Full**
Location: **2 blocks from downtown Grants Pass**	Pets: **No**
No. of Rooms: **4**	Children: **No**
Double/pb: **$60–$75**	Smoking: **No**
Single/pb: **$55–$70**	Social Drinking: **Permitted**
	Airport/Station Pickup: **Yes**

Ahlf House is located on a main street on a hill overlooking the surrounding mountains. The house dates back to 1902, and is listed on the National Register of Historic Places. The rooms are beautifully appointed and furnished in fine antiques. Guest rooms feature fluffy comforters, down pillows, fresh flowers, and candles. Enjoy a cup of fresh coffee first thing in the morning in the quiet of your room or on the sunny front porch. Your coffee is followed by a full gourmet breakfast including fruit, fresh-baked muffins, and homemade jams and jellies. There is much to explore in Grants Pass, which is set on the Rogue River and is surrounded by the beautiful Cascade Mountains. Your hosts can direct you to guided fishing, raft trips, and jet boats. In the evening, return to this lovely Victorian for evening dessert.

The Washington Inn Bed & Breakfast ✪
1002 NORTHWEST WASHINGTON BOULEVARD, GRANTS PASS, OREGON 97526

Tel: (503) 476-1131; (503) 479-3378	Single/sb: $30–$45
Hosts: Maryan and Bill Thompson	Open: All year
Location: ½ mi. from I-5	Reduced Rates: Available
No. of Rooms: 3	Breakfast: Full
No. of Private Baths: 2	Pets: No
Max. No. Sharing Bath: 2	Children: Welcome, over 14
Double/pb: $50–$65	Smoking: No
Single/pb: $40–$55	Social Drinking: Permitted
Double/sb: $40–$55	Airport/Station Pickup: Yes

The Washington Inn is a charming Victorian listed on the National Register of Historic Places. Each guest room is named for one of the Thompsons' three children and offers individual charms. Linda's is a large suite with fireplace, queen-size bed, private bath, and balcony overlooking the mountains; Pattie's Parlor is a spacious red room with fireplace and large private bath with claw-footed tub; Sally's Sunny View overlooks the mountains, has a canopied bed, and is decorated in delicate pink. Your hosts offer bicycles for exploring the area, and many interesting shops and restaurants are within easy walking distance. Fishing, rafting, and jet-boat rides can be enjoyed on the Rogue River. If you prefer, spend the afternoon relaxing on the porch swing, taking in the view.

Black Bart Bed & Breakfast ✪
94125 LOVE LAKE ROAD, JUNCTION CITY, OREGON 97448

Tel: (503) 998-1904	Breakfast: Full
Hosts: Don and Irma Mode	Credit Cards: MC, VISA
Location: 14 mi. N of Eugene	Pets: No
No. of Rooms: 2	Children: No
No. of Private Baths: 2	Smoking: No
Double/pb: $60–$70	Social Drinking: Permitted
Open: All year	Airport/Station Pickup: Yes

Don and Irma named this B&B for their National Grand Champion mammoth donkey, who strutted his stuff in a parade of equines at the 1984 Olympics; time and weather permitting, Black Bart will oblige guests by pulling them around in an antique shay. The B&B itself is a remodeled 1880s farmhouse, filled with antiques and—surprise!—lots of donkey collectibles. Nearby, you'll find lots of wineries and farmers markets, plus golf courses and antique shops. Ableskivers, eggs, bacon or sausage, fruit, and juice constitute the hearty farm breakfasts.

Marjon Bed and Breakfast Inn ✪

44975 LEABURG DAM ROAD, LEABURG, OREGON 97489

Tel: **(503) 896-3145**	Open: **All year**
Host: **Marguerite Haas**	Breakfast: **Full**
Location: **24 mi. E of Eugene**	Pets: **No**
No. of Rooms: **2**	Children: **No**
No. of Private Baths: **2**	Smoking: **Permitted**
Double/pb: **$95**	Social Drinking: **Permitted**
Suites: **$125**	Airport/Station Pickup: **Yes**

This cedar chalet is located on the banks of the McKenzie River. The suite overlooks the river and a secluded Japanese garden, and features a sunken bath. The other has a fish bowl shower and a view of a 100-year-old apple tree. Relax in the living room with its wraparound seating and massive stone fireplace. One of the walls is made entirely of glass with sliding doors that lead to a terrace that faces the river. A multicourse breakfast is served there on balmy days. Waterfalls, trout fishing, white-water rafting, and skiing are all nearby.

Secluded B&B ✪

19719 NORTHEAST WILLIAMSON ROAD, NEWBERG, OREGON 97132

Tel: **(503) 538-2635**	Hosts: **Del and Durell Belanger**
Best Time to Call: **8 AM**	Location: **27 mi. SW of Portland**

No. of Rooms: **2**	Breakfast: **Full**
No. of Private Baths: **1**	Pets: **No**
Max. No. Sharing Bath: **4**	Children: **Welcome, under 1 and**
Double/pb: **$50**	**over 6**
Double/sb: **$40**	Smoking: **No**
Single/sb: **$40**	Social Drinking: **No**
Open: **All year**	

A rustic home with a gambrel roof and sunny decks, this B&B is secluded, but not isolated. Set on 10 wooded acres, it is near several notable wineries. George Fox College is also in the area. Your hosts' hobbies include gardening, cooking, and carpentry; Durell made the stained-glass windows that accent the house. The mouth-watering breakfasts might include fresh shrimp omelets, Grand Marnier French toast, or Dutch babies swathed in apple-huckleberry sauce and whipped cream, accompanied by juice, fruit, and coffee or tea.

The Highlands Bed and Breakfast ✪
608 RIDGE ROAD, NORTH BEND, OREGON 97459

Tel: **(503) 756-0300**	Breakfast: **Full**
Hosts: **Jim and Marilyn Dow**	Credit Cards: **MC, VISA**
Location: **4 mi. from Hwy. 101**	Pets: **No**
No. of Rooms: **2**	Children: **Welcome, over 10**
No. of Private Baths: **2**	Smoking: **No**
Double/pb: **$65–$75**	Social Drinking: **Permitted**
Single/pb: **$60–$70**	Airport/Station Pickup: **Yes**
Open: **All year**	

This uniquely designed contemporary cedar home, with its wide expanses of glass and wraparound deck, has a spectacular view of the valley, inlet, and bay. From the floor-to-ceiling windows of the family room you'll be able to watch unforgettable sunrises and sunsets. Dark oak-pegged flooring, beamed vaulted ceilings, and cedar paneling make a perfect setting for the Dows' antiques. A separate entrance for guests ensures privacy, and separate heat controls assure comfort. Breakfast includes fresh-squeezed juice, fruit compote with special sauce, baked eggs on rice with cheese, ham or bacon, and freshly baked muffins or popovers. A short drive away are Oregon's beaches, sand dunes, and many fine restaurants. The Dows are retired and like to fly, sail, and garden.

Inn of the Oregon Trail ✪
416 SOUTH MCLOUGHLIN, OREGON CITY, OREGON 97045

Tel: **(503) 656-2089**	No. of Rooms: **4**
Best Time to Call: **8 AM–9 PM**	No. of Private Baths: **4**
Hosts: **Mary and Tom DeHaven**	Double/pb: **$47.50–$85**
Location: **13 mi. SE of Portland**	Suites: **$75–$85**

Open: **All year**	Children: **Welcome, over 12**
Breakfast: **Full**	Smoking: **No**
Credit Cards: **MC, VISA**	Social Drinking: **Permitted**
Pets: **No**	

A superb Gothic Revival home built in 1867 by a Willamette River captain, Inn of the Oregon Trail is listed on the National Register of Historic Places. In fact, this Oregon City neighborhood is filled with distinctive buildings and museums—ask your hosts to recommend walking and driving tours. You'll have plenty of energy for sightseeing after one of Tom's ample breakfasts of juice, coffee, eggs, pancakes, or French toast.

Oak Ridge Bed & Breakfast ✪
3010 WEST MILITARY ROAD, ROSEBURG, OREGON 97470

Tel: **(503) 672-2168; (800) 428-2428**	Open: **All year**
Best Time to Call: **AM**	Breakfast: **Full**
Hosts: **Bob and Nita Butcher**	Pets: **No**
Location: **60 mi. S of Eugene**	Children: **No**
No. of Rooms: **2**	Smoking: **No**
No. of Private Baths: **2**	Social Drinking: **Permitted**
Double p/b: **$55**	

Tall windows, a spiral staircase, and Indian crafts highlight the living room of this cedar mansard house shaded by native oaks. Each of the airy corner bedrooms has a ceiling fan, chairs, and a comfortable, handcrafted bed. You'll awaken to coffee brought to your door. Follow it up with Continental breakfast in your room, or a heartier, full-course meal in the kitchen, decorated with old cooking utensils. Even the jam is homemade, from fruit your hosts picked themselves. Wineries, rafting, fishing, and Wildlife Safari number among the local attractions. Originally a schoolteacher, Bob spent twenty-five years with the National Park Service, working from Puerto Rico to Alaska; Nita is a full-time homemaker.

The Boarding House Bed & Breakfast ✪
208 NORTH HOLLADAY DRIVE, SEASIDE, OREGON 97138

Tel: **(503) 738-9055; (800) 995-4013**	Open: **All year**
Host: **Barb Edwards**	Reduced Rates: **Available**
Location: **½ mi. from Rte. 101**	Breakfast: **Full**
No. of Rooms: **6**	Credit Cards: **MC, VISA**
No. of Private Baths: **6**	Pets: **No**
Double/pb: **$70–$80**	Children: **Welcome**
Single/pb: **$65–$75**	Smoking: **No**
Guest Cottage: **$110; sleeps 6, $600 weekly**	Social Drinking: **Permitted**
	Airport/Station Pickup: **Yes**

Located on the banks of the Necanicum River, this rustic Victorian was built as a private residence in 1898. During World War I, the house became a boarding home. After an extensive renovation, the wood walls and beamed ceilings have been restored to their original charm. Guest rooms feature brass or white iron beds, down quilts, family heirlooms, wicker, and wood. Claw-footed tubs, window seats, antiques, and a picture of grandma make you feel as if this house is your own. A fire is often burning in the fir-paneled parlor, and an old melody sounds just right on the old-fashioned Victrola. A 100-year-old guest cottage with wood paneling, country furnishings, bedroom, loft, and river view is also available. Breakfast specialties such as cheese-and-egg strata, orange French toast, and blueberry scones are served in the dining room or outside on the wraparound porch. The house is just four blocks from the ocean and two blocks from downtown.

Summer House—A Bed & Breakfast ○
1221 NORTH FRANKLIN STREET, SEASIDE, OREGON 97138

Tel: (503) 738-5740; (800) 745-2378	Reduced Rates: 10% seniors
Best Time to Call: 9 AM–9 PM	Breakfast: Full
Hosts: Jerry and Leslee Newsome	Credit Cards: MC, VISA
Location: 70 mi. W of Portland	Pets: No
No. of Rooms: 4	Children: No
No. of Private Baths: 4	Smoking: No
Double/pb: $70	Social Drinking: Permitted
Single/pb: $60	Minimum Stay: Holidays, July–Sept.;
Suites: $90	most weekends
Open: All year	Airport/Station Pickup: Yes

In bustling Seaside, quiet is a luxury and Summer House offers a quiet retreat just one block from the beach and its famous promenade. Trellised gardens surround this completely renovated, gray shingled home; the interior is light and airy, finished in warm Southwestern colors. After a day of exploring the Oregon coast, unwind in the Garden Room, with its separate sitting area and fireplace. A breakfast of fresh seasonal fruit, soufflé, waffles, crepes, or other delectables can be enjoyed by a crackling fire in winter or on the flower-adorned deck in summer. Please mention any special dietary needs—your hosts will be happy to accommodate you.

Horncroft ○
42156 KINGSTON LYONS DRIVE, STAYTON, OREGON 97383

Tel: (503) 769-6287	Max. No. Sharing Bath: 4
Hosts: Dorothea and Kenneth Horn	Double/pb: $45
Location: 17 mi. E of Salem	Single/pb: $40
No. of Rooms: 3	Double/sb: $35
No. of Private Baths: 1	Single/sb: $30

Open: **All year**   Children: **Sometimes**
Breakfast: **Full**   Smoking: **No**
Pets: **No**   Social Drinking: **Permitted**

This lovely home is situated in the foothills of the Cascade Mountains on the edge of Willamette Valley. In summer, swim in the heated pool or hike on one of the scenic nature paths. The area is dotted with farms, and the valley is abundant in fruits, berries, and vegetables. Willamette and Oregon State universities are nearby. The Mount Jefferson Wilderness hiking area is an hour away. A guest comments, "The hospitality and breakfasts were topnotch!"

Old Welches Inn ○
26401 EAST WELCHES ROAD, WELCHES, OREGON 97067

Tel: **(503) 622-3754**   Open: **All year**
Best Time to Call: **After 6 PM**   Breakfast: **Full**
Hosts: **Judith and Ted Mondun**   Credit Cards: **AMEX, MC, VISA**
Location: **50 mi. E of Portland**   Pets: **Dogs welcome**
No. of Rooms: **3**   Children: **Welcome, over 12**
Max. No. Sharing Bath: **3**   Smoking: **No**
Double/sb: **$65–$75**   Social Drinking: **Permitted**
Cottage: **$100–$175; sleeps 5**   Minimum Stay: **2 nights holidays**

Built as a resort in the late 19th century, the Old Welches Inn is a large white Colonial with blue shutters. The house stands on the edge of the Mt. Hood wilderness area, crisscrossed by miles of hiking and ski trails. Fishermen may carry poles to the back of the B&B property, where they can drop lines in the Salmon River. And just across the road, golfers will find that 27 holes await. You'll be ready for action after a full, Southern-style breakfast, highlighted by home-baked muffins, biscuits, and breads.

The Carriage House ○
515 SOUTH PACIFIC HIGHWAY, WOODBURN, OREGON 97071

Tel: **(503) 982-6321**   Open: **All year**
Best Time to Call: **Before 9 AM; after**   Breakfast: **Full**
  6 PM   Credit Cards: **MC, VISA**
Hosts: **Lawrence and Marilyn Paradis**   Pets: **Sometimes**
Location: **30 mi. S of Portland**   Children: **Welcome**
No. of Rooms: **2**   Smoking: **No**
Max. No. Sharing Bath: **4**   Social Drinking: **Permitted**
Double/sb: **$50**   Airport/Station Pickup: **Yes**
Single/sb: **$45**   Foreign Languages: **French**

The Carriage House is a 1906 Victorian known for its peaceful country elegance. Completely restored, it is furnished with family treasures and heirloom quilts. Lawrence and Marilyn keep horses and an antique buggy in a carriage house next to the inn. This is an excellent location for visiting the Enchanted Forest, the Oregon State Fair, the Octoberfest in Mt. Angel, the Bach Festival, historic Champoeg, and numerous antique shops and wineries.

For key to listings, see inside front or back cover.

✪ This star means that rates are guaranteed through December 31, 1995, to any guest making a reservation as a result of reading about the B&B in *Bed & Breakfast U.S.A.*—1995 edition.

Important! To avoid misunderstandings, always ask about cancellation policies when booking.

Please enclose a self-addressed, stamped, business-size envelope when contacting reservation services.

For more details on what you can expect in a B&B, see Chapter 1.

Always mention *Bed & Breakfast U.S.A.* when making reservations!

If no B&B is listed in the area you'll be visiting, use the form on page 743 to order a copy of our "List of New B&Bs."

We want to hear from you! Use the form on page 745.

PENNSYLVANIA

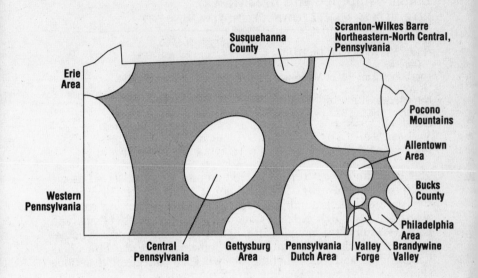

Erie Area

Susquehanna County

Scranton-Wilkes Barre Northeastern-North Central, Pennsylvania

Pocono Mountains

Allentown Area

Bucks County

Western Pennsylvania

Philadelphia Area
Brandywine Valley

Central Pennsylvania

Gettysburg Area

Pennsylvania Dutch Area

Valley Forge

ALLENTOWN AREA

Brennans B&B ○
3827 LINDEN STREET, ALLENTOWN, PENNSYLVANIA 18104

Tel: **(215) 395-0869**
Best Time to Call: **7 AM–11 PM**
Hosts: **Lois and Edward Brennan**
Location: **1 mi. from 78 and 22**
No. of Rooms: **2**
No. of Private Baths: **1**
Max. No. Sharing Bath: **2**
Double/pb: **$40**
Single/pb: **$35**

Double/sb: **$30**
Single/sb: **$25**
Open: **Apr.–Dec.**
Breakfast: **Full**
Pets: **Sometimes**
Children: **Welcome**
Smoking: **Permitted**
Social Drinking: **Permitted**
Airport/Station Pickup: **Yes**

Furnished in Early American fashion, accented with lush plants and family treasures, this comfortable brick ranch-style house can be your home away from home. The Brennans are history buffs who, now that they're retired, enjoy traveling and entertaining travelers. Breakfast features bacon and eggs with home fries, or sausages and pancakes, or delicious muffins to go with the homemade jam. You can walk off the calories on your way to the Haines Mill, Dorney Park, or one of the area's many museums.

Longswamp Bed and Breakfast ❂
RD 2, BOX 26, MERTZTOWN, PENNSYLVANIA 19539

Tel: **(215) 682-6197**	Single/sb: **$60**
Hosts: **Elsa Dimick and Dr. Dean Dimick**	Open: **All year**
	Breakfast: **Full**
Location: **12 mi. SW of Allentown**	Credit Cards: **MC, VISA**
No. of Rooms: **10**	Pets: **No**
No. of Private Baths: **6**	Children: **Welcome**
Max. No. Sharing Bath: **4**	Smoking: **No**
Double/pb: **$75–$78**	Social Drinking: **Permitted**
Single/pb: **$60**	Airport/Station Pickup: **Yes**
Double/sb: **$75–$78**	Foreign Languages: **French**

This guest house was originally built around 1750 and served as the first post office in town. The main house, completed in 1863, was a stop on the Underground Railroad. Today, Longswamp is a comfortable place with high ceilings, antiques, large fireplaces, plants, and bookcases full of reading pleasure. Breakfast specialties include home-dried fruits, *pain perdu*, quiche, and homemade breads. Elsa offers wine, cheese, and coffee anytime. She will gladly direct you to antique shops, auction houses, Reading, and the Amish country.

BRANDYWINE VALLEY

Bed & Breakfast of Chester County
P.O. BOX 825, KENNETT SQUARE, PENNSYLVANIA 19348

Tel: **(610) 444-1367**	Rates (Single/Double):
Coordinator: **Doris Passante**	Modest: **$40 / $45–$55**
States/Regions Covered: **Chester County, Chadds Ford, Valley Forge**	Average: **$45 / $55–$65**
	Luxury: **$50 / $70 and up**
	Credit Cards: **No**

Doris has a wide selection of homes located in the beautiful and historic Brandywine Valley, which is known for the River Museum, Longwood Gardens, Winterthur, Brandywine Battlefield, and Valley Forge. The area is convenient to the Pennsylvania Dutch country. Send for her brochure, which fully describes each B&B. The University of Delaware, Lincoln University, and West Chester University are close by. There's a $5 surcharge for one-night stays.

Bed & Breakfast at Walnut Hill
541 CHANDLER'S MILL ROAD, AVONDALE, PENNSYLVANIA 19311

Tel: **(610) 444-3703**	Single/sb: **$65**
Best Time to Call: **Anytime**	Open: **All year**
Hosts: **Sandy and Tom Mills**	Breakfast: **Full**
Location: **2 mi. S of Kennett Square**	Pets: **No**
No. of Rooms: **2**	Children: **Welcome, over 8**
Max. No. Sharing Bath: **4**	Smoking: **Permitted**
Double/sb: **$80**	Social Drinking: **Permitted**

Sandy and Tom's 1844 mill house is in Kennett Square (despite the mailing address above) in the heart of the Brandywine Valley, midway between Philadelphia and Amish country. Longwood Gardens, Chadds Ford Winery, Winterthur, and other museums are all within an eight-mile radius. But nature lovers may want to stay on the B&B grounds, where horses graze in the meadow and a great blue heron fishes in the stream. Deer, Canada geese, and the occasional red fox also put in appearances. Guests enjoy walking along the country road, sitting on the wicker-filled porch, or relaxing in the hot tub. However you plan to spend your day, you'll begin it with breakfast specialties like cottage cheese pancakes with blueberry sauce, fresh mushroom omelets, and French toast. Sandy welcomes guests with lemonade, iced tea, hot cider, and homemade sweets.

BUCKS COUNTY

Maplewood Farm Bed & Breakfast ○
5090 DURHAM ROAD, P.O. BOX 239, GARDENVILLE, PENNSYLVANIA 18926

Tel: **(215) 766-0477**	Reduced Rates: **Mon.–Thurs.**
Best Time to Call: **10 AM–10 PM**	Breakfast: **Full**
Hosts: **Cindy and Dennis Marquis**	Credit Cards: **AMEX, DISC, MC, VISA**
Location: **45 mi. NW of Philadelphia**	Pets: **No**
No. of Rooms: **4**	Children: **Welcome, Sun.–Thurs.**
No. of Private Baths: **5**	Smoking: **No**
Double/pb: **$85**	Social Drinking: **Permitted**
Suites: **$135**	Minimum Stay: **2 nights weekends, 3 nights holidays**
Open: **All year**	

Hundred-year-old maples shelter this fieldstone farmhouse, dated 1792. The five-acre property includes a tranquil stream, sheep-filled pastures, and a two-story bank barn that houses playful barnyard cats. Inn rooms feature local antiques, cozy comforters, and handmade quilts. Choose Victoria's Room, with a four-poster bed and ceiling fan, or the two-story loft suite, with its exposed beams and sitting room. Upon your arrival, Cindy and Dennis will offer you refreshments in the antique summer kitchen, which boasts a double walk-in fireplace. For year-round fun, your hosts will direct you to Peddler's Village, New Hope, and lots of charming river towns. In the morning, gather eggs fresh from the source and have them turned into fluffy omelets, crisp waffles, fruit-filled pancakes, or Dennis' famous French toast. Breakfast is served in the country dining room with random-width floors, beamed ceilings, and an exposed stone wall. After dinner, return to the inn to enjoy conversation and a nightcap with your hosts, and exchange tales of your day with the other guests. For those of you who don't mind paying a higher rate, 3 rooms are available.

Aaron Burr House ✪

80 WEST BRIDGE STREET, NEW HOPE, PENNSYLVANIA 18938

Tel: **(215) 862-2343**
Best Time to Call: **10 AM–10 PM**
Host: **Carl Glassman**
Location: **20 mi. N of Philadelphia**
No. of Rooms: **6**
No. of Private Baths: **6**
Double/pb: **$75**
Single/pb: **$70**
Suites: **$95–$145; sleeps 3**
Open: **All year**

Reduced Rates: **Mon.–Thurs.,
  corporate guests**
Breakfast: **Continental**
Pets: **Sometimes**
Children: **Welcome**
Smoking: **No**
Social Drinking: **Permitted**
Minimum Stay: **2 nights on weekends,
  3 nights holidays**
Station Pickup: **Yes**

This 1854 Victorian is tucked onto a tree-lined street in the town's historic district, just steps from the village center. New Hope was founded in 1681, so visitors can absorb three centuries of architecture and American history, plus fine antique shops, excellent restaurants, and art galleries and crafts shops. At the end of the day, join your hosts in the parlor for reading, games, refreshments, and friendly conversation. After a peaceful night's rest in a canopy bed, you'll wake up to the aroma of fresh coffee and home-baked muffins.

Wedgwood Inn of New Hope ✪
111 WEST BRIDGE STREET, NEW HOPE, PENNSYLVANIA 18938-1401

Tel: **(215) 862-2520**	Reduced Rates: **Available**
Best Time to Call: **10 AM–10 PM**	Breakfast: **Continental, plus**
Hosts: **Carl Glassman and Nadine**	Credit Cards: **AMEX, MC, VISA**
Silnutzer	Pets: **Sometimes**
Location: **62 mi. SW of New York City**	Children: **Welcome**
No. of Rooms: **12**	Smoking: **No**
No. of Private Baths: **12**	Social Drinking: **Permitted**
Double/pb: **$70–$125**	Minimum Stay: **3 holiday weekends, 2**
Single/pb: **$65–$115**	**nights if stay includes Saturday**
Double/sb: **$65–$85**	Station Pickup: **Yes**
Single/sb: **$60–$80**	Foreign Languages: **French, Hebrew,**
Suites: **$90–$185**	**Spanish**
Open: **All year**	

Wedgwood pottery is displayed throughout this aptly named two-and-a-half-story home with lots of nineteenth-century details: a gabled roof, veranda, porte cochere, and gazebo. Rooms are decorated with antiques, original art, handmade quilts, and fresh flowers. You can breakfast on house specialties like lemon yogurt poppyseed bread and ricotta pineapple muffins on the sun porch, in the gazebo, or in the privacy of your room. Carl and Nadine are such accomplished hosts that they conduct workshops and seminars on innkeeping, and Carl has taught courses on buying and operating country inns.

CENTRAL PENNSYLVANIA

Rest & Repast Bed & Breakfast Service ✪
P.O. BOX 126, PINE GROVE MILLS, PENNSYLVANIA 16868

Tel: **(814) 238-1484**	**Phillipsburg, Potters Mills, Spruce**
Best Time to Call: **8:30–11:30 AM**	**Creek, State College, Tyrone**
Mon.–Fri.	Rates (Single/Double):
Coordinators: **Linda and Brent Peters**	Average: **$40–$45 / $50–$60**
States/Regions Covered: **Aaronsburg,**	Luxury: **$65–$80 / $65–$80**
Bellefonte, Boalsburg, Clearfield,	Credit Cards: **No**

You will enjoy touring historic mansions, Penns Cave, Woodward Cave, and several Civil War museums in this lovely area. A two-day minimum stay is required for the second week in July, the time of the annual Central Pennsylvania Festival of the Arts, and for most Penn State University home games in autumn. Rates are increased during peak weekends to a maximum of $80 per night double. (No single rates on peak PSU weekends.) Pennsylvania State University is close by.

Bedford House ✪
203 W. PITT STREET, BEDFORD, PENNSYLVANIA 15522

Tel: (814) 623-7171
Best Time to Call: 10 AM–10 PM
Hosts: Lyn and Linda Lyon
Location: 107 mi. E of Pittsburgh
No. of Rooms: 7
No. of Private Baths: 7
Double/pb: $55–$85
Single/pb: $35–$75
Open: All year
Reduced Rates: Available

Breakfast: Full
Credit Cards: AMEX, DISC, MC, VISA
Pets: No
Children: Welcome, over 12
Smoking: No
Social Drinking: Permitted
Minimum Stay: 2 nights first 2
   weekends Oct.
Airport/Station Pickup: Yes

Situated halfway between Pittsburgh and Harrisburg, Bedford is a lovely little town that sprang up around Fort Bedford, built in 1758. Bedford House, constructed some forty years later, is a large brick village home on one of the National Historic District's original town lots. Guest rooms are furnished with a mixture of antiques, reproductions, and family heirlooms. This B&B is a five-minute stroll from Fort Bedford Museum and Park, shops, restaurants, and churches. Other area attractions include Old Bedford Village, Shawnee State Park, Coral Caverns, and Blue Knob Ski Area.

Highland House ✪
108 BUCHER HILL, BOILING SPRINGS, PENNSYLVANIA 17007

Tel: (717) 258-3744
Best Time to Call: 3 PM–10 PM
Host: Barry Buchter
Location: 17 mi. S of Harrisburg
No. of Rooms: 3
No. of Private Baths: 1
Max. No. Sharing Bath: 4
Double/pb: $85
Single/pb: $70

Double/sb: $75
Single/sb: $65
Open: All year
Breakfast: Full
Pets: No
Children: No
Smoking: Permitted
Social Drinking: Permitted
Airport Pickup: Yes

Local ironmaster Michael Ege, who supplied cannons and cannonballs to George Washington at Valley Forge, built this Federal brick house sometime around 1776. Robert Morris and John Hancock are said to have been among Ege's overnight guests. In the next century, Highland House allegedly served as a stop for escaped slaves traveling the Underground Railroad. Your host, a retired TV executive who bought the property in 1990, can show you the secret third-floor compartment where slaves are thought to have been concealed. He also promises that the best trout fishing in the eastern seaboard is in the area. If you don't get any bites, you can always take a short drive to Harrisburg, Gettysburg Battlefield, or Hershey Theme Park.

Victorian Loft Bed & Breakfast ✪
216 SOUTH FRONT STREET, CLEARFIELD, PENNSYLVANIA 16830

Tel: **(814) 765-4805**	Suites: **$80–$100**
Best Time to Call: **Evenings**	Open: **All year**
Hosts: **Tim and Peggy Durant**	Reduced Rates: **10% over 3 nights**
Location: **40 mi. NW of State College**	Breakfast: **Full**
No. of Rooms: **2**	Credit Cards: **MC, VISA**
No. of Private Baths: **1**	Pets: **Sometimes**
Max. No. Sharing Bath: **4**	Children: **Welcome**
Double/pb: **$55–$65**	Smoking: **No**
Single/pb: **$45–$55**	Social Drinking: **No**
Double/sb: **$45–$55**	Airport/Station Pickup: **Yes**
Single/sb: **$35–$45**	

Victorian charm fills this elegant 1894 riverfront home in the historic district, from the double-decker gingerbread porches to the grand staircase and original stained windows. Yet it's only minutes to myriad outdoor recreational activities—the B&B is just three miles off Exit 19 on I-80. Amenities, in addition to warm hospitality, include a memorable full breakfast, air-conditioned rooms with skylights, a private kitchen and dining room, a guest entertainment center and a whirlpool bath. For those interested in clothing and textile design, Peggy, a fiber enthusiast, gives spinning demonstrations on request.

Split Pine Farmhouse B&B ✪
BOX 326, 347 WEST PINE GROVE ROAD, PINE GROVE MILLS, PENNSYLVANIA 16868

Tel: **(814) 238-2028**	Open: **All year**
Best Time to Call: **10 AM–8 PM**	Reduced Rates: **10% Jan. 15–March 15; 10% entire house**
Host: **Mae McQuade**	Breakfast: **Full**
Location: **5 mi. SW of State College**	Credit Cards: **DISC, MC, VISA**
No. of Rooms: **5**	Pets: **No**
No. of Private Baths: **1**	Children: **Welcome, over 12**
Max. No. Sharing Bath: **4**	Smoking: **No**
Double/pb: **$85**	Social Drinking: **Permitted**
Single/pb: **$50**	Minimum Stay: **2 nights, holidays and special events**
Double/sb: **$70**	
Single/sb: **$50**	

Split Pine Farmhouse is a simple Federal-style home, circa 1830, with spacious rooms in a pastoral, sylvan setting. The B&B is near Penn State and the historic towns of Boalsburg and Bellefonte. Local events include the Pennsylvania Arts Festival, Victorian and Colonial Christmas celebrations, Memorial Day in Boalsburg, as well as outdoor activities in all seasons. The house is shaded by many venerable evergreens, while the interior holds antique and vintage furnishings collected from military travels at home and abroad. Mae's interests outside the domestic vein are Spanish and Brazilian literature, especially *Don Quixote* by Cervantes.

ERIE AREA

Raspberry House Bed & Breakfast ○

118 ERIE STREET, ROUTE 99, EDINBORO, PENNSYLVANIA 16412

Tel: (814) 734-8997	Reduced Rates: **Available**
Best Time to Call: **After 6 PM weekdays, anytime on weekends**	Breakfast: **Full, Continental; weekdays only**
Hosts: **Betty and Hal Holmstrom**	Pets: **Sometimes**
Location: **20 mi. S of Erie**	Children: **Welcome**
No. of Rooms: **3**	Smoking: **No**
No. of Private Baths: **3**	Social Drinking: **Permitted**
Double/pb: **$55–$75**	Minimum Stay: **2 nights on Edinboro homecoming weekend**
Single/pb: **$45–$65**	
Open: **All year**	Airport/Station Pickup: **Yes**

Raspberry House is a Victorian home that retains its original charm. Wake-up coffee is brought to your room each morning. A full breakfast, including raspberry delight, is served on weekends; a generous Continental breakfast, prepared to match your appetite and schedule, is served on weekdays. This B&B is located in the heart of Edinboro, within easy walking distance of Edinboro University, a lake, restaurants, and entertainment. Four golf courses and a ski resort are minutes away. Cyclists may borrow bikes for daytime use.

GETTYSBURG AREA

The Brafferton Inn ○

44 YORK STREET, GETTYSBURG, PENNSYLVANIA 17325

Tel: (717) 337-3423	Suites: **$110–$125**
Best Time to Call: **9 AM–9 PM**	Open: **All year**
Hosts: **Jane and Sam Back**	Breakfast: **Full**
Location: **90 mi. N of Washington, D.C.; 2 mi. from Rte 15 York Street exit**	Credit Cards: **MC, VISA**
	Pets: **No**
No. of Rooms: **10**	Children: **Welcome, over 7**
No. of Private Baths: **10**	Smoking: **No**
Double/pb: **$70–$95**	Social Drinking: **Permitted**

This Early American stone structure is listed on the National Register of Historic Places. The clapboard addition dates back to pre–Civil War days. Six of the guest rooms, decorated with hand-painted stencils, area. Each of the four bedrooms has private baths and three have queen-size beds. Guests have full use of the house including the always full cookie jar. Barbecue facilities are also provided. Whitetail Ski Resort, Mercersburg Academy, State Parks, Antietam Battlefield, country auctions and antique shops, and Fort Frederick are among the nearby attractions.

PENNSYLVANIA DUTCH AREA

Adamstown Inn ✪

62 WEST MAIN STREET, ADAMSTOWN, PENNSYLVANIA 19501

Tel: **(717) 484-0800; (800) 594-4808**	Reduced Rates: **10% after 4th night**
Hosts: **Tom and Wanda Berman**	Breakfast: **Continental, plus**
Location: **10 mi. SW of Reading**	Credit Cards: **MC, VISA**
No. of Rooms: **4**	Pets: **No**
No. of Private Baths: **4**	Children: **Welcome, over 12**
Double/pb: **$65–$85**	Smoking: **Restricted**
Suite: **$95**	Social Drinking: **Permitted**
Open: **All year**	

In the heart of Adamstown's antique district, and just a short drive from Pennsylvania Dutch country and Reading's factory outlets, you'll find this handsome brick Victorian. Inside, lace and balloon curtains and oriental rugs complement the chestnut woodwork and leaded-glass doors. Two rooms feature two-person Jacuzzis. Your hosts are avid antiquers and will gladly direct you to their favorite haunts. Coffee or tea will be brought to your door in the morning; refills, as well as juice, fresh fruit, cheese, and home-baked goodies are served during a Continental breakfast.

Umble Rest ✪

RD 1, BOX 79, ATGLEN, PENNSYLVANIA 19310

Tel: **(610) 593-2274**	Open: **May 15–Oct. 15**
Best Time to Call: **7–10 AM; 3–7 PM**	Breakfast: **No**
Hosts: **Ken and Marilyn Umble**	Pets: **No**
Location: **15 mi. E of Lancaster**	Children: **Welcome**
No. of Rooms: **3**	Smoking: **No**
Max. No. Sharing Bath: **6**	Social Drinking: **No**
Double/sb: **$25–$30**	Minimum Stay: **Holiday weekends**

Ken and Marilyn are busy Mennonite farmers with interests in crafts, quilting, and restoring their 1800 farmhouse. You are invited to watch the milking of their 50 cows, stroll a country lane to their pond, and participate in the simple life-style. Bring your children to play with their boys, ages thirteen, ten and six. All the popular tourist attractions are nearby.

are separated from the main house by an atrium where one may sit and enjoy the pretty plantings during the warm months. The sumptuous breakfast is served in the dining room on antique tables. There are hosts of activities to whet the appetite of the history buff, sportsman, antique collector, or nature lover.

Keystone Inn ✪

231 HANOVER STREET, GETTYSBURG, PENNSYLVANIA 17325

Tel: **(717) 337-3888**	Open: **All year**
Best Time to Call: **7 AM–10 PM**	Reduced Rates: **Available**
Hosts: **Wilmer and Doris Martin**	Breakfast: **Full**
Location: **35 mi. S of Harrisburg**	Credit Cards: **MC, VISA**
No. of Rooms: **4**	Pets: **No**
No. of Private Baths: **2**	Children: **Welcome**
Max. No. Sharing Bath: **4**	Smoking: **No**
Double/pb: **$75**	Social Drinking: **No**
Double/sb: **$59**	

Keystone Inn is a large Victorian built in 1913 by Clayton Reaser, a local furniture maker. His talents as a craftsman are evident in the natural oak and chestnut found throughout the house. The beautiful woodwork is complemented with lace, ruffles, and floral designs favored by the Martin family. The guest rooms are decorated with brass or antique wood beds and soft pastel wallpapers, and each bedroom has a reading nook and windowside writing table overlooking historic Gettysburg. A full breakfast features such specialties as cinnamon-apple or blueberry pancakes, waffles, eggs, and fruits. Afternoon lemonade is served on the front porch in summer; in winter guests can enjoy a hot drink by the fireplace. The inn is close to historic sites and Civil War battlefields, antique shops, state parks, and is nine miles from the Liberty ski area.

The Doubleday Inn ✪

104 DOUBLEDAY AVENUE, GETTYSBURG BATTLEFIELD, PENNSYLVANIA 17325

Tel: **(717) 334-9119**	Open: **All year**
Hosts: **Joan and Sal Chandon, and Olga Krossick**	Breakfast: **Full**
	Credit Cards: **MC, VISA**
No. of Rooms: **9**	Pets: **No**
No. of Private Baths: **5**	Children: **Welcome, over 10**
Max. No. Sharing Bath: **4**	Smoking: **No**
Double/pb: **$89–$99**	Social Drinking: **Permitted**
Double/sb: **$79**	

The only B&B located on the battlefield, this beautifully restored Colonial recalls past-century charms with Civil War furnishings and antique accessories. Afternoon tea is served with country-style drinks and hors d'oeuvres on the outdoor patio, or by the fireplace in the main parlor. One of the largest known library collections devoted exclusively to the Battle of Gettysburg is available to you. On selected evenings, you are welcome to participate in a discussion with a Civil War historian who brings the battle alive with accurate accounts and displays of authentic memorabilia and weaponry.

Phaeton Farm ✪

9762 BROWNS MILL ROAD, GREENCASTLE, PENNSYLVANIA 17225

Tel: **(717) 597-8656**	Guest Cottage: **$55–$65 summer only**
Best Time to Call: **7–9 PM**	Open: **All year**
Host: **Sandy Kirkpatrick**	Breakfast: **Full, Continental**
Location: **80 mi. NW of Washington,**	Credit Cards: **MC, VISA**
D.C.	Pets: **Sometimes**
No. of Rooms: **4**	Children: **Welcome**
No. of Private Baths: **2**	Smoking: **No**
Max. No. Sharing Bath: **4**	Social Drinking: **Permitted**
Double/pb: **$65**	Airport Pickup: **Yes**
Single/pb: **$55**	

Phaeton Farm was probably built at four different times, the earliest section dating from the late 1700s. Wide floorboards, fireplaces, and unique stairways add country charm. The charm is accompanied by twentieth-century comforts—modern bathrooms, central heat, and air-conditioning in some rooms. The house sits on a 100-acre farm, which has beef cattle on pasture in summer. Sandy will be happy to show you her collection of horse-drawn carriages if you are interested. She will also explain the origin of the name of the farm. Located 1½ miles from Pa. exit 3 off I-81.

Welsh Run Inn Bed and Breakfast ✪

11299 WELSH RUN ROAD (VILLAGE OF WELSH RUN)
GREENCASTLE, PENNSYLVANIA 17225

Tel: **(717) 328-9506**	Reduced Rates: **10%, 3rd night**
Best Time to Call: **Anytime**	Breakfast: **Full**
Hosts: **Bob and Ellie Neff**	Credit Cards: **MC, VISA**
Location: **65 mi. S of Harrisburg**	Pets: **No**
No. of Rooms: **4**	Children: **Welcome, over 12**
No. of Private Baths: **1**	Smoking: **Permitted**
Max. No. Sharing Bath: **4**	Social Drinking: **Permitted**
Double/pb: **$65**	Minimum Stay: **2 nights ski season**
Double/sb: **$55**	**weekends**
Open: **All year**	

Large maple trees surround this turn-of-the-century farm home with molded wood siding and a generous, wraparound porch. The interior is rich in original details like oak woodwork, oak and marble fireplaces

and pocket doors. Two living rooms are available for guests' ... Breakfast is served by candlelight in the formal dining room ... hand-stenciled walls. Bob, a retired businessman and dairy farm... and Ellie, a floral designer, can direct you to the area's numer... attractions, such as Whitetail Ski Area, Greencastle Greens ... Course, and historic Mercersburg, the birthplace of James Buchan... Civil War buffs take note: this B&B is only twenty minutes f... Antietam Battlefield and fifty minutes from Gettysburg. Harp... Ferry, antique shops, and malls are also nearby.

Beechmont Inn ✪

315 BROADWAY, HANOVER, PENNSYLVANIA 17331

Tel: **(717) 632-3013; (800) 553-7009**	Open: **All year**
Best Time to Call: **9 AM–9 PM**	Breakfast: **Full**
Hosts: **William and Susan Day**	Credit Cards: **AMEX, DC, MC, VIS**
Location: **13 mi. E of Gettysburg**	Pets: **No**
No. of Rooms: **4**	Children: **Welcome, over 12**
No. of Private Baths: **4**	Smoking: **Permitted**
Double/pb: **$70–$85**	Social Drinking: **Permitted**

This Georgian house, restored to its Federal-period elegance, off... the visitor a bridge across time. Climb the winding staircase to fres... decorated rooms named in honor of the gallant heroes of the C... War. At breakfast time, enjoy homemade granola, baked goods, a... entrée, and fruit. Join the other guests in the dining room, or ta... tray to your room for breakfast in bed. Visit nearby Gettysburg... Eisenhower Farm, Hanover Shoe Farms, Codorus State Park for ... ing and fishing, or go antique hunting in New Oxford. Upon... return, you may relax in the quiet comfort of the parlor. The ... look forward to pampering you.

Fox Run Inn ✪

14873 BAIN ROAD, MERCERSBURG, PENNSYLVANIA 17236

Tel: **(717) 328-3570**	Reduced Rates: **10% April–/**
Best Time to Call: **After 8 PM**	**families**
Hosts: **Dick and Elsie Secrest**	Breakfast: **Full**
Location: **54 mi. NW of Washington,**	Credit Cards: **MC, VISA**
D.C.	Pets: **No**
No. of Rooms: **4**	Children: **Welcome, over 1**
No. of Private Baths: **4**	Smoking: **No**
Double/pb: **$59**	Social Drinking: **Permitted**
Open: **All year**	

Built in 1786, this authentically restored farmhouse is sur... 170 acres of fields with walking trails. The inn's views of t... side and Tuscarora Mountain are spectacular. The kitchen... area have open beamed ceilings and an exposed log wall ...

Sunday's Mill Farm B&B ✪
RD 2, BOX 419, BERNVILLE, PENNSYLVANIA 19506

Tel: (610) 488-7821
Hosts: Sally and Len Blumberg
Location: 11 mi. N of Reading
No. of Rooms: 5
Max. No. Sharing Bath: 4
Double/sb: $45–$60
Single/sb: $35–$45
Suite: $160; sleeps 6
Open: All year

Reduced Rates: 10% 3 or more
  nights; families
Breakfast: Full
Pets: Horses welcome
Children: Welcome
Smoking: No
Social Drinking: Permitted
Airport/Station Pickup: Yes

With a grist mill dating to 1820 and main buildings that are thirty years younger, this pastoral property is part of a National Historic District. Sunday's Mill Farm looks like a farmhouse should: exposed beams, rich woodwork, a brick dining room fireplace, quilts on the beds. Bring your fishing pole—Len stocks the pond. This is the rare B&B that accommodates both horseback riders and their mounts. Guests who prefer to use their own legs can explore the area's antique shops and factory outlets; Sally is active in historic preservation and can tell you a lot about the region over a breakfast of deep dish apple pancakes and sausage.

The Enchanted Cottage ✪
RD 4, 22 DEER RUN ROAD, BOYERTOWN, PENNSYLVANIA 19512

Tel: (610) 845-8845
Hosts: Peg and Richard Groff
Location: 16 mi. S of Allentown
No. of Private Baths: 1
Double/pb: $80
Single/pb: $70
Open: All year

Reduced Rates: $5 less Mon.–Thurs.
  except holidays and special events
Breakfast: Full
Pets: No
Children: Welcome, over 12
Smoking: Permitted
Social Drinking: Permitted

Complete privacy awaits you in this cozy cottage nestled in a clearing in the woods. Downstairs, the exposed beams, wood-burning fireplace, quilts, and antique furniture lend themselves to quiet, romantic evenings. On the second floor you'll find an air-conditioned double bedroom and a Laura Ashley bathroom. Gourmet breakfasts are served in the main house in front of either the garden or a cheerful fire, depending on the season. While the cottage is a destination in itself, you'll have easy access to the Pennsylvania Dutch area, the Reading factory outlets, antique shops, historic sites, and country auctions. An excellent restaurant is within walking distance.

Twin Turrets Inn ✪
11 EAST PHILADELPHIA AVENUE, BOYERTOWN, PENNSYLVANIA 19512

Tel: **(610) 367-4513**	Reduced Rates: **Corp. rate $60 single;**
Best Time to Call: **7 AM–7 PM**	**10% seniors**
Host: **Gary Slade**	Breakfast: **Continental**
Location: **40 mi. NW of Philadelphia**	Credit Cards: **AMEX, DISC, MC, VISA**
No. of Rooms: **10**	Pets: **No**
No. of Private Baths: **10**	Children: **Welcome, over 12**
Double/pb: **$80**	Smoking: **No**
Single/pb: **$70**	Social Drinking: **Permitted**
Open: **All year**	Airport/Station Pickup: **Yes**

The Twin Turrets is a wonderful Victorian mansion in all its restored glory: stained-glass windows, chandeliers, elegant wallpaper, period furniture, and drapery. If this whets your appetite, an antique shop on the first floor sells sterling silver, glass, china, and furniture. Guests have use of the parlor piano. Each room has cable TV and telephone.

Danmar House ✪
RD 21, BOX 107, DOVER, PENNSYLVANIA 17315

Tel: **(717) 292-5128**	Open: **All year**
Best Time to Call: **Anytime**	Breakfast: **Full**
Hosts: **Marilyn and Danny Muir**	Pets: **No**
Location: **8 mi. W of York**	Children: **Welcome, over 12**
No. of Rooms: **3**	Smoking: **Permitted**
Max. No. Sharing Bath: **3**	Social Drinking: **Permitted**
Double/sb: **$55**	Airport/Station Pickup: **Yes**
Suites: **$85**	

This twelve-room country house, built in three stages from the mid-1700s, was completely overhauled in 1988: the interior and exterior were restored, and modern plumbing and electrical systems were installed. Guest quarters are air-conditioned and comfortably furnished with antiques. After breakfasting on entrées such as cheese and bacon soufflé or apple sausage ring, you can head out for ski slopes, golf courses, parks, antique shops, or York and Gettysburg—all less than a half hour away.

Detters Acres Bed and Breakfast ✪
6631 OLD CARLISLE ROAD, DOVER, PENNSYLVANIA 17315

Tel: **(717) 292-3172**	No. of Rooms: **3**
Best Time to Call: **Anytime**	No. of Private Baths: **1**
Hosts: **Lorne and Ailean Detter**	Max. No. Sharing Bath: **4**
Location: **7 mi. N of York**	Double/pb: **$65**

Single/pb: **$55**
Double/sb: **$55**
Single/sb: **$45**
Open: **All year**
Breakfast: **Full**
Other Meals: **Available**

Pets: **No**
Children: **Welcome**
Smoking: **No**
Social Drinking: **Permitted**
Airport/Station Pickup: **Yes**

Visit a 76-acre working beef cattle farm in northern York County. For a nominal fee, your hosts will take you for a ride in one of their three Amish buggies. Or get behind the wheel of a more modern vehicle for the short drive to Gettysburg, Hershey Amusement Park and Zoo, Amish country, Hanover Shoe Farms Standardbred Stables, Roundtop's ski slopes, and innumerable farmers markets and shopping malls. On a chilly evening, gather around the fireplace in the recreation room, where you can play games or the piano. Weather permitting, full breakfasts, including fruit and homemade breads, are served in the gazebo.

Red Door Studio B&B ✪
6485 LEMON STREET, EAST PETERSBURG, PENNSYLVANIA 17520

Tel: **(717) 569-2909**
Best Time to Call: **8–9 AM**
Host: **Mary Elizabeth Patton**
Location: **1½ mi. N of Lancaster**
No. of Rooms: **3**

Max. No. Sharing Bath: **4**
Double/sb: **$40–$45**
Open: **All year**
Breakfast: **Continental**
Pets: **Sometimes**

Children: **Welcome**	Social Drinking: **Permitted**
Smoking: **No**	Airport/Station Pickup: **Yes**

Open the red door and you instantly know you're in an artist's home. A former teacher of art history, Mary Elizabeth is now a full-time artist and portrait painter. Her B&B is warm, bright, and inviting, with many souvenirs and paintings of her world travels. Of special interest is her collection of Indian and African works. Breakfast is an inviting spread of fresh fruit, yogurt, granola, Danish pastry, coffee, or herb tea. You are welcome to relax in the backyard, use the barbecue, or watch TV.

Elm Country Inn Bed & Breakfast ○

P.O. BOX 37, ELM AND NEWPORT ROADS, ELM, PENNSYLVANIA 17521

Tel: **(717) 664-3623; (800) 245-0532**	Reduced Rates: **10% seniors, Sun.–Thurs.**
Best Time to Call: **After 4:30 PM**	Breakfast: **Full**
Hosts: **Betty and Melvin Meck**	Credit Cards: **MC, VISA**
Location: **12 mi. N of Lancaster**	Pets: **No**
No. of Rooms: **2**	Children: **Welcome**
Max. No. Sharing Bath: **4**	Smoking: **No**
Double/sb: **$50–$55**	Social Drinking: **Permitted**
Single/sb: **$35**	Airport/Station Pickup: **Yes**
Open: **All year**	

Located in a small country village, this 1860 brick farmhouse overlooks beautiful farmland. The large, sunny rooms feature original wood trim and are furnished with a pleasing blend of antiques and collectibles. Antique shops, crafts shops, and opportunities to fish or canoe are available. Betty and Melvin thoroughly enjoy having visitors and do their best to make them feel instantly at home.

Historic Smithton Country Inn ○

900 WEST MAIN STREET, EPHRATA, PENNSYLVANIA 17522

Tel: **(717) 733-6094**	Breakfast: **Full**
Best Time to Call: **9 AM–10 PM**	Credit Cards: **AMEX, MC, VISA**
Host: **Dorothy Graybill**	Pets: **By arrangement**
Location: **12 mi. NE of Lancaster**	Children: **By arrangement**
No. of Rooms: **8**	Smoking: **No**
No. of Private Baths: **8**	Social Drinking: **Permitted**
Double/pb: **$65–$115**	Minimum Stay: **2 nights weekends, holidays**
Single/pb: **$55–$105**	Airport/Station Pickup: **Yes**
Suites: **$125–$170**	
Open: **All year**	

The inn has been serving guests since 1763. Picture yourself returning "home" after seeing the Pennsylvania Dutch sights and trudging wearily to your bedroom. Waiting for you are candle sconces, canopy beds, Amish quilts, down pillows, and on cool nights, a cozy fire. There's even a flannel nightshirt to snuggle in. And after a restful sleep, come down to an all-you-can-eat breakfast that often features blueberry waffles.

Martin House ✪
265 RIDGE AVENUE, EPHRATA, PENNSYLVANIA 17522

Tel: **(717) 733-6804**
Best Time to Call: **Noon**
Hosts: **Moses and Vera Martin**
Location: **10 mi. N of Lancaster**
No. of Rooms: **2**
Max. No. Sharing Bath: **4**
Double/sb: **$59**
Open: **All year**

Reduced Rates: **5% families**
Breakfast: **Continental**
Pets: **No**
Children: **Welcome**
Smoking: **No**
Social Drinking: **No**
Airport/Station Pickup: **Yes**

Gray stone and tall, arch-tapped windows are the first things you'll notice as you follow the curved drive leading to this contemporary home. Then, walking into the foyer, with its dramatic cathedral ceiling, you'll see modern furnishings complemented by a few choice antiques. In the back, a spacious deck overlooks the tranquil, semi-secluded grounds. From this Lancaster County location, it's easy to get to Pennsylvania Dutch country, antique markets and restaurants. Hershey Park and Chocolate World are 45 minutes away. Your hosts love to travel and appreciate the great outdoors. Moses is a supervisor for a dairy herd improvement association, while Vera is a full-time hostess.

Hershey Bed & Breakfast Reservation Service ○
P.O. BOX 208, HERSHEY, PENNSYLVANIA 17033

Tel: **(717) 533-2928**
Best Time to Call: **10 AM–4 PM**
Coordinator: **Renee Deutel**
States/Regions Covered: **Hanover, Harrisburg, Hershey, Lancaster, Palmyra**

Rates (Single/Double):
Modest: **$50 / $55**
Average: **$60 / $65**
Luxury: **$70 / $85**
Credit Cards: **MC, VISA**

Renee has a small roster of lovely homes close to main thoroughfares. Hosts come from a variety of interesting backgrounds, and all share a common enthusiasm to share their homes and communities. You may choose a cozy farmhouse, a large older home with beautiful furnishings, or a country inn. Whatever your wishes, the town that chocolate made famous will welcome you.

Gibson's Bed & Breakfast ○
141 WEST CARACAS AVENUE, HERSHEY, PENNSYLVANIA 17033

Tel: **(717) 534-1305**
Hosts: **Frances and Bob Gibson**
Location: **One block off Rte. 422**
No. of Rooms: **3**
Max. No. Sharing Bath: **3**
Double/sb: **$45**
Single/sb: **$35**
Open: **All year**

Breakfast: **Full**
Pets: **No**
Children: **Welcome, over 5**
Smoking: **No**
Social Drinking: **Permitted**
Airport/Station Pickup: **Yes**
Foreign Languages: **Italian**

Bob and Frances Gibson have a 50-year-old Cape Cod, located in the center of Hershey, walking distance from many local attractions. The house has been recently renovated to enhance the charm of the hardwood floors, wood trim, and original windows. The atmosphere is friendly and informal, and your hosts are glad to offer complimentary nibbles. The Gibsons will gladly help you find local sights such as Hershey Park, Chocolate World, Founders Hall, and the Amish country.

Bed & Breakfast—The Manor ○
830 VILLAGE ROAD, P.O. BOX 416, LAMPETER, PENNSYLVANIA 17537

Tel: **(717) 464-9564**
Best Time to Call: **9 AM–9 PM**
Coordinator: **Jackie Curtis**
States/Regions Covered: **Ardmore, Bird-in-Hand, Bryn Mawr, Intercourse, Lampeter, Lancaster, Merlon, Philadelphia, Strasburg, Villanova**

Rates (Single/Double):
Modest: **$45 / $55**
Average: **$60 / $65**
Luxury: **$70 / $75**
Credit Cards: **MC, VISA**

Bed & Breakfast—The Manor gives you access to selected B&Bs throughout Philadelphia and the outlying areas including the Main Line and Lancaster County. Featured is a cozy farmhouse with a deluxe in-ground pool in the heart of Amish country. Stay in a city apartment or town house, a suburban home, a Main Line mansion, or a country cottage. Hosts are anxious to share their knowledge and expertise about their particular locales and provide guests with cozy, quiet bedrooms and hearty breakfasts.

Bed & Breakfast—The Manor ✪

830 VILLAGE ROAD, P.O. BOX 416, LAMPETER (LANCASTER COUNTY), PENNSYLVANIA 17537

Tel: (717) 464-9564	Single/sb: $60
Best Time to Call: 9 AM–9 PM	Open: All year
Hosts: Mary Lou Paolini and Jackie	Reduced Rates: 25% seniors
Curtis	Oct.–Mar.
Location: 3 mi. SE of Lancaster	Breakfast: Full
No. of Rooms: 5	Credit Cards: MC, VISA
No. of Private Baths: 3	Pets: No
Max. No. Sharing Bath: 4	Children: Welcome
Double/pb: $75	Smoking: No
Single/pb: $70	Social Drinking: No
Double/sb: $65	Airport/Station Pickup: Yes

Set on four and a half acres of lush Amish farmland, this cozy farmhouse is just minutes away from Lancaster's historical sights and attractions. Dutch Wonderland, the Strasburg Railroad, Amish farms, and Hershey are but a few of the don't-miss sights nearby. Guests delight in Mary Lou's delicious breakfasts, which often feature gourmet treats such as Eggs Mornay, crêpes or strata, apple cobbler, and her homemade jams and breads. In summer, a swim in the pool or a nap under one of the many shade trees is the perfect way to cap a day of touring. There is a conference room now available.

Walkabout Inn ✪

837 VILLAGE ROAD, LAMPETER (LANCASTER COUNTY), PENNSYLVANIA 17537

Tel: (717) 464-0707	Reduced Rates: Available
Hosts: Richard and Maggie Mason	Breakfast: Full
Location: 3 mi. S of Lancaster	Other Meals: Available
No. of Rooms: 5	Credit Cards: AMEX, MC, VISA
No. of Private Baths: 5	Pets: No
Double/pb: $79	Children: Welcome, over 10
Single/pb: $60	Smoking: No
Suites: $169; sleeps 5	Social Drinking: Permitted
Open: All year	Airport/Station Pickup: Yes

The Walkabout Inn takes its name from the Australian word, which means to go out and discover new places. Australian-born host Richard Mason and his wife, Maggie, will help you explore the Amish country that surrounds their brick Mennonite farmhouse. The twenty-two-room house was built in 1925 and features wraparound porches, balconies, and chestnut woodwork. Guest rooms feature Maggie's hand stenciling and are decorated with antiques, oriental rugs, and Pennsylvania Dutch quilts. When it's time to say "good day," a candlelight gourmet breakfast is served on silver and crystal in the dining room. Homemade Australian bread, pastries, and tea imported from Down Under are always on the menu. You can choose a romantic honeymoon or anniversary suite that comes with a gift. Special packages include dinner with the Amish, 3-hour scenic bus tour, and free maps and information.

Hollinger House Bed and Breakfast
2336 HOLLINGER ROAD, LANCASTER, PENNSYLVANIA 17602

Tel: (717) 464-3050	Breakfast: **Full**
Best Time to Call: **Anytime**	Credit Cards: **DISC, MC, VISA**
Hosts: **Gina and Jeffrey Trost**	Pets: **No**
No. of Rooms: 5	Children: **Welcome, over 12**
No. of Private Baths: 5	Smoking: **No**
Double/pb: **$60–$90**	Social Drinking: **Permitted**
Open: **All year**	Minimum Stay: **2 nights holiday**
Reduced Rates: **Available**	**weekends**

This Adams-period, three-story brick home was built in 1870 for the Hollinger family, whose outstanding harness leather won them an international reputation. This B&B is romantic and friendly, with hardwood floors, fireplaces, high ceilings, king- and queen-size beds, and air-conditioning. Gina and Jeff offer hors d'oeuvres upon guests' arrival, afternoon tea, and goodnight goodies. Hollinger House is located only minutes from downtown Lancaster, shopping outlets, historic attractions, farmers markets, and Amish country. Train buffs will want to ride the Strasburg Rail Road, the time-honored short line through Dutch country. Golfing, swimming, hiking, and tennis are also available nearby.

Lincoln Haus Inn Bed & Breakfast
1687 LINCOLN HIGHWAY EAST, LANCASTER, PENNSYLVANIA 17602

Tel: (717) 392-9412	Single/pb: **$43–$53**
Best Time to Call: **Before 11 PM**	Suites: **$50–$90**
Host: **Mary K. Zook**	Open: **All year**
Location: **2 mi. E of Lancaster**	Reduced Rates: **Available**
No. of Rooms: 5	Breakfast: **Full**
No. of Private Baths: 5	Other Meals: **Available**
Double/pb: **$45–$55**	Pets: **No**

Children: **Welcome**   Social Drinking: **No**
Smoking: **No**   Station Pickup: **Yes**

Ten minutes east of historic Lancaster and five minutes from Route 30 and the Pennsylvania Dutch Visitors Bureau in Lancaster County, you'll find this 1915 stucco home with distinctive hip roofs and black trim. Above the living room door, your host has hung a "Welcome" sign. Mary prides herself on giving guests a glimpse of the Amish lifestyle; the farmers market, horse auctions, buggy rides, quilt sales, and traditional Amish farmlands are all within ten to twenty minutes by car. But before you set out, you'll have a hearty family-style breakfast including juice, fruit, quiche, sausage, and different kinds of muffins.

Meadowview Guest House ○
2169 NEW HOLLAND PIKE, LANCASTER, PENNSYLVANIA 17601

Tel: **(717) 299-4017**   Reduced Rates: **$3 less 3rd night; off-**
Best Time to Call: **Before 10:30 PM**   **season**
Hosts: **Edward and Sheila Christie**   Open: **All year**
No. of Rooms: **3**   Breakfast: **Continental**
No. of Private Baths: **1**   Pets: **No**
Max. No. Sharing Bath: **4**   Children: **Welcome, over 7**
Double/pb: **$50**   Smoking: **No**
Single/pb: **$40**   Social Drinking: **Permitted**
Double/sb: **$30–$35**   Airport/Station Pickup: **Yes**

Situated in the heart of Pennsylvania Dutch country, the house has a pleasant blend of modern and traditional furnishings. Your hosts offer a fully equipped guest kitchen where you can store and prepare your own light meals. Ed and Sheila supply coffee and tea. The area is known for great farmers markets, antique shops, crafts shops, country auctions, and wonderful restaurants.

O'Flaherty's Dingeldein House ○
1105 EAST KING STREET, LANCASTER, PENNSYLVANIA 17602

Tel: **(717) 293-1723, (800) 779-7765**   Reduced Rates: **Weekly**
Best Time to Call: **9 AM–9 PM**   Breakfast: **Full**
Hosts: **Jack and Sue Flatley**   Credit Cards: **DISC, MC, VISA**
Location: **1 mi. E of Lancaster**   Pets: **No**
No. of Rooms: **4**   Children: **Welcome**
No. of Private Baths: **2**   Smoking: **No**
Max. No. Sharing Bath: **4**   Social Drinking: **Permitted**
Double/pb: **$70**   Minimum Stay: **2 nights weekends July**
Double/sb: **$60**   **thru Oct.**
Open: **All year**   Airport/Station Pickup: **Yes**

One visit to O'Flaherty's and it's sure to become your home away from home. Hospitality abounds at this traditionally furnished 1912

Dutch Colonial—originally the home of the Armstrong (floor tile) family—surrounded by a lovely landscaped garden. As co-chef and tour planner, Jack explored side roads and found Amish friends: a toymaker who lives on a farm and loves to meet guests, a family that may have you to dinner. But before you set out, you'll have a hearty breakfast of seasonal fruit and home-baked muffins followed by the chef's choice of such morsels as Sue's potato pie, cinnamon-oat pancakes topped with brandied lemon apples, or peaches and cream French toast. Specially brewed coffee accompanies your meal.

Patchwork Inn Bed & Breakfast ✪
2319 OLD PHILADELPHIA PIKE, LANCASTER, PENNSYLVANIA 17602

Tel: **(717) 293-9078**
Best Time to Call: **Mornings**
Hosts: **Lee and Anne Martin**
No. of Rooms: **4**
No. of Private Baths: **2**
Max. No. Sharing Bath: **4**
Double/pb: **$70**
Double/sb: **$60**
Suites: **$80**

Open: **All year**
Breakfast: **Full**
Credit Cards: **DISC, MC, VISA**
Pets: **No**
Children: **Welcome, over 10**
Smoking: **No**
Social Drinking: **Permitted**
Airport/Station Pickup: **Yes**

Upon entering this lovely 19th-century farmhouse, you won't be surprised to discover that quilts are the innkeeper's hobby. Gorgeous quilts cover the queen-size beds, art and posters feature quilts, and several adorn the walls as hangings. Lee and Anne will be happy to direct you to special shops where quilting material or completed quilts are sold. The inn features a handsome collection of fine oak furniture including an oak phone booth where Lee displays a collection of interesting antique telephones. Breakfast, served in the dining room decorated with Holland Delft, is a generous repast.

The Loom Room ✪
RD 1, BOX 1420, LEESPORT, PENNSYLVANIA 19533

Tel: **(610) 926-3217**
Hosts: **Mary and Gene Smith**
Location: **4 mi. N of Reading**
No. of Rooms: **3**
No. of Private Baths: **1**
Max. No. Sharing Bath: **4**
Double/pb: **$50**
Single/pb: **$50**
Double/sb: **$45**

Single/sb: **$45**
Open: **All year**
Breakfast: **Full**
Reduced Rates: **Weekly**
Pets: **No**
Children: **Welcome (crib)**
Smoking: **No**
Social Drinking: **Permitted**
Airport/Station Pickup: **Yes**

The Loom Room is a stucco-covered stone farmhouse dating back more than 175 years. It is located in the countryside surrounded by shade trees, flowers, and herb gardens. Inside, the spacious rooms feature country antiques, open beams, fireplaces, and handwoven accessories. Mary invites you to her studio, where her work is on display. Her talents also extend to the kitchen, where she helps Gene cook up eggnog French toast, homemade jams, muffins, and chipped beef. Breakfast may be served in the sunny kitchen or outside in the gazebo. This lovely farm is near Reading's outlet complexes, Blue Marsh Lake Recreation Area, antique shops, and many historic sights.

Alden House ✪
62 EAST MAIN STREET, LITITZ, PENNSYLVANIA 17543

Tel: **(717) 627-3363; (800) 584-0753**
Best Time to Call: **1–9 PM**
Host: **Leanne Schweitzer**
Location: **7 mi. N of Lancaster**
No. of Rooms: **7**
No. of Private Baths: **5**
Max. No. Sharing Bath: **4**
Double/pb: **$75–$85**
Double/sb: **$65–$70**
Suites: **$95; sleeps 4**

Open: **All year**
Reduced Rates: **10% after 2nd night
Nov. 1–Apr. 30**
Breakfast: **Continental**
Credit Cards: **MC, VISA**
Pets: **No**
Children: **Welcome, over 6**
Smoking: **Permitted**
Social Drinking: **Permitted**

Built in 1850 and fully restored, this brick town house has lots of old-fashioned appeal. At the end of the day, grab a chair on one of the three porches and savor the chocolate aroma wafting over from the local candy factory. The farmers markets and crafts shops of Amish country are a short drive away, and numerous restaurants are within walking distance. Breakfast includes juice, coffee or tea, cereal, fresh seasonal fruit, and baked goods.

Dot's Bed & Breakfast ✪
435 WOODCREST AVENUE, LITITZ, PENNSYLVANIA 17543

Tel: **(717) 627-0483**
Best Time to Call: **7–9 AM; 6–11 PM**
Hosts: **Dorothy and Erwin Boettcher**
Location: **7 mi. N of Lancaster**
No. of Rooms: **2**
Max. No. Sharing Bath: **4**
Double/sb: **$40**
Single/sb: **$30**

Open: **All year**
Breakfast: **Continental**
Pets: **Sometimes**
Children: **Welcome (crib)**
Smoking: **No**
Social Drinking: **Permitted**
Foreign Languages: **German**

Dot's is located in a quiet residential suburb of Lititz, home of the country's first pretzel bakery. Much of this quaint little town has stayed the way it was in 1756, the year it was founded. You are sure to enjoy an easy stroll past Lititz Springs Park, the historic buildings on Main Street, and the Linden Hall Girl's School. After a busy day, you'll be glad to return to Dot's, where you'll find a quiet guest room furnished with a cozy bed, lounge chair, rocker, and plenty of books. Awake to the birds singing and join your hosts for some of Dot's homemade muffins or shoofly pie. Your hosts will gladly direct you to the nearby sights, including the Wilbur Chocolate Factory.

Market Sleigh Bed & Breakfast ✪
BOX 99, 57 SOUTH MAIN STREET, LOGANVILLE, PENNSYLVANIA 17342-0099

Tel: **(717) 428-1440**
Best Time to Call: **3–6 PM**
Hosts: **Judy and Jerry Dietz**
Location: **7 mi. S of York**
No. of Rooms: **1**
No. of Private Baths: **1**
Suite: **$55–$100**
Open: **All year**
Reduced Rates: **Corporate travelers Mon.–Thurs.**

Breakfast: **Full**
Credit Cards: **MC, VISA**
Pets: **No**
Children: **Welcome, over 12**
Smoking: **No**
Social Drinking: **Permitted**
Minimum Stay: **2 nights convention weekends**

This bed and breakfast takes its name from the large 19th-century sleigh parked by the main entrance, as if stranded when the snow melted. Guests are encouraged to wander around the 22-acre property, or just sit with a book in the back porch swing. The many local attractions range from parks and wineries to museums and malls. Judy dishes out a hearty farmer's breakfast of fruit, homemade breads, eggs, cheese, bacon, and French toast or pancakes.

Herr Farmhouse Inn ✪
2256 HUBER DRIVE, MANHEIM, PENNSYLVANIA 17545

Tel: **(717) 653-9852**
Best Time to Call: **After 4 PM**
Host: **Barry A. Herr**
Location: **9 mi. W of Lancaster; ¼ mi.**
from Rte. 283
No. of Rooms: **4**
No. of Private Baths: **2**
Max. No. Sharing Bath: **4**
Double/pb: **$85**

Double/sb: **$70**
Suites: **$95**
Open: **All year**
Breakfast: **Full**
Credit Cards: **MC, VISA**
Pets: **No**
Children: **Welcome, over 6**
Smoking: **Permitted**
Social Drinking: **Permitted**

Nestled on more than 11 acres of rolling farmland, this farmhouse, dating back to 1738, has been restored with the greatest of care and attention to detail. Fanlights adorn the main entrance, there are six working fireplaces, and it has the original pine floors. Whether spending a winter's night by a cozy fire, or a bright summer morning sipping tea in the sun room, it is the perfect retreat. It is less than 20 minutes to the sights, shops, and restaurants of Amish country.

The Noble House ✪
113 WEST MARKET STREET, MARIETTA, PENNSYLVANIA 17547

Tel: **(717) 426-4389**
Best Time to Call: **Before noon; after**
4 PM
Hosts: **Elissa and Paul Noble**
Location: **12 mi. W of Lancaster**
No. of Rooms: **2**
No. of Private Baths: **1**
Max. No. Sharing Baths: **4**
Double/pb: **$75**
Double/sb: **$55**

Suites: **$75**
Open: **All year**
Reduced Rates: **Extended stays**
Breakfast: **Full**
Pets: **No**
Children: **Welcome**
Smoking: **No**
Social Drinking: **Permitted**
Airport/Station Pickup: **Yes**

A 170-year-old Federal style home, Noble House offers a private, romantic getaway. Intimate catered dinners can be arranged and served in this home filled with fresh flowers, antiques, and collectibles. Rooms are on the second floor, one with a queen-size, brass four-poster, and the other with a king/twin bed option and a gas log fireplace. Breakfast is served in the candlelit dining room. The side porch overlooks lush gardens and the living room includes a library, piano, cable TV, and a fireplace for your enjoyment.

Cedar Hill Farm ✪
305 LONGENECKER ROAD, MOUNT JOY, PENNSYLVANIA 17552

Tel: **(717) 653-4655**
Best Time to Call: **Anytime**

Hosts: **Russel and Gladys Swarr**
Location: **10 mi. W of Lancaster**

No. of Rooms: **5**
No. of Private Baths: **5**
Double/pb: **$60–$70**
Single/pb: **$50–$60**
Open: **All year**
Reduced Rates: **Weekly**
Breakfast: **Continental, plus**

Credit Cards: **AMEX, DISC, MC, VISA**
Pets: **No**
Children: **Welcome (crib)**
Smoking: **No**
Social Drinking: **Permitted**
Airport/Station Pickup: **Yes**

Russel was born in this restored 1817 farmhouse and can tell you all about its history. It has an open, winding staircase, original pine floors, and an Indian door; breakfast is served beside a walk-in fireplace. Stroll the acreage or relax on the large porch overlooking a peaceful stream. Beautiful wallpapers and family heirlooms enhance the comfortable, air-conditioned bedrooms; the honeymoon suite has a private balcony. Quilt auctions and other attractions for collectors are plentiful year-round. Every Tuesday a farmers market and antiques auction take place just minutes away. Amish country, Hershey Park, and Chocolate World are nearby attractions.

Country Gardens Farm Bed & Breakfast ✪
686 ROCK POINT ROAD, MOUNT JOY, PENNSYLVANIA 17552

Tel: **(717) 426-3316**
Best Time to Call: **Anytime**
Hosts: **Andy and Dottie Hess**
Location: **16 mi. W of Lancaster**
No. of Rooms: **3**
No. of Private Baths: **3**
Double/pb: **$60–$70**
Single/pb: **$50–$60**

Open: **All year**
Reduced Rates: **Available**
Breakfast: **Full**
Credit Cards: **AMEX, MC, VISA**
Pets: **No**
Children: **Welcome**
Smoking: **No**

Country Gardens offers the friendly down-home hospitality which made Lancaster County famous. Colorful flower gardens accent the 1860s brick farmhouse with large porches and spacious lawns. The farmhouse is graced with handmade crafts, houseplants, original oil paintings, and family heirlooms. The host and hostess spent most of their lives working on the farm and delight in sharing it with you. Relax in clean comfortable bedrooms, air-conditioning, electric heat, and private baths. There's easy access to farmers markets, quilt shops, antique shops, and historic sites, and other attractions are available year-round. County Gardens is also close to Amish country and Hershey Park.

Hillside Farm B&B ✪
607 EBY CHIQUES ROAD, MOUNT JOY, PENNSYLVANIA 17552-8819

Tel: **(717) 653-6697**
Best Time to Call: **Anytime**

Hosts: **Gary and Deb Lintner/Bob and Wilma Lintner**
Location: **10 mi. W of Lancaster**

No. of Rooms: **5**
No. of Private Baths: **3**
Max. No. Sharing Bath: **4**
Double/pb: **$62.50**
Single/pb: **$62.50**
Double/sb: **$50**
Single/sb: **$50**

Open: **All year**
Reduced Rates: **Available**
Breakfast: **Full**
Pets: **No**
Children: **Welcome, over 10**
Smoking: **No**
Social Drinking: **Permitted**

Quiet and secluded, this 1863 brick homestead overlooks Chickies Creek, a dam and waterfall. Amish country, Hershey Park, antique shops, flea markets, auctions, wineries, and hiking and biking trails are all nearby. (Bike trail maps are available.) Although it is located near downtown Lancaster, the B&B is entirely surrounded by farmland. Guests can explore a large barn or watch milking at a neighborhood farm; dinner with an Amish family can be arranged. Hillside Farm is filled with cozy country furnishings, dairy antiques, and milk bottles. Gary, an electrical project superintendent, and Deb, an executive secretary, run this special inn along with Gary's parents Bob and Wilma.

Churchtown Inn B&B ⊘
21 MAIN STREET, ROUTE 23 W, NARVON, PENNSYLVANIA 17555

Tel: **(215) 445-7794**
Best Time to Call: **9 AM–9 PM**
Hosts: **Jim Kent Hermine and Stuart Smith**
Location: **4 mi. off Pennsylvania Turnpike, Exit 22**
No. of Rooms: **8**
No. of Private Baths: **6**
Max. No. Sharing Bath: **4**
Double/pb: **$75–$85**
Single/pb: **$65–$85**

Double/sb: **$49–$55**
Open: **All year**
Reduced Rates: **Weekly**
Breakfast: **Full**
Other Meals: **Available**
Credit Cards: **MC, VISA**
Pets: **No**
Children: **Welcome, over 12**
Smoking: **No**
Social Drinking: **Permitted**
Foreign Languages: **German**

Churchtown Inn is a lovely fieldstone Federal Colonial mansion built in 1735. Located in the heart of Pennsylvania Dutch country, this B&B is close to Amish attractions, antique markets, and manufacturers' outlets. Rooms are decorated with the hosts' personal treasures: antique furniture, original art, and music boxes. Stuart (a former music director) and Jim (a former accountant who moonlighted as a ballroom dance instructor) stage events throughout the year. The schedule includes concerts, costume balls, carriage rides, walks, and holiday celebrations. Every Saturday, guests have the opportunity of joining Amish or Mennonite families for dinner at an additional fee. Of course, after a Churchtown Inn breakfast, you may not have room for any more meals; the table groans with English oatmeal custard, apple pancakes, Grand Marnier French toast, homemade coffee cake, and other delectables.

The "Hen-Apple" Bed and Breakfast ○
409 SOUTH LINGLE AVENUE, PALMYRA, PENNSYLVANIA 17078

Tel: (717) 838-8282
Best Time to Call: 10 AM–11 PM
Hosts: Flo and Harold Eckert
Location: E of Hershey
No. of Rooms: 6
No. of Private Baths: 6
Double/pb: $65
Single/pb: $55
Open: All year

Reduced Rates: Available
Breakfast: Full
Credit Cards: MC, VISA
Pets: No
Children: No
Smoking: No
Social Drinking: Permitted
Airport/Station Pickup: Yes

Wood floors, stenciling, antiques, and candlelit windows create a cozy country atmosphere at this 1825 farmhouse five minutes from Hershey. Flo will offer you complimentary snacks upon your arrival or later in the afternoon. Home-baked breads and muffins, served on old china, make breakfast a treat, whether you enjoy it on the screened porch or in the dining room. In warm weather, guests may relax in the orchard on lawn furniture, a swing, and a hammock. The local attractions are many and varied: antique and crafts shops, horse racing and ice hockey, theaters and museums, even a winery and a bologna factory that welcome visitors.

Maple Lane Guest House
505 PARADISE LANE, PARADISE, PENNSYLVANIA 17562

Tel: (717) 687-7479
Best Time to Call: Anytime
Hosts: Edwin and Marion Rohrer
Location: 10 mi. E of Lancaster
No. of Rooms: 4
No. of Private Baths: 1
Max. No. Sharing Bath: 4
Double/pb: $40–$60
Single/pb: $40–$48

Double/sb: $40–$55
Single/sb: $40–$45
Open: All year
Breakfast: Continental, plus
Pets: No
Children: Welcome (crib)
Smoking: No
Social Drinking: Permitted

For an unusual experience, travel along a back country road to this 200-acre dairy farm with woodland and a winding stream. Relax, watch the dairy in operation, or hike up the hill for a 40-mile panoramic view. Nearby are excellent restaurants, farmers markets, Amish crafts and quilt shops, historic sites, and the Strasburg train museum. Air-conditioned rooms are pleasantly furnished with poster and canopy beds, quilts, crafts, and wall stenciling. Breakfast includes fresh fruit, cheese, coffee, tea, cereal, and homemade breads.

The Forge Bed & Breakfast Inn ○
RD 1, BOX 438, PINE GROVE, PENNSYLVANIA 17963

Tel: (717) 345-8349
Best Time to Call: 9 AM–12 noon

Owners: Margo and Dick Ward
Host: Mabel Stump

Location: **34 mi. NE of Harrisburg**
No. of Rooms: **6**
No. of Private Baths: **2**
Max. No. Sharing Bath: **4**
Double/pb: **$70–$75**
Single/pb: **$70**
Double/sb: **$65**
Single/sb: **$60**

Open: **All year**
Breakfast: **Full**
Credit Cards: **MC, VISA**
Pets: **No**
Children: **Welcome, over 14**
Smoking: **No**
Social Drinking: **Permitted**
Airport/Station Pickup: **Yes**

This magnificent three-story fieldstone mansion dates to 1830, and has been in Margo's family since 1860. Many of the antique furnishings are treasured heirlooms. Picturesque hiking paths crisscross the 250-acre property, and fishermen are welcome to try their luck in the stream in front of the house. Visitors can also avail themselves of the swimming pool and the library. Home-baked goods, such as sticky buns and blueberry muffins, highlight breakfast.

The House on the Canal ✪
4020 RIVER ROAD, READING, PENNSYLVANIA 19605

Tel: **(610) 921-3015**
Best Time to Call: **Anytime**
Hosts: **Mr. and Mrs. Robert Yenser**
No. of Rooms: **2**
No. of Private Baths: **2**
Double/pb: **$75**
Suites: **$85**

Open: **All year**
Breakfast: **Full**
Pets: **Welcome**
Children: **Welcome**
Smoking: **Restricted**
Social Drinking: **Permitted**

This secluded old lockkeeper's house was built back in the late 1700s and recently restored. The property's two-foot stone walls and 200-year-old trees are nestled along the banks of the Schuylkill River, and fishing, hiking, and biking are literally at your doorstep. Depending on the season, you might even catch a glimpse of the Canadian wild geese who have made their home by the old wooden dam nearby. Whatever your interests, you'll find something to do here. It's 5 minutes to Reading Airport and the Reading outlets; 10 minutes to the campuses of Albright, Alvernia, and Penn State; and 30 minutes to Redners Antique Market and Black Angus Beer Fest.

PJ's Guest Home ✪
101 WEST MAIN STREET, STRASBURG, PENNSYLVANIA 17579

Tel: **(717) 687-8800**
Best Time to Call: **Anytime**
Hosts: **Pat and John Settle**
Location: **5 mi. E of Lancaster, Route 741**
No. of Rooms: **3**
No. of Private Baths: **2**
Max. No. Sharing Bath: **4**
Double/pb: **$48**
Double/sb: **$38**

Open: **Feb. 15–Dec. 31**
Reduced Rates: **$6 less Sept. 4–May 24**
Breakfast: **Continental**
Credit Cards: **DISC, MC, VISA**
Pets: **No**
Children: **Welcome**
Smoking: **No**
Social Drinking: **Permitted**
Airport/Station Pickup: **Yes**

The serene Amish countryside of Lancaster County surrounds this lovely guest home, built in 1824. Your hosts, Pat and John, are longtime residents whose knowledge of this special area can help you plan a fun-filled vacation. Attractions include the Strasburg Railroad Museum, Amish crafts shops, antique shops, and numerous historic sites. There is a swimming pool and off-street parking.

Hiwwelhaus ✪
R.D. #1 BOX 456, WOMELSDORF, PENNSYLVANIA 19567

Tel: (215) 589-4660	Reduced Rates: 10% seniors
Best Time to Call: 8–10 AM, 6–9 PM	Breakfast: Full
Host: Mary E. Keeler	Pets: No
Location: 15 mi. NW of Reading	Children: Welcome, over 6
No. of Rooms: 2	Smoking: No
No. of Private Baths: 2	Social Drinking: No
Double/pb: $55	Station Pickup: Yes
Single/pb: $45	Foreign Languages: German
Open: Apr.–Dec.	

In 1743 this area was part of a thousand-acre plantation purchased from the Penn family. On a corner of the original property stands a log home known as "Hiwwelhaus"—"house on a hill" in the local Pennsylvania German dialect. From its hilltop perch, this B&B overlooks a lovely rural landscape. After a country breakfast, relax on the spacious porch and plan your day. Reading outlets, Hershey Park, Lancaster County's Amish country, Hawk Mountain, the Appalachian Trail and many other attractions are close by. The area also boasts an abundance of excellent restaurants. Attend a country auction, browse antique and crafts shops; the sports-minded can go fishing, boating, swimming, biking, hiking, or skiing. An easy drive takes you to a wildlife area with birds and deer in residence.

PHILADELPHIA AREA

Bed and Breakfast Connections ✪
P.O. BOX 21, DEVON, PENNSYLVANIA 19333

Tel: (215) 687-3565; (800) 448-3619	suburbs; Reading, Valley Forge, York County
Best Time to Call: 9 AM–9 PM Mon.–Sat.	Rates (Single/Double):
Coordinators: Peggy Gregg and Lucy Scribner	Modest: $30 / $40
	Average: $45 / $85
States/Regions Covered: Amish country, Philadelphia and Main Line	Luxury: $75 / $175
	Credit Cards: AMEX, MC, VISA

Bed and Breakfast Connections invites you to select a personally inspected host home in the greater Philadelphia area, from historic Center City to revolutionary Valley Forge. It also serves the scenic Brandywine Valley and Pennsylvania Dutch country. While the locations range from country farmhouses to downtown high-rises, they all offer an inviting atmosphere and dedicated, attentive hosts.

Bed & Breakfast of Philadelphia ✪
1530 LOCUST STREET, SUITE K, PHILADELPHIA, PENNSYLVANIA 19102

Tel: (215) 735-1917; (800) 220-1917	Descriptive Directory: **Free**
Best Time to Call: **9 AM–5 PM**	Rates (Single/Double):
Coordinator: **Debra Wiggins**	Modest: **$25–$35 / $35–$45**
States/Regions Covered: **Philadelphia**	Average: **$45–$55 / $55–$65**
and suburbs, Amish country,	Luxury: **$65–$125 / $75–$150**
Brandywine Valley, Bucks County;	Credit Cards: **AMEX, MC, VISA**
New Hope, Valley Forge	

Debra represents over 60 host homes in Center City, the Main Line suburbs, Valley Forge, Chester County, the Brandywine Valley, and New Hope. The accommodations vary from city town houses to country manors or farms to suburban mansions. Several historic properties are available, including several listed on the National Register of Historic Places.

Bed & Breakfast of Valley Forge and Subsidiaries
All About Town—B&B in Philadelphia
All About the Brandywine Valley B&B
P.O. BOX 562, VALLEY FORGE, PENNSYLVANIA 19481

Tel: (215) 783-7838; (800) 344-0123;	Descriptive Directory of B&Bs: **$3**
fax: (215) 783-7783	Rates (Single/Double):
Best Time to Call: **9 AM–9 PM**	Modest: **$35–$45 / $45–$55**
Coordinator: **Carolyn J. Williams**	Average: **$50–$65 / $60–$75**
States/Regions Covered: **Philadelphia,**	Luxury: **$70–$85 / $85–up**
Valley Forge, Main Line, Brandywine	Credit Cards: **AMEX, VISA, MC, DISC**
Valley, Bucks County, Lancaster	

Even George Washington would applaud the manner in which Carolyn has brought the British tradition of bed and breakfast to his former headquarters. Choose from more than 130 sites in southeast Pennsylvania. Whether you are on vacation, business, personal getaway or using a gift certificate, Carolyn says, "There is a B&B for you!" Her roster includes modest homestays, city/country inns and town houses, historic and farm homes, ski lodges, guest cottages, carriage houses and elegant, grand estates close to where you need to be.

Guesthouses ✪
BOX 2137, WEST CHESTER, PENNSYLVANIA 19380

Tel: (215) 692-4575;
  fax: (215) 692-4451
Best Time to Call: Noon–4 PM
  Mon.–Fri.
Coordinator: Janice K. Archbold
States/Regions Covered:
  Pennsylvania—Amish country,
  Brandywine Valley, Bucks County,
  Carlisle, Chesapeake Bay,

Gettysburg, Harrisburg, Main Line
Philadelphia, Poconos; Delaware;
Maryland; New Jersey
Rates (Single/Double):
  Modest: $55–$65
  Average: $70–$95
  Luxury: $100–$200
Credit Cards: AMEX, MC, VISA

With more than 200 locations in the mid-Atlantic region, Guesthouses provides a choice among various accommodations even during the busiest seasons. Guesthouses specializes in historic National Register or landmark sites, with four categories of offerings: separate guest houses for two on private estates; private one- to three-guest-room homes; private manor houses with four to twelve guest rooms and suites; and small, owner-occupied bed-and-breakfast inns and hotels with up to 40 rooms. Guest stays can last from one night to one year. Packages are available, including tickets to an area's museums, gardens, and historic sites.

The Benjamin Cox House ✪
310 BLACK ROCK ROAD, COLLEGEVILLE, PENNSYLVANIA 19426

Tel: (215) 933-5036
Hosts: Robert and Rosemary French
No. of Rooms: 2
No. of Private Baths: 1
Max. No. Sharing Bath: 3
Double/pb: $85
Single/pb: $70
Double/sb: $70

Single/sb: $60
Open: All year
Reduced Rates: 10% seniors
Breakfast: Full
Pets: No
Children: Welcome, over 12
Smoking: No
Social Drinking: Permitted

Nestled in a small Philadelphia suburb, Benjamin Cox House is located minutes away from Valley Forge National Park, Mill Grove, King of Prussia (a shopper's paradise), and Ursinus College. This three-story stone farmhouse is decorated with Pennsylvania antiques and period accessories. Winding open stairways, random-width floors, original handcrafted woodwork, colorful stencil art, and five fireplaces all serve as reminders of a bygone era. Bob works in commercial construction and collects antique wooden tools, while Rosemary is an antique dealer and shopkeeper, who, true to her name, loves herbs. Both of your hosts love to share their knowledge of the area and of the 19th century with guests.

POCONO MOUNTAINS

La Anna Guest House ✪

RD 2, BOX 1051, CRESCO, PENNSYLVANIA 18326

Tel: **(717) 676-4225**
Host: **Kay Swingle**
Location: **9 mi. from I-80 and I-84**
No. of Rooms: **2**
Max. No. Sharing Bath: **4**
Double/sb: **$30**
Single/sb: **$25**

Open: **All year**
Breakfast: **Continental**
Pets: **No**
Children: **Welcome (crib)**
Smoking: **Permitted**
Social Drinking: **Permitted**

This Victorian home has large rooms furnished with antiques; it is nestled on 25 acres of lush, wooded land, and has its own pond. Kay will happily direct you to fine dining spots that are kind to your wallet. Enjoy scenic walks, waterfalls, mountain vistas, Tobyhanna and Promised Land state parks; there's cross-country skiing right on the property. Lake Wallenpaupack is only 15 minutes away.

The Shepard House ✪

P.O. BOX 486, 108 SHEPARD AVENUE, DELAWARE WATER GAP, PENNSYLVANIA 18327

Tel: **(717) 424-9779**
Best Time to Call: **9 AM–noon**
Host: **Jeanni Buonura**

Location: **3 mi. E of Stroudsburg**
No. of Rooms: **6**
Max. No. Sharing Bath: **4**

Double/sb: **$75–$85**	Pets: **No**
Single/sb: **$65–$75**	Children: **Welcome, over 8**
Open: **All year**	Smoking: **No**
Reduced Rates: **Available**	Social Drinking: **Permitted**
Breakfast: **Full**	Minimum Stay: **2 nights holidays**

Originally called "the Far View House," this large Victorian operated as a summer vacation boarding house in the early 1900s. Today, from its site just off the Appalachian Trail, the Shepard House greets visitors year-round. Guest rooms are filled with antiques and special touches. Take a seat in the comfortable parlor, or on the veranda that wraps around the entire house. Your host serves a four-course breakfast and offers afternoon tea and refreshments.

Academy Street Bed & Breakfast ✪
528 ACADEMY STREET, HAWLEY, PENNSYLVANIA 18428

Tel: **(717) 226-3430**	Double/sb: **$75**
Hosts: **Judith and Sheldon Lazan**	Single/sb: **$45**
Location: **100 mi. NW of New York City**	Open: **May–Oct.**
	Breakfast: **Full**
No. of Rooms: **7**	Credit Cards: **MC, VISA**
No. of Private Baths: **4**	Pets: **No**
Max. No. Sharing Bath: **3**	Children: **Welcome, over 14**
Double/pb: **$75**	Smoking: **Permitted**
Single/pb: **$40**	Social Drinking: **Permitted**

This Italian-style Victorian, circa 1865, is situated on a rise near the Lackawaxen River. Judith and Sheldon have done a marvelous job of restoring the rare and beautiful woodwork, paneling, and inlay to make a fitting background for their lovely antiques and furnishings. You'd better diet before you arrive because you won't be able to resist the culinary delights at breakfast or the complimentary high tea. It's only minutes away from famed Lake Wallenpaupack.

Morning Glories ✪
204 BELLEMONTE AVENUE, HAWLEY, PENNSYLVANIA 18428

Tel: **(717) 226-0644**	Double/sb: **$45**
Best Time to Call: **6 PM–10 PM**	Single/sb: **$45**
Hosts: **Becky and Roberta Holcomb**	Open: **All year**
Location: **35 mi. E of Scranton**	Reduced Rates: **Weekly**
No. of Rooms: **2**	Breakfast: **Full**
No. of Private Baths: **1**	Pets: **No**
Max. No. Sharing Bath: **4**	Children: **No**
Double/pb: **$50**	Smoking: **Permitted**
Single/pb: **$50**	Social Drinking: **Permitted**

From this B&B's location in the small town of Hawley, you can walk to the downtown shopping area, summer theater, and several fine restaurants. Your own transportation will allow you to enjoy the area's attractions, such as Lake Wallenpaupack, the Delaware River, train rides, canoeing, rafting, skiing, horseback riding, antiquing, hunting, and fishing. The house has a front porch and a deck in the rear for relaxation, and the living room makes a nice gathering place. The oak staircase leads to the guest rooms on the second floor.

Bonny Bank ✪
P.O. BOX 481, MILLRIFT, PENNSYLVANIA 18340

Tel: (717) 491-2250	Open: May 15–Sept. 15
Best Time to Call: 9 AM–9 PM	Reduced Rates: 10% weekly
Hosts: Doug and Linda Hay	Breakfast: Full
Location: 5 mi. from I-84	Pets: No
No. of Rooms: 1	Children: No
No. of Private Baths: 1	Smoking: No
Double/pb: $40	Social Drinking: Permitted
Single/pb: $30	

Stay in a picture-book small town on a dead-end road. The sound of the rapids will lull you to sleep in this charming bungalow perched on the banks of the Delaware River. Doug and Linda invite you to use their private swimming area and will lend you inner tubes for float trips. Nearby attractions include the Zane Grey house, Minisink Battlefield, Grey Towers Historical Site, the Victorian village of Milford, and all the sports and variety of restaurants the Poconos are known for.

Elvern Country Lodge ✪
RR 2, BOX 2099A, STONE CHURCH–FIVE POINTS ROAD, MOUNT BETHEL, PENNSYLVANIA 18343-9614

Tel: (610) 588-7922	Double/sb: $50
Best Time to Call: Before 11 PM	Single/sb: $30
Host: Doris Deen	Open: All year
Location: 16 mi. N of Easton; 7 mi. S of Delaware Water Gap	Reduced Rates: 10% seniors; weekly; former guests
No. of Rooms: 4	Breakfast: Full
No. of Private Baths: 2	Pets: No
Max. No. Sharing Bath: 4	Children: Welcome
Double/pb: $60	Smoking: Permitted downstairs only
Single/pb: $35	

Enjoy the country atmosphere of a working farm in the foothills of the Pocono Mountains. The house, which dates to the early 1800s, includes a shaded second-floor deck where guests can relax in the summer months. Your hostess's breakfasts typically include country bacon or sausage, fresh eggs, and a variety of homemade breads and jams. You are invited to visit the farm animals, stroll through the fruit orchards, and fish on the property's two-acre lake. In the autumn, visitors have the opportunity to watch apple cider being pressed. The

Delaware Water Gap Recreation Area, Appalachian Trail, and Pocono Recreation Area are a short drive away.

The Lampost Bed & Breakfast ○

HCR BOX 154, ROUTE 507, PAUPACK, PENNSYLVANIA 18451

Tel: **(717) 857-1738**	Single/sb: **$50**
Best Time to Call: **9 AM–6 PM**	Open: **Apr.–Oct.**
Hosts: **Lily, Karen, and David Seagaard**	Reduced Rates: **10% Mon.–Thurs.**
Location: **9 mi. S of Hawley**	Breakfast: **Continental**
No. of Rooms: **3**	Credit Cards: **MC, VISA**
No. of Private Baths: **2**	Pets: **Sometimes**
Max. No. Sharing Bath: **4**	Children: **Welcome, over 10**
Double/pb: **$70**	Smoking: **No**
Double/sb: **$60**	Social Drinking: **Permitted**

An assortment of lampposts line the driveway leading to this white Colonial home on two acres overlooking Lake Wallenpaupack. This is an ideal stopover for those who love waterfront activities—swimming, boating, fishing, and water skiing. If you'd rather stay high and dry, there are facilities for golfing, tennis, and horseback riding nearby. Other recreational options include scenic train excursions and balloon rides.

High Hollow

STAR ROUTE, BOX 9-A1, SOUTH STERLING, PENNSYLVANIA 18460

Tel: **(717) 676-4275**	Open: **All year**
Best Time to Call: **10 AM–10 PM**	Reduced Rates: **Available**
Hosts: **Tex and Robbie Taylor**	Breakfast: **Continental**
Location: **From I-80, 12 mi. N of**	Pets: **Sometimes**
Mount Pocono; from I-84, 5.4 mi.	Children: **Sometimes**
No. of Rooms: **1 Suite**	Smoking: **No**
No. of Private Baths: **1**	Social Drinking: **Permitted**
Suite: **$40–$67**	

This tranquil rustic home overlooks a pond and mountain stream. Walk into the guest suite by its separate entrance and inside you'll find a decorative fireplace, TV, kitchenette with refrigerator and microwave, and private bath. There are woodlands for strolling, with a BBQ grill and picnic tables, and a secluded streamside area where guests can relax to the sounds of rippling water. Lakes, state parks, nighttime entertainment, and fine dining are all nearby.

The Redwood House ○

BOX 9B, EAST SIDE BORO, WHITE HAVEN, PENNSYLVANIA 18661

Tel: **(717) 443-7186; (215) 355-1754**	No. of Private Baths: **2**
Hosts: **John and Emma Moore**	Max. No. Sharing Bath: **4**
No. of Rooms: **4**	Double/pb: **$35**

Single/pb: **$25**
Double/sb: **$30**
Single/sb: **$20**
Suites: **$60**
Open: **All year**
Reduced Rates: **5% seniors**

Breakfast: **Continental**
Pets: **No**
Children: **Welcome**
Smoking: **Permitted**
Social Drinking: **Permitted**

This frame chalet is minutes from the slopes at Big Boulder and Jack Frost. In summer enjoy sunning and swimming at Hickory Run State Park. Nearby Lehigh River offers fishing and rafting. Your hosts recommend a visit to Eckley, where the movie *The Molly Maguires* was filmed—a true example of what life was like in a 19th-century mining community. After a day of touring, come and relax on the large, comfortable porch.

SCRANTON/WILKES-BARRE/NORTHEASTERN/ NORTH CENTRAL PENNSYLVANIA

Irondale Inn Bed & Breakfast ✪
100 IRONDALE AVENUE, BLOOMSBURG, PENNSYLVANIA 17815

Tel: **(717) 784-1977**
Best Time to Call: **After 4 PM**
Host: **Linda Wink**
Location: **100 mi. S of New York City; 135 mi. N of Philadelphia**
No. of Rooms: **4**
Max. No. Sharing Bath: **4**
Double/sb: **$85**
Single/sb: **$65**
Open: **All year**

Breakfast: **Full**
Other Meals: **Available**
Pets: **No**
Children: **Welcome, over 10**
Smoking: **Permitted**
Social Drinking: **Permitted**
Minimum Stay: **2 nights special college weekends**
Airport/Station Pickup: **Yes**

Relax and let the world go by in Linda's charming home, built in 1838. Gracious extras include a sun porch for reading or watching TV, a billiard room with a regulation-size table, and two living rooms where you can sit around a hearth and enjoy a rousing fire and conversation. In each guest room, "terrific mattresses" and fine bedding ensure a restful night's sleep. The carefully groomed grounds offer leisurely strolls amid several gardens, while the covered patio beckons you to sit down with a cool drink at sunset. Within walking distance lie Bloomsburg University, unique shops, and fine restaurants. An added attraction is the annual Bloomsburg Fair, which runs during the last week of September.

Ponda-Rowland Bed & Breakfast Inn ✪
RR 1, BOX 349, DALLAS, PENNSYLVANIA 18612

Tel: **(717) 639-3245; (800) 854-3286**
Best Time to Call: **11 AM–10 PM**

Hosts: **Jeanette and Cliff Rowland**
Location: **7 mi. N of Wilkes-Barre**

No. of Rooms: 5
No. of Private Baths: 5
Double/pb: $55–$85
Single/sb: $55–$85
Open: All year
Reduced Rates: $15, after 3 days
Breakfast: Full

Credit Cards: AMEX, DISC, MC, VISA
Pets: Yes (outside)
Children: Welcome
Smoking: No
Social Drinking: Permitted
Airport Pickup: Yes

You'll have a memorable stay at this large scenic farm in the Endless Mountains region of northeast Pennsylvania. The farmhouse (circa 1850) features a big stone fireplace, beamed ceilings, and museum-quality antiques. Outside you'll see farm animals as well as the less domesticated kind—the property includes a private 34-acre wildlife refuge with six ponds and walking and skiing trails. Athletic types can go canoeing, swimming, ice skating and ice fishing, or play horseshoes, volleyball, and badminton. Over a full breakfast, your hosts can tell you about local horse rentals, air tours, state parks, hunting and trout fishing sites, restaurants, country fairs, and ski slopes. They now have horses and give free pony rides.

Harts' Content ✪
P.O. BOX 97, HUNTINGTON MILLS, PENNSYLVANIA 18622

Tel: (717) 864-2499
Best Time to Call: After 5 PM
Hosts: Kenneth and Gerry Hart
Location: 25 mi. SW of Wilkes-Barre
No. of Rooms: 3
No. of Private Baths: 3
Double/pb: $45–$50

Open: All year
Breakfast: Full
Pets: No
Children: Welcome
Smoking: No
Social Drinking: Permitted
Airport/Station Pickup: Yes

Harts' Content is nestled on twenty-seven wooded acres in the old 19th-century mill town of Huntington Mills. The area abounds in wildlife. Fish in the B&B's private pond or quietly wander through the woods to Huntington Mills Creek. Delight in a leisurely country breakfast with friendly conversation around an oak table. Nearby, enjoy golf, Rickett's Glen State Park, covered bridges, and antiquing. Gerry and Ken will gladly help you plan your stay.

Sommerville Farms ✪
R.R. 4, BOX 22, JERSEY SHORE, PENNSYLVANIA 17740

Tel: (717) 398-2368
Best Time to Call: Noon–11 PM
Hosts: Bill and Jane Willams
Location: 12 mi. W of Williamsport
No. of Rooms: 4
Max. No. Sharing Bath: 4
Double/sb: $45
Single/sb: $35
Open: Apr.–Dec.

Reduced Rates: Available
Breakfast: Continental
Credit Cards: MC, VISA
Pets: No
Children: Welcome, over 6
Smoking: No
Social Drinking: Permitted
Minimum Stay: Holidays and October

As part of a 200-acre working farm, this large white nineteenth-century farmhouse looks the way it's supposed to, from the gabled roof to the side porch. The living room fireplace has an imposing hand-rubbed cherry mantel, and hand-painted scenes decorate the ceiling. Jane, a former antiques dealer, has furnished the house in period style. This area draws hunters, fishermen, skiers, canoeists, and shoppers—Woolrich Woolen Mills Outlet Store is a notable attraction. You'll be ready for any activity after breakfasting on a variety of muffins, breads, and coffee cake.

The Carriage House at Stonegate ✪
RD 1, BOX 11A, MONTOURSVILLE, PENNSYLVANIA 17754

Tel: **(717) 433-4340**	Open: **All year**
Best Time to Call: **5:30–9:30 PM**	Breakfast: **Continental**
Hosts: **Harold and Dena Mesaris**	Pets: **Welcome**
Location: **6 mi. E of Williamsport**	Children: **Welcome**
No. of Rooms: **2**	Smoking: **Permitted**
No. of Private Baths: **1**	Social Drinking: **Permitted**
Guest Cottage: **$50 for 2; $70 for 4**	Airport/Station Pickup: **Yes**

This self-contained facility was converted from the original carriage house of an 1830 farmhouse. Perfect for a family, there are two bedrooms, a bathroom, a living room with cable television, a dining area, and a kitchen equipped with all your breakfast needs. Decorated in country fashion, with some antiques, it offers complete privacy just 30 yards from your hosts' home. You'll have access to a creek, a barn complete with a variety of animals, and 30 acres on which to roam. It's close to the Little League Museum and Loyalsock Creek for swimming, canoeing, tubing, and fishing.

The Bodine House ✪
307 SOUTH MAIN STREET, MUNCY, PENNSYLVANIA 17756

Tel: **(717) 546-8949**	Single/pb: **$50–$60**
Best Time to Call: **Evenings**	Open: **All year**
Hosts: **David and Marie Louise Smith**	Credit Cards: **AMEX, MC, VISA**
Location: **15 mi. S of Williamsport;**	Breakfast: **Full**
10 mi. from I-80, Exit 31B	Pets: **No**
No. of Rooms: **4**	Children: **Welcome, over 6**
No. of Private Baths: **4**	Smoking: **No**
Double/pb: **$60–$70**	Social Drinking: **Permitted**

This restored town house dates back to 1805. A baby grand piano, four fireplaces, and a candlelit living room add to its old-fashioned appeal. A full country breakfast and wine and cheese are on the house. Local attractions include the Susquehanna River, the Endless Mountains, and the fall foliage.

VALLEY FORGE AREA

Amsterdam Bed & Breakfast ✪
P.O. BOX 1139, VALLEY FORGE, PENNSYLVANIA 19482

Tel: **(800) 952-1580**	Open: **All year**
Best Time to Call: **Anytime**	Reduced Rates: **10%, Nov.–Jan. 10%**
Hosts: **Pamela and Ino Vandersteur**	**seniors**
Location: **5 mi. W of Valley Forge**	Breakfast: **Full**
No. of Rooms: **3**	Credit Cards: **MC, VISA**
No. of Private Baths: **1**	Pets: **No**
Max. No. Sharing Bath: **4**	Children: **No**
Double/pb: **$75**	Smoking: **No**
Single/pb: **$65**	Social Drinking: **Permitted**
Double/sb: **$65**	Foreign Languages: **Dutch, French,**
Single/sb: **$55**	**German**

Formerly a general store, as well as a stop on the Underground Railroad, this nineteenth-century building underwent extensive renovations before debuting as a guest house in 1989. Despite this very American background, Amsterdam B&B takes its name and its decor from the Netherlands, Ino's birthplace. Appropriately enough, the Vandersteurs draw a mixture of American and European visitors, which makes for stimulating discussions. If you can tear yourself away from conversation, there is much to explore here, such as the Audubon Wildlife Sanctuary, Valley Forge Historical Park, King of Prussia Mall, the Reading Outlets, and Adamstown Antique Markets. Amish country, Brandywine Valley, and Philadelphia all lie within a twenty-mile radius.

WESTERN PENNSYLVANIA

Weatherbury Farm
RR 1, BOX 250, AVELLA, PENNSYLVANIA 15312

Tel: **(412) 587-3763**	Breakfast: **Full**
Hosts: **Dale, Marcy, and Nigel Tudor**	Credit Cards: **MC, VISA**
Location: **20 mi. SW of Pittsburgh**	Pets: **No**
No. of Rooms: **2**	Children: **Welcome**
No. of Private Baths: **2**	Smoking: **No**
Double/pb: **$60**	Social Drinking: **Permitted**
Single/pb: **$55**	Airport Pickup: **Yes**
Open: **All year**	Foreign Languages: **German**

One hundred acres of meadows, gardens, fields, and valleys create a tranquil setting at the Tudors' B&B, the perfect getaway from everyday pressures. Guest rooms at this 1860s farmhouse have been lovingly furnished with an old-fashioned country charm. Awake to a bountiful farm breakfast which might include apple cinnamon pancakes, garden vegetable eggs, or creamy peach-filled French toast. Later, get acquainted with the chickens, sheep, and cattle. Opportunities for golf, fishing, boating, and antiquing abound. Or visit the historic nineteenth-century Meadowcroft Village, Starlake Amphitheater, or West Virginia attractions nearby.

Mountain View Bed and Breakfast and Antiques ✪
MOUNTAIN VIEW ROAD, DONEGAL, PENNSYLVANIA 15628

Tel: (412) 593-6349; (800) 392-7773	Open: All year
Hosts: Lesley and Jerry O'Leary	Breakfast: Full
Location: 1 mi. E of Pa. Tpke. Exit 9	Credit Cards: AMEX, DC, DISC, MC,
No. of Rooms: 6	VISA
No. of Private Baths: 3	Pets: No
Max. No. Sharing Bath: 4	Children: Welcome, over 10
Double/pb: $105–$135	Smoking: No
Double/sb: $75–$105	Social Drinking: Permitted

In a quiet pastoral setting in the heart of the Laurel Highlands, you can enjoy lodging and breakfast in a restored 1850s farmhouse and barn furnished with period American furniture. Mountain View is a Westmoreland County historic landmark which affords a magnificent view of the Laurel Ridge. This location is convenient to several mountain resorts, state parks, white-water rafting, and Frank Lloyd Wright's Fallingwater.

The Lamberton House ✪
1331 OTTER STREET, FRANKLIN, PENNSYLVANIA 16323-1530

Tel: (814) 432-7908	Max. No. Sharing Bath: 4
Hosts: Jack and Sally Clawson	Double/pb: $65
Location: 80 mi. N of Pittsburgh	Single/pb: $55
No. of Rooms: 6	Double/sb: $55
No. of Private Baths: 2	Single/sb: $40

Open: **All year**
Reduced Rates: **Available**
Breakfast: **Full**
Pets: **Sometimes**

Children: **Welcome**
Smoking: **Restricted**
Social Drinking: **Permitted**

Named for its original occupant, this Queen Anne Victorian was built in 1874 and is listed in the National Register of Historic Places. The rooms feature beautiful glass, original brass chandeliers, and woodwork of old-world craftsmanship. When they aren't exploring nearby recreational and historic sites, guests can relax in the drawing room, watch TV, play the piano, read in the library, swing on the front porch, or walk in the flower garden. A full country breakfast is served in the elegant dining room each morning.

Snow Goose Inn ✪
112 EAST MAIN STREET, GROVE CITY, PENNSYLVANIA 16127

Tel: **(412) 458-4644**
Best Time to Call: **10 AM–10 PM**
Hosts: **Orvil and Dorothy McMillen**
Location: **60 mi. N of Pittsburgh**
No. of Rooms: **4**
Max. No. Sharing Bath: **4**
Double/sb: **$55**
Single/sb: **$55**

Open: **All year**
Breakfast: **Full**
Credit Cards: **MC, VISA**
Pets: **Sometimes**
Children: **Welcome**
Smoking: **No**
Social Drinking: **Permitted**
Airport/Station Pickup: **Yes**

Formerly a country doctor's home and office, the Snow Goose Inn, built around 1895, has a large porch with an old-fashioned swing. Inside, you'll find tastefully furnished bedrooms with a cozy, warm atmosphere. Each morning, freshly brewed coffee and a complete breakfast, including homemade muffins and nut breads, await guests in the dining room. The inn is conveniently located across from Grove City College, next door to a restaurant, and two blocks from the business district. Orvil and Dorothy will be glad to direct you to all the local points of interest.

Neff House ✪
P.O. BOX 67, 552 MAIN STREET, HARMONY, PENNSYLVANIA 16037

Tel: **(412) 452-7512**
Host: **Sally Jones**
Location: **N of Pittsburgh**
No. of Rooms: **2**
No. of Private Baths: **2**
Double/pb: **$45–$50**
Single/pb: **$30–$35**
Open: **All year**

Reduced Rates: **Available**
Breakfast: **Full**
Pets: **No**
Children: **Welcome, under 1½ or over
12**
Smoking: **No**
Social Drinking: **Permitted**
Airport Pickup: **Yes**

You will find a cozy atmosphere in this 1808 home located in the national historic district of Harmony, founded as a religious commune in 1805. Museums, antique shops, and fine restaurants are within walking distance. For Amish country, state parks, universities, and the hustle and bustle of Pittsburgh, you will have only a thirty-minute drive. Upon your arrival, Sally, owner and restorer of Neff House, will greet you with cold drinks, wine, and cheese. Good weather may find you savoring her special breakfast on her garden patio.

Gillray Bed and Breakfast ✪
215 N. MAIN STREET, P.O. BOX 493, HARRISVILLE, PENNSYLVANIA 16038

Tel: **(412) 735-2274**	Open: **All year**
Best Time to Call: **Anytime**	Reduced Rates: **10% seniors, families; weekly**
Hosts: **Dick and Wendy Christner**	
Location: **5 mi. S of Exit 3 on I-80**	Breakfast: **Full**
No. of Rooms: **3**	Pets: **No**
No. of Private Baths: **3**	Children: **Welcome, over 4**
Double/pb: **$50**	Smoking: **Restricted**
Single/pb: **$40**	Social Drinking: **Permitted**

Old-fashioned hospitality is the hallmark of this restored mid-nineteenth-century home, which is furnished with antiques. The gracious decor is enhanced by the tall arched windows and the original staircase. You can relax with a book in the formal parlor or watch television in the Sherlockian Parlor. A tempting country breakfast is served by candlelight. Slippery Rock University and Grove City College are nearby.

Foursquare B&B ✪
250 SOUTH FIFTH STREET, INDIANA, PENNSYLVANIA 15701

Tel: **(412) 465-6412**	Open: **All year**
Best Time to Call: **After 5 PM**	Breakfast: **Full**
Hosts: **Mary Ann and Walt Ballard**	Credit Cards: **MC, VISA**
Location: **60 mi. NE of Pittsburgh**	Pets: **No**
No. of Rooms: **3**	Children: **Welcome**
Max. No. Sharing Bath: **4**	Smoking: **Restricted**
Double/sb: **$47**	Social Drinking: **Permitted**
Single/sb: **$37**	

Come stay at this buff brick American Foursquare house, built in the 1920s. Children will adore Sam, the resident collie, adults will admire Mary Ann's handmade quilts, and everyone will enjoy Walt's breakfast specialties. Indiana, the "Christmas Tree Capital of the World," is also Jimmy Stewart's birthplace and the home of Indiana University of Pennsylvania. Local attractions include an Amish community and a fine winery.

Eagle's Mere Gardens B&B ✪
1199 EAST LAKE ROAD, JAMESTOWN, PENNSYLVANIA 16134

Tel: **(412) 932-3572**
Best Time to Call: **8 AM–9 PM**
Hosts: **Richard and Doris Ostermeyer**
No. of Rooms: **1**
No. of Private Baths: **1**
Double/pb: **$45**
Single/pb: **$35**

Open: **Spring–Fall**
Reduced Rates: **10% seniors**
Breakfast: **Full**
Pets: **Sometimes**
Smoking: **No**
Social Drinking: **Permitted**

From the wraparound porch of this rustic home, you can look down on gardens, trees, and Pymatuning State Park Lake—the view is especially picturesque in autumn. Inside, the decor is primitive, with country motifs. Since the guest room is detached from the main house, you'll have complete privacy, but you can join your hosts for conversation and breakfast. Gardeners take note: both Dick and Doris love cultivating dahlias. For athletic sorts, fishing and nature trails are within walking distance, and five golf courses are nearby.

Beighley Flower Cottage ✪
515 WEST SIXTH STREET, OIL CITY, PENNSYLVANIA 16301

Tel: **(814) 677-3786**
Hosts: **Martha and Jack Beighley**
Location: **60 mi. S of Erie**
No. of Rooms: **2**
Max. No. Sharing Bath: **4**
Double/sb: **$45**
Open: **All year**
Reduced Rates: **Long stays; families
  with children**

Breakfast: **Full**
Pets: **No**
Children: **Welcome, over 10**
Smoking: **No**
Social Drinking: **Permitted**
Airport/Station Pickup: **Yes**

Welcome to Pennsylvania's oil country, where you can see some of the world's oldest producing oil wells. The Beighleys are avid gardeners, which accounts for the name of this B&B. For the best view of the flowers, your hosts will pour you a beverage and settle you on the back porch of their white ranch house. Full breakfasts are served in the country-style kitchen, with its exposed beams and hanging wicker baskets. While the menu varies, you can expect to sample homemade bran-raisin muffins and peach honey.

Blackberry Inn Bed & Breakfast
820 WEST MAIN STREET, SMETHPORT, PENNSYLVANIA 16749

Tel: **(814) 887-7777**
Hosts: **Marilyn and Arnie Bolin**
Location: **100 mi. E of Erie**
No. of Rooms: **5**

Max. No. Sharing Bath: **4**
Double/sb: **$45–$50**
Single/sb: **$40–$45**
Open: **All year**

Breakfast: **Full**   Smoking: **No**
Pets: **No**   Airport Pickup: **Yes**
Children: **Welcome**

Built in 1881 and completely restored in 1988–89, Blackberry Inn is a Victorian home set in a friendly little borough in the Allegheny Mountains. Marilyn and Arnie are retired professionals devoting all their time to providing warm hospitality to visitors. Nearby attractions include the Kinzua Bridge State Park, the Allegheny National Forest, America's First Christmas Store, and miles of country roads winding through forested mountains. Outdoor activities include hiking, fishing, biking, hunting, cross-country skiing, picnicking and swimming. Or relax in the guest parlor or on one of the large front porches. Breakfast is served at the time chosen by the guest.

H.B.'s Cottage ✪
231 WEST CHURCH STREET, SOMERSET, PENNSYLVANIA 15501

Tel: **(814) 443-1204**   Breakfast: **Full, Continental**
Best Time to Call: **Evenings**   Credit Cards: **MC, VISA**
Hosts: **Phyllis and Hank Vogt**   Pets: **Sometimes**
Location: **70 mi. E of Pittsburgh** Children: **No**
No. of Rooms: **1**   Smoking: **No**
No. of Private Baths: **1**   Social Drinking: **Permitted**
Double/pb: **$65**   Minimum Stay: **2 nights on holiday**
Single/pb: **$65**   **weekends**
Open: **All year**   Airport Pickup: **Yes**

H.B.'s Cottage, an exclusive and elegant B&B located within the Borough of Somerset, is a 1920s stone and frame house with an oversized fireplace in the living room. Pieces acquired in the Vogts' overseas travels—Hank is a retired naval officer—and teddy bears from Phyllis's extensive collection accent the traditional furnishings. The warm, romantic guest room has a private porch. Downhill and cross-country skiing, mountain biking, and tennis are the hosts' specialties. Fortunately for them, and their guests, H.B.'s Cottage is to 7 Springs Mountain Resort, Falling Water, Hidden Valley t, biking and hiking trails, and white water sports.

RHODE ISLAND

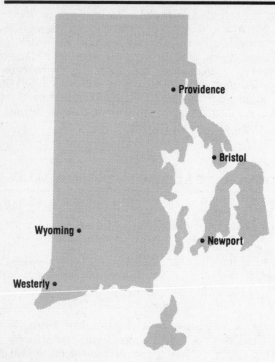

- • Providence
- • Bristol
- Wyoming •
- • Newport
- Westerly •

Rockwell House Inn ✪
610 HOPE STREET, BRISTOL, RHODE ISLAND 02809

Tel: **(401) 253-0040**
Hosts: **Debra and Steve Krohn**
Location: **15 mi. SE of Providence; 12 mi. NE of Newport**
No. of Rooms: **4**
No. of Private Baths: **4**
Double/pb: **$75–$95**
Open: **All year**
Reduced Rates: **Weekly; off-season, corporate**

Breakfast: **Continental, plus**
Credit Cards: **AMEX, MC, VISA**
Pets: **No**
Children: **Welcome, over 12**
Smoking: **No**
Social Drinking: **Permitted**
Minimum Stay: **Only major holi**
Foreign Languages: **Spanish**

This beautifully restored Federal-style home, built in 1809 and l
on the National Register of Historic Places, is located in the hea
Bristol's historic waterfront district, 20 minutes from Newport
within walking distance of museums and antique shops. Ro
feature fireplaces, king-size beds, and a casual elegance that

immediately put you at ease. Enjoy afternoon tea in the garden, read in one of the parlors, and meet new friends over evening sherry. Your hosts Steve and Debra will share their passion for wines, cooking, and entertaining.

William's Grant Inn ✪
154 HIGH STREET, BRISTOL, RHODE ISLAND 02809

Tel: **(401) 253-4222**
Best Time to Call: **8 AM–9 PM**
Hosts: **Mary and Michael Rose**
Location: **15 mi. SE of Providence**
No. of Rooms: **5**
No. of Private Baths: **3**
Max. No. Sharing Bath: **4**
Double/pb: **$65–$95**
Double/sb: **$55–$85**
Suites: **$85**
Open: **All year**

Reduced Rates: **Off-season**
Breakfast: **Full**
Credit Cards: **AMEX, DISC, DC, MC, VISA**
Pets: **No**
Children: **Welcome, over 12**
Smoking: **No**
Social Drinking: **Permitted**
Minimum Stay: **2 nights, holidays and graduation**

Just two blocks from Bristol's unspoiled harbor you'll find the sea captain's house that Deputy Governor William Bradford granted to his grandson in 1808. Mary and Mike restored and remodeled the five-bay Federal house, turning it into a gracious, beautifully appointed inn decorated with traditional and folk art. Breakfasts are always a treat, with home-baked goodies, granola, and perhaps Mike's huevos rancheros or Mary's pesto omelets. Each guest room has a firm queen-size bed, a comfortable chair to read in, and a fireplace. Within a 3-mile radius you'll find seven museums and a 30-mile bike/walking path. Your hosts are Mary, a full-time innkeeper and animal shelter

volunteer and Mike, an accountant and part-time innkeeper. They enjoy kayaking, exercise, gardening, and many other activities too numerous to mention.

The Melville House ✪
39 CLARKE STREET, NEWPORT, RHODE ISLAND 02840

Tel: **(401) 847-0640**
Hosts: **Vince DeRico and David Horan**
Location: **35 mi. from I-95, Exit 3**
No. of Rooms: **7**
No. of Private Baths: **5**
Max. No. Sharing Bath: **4**
Double/pb: **$55–$110**
Double/sb: **$50–$95**

Open: **Mar. 1–Jan. 1**
Breakfast: **Continental, plus**
Credit Cards: **AMEX, MC, VISA**
Pets: **No**
Children: **Welcome, over 12**
Smoking: **Permitted**
Social Drinking: **Permitted**
Minimum Stay: **2 nights weekends**

The Melville House is a 1750s shingled home set in Newport's historic Hill section. This quiet street is just one block from the Brick Market and wharfs, and around the corner from Touro Synagogue and Trinity Church. Vince and Dave welcome you to guest rooms decorated with oak furnishings, braided rugs, and lace curtains, with special touches such as fresh flowers and a bowl of fruit. Your hosts will start your day off with homemade muffins, granola and other home-baked items served at polished wood tables in the sunny breakfast room. When you want to relax, the country parlor with its collection of old grinders and gadgets and comfortable wing chairs awaits. Vince and Dave will be glad to provide sightseeing advice, and when the day is at a close, enjoy a 4 o'clock sherry at the house.

Cady House ○

127 POWER STREET, PROVIDENCE, RHODE ISLAND 02906

Tel: **(401) 273-5398**	Open: **All year**
Hosts: **Anna and Bill Colaiace**	Breakfast: **Continental**
Location: **1 mi. from Rte. I-95 E, Exit 2**	Other Meals: **Available**
No. of Rooms: **3**	Pets: **Sometimes**
No. of Private Baths: **3**	Children: **Welcome**
Double/pb: **$65**	Smoking: **No**
Single/pb: **$60**	Social Drinking: **Permitted**
Suites: **$75; sleeps 4**	Airport/Station Pickup: **Yes**

Cady House is a beautiful Classical Revival house (circa 1839) on College Hill, in the heart of the Brown University campus and within walking distance of the Rhode Island School of Design and Johnson and Wales University. The interior is decorated with antique furnishings, oriental carpets, and the owners' extensive collection of American and international folk art. A screened veranda overlooks a large landscaped garden and patio for warm weather relaxation. The hosts are health professionals, cooks, and musicians. They enjoy helping guests discover the attractions of Providence and Rhode Island.

Woody Hill B&B ○

149 SOUTH WOODY HILL ROAD, WESTERLY, RHODE ISLAND 02891

Tel: **(401) 322-0452**	Open: **All year**
Best Time to Call: **After 5 PM during school year**	Reduced Rates: **Off-season**
	Breakfast: **Full**
Host: **Ellen L. Madison**	Pets: **No**
Location: **¾ mi. from Rte. 1**	Children: **Welcome**
No. of Rooms: **3**	Smoking: **No**
No. of Private Baths: **3**	Social Drinking: **Permitted**
Double/pb: **$65–$85**	

This Colonial reproduction is set on a hilltop among informal gardens and fields. Antiques, wide-board floors, and handmade quilts create an Early American atmosphere. Your hostess may serve homemade jams, muffins, and fresh raspberries in the morning. She can direct you to Mystic Seaport, Block Island, and historic areas. Watch Hill and Westerly beaches are two miles away.

The Cookie Jar B&B ✪

64 KINGSTOWN ROAD, ROUTE 138, WYOMING, RHODE ISLAND 02898

Tel: **(401) 539-2680; (800) 767-4262**	Single/sb: **$54**
Best Time to Call: **After 5 PM**	Open: **All year**
Hosts: **Dick and Madelein Sohl**	Reduced Rates: **20% Nov. 15–Apr. 15,**
Location: **7/10 mi. off I-95, exit 3A**	**4th night 10%, 7th night free**
No. of Rooms: **3**	Breakfast: **Full**
No. of Private Baths: **1**	Pets: **No**
Max. No. Sharing Bath: **4**	Children: **Welcome**
Double/pb: **$65**	Smoking: **No**
Double/sb: **$60**	Social Drinking: **Permitted**

The heart of this house, the living room, was a blacksmith's shop built in 1732; the original ceiling, hand-hewn beams, and granite walls are still in use. Fittingly, Dick and Madelein have furnished their home with a mixture of antique, country, and contemporary pieces. You'll enjoy strolling around their property, which includes a barn, swimming pool, flower garden, and lots of fruit trees, berry bushes, and grapevines. Despite the rural setting, you'll have only a short drive to the University of Rhode Island, the beaches, and cities like Mystic and Providence. Golfing, horseback riding, bicycling, and waterfront sports are all close at hand.

SOUTH CAROLINA

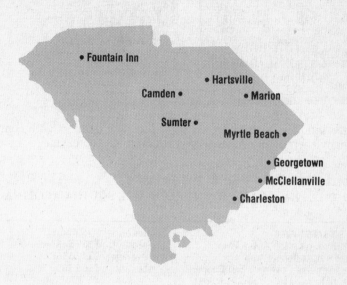

- Fountain Inn
- Hartsville
- Camden •
- Marion
- Sumter •
- Myrtle Beach •
- Georgetown
- McClellanville
- Charleston

The Carriage House ✪
1413 LYTTLETON STREET, CAMDEN, SOUTH CAROLINA 29020

Tel: **(803) 432-2430**
Best Time to Call: **9 AM–7 PM**
Hosts: **Appie and Bob Watkins**
Location: **30 mi. N of Columbia**
No. of Rooms: **2**
No. of Private Baths: **1½**
Double/pb: **$65**

Open: **All year**
Breakfast: **Full**
Pets: **No**
Children: **Welcome, over 6**
Smoking: **Permitted**
Social Drinking: **Permitted**

The Carriage House is an antebellum cottage with window boxes and a picket fence. Located in the center of historic Camden, it is within walking distance of tennis, parks, and shops. The guest rooms have twin or queen-size beds and are decorated with colorful fabrics and

lovely antiques. Visitors are welcomed to their quarters with complimentary sherry. Your hosts serve a Southern-style breakfast.

Charleston East Bed & Breakfast

1031 TALL PINE ROAD, MOUNT PLEASANT, SOUTH CAROLINA 29464

Tel: **(803) 884-8208**
Best Time to Call: **9 AM–6 PM**
Coordinator: **Bobbie Auld**
States/Regions Covered: **East Cooper, Isle of Palms, McClellanville, Mount Pleasant, Sullivans Island**

Rates (Single/Double):
Modest: **$20 / $40**
Average: **$35 / $50**
Luxury: **$50 / $80**

East Cooper is an historic area dating back to 1767. Fort Moultrie, on Sullivans Island, stands guard over quiet beaches. Bobbie's hosts are convenient to the historic district of Charleston and close to the sights that have made this city famous. The B&Bs range from quiet village homes near the harbor to modern suburban homes.

Historic Charleston Bed & Breakfast ✪

60 BROAD STREET, CHARLESTON, SOUTH CAROLINA 29401

Tel: **(803) 722-6606; (800) 743-3583**
Best Time to Call: **9:30 AM–6 PM Mon.–Fri.**
Coordinator: **Douglas B. Lee**
States/Regions Covered: **South Carolina**
Descriptive Directory: **Free**

Rates (Single/Double):
Modest: **$65 / $75**
Average: **$80 / $95**
Luxury: **$100 / $135**
Credit Cards: **AMEX, MC, VISA**
Minimum Stay: **2 nights Mar. 15–June 15, Oct.**

This port city is one of the most historic in the United States. Through the auspices of Douglas, you will enjoy your stay in a private home, carriage house, or mansion in a neighborhood of enchanting walled gardens, cobblestoned streets, and moss-draped oak trees. Each home is unique, yet each has a warm and friendly atmosphere provided by a host who sincerely enjoys making guests welcome. All are historic properties dating from 1720 to 1890, yet all are up to date with air-conditioning, phones, and television. Reduced rates may be available for weekly stays. There is a onetime $15 reservation fee charged with each reservation.

Ann Harper's Bed & Breakfast

56 SMITH STREET, CHARLESTON, SOUTH CAROLINA 29401

Tel: **(803) 723-3947**	Single/pb: **$55–$60**
Best Time to Call: **Before 10 AM; after 6 PM**	Open: **All year**
Host: **Ann D. Harper**	Breakfast: **Full**
Location: **1 mi. from I-26**	Pets: **No**
No. of Rooms: **2**	Children: **Welcome, over 10**
Max. No. Sharing Bath: **3**	Smoking: **Restricted**
Double/pb: **$65–$70**	Social Drinking: **Permitted**

This attractive home, circa 1870, is located in Charleston's historic district. The rooms, ideally suited for two friends traveling together, are decorated with wicker pieces and family treasures. Take a moment to relax on the porch or in the intimate walled garden out back. Ann serves a hot, Southern-style breakfast each morning featuring homemade bread and hominy grits. She will gladly direct you to the interesting sights of this historic area. There is a $5 surcharge for one-night stays; no single rates March 15 to June 15.

Country Victorian Bed and Breakfast ✪

105 TRADD STREET, CHARLESTON, SOUTH CAROLINA 29401

Tel: **(803) 577-0682**	Suites: **$100–$115**
Host: **Diane Deardurff Weed**	Open: **All year**
Location: **96 mi. S of Myrtle Beach**	Breakfast: **Continental**
No. of Rooms: **2**	Pets: **No**
No. of Private Baths: **2**	Children: **Welcome, over 8**
Double/pb: **$65–$85**	Smoking: **No**
Single/pb: **$65–$85**	Social Drinking: **Permitted**

As tourists pass in horse-drawn carriages, their eyes are drawn to the beautiful screen doors of this Victorianized house, built in 1820. Rooms have private entrances and are comfortably decorated with antique iron and brass beds, old quilts, and antique oak and wicker furniture. You'll find homemade cookies waiting for you when you arrive. Coffee and tea can be prepared in your room at any time, and snacks are served in the afternoon. Restaurants, churches, antique shops, museums, and art galleries are all within walking distance.

Johnson's Six Orange Street B&B
6 ORANGE STREET, CHARLESTON, SOUTH CAROLINA 29401

Tel: **(803) 722-6122**
Hosts: **Becky and Bill Johnson**
Location: **Located in historic district of Charleston**
No. of Rooms: **1**
No. of Private Baths: **1**
Apartment: **$90**
Open: **All year**

Breakfast: **Continental**
Credit Cards: **No**
Pets: **No**
Children: **Welcome (crib)**
Smoking: **No**
Social Drinking: **Permitted**
Foreign Languages: **French, German**

Within Charleston's historical district, Becky and Bill maintain an attached guest house complete with sitting room, efficiency kitchen, upstairs bedroom, and private bath and entrance. The bedroom sleeps three and features an antique sleigh bed plus an iron and brass single bed. A crib is also available for families with an infant. Enjoy scrumptious home-baked coffee cakes, pastries, and breads before you explore the numerous sights and attractions this city has to offer.

Hollydale Farm Bed & Breakfast
1603 FAIRVIEW ROAD, FOUNTAIN INN, SOUTH CAROLINA 29644

Tel: **(803) 862-4077**
Host: **Byrd Hammett**
Location: **16 mi. S of Greenville**

No. of Rooms: **4**
No. of Private Baths: **2**
Max. No. Sharing Bath: **4**

Double/pb: **$60**
Single/pb: **$45**
Double/sb: **$50**
Single/sb: **$35**
Open: **All year**

Breakfast: **Continental**
Pets: **No**
Children: **Welcome, over 10**
Smoking: **No**
Social Drinking: **Permitted**

Hollydale Farm House, built in 1887, is a classic example of early Victorian architecture, with a tin roof, wraparound porch, and stained glass windows. The holly tree in front is reported to be the largest in the state. In the back, you can relax on the porch overlooking pastures, fruit trees, and berry bushes on the surrounding forty-two acres. All bedrooms are furnished with antiques. Tea or coffee is available in your room, and you can request a picnic lunch to take on the day's adventures, whether you're hitting mountain trails or shopping malls. Your hostess, a retired retail buyer and pet shop owner, now owns a gift-furniture consignment shop.

1790 House ✪

630 HIGHMARKET STREET, GEORGETOWN, SOUTH CAROLINA 29440

Tel: **(803) 546-4821**
Best Time to Call: **9 AM–6 PM**
Hosts: **Patricia and John Wiley**
Location: **60 mi. N of Charleston**
No. of Rooms: **6**
No. of Private Baths: **6**
Double/pb: **$70–$80**
Guest Cottage: **$115**
Suites: **$95**
Open: **All year**

Reduced Rates: **Nov.–Feb. $10 less Sun.–Thurs., 10% seniors**
Breakfast: **Full**
Credit Cards: **AMEX, MC, VISA**
Pets: **No**
Children: **Welcome, over 12**
Smoking: **No**
Social Drinking: **Permitted**
Minimum Stay: **Holiday weekends**

This meticulously restored, 200-year-old Colonial plantation-style inn in Georgetown's historic district has spacious, luxurious rooms, 11-foot ceilings, and seven fireplaces. Slaves once slept in the Slave Quarters, while the elegant Rice Planters and Indigo Rooms have four-poster beds, sitting areas, and fireplaces. Your other options include the Prince George Suite, a hideaway under the eaves; Gabriella's Library, with built-in bookcases and a fireplace; and the Dependency Cottage, with its private entrance, patio, and spacious bath with a Jacuzzi. Whichever you pick, you can walk to shops, restaurants, and historic sites. Or take a short drive to Myrtle Beach, golfing at the Grand Strand, the Brookgreen Gardens, Pawleys Island, and downtown Charleston.

Shaw House ✪

613 CYPRESS COURT, GEORGETOWN, SOUTH CAROLINA 29440

Tel: **(803) 546-9663**
Best Time to Call: **Anytime**
Host: **Mary Shaw**

Location: **1 block off Hwy. 17**
No. of Rooms: **3**
No. of Private Baths: **3**

Double/pb: **$45–$55**	Pets: **No**
Single/pb: **$45**	Children: **Welcome**
Open: **All year**	Smoking: **Permitted**
Reduced Rates: **10% after 4th night**	Social Drinking: **Permitted**
Breakfast: **Full**	Airport/Station Pickup: **Yes**

Shaw House is a two-story Colonial with a beautiful view of the Willowbank Marsh. Your host is knowledgeable about antiques and has filled the rooms with them. The rocking chairs and cool breeze will tempt you to the porch. Each morning a pot of coffee and Southern-style casserole await you. Fresh fruit and homemade snacks are available all day. The house is within walking distance of the historic district and is near Myrtle Beach, Pawleys Island, golf, tennis, and restaurants.

Missouri Inn B&B ○

314 EAST HOME AVENUE, HARTSVILLE, SOUTH CAROLINA 29550

Tel: **(803) 383-9553**	Open: **All year**
Best Time to Call: **Noon–9 PM**	Reduced Rates: **Corporate**
Hosts: **Kyle and Kenny Segars, and**	Breakfast: **Full**
Lucy Brown	Credit Cards: **AMEX, MC, VISA**
Location: **28 mi. NW of Florence**	Pets: **No**
No. of Rooms: **5**	Children: **No**
No. of Private Baths: **5**	Smoking: **Permitted**
Double/pb: **$85**	Social Drinking: **Permitted**
Single/pb: **$75**	

An elegant Southern mansion built around the turn of the century and completely renovated in 1990, the Missouri Inn offers discriminating guests exceptional peace, quiet, and privacy in a small, luxurious setting. Located in Hartsville's official historic district, the inn stands opposite the lovely Coker College campus, on about five acres landscaped with stately trees and flowering shrubs. The distinctively furnished rooms not only have telephones and TVs, but terry robes, bath sheets, towel warmers, hair dryers, and fresh floral arrangements. Amenities include afternoon tea and complimentary beverages at all times.

Ambiance Bed & Breakfast

8 WREN DRIVE, HILTON HEAD, SOUTH CAROLINA 29928

Tel: **(803) 671-4981**	Single/pb: **$70**
Best Time to Call: **Anytime**	Open: **All year**
Host: **Marny Kridel Daubenspeck**	Breakfast: **Continental**
Location: **40 mi. from I-95, Exit 28**	Pets: **No**
No. of Rooms: **2**	Children: **Welcome, over 12**
No. of Private Baths: **2**	Smoking: **No**
Double/pb: **$75**	Social Drinking: **Permitted**

This contemporary cypress home is nestled in subtropical surroundings within Sea Pines Plantation. Ambiance reflects the hostess's interior decorating business of the same name. The climate is favorable year-round for outdoor sports. To get to a beautiful Atlantic Ocean beach, just walk across the street.

Montgomery's Grove ✪
408 HARLEE STREET, MARION, SOUTH CAROLINA 29571

Tel: **(803) 423-5220**
Hosts: **Coreen and Rick Roberts**
Location: **20 mi. E of Florence**
No. of Rooms: **4**
No. of Private Baths: **2**
Max. No. Sharing Bath: **4**
Double/pb: **$70**
Single/pb: **$60**
Double/sb: **$70**
Single/sb: **$60**

Open: **All year**
Reduced Rates: **10% weekly; 10% seniors**
Breakfast: **Full**
Other Meals: **Available**
Pets: **No**
Children: **Welcome**
Smoking: **No**
Social Drinking: **Permitted**

Nestled among five acres of century-old trees and gardens, Montgomery's Grove is a beautiful Victorian mansion known for its exceptional architectural features. Dramatic fourteen-foot archways and elaborate woodwork greet all guests. Yet it is easy to relax in the five beautifully decorated rooms, on the wraparound porches, or with a stroll through the woods. Walk beneath the Spanish moss to historic downtown Marion, or travel just thirty minutes to Myrtle Beach. Only 15 minutes from I-95, Montgomery's Grove is the perfect midway stopping point to and from Florida. Visit Marion, the pretty little town on the way to the beach. It'll be a visit you won't forget.

Laurel Hill Plantation ❂

8913 NORTH HIGHWAY 17, P.O. BOX 190, McCLELLANVILLE, SOUTH CAROLINA 29458

Tel: **(803) 887-3708**	Single/pb: **$65**
Best Time to Call: **Before 9 PM**	Open: **All year**
Hosts: **Jackie and Lee Morrison**	Breakfast: **Full**
Location: **30 mi. N of Charleston**	Pets: **No**
No. of Rooms: **4**	Children: **Welcome, over 6**
No. of Private Baths: **4**	Smoking: **No**
Double/pb: **$75**	Social Drinking: **Permitted**

The original Laurel Hill, an 1850s plantation house listed on the National Register of Historic Places, was destroyed by Hurricane Hugo in 1989. Nestled in a nook by a picturesque tidal creek, the spacious reconstruction retains the romance of the past while affording the convenience of the contemporary. Wraparound porches provide a sweeping panorama of the Atlantic Ocean and Cape Romain's salt marches, islands, and waterways. Four charming guest rooms feature fascinating views of the landscape and are furnished with carefully chosen primitives and antiques reflecting the renowned hospitality of South Carolina's low country.

Brustman House

400 25TH AVENUE SOUTH, MYRTLE BEACH, SOUTH CAROLINA 29577

Tel: **(803) 448-7699**	Open: **All year**
Best Time to Call: **11 AM–8 PM**	Reduced Rates: **Extended stay; Oct.**
Host: **Dr. Wendell C. Brustman**	**1–Mar. 31**
Location: **90 mi. N of Charleston**	Breakfast: **Full**
No. of Rooms: **4**	Pets: **No**
No. of Private Baths: **4**	Children: **Welcome, over 10**
Double/pb: **$55–$75**	Smoking: **No**
Single/pb: **$50–$70**	Social Drinking: **Permitted**
Suites: **$80–$95**	Airport/Station Pickup: **Yes**

Maybe you can't have it all, but Brustman House comes close. This Georgian-style home is two short blocks from the beach, and without leaving the one-acre property, you can play badminton or croquet, admire the rose garden, or follow the pine-straw path to the woods behind the house. Golf courses, seafront restaurants, discount shopping, and the Pavilion amusement complex are close at hand, and Brookgreen Gardens and the Carolina Opry are also nearby. Afternoon tea includes wines, waters, and sweets served on exquisite

Scandinavian dinnerware. Sleep late in your quiet room, its snug bed warmed by a down or Laura Ashley comforter; breakfast can be served at almost any morning hour, and the menu includes healthful specialties, such as ten-grain buttermilk pancakes.

Serendipity, An Inn ✪
407 71ST AVENUE NORTH, MYRTLE BEACH, SOUTH CAROLINA 29577

Tel: **(803) 449-5268**	Open: **All year**
Best Time to Call: **8 AM–10 PM**	Breakfast: **Continental**
Hosts: **Cos and Ellen Ficarra**	Credit Cards: **AMEX, MC, VISA**
Location: **60 mi. from Rte. 95**	Pets: **No**
No. of Rooms: **15**	Children: **Welcome**
No. of Private Baths: **15**	Smoking: **Permitted**
Double/pb: **$67–$80**	Social Drinking: **Permitted**
Suites: **$70–$92**	Foreign Languages: **Italian, Spanish**

Serendipity is a Spanish Mission-style inn surrounded by lush tropical plants and flowers. The setting is peaceful, the street is quiet, and the ocean is less than 300 yards away. Bedrooms are highlighted with antiques drawing from Art Deco, Oriental, wicker, and pine motifs. The Garden Room is the place for a generous breakfast of homemade breads, fresh fruit, eggs, and cereal. Guests also gather here for afternoon drinks and conversation. Your hosts invite you to use the heated pool and spa, play shuffleboard, Ping-Pong, or just share a quiet moment beside the patio fountain. Myrtle Beach is known for its fine restaurants, but the Ficarras have a gas grill if you want to do your own cooking. Cos and Ellen will gladly direct you to nearby shops, fishing villages, golf courses, miles of beaches, and music theaters.

The Bed & Breakfast of Sumter ✪
6 PARK AVENUE, SUMTER, SOUTH CAROLINA 29150

Tel: **(803) 773-2903**	Reduced Rates: **10% for 3 nights or**
Best Time to Call: **10 AM–9 PM**	**longer**
Hosts: **Suzanne and Jess Begley**	Breakfast: **Full**
Location: **40 mi. E of Columbia**	Credit Cards: **MC, VISA**
No. of Rooms: **5**	Pets: **No**
No. of Private Baths: **5**	Children: **Welcome, over 12**
Double/pb: **$60–$65**	Smoking: **No**
Single/pb: **$50**	Social Drinking: **Permitted**
Open: **All year**	

A charming, traditional Southern home built in 1896, this B&B is located in Sumter's historic district, facing a lush, quiet park. Enjoy the large front porch, with its swing and rocking chairs, or head indoors to read in the Victorian parlor and watch TV in the upstairs sitting room. (HBO is available, as is fax service.) Guest rooms are decorated with antiques; some have fireplaces. A gourmet breakfast awaits you in the morning, with home-baked breads and muffins and entrees like Eggs Benedict, Belgian waffles, and artichoke soufflé. You won't have to travel far to find tennis courts, antique shops, fifteen golf courses, and Swan Lake and Gardens. Suzanne and Jess, who left the corporate world to become full-time innkeepers, look forward to sharing Sumter's many pleasures.

For key to listings, see inside front or back cover.

❍ This star means that rates are guaranteed through December 31, 1995, to any guest making a reservation as a result of reading about the B&B in *Bed & Breakfast U.S.A.—1995* edition.

Important! To avoid misunderstandings, always ask about cancellation policies when booking.

Please enclose a self-addressed, stamped, business-size envelope when contacting reservation services.

For more details on what you can expect in a B&B, see Chapter 1.

Always mention *Bed & Breakfast U.S.A.* when making reservations!

If no B&B is listed in the area you'll be visiting, use the form on page 743 to order a copy of our "List of New B&Bs."

We want to hear from you! Use the form on page 745.

SOUTH DAKOTA

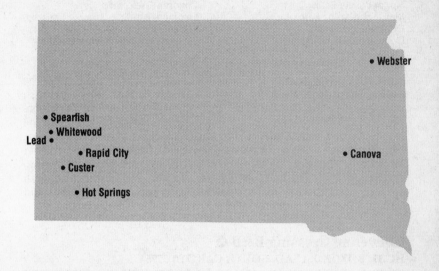

• Webster

• Spearfish
• Whitewood
Lead •
• Rapid City
• Custer

• Hot Springs

• Canova

Skoglund Farm ✪
CANOVA, SOUTH DAKOTA 57321

Tel: **(605) 247-3445**
Best Time to Call: **Early mornings;
  evenings**
Hosts: **Alden and Delores Skoglund**
Location: **12 miles from I-90**
No. of Rooms: **5**
Max. No. Sharing Bath: **3**
Double/sb: **$50**
Single/sb: **$30**

Open: **All year**
Reduced Rates: **Under 18**
Breakfast: **Full**
Other Meals: **Dinner included**
Pets: **Welcome**
Children: **Welcome (crib)**
Smoking: **Permitted**
Social Drinking: **Permitted**
Airport/Station Pickup: **Yes**

This is a working farm where the emphasis is on the simple, good life. It is a welcome escape from urban living. You may, if you wish, help with the farm chores, or just watch everyone else work; the family raises cattle, fowl, and peacocks. You are welcome to use the laundry facilities or play the piano. The coffeepot is always on.

Custer Mansion Bed & Breakfast ○
35 CENTENNIAL DRIVE, CUSTER, SOUTH DAKOTA 57730

Tel: (605) 673-3333
Hosts: Millard and Carole Seaman
Location: 42 mi. W of Rapid City
No. of Rooms: 6
No. of Private Baths: 2
Max. No. Sharing Bath: 4
Double/pb: $60–$75
Double/sb: $47.50–$60
Open: All year

Reduced Rates: Off-season, extended stays
Breakfast: Full
Pets: No
Children: Welcome
Smoking: No
Social Drinking: No
Foreign Languages: Spanish

Soon after it was built in 1891, this Victorian Gothic house became the center of many community activities. Today, antique light fixtures, ceiling fans, and the transoms and stained glass above the doors preserve the turn-of-the-century mood. There is a guest lounge in the front parlor, a tree-shaded patio, and a spacious yard. Located near Mt. Rushmore, Crazy Horse, Custer State Park, and many other attractions, the area offers swimming, fishing, hiking, golf, biking, and skiing. Mill, a retired school administrator, and Carole, mother of six and grandmother of ten, specialize in friendly hospitality and delicious home-cooked breakfasts.

Cheyenne Crossing B&B ○
HC 37, BOX 1220, LEAD, SOUTH DAKOTA 57754

Tel: (605) 584-3510, 584-2636
Hosts: Jim and Bonnie LeMar
Location: Junction Hwys. 85 and 14A
No. of Rooms: 3
Max. No. Sharing Bath: 4
Double /pb: $85
Double/sb: $69
Single/sb: $59
Open: All year

Reduced Rates: Families; groups
Breakfast: Full
Other Meals: Available
Credit Cards: DISC, MC, VISA
Pets: No
Children: Welcome, over 6
Smoking: No
Social Drinking: Permitted

This two-story frame building with its facade of rough-sawed pine is situated in the heart of Spearfish Canyon. The main floor houses a typical country general store and café; the guest quarters are upstairs. From 1876 to 1885 the original building was a stop for the Deadwood–Cheyenne stagecoach. After it burned down in 1960, the present building was built to replace it. Jim and Bonnie will be delighted to map out special trips tailored to your interests. Spend the day visiting Mt. Rushmore and Crazy Horse Monument, pan for gold, hike, or fish for trout on Spearfish Creek, which flows behind the store. It's also close to the Black Hills Passion Play. Sourdough pancakes are a frequent breakfast treat.

Abend Haus Cottage & Audrie's Cranbury Corner Bed & Breakfast ✪

23029 THUNDERHEAD FALLS ROAD, RAPID CITY, SOUTH DAKOTA 57702-8524

Tel: **(605) 342-7788**
Best Time to Call: **9 AM–9 PM MST**
Hosts: **Hank and Audrie Kuhnhauser**
Location: **¼ mi. from Hwy. 44**
No. of Rooms: **6**
No. of Private Baths: **6**
Double/pb: **$85**
Guest Cottage: **$85–$125**

Suites: **$85**
Open: **All year**
Breakfast: **Full**
Pets: **No**
Children: **No**
Smoking: **No**
Social Drinking: **Permitted**

At this country home and five-acre estate in a secluded Black Hills setting just 30 miles from Mt. Rushmore and 7 miles from Rapid City, you can experience charm and old-world hospitality. There are free trout fishing, biking, and hiking on the property, which is surrounded by thousands of acres of national forest land. Each room, suite, and cottage has a private entrance, bath, hot tub, patio, cable TV, and refrigerator. Full breakfasts are served.

Cliff Creek Bed & Breakfast ✪

R.R. 8, BOX 975, RAPID CITY, SOUTH DAKOTA 57702

Tel: **(605) 399-9970**
Hosts: **Dave and Judy Knecht**
Location: **10 mi. W of Rapid City**
No. of Rooms: **3**
No. of Private Baths: **2**
Max. No. Sharing Bath: **2**
Double/pb: **$85**
Guest Cottage: **$85; sleeps 4**

Suite: **$85**
Open: **All year**
Breakfast: **Continental**
Pets: **No**
Children: **No**
Smoking: **No**
Social Drinking: **Permitted**
Minimum Stay: **2 nights, in cottage**

Experience country pleasures in a spectacular setting: this B&B is located on Rapid Creek, below a slate cliff that crosses the stream. Spend the day watching as bald eagles soar overhead, deer graze in the meadow, ducks splash in the water, and wild birds dine at the feeders. Fish from your hosts' barbecue-equipped deck or practice your putting stroke on their green. From this Black Hills location, Mt. Rushmore, Deadwood, and Pactola Lake are easily accessible, and recreational options include hiking, biking, hunting, boating, golfing, skiing, and gambling. The main house offers two accommodations. The guest room has a balcony overlooking the stream, a queen-size

bed, and cable TV; the suite has a king-size bed and two twin beds.
There is also a separate guest cottage.

Bed and Breakfast Domivara ✪
2760 DOMIVARA ROAD, RAPID CITY, SOUTH DAKOTA 57702-6008

Tel: **(605) 574-4207**
Best Time to Call: **Mornings; 6–8 PM**
Host: **Betty Blount**
Location: **26 mi. SW of Rapid City**
No. of Rooms: **3**
No. of Private Baths: **3**
Double/pb: **$70–$75**
Single/pb: **$60–$65**

Open: **All year**
Breakfast: **Full**
Pets: **Sometimes**
Children: **Welcome**
Smoking: **Permitted**
Social Drinking: **Permitted**
Minimum Stay: **2 nights**

Enjoy Western hospitality in a unique log home located in the picturesque Black Hills of South Dakota. The homey wood interior is
decorated with comfortable antiques and accents of stained glass. A
large picture window overlooks the countryside where you may see
an occasional wild turkey or deer. Betty Blount offers complimentary
snacks served with wine or coffee. She prepares a variety of special
breakfast dishes including sourdough pancakes, egg soufflés, fresh
trout, and homemade blueberry muffins. There are good restaurants
nearby, or if you prefer home cooking, your host will be glad to

prepare dinner for you. Domivara is conveniently located just 20 minutes from Mt. Rushmore and the Crazy Horse memorial.

Eighth Street Inn ✪
735 EIGHTH STREET, SPEARFISH, SOUTH DAKOTA 57783

Tel: **(605) 642-9812; (800) 642-9812**	Reduced Rates: **Available**
Hosts: **Sandy Snyder and Brad Young**	Breakfast: **Full**
Location: **44 mi. W of Rapid City**	Other Meals: **Available**
No. of Rooms: **4**	Credit Cards: **MC, VISA**
No. of Private Baths: **2**	Pets: **Sometimes**
Max. No. Sharing Bath: **4**	Children: **Welcome**
Double/pb: **$45–$70**	Smoking: **No**
Double/sb: **$35–$55**	Social Drinking: **Permitted**
Open: **All year**	Airport/Station Pickup: **Yes**

A Queen Anne–style home (circa 1900) listed on the National Register of Historic Places, the inn is filled with family heirlooms that possess character as well as beauty. Each guest room has special features like bay windows, brass beds, and cozy comforters. The original fir woodwork and open staircase are rare finds. From the B&B's location three blocks from downtown, guests can enjoy shopping, fine dining, antique shops, parks, and the historic fish hatchery. Athletic types can go hiking, nordic and alpine skiing, and snowmobiling. Movie fans will want to visit nearby Spearfish Canyon, site of the winter scene in *Dances with Wolves*. As avid hikers, cyclists and skiers, Sandy and Brad are eager to help guests plan outdoor adventures. Moreover, Sandy promises to prepare a healthful and mouthwatering breakfast to suit any appetite.

Lakeside Farm ✪
RR 2, BOX 52, WEBSTER, SOUTH DAKOTA 57274

Tel: **(605) 486-4430**	Single/sb: **$30**
Hosts: **Joy and Glenn Hagen**	Open: **All year**
Location: **60 mi. E of Aberdeen on**	Breakfast: **Full**
Hwy. 12	Pets: **No**
No. of Rooms: **2**	Children: **Welcome**
Maximum No. Sharing Bath: **4**	Smoking: **No**
Double/sb: **$40**	Social Drinking: **No**

This 750-acre farm where Joy and Glenn raise oats, and corn, is located in the Lake Region where recreational activities abound. You are certain to be comfortable in their farmhouse, built in 1970 and furnished in a simple, informal style. You will awaken to the delicious aroma of Joy's heavenly cinnamon rolls or bread and enjoy breakfast served on the enclosed porch. Nearby attractions include Fort Sisseton and the June festival that recounts Sam Brown's historic ride. You will also enjoy the Blue Dog fish hatchery, and the Game Reserve. Dakotah, Inc., manufacturers of linens and wall hangings, is located in Webster. They have an outlet shop where great buys may be found.

Rockinghorse Bed & Breakfast ✪
RR 1, BOX 133, WHITEWOOD, SOUTH DAKOTA 57793

Tel: **(605) 269-2625**	Double/sb: **$50**
Hosts: **Jerry and Sharleen Bergum**	Single/sb: **$45**
Location: **35 mi. N of Rapid City**	Open: **All year**
No. of Rooms: **3**	Reduced Rates: **10% seniors, families**
No. of Private Baths: **1**	Breakfast: **Full**
Max. No. Sharing Bath: **4**	Pets: **Sometimes**
Double/pb: **$55**	Children: **Welcome**
Single/pb: **$50**	Smoking: **No**

A cedar clapboard–sided house, built in 1914 to accommodate local timber teams, Rockinghorse was moved one and a half miles from its first site by Jerry and Sharleen, who have lovingly restored much of the interior. Handsome wood floors, columns, and trims grace the living and dining areas, and the original stairway is still usable. This B&B is situated at the base of the rustic Black Hills; deer graze in nearby fields and wild turkeys strut across the valley below the house. Domestic animals abound, too: after a rooster's crow awakens you, you may pet a bunny in your hosts' petting zoo or visit their horses.

TENNESSEE

Goodlettsville •
Rugby •
Fairview •   Johnson City
Limestone •   • •
• • Chuckey
Arrington • Nashville
• • Murfreesboro
Hampshire •
McMinnville •
Dandridge • Greeneville
Knoxville • •
Loudon
• Kodak
• Sevierville
• Gatlinburg
• Memphis
• Savannah
Pikeville •
Chattanooga •   • Cleveland

Bed & Breakfast—About Tennessee
P.O. BOX 110227, NASHVILLE, TENNESSEE 37222-0227

Tel: **(615) 331-5244 for information;**
fax: **(615) 833-7701; (800) 458-2421**
for reservations
Coordinator: **Fredda Odom**
States/Regions Covered: **Statewide**

Rates (Single/Double):
Average: **$40–$50 / $65**
Luxury: **$80–$100 / $80–$150**
Credit Cards: **AMEX, DISC, MC, VISA**
Descriptive Directory: **$5**

From the Great Smoky Mountains to the Mississippi, here is a diversity of attractions that includes fabulous scenery, Tennessee's Grand Ole Opry and Opryland, universities, Civil War sites, horse farms, and much more. Fredda will arrange sightseeing tours, car rentals, tickets to events, and everything she can to assure you a pleasant stay. There is a $5 booking fee.

Xanadu Farm ○
8155 HORTON HIGHWAY, ARRINGTON, TENNESSEE 37014

Tel: **(615) 395-4771; 395-4040**
Best Time to Call: **8 AM–7 PM**
Hosts: **Susan L. Freeman and Lisa Smith**
Location: **35 mi. SE of Nashville**
Guest Cottage: **$75 for 2; $7.50 each**
additional person; sleeps 6

Open: **All year**
Breakfast: **Continental**
Pets: **Yes**
Children: **Welcome**
Smoking: **No**
Social Drinking: **Permitted**

This cowboy cottage, located on 130 acres of rolling Tennessee hills, has a full-service kitchen, laundry facilities, master bedroom and bath, queen-size sleeper sofa, and an upstairs loft containing two twin beds. A Continental breakfast is provided, or you may feel free to cook up your own. This is the perfect place to vacation with your equine friend, thanks to the miles of trails and comfortable stalls. And there's a stocked, one and a half acre pond for fishing. In Nashville, only a forty-minute drive, visit Opryland, Music Row, or take a ride on the General Jackson Showboat. You'll be sure to enjoy this beautiful environment.

Forrest Ridge B&B ✪

207 FORREST AVENUE, ATHENS, TENNESSEE 37303

Tel: **(615) 744-9918**	Single/sb: **$30**
Best Time to Call: **9 AM–6 PM**	Open: **Apr. 30–Dec. 31**
Hosts: **Willy Halder and Mildred Hardison**	Reduced Rates: **5% seniors; 10% families; July and Aug.**
Location: **57 mi. E of Chattanooga**	Breakfast: **Full, Continental**
No. of Rooms: **4**	Credit Cards: **MC, VISA**
No. of Private Baths: **2**	Pets: **Sometimes**
Max. No. Sharing Bath: **4**	Children: **Welcome, over 12**
Double/pb: **$35**	Smoking: **No**
Single/pb: **$32.50**	Social Drinking: **Permitted**
Double/sb: **$32.50**	Minimum Stay: **2 nights, weekends**

Athens, tucked into the lovely Sweetwater Valley, lies halfway between Knoxville and Chattanooga. It's 30 miles from the Appalachian Trail, and less than an hour's drive from attractions like Gatlinburg, Pigeon Forge, Dollywood, the Appalachian Museum, and numerous Civil War sites. Great Smokies National Park and the Cherokee Indian Reservation Park are also within easy reach. Athens itself boasts fine old homes, farmers markets, and flea markets. Mildred traveled extensively as a short-term missionary; today she writes fiction and recreates her blue-ribbon recipes for her guests. Her son William is an expert in organic gardening, specializing in plants native to the area.

Captain's Quarters B&B Inn ✪

P.O. BOX 71713, CHATTANOOGA, TENNESSEE 37407

Tel: **(706) 858-0624**	Reduced Rates: **10% Seniors**
Hosts: **Ann Gilbert and Pam Humphrey**	Breakfast: **Full**
Location: **5 mi. S of Chattanooga**	Credit Cards: **AMEX, MC, VISA**
No. of Rooms: **6**	Pets: **No**
No. of Private Baths: **6**	Children: **By arrangement**
Double/pb: **$60–$85**	Smoking: **No**
Open: **All year**	Social Drinking: **No**

This grand home, with its twin porches and winding staircase, was originally built for two army officers and their families when Fort Oglethorpe was regarded as one of the army's most elite posts. Ann and Pam have transformed and restored it to a vision that could easily grace the pages of any magazine. All rooms have color TV and a private bath. Breakfast is served in the large dining room, where one can imagine officers and their ladies being graciously served. The Tennessee Aquarium, Chickamauga battlefield, and Lookout Mountain are close by.

Harmony Hill Inn ✪
85 PLEASANT HILL ROAD, CHUCKEY, TENNESSEE 37641

Tel: **(615) 257-3893**	Single/pb: **$45**
Best Time to Call: **8 AM–10 PM**	Open: **All year**
Host: **Dodie Melton**	Breakfast: **Full**
Location: **8 mi. NE of Greeneville, and**	Pets: **Sometimes**
20 mi. from Jonesborough	Children: **Welcome**
No. of Rooms: **2**	Smoking: **No**
No. of Private Baths: **2**	Social Drinking: **No**
Double/pb: **$55**	

Located on Horse Creek in the foothills of the Appalachian Mountains, this two-story 1850 farmhouse has a soothing, country atmosphere. Dodie, a registered nurse, is also a skilled woodworker and has renovated much of the house herself. After a full breakfast featuring her homemade sourdough bread—special diets considered upon request—take an easy drive to some of the area's attractions, such as Davy Crockett's birthplace, historic Jonesborough, Andrew Johnson's home and tailor shop, Bristol Caverns, Roan Mountain's rhododendron gardens, Smoky Mountain National Park, Dollywood, and North

Carolina's Hot Springs Spa. For your greater relaxation, therapeutic massage is available by appointment.

Chadwick House ✪

2766 MICHIGAN AVENUE RD NORTH EAST, CLEVELAND, TENNESSEE 37312

Tel: **(615) 339-2407**	Open: **All year**
Host: **Winnie A. Chadwick**	Reduced Rates: **10% seniors**
Location: **35 mi. N of Chattanooga**	Breakfast: **Full**
No. of Rooms: **3**	Other Meals: **Available**
No. of Private Baths: **1**	Pets: **No**
Max. No. Sharing Bath: **4**	Children: **Welcome**
Double/pb: **$52**	Smoking: **Permitted**
Double/sb: **$43**	Social Drinking: **Permitted**
Single/sb: **$35**	Airport/Station Pickup: **Yes**

White shutters and trim accent the multicolored bricks of this handsome ranch home just a half hour from Chattanooga. White-water rafting, Red Clay's historic Indian meeting grounds, and Cherokee National Forest are close by, and golfing and tennis are available right in Cleveland. In their spare moments B&B guests can watch the squirrels and birds in the back garden or relax by the fireplace with a glass of locally made wine. Winnie's full country breakfasts include homemade rolls and muffins.

Sugarfork Bed & Breakfast ✪

743 GARRETT ROAD, DANDRIDGE, TENNESSEE 37725

Tel: **(615) 397-7327; (800) 487-5634**	Single/sb: **$45**
Hosts: **Mary and Sam Price**	Open: **All year**
Location: **30 mi. E of Knoxville**	Reduced Rates: **Available**
No. of Rooms: **3**	Breakfast: **Full**
No. of Private Baths: **1**	Credit Cards: **MC, VISA**
Max. No. Sharing Bath: **4**	Pets: **No**
Double/pb: **$65**	Children: **Welcome, over 6**
Single/pb: **$55**	Smoking: **Permitted**
Double/sb: **$55**	Social Drinking: **Permitted**

Guests will appreciate the tranquil setting of Sugarfork Bed & Breakfast, located on Douglas Lake in the foothills of the Great Smoky Mountains. Your hosts have private lake access and their own floating dock. Swimming, water skiing, and boating are the main warm-weather activities here, while fishing is a year-round sport. On chilly mornings sit by the stone fireplace in the downstairs common room, or study the lake and mountains from the wall of windows upstairs. A hearty breakfast featuring homemade biscuits, country ham, and Mary's own special egg casseroles is served in the spacious dining room or, weather permitting, on the deck.

Sweet Annie's Bed, Breakfast & Barn ✪
7201 CROW CUT ROAD S.W., FAIRVIEW, TENNESSEE 37062

Tel: **(615) 799-8833**
Best Time to Call: **Early mornings or late evenings**
Hosts: **Ann and Charles Murphy**
Location: **27 mi. SW of Nashville**
No. of Rooms: **2**
No. of Private Baths: **1**
Double/pb: **$50**
Open: **All year**

Reduced Rates: **10% seniors; 15% weekly**
Breakfast: **Full**
Other Meals: **Available**
Pets: **Sometimes**
Children: **By arrangement**
Smoking: **No**
Social Drinking: **Permitted**
Airport/Station Pickup: **Yes**

Located one mile from an 800-acre park with hiking, biking, and bridle trails, this B&B also offers easy access to Opryland, the Hermitage, Dollywood, Twitty City, and Gatlinburg. Annie's is a modern brick home with a pool and a huge yard for guests to enjoy; horses occupy the back pasture. Your hosts are outdoor people. Ann, a fitness instructor, specializes in delicious, healthful meals, and her breakfasts usually feature fruit muffins, casseroles, and rich flavored coffees.

Butcher House in the Mountains ✪
1520 GARRETT LANE, GATLINBURG, TENNESSEE 37738

Tel: **(615) 436-9457**
Best Time to Call: **10 AM–9 PM**
Hosts: **Hugh and Gloria Butcher**
Location: **50 mi. SE of Knoxville**
No. of Rooms: **5**
No. of Private Baths: **5**
Double/pb: **$70–$85**
Open: **All year**
Reduced Rates: **$10 less after 2nd night, Mon.–Thurs.**

Breakfast: **Full**
Credit Cards: **AMEX, MC, VISA**
Pets: **No**
Children: **Welcome, over 12**
Smoking: **No**
Social Drinking: **Permitted**
Minimum Stay: **Weekends**
Foreign Languages: **Italian**

The ambiance at Butcher House is one of elegance, warmth, and beauty. Hugh and Gloria's years of collecting have resulted in a home filled with one-of-a-kind antique treasures. Guest rooms are decorated with unique linens and furniture from various eras. Nearby attractions include Pigeon Forge, Dollywood, and Smoky Mountains National Park. Guests can enjoy hiking, fishing, skiing, golfing, or visiting the many crafts shops. Your hosts will send you on your way after a gourmet breakfast that may consist of eggs Sebastian, Italian crepes, or eggs cardamom.

Olde English Tudor Inn ✪

135 WEST HOLLY RIDGE ROAD, GATLINBURG, TENNESSEE 37738

Tel: **(615) 436-7760**	Open: **All year**
Best Time to Call: **11 AM–9 PM**	Reduced Rates: **10% seniors**
Hosts: **Kathy and Larry Schuh**	Breakfast: **Full**
Location: **45 mi. SE of Knoxville**	Credit Cards: **MC, VISA**
No. of Rooms: 7	Pets: **No**
No. of Private Baths: 7	Children: **Welcome**
Double/pb: **$69–$79**	Smoking: **No**
Single/pb: **$65**	Social Drinking: **Permitted**
Suites: **$89–$99**	Airport Pickup: **Yes**

From the Olde English Tudor Inn's ideal downtown location, it's just a few minutes' walk to the attractions of Gatlinburg, and only a brief drive to Dollywood, Craft Community, outlet malls, and Great Smoky National Park. Handsomely decorated bedrooms have cable TV with HBO. Guests are invited to relax in the large, comfortably furnished community room with a TV/VCR and free-standing wood burning stove, or enjoy the peaceful seclusion of the rear patio. Generous breakfasts typically include fresh fruit, pancakes or French toast, and eggs, bacon, sausage, or ham. Make sure to save room for freshly baked breads with jams and jellies. Kathy and Larry want your visit to be memorable and will be happy to assist you with your touring, dining, and shopping questions.

Woodshire B&B ✪

600 WOODSHIRE DRIVE, GOODLETTSVILLE, TENNESSEE 37072

Tel: **(615) 859-7369**	Guest Cabin: **$60–$70**
Best Time to Call: **Before 9 AM; after**	Open: **All year**
9 PM	Breakfast: **Continental**
Hosts: **Beverly and John Grayson**	Pets: **No**
Location: **11 mi. N of Nashville**	Children: **Welcome**
No. of Rooms: 2	Smoking: **No**
No. of Private Baths: 2	Social Drinking: **No**
Double/pb: **$50**	Airport/Station Pickup: **Yes**
Single/pb: **$40**	

A blue clapboard house inspired by New England saltboxes, Woodshire B&B is 20 minutes from downtown Nashville and its attractions—Opryland Park, Andrew Jackson's Hermitage, and the homes and museums of country music stars. Beverly will gladly tell you the stories behind the antique family furniture. She's a retired art teacher, and as you look around you'll see her paintings and weavings, and John's woodcrafts. Continental breakfast features homemade preserves.

Hilltop House Bed and Breakfast Inn ✪
6 SANFORD CIRCLE, GREENEVILLE, TENNESSEE 37743

Tel: **(615) 639-8202**
Best Time to Call: **5 PM–7 PM**
Host: **Denise M. Ashworth**
Location: **7 mi. S. of Greeneville**
No. of Rooms: **3**
No. of Private Baths: **3**
Double/pb: **$70**
Single/pb: **$65**
Open: **All year**

Reduced Rates: **Available**
Breakfast: **Full**
Other Meals: **Available**
Credit Cards: **AMEX, MC, VISA**
Pets: **No**
Children: **Welcome, over 3 years**
Smoking: **No**
Social Drinking: **Permitted**
Airport/Station Pickup: **Yes**

Hilltop House is a 1920s Victorian manor on a hillside above the Nolichucky River Valley, with the Appalachian Mountains in the background. All the guest rooms, which are furnished in eighteenth-century English antiques and period reproductions, have mountain views; two have verandas. In keeping with her British birth, the innkeeper sets out a proper English tea every afternoon. The family-style breakfast consists of fruit, cereal, egg dishes, and homemade biscuits or muffins. Then it's time to explore the great outdoors: white-water rafting, hiking, biking, trout fishing, golfing, hunting, and bird-watching are among your options. Cherokee National Forest is within striking distance, as are the Great Smoky Mountains and the Blue Ridge Parkway.

Natchez Trace B&B Reservation Service ✪
P.O. BOX 193, HAMPSHIRE, TENNESSEE 38461

Tel: (800) 377-2770
Best Time to Call: **Evening; weekends**
Coordinator: **Kay Jones**
States/Regions Covered:
  Alabama—**Florence;**
  Mississippi—**Corinth, French Camp,**
  Jackson, Kosciusko, Lorman,
  Natchez, Vicksburg;

Tennessee—**Ashland City, Columbia,**
  Hampshire, Liepers Fork, Nashville
Descriptive Directory of B&Bs: **Free**
Rates (Single/Double):
  Modest: **$45 / $50**
  Average: **$60 / $75**
  Luxury: **$75 / $100**
Credit Cards: **MC, VISA**

Kay's reservation service is unique in that the homes are all convenient to the Natchez Trace National Parkway, the historic Nashville-to-Natchez route that was first designated by President Thomas Jefferson. The parkway is known for both its natural beauty and the charming Southern towns along the way. Kay can help you plan your trip and give you access to homes ranging from rustic, woodsy sites to fine antebellum mansions. Call her for a free list of homes, as well as literature about the Natchez Trace.

Hart House Bed and Breakfast ✪
207 EAST HOLSTON AVENUE, JOHNSON CITY, TENNESSEE 37601

Tel: **(615) 926-3147**
Hosts: **Francis and Vanessa Gingras**
Location: **90 mi. NE of Knoxville**

No. of Rooms: **3**
No. of Private Baths: **3**
Double/pb: **$60**

Single/pb: **$50**
Open: **All year**
Reduced Rates: **10% seniors**
Breakfast: **Full**
Credit Cards: **MC, VISA**

Pets: **Sometimes**
Children: **Welcome**
Smoking: **No**
Social Drinking: **Permitted**

Hart House is named after the original owner of this 1910 Dutch Colonial, which Francis and Vanessa have filled with antiques and collectibles. Johnson City is located in the heart of upper northeast Tennessee, an area brimming with both notable sites and scenic beauty. For history buffs, Jonesborough, the oldest town in the state, is five miles away, and those who love the great outdoors—camping, hiking, fishing, white-water rafting—will find plenty to do here. Each morning, guests wake up to an elegant breakfast of fresh fruit, homemade muffins, eggs, and fresh brewed coffee.

Windy Hill B&B ○
1031 WEST PARK DRIVE, KNOXVILLE, TENNESSEE 37909

Tel: **(615) 690-1488**
Host: **Mary M. Mitchell**
Location: **1.6 mi. from I-75-40, Exit 380**
No. of Rooms: **1**
No. of Private Baths: **1**
Double/pb: **$40**
Single/pb: **$35**

Open: **All year**
Breakfast: **Continental**
Pets: **Sometimes**
Children: **Welcome**
Smoking: **Permitted**
Social Drinking: **Permitted**
Airport/Station Pickup: **Yes**

Located in a pleasant, quiet neighborhood with numerous shade trees, Mary's B&B is air-conditioned and has a private entrance with no steps to climb. There's a double bed and a rollaway is available. Breakfast features homemade muffins or cinnamon rolls with coffee. Windy Hill is convenient to the University of Tennessee; Oak Ridge is only a 15-minute drive while Great Smoky Mountains National Park is an hour away.

Grandma's House ○
734 POLLARD ROAD, KODAK, TENNESSEE 37764

Tel: **(615) 933-3512; reservations: (800) 676-3512**
Best Time to Call: **Anytime**
Hosts: **Charlie and Hilda Hickman**
Location: **8 mi. N of Sevierville; 2 mi. from I-40, Exit 407**
No. of Rooms: **3**
No. of Private Baths: **3**

Double/pb: **$65**
Open: **All year**
Breakfast: **Full**
Credit Cards: **MC, VISA**
Pets: **No**
Children: **Welcome, over 12**
Smoking: **No**
Social Drinking: **No**

Grandma's House is located on a quiet country lane in Dumplin Valley at the base of the Great Smoky Mountains. Nearby attractions include: Great Smoky Mountains National Park, Dollywood in Pigeon Forge, Museum of Science and Energy in Oak Ridge, and much more. The farm-style house is furnished with country antiques, handmade quilts, and interesting family heirlooms. The hearty farm breakfast features buttermilk biscuits, Hilda's own homemade jams and jellies, and the house specialty, Apple Stack Cake. Both hosts are native East Tennesseans with lots of down-home friendliness to share with their guests. Death by Design Murder Mystery weekends are available in November, January, February, and March.

Snapp Inn B&B ✪
1990 DAVY CROCKETT PARK ROAD, LIMESTONE, TENNESSEE 37681

Tel: **(615) 257-2482**	Single/pb: **$40**
Best Time to Call: **Before 10 AM; after 7 PM**	Open: **All year**
	Breakfast: **Full**
Hosts: **Dan and Ruth Dorgan**	Pets: **Welcome**
Location: **4 mi. from Rte. 11 E**	Children: **Welcome (one at a time)**
No. of Rooms: **2**	Smoking: **No**
No. of Private Baths: **2**	Social Drinking: **Permitted**
Double/pb: **$50**	Airport/Station Pickup: **Yes**

Built in 1815 and situated in farm country, this Federal brick home has lovely mountain views. The house is decorated with antiques, including a Victorian reed organ. Now retired, Ruth and Dan have the time to pursue their interests in antiques restoration, history, needlework, and bluegrass music. It is an easy walk to Davy Crockett Birthplace State Park, and 15 minutes to historic Jonesboro or the Andrew Johnson Home in Greeneville. A swimming pool, golf, and fishing are close by. You are welcome to use the laundry facilities, television, and pool table.

The Mason Place ○
600 COMMERCE STREET, LOUDON, TENNESSEE 37774

Tel: **(615) 458-3921**	Breakfast: **Full**
Hosts: **Bob and Donna Siewert**	Credit Cards: **MC, VISA**
Location: **25 mi. SW of Knoxville**	Pets: **No**
No. of Rooms: **5**	Children: **No**
No. of Private Baths: **5**	Smoking: **No**
Double/pb: **$96**	Social Drinking: **Permitted**
Open: **All year**	Airport/Station Pickup: **Yes**
Reduced Rates: **Long-term stays**	

This impeccably restored 1865 plantation home is nestled in a quaint Civil War town along the Tennessee River. Civil War bullets and artifacts are still being found on the property's three acres of lawns and gardens. Inside, Mason Place offers quality lodging and an opportunity to wander back to yesteryear. A grand entrance hall, ten working fireplaces, authentic feather beds, period antiques, a Grecian swimming pool, a gazebo, and a wisteria-covered arbor are only a few of the amenities at your disposal. Bountiful breakfasts are included. Cheese plates, local wine, and picnic lunches are available by prior arrangement.

Falcon Manor Bed and Breakfast ○
2645 FAULKNER SPRINGS ROAD, McMINNVILLE, TENNESSEE 37110

Tel: **(615) 668-4444**	Single/sb: **$75**
Best Time to Call: **Anytime**	Open: **All year**
Hosts: **George and Charlien McGlothin**	Reduced Rates: **$5 off per day, 3 days**
Location: **72 mi. SE of Nashville**	**or more**
No. of Rooms: **5**	Breakfast: **Full**
No. of Private Baths: **1**	Credit Cards: **MC, VISA**
Max. No. Sharing Bath: **4**	Pets: **No**
Double/pb: **$75**	Children: **Welcome, over 12**
Single/pb: **$75**	Smoking: **No**
Double/sb: **$75**	Social Drinking: **Permitted**

This historic Victorian mansion recreates the romance of the 1890s. Relax in the friendly warmth of this fine old house and savor the luxury of its museum-quality antiques. The huge gingerbread veranda is well-stocked with rocking chairs and shaded by giant trees. Falcon Manor is a favorite for couples celebrating anniversaries. It's also the ideal base for a middle Tennessee vacation—halfway between Nashville and Chattanooga and just thirty minutes from four state parks. McMinnville is "the nursery capital of the world" and the home of America's second largest cave. George left a career in retail management to spend four years restoring the house, while Charlien pitched in during time off from her job as a NASA public affairs writer. They love sharing stories about Falcon Manor's history and their adventures bringing it back to life.

Clardy's Guest House ✪
435 EAST MAIN STREET, MURFREESBORO, TENNESSEE 37130

Tel: (615) 893-6030
Best Time to Call: After 4 PM
Hosts: Robert and Barbara Deaton
Location: 2 mi. from I-24
No. of Rooms: 3
No. of Private Baths: 2
Max. No. Sharing Bath: 4
Double/pb: $45
Single/pb: $35

Double/sb: $35
Single/sb: $30
Open: All year
Breakfast: Continental
Pets: Sometimes
Children: Welcome (crib)
Smoking: Permitted
Social Drinking: Permitted

This Romanesque-style Victorian dates back to 1898. The 20 rooms are filled with antiques; with 40 antiques dealers in town, you can guess what Murfreesboro is best known for. The world championship horse show at Shelbyville is 30 minutes away. Your hosts will be glad to advise on local tours and can direct you to the home of Grand Ole Opry, one hour away in Nashville, and fine eating places. Middle Tennessee State University is close by.

Quilts and Croissants
2231 RILEY ROAD, MURFREESBORO, TENNESSEE 37130

Tel: (615) 893-2933
Hosts: Robert and Mary Jane Roose
Location: 28 mi. S of Nashville
No. of Rooms: 1
No. of Private Baths: 1
Double/pb: $40
Single/pb: $35

Open: All year
Reduced Rates: Seniors
Breakfast: Continental
Pets: No
Smoking: No
Social Drinking: Permitted

This unusual home, constructed out of logs hewn in 1834, combines old-fashioned country charm and modern efficiency. Stencils and folk art ornament the walls of the guest room, and patchwork quilts drape the twin beds. Don't be fooled by the appearance of the quaint icebox in the kitchenette—it's really a refrigerator stocked with juice, breakfast foods, and soda. Quilts and Croissants is less than an hour's drive from Nashville, but your hosts can steer you to the notable sights of Murfreesboro, such as Oaklands Mansion (a mid-19th-century landmark) and Canonsburgh (a restored Civil War–era village). Breakfast here is a do-it-yourself affair; take whatever you want from the refrigerator.

Bed and Breakfast Adventures ✪
P.O. BOX 150586, NASHVILLE, TENNESSEE 37215

Tel: **(615) 383-6611; (800) 947-7404**
Best Time to Call: **9 AM–6 PM Mon.–Sat.**
Coordinator: **Carol Montgomery**
States/Regions Covered:
Chattanooga, Clarkeville, Franklin, Gatlinburg, Jackson, Knoxville, Memphis, Monteagie, Nashville, Townsend

Descriptive Directory of B&Bs: **$3**
Rates (Single/Double):
Modest: **$40–$50**
Average: **$50–$85**
Luxury: **$85–$135**
Credit Cards: **AMEX, DC, DISC, MC, VISA**
Minimum Stay: **In some areas**

Carol's world-wide travels, as well as her experience in hosting and entertaining business associates, relatives, and friends, has given her insight into people's needs and wants when traveling. The ambience of individual bed and breakfasts is very important, so Carol's policy is to see every bed and breakfast she represents, and to meet the owners/innkeepers. Her hosts are warm and gracious, knowledgeable of their area, and ready to help you have a memorable experience in Tennessee! Whether you're looking for that secluded hideaway, romantic weekend, or convenience to all the activities in a particular area, Carol will give you personalized service.

Fall Creek Falls Bed & Breakfast ✪
ROUTE 3, BOX 298B, PIKEVILLE, TENNESSEE 37367

Tel: **(615) 881-5494**
Hosts: **Doug and Rita Pruett**
Location: **50 mi. N of Chattanooga**
No. of Rooms: **8**
No. of Private Baths: **6**
Max. No. Sharing Bath: **4**
Double/pb: **$64–$79**
Single/pb: **$53**
Double/sb: **$50**
Open: **All year (except Jan.)**

Reduced Rates: **$10 less per night, Feb. 1–April 30**
Breakfast: **Full**
Pets: **No**
Children: **Welcome, over 8**
Smoking: **No**
Social Drinking: **Permitted**
Minimum Stay: **2 nights, weekends and holidays**

Enjoy the relaxing atmosphere of a new country manor home on forty acres of rolling hillside one mile from the nationally acclaimed Fall Creek Falls State Resort Park. Beautiful guest rooms have pickled oak floors and antique furniture with two common sitting areas. Lodging includes a full breakfast served in a cozy country kitchen or an elegant dining room. Doug enjoys grouse hunting and trout fishing and is a licensed Tennessee building contractor. Rita is an insurance executive who enjoys bargain hunting and antique auctions. Touring, dining, and shopping information is always available.

Clear Fork Farm ✪
328 SHIRLEY FORD ROAD, RUGBY, TENNESSEE 37852

Tel: (615) 628-2967
Best Time to Call: Anytime
Hosts: Ted and Barbara Lankford
Location: 65 mi NW of Knoxville
No. of Rooms: 3
No. of Private Baths: 3
Double/pb: $65

Open: All year
Breakfast: Continental
Pets: No
Children: Welcome, over 12
Smoking: No
Social Drinking: Permitted

This large brick farmhouse, sitting high above the Clear Fork River on 200 acres, is furnished with antiques and period reproductions, with four fireplaces for guests to enjoy. Bedrooms contain locally made quilts. A private sitting room is located off the bedrooms upstairs, and a large screen television and VCR is available in the den. Admire the view from two large porches; one is screened with an adjacent hot tub. Continental breakfast is served on antique china in the dining room with its own fireplace. Hiking, biking, and horseback riding trails are on the property, as well as in the adjoining park, Big South Fork National Recreational Area. A four-stall horse barn is provided for your horse. Historical Rugby, an English settlement built in the 1880s by social reformer Thomas Hughes, is three miles away.

Ross House Bed and Breakfast ✪
504 MAIN STREET, P.O. BOX 398, SAVANNAH, TENNESSEE 38372

Tel: (901) 925-3974; (800) 467-3174
Best Time to Call: 9 AM–5 PM
Hosts: John and Harriet Ross
Location: 110 mi. E of Memphis
Suites: $60–$115
Open: All year
Breakfast: Continental

Credit Cards: MC, VISA
Pets: No
Children: Welcome, over 10
Smoking: No
Social Drinking: Permitted
Foreign Languages: French, Spanish

Part of Savannah's National Register Historic District, which contains residences from the late 1860s to the 1920s, this B&B is a Neoclassical brick house built in 1908 by John's grandparents. Inside you'll see the original owners' furniture, books, paintings, and photographs. It is a short walk to the Cherry Mansion and Tennessee River and a short drive to Shiloh National Military Park and Pickwick Lake, for fishing and boating. If you'd rather paddle your canoe, take the 45-minute drive to the Buffalo River. John practices law next door where his grandfather once did, but when time permits, he accompanies guests on bicycle tours. Harriet is a full-time hostess.

Blue Mountain Mist Country Inn
1811 PULLEN ROAD, SEVIERVILLE, TENNESSEE 37862

Tel: **(800) 497-2335**
Best Time to Call: **10 AM–4 PM**
Hosts: **Norman and Sarah Ball**
Location: **4 mi. E of Pigeon Forge**
No. of Rooms: **12**
No. of Private Baths: **12**
Double/pb: **$79**
Guest Cottage: **$125**
Suites: **$95–$115**

Open: **All year**
Breakfast: **Full**
Pets: **No**
Children: **Welcome (2 rooms)**
Smoking: **No**
Social Drinking: **Permitted**
Minimum Stay: **2–3 nights holiday weekends and Oct.**

This Victorian-style inn is remote from congestion and noise, yet has easy access to Pigeon Forge, Dollywood, factory outlets, and the crafts community. A view of rolling meadows framed by the Great Smoky Mountains can be enjoyed from rocking chairs on the huge front porch or from the backyard hot tub and patio. Country antiques, claw-foot tubs, handmade quilts and accessories, all make for a homey atmosphere. Two suites have in-room Jacuzzis. The large, fireplaced living room is the gathering spot on cool evenings. The Southern breakfast often features fresh fruit, sausages and eggs, grits and gravy, and homemade biscuits.

Von-Bryan Inn
2402 HATCHER MOUNTAIN ROAD, SEVIERVILLE, TENNESSEE 37862

Tel: **(800) 633-1459**
Best Time to Call: **Anytime**
Hosts: **D. J. and Joann Vaughn**
Location: **9½ mi. S of Pigeon Forge**
No. of Rooms: **6**
No. of Private Baths: **6**
Double/pb: **$80–$125**
Single/pb: **$70–$115**
Guest Chalet: **160; sleeps 4**
Open: **All year**
Reduced Rates: **10% 2 nights or more, Sun.–Thurs.**

Breakfast: **Full**
Other Meals: **Available**
Credit Cards: **AMEX, DISC, MC, VISA**
Pets: **No**
Children: **Welcome, over 10 in main house, any age in chalet**
Smoking: **No**
Social Drinking: **Permitted**
Minimum Stay: **2 nights in chalet**
Airport/Station Pickup: **Yes**

A curving, climbing gravel road leads to a mountaintop hideaway with sensational views of spectacular mountain ranges and peaceful valley farmland. The log structure has cathedral ceilings of warm wood, skylights, and big windows framing breathtaking views. There are six guest rooms, a two-bedroom chalet, and several common areas. Enjoy the pool, hot tub, rockers, telescope, Jacuzzis, books, music, and full breakfast in addition to hiking, birdwatching, or simply relaxing. Within minutes of Great Smoky National Park, Cades Cove, Gatlinburg, Pigeon Forge, and Townsend, which offer crafts, outlet shopping, and Dollywood.

TEXAS

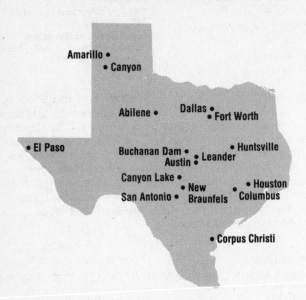

The Bed & Breakfast Society of Texas ✪
1200 SOUTHMORE AVENUE, HOUSTON, TEXAS 77004

Tel: **(713) 523-1114**
Best Time to Call: **9 AM–5 PM**
Coordinator: **Pat Thomas**
States/Regions Covered: **Statewide**

Rates (Single/Double):
Modest: **$40 / $45**
Average: **$45 / $60**
Luxury: **$65 / $85**

Whether you're traveling for business or pleasure, Pat's hosts offer the kind of friendliness and individualized care that will make your stay pleasant. The area is known for the Astrodome, Galveston Bay, NASA, and the Texas Medical Center. There are wonderful restaurants, shops, museums, and historic sights, and Baylor, Rice, and the University of Houston are nearby. Many are conveniently located urban homes, serene country houses, historic inns, waterfront cottages, and one is a 42-foot yacht.

Bed & Breakfast Texas Style ✪
4224 WEST RED BIRD LANE, DALLAS, TEXAS 75237

Tel: **(214) 298-8586**	Descriptive Directory: **$6**
Best Time to Call: **9 AM–4:30 PM CST**	Rates (Single/Double):
Coordinator: **Ruth Wilson**	Modest: **$50 / $70**
States/Regions Covered: **Austin,**	Average: **$70 / $90**
Dallas, Houston, Lake Texoma, San	Luxury: **$100 / $150**
Antonio, Santa Fe, Tyler	Credit Cards: **MC, VISA**

The above cities are only a small sample of the locations of hosts waiting to give you plenty of warm hospitality. Ruth's register includes comfortable accommodations in condos, restored Victorians, lakeside cottages, and ranches. Texas University, Southern Methodist University, Baylor University, Rice University, and Texas Christian University are convenient to many B&Bs.

Bolin's Prairie House Bed & Breakfast ✪
508 MULBERRY, ABILENE, TEXAS 79601

Tel: **(915) 675-5855**	Single/sb: **$30–$40**
Best Time to Call: **8AM–8 PM**	Open: **All year**
Mon.–Sat.	Breakfast: **Full**
Hosts: **Sam and Ginny Bolin**	Other Meals: **Available**
Location: **180 mi. W of Dallas**	Credit Cards: **AMEX, DISC, DC, MC,**
No. of Rooms: **4**	**VISA**
No. of Private Baths: **2**	Pets: **Sometimes**
Max. No. Sharing Bath: **4**	Children: **Welcome, over 12**
Double/pb: **$60–$65**	Smoking: **No**
Double/sb: **$50–$55**	Station Pickup: **Yes**

Tucked into the heart of this famous frontier town is Bolin's Prairie House, a 1902 house furnished with antiques and modern luxuries. The warm, homey atmosphere puts guests at their ease. Relax in the living room with its wood-burning stove, or settle in the den for a little TV. Each of the four bedrooms—named Love, Joy, Peace, and Patience—has its own special charm. Breakfast features Ginny's delicious baked egg dishes, fresh fruit, and homemade bread, all lovingly served in the dining room, where fine china and cobalt Depression glass are displayed.

Parkview House
1311 SOUTH JEFFERSON, AMARILLO, TEXAS 79101

Tel: **(806) 373-9464**	No. of Private Baths: **3**
Best Time to Call: **9 AM–9 PM**	Max. No. Sharing Bath: **4**
Hosts: **Nabil and Carol Dia**	Double/pb: **$60**
Location: **½ mi. from I-40**	Double/sb: **$50**
No. of Rooms: **5**	Suite: **$75**

Open: **All year**
Breakfast: **Continental**
Credit Cards: **MC, VISA**
Pets: **No**
Children: **No**

Smoking: **No**
Social Drinking: **Permitted**
Foreign Languages: **Arabic**
Airport/Station Pickup: **Yes**

Carol is a full-time host; Nabil a civil engineer. Both share interests in restoration and antiques, which is evident in their charming Prairie Victorian located in the historic district. The guest rooms are furnished with selected antiques, lace, and luxurious linens. The large columned porch is a fine place to start the day with breakfast or to relax. Carol will lend you a bike and be glad to prepare a picnic basket to take to nearby Palo Duro Canyon State Park or Lake Meredith. West Texas A and M University is nearby. They enjoy having guests join them for a "social hour" before dinner.

Aunt Dolly's Attic B&B ✪
12023 ROTHERHAM DRIVE, AUSTIN, TEXAS 78753

Tel: **(512) 837-5320; (800) 290-0294**
Best Time to Call: **Anytime**
Host: **Mary B. Rolan**
Location: **10.5 mi. NE of Austin**
No. of Rooms: **2**
Max. No. Sharing Bath: **4**
Double/sb: **$65**
Single/sb: **$55**

Open: **All year**
Reduced Rates: **Available**
Breakfast: **Full, Continental**
Pets: **Sometimes**
Children: **Welcome, infants and over 8**
Smoking: **No**
Social Drinking: **Permitted**

Aunt Dolly's Attic is located in a quiet, safe neighborhood. Once inside, you'll think you've stepped back in time: Throughout the house you'll find antiques, quilts, collectables, and other treasures. Businessmen and -women can receive clients in the parlor, with its Victorian armoire, decorative mantelpiece, washstand, and mirrors. Guests may lounge on the back deck, take a dip in the pool, lie in the hammock, sway on the porch swing, or chat with other guests in the common room, which has a TV and VCR. Stroll to the edge of the property and you'll see a natural pond and greenbelt. Continental breakfast is served weekdays, full breakfast on weekends; specialties include quiche, omelettes, casseroles, scones, and biscuits.

Carrington's Bluff B&B ✪
1900 DAVID STREET, AUSTIN, TEXAS 78705

Tel: **(512) 479-0638**
Best Time to Call: **8 AM–9 PM**
Hosts: **Gwen and David Fullbrook**
No. of Rooms: **8**
No. of Private Baths: **6**
Max. No. Sharing Bath: **4**

Double/pb: **$69–$85**
Single/pb: **$65–$80**
Double/sb: **$60–$65**
Single/sb: **$55–$60**
Open: **All year**

Reduced Rates: **Midweek business rate
$10 less**
Breakfast: **Full**
Credit Cards: **AMEX, DC, MC, VISA**

Pets: **No**
Children: **Welcome, over 10**
Smoking: **No**
Social Drinking: **Permitted**

After operating other B&Bs in Vermont and Texas, Gwen and David are experienced innkeepers who know how to pamper their guests. Their 1877 farmhouse has an enviable downtown Austin location seven blocks from the University of Texas and nine blocks from the State Capitol. Still, you'll feel like you're in the country, since the 35-foot front porch faces a tree-covered bluff. The interior is decorated in an English country style, with English and American antiques. Full breakfasts feature homemade muffins or breads, egg dishes, and homemade granola.

The McCallum House
613 WEST 32ND, AUSTIN, TEXAS 78705

Tel: **(512) 451-6744; fax: (512) 451-6744**
Best Time to Call: **10 AM–9 PM**
Hosts: **Roger and Nancy Danley**
Location: **2 mi. W of I-35**
No. of Rooms: **5**
No. of Private Baths: **5**
Double/pb: **$75**
Single/pb: **$65**
Suites: **$95**

Open: **All year**
Reduced Rates: **Weeknights, $15 nightly with 2 nights or more**
Breakfast: **Full**
Credit Cards: **MC, VISA (reservations only)**
Pets: **No**
Children: **Welcome, over 8**
Smoking: **No**
Social Drinking: **Permitted**

This late Victorian home is just 10 blocks north of the University of Texas and 20 blocks north of the capitol and downtown. Air-conditioned and furnished with antiques, the house has four guest rooms with private verandas. All facilities have phones, color TVs, sitting areas, and kitchens or mini-kitchens. McCallum House has a Texas historic marker, an Austin landmark designation and a preservation award from the Austin Heritage Society. Guests breakfast daily on fresh fruits and homemade egg dishes, muffins, and coffeecakes.

Peaceful Hill Bed & Breakfast ✪
6401 RIVER PLACE BOULEVARD, AUSTIN, TEXAS 78730-1102

Tel: (512) 338-1817	Open: **All year**
Best Time to Call: **Anytime**	Reduced Rates: **$50, 7 nights**
Host: **Peninnah Thurmond**	Breakfast: **Full**
Location: **15 min. W of Austin**	Credit Cards: **MC, VISA**
No. of Rooms: **2**	Pets: **No**
No. of Private Baths: **2**	Children: **Welcome**
Double/pb: **$60**	Smoking: **No**
Single/pb: **$60**	Social Drinking: **Permitted**

Deer watch you come to a small country inn located on ranchland high in the beautiful rolling hills fifteen minutes from Austin and ten minutes from Lake Travis and the Oasis. In springtime, settle on the porch with a cup of coffee and admire the countryside and the city below. Laze away the summer in a hammock built for two, or hike and bicycle; golf, swimming, and tennis are only two miles away. In the winter, warm up by a crackling fire in the grand stone fireplace in the living room, where a glass wall looks over both the country and the city. All this and a home-cooked breakfast. Peaceful is the name and peaceful is the game. Deer watch you go.

Austin's Wildflower Inn ✪
1200 WEST 22½ STREET, AUSTIN, TEXAS 78705

Tel: (512) 477-9639	Double/sb: **$59**
Best Time to Call: **Anytime**	Single/sb: **$50**
Hosts: **Kay Jackson and Claudean Schultz**	Open: **All year**
	Reduced Rates: **10% seniors**
Location: **2 mi. from Rte. IH35, Exit MLK**	Breakfast: **Full**
	Credit Cards: **AMEX, MC, VISA**
No. of Rooms: **4**	Pets: **No**
No. of Private Baths: **2**	Smoking: **No**
Max. No. Sharing Bath: **4**	Social Drinking: **Permitted**
Double/pb: **$69–$75**	Airport/Station Pickup: **Yes**
Single/pb: **$60–$65**	

Nestled on a quiet, tree-lined street, this fifty-year-old central Austin home is within a few blocks of the University of Texas and within minutes of the State Capitol complex. Outdoor enthusiasts will love the hike and bike trails at Shoal Creek or tennis at Caswell Courts.

Kay and Claudean pride themselves on their warm Texas hospitality and delight in serving you their hearty gourmet specialties each morning.

Mystic Cove Bed & Breakfast ○
RR 1, BOX 309B, BUCHANAN DAM, TEXAS 78609

Tel: **(512) 793-6642**
Best Time to Call: **8 AM–8 PM**
Hosts: **Ralph and Loretta Dueweke**
Location: **73 mi. NW of Austin**
No. of Rooms: **3**
No. of Private Baths: **3**
Double/pb: **$65–$75**
Single/pb: **$50**
Guest Cottage: **$75, sleeps 2–6**
Open: **All year**

Reduced Rates: **10% seniors**
Breakfast: **Full**
Other Meals: **Available**
Pets: **No**
Children: **Welcome, over 10**
Smoking: **No**
Social Drinking: **Permitted**
Minimum Stay: **2 nights, summer weekends**

Here's the perfect spot for artists, writers, mystics, and anyone else to relax and enjoy nature. Choose a room in the main house with either a king- or queen-size bed, or reserve the private guest house that can accommodate six. All rooms have beautiful lake views. Awaken to the smell of the best breakfast in the Texas hills. Afterwards, relax on the beach, fish from the dock, or enjoy a yoga class or a massage. You'll still have plenty of time to take a Texas River cruise or visit sights such as Longhorn Caverns, the LBJ ranch, and Fall Creek Vineyard.

Hudspeth House ○
1905 4TH AVENUE, CANYON, TEXAS 79015

Tel: **(806) 655-9800**
Hosts: **Sally and David Haynie**
Location: **14 mi. S of Amarillo**
No. of Rooms: **8**
No. of Private Baths: **4**
Max. No. Sharing Bath: **4**
Double/pb: **$50–$75**
Double/sb: **$45–$50**
Suites: **$90–$110**
Open: **All year**

Reduced Rates: **15% Jan. 1–Apr. 30; 20% weekly**
Breakfast: **Full**
Other Meals: **Available**
Credit Cards: **MC, VISA**
Pets: **No**
Children: **Welcome (crib)**
Smoking: **Restricted**
Social Drinking: **Permitted**
Airport/Station Pickup: **Yes**

Named for Mary E. Hudspeth, a leading Texas educator, this landmark home is rich in local history. Restored several times, the house was bought by Sally and Dave in 1987, and they have again refurbished it while retaining much of the original stained glass and chandeliers. In keeping with the elegant tone, breakfast features such delights as eggs Benedict. Sally, a former manager of the chic Zodiac Dining Room at Neiman-Marcus in Dallas, knows all about elegance with comfort. Within walking distance are Canyon Square, West Texas State University, and the Panhandle Plains Museum.

Aunt Nora's Bed and Breakfast ⊘
120 NAKED INDIAN TRAIL (NEW BRAUNFELS), CANYON LAKE, TEXAS 78132-1865

Tel: (210) 905-3989
Best Time to Call: 9 AM–5 PM
Hosts: Iralee and Alton Haley
Location: 15 mi. NW of New Braunfels
No. of Rooms: 3
No. of Private Baths: 2
Max. No. Sharing Bath: 4
Double/sb: $65–$75
Guest Cottage: $95–$125

Open: All year
Reduced Rates: Available
Breakfast: Full, Continental
Pets: Sometimes
Children: Welcome, over 14
Smoking: No
Social Drinking: Permitted
Airport Pickup: Yes

In the Texas hill country at Canyon Lake, just minutes from New Braunfels and Guadalupe River, is a country house with old-time Victorian charm, nestled on four tree-covered acres with a meadow. Walk to the top of the hill to view Canyon Lake, or breathe the fresh country air from the front porch swing. Relax amid handmade furnishings, antiques, a woodstove, and natural wood floors. Tastefully decorated Queen rooms have ruffled curtains, handmade quilts, private or semi-private baths and views. The cottages have private decks, sofa sleepers, kitchens, beautiful decor, private baths, and a view.

Magnolia Oaks ⊘
634 SPRING STREET, COLUMBUS, TEXAS 78934

Tel: (409) 732-2726
Best Time to Call: Evenings
Hosts: Bob and Nancy Stiles
Location: 70 mi. W of Houston
No. of Rooms: 4
No. of Private Baths: 4
Efficiency Apt.: $80–$120
Open: All year

Reduced Rates: Available
Breakfast: Full
Pets: No
Children: No
Smoking: No
Social Drinking: Permitted
Minimum Stay: Homes Tour Weekend
Airport Pickup: Yes

Magnolia Oaks is an Eastlake Victorian jewel two blocks from the historic square in Columbus. This landmark home was built in 1890 by Senator Marcus Townsend. Bob and Nancy Stiles restored the house and furnished it with Victorian Texana; they opened the B&B in 1990. Featured are two fireplaces, stained-glass windows, carved woodwork, gingerbread porches, a summer room, generous breakfasts, private baths, horseshoes, croquet, and a tandem bike. Columbus, on Interstate 10, is in the heart of wildflower country. It has museums, antique shops, and Stafford Opera House.

Bay Breeze Bed & Breakfast ✪
201 LOUISIANA, CORPUS CHRISTI, TEXAS 78404

Tel: **(512) 882-4123**	Treehouse: **$85**
Best Time to Call: **Anytime**	Open: **All year**
Hosts: **Perry and Frank Tompkins**	Reduced Rates: **Available**
Location: **145 mi. S of San Antonio**	Breakfast: **Full**
No. of Rooms: **4**	Pets: **No**
No. of Private Baths: **4**	Children: **Welcome, over 13**
Double/pb: **$60–$75**	Smoking: **No**
Single/pb: **$72**	Social Drinking: **Permitted**

Standing within view of the sparkling bay waters, this fine older home radiates the charm and ambiance of days gone by. It's only a stroll to the city's finest park and fishing pier; nearby is Oleander Point, one of the world's premier sailboarding sites, with windsurfers flitting like butterflies on the waves. A five-minute drive takes you to the business district and city marinas, where sea vessels of every description are berthed and shrimp are sold directly from the net. Then travel the short distance to the Bayfront Convention Center, art and science museums, and the Harbor Playhouse Community Theater. Cross the High Bridge to the Texas State Aquarium and the USS Lexington Floating Museum. After experiencing Bay Breeze's many pleasures, you will want to return again and again.

B & G's ✪
15869 NEDRA WAY, DALLAS, TEXAS 75248

Tel: **(214) 386-4323**	Reduced Rates: **Available**
Best Time to Call: **Before 8 AM**	Breakfast: **Full**
Hosts: **George and Betty Hyde**	Other Meals: **Available**
No. of Rooms: **2**	Pets: **No**
No. of Private Baths: **2**	Children: **Welcome**
Double/pb: **$50**	Smoking: **No**
Single/pb: **$45**	Social Drinking: **Permitted**
Open: **All year**	Airport/Station Pickup: **Yes**

Betty and George are retirees who have had visitors from around the world since 1980. They want you to think of their home—furnished with "an eclectic collection of family heirlooms and junk"—as your own. Upon your arrival, they'll pour you something to drink, ascertain your interests, and direct you to appropriate activities in the Dallas-Fort Worth area. This B&B is close to prestigious shopping malls, the University of Texas at Dallas, Southern Methodist University, and the sights of downtown Dallas, such as the Kennedy Assassination Museum and the new Arts District. You'll start the day with conversation and a three-course breakfast at a lovely table set with grandma's antique silver and good crystal.

Bergmann Inn ✪
10009 TRINIDAD DRIVE, EL PASO, TEXAS 79925

Tel: **(915) 599-1398**	Breakfast: **Continental**
Host: **David Bergmann**	Other Meals: **Available**
No. of Rooms: **2**	Pets: **No**
Max. No. Sharing Bath: **4**	Smoking: **No**
Double/sb: **$50**	Social Drinking: **Permitted**
Single/sb: **$35**	Airport Pickup: **Yes**
Open: **All year**	

David has a spacious, two-story home with two large bedrooms, a sizable living room, a den with a fireplace, and air-conditioning. Guests will enjoy the back patio overlooking a yard with flower beds and fruit trees that provide shade in the summertime. Bergmann Inn offers easy access to the east-west freeway and the northbound highways leaving El Paso.

The Texas White House ✪
1417 8TH AVENUE, FORT WORTH, TEXAS 76104

Tel: **(817) 923-3597**	Reduced Rates: **Available**
Best Time to Call: **7 AM–10:30 PM**	Breakfast: **Full**
Host: **Jamie Sexton**	Other Meals: **Available**
Location: **2 mi. SW of downtown Fort Worth**	Credit Cards: **AMEX, MC, VISA**
	Pets: **No**
No. of Rooms: **3**	Children: **Welcome**
No. of Private Baths: **3**	Smoking: **Restricted**
Double/pb: **$85**	Social Drinking: **Permitted**
Open: **All year**	Airport/Station Pickup: **Yes**

Texas White House is a 1910 Colonial Revival home with a large wraparound porch on the first floor. The parlor, living room with a fireplace, and formal dining room may be rented for business conferences and luncheons. Secretarial and notary services can also be arranged. Each guest room features a queen-size bed, desk, and chair, and sitting area. You'll receive keys both to your room and the front door, so you can come and go at your leisure. Full breakfasts are served; you may eat either in your bedroom or in the dining room. Architecture buffs will want to tour the area's historical districts and landmark homes, while flora and fauna fans may prefer the Botanical Gardens and the Fort Worth Zoo.

Durham House Bed & Breakfast ✪
921 HEIGHTS BOULEVARD, HOUSTON, TEXAS 77008

Tel: **(713) 868-4654**	No. of Rooms: **6**
Best Time to Call: **Anytime**	No. of Private Baths: **5**
Host: **Marguerite Swanson**	Max. No. Sharing Bath: **3**

Double/pb: **$65–$85**
Single/pb: **$50–$75**
Double/sb: **$60**
Single/sb: **$50**
Open: **All year**
Reduced Rates: **10% seniors; 10% weekly**

Breakfast: **Full**
Credit Cards: **AMEX, MC, VISA**
Pets: **No**
Children: **Welcome, infants and over 12**
Smoking: **No**
Social Drinking: **Permitted**

A Queen Anne Victorian listed on the National Register of Historic Places, Durham House is conveniently located just five minutes from downtown Houston. Antique-filled rooms, a player piano, a solarium, and a gazebo make this the perfect setting for both business travelers and weekend visitors in search of a romantic getaway. The amenities include a bicycle built for two. Memorable full breakfasts are served at the time and location requested. Marguerite, a former school counselor, now devotes all her time to her guests and her murder-mystery dinner parties.

The Lovett Inn ✪

501 LOVETT BOULEVARD, HOUSTON, TEXAS 77006

Tel: **(713) 522-5224; (800) 779-5224; fax: (713) 528-6708**
Best Time to Call: **10 AM–6 PM**
Host: **Tom Fricke**
Location: **Downtown Houston**
No. of Rooms: **7**
No. of Private Baths: **7**
Double/pb: **$55–$85**
Single/pb: **$55–$80**
Townhouse: **$75–$150**

Suites: **$50–$100**
Open: **All year**
Reduced Rates: **Weekly**
Breakfast: **Continental**
Credit Cards: **AMEX, MC, VISA**
Pets: **Sometimes**
Children: **By arrangement**
Smoking: **Restricted**
Social Drinking: **Permitted**

It's easy to be fooled by the Lovett Inn: although it looks far older, this stately Federalist-style mansion, attractively furnished with 19th-century reproductions, was actually built in 1924. Its convenient museum-district location puts visitors within easy striking distance of downtown Houston, the Galleria, and the Houston Medical Center. After spending the day in the city, guests are sure to appreciate a dip in the pool. Each room has a color TV.

Sara's Bed & Breakfast Inn ✪

941 HEIGHTS BOULEVARD, HOUSTON, TEXAS 77008

Tel: **(713) 868-1130; (800) 593-1130**
Best Time to Call: **Anytime**
Hosts: **Donna and Tillman Arledge**
Location: **6 blocks from I-10**
No. of Rooms: **13**
No. of Private Baths: **11**
Max. No. Sharing Bath: **4**

Double/pb: **$50–$75**
Double/sb: **$57**
Suites: **$120 for 4**
Open: **All year**
Breakfast: **Continental, plus**
Credit Cards: **AMEX, CB, DC, MC, VISA**

Pets: **No**	Smoking: **Restricted**
Children: **Welcome**	Social Drinking: **Permitted**

This Queen Anne Victorian, with its turret and widow's walk, is located in Houston Heights, a neighborhood of historic homes, many of which are on the National Historic Register. Each bedroom is uniquely furnished, having either single, double, queen- or king-size beds. The Balcony Suite consists of two bedrooms, two baths, full kitchen and living area. Cool drinks or hot coffee are graciously offered in the afternoon. The sights and sounds of downtown Houston are four miles away.

Blue Bonnet Bed & Breakfast ✪
1215 AVENUE G #4, HUNTSVILLE, TEXAS 77340

Tel: **(409) 295-2072**	Suite: **$48**
Hosts: **John and Bette Nelson**	Open: **All year**
Location: **70 mi. N of Houston**	Breakfast: **Continental**
No. of Rooms: **4**	Pets: **Sometimes**
No. of Private Baths: **3**	Children: **Welcome**
Max. No. Sharing Bath: **4**	Smoking: **No**
Double/sb: **$38**	Social Drinking: **Permitted**

Seven tree-shaded acres frame this appealing blue Victorian-style house, with its white trim and wraparound porch. Try your luck fishing in the pond, sit on the porch, or play horseshoes and croquet on the lawn. The house is less than five minutes from Sam Houston State University and the adjacent Sam Houston Grave and Museum complex. Antique lovers will find plenty of shops in the neighborhood; Bette, who owns and manages two antique malls, can give you some good suggestions. Continental breakfast may include apple fritters, poppyseed muffins, filled croissants, and fruit compote.

Trails End Bed & Breakfast ✪
12223 TRAILS END ROAD #7, LEANDER, TEXAS 78641

Tel: **(512) 267-2901**	Open: **All year**
Best Time to Call: **10 AM–10 PM**	Reduced Rates: **Over 2 nights**
Hosts: **JoAnn and Tom Patty**	Breakfast: **Full**
Location: **20 mi. NW of Austin**	Pets: **No**
No. of Rooms: **2**	Children: **Welcome**
No. of Private Baths: **2**	Smoking: **No**
Double/pb: **$68.90**	Social Drinking: **Permitted**
Single/pb: **$58.30**	
Guest House: **$79.50–$180.20,** sleeps 6	

JoAnn designed this colonial Texas-style home with the intention of opening a B&B. The main house has two guest rooms furnished with

mahogany pieces. For greater privacy, stay in the guest house and save money by preparing your own meals in the fully furnished kitchen. Banana pancakes and cheese-and-bacon biscuits are among the highlights of breakfast, served in the main house. After your morning meal, walk around the Pattys' six-acre property or visit local points of interest, such as Zilker Gardens, Texas Memorial Museum, and Erwin Special Events Center. Golfers are urged to go to Lago Vista, while fans of water sports can swim, ski, fish, or sail on Lake Travis.

River Haus Bed & Breakfast ☉

817 EAST ZIPP ROAD, NEW BRAUNFELS, TEXAS 78130

Tel: **(210) 625-6411**	Reduced Rates: **10% Sun.–Thurs.**
Hosts: **Dick and Arlene Buhl**	Breakfast: **Full**
Location: **25 mi. NE of San Antonio**	Pets: **Sometimes**
No. of Rooms: **1**	Children: **No**
No. of Private Baths: **1**	Smoking: **No**
Double/pb: **$65**	Social Drinking: **No**
Single/pb: **$60**	Foreign Languages: **German**
Open: **All year**	

Historic New Braunfels, a major tourist destination, offers museums, antique shopping, and unparalleled canoeing and river sports, all in the charming setting of the German Hill Country. River Haus is a delightful hill country–style home located on the Guadalupe River at Lake Dunlap. Watch the sun set over the lake from your spacious bedroom or sitting room. On the enclosed porch, with its deck overlooking the lake, you can sip a cool drink or enjoy the warmth of a wood stove fire. The complete gourmet breakfasts include local specialties and homemade bread and preserves.

The Rose Garden ✪
195 SOUTH ACADEMY, NEW BRAUNFELS, TEXAS 78130

Tel: **(210) 629-3296**	Open: **All year**
Best Time to Call: **Before 8 PM**	Reduced Rates: **Available**
Host: **Dawn Mann**	Breakfast: **Full**
Location: **1½ mi. from I-35, Exit 187**	Pets: **No**
No. of Rooms: **2**	Children: **No**
Max. No. Sharing Bath: **4**	Smoking: **No**
Double/sb: **$65**	Social Drinking: **Permitted**
Single/sb: **$60**	Foreign Languages: **German**

This half-century-old white brick Colonial is located one block from historic downtown New Braunfels. Enjoy a movie, browse the antique shops, or stroll along the Comal Springs. Then relax by the fireplace in the parlor, or in the formal dining room with a flavored cup of coffee. The Royal Rose Room features a four-poster bed; you'll also find English and German books, pictures, and magazines concerning the royal family. The Romantic Country Rose Room has a Victorian wrought-iron and brass bed, an antique English dresser.

The White House
217 MITTMAN CIRCLE, NEW BRAUNFELS, TEXAS 78130

Tel: **(210) 629-9354**	Open: **All year, except Thanksgiving, Christmas, and New Years Day**
Best Time to Call: **9 AM–9 PM**	
Hosts: **Beverly and Jerry White**	Breakfast: **Full**
Location: **25 mi. N of San Antonio**	Other Meals: **Available**
No. of Rooms: **2**	Pets: **Sometimes**
Max. No. Sharing Bath: **4**	Children: **Welcome (crib)**
Double/sb: **$45–$50**	Smoking: **No**
Single/sb: **$40–$45**	Social Drinking: **Permitted**

This Spanish-style white-brick ranch home is nestled among cedar and oaks in Texas hill country. Guests are welcomed here with tea and pastries and shown to comfortable rooms with antique iron beds and oak dressers. A large fishing pond is located on the premises, and a few miles away you may enjoy a refreshing tube or raft ride down the Guadalupe River. Your hosts have giant inner tubes to lend. Other attractions include the Alamo, the Riverwalk, and the many old missions located in nearby San Antonio.

Beckmann Inn and Carriage House ✪
222 EAST GUENTHER STREET, SAN ANTONIO, TEXAS 78204

Tel: (210) 229-1449
Best Time to Call: 8 AM–10 PM
Hosts: Betty Jo and Don Schwartz
Location: 1 mi. N of San Antonio
No. of Rooms: 5
No. of Private Baths: 5
Double/pb: $80–$130
Single/pb: $70–$120
Open: All year

Reduced Rates: Available
Breakfast: Full
Credit Cards: AMEX, DC, MC, VISA
Pets: No
Children: Welcome, over 12
Smoking: No
Social Drinking: Permitted
Minimum Stay: 2 nights, weekends

Enjoy gracious hospitality in an elegant Victorian inn located in San Antonio's King William historic district. The beautiful wraparound porch welcomes guests. Inside, rooms are colorfully decorated, with high-back, queen-size, antique Victorian beds. Gourmet breakfast, complete with dessert, is served in the formal dining room on a table set with china, crystal, and silver. Then guests may stroll over to the Riverwalk or ride the ten-cent trolley to the sights of San Antonio.

The Belle of Monte Vista ✪
505 BELKNAP PLACE, SAN ANTONIO, TEXAS 78212

Tel: (210) 732-4006
Hosts: Joann and David Bell and Jim
  Davis
No. of Rooms: 5
No. of Private Baths: 3
Max. No. Sharing Bath: 4
Double/sb: $60–$75
Single/sb: $50

Open: All year
Breakfast: Full
Pets: No
Children: Welcome
Smoking: No
Social Drinking: Permitted
Airport/Station Pickup: Yes

J. Riely Gordon designed this Queen Anne Victorian as a model house for a local developer. Built in 1890 with limestone that was quarried less than half a mile away, the house has been beautifully restored and is located in the elegant Monte Vista historic district. Inside, you'll find eight fireplaces, stained-glass windows, a hand-carved oak staircase, and Victorian furnishings. Jim serves a Southern breakfast with homemade muffins and jellies each morning. They are happy to help you plan your day and will direct you to nearby attractions such as Alamo Plaza, the Riverwalk, and El Mercado Market Place.

Brookhaven B&B ✪
128 WEST MISTLETOE, SAN ANTONIO, TEXAS 78212

Tel: (210) 733-3939
Hosts: Gene and Henna Siler
Location: Downtown San Antonio

No. of Rooms: 4
No. of Private Baths: 4
Double/pb: $75

Single/pb: **$70**
Suites: **$85; sleeps 4**
Open: **All year**
Reduced Rates: **50% seniors; 10% weekly**
Breakfast: **Full**
Credit Cards: **AMEX, DISC**

Pets: **No**
Children: **Welcome**
Smoking: **No**
Social Drinking: **Permitted**
Minimum Stay: **2 nights, weekends**
Foreign Languages: **Dutch, Spanish**

Located in the city's Monte Vista Historic District, this B&B is only five minutes from the Alamo, Riverwalk, the cathedral, botanical gardens, Trinity University, and Incarnate Word College. The house, a three-story Queen Anne built in 1914, is furnished in period style and contains many fine antiques. Guests are invited to sit on the large wraparound porch's wicker chairs and enjoy the view or read a book. Your hosts are Gene, a retired California fire fighter interested in horticulture, and Henna, his Dutch-born wife.

Falling Pines B&B ✪
300 WEST FRENCH PLACE, SAN ANTONIO, TEXAS 78212

Tel: **(210) 733-1998; (800) 880-4580**
Best Time to Call: **9 AM–noon**
Hosts: **Grace and Bob Daubert**
No. of Rooms: **4**
No. of Private Baths: **4**
Double/pb: **$100**
Single/pb: **$65**
Suite: **$150**

Open: **All year**
Reduced Rates: **15% families; weekly**
Breakfast: **Full**
Pets: **No**
Children: **Welcome, over 10**
Smoking: **No**
Social Drinking: **Permitted**
Minimum Stay: **2 nights**

When you enter Falling Pines through the magnificent front archway, you realize that they don't make estates like this anymore. Pines, oaks, and pecan trees shade the one-acre property. Inside, the brick-and-limestone mansion is sumptuously decorated with oak paneling, oriental rugs, and antique furnishings. Tennis courts, a swimming pool, and a zoo are all a short walk away, or you can ride over on the bikes Grace and Bob will lend you. A breakfast of fresh fruit, pastries, and hot and cold cereals is served in the tiled solarium.

For key to listings, see inside front or back cover.

✪ This star means that rates are guaranteed through December 31, 1995, to any guest making a reservation as a result of reading about the B&B in *Bed & Breakfast U.S.A.*—1995 edition.

Important! To avoid misunderstandings, always ask about cancellation policies when booking.

Please enclose a self-addressed, stamped, business-size envelope when contacting reservation services.

For more details on what you can expect in a B&B, see Chapter 1.

Always mention *Bed & Breakfast U.S.A.* when making reservations!

If no B&B is listed in the area you'll be visiting, use the form on page 743 to order a copy of our "List of New B&Bs."

We want to hear from you! Use the form on page 745.

UTAH

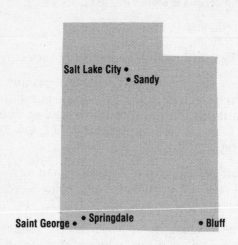

Salt Lake City •
• Sandy

Saint George • • Springdale   • Bluff

Bluff Bed and Breakfast ✪
BOX 158, BLUFF, UTAH 84512

Tel: **(801) 672-2220**
Host: **Rosalie Goldman**
Location: **On Rtes. 163 and 191**
No. of Rooms: **2**
No. of Private Baths: **2**
Double/pb: **$70–$75**
Single/pb: **$65–$70**
Open: **All year**

Breakfast: **Full**
Other Meals: **Available**
Pets: **No**
Children: **Welcome**
Smoking: **No**
Social Drinking: **Permitted**
Airport/Station Pickup: **Yes**
Foreign Languages: **French**

Close to the Four Corners (the junction of Colorado, New Mexico, Arizona, and Utah), this Frank Lloyd Wright–style home is nestled among huge boulders at the foot of redrock cliffs, near the San Juan River. On the main highway between Grand Canyon and Mesa Verde, it is secluded on seventeen desert acres. Across the river is the Navajo Reservation, and prehistoric ruins have been discovered nearby. Simply furnished, it is bright and tidy; large picture windows frame four different spectacular views. Rosalie prepares your breakfast of choice, from oatmeal to steak.

Seven Wives Inn
217 NORTH 100 WEST, ST. GEORGE, UTAH 84770

Tel: (801) 628-3737; (800) 600-3737, Code, 0165
Best Time to Call: After 9 AM
Hosts: Jay and Donna Curtis, and Alison and Jon Bowcutt
Location: 125 mi. NE of Las Vegas
No. of Rooms: 12
No. of Private Baths: 12
Double/pb: $50–$75
Single/pb: $50–$70

Suites: $100–$110
Open: All year
Reduced Rates: Special business rate (single occupancy) $45
Breakfast: Full
Credit Cards: AMEX, DC, MC, VISA
Children: By arrangement
Smoking: No
Social Drinking: Permitted
Airport/Station Pickup: Yes

This delightful inn is featured on the walking tour of St. George; it is just across from the Brigham Young home and two blocks from the historic Washington County Court House. Your hosts offer traditional Western hospitality. Their home is decorated with antiques collected in America and Europe. Some bedrooms are named after one of the seven wives of Donna's polygamous great-grandfather. A gourmet breakfast is served in the elegant dining room that will give you a hint of the past. St. George is located near Zion and Bryce national parks, boasts eight golf courses, and is noted for its mild winters. Dixie College is nearby. There's a swimming pool for your pleasure.

Anton Boxrud Bed & Breakfast Inn ✪
57 SOUTH 600 EAST, SALT LAKE CITY, UTAH 84102

Tel: (801) 363-8035; (800) 524-5511
Best Time to Call: 5 PM–9 PM
Hosts: C. Keith Lewis and Mark A. Brown
Location: 5 blocks from downtown
No. of Rooms: 6
No. of Private Baths: 3
Max. No. Sharing Bath: 4
Double/pb: $79–$89
Single/pb: $79–$89
Double/sb: $49–$59

Single/sb: $38–$48
Suites: $99–$109
Open: All year
Reduced Rates: 10% weekly
Breakfast: Full
Credit Cards: AMEX, MC, VISA
Pets: By arrangement
Children: Welcome
Smoking: No
Social Drinking: Permitted

The Anton Boxrud Bed & Breakfast is a charming, restored Victorian inn, located in a historic district of Salt Lake City, just half a block from the governor's mansion. A hearty breakfast and you're on your way to Utah's many cultural events and world-renowned outdoor activities. Within walking distance, you will find three large shopping malls, the world famous Mormon Temple Square and Geneological Library, museums, galleries, restaurants, and more. During the summer months, join your hosts on the veranda for evening hors d'oeuvres and great conversation.

Dave's Cozy Cabin Bed & Breakfast ✪
2293 EAST 6200 SOUTH, SALT LAKE CITY, UTAH 84121

Tel: **(801) 278-6136**	Suites: **$65**
Best Time to Call: **8 AM–8 PM**	Open: **All year**
Hosts: **Dave and Dorothy Moore**	Reduced Rates: **5% seniors; 5%**
Location: **11 mi. S of Salt Lake City**	**families**
No. of Rooms: **4**	Breakfast: **Full**
No. of Private Baths: **2**	Pets: **No**
Max. No. Sharing Bath: **4**	Children: **Welcome, over 12**
Double/pb: **$55**	Smoking: **No**
Single/pb: **$45**	Social Drinking: **Permitted**
Double/sb: **$45**	Minimum Stay: **2 nights**
Single/sb: **$35**	

This log cabin at the base of the Wasatch Mountains is a handsome retreat, with its knotty pine paneling, large fireplace, and lovely garden patio. For that extra bit of relaxation, hop into the redwood hot tub. Between the nearby ski slopes and the sights of Salt Lake City, visitors will find plenty to do. You'll start the day off right with a full breakfast highlighted by oven-fresh muffins with homemade jams and jellies.

Alta Hills Farm ✪
10852 SOUTH 20TH EAST SANDY, SANDY, UTAH 84092

Tel: **(801) 571-1712**	Reduced Rates: **10% weekly, seniors**
Hosts: **Blaine and Diane Knight**	Breakfast: **Continental**
Location: **15 mi. S of Salt Lake**	Credit Cards: **DISC, MC, VISA**
No. of Rooms: **4**	Pets: **Yes**
No. of Private Baths: **2**	Children: **Welcome**
Max. No. Sharing Bath: **4**	Smoking: **No**
Double/pb: **$78**	Social Drinking: **No**
Double/sb: **$58**	Airport/Station Pickup: **Yes**
Open: **Sept. 1–May 31**	

This B&B is nestled at the base of the Rocky Mountains fifteen minutes from the Alta and Snow Bird ski resorts. Alta Hills Farm has been an English Huntseat Equestrian Center for the past twenty years. In the summer the Knights run a riding camp for children of all ages. Their home has a warm, spacious English country style. Every evening, guests can relax with hot apple cider in a private living room with a fireplace. You are also invited to join the Knights downstairs. Blaine and Diane love kids and welcome families who come to ski or to enjoy beautiful Salt Lake.

O'Toole's Under the Eaves
P.O. BOX 29, 980 ZION PARK BOULEVARD, SPRINGDALE, UTAH 84767

Tel: **(801) 772-3457**	Suites: **$115**
Hosts: **Rick and Michelle O'Toole**	Open: **All year**
Location: **45 mi. E of St. George**	Reduced Rates: **Available**
No. of Rooms: **5**	Breakfast: **Full**
No. of Private Baths: **3**	Credit Cards: **MC, VISA**
Max. No. Sharing Bath: **4**	Pets: **Sometimes**
Double/pb: **$75**	Children: **By arrangement**
Single/pb: **$65**	Smoking: **No**
Double/sb: **$60**	Social Drinking: **Permitted**
Single/sb: **$50**	

Under the Eaves is a historic stone-and-stucco cottage located at the gate of Zion National Park. Constructed of massive sandstone blocks from the canyon, the guest house has served as a landmark for visitors to Zion for more than 50 years. Choose from two antique-filled bedrooms or a luxurious suite. The garden cottage dates from the 1920s and has two nonconnecting private bedrooms and baths.

VERMONT

Montgomery ·   North Troy ·   Derby Line ·
North Hero ·   · Morgan
            Swanton ·   · Barton
           Craftsbury ·   · East Haven
           Common
Jericho ·   · Stowe
Waterbury ·   · Cabot
   Waitsfield ·   · Northfield
     Bristol ·   Northfield Falls
Middlebury ·   Warren   · Fairlee
        Brookfield ·   · Chelsea
         Bethel ·

Brandon ·
Cuttingsville · Rutland
Fair Haven ·   · Wallingford
        · Belmont

Dorset · · East Dorset
Manchester ·   · Chester
Manchester Center ·
         · Townshend

      · West Dover

American Country Collection—Bed & Breakfast Vermont
4 GREENWOOD LANE, DELMAR, NEW YORK 12054

Tel: (518) 439-7001
Best Time to Call: 10 AM–5 PM
  Mon.–Fri.
Coordinator: **Arthur Copeland**
States/Regions Covered: **Bennington,
Brattleboro, Burlington, Fairfax,
Fairhaven, Ludlow, Manchester,
Middle Springs, Newport, Stowe,**

**Waterbury, Woodstock, Rutland;
Northern New Hampshire**
Descriptive Directory of B&Bs: **$6**
Rates (Single/Double):
  Modest: **$35–$50 / $35–$55**
  Average: **$50–$60 / $55–$85**
  Luxury: **$60–$95 / $85–$135**
Credit Cards: **AMEX, MC, VISA**

The American Country Collection offers comfortable lodging in private homes and country inns throughout northern, central, and southern Vermont. Accommodations include an 1850 Colonial on eight acres in Turnbridge with full breakfast, a luxurious inn (with all meals provided) in Weathersfield, a tranquil home bordered by a brook in

Manchester, and a farmhouse inn with solarium, pool, farm animals, and complete play area for children in Fairfax. Many locations are also equipped to serve the needs of small business meetings. In addition, reservations through the American Country Collection are handled for the Massachusetts Berkshire area, as well as eastern New York and the Island of St. Thomas, U.S.V.I.

Anglin' B&B ✪
CRYSTAL LAKE, P.O. BOX 403, BARTON, VERMONT 05822

Tel: **(802) 525–4548**	Single/sb: **$35**
Best Time to Call: **8 AM**	Open: **All year**
Host: **Fay Valley**	Breakfast: **Continental, plus**
Location: **18 mi. S of Newport**	Other Meals: **Available**
No. of Rooms: **4**	Pets: **No**
No. of Private Baths: **2**	Children: **Welcome**
Max. No. Sharing Bath: **2**	Smoking: **No**
Double/pb: **$45**	Social Drinking: **Permitted**
Single/pb: **$35**	Station Pickup: **Yes**
Double/sb: **$45**	

This scenic cottage is located on the shore of Crystal Lake, in the heart of Northeast Kingdom. Swim in clear clean water, lounge on the decks, fish from the docks, and go boating or canoeing. Landlubbers may opt for biking, hiking, and birdwatching; there are also four golf courses and free tennis courts. Snowbirds may ride sleighs and snowmobiles, or exert themselves in downhill and cross-country skiing at Burke Mountain, Stowe, and Jay Peak. If you still have time, visit antique shops and tour working farms. Then relax on the glassed-in porch and listen to the loons call; in the fall, you'll be able to admire the foliage and watch flocks of Canada geese settle for a rest before flying south. If you get the urge to travel, this B&B is a pivotal point for Canada, New Hampshire or Lake Champlain.

The Parmenter House ✪
BOX 106, BELMONT, VERMONT 05730

Tel: **(802) 259-2009; (800) 785-7468**	Single/pb: **$45**
Best Time to Call: **7:30 AM–noon;** **evenings**	Open: **All year**
	Reduced Rates: **Available**
Hosts: **Robin and Joe Phelan**	Breakfast: **Continental**
Location: **25 mi. SE of Rutland; 2 mi.** **from Rte. 155**	Credit Cards: **MC, VISA**
	Pets: **No**
No. of Rooms: **4**	Children: **Welcome**
No. of Private Baths: **4**	Smoking: **No**
Double/pb: **$55–$85**	Social Drinking: **Permitted**

You are certain to benefit from the clear mountain air of this idyllic lakeside village. In summer, swim or canoe on Star Lake by day, stargaze from the large deck by night. Explore a country lane on a crisp autumn morning or rent an all-terrain bike for an excursion, followed with mulled cider from the wood stove. Robin and Joe invite you to relax in the serene atmosphere of their parlor. Retire to your bedroom furnished with Victorian antiques, handmade quilts, and herbal wreaths. The bountiful breakfast buffet of fruit, local cheeses, homemade granola, and freshly baked breads is a gastronomic treat.

Greenhurst Inn
RIVER STREET, BETHEL, VERMONT 05032

Tel: **(802) 234-9474**	Single/sb: **$40–$55**
Hosts: **Lyle and Claire Wolf**	Open: **All year**
Location: **30 mi. E of Rutland**	Breakfast: **Continental**
No. of Rooms: **13**	Credit Cards: **DISC, MC, VISA**
No. of Private Baths: **7**	Pets: **Welcome (no cats)**
Max. No. Sharing Bath: **4**	Children: **Welcome (crib)**
Double/pb: **$75–$95**	Smoking: **Permitted**
Single/pb: **$65–$85**	Social Drinking: **Permitted**
Double/sb: **$50–$65**	

Located 100 yards from the White River, this elegant Queen Anne mansion, built in 1890, is listed on the National Register of Historic Places. The heavy brass hinges, embossed floral brass doorknobs, and etched windows at the entry have withstood the test of time. The cut-crystal collection is magnificent, and the stereoscope and old Victrola add to the old-fashioned atmosphere. The mansion is close to many points of historic interest, and seasonal recreational activities are abundant. Vermont Law School is close by.

Rosebelle's Victorian Inn ✪
31 FRANKLIN STREET, ROUTE 7, BRANDON, VERMONT 05733

Tel: **(802) 247-0098**	Breakfast: **Full**
Best Time to Call: **9 AM–9 PM**	Other Meals: **Available**
Hosts: **Ginette and Norman Milot**	Credit Cards: **MC, VISA**
Location: **14 mi. N of Rutland**	Pets: **No**
No. of Rooms: **6**	Children: **Welcome, over 12**
No. of Private Baths: **3**	Smoking: **No**
Max. No. Sharing Bath: **4**	Social Drinking: **Permitted**
Double/pb: **$65–$85**	Minimum Stay: **During foliage**
Double/sb: **$60–$75**	Airport/Station Pickup: **Yes**
Single/sb: **$50**	Foreign Languages: **French**
Open: **All year**	
Reduced Rates: **10% Mar., Apr., Nov.;**	
10% seniors	

In a village known for beautiful antique homes, this French Second Empire–style manor stands out with its stunning mansard roof, Italianate porch, and artistic exterior filigree. Inside you'll find folding doors, high ceilings, large windows, wide soft pine floors, and a sitting room with a fireplace. The furniture, wallpaper, and drapes enhance the nineteenth-century atmosphere. Visit your hosts' gift shop with Victorian and country crafts, read a book in the flower garden, or play croquet on the lawn. The village center is within walking distance; hiking, biking, cross-country and downhill skiing, museums, and antique shops are only minutes away, also near Middleburg College. Gift certificates and packages available.

The Cliff Hanger
RD 3, BOX 2027, BRISTOL, VERMONT 05443

Tel: **(802) 453-2013**	Open: **All year**
Best Time to Call: **Anytime**	Reduced Rates: **10% seniors**
Hosts: **Kim and Ken Hewitt**	Breakfast: **Full**
Location: **30 mi. S of Burlington**	Pets: **Sometimes**
No. of Rooms: **2**	Children: **Welcome**
No. of Private Baths: **1**	Smoking: **No**
Max. No. Sharing Bath: **3**	Social Drinking: **Permitted**
Double/pb: **$60**	Airport/Station Pickup: **Yes**
Single/sb: **$40**	

The Cliff Hanger is located on four acres with views of the Bristol Cliffs, beautiful perennial, wildflower, herb and vegetable gardens, and much wilderness to explore. The gardens attract birds, butterflies, and other fascinating creatures. There are many noted hiking and cross-country trails within walking distance of the house, which is about 30 minutes from Sugarbush Ski Resort and Mad River Glen (ski it if you can) for those who like downhill skiing. This is the part of the country that inspired Robert Frost and with little assistance you will be awed also. One of the ski trails nearby is called "Paradise"—and that it is. *Yankee Magazine* rated Mary's Restaurant in downtown Bristol as the "best restaurant in Vermont." Other attractions include Prayer Rock, Bartlett Falls on the New Haven River—which also has many nice, cool swimming holes—the Bristol Cliffs, where they say gold is still buried, and Deer Leap.

Green Trails Country Inn ✪
POND VILLAGE, BROOKFIELD, VERMONT 05036

Tel: **(802) 276-3412; (800) 243-3412**	Open: **May–Mar.**
Hosts: **Peter and Pat Simpson**	Reduced Rates: **Groups, AARP**
Location: **8 mi. from I-89, Exit 4**	Breakfast: **Full**
No. of Rooms: **15**	Other Meals: **Available**
No. of Private Baths: **9**	Pets: **No**
Max. No. Sharing Bath: **4**	Children: **Welcome (crib)**
Double/pb: **$77–$90**	Smoking: **No**
Single/pb: **$56–$66**	Social Drinking: **Permitted**
Double/sb: **$69–$80**	Airport/Station Pickup: **Yes**
Single/sb: **$50–$56**	

The inn consists of two buildings. One is an 1840 farmhouse; the other was built in the late 1700s and has pumpkin pine floorboards. They are located across from the famous Floating Bridge and Sunset Lake. Furnished in antiques and "early nostalgia," the rooms have stenciling, circa 1800, handmade quilts, and fresh flowers. The historic village is a perfect base for seasonal excursions to the Shelburne Museum or Woodstock. Cross-country skiers can start at the doorstep, while downhill enthusiasts can try Sugarbush and Killington.

Creamery Inn Bed & Breakfast ✪
P.O. BOX 187, CABOT, VERMONT 05647

Tel: (802) 563-2819
Hosts: Dan and Judy Lloyd
Location: 18 mi. NE of Montpelier
No. of Rooms: 3
No. of Private Baths: 1
Max. No. Sharing Bath: 4
Double/pb: $60
Single/pb: $35
Double/sb: $55
Single/sb: $35

Suites: $60
Open: All year
Reduced Rates: Families, Nov.–July
Breakfast: Full
Other Meals: Available
Pets: Sometimes
Children: Welcome
Smoking: No
Social Drinking: Permitted

Enjoy lovely year-round accommodations in this Federal-style home, circa 1835. Guest rooms are tastefully decorated, with stenciling, old-fashioned wallpaper, a canopy bed, and old trunks. Located one mile from Cabot Creamery, the inn is on two acres in a country setting beautiful in any season. New lambs each spring attract many visitors. It's a great area for joggers, hikers, bicyclists, and nature lovers—walk up the road and delight in ponds and waterfalls along the way. Full breakfasts include Finnish pancakes and other homemade fare.

Shire Inn ✪
MAIN STREET, CHELSEA, VERMONT 05038

Tel: **(802) 685-3031; (800) 441-6908**	Breakfast: **Full**
Hosts: **Jay and Karen Keller**	Other Meals: **Available**
Location: **20 mi. from I-89**	Credit Cards: **MC, VISA**
No. of Rooms: **6**	Pets: **No**
No. of Private Baths: **6**	Children: **Welcome, over 6**
Double/pb: **$80–$118**	Smoking: **No**
Open: **All year**	Social Drinking: **Permitted**

In 1832 a successful Chelsea businessman built this stately home entirely of Vermont brick. The Federal-style house was made to last, from the unusually high ceilings above to the pine floors below, now carefully restored and gleaming under coats of varnish. Enter through the granite front archway and step into the parlor, where a crackling fire and a warm welcome await. Your hosts are transplanted professionals who have left the city life for a white picket fence and a river flowing out back. They invite you to antique-filled bedrooms, several with fireplaces, and modern baths with fluffy, oversize towels. A typical Shire breakfast features German pancakes served with apricot sauce. Home cooking can also be enjoyed in the evening, when a five-course meal is served in the dining room. The inn is set on 23 acres in a quiet country village that is said to have the state's oldest general store.

Stone Hearth Inn ✪
ROUTE 11, CHESTER, VERMONT 05143

Tel: **(802) 875-2525**	Breakfast: **Full**
Hosts: **Janet and Don Strohmeyer**	Pets: **No**
Location: **10 mi. from I-91, Exit 6**	Children: **Welcome (crib)**
No. of Rooms: **10**	Smoking: **Restricted**
No. of Private Baths: **10**	Social Drinking: **Licensed pub**
Double/pb: **$60–$95**	Airport/Station Pickup: **Yes**
Single/pb: **$40–$65**	Foreign Languages: **Dutch, French,**
Open: **All year**	**German**
Reduced Rates: **Available**	

This white 19th-century Colonial is set on seven acres of fields and wooded land. The rooms have been lovingly restored and feature wide-board pine floors and open beams, floral wallpapers, antiques, quilts, and a player piano. A fire-warmed living room and library are available. After a busy day, relax in the licensed pub and recreation room, or enjoy the whirlpool spa. Horseback riding, downhill and cross-country skiing, and swimming in the river across the road are but a handful of the local pleasures. Your hosts offer fresh-baked breads, pancakes, and French toast for breakfast. The dining room and licensed pub are open to the public.

Craftsbury Bed & Breakfast on Wylie Hill ✪
CRAFTSBURY COMMON, VERMONT 05827

Tel: **(802) 586-2206**	Open: **All year**
Best Time to Call: **Mornings; evenings**	Breakfast: **Full**
Host: **Margaret Ramsdell**	Pets: **No**
Location: **40 mi. N of Montpelier**	Children: **Welcome (crib)**
No. of Rooms: **5**	Smoking: **No**
Max. No. Sharing Bath: **4**	Social Drinking: **Permitted**
Double/sb: **$60–$70**	Foreign Languages: **French**
Single/sb: **$45**	

This 1860 Georgian hilltop farmhouse has beautiful views. The homey guest rooms adjoin the living room with its wood stove, where you are welcome to relax and visit. You may use Margaret's kitchen, barbecue, and picnic table should the crisp mountain air stoke your appetite. You're sure to enjoy the bountiful breakfast that often features cinnamon apple pancakes with fresh maple syrup. Dinner is served only by prior arrangement. The ski slopes of Stowe are 30 miles away, and lakes and rivers are within a two-mile radius. Cross-country skiing starts at the door.

Buckmaster Inn ✪
LINCOLN HILL ROAD, CUTTINGSVILLE, VERMONT 05738

Tel: **(802) 492-3485**	Single/sb: **$40–$50**
Best Time to Call: **8 AM–8 PM**	Open: **All year**
Hosts: **Sam and Grace Husselman**	Reduced Rates: **Weekly**
Location: **8 mi. SE of Rutland**	Breakfast: **Full**
No. of Rooms: **3**	Pets: **No**
No. of Private Baths: **2**	Children: **Welcome, over 8**
Max. No. Sharing Bath: **4**	Smoking: **No**
Double/pb: **$60–$65**	Social Drinking: **Permitted**
Single/pb: **$50–$65**	Airport/Station Pickup: **Yes**
Double/sb: **$50**	Foreign Languages: **Dutch**

The Buckmaster Inn, located near Cuttingsville in the Green Mountains, is a Federal clapboard Colonial overlooking a picturesque valley. Its center hall, grand staircase, and wide pine floors are typical of 19th-century style. This is New England relaxation at its best: fireplaces, wood-burning stove, library, and two porches. Homemade muffins, casseroles, and jams are among the specialties served in the country kitchen each morning. A pond for skating and fishing is within walking distance, and ski slopes, hiking trails, and craft shops are nearby.

The Quail's Nest Bed and Breakfast
P.O. BOX 221, MAIN STREET, DANBY, VERMONT 05739

Tel: (802) 293-5099	Open: All year
Best Time to Call: 11 AM–10 PM	Reduced Rates: $10 less April, May,
Hosts: Greg and Nancy Diaz	June and Nov.
Location: 13 mi. N of Manchester	Breakfast: Full
No. of Rooms: 6	Credit Cards: MC, VISA
No. of Private Baths: 4	Pets: No
Double/pb: $75	Children: Welcome, over 8
Single/pb: $55	Smoking: No
Double/sb: $60	Social Drinking: Permitted
Single/sb: $45	

The Quail's Nest is a Greek Revival-style inn (circa 1835) nestled in the quiet village of Danby. Guest rooms are furnished with antiques and handmade country quilts. Your hosts love entertaining and offer such homemade breakfast specialties as assorted breads, muffins, and quiches; catering to special dietary requirements and tastes is never a problem. The Green Mountains are just east of here, offering some of the finest swimming, fishing, hiking, and downhill and cross-country skiing in the state. The inn is centrally located just minutes from the alpine ski slopes of Stratton, Bromley, Killington, Pico, and Okemo.

Derby Village Inn ☉
46 MAIN STREET, DERBY LINE, VERMONT 05830

Tel: (802) 873-3604	Open: All year
Hosts: Tom and Phyllis Moreau	Breakfast: Full
Location: 45 mi. N of St. Johnsbury	Credit Cards: MC, VISA
No. of Rooms: 5	Pets: No
No. of Private Baths: 5	Children: Welcome
Double/pb: $55–$65	Smoking: No
Single/pb: $45–$55	Social Drinking: Permitted

The village of Derby Line straddles the U.S.–Canadian border. Phyllis and Tom's home is a rambling Victorian mansion boasting beautiful wood wainscoting. The immaculate, airy bedrooms are furnished with select antiques, braided rugs, charming wallpaper and tieback curtains. Breakfast menus may feature cheddar cheese strata apple pancakes with cider syrup. It's an easy walk to the town's unique international library and opera house. Downhill or cross-country skiing, water sports, golf, fishing, and antiquing are just some of the seasonal activities.

The Little Lodge at Dorset ☺
ROUTE 30, BOX 673, DORSET, VERMONT 05251

Tel: **(802) 867-4040**
Best Time to Call: **Anytime**
Hosts: **Allan and Nancy Norris**
Location: **6 mi. N of Manchester**
No. of Rooms: **5**
No. of Private Baths: **5**
Double/pb: **$80–$100**
Single/pb: **$70–$90**

Open: **All year**
Breakfast: **Continental, plus**
Credit Cards: **AMEX, DISC**
Pets: **No**
Children: **Welcome**
Smoking: **No**
Social Drinking: **Permitted**

Situated in one of the prettiest little towns in Vermont, this delightful 1820 Colonial house, on the Historic Register, is perched on a hillside way back from the road, overlooking the mountains and its own trout pond that's used for skating in winter or swimming in summer. The original paneling and wide floorboards set off the splendid antiques. After skiing at nearby Stratton or Bromley, toast your feet by the fireplace while sipping hot chocolate. If you prefer, bring your own liquor, and Nancy and Allan will provide Vermont cheese and crackers.

Christmas Tree Bed & Breakfast
BENEDICT ROAD, EAST DORSET, VERMONT 05253

Tel: **(802) 362-4889**
Hosts: **Dennis and Catherine Conroy**
Location: **4.5 mi. N of Manchester**
No. of Rooms: **4**
Max. No. Sharing Bath: **4**
Double/pb: **$50–$55**
Single/pb: **$30–$35**
Double/sb: **$45**

Single/sb: **$25**
Open: **All year**
Breakfast: **Continental**
Pets: **Sometimes**
Children: **Welcome**
Smoking: **No**
Social Drinking: **Permitted**

Dennis and Catherine invite you to share their contemporary wood-paneled home where you are welcome to relax on the deck or in front of the wood stove, depending upon the season. There's a pond and a stream for fishing, and it is located close to Emerald Lake State Park. It is 15 minutes from the slopes at Bromley; 30 minutes from Stratton. The coffeepot is always on, and pretzels and chips are complimentary. The generous breakfast may let you skip lunch.

Hansel & Gretel Haus ☺
BOX 95, TOWN HIGHWAY 34, EAST HAVEN, VERMONT 05837

Tel: **(802) 467-8884**
Hosts: **Eileen and John Hombach**
Location: **20 mi. N of St. Johnsbury**
No. of Rooms: **3**

Max. No. Sharing Bath: **4**
Double/sb: **$45**
Single/sb: **$35**
Open: **Jan.–Nov.**

Reduced Rates: **10% seniors; 10% after 3 nights**
Breakfast: **Full**
Other Meals: **Available**
Credit Cards: **MC, VISA**

Pets: **No**
Children: **Welcome, over 10**
Smoking: **No**
Social Drinking: **Permitted**

Appropriately enough, Hansel & Gretel Haus is located in the forest of Vermont's Northeast Kingdom. Your hosts strive for coziness in their rooms and decor; they also operate a small gift and crafts shop on the premises. For downhill and cross-country skiers, nearby Burke Mountain Ski Area is a promising destination. Numerous lakes will appeal to swimmers and fishermen. Other outdoor types, from golfers and bicyclists to hikers and snowmobilers, will find plenty to do here.

Maplewood Inn & Antiques
ROUTE 22A SOUTH, FAIR HAVEN, VERMONT 05743

Tel: **(802) 265-8039; (800) 253-7729**
Best Time to Call: **9 AM–9 PM**
Hosts: **Cindy and Doug Baird**
Location: **18 mi. W of Rutland**
No. of Rooms: **5**
No. of Private Baths: **5**
Double/pb: **$70–$85**
Suites: **$105**
Open: **All year**
Reduced Rates: **After 5th night**

Breakfast: **Continental, plus**
Credit Cards: **AMEX, CB, DC, DISC, MC, VISA**
Pets: **No**
Children: **Welcome, over 5**
Smoking: **Permitted**
Social Drinking: **Permitted**
Minimum Stay: **Parents college weekends, holidays**

The inn is a beautifully restored Greek Revival–style home, built in 1850, with lovely country views from every window. Chippendale furnishings, original pine floors polished to a warm glow, four-poster or brass beds, wingback chairs, and carefully chosen accessories provide a soothing backdrop for a relaxing visit. Cindy and Doug have added air-conditioning, TVs, and phones, and four out of the five rooms have fireplaces. After a multicourse breakfast, enjoy a walk in the historic village or participate in the recreational activities at nearby

Lakes Bomoseen and St. Catherine, or take a short drive to ski the slopes of Killington or Pico. Linger on the porch, play croquet on the lawn, enjoy a board game or a book in the parlor. The gourmet restaurants and shops of Rutland are close by. Reserve early for the fall foliage season. Don't forget to visit their shops in the Red Barn behind Maplewood Inn!

Silver Maple Lodge and Cottages ✪
SOUTH MAIN STREET, RR1, BOX 8, FAIRLEE, VERMONT 05045

Tel: (802) 333-4326; (800) 666-1946	Single/sb: $44
Hosts: Scott and Sharon Wright	Open: All year
Location: 20 mi. N of White River Junction	Reduced Rates: 10% seniors, AAA
	Breakfast: Continental
No. of Rooms: 14	Credit Cards: AMEX, MC, VISA
No. of Private Baths: 12	Pets: Sometimes
Max. No. Sharing Bath: 4	Children: Welcome
Double/pb: $58–$70	Smoking: Permitted
Single/pb: $56–$68	Social Drinking: Permitted
Double/sb: $48	Airport/Station Pickup: Yes

Built as a farmhouse in 1855, Silver Maple Lodge became an inn some seventy years later. To accommodate extra guests, several cottages were added, constructed from lumber cut on the property. It's easy to see why this B&B remains popular. There's swimming, boating, and fishing at two local lakes. Other outdoor activities in the area include golf, tennis, horseback riding, canoeing, hiking, and skiing. If you're tired of feeling earthbound, Post Mills Airport, seven miles away, offers flights in a hot-air balloon and gliding rides. (Special packages, combining a flight in a hot-air balloon and other activities of your choice, can be arranged.) And for concerts, theater, and art exhibits, it's an easy drive to Dartmouth College, in Hanover, New Hampshire.

Heron House Bed & Breakfast ✪
HIGHGATE SPRINGS, VERMONT (MAILING ADDRESS: RR 2, BOX 174-2, SWANTON, VERMONT 05488)

Tel: (802) 868-7433	Single/pb: $45
Best Time to Call: Anytime before 10 PM	Open: All year
	Reduced Rates: 10% seniors
Hosts: Shirley and Ray Henderson	Breakfast: Full
Location: 42 mi. N of Burlington	Pets: No
No. of Rooms: 1	Children: No
No. of Private Baths: 1	Smoking: No
Double/pb: $50	Social Drinking: Permitted

It's a short stroll to Lake Champlain from Shirley and Ray's recently built country home, which lies off a secluded private road, surrounded by trees and wildlife. The pleasant mauve-and-lavender color scheme lends a fresh, airy feeling to the carpeted bedroom, which has a four-poster bed and an indoor balcony overlooking the cathedral-style living room (a favorite place for their fluffy orange cat, Fritz). Shirley's generous breakfast features freshly baked muffins, bacon, and oat pancakes served with Vermont's celebrated maple syrup. The Canadian border is a short drive away, while Montreal and Jay and Smuggler's ski areas are within one hour by car.

Henry M. Field House Bed & Breakfast
ROUTE 15, RR2, BOX 395, JERICHO, VERMONT 05452

Tel: **(802) 899-3984**
Best Time to Call: **After 5 PM**
Hosts: **Mary Beth and Terrence L. Horan**
Location: **12 mi. E of Burlington**
No. of Rooms: **3**
No. of Private Baths: **3**
Double/pb: **$60–$70**

Open: **All year**
Breakfast: **Full**
Credit Cards: **MC, VISA**
Pets: **No**
Children: **Welcome, over 8**
Smoking: **No**
Social Drinking: **Permitted**

This is an opulent, Italian-style Victorian with all the trimmings: high ceilings, ornamental plaster, etched glass, and chestnut and walnut woodwork. Guests may relax on one of three porches or stroll along the Browns River, which borders the lovely three-and-a-half-acre property. Jericho is convenient to skiing at Bolton Valley or Smuggler's Notch; hiking, biking, golf, and water sports are all within a 30-minute drive. The Henry M. Field House also offers easy access to Burlington, home of the University of Vermont, and many fine shops and restaurants.

Milliken's ✪
RD 2, BOX 397, JERICHO, VERMONT 05465

Tel: **(802) 899-3993**
Best Time to Call: **Mornings; evenings**
Hosts: **Rick and Jean Milliken**
Location: **12 mi. E of Burlington**
No. of Rooms: **2**
Max. No. Sharing Bath: **4**
Double/sb: **$45**
Single/sb: **$35**

Suites: **$60**
Open: **All year**
Breakfast: **Full**
Pets: **No**
Children: **Welcome**
Smoking: **No**
Social Drinking: **Permitted**
Airport/Station Pickup: **Yes**

This Second Empire early Victorian was built in 1867 by a lumber magnate. The house has a graceful mansard roof, original woodwork, and floors of alternating cherry and white maple. The spaciousness of the rooms is enhanced by high ceilings, large windows, and gracious decor. Rick is a hotel manager and Jean is a choreographer and host. She prepares such breakfast specialties as French toast with maple syrup and hot mulled cider. In the evening, a good-night brandy and snack are offered. Your family is sure to enjoy its stay with the Millikens, their two children, and a friendly dog named Bailey. Nearby attractions are hiking trails on Mt. Mansfield, skiing, and fabulous fall foliage.

Minterhaus Bed & Breakfast ✪
P.O. BOX 226, JERICHO, VERMONT 05465

Tel: **(802) 899-3900**
Best Time to Call: **9 AM–9 PM**
Host: **Ruth Minter**

Location: **12 mi. NE of Burlington**
No. of Rooms: **3**
Max. No. Sharing Bath: **4**

Double/sb: **$45**
Single/sb: **$40**
Suite: **$65**
Open: **Aug. 1–June 30**
Breakfast: **Continental**

Pets: **No**
Children: **Welcome**
Smoking: **No**
Social Drinking: **Permitted**

Minterhaus is located on two riverfront acres in the historic village of Jericho, within walking distance of Old Red Mill Museum and Craft Shop and Old Mill Park. It is also near Mt. Mansfield, a source of year-round recreation with its hiking paths and ski areas. Lake Champlain and Burlington are a half hour away by car. This home, built in the mid–1800s, is on the National Register of Historic Places. Guests appreciate the warmth of its butternut woodwork, pine floors and many antique furnishings. A generous Continental breakfast of juice, fruits, cereals, home-baked breads, and other specialties is served.

Brook 'n' Hearth ✪
STATE ROAD 11/30, BOX 508, MANCHESTER CENTER, VERMONT 05255

Tel: **(802) 362-3604**
Best Time to Call: **10 AM–10 PM**
Hosts: **Larry and Terry Greene**
Location: **1 mi. E of US 7**
No. of Rooms: **3**
No. of Private Baths: **3**
Double/pb: **$70**
Single/pb: **$46**
Suites: **$80 for 2**

Open: **May 22–Oct. 30; Nov. 20–Apr. 17**
Reduced Rates: **Available**
Breakfast: **Full**
Credit Cards: **AMEX, DISC, MC, VISA**
Pets: **No**
Children: **Welcome (crib)**
Smoking: **Restricted**
Social Drinking: **Permitted**

True to its name, a brook runs through the property and a fire warms the living room of this country home. Terry and Larry offer setups and happy-hour snacks for your self-supplied cocktails. You're within five miles of the ski slopes at Bromley and Stratton; it is also convenient to art centers, summer theater, restaurants, and a score of sports that include hiking on the Long Trail. Air-conditioned in summer, enjoy the pool, lawn games, and barbecue. The game room, with its VCR, pocket billiards, and Ping-Pong, is always available.

Brookside Meadows Country Bed & Breakfast ✪
RD 3, BOX 2460, MIDDLEBURY, VERMONT 05753-8751

Tel: **(802) 388-6429;**
  reservations only: **(800) 442-9887**
Hosts: **Linda and Roger Cole**
Location: **2½ mi. from Rte. 7**
No. of Rooms: **5**
No. of Private Baths: **5**

Double/pb: **$75–$90**
Suites: **$90–$105**
Open: **All year**
Breakfast: **Full**
Credit Cards: **MC, VISA**
Pets: **No**

Children: **Welcome, over 5**	Minimum Stay: **2 nights weekends and**
Smoking: **No**	**peak times**
Social Drinking: **Permitted**	Airport/Station Pickup: **Yes**

This handsome farmhouse was built in 1979, based on a nineteenth-century design. Located on a country road, on twenty acres of meadowland, the property borders a brook. The two-bedroom suite has a living room with wood stove, dining area, and kitchen as well as a private entrance and bath. Relax and enjoy spacious lawns, perennial gardens, a spectacular view of the Green Mountains, and only country sounds. Area attractions include excellent downhill and cross-country skiing, hiking, swimming, Lake Champlain ferryboat trips, maple syrup operations, Middlebury College, the University of Vermont, Morgan Horse Farm, Fort Ticonderoga, and Shelburne Museum.

Phineas Swann
P.O. BOX 43, MONTGOMERY CENTER, VERMONT 05471

Tel: **(802) 326-4306**	Single/sb: **$45**
Best Time to Call: **9 AM–9 PM**	Open: **All year**
Hosts: **Glen Bartolomeo and Michael**	Reduced Rates: **15% weekly**
Bindler	Breakfast: **Full**
Location: **56 mi. NE of Burlington**	Credit Cards: **MC, VISA**
No. of Rooms: **4**	Pets: **No**
No. of Private Baths: **2**	Children: **Welcome, over 6**
Max. No. Sharing Bath: **4**	Smoking: **No**
Double/pb: **$70**	Social Drinking: **Permitted**
Single/pb: **$50**	Airport/Station Pickup: **Yes**
Double/sb: **$65**	

A Victorian house with a country flavor, Phineas Swann has an enclosed porch and lots of gingerbread trim. Inside, the house is decorated in pastels, with overstuffed chairs and sofas and period antiques. Each bedroom has its own distinct style and flair. Outside the B&B, you're close to all of the wonderful recreational possibilities that Montgomery Center has to offer—downhill and cross-country skiing, hiking, biking, boating, lots of fishing, and more. Sedentary types will want to visit the many antique shops and restaurants in the area. Breakfasts consist of home-baked breads and muffins, with an entrée like raspberry French toast or blueberry buttermilk pancakes with local Vermont maple syrup.

Betsy's B&B ✪
74 EAST STATE STREET, MONTPELIER, VERMONT 05602

Tel: **(802) 229-0466**	No. of Private Baths: **5**
Hosts: **Jon and Betsy Anderson**	Double/pb: **$60–$75**
Location: **¼ mi. E of Montpelier**	Single/pb: **$55–$70**
No. of Rooms: **5**	Suites: **$105**

Open: **All year**
Reduced Rates: **Available**
Breakfast: **Full**
Credit Cards: **MC, VISA**
Pets: **No**

Children: **Welcome**
Smoking: **No**
Social Drinking: **Permitted**
Airport/Station Pickup: **Yes**

This fancy Queen Anne B&B in the historic district near downtown, Statehouse, Vermont College, and history and art museums is a real find. It is lavishly furnished with period antiques. Great restaurants and interesting book, crafts and sporting goods shops are nearby. Walk or run in nearby park or neighborhoods with Victorian homes, then relax on the porch or decks. Betsy's boasts award-winning building restoration and landscaping. Amenities include in-room cable TV and telephone, exercise room, hot tub, and fax. Choose from three rooms in main house plus a two-bedroom carriage house suite with full kitchen, dining and living areas. Your hosts are two lawyers interested in historic preservation, gardening, antiques, and politics.

Hunt's Hideaway ✪
RR 1, BOX 570, WEST CHARLESTON, MORGAN, VERMONT 05872

Tel: **(802) 895-4432, 334-8322**
Best Time to Call: **7 AM–11 PM**
Host: **Pat Hunt**
Location: **6 mi. from I-91**
No. of Rooms: **3**
Max. No. Sharing Bath: **4**
Double/sb: **$35**
Single/sb: **$25**

Open: **All year**
Reduced Rates: **Available**
Breakfast: **Full**
Pets: **Sometimes**
Children: **Welcome**
Smoking: **Permitted**
Social Drinking: **Permitted**

This modern, split-level home is located on 100 acres of woods and fields, with a brook, pond, and large swimming pool. Pancakes with Vermont maple syrup are featured at breakfast. Ski Jay Peak and Burke, or fish and boat on Lake Seymour, two miles away. Visiting antique shops or taking a trip to nearby Canada are other local possibilities.

Charlie's Northland Lodge ✪
BOX 88, NORTH HERO, VERMONT 05474

Tel: **(802) 372-8822**
Best Time to Call: **Before 8 PM**
Hosts: **Charles and Dorice Clark**
Location: **60 mi. S of Montreal, Canada**
No. of Rooms: **3**
Max. No. Sharing Bath: **5**
Double/sb: **$45–$50**
Guest Cottage: **$350–$550 weekly;**
  sleeps 6

Open: **All year**
Breakfast: **Continental**
Pets: **No**
Children: **Welcome, over 5**
Smoking: **Permitted**
Social Drinking: **Permitted**

The lodge is a restored Colonial, circa 1850, located on Lake Champlain, where bass and walleye abound. A sport and tackle shop is on the premises. Fall and winter fishing should appeal to all anglers. In summer, hiking, biking, fishing, boating, or relaxing in the reading room are pleasant activities.

Rose Apple Acres Farm ✪
RR 2, BOX 300, EAST HILL ROAD, NORTH TROY, VERMONT 05859

Tel: **(802) 988-4300**	Single/sb: **$35**
Best Time to Call: **Evenings**	Open: **All year**
Hosts: **Jay and Camilla Mead**	Breakfast: **Full**
Location: **60 mi. N of St. Johnsbury**	Pets: **No**
No. of Rooms: **3**	Children: **Welcome, over 6**
No. of Private Baths: **1**	Smoking: **No**
Max. No. Sharing Bath: **4**	Social Drinking: **Permitted**
Double/pb: **$60**	Airport/Station Pickup: **Yes**
Double/sb: **$50**	

Located 2 miles from the Canadian border and 2 hours from Montreal or Burlington, the farm is situated on 52 acres of fields, woods, and streams. The farmhouse has a bright and friendly atmosphere, enhanced by panoramic mountain views. Hiking, cross-country skiing, and snowshoeing may be enjoyed on-premises. Horse-drawn carriage and sleigh rides are offered. It is only 10 miles to Jay Peak for skiing. Camilla and Jay are interested in classical music and gardening.

Northfield Inn ✪
27 HIGHLAND AVENUE, NORTHFIELD, VERMONT 05663

Tel: **(802) 485-8558**	Open: **All year**
Best Time to Call: **Day**	Breakfast: **Full**
Hosts: **Aglaia and Alan Stalb**	Other Meals: **Available**
Location: **9 mi. S of Montpelier**	Pets: **No**
No. of Rooms: **8**	Children: **Welcome, over 15**
No. of Private Baths: **8**	Smoking: **No**
Double/pb: **$85**	Social Drinking: **Permitted**
Single/pb: **$75**	Minimum Stay: **During special events**
Double/sb: **$75**	Airport/Station Pickup: **Yes**
Single/sb: **$55**	Foreign Languages: **Greek**
Suites: **$130–$140; sleeps 2–3**	

This fully restored Victorian mansion is nestled on a sun-bathed hillside with a magnificent view of the Green Mountains and the valley below. Visit here for a romantic interlude that refreshes and rejuvenates your spirit. The luxurious furnishings include antiques, brass and carved wooden beds, European feather bedding, and oriental rugs. A hearty breakfast, afternoon tea, snacks, and beverages are yours to enjoy.

Four Bridges Inn ✪

P.O. BOX 117, SCHOOL STREET, NORTHFIELD FALLS, VERMONT 05664

Tel: **(802) 485-8995**
Best Time to Call: **Anytime**
Hosts: **John and Sue Fisher**
Location: **8 mi. S of Montpelier**
No. of Rooms: **2**
No. of Private Baths: **2**
Double/pb: **$65**
Single/pb: **$60**
Open: **All year**

Reduced Rates: **Available**
Breakfast: **Full**
Credit Cards: **MC, VISA**
Pets: **No**
Children: **Welcome**
Smoking: **No**
Social Drinking: **Permitted**
Minimum Stay: **2 nights graduation, Quilt Festival**

Here is just what you are looking for: a wonderful place in a picturesque village, and close to everything—two miles to Northfield, eight miles to Montpelier. Almost every corner in Vermont is within two hours. This inn is an award-winning 1896 Victorian decorated with beautiful antiques, romantic touches and lovely gardens. Breakfast is always an adventure of bountiful, great food, and great information. Tips on six golf courses, fly fishing, skiing, waterfall hunting, covered bridges, granite statutes, sugaring, and much more is available, whether you have lots to do or nothing at all.

Hillcrest Guest House ✪

RR 1, BOX 4459, RUTLAND, VERMONT 05701

Tel: **(802) 775-1670**
Hosts: **Bob and Peg Dombro**
Location: **³⁄₁₀ mi. from Rte. 7**
No. of Rooms: **3**
Max. No. Sharing Bath: **5**

Double/sb: **$45**
Single/sb: **$40**
Open: **All year**
Breakfast: **Continental**
Pets: **No**

Children: **Welcome, over 5**
Smoking: **No**

Social Drinking: **Permitted**
Airport/Station Pickup: **Yes**

This 150-year-old farmhouse, with a comfortable screened porch for warm-weather relaxing, is furnished with country antiques. Pico and Killington ski areas are 7 and 16 miles away, respectively. Summer brings the opportunity to explore charming villages, covered bridges, and antiques and crafts centers. Country auctions, marble quarries, trout streams, and Sunday-evening band concerts are pleasant pastimes. Bob and Peg always offer something in the way of between-meal refreshments.

Bittersweet Inn
692 SOUTH MAIN STREET, STOWE, VERMONT 05672

Tel: **(802) 253-7787**
Best Time to Call: **7 AM–10 PM**
Hosts: **Barbara and Paul Hansel**
Location: **36 mi. E of Burlington**
No. of Rooms: **8**
No. of Private Baths: **5**
Max. No. Sharing Bath: **4**
Double/pb: **$64–$80**
Double/sb: **$54–$68**

Suites: **$135–$165**
Open: **All year**
Reduced Rates: **5-night stays**
Breakfast: **Continental, plus**
Credit Cards: **AMEX, DISC, MC, VISA**
Children: **Welcome (play area)**
Smoking: **Permitted**
Social Drinking: **Permitted**

Bittersweet Inn is a brick Cape with converted clapboard carriage house, dating back to 1835. The house is set on eleven and a half acres, overlooking Camel's Hump Mountain. Inside you'll find comfortable rooms decorated with a combination of antiques and family pieces. It's just a half mile to the center of town and minutes to ski lifts and a cross-country touring center. A good-size swimming pool is located out back with plenty of room for laps or just taking it easy. In the winter season, hot soup and the indoor hydro-spa will be waiting after your last ski run. Your hosts, Barbara and Paul, invite you to relax in the game room with BYOB bar and will help you plan your evening.

The Inn at the Brass Lantern ✪
717 MAPLE STREET, STOWE, VERMONT 05672

Tel: **(802) 253-2229; (800) 729-2980**
Best Time to Call: **9 AM–9 PM**
Host: **Andy Aldrich**
Location: **10 mi. from I-89, Exit 10**
No. of Rooms: **9**
No. of Private Baths: **9**
Double/pb: **$70–$150**
Single/pb: **$60–$140**
Open: **All year**

Reduced Rates: **Available**
Breakfast: **Full**
Credit Cards: **AMEX, MC, VISA**
Pets: **No**
Children: **Welcome**
Smoking: **No**
Social Drinking: **Permitted**
Minimum Stay: **Weekends, foliage, and holidays**

The inn was originally built as a farmhouse and carriage barn around 1800. Andy won an award for his efforts in its restoration by maintaining its character with the artful use of period antiques, handmade quilts, and handmade accessories. Its setting provides panoramic views of Mt. Mansfield and the valley. You are invited to join your host for wine, tea, and dessert while watching the sun set over the Green Mountains.

Ski Inn ✪
ROUTE 108, STOWE, VERMONT 05672

Tel: **(802) 253-4050**
Best Time to Call: **Before 10 AM, after 7:30 PM**
Hosts: **The Heyer Family**
Location: **47 mi. NE of Burlington**
No. of Rooms: **10**
No. of Private Baths: **5**
Max. No. Sharing Bath: **5**
Double/pb: **$50–$60**
Double/sb: **$40–$45**

Single/sb: **$30–$45**
Open: **All year**
Reduced Rates: **Off-season**
Breakfast: **Continental**
Other Meals: **In winter, full breakfast and dinner (additional fee)**
Pets: **Sometimes**
Children: **Welcome**
Smoking: **No**
Social Drinking: **Permitted**

This traditional New England inn, set back from the highway among evergreens on a gentle sloping hillside, is a quiet place to relax and sleep soundly. In winter, it's a skier's delight, close to Mt. Mansfield's downhill and cross-country trails. In summer, the rates drop and include just Continental breakfast. The Heyer Family offers warm hospitality in all seasons.

Boardman House Bed & Breakfast ✪
P.O. BOX 112, TOWNSHEND, VERMONT 05353

Tel: **(802) 365-4086**
Hosts: **Sarah Messenger and Paul Weber**
Location: **125 mi. N of Boston**
No. of Rooms: **6**
No. of Private Baths: **5**
Max. No. Sharing Bath: **4**
Double/pb: **$70–$80**
Single/pb: **$65–$75**

Suites: **$90–$100**
Open: **All year**
Reduced Rates: **10–15% seniors; off-season; weekly**
Breakfast: **Full**
Pets: **Sometimes**
Children: **Welcome**
Smoking: **Restricted**
Social Drinking: **Permitted**

If you tried to imagine an idealized New England home, it would resemble this white 19th-century farmhouse set on Townshend's Village Green. This is a prime foliage and antiquing area. Direct access to State Routes 30 and 35 allows you to pursue other interests, from skiing at Stratton to canoeing on the West River. Gourmet breakfasts feature pear pancakes, individual soufflés, hot fruit compotes, and more.

Newton's 1824 House Inn
ROUTE 100, BOX 159, WAITSFIELD, VERMONT 05673

Tel: (802) 496-7555; (800) 42-
  NEWTON; fax: (802) 496-5558
Best Time to Call: 9:30 AM
Hosts: Nick and Joyce Newton
Location: 18 mi. SE of Montpelier
No. of Rooms: 6
No. of Private Baths: 6
Double/pb: $85–$125
Single/pb: $75–$115
Open: All year

Breakfast: Full
Credit Cards: DISC, MC, VISA
Pets: No
Children: By arrangement
Smoking: No
Social Drinking: Permitted
Minimum Stay: 2 nights Sept. 17–
  Oct. 17, holidays
Airport/Station Pickup: Yes
Foreign Languages: Spanish

Surrounded by original art, oriental rugs, select antiques, and period furniture, guests enjoy a relaxed elegance at this two-story clapboard farmhouse crowned with ten gables. Built in 1824, it was recently recommended for National Register status. The farm's 52 acres include scenic hills, pastures, stands of pines and sugarbush. The Mad River runs through the property and feeds a great private swimming hole. It's only minutes from Sugarbush Resort and Mad River Glen ski areas. After a good night's sleep in one of the cozy bedrooms, one can look forward to such breakfast treats as baked stuffed pears with nuts and currants, oatmeal soufflé, or apple muffins.

White Rocks Inn ○
RR 1, BOX 297, ROUTE 7, WALLINGFORD, VERMONT 05773

Tel: (802) 446-2077
Best Time to Call: Mornings; evenings
Hosts: June and Alfred Matthews
Location: 20 mi. N of Manchester
No. of Rooms: 5
No. of Private Baths: 5
Double/pb: $70–$110
Single/pb: $65–$100
Guest Cottage: $130–$140
Open: Dec. 1–Oct. 31

Breakfast: Full
Credit Cards: MC, VISA
Pets: No
Children: Welcome, over 10
Smoking: No
Social Drinking: Permitted
Minimum Stay: 2 nights holidays, fall
  foliage season
Foreign Languages: French, Spanish

If your idea of paradise is a pasture, a creek stocked with trout, an old-fashioned swimming hole, and a peaceful valley surrounded by mountains, then reserve a room here. June and Alfred have renovated their vintage 1800 farmhouse with care, preserving the charm of wide-board floors, wainscoting, ornate moldings, and high ceilings, while enhancing it with antiques, oriental rugs, and canopied beds. In summer, such breakfast delights as banana pancakes or raisin bread French toast is served on the large veranda overlooking the meadows. In cooler weather, this feast is presented in the dining room. Five downhill ski areas are a short drive away, and miles of cross-country ski trails are adjacent to the inn.

West Hill House
RR1, BOX 292, WEST HILL ROAD, WARREN, VERMONT 05674

Tel: (802) 496-7162	Reduced Rates: Available
Best Time to Call: 7 AM–10 PM	Breakfast: Full
Hosts: Dotty Kyle and Eric Brattstrom	Credit Cards: MC, VISA
Location: 25 mi. SW of Montpelier	Pets: No
No. of Rooms: 4	Children: Welcome, over 10
No. of Private Baths: 4	Smoking: No
Double/pb: $85–$95	Social Drinking: Permitted
Single/pb: $55–$70	Minimum Stay: 2 nights weekends
Open: All year	

Up a quiet country lane, on nine wooded and open acres with stunning mountain views, gardens, pond and apple orchard, this 1860s farmhouse is one mile from Sugarbush Ski Resort, adjacent to its golf course and cross-country ski trails. Take advantage of an outdoor sports paradise near fine restaurants, quaint villages, covered bridges and unique shops. After a busy day, enjoy the comfortable front porch or a roaring fire, eclectic library, oriental rugs, art, antiques, and the interesting company of other guests. Bedrooms feature premium linens, down comforters, and good reading lights. The guest pantry has a wet bar and fridge. Dotty and Eric pride themselves on their memorable breakfasts, afternoon and bedtime snacks.

Grünberg Haus ✪
RR2, BOX 1595, WATERBURY, VERMONT 05676

Tel: (802) 244-7726; (800) 800-7760	Open: All year
Hosts: Christopher Sellers and Mark Frohman	Reduced Rates: 10% after 3rd night
	Breakfast: Full
Location: 25 mi. E of Burlington	Other Meals: Available
No. of Rooms: 15	Credit Cards: AMEX, DISC, MC, VISA
Max. No. Sharing Bath: 4	Pets: No
Double/pb: $80–$150	Children: Welcome
Single/pb: $55–$105	Smoking: No
Double/sb: $55–$75	Social Drinking: Permitted
Single/sb: $35–$55	Airport/Station Pickup: Yes

You'll think you're in the Alps when you see this hand-built Tyrolean chalet perched on a secluded hillside. The living room features an eight-foot grand piano, a massive fieldstone fireplace, and a long breakfast table overlooking the valley and distant forest. All fifteen guest rooms open onto the quaint balcony that surrounds the chalet. The BYOB rathskeller features hand-stenciled booths; the formal dining room is furnished with antiques. Outside, cleared logging trails provide cross-country skiing and hiking access to hundreds of acres of meadows and woodlands. And Waterbury's central location makes it easy to get to ski resorts like Stowe and Sugarbush. Whatever you plan to do, bring an appetite; Grünberg Haus serves memorable gourmet breakfasts, and other meals can be arranged.

Inn at Blush Hill ✪

BOX 1266, BLUSH HILL ROAD, WATERBURY, VERMONT 05676

Tel: (802) 244-7529; (800) 736-7522
Hosts: Gary and Pam Gosselin
Location: 22 mi. E. of Burlington
No. of Rooms: 6
No. of Private Baths: 2
Max. No. Sharing Bath: 4
Double/pb: $75–$90
Double/sb: $50–$70
Open: All year

Reduced Rates: Available
Breakfast: Full
Credit Cards: AMEX, DISC, MC, VISA
Pets: No
Children: Welcome, over 6
Smoking: No
Social Drinking: Permitted
Airport/Station Pickup: Yes

This 1790 brick farmhouse is located halfway between the Stowe and Sugarbush ski areas. The atmosphere is warm and homey, with antiques, old-time rockers, books, and lots of fireplaces. Your host is a gourmet cook and enjoys making her own bread and muffins each morning. A huge lake with boating, swimming, and fishing is located just one and a half miles from the house, and a nine-hole golf course is located directly across the street. At the end of the day, sit back and enjoy the surroundings, relaxing on the large, old-fashioned porch. Afternoon and evening refreshments are served.

The Weathervane Lodge B&B ✪

BOX 57, DORR FITCH ROAD, WEST DOVER, VERMONT 05356

Tel: (802) 464-5426
Hosts: Liz and Ernie Cabot
Location: 1 mi. from Rte. 100
No. of Rooms: 10
No. of Private Baths: 3
Max. No. Sharing Bath: 4
Double/pb: $64–$72
Single/pb: $42–$56
Double/sb: $42–$56
Single/sb: $39–$42

Suites: $88–$160; sleeps 2–4
Open: All year
Breakfast: Full
Pets: Sometimes
Children: Welcome
Smoking: Permitted
Social Drinking: Permitted
Minimum Stay: 2 nights weekends; ski
  and foliage seasons

Only four miles from Haystack, Mount Snow, and Corinthia, this Tyrolean-style ski lodge is decorated with authentic antiques and Colonial charm. The lounge and recreation room have fireplaces and a bring-your-own bar. Winter rates include cross-country ski equipment, sleds, and snowshoes, so that you may explore the lovely marked trails. Summer brings lakeshore swimming, boating, fishing, tennis, riding, museums, and the Marlboro Music Festival.

Golden Maple Inn ✪
ROUTE 15, WOLCOTT VILLAGE, VERMONT 05680

Tel: **(802) 888-6614**	Suites: **$74**
Hosts: **Dick and Jo Wall**	Open: **All year**
Location: **45 mi. NE of Burlington**	Reduced Rates: **10% Nov.–July; 10% seniors**
No. of Rooms: **3**	
No. of Private Baths: **1**	Breakfast: **Full**
Max. No. Sharing Bath: **4**	Credit Cards: **AMEX, DISC, MC, VISA**
Double/pb: **$74**	Pets: **No**
Single/pb: **$59**	Children: **Welcome, over 12**
Double/sb: **$64**	Smoking: **No**
Single/sb: **$49**	Social Drinking: **Permitted**

Originally the home of mill owner William Bundy, this 1865 Greek Revival inn has been designated one of Vermont's historically significant structures. The large common rooms and spacious bedchambers are furnished with antiques and cozy comforters. Dick and Jo serve a scrumptious breakfast on a table set with linen tablecloths and sterling silverware; entrées include oven-baked French toast and baked holiday eggs, accompanied by juice, fruit, cereal, tea, hot chocolate, or freshly ground coffee. Guests canoe, fish, hike, bike, and cross-country ski right from the inn or simply enjoy the gardens and lawns which roll down to the river's edge. Stowe, Craftsbury, Bread & Puppet, and Ben & Jerry's are all in the area.

VIRGINIA

Woodstock •
• Flint Hill   • Alexandria
New Market •
Harrisonburg •   Manassas   Chincoteague
          • Weyers Cave   • Montross   Island
          Gordonsville • Fredericksburg
          Staunton •   • Charlottesville   • Onancock
          Goshen •   • Mollusk
                    Richmond   • Morattico
Buchanan •   • Lexington   Lynchburg   Rockville   • Urbanna   • Cape
                              Williamsburg   Charles
Pulaski • Roanoke • Smith Mountain Lake   Smithfield •
Abingdon • • Chilhowie   Capron •
                                        • Virginia Beach

River Garden ✪
19080 NORTH FORK, RIVER ROAD, ABINGDON, VIRGINIA 24210

Tel: **(703) 676-0335; (800) 952-4296**
Best Time to Call: **Evenings and weekends**
Hosts: **Bill Crump and Carol Schoenherr-Crump**
Location: **9 mi. NE of Abingdon**
No. of Rooms: **4**
No. of Private Baths: **4**
Double/pb: **$60–$65**

Single/pb: **$55–$60**
Open: **All year**
Reduced Rates: **10%, over 2 nights**
Breakfast: **Full**
Pets: **No**
Children: **Welcome, infants, over 4**
Smoking: **No**
Social Drinking: **Permitted**
Airport/Station Pickup: **Yes**

River Garden is tucked into the foothills of the Clinch Mountains, on the bank of the Holston River's North Fork. Each room has its own riverside deck, private entrance, and a king- or queen-size bed. Guests are encouraged to try their hand at weaving on the antique loom. More contemporary challenges can be had in the recreation room, which is equipped with a Ping-Pong table, board games, and exercise equipment. Fishing equipment, a picnic table, a canoe, and inner tubes are also at your disposal. The center of Abingdon, fifteen minutes away, is home to the historic Barter Theater, as well as many eateries. Lovers of the outdoors will want to head for the Virginia Creeper Trail—34 miles of scenic mountain trails for hikers, bikers, and horseback riders.

Summerfield Inn
101 WEST VALLEY STREET, ABINGDON, VIRGINIA 24210

Tel: (703) 628-5905
Best Time to Call: **Mornings; after 3 PM**
Hosts: **Champe and Don Hyatt**
Location: **15 mi. NE of Bristol**
No. of Rooms: **4**
No. of Private Baths: **4**
Double/pb: **$65–$75**
Single/pb: **$55**

Open: **Apr. 1–Nov. 1**
Breakfast: **Continental**
Credit Cards: **AMEX, MC, VISA**
Pets: **No**
Children: **Welcome, over 12**
Smoking: **Permitted**
Social Drinking: **Permitted**
Airport/Station Pickup: **Yes**

A large covered porch with comfortable rockers graces the front and side of this meticulously restored Victorian residence. Guests are welcome to share the large living room, handsomely appointed morning room, and refreshing sun room. A guest pantry is also available for the preparation of light snacks. Summerfield Inn is but a short walk from Barter Theatre, Abingdon's historic district, the Virginia Creeper Trail, and excellent dining. Set at 2,300 feet above sea level and surrounded by mountains, Abingdon, chartered in 1778, is the jumping-off point to the Mt. Rogers National Recreational Area and the Appalachian Trail.

Princely B&B Ltd. ✪
819 PRINCE STREET, ALEXANDRIA, VIRGINIA 22314

Tel: (703) 683-2159
Best Time to Call: **10 AM–6 PM Mon.–Fri.**
Coordinator: **E. J. Mansmann**

States/Regions Covered: **Alexandria**
Rates (Single/Double):
Modest: **$75–$90**
Minimum Stay: **2 nights**

This reservation service lists more than thirty privately owned historic homes, circa 1750 to 1890, many furnished with fine antiques, located in the heart of the Old Town area of Alexandria. All are within eight miles of the White House or Mount Vernon and afford easy access to shopping, dining, and monuments in and around Washington, D.C.

The Berkley House ✪
ROUTE 2, BOX 220A, BUCHANAN, VIRGINIA 24066

Tel: (703) 254-2548; (800) 466-1891
Best Time to Call: **After 4 PM**
Hosts: **John and Sue Shotwell**

Location: **13 mi. N of Roanoke**
No. of Rooms: **4**
No. of Private Baths: **1**

Max. No. Sharing Bath: **4**
Double/pb: **$65**
Single/pb: **$55**
Double/sb: **$55–$65**
Single/sb: **$45–$55**
Suites: **$95–$125**
Open: **All year**
Reduced Rates: **Available**

Breakfast: **Full**
Credit Cards: **AMEX, MC, VISA**
Pets: **No**
Children: **Welcome, over 8**
Smoking: **No**
Social Drinking: **Permitted**
Airport/Station Pickup: **Yes**

Farmland surrounds this 1887 Victorian country home, located within minutes of the Peaks of Otter on the Blue Ridge Parkway. Three porches, a guest kitchen, and a TV/VCR room are at your disposal. Golfers have a choice of several excellent courses in the immediate area. Sue's breakfast menu features homemade pancakes, waffles, and breads; complimentary refreshments, served from 4 to 5 PM, will tide visitors over until dinnertime.

Nottingham Ridge

28184 NOTTINGHAM RIDGE LANE, CAPE CHARLES, VIRGINIA 23310

Tel: **(804) 331-1010**
Best Time to Call: **Anytime**
Hosts: **Bonnie Nottingham and M.S. Scott**
Location: **20 mi. N of Norfolk**
No. of Rooms: **4**
No. of Private Baths: **4**
Double/pb: **$80**
Single/pb: **$60**

Open: **All year**
Breakfast: **Full**
Other Meals: **Available**
Pets: **No**
Children: **Welcome, over 7**
Smoking: **No**
Social Drinking: **Permitted**
Airport/Station Pickup: **Yes**

Reflecting the beauty and charm of Virginia's historic eastern shore, this lovely home boasts a private secluded beach on the Chesapeake Bay, bordered by tall trees, sand dunes, and abundant wildlife. Guests can savor breakfast on the porch while watching boats and birds; at day's end, the sunsets are spectacular. Cooler times can be spent in the den by a crackling fire. Biking, fishing, tennis, golf, running, birdwatching, crabbing, swimming, and sightseeing are just a few pastimes guests can enjoy. Visitors to Nottingham Ridge can look forward to an informal, relaxed atmosphere with emphasis on the small details that create a memorable stay.

Picketts Harbor ○

BOX 97AA, CAPE CHARLES, VIRGINIA 23310

Tel: **(804) 331-2212**
Best Time to Call: **After 5 PM**
Hosts: **Sara and Cooke Goffigon**
Location: **21 mi. E of Virginia Beach**
No. of Rooms: **6**

Max. No. Sharing Bath: **4**
Double/pb: **$85–$125**
Single/pb: **$65–$85**
Double/sb: **$75–$85**
Single/sb: **$65–$75**

Suites: $125
Open: **All year**
Breakfast: **Full**
Other Meals: **Available**
Pets: **Sometimes**

Children: **Welcome**
Smoking: **No**
Social Drinking: **Permitted**
Airport/Station Pickup: **Yes**

Picketts Harbor is a real find on Virginia's eastern shore, with twenty-seven acres of private beach and views of the Chesapeake Bay from all rooms. Set amid pine trees, the home is built to an Eighteenth-century design; central air-conditioning, fireplaces and antique pieces complement the two-hundred-year-old red heart-pine floors and cup-boards. One wing of the house has a private entrance. A country breakfast is served on the porch, in the country kitchen, or in the dining room. Seasonal fruit, homemade breads with jam, and Virginia ham tempt guests. Things to do include fishing, birdwatching, and antiquing, and reasonable restaurants are nearby. Williamsburg and Chincoteague lie within a short drive.

Sunset Inn Bed & Breakfast ✪
108 BAY AVENUE, CAPE CHARLES, VIRGINIA 23310

Tel: **(804) 331-2424**
Hosts: **Al Longo and Joyce Tribble**
Location: **35 mi. N of Norfolk**
No of Rooms: **4**
No. of Private Baths: **3**
Max. No. Sharing Bath: **4**
Double/pb: **$65–$85**
Single/pb: **$65–$70**
Double/sb: **$55**
Open: **All year**

Reduced Rates: **Available**
Breakfast: **Full**
Credit Cards: **MC, VISA**
Pets: **No**
Children: **Welcome, over 10**
Smoking: **Restricted**
Social Drinking: **Permitted**
Minimum Stay: **2 nights, holiday
   weekends**
Airport Pickup: **Yes**

Enjoy a waterfront getaway on the unspoiled Eastern Shore. Cape Charles is directly on the Chesapeake Bay, at the southernmost part of the Delmarva Peninsula; this picturesque town has no traffic lights or parking meters. You'll be able to watch spectacular unobstructed sunsets from the inn's breezy porch or common area. Sun, swim, and relax—a hot tub is available. Then walk the beach, explore the historic district, and visit quaint shops. Birdwatching and charter fishing are nearby. A hearty full breakfast features homemade baked goods and fresh fruit.

Sandy Hill Farm B&B ✪
11307 RIVERS MILL ROAD, CAPRON, VIRGINIA 23829

Tel: **(804) 658-4381**
Best Time to Call: **6:30–8 AM;
   7:30–11:30 PM**
Host: **Anne Kitchen**

Location: **11 mi. from I-95**
No. of Rooms: **2**
Max. No. Sharing Bath: **3**
Double/pb: **$50**

Single/pb: **$40**
Open: **Mar. 20–Dec. 5**
Reduced Rates: **Families; 5 nights**
Breakfast: **Full**
Other Meals: **Available**

Pets: **Welcome**
Children: **Welcome**
Smoking: **Permitted**
Social Drinking: **Permitted**

Experience the pleasures of an unspoiled rural setting at this ranch-style farmhouse. There are animals to visit, quiet places to stroll, and a lighted tennis court on the grounds. This is an ideal hub from which to tour southeastern and central Virginia. Day trips to Williamsburg, Norfolk, and Richmond are possibilities. Fresh fruits and homemade breads are served at breakfast.

Guesthouses Reservation Service ✪
P.O. BOX 5737, CHARLOTTESVILLE, VIRGINIA 22905

Tel: **(804) 979-7264**
Best Time to Call: **12–5 PM Mon.–Fri.**
Coordinator: **Mary Hill Caperton**
States/Regions Covered: **Albemarle County, Charlottesville**
Descriptive Directory: **$1**

Rates (Single/Double):
  Modest: **$48 / $60**
  Average: **$68 / $72**
  Luxury: **$80 / $150**
  Estate Cottages: **$100 up**
Credit Cards: **AMEX, MC, VISA**

Charlottesville is a gracious town. The hosts in Mary's hospitality file offer you a genuine taste of Southern hospitality. All places are close to Thomas Jefferson's Monticello and James Madison's Ash Lawn, as well as the University of Virginia. Unusual local activities include ballooning, steeplechasing, and wine festivals. Please note that the office is closed from Christmas through New Year's Day. Reduced rates are available for extended stays, and most hosts offer a full breakfast.

Clarkcrest Bed and Breakfast ✪
STAR ROUTE BOX 60, CHILHOWIE, VIRGINIA 24319

Tel: **(703) 646-3707**
Hosts: **Doug and Mary Clark**
Location: **35 mi. E of Bristol, Virginia-Tennessee**
No of Rooms: **4**
No. of Private Baths: **2**
Max. No. Sharing Bath: **4**
Double/pb: **$60–$70**
Single/pb: **$55**
Double/sb: **$50**

Single/sb: **$45**
Open: **Apr. 15–Nov. 15**
Reduced Rates: **$5 off 2nd night**
Breakfast: **Continental**
Credit Cards: **MC, VISA**
Pets: **No**
Children: **Welcome, over 12**
Smoking: **Permitted**
Social Drinking: **No**

Doug and Mary invite you to their brick farmhouse in one of western Virginia's oldest communities. Hikers, bikers, and horseback riders will find several likely destinations within a twenty- to thirty-minute

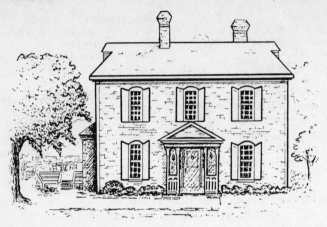

drive: Mount Rogers National Recreation Area, Hungry Mother State Park, the Appalachian Trail, and the Virginia Creeper Trail. For dining and entertainment, try the nearby town of Abingdon. Continental breakfast is served from 7 to 9 each morning.

Miss Molly's Inn ✪
4141 MAIN STREET, CHINCOTEAGUE ISLAND, VIRGINIA 23336

Tel: **(804) 336-6686; (800) 221-5620**
Best Time to Call: **10 AM–10 PM**
Hosts: **Barbara and David Wiedenheft**
Location: **50 mi. S of Salisbury,
    Maryland**
No. of Rooms: **7**
No. of Private Baths: **5**
Max. No. Sharing Bath: **4**
Double/pb: **$69–$135**
Single/pb: **$59–$109**
Double/sb: **$75–$109**
Single/sb: **$65–$99**
Open: **Mid-February–New Year's day**

Reduced Rates: **10% seniors; Oct.
    1–Memorial Weekend**
Breakfast: **Full**
Other Meals: **Available**
Pets: **No**
Children: **Welcome, over 8**
Smoking: **No**
Social Drinking: **Permitted**
Minimum Stay: **2 days, weekends**
Airport/Station Pickup: **Yes**
Foreign Languages: **French, Dutch,
    German**

This bayside Victorian inn has been lovingly restored to its nineteenth-century charm; lace curtains, stained glass windows, and period pieces add to the ambience. While writing her book *Misty of Chinco-teague*, Marguerite Henry stayed here. The ponies celebrated by that story roam wild at the nearby National Wildlife Refuge close to the unspoiled beaches of Assateague Island. You, too, may find Miss Molly's cool breezes, five porches, and traditional English tea—complete with superlative scones—worth writing about.

The Watson House ☉
4240 MAIN STREET, CHINCOTEAGUE, VIRGINIA 23336

Tel: **(804) 336-1564**
Hosts: **Tom and Jacque Derrickson,
   David and Joanne Snead**
Location: **180 mi. SE of Washington,
   DC**
No. of Rooms: **6**
No. of Private Baths: **6**
Double/pb: **$59–$85**
Suites: **$79–$99**
Open: **Apr.–Nov.**

Reduced Rates: **Available**
Breakfast: **Full**
Credit Cards: **MC, VISA**
Pets: **No**
Children: **Welcome, over 10**
Smoking: **No**
Social Drinking: **Permitted**
Minimum Stay: **2 nights, weekends; 3
   nights, holidays**

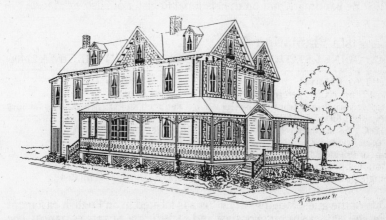

Friendly hosts and Southern hospitality await you at this newly restored country Victorian home. Guest rooms are tastefully decorated with antiques, wicker, and nostalgic pieces; each room has a ceiling fan and air conditioning. Watson House is within biking distance of Assateague National Wildlife Refuge, where you can enjoy numerous nature trails, guided tours, crabbing, fishing, clamming, or swimming. Your hosts will equip you with bicycles, beach chairs, and towels. In the mornings, you can mingle with other guests over a hearty breakfast which includes fruit, eggs, breads, pastries, and aromatic coffee and tea.

Caledonia Farm–1812 ☉
ROUTE 1, BOX 2080, FLINT HILL, VIRGINIA 22627

Tel: **(703) 675-3693; (800) BNB-1812**
Best Time to Call: **10 AM–6 PM**
Host: **Phil Irwin**
Location: **68 mi. SW of Washington,
   D.C.; 4 mi. N of Washington, Va.**

No. of Rooms: **3**
Max. No. Sharing Bath: **4**
Double/sb: **$80**
Suite: **$140**
Open: **All year**

Breakfast: **Full**
Credit Cards: **DISC, MC, VISA**
Pets: **No**

Children: **Welcome, over 12**
Smoking: **No**
Social Drinking: **Permitted**

This charming 1812 stone manor house and its companion "summer kitchen" are located on a working beef cattle farm adjacent to Shenandoah National Park. Each accommodation has a fireplace, period furnishings, individual temperature controls for heat or air-conditioning, and spectacular views of the Blue Ridge Mountains. A candlelight breakfast is served from a menu that offers a choice of omelet, smoked salmon, or eggs Benedict. The Skyline Drive, fine dining, caves, wineries, hayrides, antiquing, historic sites, and sporting activities are a few of the possible diversions. Caledonia Farm is now a Virginia Historic Landmark and on the National Register of Historic Places.

La Vista Plantation ☉
4420 GUINEA STATION ROAD, FREDERICKSBURG, VIRGINIA 22408

Tel: **(703) 898-8444**
Best Time to Call: **Before 9:30 PM**
Hosts: **Michele and Edward Schiesser**
Location: **60 mi. S of Washington,
    D.C.; 4.5 mi. from I-95**
No. of Rooms: **2**
No. of Private Baths: **2**
Double/pb: **$85**
Single/pb: **$65**

Suite: **$85; sleeps 6**
Open: **All year**
Reduced Rates: **7th night free; families**
Breakfast: **Full**
Credit Cards: **MC, VISA**
Pets: **No**
Children: **Welcome**
Smoking: **No**
Social Drinking: **Permitted**

One of the guest lodgings at La Vista is located in an English basement blessed with a sunny exposure and featuring a private entrance. The spacious, air-conditioned suite has a large living room with fireplace, full kitchen, sitting room, and bath. Ten acres surround the manor house, circa 1838, and you are welcome to stroll, bird-watch, or fish in a pond stocked with bass and sunfish.

Selby House Bed & Breakfast ☉
226 PRINCESS ANNE STREET, FREDERICKSBURG, VIRGINIA 22401

Tel: **(540) 373-7037**
Hosts: **Jerry and Virginia Selby**
Location: **54 mi. S of Washington, D.C.**
No. of Rooms: **4**
No. of Private Baths: **4**
Double/pb: **$70**
Single/pb: **$60**
Open: **All year**

Reduced Rates: **Available**
Breakfast: **Full**
Credit Cards: **MC, VISA**
Pets: **No**
Children: **Welcome**
Smoking: **No**
Social Drinking: **Permitted**
Station Pickup: **Yes**

Warm Southern hospitality is the order every day at this restored, late 19th-century Colonial located in Fredericksburg's historic district.

Selby House is decorated throughout with late American Empire furniture. Just two blocks from the railroad station and with off-street parking provided, this B&B assures easy access to good restaurants, museums, art galleries, fine antique shops, and the numerous historic attractions Fredericksburg offers. Civil War buffs will enjoy talking with Jerry and perhaps signing up for one of his Civil War seminars. Virginia, a Richmond local, will have you raving over her full Southern breakfasts with all the trimmings.

The Spooner House Bed and Breakfast
1300 CAROLINE STREET, FREDERICKSBURG, VIRGINIA 22401

Tel: **(703) 371-1267**
Best Time to Call: **After 6 PM**
Hosts: **Peggy and John Roethel**
Location: **54 mi. S of Washington, D.C.**
Suites: **$85; sleeps 2, $15 each additional person**
Open: **All year**

Reduced Rates: **10% weekly**
Breakfast: **Continental, plus**
Pets: **No**
Children: **Welcome**
Smoking: **No**
Social Drinking: **Permitted**
Station Pickup: **Yes**

Built in 1793 on land once owned by George Washington's youngest brother, Charles, the Spooner House operated as a general store and later a tavern. Located in Fredericksburg's historic district, it is within walking distance of museums, restaurants, shops, and the Amtrak station. The lovely two-room suite has its own private entrance and private bath. Breakfast, along with the morning paper, is delivered to guests at their convenience. A complimentary guided tour of the Rising Sun Tavern, the National Historic Landmark that is adjacent to the Spooner House, is available to guests.

Sleepy Hollow Farm Bed & Breakfast ✪
16280 BLUE RIDGE TURNPIKE, ROUTE 231 N, GORDONSVILLE, VIRGINIA 22942

Tel: **(703) 832-5555; (800) 215-4804**
Best Time to Call: **8 AM–noon; 5–10 PM**
Host: **Beverley Allison**
Location: **25 mi. N of Charlottesville**
No. of Rooms: **6**
No. of Private Baths: **6**
Double/pb: **$60–$95**
Single/pb: **$50–$75**
Guest Cottage: **$95–$225; sleeps 4–8**
Suites: **$85–$125**

Open: **All year**
Reduced Rates: **Weekly**
Breakfast: **Full**
Credit Cards: **MC, VISA**
Pets: **Sometimes**
Children: **Welcome**
Smoking: **Permitted**
Social Drinking: **Permitted**
Minimum Stay: **2 nights weekends Sept.–Nov. and May–June**

Sleepy Hollow Farm lies in the heartland of American history, where evidence of Indians and the Revolutionary and Civil War periods still exists. The air-conditioned brick farmhouse evolved from an 18th-century structure, and today boasts terraces, porches, gazebo, pond, a croquet lawn, and rooms with fireplaces. Furnished with antiques and carefully chosen accessories, the decor is picture pretty. Beverley, a retired missionary and journalist, is a fine cook as evidenced by breakfast treats such as sausage pie, fried apples, apple cake, and fruit compote. While in the area, you may want to visit Montpelier, home of James and Dolley Madison, local wineries, a church dating back to 1769, or fish at Lake Orange.

The Hummingbird Inn ✪
WOOD LANE, P.O. BOX 147, GOSHEN, VIRGINIA 24439

Tel: (703) 997-9065
Best Time to Call: 8 AM–5 PM
Hosts: Jeremy and Diana Robinson
Location: 23 mi. NW of Lexington
No. of Rooms: 4
No. of Private Baths: 4
Double/pb: $50–$65
Open: All year
Reduced Rates: 10% seniors; Nov. 1–Mar. 31

Breakfast: Full
Other Meals: Available
Credit Cards: MC, VISA
Pets: Sometimes
Children: Welcome, over 14
Smoking: No
Social Drinking: Permitted

Located on an acre of landscaped grounds in the Shenandoah Valley, this Victorian Carpenter Gothic villa has accommodated Eleanor Roosevelt and Ephraim Zimbalist, Sr. Wraparound verandas, original pine floors, a rustic den, a solarium, and a music room give Hummingbird Inn an old-fashioned ambiance. In keeping with its architecture, the B&B is decorated in an early Victorian style and furnished with antiques. Nearby recreational facilities offer golf, swimming, hiking, skiing, canoeing, tubing, fishing, and hunting. Head out in your car for scenic routes like the Blue Ridge Parkway and Skyline Drive. Or visit the Garth Newell Music Center, historic Staunton, the Museum of American Frontier Culture, Virginia Military Institute, and Washington and Lee University.

The Inn at Keezletown Road ✪
P.O. BOX 341, HARRISONBURG, VIRGINIA 22801

Tel: (703) 234-0644
Best Time to Call: 8 AM–8 PM
Hosts: Sandy and Alan Inabinet
Location: 10 mi. S of Harrisonburg
No. of Rooms: 3
No. of Private Baths: 3
Double/pb: $75–$85
Single/pb: $65–$75
Open: All year

Breakfast: Full
Other Meals: Available
Credit Cards: MC, VISA
Pets: No
Children: Welcome, over 14
Smoking: No
Social Drinking: Permitted
Airport Pickup: Yes

The quaint village of Weyers Cave provides the setting for this elegant, 100-year-old lavender pink Victorian. The inn is furnished with antiques, wonderfully comfortable beds and oriental rugs, intimate sitting areas have been arranged in each guest room. There is a swing on the porch for relaxation, a sunroom for intimate dinners by reservation, and a terrace for warm weather breakfasts. Morning specialties include pumpkin pancakes, Grand Marnier French toast, and omelettes made with the freshest eggs from the inn's own chickens. Air-conditioning, cable TV, and room phones available upon request ensure modern comfort.

Kingsway Bed & Breakfast ✪
3581 SINGERS GLEN ROAD, HARRISONBURG, VIRGINIA 22801

Tel: **(703) 867-9696**	Open: **All year**
Hosts: **Chester and Verna Leaman**	Reduced Rates: **Available**
Location: **2.5 mi. NW of Harrisonburg**	Breakfast: **Continental, plus**
No. of Rooms: 3	Pets: **Yes**
No. of Private Baths: 1	Children: **Welcome**
Max. No. Sharing Bath: 4	Smoking: **No**
Double/pb: **$50–$55**	Social Drinking: **No**
Single/pb: **$40**	Airport Pickup: **Yes**
Double/sb: **$50**	

This modern country home reveals the carpentry and decorating skills of Chester, a cabinet builder, and Verna, a full-time hostess. Enjoy the gardens or take a dip in the pool. If you're up for an excursion, visit George Washington National Forest, Shenandoah National Park with picturesque Skyline Drive, Thomas Jefferson's home at Monticello, or New Market Battlefield. Local sports range from hiking, skiing, and caverning, to pricing the wares at the antique shops, flea markets, and the Valley Mall.

Asherowe ✪

314 SOUTH JEFFERSON STREET, LEXINGTON, VIRGINIA 24450

Tel: **(703) 463-4219**
Best Time to Call: **Early mornings**
Host: **Yvonne Emerson**
Location: **45 mi. N of Roanoke**
No. of Rooms: **2**
Max. No. Sharing Bath: **4**
Double/sb: **$53.75**
Single/sb: **$30**

Open: **Closed July**
Breakfast: **Continental**
Pets: **Sometimes**
Children: **Welcome, over 15**
Smoking: **No**
Social Drinking: **Permitted**
Foreign Languages: **French, German**

This comfortable 1904 wooden home lies only minutes from downtown, in the Golden Triangle section of Lexington's historic district. Sights include the Marshall Library, Washington and Lee University, the Virginia Horse Center, and the Virginia Military Institute, formerly the home of Stonewall Jackson. Guests from both sides of the Atlantic will feel right at home here, since Yvonne speaks fluent French and German as well as English. With the Blue Ridge Parkway to the east, and the Allegheny Mountains to the west, the breathtaking scenery is sure to entice any outdoor enthusiast. Lady Calypso, the resident cat, greets all guests on arrival as any good Southern hostess would.

Brierley Hill

RT 6, BOX 21, LEXINGTON, VIRGINIA 24450

Tel: **(703) 464-8421; (800) 422-4925**
Best Time to Call: **8 AM–8 PM**
Hosts: **Barry and Carole Speton**
Location: **50 mi. N of Roanoke**
No. of Rooms: **5**
No. of Private Baths: **5**
Double/pb: **$70–$95**
Single/pb: **$60–$85**
Open: **All year**

Reduced Rates: **Available**
Breakfast: **Full**
Other Meals: **Available**
Credit Cards: **AMEX, MC, VISA**
Pets: **No**
Children: **Welcome, over 14**
Smoking: **No**
Social Drinking: **Permitted**

This charming B&B sits on eight acres of farmland. Guests are sure to appreciate the spectacular views of the Blue Ridge Mountains and the Shenandoah Valley. Located nearby are Blue Ridge Parkway, the Natural Bridge area and historic Lexington. All rooms are furnished with antique brass or canopy beds, plus Laura Ashley wall coverings and linens. A TV room and a sitting room with a fireplace are at your disposal, and the dining room also has a fireplace. Barry, a retired Canadian lawyer, is interested in antique prints and refinishing furniture. Carole likes cooking, gardening, and quilting. Together, they offer relaxed comfort, wonderful food, and friendly hospitality.

Lavender Hill Farm B&B ✪
ROUTE 1, BOX 515, LEXINGTON, VIRGINIA 24450

Tel: (703) 464-5877; (800) 446-4240
Best Time to Call: 9 AM–6 PM
Hosts: Cindy and Colin Smith
Location: 50 mi. N of Roanoke
No. of Rooms: 3
No. of Private Baths: 3
Double/pb: $60–$75
Single/pb: $50–$60
Suites: $110
Open: All year

Reduced Rates: Available
Breakfast: Full
Other Meals: Available
Credit Cards: MC, VISA
Pets: No
Children: Welcome
Smoking: No
Social Drinking: Permitted
Minimum Stay: 2 nights, holidays, special events

Situated on a 20-acre working farm in the beautiful Shenandoah Valley, this restored farmhouse (circa 1790) is located five miles from historic Lexington. It has been carefully renovated to blend old and new for your comfort and relaxation. Enjoy the large front porch, fishing, hiking, birdwatching, panoramic mountain views, and lambs frolicking on the hillside. Breakfast specialties include homemade bread, stuffed French toast, fresh farm eggs, and much more. Dinner, served to guests by advance reservation, is highly recommended. Colin, the English half of the family, is the chef whose specialties involve fresh herbs and vegetables from the garden. Cindy will be glad to direct you to nearby attractions, give a spinning demonstration, or arrange a horseback riding package for you.

Llewellyn Lodge at Lexington ✪
603 SOUTH MAIN STREET, LEXINGTON, VIRGINIA 24450

Tel: (703) 463-3235; (800) 882-1145
Best Time to Call: 9:30 AM–7:30 PM
Hosts: Ellen and John Roberts
Location: 50 mi. N of Roanoke
No. of Rooms: 6
No. of Private Baths: 6
Double/pb: $68–$80
Single/pb: $58–$70

Open: All year
Breakfast: Full
Credit Cards: AMEX, MC, VISA
Pets: No
Children: Welcome, over 10
Smoking: Restricted
Social Drinking: Permitted
Airport/Station Pickup: Yes

A warm and friendly atmosphere, combining country charm with a touch of class, awaits you at this lovely brick Colonial furnished in traditional and antique pieces. Guests are welcomed with a cool drink on the deck in warm months, or with a refreshment by the fire in the winter. Ellen spent twenty years in the airline, travel, and hospitality business before moving to Lexington in 1985 to start her B&B. John, a native Lexingtonian, is acquainted with the hiking and biking trails and knows where the fish are hiding. A hearty gourmet breakfast is offered each morning, including omelets, Belgian waffles, Virginia maple syrup, sausage, bacon, and Ellen's famous blueberry muffins.

The lodge is an easy walk to the Robert E. Lee Chapel, the Stonewall Jackson House, Washington and Lee University, and the Virginia Military Institute.

Lynchburg Mansion Inn B&B ✪
405 MADISON STREET, LYNCHBURG, VIRGINIA 24504

Tel: **(804) 528-5400; (800) 352-1199**
Hosts: **Bob and Mauranna Sherman**
Location: **65 mi. S of Charlottesville**
No. of Rooms: **5**
No. of Private Baths: **5**
Double/pb: **$85**
Suites: **$119**
Open: **All year**

Reduced Rates: **Available**
Breakfast: **Full**
Credit Cards: **AMEX, DC, MC, VISA**
Pets: **No**
Children: **Welcome**
Smoking: **No**
Social Drinking: **No**

Restored with your every comfort in mind, this Spanish Georgian mansion has pretty gardens, a spacious veranda, oak floors, tall ceilings, pocket doors, and cherry woodwork. Bedrooms are lavish, with either king- or queen-size beds, luxurious linens, fireplaces, TVs, and turndown service. Bob and Mauranna have also added an outdoor hot tub for guests to use. Fine china, silver, and crystal complement the sumptuous full breakfasts. The mansion surveys a half-acre in downtown Lynchburg's Garland Hill Historic District, which is listed on the National Register of Historic Places; impressive Federal and Victorian homes line Madison Street, still paved in its turn-of-the-century brick. Plus there are Civil War sites, antique shops, art galleries, and countless programs offered by the city's colleges and universities.

Winridge Bed & Breakfast ✪

ROUTE 1, BOX 362, MADISON HEIGHTS, VIRGINIA 24572

Tel: **(804) 384-7220**
Best Time to Call: **10 AM–4 PM**
Hosts: **Lois Ann and Ed Pfister**
Location: **6 mi. N of Lynchburg**
No. of Rooms: **3**
No. of Private Baths: **1**
Max. No. Sharing Bath: **4**
Double/pb: **$69**
Double/sb: **$59**

Open: **All year**
Reduced Rates: **Available**
Breakfast: **Full**
Pets: **No**
Children: **Welcome**
Smoking: **No**
Social Drinking: **No**
Airport/Station Pickup: **Yes**

Enjoy wonderful mountain views while relaxing on the large porches of this grand Colonial southern home. Swing under the shade trees and stroll through the gardens, where you'll admire the beauty of flowers, birds, and butterflies. Spacious rooms with high ceilings, large sunny windows, and a delightful mix of modern and antique furniture await you. Breakfasts are tempting, with offerings like oven baked pecan French toast and blueberry patch muffins. The Blue Ridge Parkway, Appomattox Courthouse, Poplar Forest, and much more are close by for your diversion.

Sunrise Hill Farm ✪

5590 OLD FARM LANE, MANASSAS, VIRGINIA 22110

Tel: **(703) 754-8309**
Best Time to Call: **Anytime**
Hosts: **Frank and Sue Boberek**
Location: **35 minutes W of Washington, D.C.**
No. of Rooms: **2**
No. of Private Baths: **1**
Max. No. Sharing Bath: **4**
Double/pb: **$85**
Double/sb: **$75**

Open: **All year**
Reduced Rates: **15% families using both rooms**
Breakfast: **Full**
Credit Cards: **MC, VISA**
Pets: **Horses boarded**
Children: **Welcome, over 10**
Smoking: **No**
Social Drinking: **Permitted**

Standing in the heart of the 6,000-acre Manassas National Battlefields, this Civil War treasure overlooks Bull Run Creek. Sunrise Hill Farm is an uncommonly charming, Federal-era country home furnished in period style. This B&B is a haven for Civil War buffs and guests visiting northern Virginia and the nation's capital. Situated within the renowned Virginia hunt country, it is just 35 minutes from Washington, D.C., and close to Harpers Ferry, Antietam, Skyline Drive, Luray Caverns, and numerous historic sites and antique-filled towns.

A Touch of Country Bed & Breakfast ✪
9329 CONGRESS STREET, NEW MARKET, VIRGINIA 22844

Tel: (703) 740-8030
Hosts: Jean Schoellig and Dawn Kasow
Location: 18 mi. N of Harrisonburg
No. of Rooms: 6
No. of Private Baths: 6
Double/pb: $60–$70
Single/pb: $50–$60

Open: All year
Breakfast: Full
Credit Cards: MC, VISA
Pets: No
Children: Welcome, over 12
Smoking: No
Social Drinking: Permitted

This restored 1870s home is located in a historic town in the beautiful Shenandoah Valley. It displays the original hardwood floors and is decorated with antiques and collectibles in a country motif. You'll start your day with a hearty breakfast of pancakes, meats, gravy, and biscuits. Daydream on the porch swings or stroll through town with its charming shops, dine at a variety of restaurants or visit the legendary New Market Battlefield and Park. Close by are Skyline Drive, George Washington National Forest, caverns, and vineyards.

The Spinning Wheel Bed & Breakfast ✪
31 NORTH STREET, ONANCOCK, VIRGINIA 23417

Tel: (804) 787-7311
Hosts: David and Karen Tweedie
Location: 60 mi. N of Virginia Beach
No. of Rooms: 5
No. of Private Baths: 5
Double/pb: $75–$85
Single/pb: $70–$80
Open: May–Oct.

Reduced Rates: Over 4 nights
Breakfast: Full
Credit Cards: MC, VISA
Pets: No
Children: Welcome, over 12
Smoking: No
Social Drinking: Permitted
Minimum Stay: 2 nights, weekends

This 1890s folk Victorian home is in the historic waterfront town of Onancock, on the eastern shore peninsula separating the Chesapeake Bay from the Atlantic Ocean. The B&B is decorated with antiques and, true to its name, spinning wheels. Guest rooms have queen-size beds and air conditioning. Kerr Place (a 1799 museum), restaurants, shops, the town wharf, and the ferry to Tangier Island are all within walking distance. David is a college professor and Karen is a teacher of the deaf. Their guests are greeted by Nelly, the resident old English sheepdog.

Count Pulaski Bed & Breakfast and Gardens
821 NORTH JEFFERSON AVENUE, PULASKI, VIRGINIA 24301

Tel: (703) 980-1163
Host: Dr. Flo Stevenson
Location: 55 mi S of Roanoke
No. of Rooms: 3
No. of Private Baths: 3
Double/pb: $75
Single/pb: $60

Open: All year
Breakfast: Full
Credit Cards: MC, VISA
Pets: Sometimes
Children: Welcome, over 15
Smoking: No
Social Drinking: No

In a mountain village in southwest Virginia, you'll find this spacious eighty-year-old house furnished with family antiques, paintings, and pieces your host collected around the world. Guest rooms have carpeting, air-conditioning, and king- or queen-size beds; one room has a fireplace. A television, beverage center, and games and books are inside, while garden sitting areas beckon you outside. Breakfast is served by candlelight on a one hundred fifty-year-old table set with china, crystal, and silver. From its quiet hillside perch, this B&B overlooks the town and mountains below, yet Main Street's restaurants and antique shops are only a few blocks away. A fifty-mile bike trail originates in Pulaski; other recreational options include rafting, canoeing, horseback riding, and golf.

Bensonhouse of Richmond and Williamsburg ○
2036 MONUMENT AVENUE, RICHMOND, VIRGINIA 23220

Tel: (804) 353-6900
Best Time to Call: 11 AM–6 PM
Coordinator: Lyn Benson
States/Regions Covered: Eastern
  Shore, Fredericksburg, Petersburg,
  Richmond, Williamsburg
Descriptive Directory: $3

Rates (Single/Double):
  Modest: $60 / $68
  Average: $68 / $85
  Luxury: $85–$105 / $95–$135
Credit Cards: MC, VISA
Minimum Stay: Williamsburg: 2
  nights weekends

Houses and inns on Lyn's list are of architectural or historic interest, offering charm in the relaxed comfort of a home. Most have private bath accommodations, and some have fireplaces and/or Jacuzzis. The hosts delight in guiding you to the best sights and advising you on how to get the most out of your visit.

The Emmanuel Hutzler House ✪
2036 MONUMENT AVENUE, RICHMOND, VIRGINIA 23220

Tel: **(804) 353-6900, 355-4885**
Best Time to Call: **11AM–6 PM**
Host: **John E. Richardson**
Location: **1½ mi. from Rte. I-95/64**
No. of Rooms: **3**
No. of Private Baths: **1**
Double/pb: **$85**
Open: **All year**

Reduced Rates: **Corporate, 5%, seniors**
Breakfast: **Full**
Credit Cards: **AMEX, MC, VISA**
Pets: **No**
Children: **Welcome, over 12**
Smoking: **No**
Social Drinking: **Permitted**

This spacious Italian Renaissance inn, built in 1914, recently received a total renovation. The classical interior has raised mahogany paneling, lavish wainscoting, leaded glass windows, and, on the first floor, coffered ceilings with dropped beams. Mahogany bookcases flank the marble fireplace in the living room, where guests can relax and converse. The generously sized guest rooms, all on the second floor, are furnished with antiques and handsome draperies; two rooms have fireplaces. The central location makes this an ideal location for either a midweek business trip or a weekend getaway. For those who do not mind paying a higher rate, 3 rooms are available.

The Mary Bladon House ✪
381 WASHINGTON AVENUE SOUTH WEST, ROANOKE, VIRGINIA 24016

Tel: **(703) 344-5361**
Hosts: **Mr. and Mrs W. D. Bestpitch**
Location: **220 mi. S of Washington, D.C.**
No. of Rooms: **3**
No. of Private Baths: **3**
Double/pb: **$80**
Single/pb: **$62.50**
Suites: **$110**
Open: **All year**

Reduced Rates: **Available**
Breakfast: **Full**
Credit Cards: **MC, VISA**
Pets: **No**
Children: **Welcome**
Smoking: **No**
Social Drinking: **Permitted**
Airport/Station Pickup: **Yes**
Foreign Languages: **German**

The Mary Bladon House is located in the old southwest neighborhood, just five minutes away from the Blue Ridge Parkway. This Victorian dates back to the late 1800s and has four porches. Although the original brass light fixtures are still in place, the decor in the public rooms is constantly changing, with works by local artists and craftsmen. All the rooms are elegantly appointed with antiques, and guest rooms feature fresh flowers in season.

Woodlawn ○
2211 WILTSHIRE ROAD, ROCKVILLE, VIRGINIA 23146

Tel: **(804) 749-3759**
Best Time to Call: **3–10 PM**
Host: **Ann Nuckols**
Location: **20 mi. W of Richmond**
No. of Rooms: **2**
No. of Private Baths: **2**
Double/pb: **$75**

Open: **All year**
Breakfast: **Full**
Pets: **No**
Children: **No**
Smoking: **No**
Social Drinking: **Permitted**

An ideal hub from which to tour many historic points of interest in the area, this circa 1813 farmhouse is set on 40 acres of peaceful, grassy slopes, just 3 miles from the interstate. The interior has been completely restored, tastefully decorated, and furnished with antiques. The house has central air conditioning for summer comfort. Each of the two guest rooms has its own fireplace. Both guest rooms are furnished with majestic hand-carved double beds and down pillows and comforters. Breakfasts with sourdough rolls, bran muffins, homemade jellies, and juice, are served on the screened porch or in the dining area in the English basement.

Isle of Wight Inn ○
1607 SOUTH CHURCH STREET, SMITHFIELD, VIRGINIA 23430

Tel: **(804) 357-3176**
Best Time to Call: **3–9 PM**
Hosts: **The Earls and The Harts**
Location: **27 mi. W of Norfolk**
No. of Rooms: **9**
No. of Private Baths: **9**
Double/pb: **$59**
Single/pb: **$49**

Suites: **$79–$99**
Open: **All year**
Breakfast: **Full**
Credit Cards: **AMEX, MC, VISA**
Pets: **No**
Children: **Welcome**
Smoking: **Restricted**
Social Drinking: **Permitted**

The Isle of Wight Inn is a sprawling brick Colonial, one mile from downtown Smithfield. Inside you will find antiques, reproductions, and motifs of glass, wood, and wicker. Wake up to fresh coffee and Smithfield's own ham rolls. This riverport town has numerous historic homes that will surely delight you. Williamsburg, Norfolk, and Virginia Beach are less than an hour's drive from the house. An antiques shop is on the premises.

The Manor at Taylor's Store B&B Country Inn ○
ROUTE 1, BOX 533, SMITH MOUNTAIN LAKE, VIRGINIA 24184

Tel: **(703) 721-3951; (800) 248-6267**
Hosts: **Lee and Mary Lynn Tucker**
Location: **20 mi. E of Roanoke**
No. of Rooms: **6**

No. of Private Baths: **4**
Double/pb: **$80–$125**
Guest Cottage: **$90–$150; sleeps 2–6**
Open: **All year**

Reduced Rates: **$450–up weekly for cottage**
Breakfast: **Full**
Credit Cards: **MC, VISA**
Pets: **No**

Children: **Welcome in cottage**
Smoking: **Cottage only**
Social Drinking: **Permitted**
Airport/Station Pickup: **Yes**

Situated on 100 acres in the foothills of the Blue Ridge Mountains, this elegant manor house, circa 1799, was the focus of a prosperous tobacco plantation. It has been restored and refurbished, and you'll experience the elegance of the past combined with the comfort of tasteful modernization. The estate invites hiking, swimming, and fishing. The sunroom, parlor, and hot tub are special spots for relaxing. Smith Mountain Lake, with its seasonal sporting activity, is five miles away. Breakfast, designed for the health-conscious, features a variety of fresh gourmet selections.

Frederick House
28 NORTH NEW STREET, STAUNTON, VIRGINIA 24401

Tel: **(703) 885-4220; (800) 334-5575**
Best Time to Call: **7 AM–10 PM**
Hosts: **Joe and Evy Harman**
Location: **2.7 mi. from Route I-81 exit 222**
No. of Rooms: **14**
No. of Private Baths: **14**
Double/pb: **$55–$150**
Single/pb: **$55–$135**
Suites: **$95–$150**

Open: **All year**
Reduced Rates: **Available**
Breakfast: **Full**
Credit Cards: **AMEX, DC, DISC, MC, VISA**
Pets: **No**
Children: **Welcome**
Smoking: **No**
Social Drinking: **Permitted**
Station Pickup: **Yes**

Frederick House is located across from Mary Baldwin College in downtown Staunton, the oldest city in the Shenandoah Valley. The five separate buildings that are listed in the National Register of Historic Places have been tastefully restored and furnished with antiques. The large rooms and suites feature oversize beds, modern baths, remote cable TV, air-conditioning, ceiling fans, robes, telephones, and private entrances. Some have whirlpools, fireplaces, or balconies. A full breakfast, prepared by the owners, is served in Chumley's Tearoom between 7:30 and 10:30 AM. Breakfast choices include ham and cheese pie, apple raisin quiche, waffles, strata, fresh fruit, juice, coffee, tea, warm bread and hot or cold cereal. Joe and Evy Harman previously worked in banking and insurance. Since 1984 they have enjoyed informing guests about the area and suggesting trips to many nearby interesting sights.

Kenwood ✪
235 EAST BEVERLEY STREET, STAUNTON, VIRGINIA 24401

Tel: (703) 886-0524
Hosts: Liz and Ed Kennedy
Location: 30 mi. W of Charlottesville
No. of Rooms: 3
No. of Private Baths: 3
Double/pb: $70
Single/pb: $60
Open: All year

Breakfast: Full
Credit Cards: MC, VISA
Pets: No
Children: Welcome
Smoking: No
Social Drinking: Permitted
Airport/Station Pickup: Yes

Kenwood, a stately brick Colonial revival home built in 1910, has been restored and decorated with floral wallpapers and antique furniture. The Woodrow Wilson Birthplace—and its museum and research library—are next door. Staunton boasts several other museums and numerous antique shops, and it's only a half-hour drive to attractions like Monticello and the Virginia Horse Center. Select your destinations over such breakfast fare as fresh seasonal fruit and homemade baked goods.

The Sampson Eagon Inn ✪
238 EAST BEVERLEY STREET, STAUNTON, VIRGINIA 24401

Tel: (703) 886-8200; (800) 597-9722
Best Time to Call: 10 AM–9 PM
Hosts: Laura and Frank Mattingly
Location: 35 mi. W of Charlottesville
No. of Rooms: 5
No. of Private Baths: 5
Double/pb: $80–$85
Suites: $90

Open: All year
Breakfast: Full
Pets: No
Children: Welcome, over 12
Smoking: No
Social Drinking: Permitted
Minimum Stay: Weekends in Oct. and May

This circa 1840 in-town Greek Revival mansion provides affordable luxury accommodations in a preservation award-winning setting. Comfort and hospitality are key. Guest rooms are spacious, air-conditioned, and have modern ensuite baths. Canopied beds and antique furnishings reflect various periods of this elegant building's past. Scrumptious, gourmet breakfasts are served daily. Within two blocks of shops and restaurants, the inn is adjacent to the Woodrow Wilson Birthplace and Mary Baldwin College. Nearby, guests can enjoy the natural and historic attractions and recreational activities of the central Shenandoah Valley. Charlottesville and Lexington are within a 40-minute drive.

Thornrose House at Gypsy Hill ✪
531 THORNROSE AVENUE, STAUNTON, VIRGINIA 24401

Tel: **(703) 885-7026, (800) 861-4338**	Reduced Rates: **Available**
Best Time to Call: **Anytime**	Breakfast: **Full**
Hosts: **Suzanne and Otis Huston**	Pets: **No**
Location: **3½ mi. from Rte. I-81, Exit 222**	Children: **Welcome**
	Smoking: **No**
No. of Rooms: **5**	Social Drinking: **Permitted**
No. of Private Baths: **5**	Minimum Stay: **3 days over July 4th; 2 days October weekends**
Double/pb: **$55–$75**	
Single/pb: **$45–$65**	Airport/Station Pickup: **Yes**
Open: **All year**	

This 1912 Georgian Revival home is six blocks from the center of Victorian Staunton and adjacent to 300-acre Gypsy Hill Park, which has facilities for golf, tennis, swimming, and summer concerts. A wraparound veranda and Greek colonnades grace the exterior of the house. Inside, there's a cozy parlor with a fireplace and a grand piano. A relaxed, leisurely breakfast is set out in the dining room, which offers the comfort of a fireplace on chilly mornings. Local attractions include Blue Ridge National Park, Natural Chimneys, Skyline Drive, Woodrow Wilson's birthplace, and the Museum of American Frontier Culture.

The Duck Farm Inn ✪
P.O. BOX 787, RTES. 227 AND 639, URBANNA, VIRGINIA 23175

Tel: **(804) 758-5685**	Single/sb: **$60**
Host: **Fleming Godden**	Open: **All year**
Location: **55 mi. E of Richmond**	Reduced Rates: **After first visit**
No. of Rooms: **6**	Breakfast: **Full**
No. of Private Baths: **2**	Pets: **No**
Max. No. Sharing Bath: **4**	Children: **Welcome**
Double/pb: **$85**	Smoking: **No**
Single/pb: **$60**	Social Drinking: **Permitted**
Double/sb: **$75**	Airport/Station Pickup: **Yes**

This elegant, contemporary inn is situated on Virginia's middle peninsula, surrounded by 800 secluded acres and bordered by the Rappahannock River. Guests are welcome to hike along the shore or through the woods, fish in the river, sunbathe on the private beach, lounge on the deck, or retire to the cozy library with a good book. Fleming has traveled all over the world and thoroughly enjoys her role as full-time innkeeper. One of her breakfast menus consists of seasonal fresh fruit, jumbo blueberry muffins, cheese-and-egg scramble served with spiced sausage, and a variety of hot beverages.

Hewick Plantation ✪
VSH 602/VSH 615 BOX 82, URBANNA, VIRGINIA 23175-0082

Tel: **(804) 758-4214; (800) 484-7514 code 1678**
Hosts: **Helen and Ed Battleson**
Location: **60 mi. E. of Richmond**
No. of Rooms: **2**
No. of Private Baths: **2**
Double/pb: **$85**
Single/pb: **$75**
Open: **All year**
Reduced Rates: **10% less Jan. & Feb., Seniors 10%**

Breakfast: **Continental**
Credit Cards: **MC, VISA**
Pets: **No**
Children: **Welcome, over 2**
Smoking: **No**
Social Drinking: **Permitted**
Station Pickup: **Yes**
Foreign Languages: **Spanish**

Hewick Plantation was the home of an English family that immigrated in 1670; the sixty-acre site includes an old family cemetery and an archaeological dig being conducted by the College of William and Mary. The manor house's spacious bedrooms are decorated with antiques and heirlooms, such as four-poster beds. To accommodate little ones, the twin beds come equipped with trundle beds. Among the local attractions is Christ Church and Cemetery, where General Lewis Puller, the most decorated soldier in American history, is buried. Helen runs a nearby antique shop and Ed is retired from the DEA/US Customs. Their daughter Rachel is a fifth-grader who loves horses, while her little sister Regina, a second-grader, is partial to all animals, especially her dog and cat.

Angie's Guest Cottage ✪
302 24TH STREET, VIRGINIA BEACH, VIRGINIA 23451

Tel: **(804) 428-4690**
Best Time to Call: **10 AM–10 PM**
Host: **Barbara G. Yates**
Location: **20 mi. E of Norfolk**
No. of Rooms: **6**
No. of Private Baths: **1**
Max. No. Sharing Bath: **4**
Double/pb: **$68**
Single/pb: **$58**
Double/sb: **$48–$68**
Single/sb: **$40–$58**

Guest Cottage: **$425–$550 weekly; sleeps 2–6**
Open: **Apr. 1–Oct. 1**
Reduced Rates: **Off-season**
Breakfast: **Continental, plus**
Pets: **Sometimes**
Children: **Welcome**
Smoking: **No**
Social Drinking: **Permitted**
Minimum Stay: **2 nights**

Just a block from the beach, shops, and restaurants is this bright and comfortable beach house. Former guests describe it as: "cozy, cute, and clean." Deep-sea fishing, nature trails, and harbor tours are but a few things to keep you busy. Freshly baked croissants in various flavors are a breakfast delight. You are welcome to use the sundeck, barbecue, and picnic tables.

Barclay Cottage ✪
400 16TH STREET, VIRGINIA BEACH, VIRGINIA 23451

Tel: **(804) 422-1956**	Reduced Rates: **10% seniors**
Hosts: **Peter and Claire**	Breakfast: **Full**
Location: **20 mi. E of Norfolk**	Credit Cards: **AMEX, DISC, MC, VISA**
No. of Rooms: **6**	Pets: **No**
No. of Private Baths: **2**	Children: **No**
Max. No. Sharing Bath: **2**	Smoking: **No**
Double/pb: **$80**	Social Drinking: **Permitted**
Double/sb: **$65–$70**	Minimum Stay: **2 nights**
Open: **Apr.–Oct.; Special holidays**	

The Barclay is a historic building designed in turn-of-the-century, Southern Colonial style. Your hosts bring you casual sophistication in a warm, inn-like atmosphere two blocks from the beach and fishing pier. The inn has been completely restored to add the feeling of yesterday to the comfort of today. Peter and Claire look forward to welcoming you to their B&B, where the theme is, "We go where our dreams lead us."

The Iris Inn
191 CHINQUAPIN DRIVE, WAYNESBORO, VIRGINIA 22980

Tel: **(703) 943-1991**	Location: **25 mi. W of Charlottesville**
Best Time to Call: **10 AM–8 PM**	No. of Rooms: **6**
Hosts: **Wayne and Iris Karl**	No. of Private Baths: **6**

Double/pb: **$75–$85**
Single/pb: **$65**
Open: **All year**
Reduced Rates: **Corporate,**
  Sun.–Thurs.
Breakfast: **Full**
Credit Cards: **MC, VISA**

Pets: **No**
Children: **Welcome, by arrangement**
Smoking: **No**
Social Drinking: **Permitted**
Minimum Stay: **2 nights weekends**
Airport: **Yes**

The charm and grace of southern living in a totally modern facility, nestled in a wooded tract on the western slope of the Blue Ridge overlooking the historic Shenandoah Valley—that's what awaits you at the Iris Inn in Waynesboro. It's ideal for a weekend retreat, a refreshing change for the business traveler, and a tranquil spot for the tourist to spend a night or a week. Guest rooms are spacious, comfortably furnished, and delightfully decorated in nature and wildlife motifs. Each room has private bath and individual temperature control.

The Travel Tree ✪
P.O. BOX 838, WILLIAMSBURG, VIRGINIA 23187

Tel: **(800) 989-1571**
Best Time to Call: **6–9 PM, weekdays**
Coordinator: **Joann Proper**
States/Regions Covered:
  Williamsburg, Jamestown, Yorktown
Descriptive Directory of B&Bs: **Free**

Rates (Single/Double):
  Modest: **$50–$70**
  Average: **$75–$95**
  Luxury: **$100–$125**
Credit Cards: **No**

This complimentary service offers you a broad view—a variety of choices among the B&B accommodations available in the Williamsburg area. Searching for lodgings in a historic estate, small inn, or private home becomes a one-step process when you make your reservations through The Travel Tree. Gift certificates are also available.

Blue Bird Haven B&B ✪
8691 BARHAMSVILLE ROAD, WILLIAMSBURG-TOANO, VIRGINIA 23168

Tel: **(804) 566-0177**
Best Time to Call: **Early mornings**
Host: **June Cottle**
Location: **9 mi. N of Williamsburg**
No. of Rooms: **3**
No. of Private Baths: **2**
Max. No. Sharing Bath: **4**
Double/pb: **$65**

Suites: **$76**
Open: **All year**
Breakfast: **Full**
Pets: **Sometimes**
Children: **Welcome**
Smoking: **No**
Social Drinking: **Permitted**

June and Ed welcome you to their ranch-style home, located 20 minutes from Colonial Williamsburg. Guest accommodations, located in a private wing, feature traditional furnishings. June is interested in many kinds of handcrafts and has decorated the rooms with one-of-a-kind quilts, spreads, rugs, and pictures. Breakfast includes a Southern-style assortment of Virginia ham, spoon bread, red-eye gravy, blueberry pancakes, fresh fruits, home-baked biscuits, and granola. Blue Bird Haven is convenient to Busch Gardens, James River Plantations, and Civil War battlefields. After a full day of seeing the sights, you are welcome to enjoy some of June's evening desserts.

Candlewick Inn B&B ✪
800 JAMESTOWN ROAD, WILLIAMSBURG, VIRGINIA 23185

Tel: **(804) 253-8693**	Reduced Rates: **Available**
Best Time to Call: **Anytime**	Breakfast: **Full**
Hosts: **Mary L. Peters**	Credit Cards: **MC, VISA**
Location: **2 miles from Route 64 Exit 242A**	Pets: **No**
	Children: **Welcome, over 12**
No. of Rooms: **2**	Smoking: **No**
No. of Private Baths: **2**	Social Drinking: **Permitted**
Double/pb: **$85**	Minimum Stay: **2 nights**
Single/pb: **$75**	Station Pickup: **Yes**
Open: **All year**	Foreign Languages: **German**

Mary restored and redecorated this 1946 two-story frame house so that it looks like a farmhouse from the previous century, with beam ceilings, chair rails, and beautiful canopy beds. She also sets out wonderful country breakfasts featuring home-baked bread and muffins. Then it's an easy four-block walk or bike ride to the historic area; first stop is William and Mary College, just across the way.

Colonial Capital Bed & Breakfast ✪
501 RICHMOND ROAD, WILLIAMSBURG, VIRGINIA 23185

Tel: **(800) 776-0570**	Breakfast: **Full**
Hosts: **Barbara and Phil Craig**	Credit Cards: **AMEX, MC, VISA**
Location: **2.5 mi. from I-64 Exit 238**	Pets: **No**
No. of Rooms: **5**	Children: **Welcome, over 6**
No. of Private Baths: **5**	Smoking: **Permitted**
Double/pb: **$85–$105**	Social Drinking: **Permitted**
Suites: **$135**	Airport/Station Pickup: **Yes**
Open: **All year**	

Barbara and Phil offer a warm welcome to guests in their three-story Colonial revival (c.1926) home only three blocks from the historic area. The B&B is decorated with period antiques, oriental rugs, and many of the original lighting and plumbing fixtures, all guest rooms feature four-poster beds crowned with charming canopies. In the morning you can look forward to such treats as a soufflé, French toast, fluffy omelet, or yeast waffles complimented with a choice of juices, fresh fruits, and specially blended coffees and tea. The sunny solarium or formal dining room invites guests to linger over breakfast and get to know one another as does the plantation parlor where tea and wine are served during afternoons and evenings. Games, books and puzzles are provided for your pleasure. Jamestown, Yorktown, some of the state's finest plantations, Busch Gardens, and Water Country USA are only a few minutes away. Personalized gift certificates are available.

For Cant Hill Guest Home
4 CANTERBURY LANE, WILLIAMSBURG, VIRGINIA 23185

Tel: **(804) 229-6623**	Open: **All year**
Best Time to Call: **Anytime**	Breakfast: **Continental**
Hosts: **Martha and Hugh Easler**	Pets: **No**
No. of Rooms: **2**	Children: **Welcome, over 10**
No. of Private Baths: **2**	Smoking: **No**
Double/pb: **$65–$75**	Social Drinking: **Permitted**

Situated in the heart of town, overlooking Lake Matoaka, a part of the campus of the College of William and Mary, the home is only a few blocks from the restored area of Colonial Williamsburg, yet very secluded and quiet in a lovely wooded setting. Both rooms are tastefully decorated, accented in winter with homemade quilts. Each room has a TV and a hearty Continental breakfast is served in the room. The hosts are happy to make dinner reservations for guests and provide very helpful information on the many attractions in the entire area.

Fox Grape Bed & Breakfast ✪
701 MONUMENTAL AVENUE, WILLIAMSBURG, VIRGINIA 23185

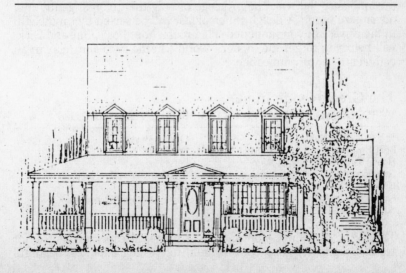

Tel: **(804) 229-6914; (800) 292-3699**
Best Time to Call: **9 AM–9 PM**
Hosts: **Bob and Pat Orendorff**
Location: **2 mi. from I-64, Exit 238**
No. of Rooms: **4**
No. of Private Baths: **4**
Double/pb: **$68–$84**
Single/pb: **$68–$84**

Open: **All year**
Reduced Rates: **10% seniors**
Breakfast: **Continental**
Pets: **No**
Children: **Welcome**
Smoking: **Permitted**
Social Drinking: **Permitted**
Station Pickup: **Yes**

Warm hospitality awaits you just a seven-minute walk north of Virginia's restored Colonial capital. Furnishings include counted cross-stitch pieces, antiques, stained glass, stenciled walls, duck decoys, and a cup-plate collection. Pat enjoys doing counted cross-stitch. Bob carves walking sticks and makes stained-glass windows.

Governor's Trace ✪
303 CAPITOL LANDING ROAD, WILLIAMSBURG, VIRGINIA 23185

Tel: **(804) 229-7552; (800) 303-7562**
Best Time to Call: **9 AM–10 PM**
Hosts: **Sue and Dick Lake**
Location: **2 mi. from I-64, exit 238**
No. of Rooms: **3**
No. of Private Baths: **3**
Double/pb: **$85**
Single/pb: **$85**

Suites: **$95–$115**
Open: **All year**
Breakfast: **Continental**
Credit Cards: **MC, VISA**
Pets: **No**
Children: **No**
Smoking: **No**
Social Drinking: **Permitted**

This Georgian brick home, featured on the back cover of the 1992 edition of *Bed & Breakfast U.S.A.*, is Colonial Williamsburg's closest B&B neighbor—just one door away. Choose a king-size bed and fireplace, a double canopy bed with a screened-in porch, or experience the ambiance that was the privilege of only the Colonial gentry in a queen-size room. A delightful breakfast will be served by candlelight in the privacy of your antiqued-filled room. Your hosts, Sue and Dick, will help you forget the modern world's hectic pace and relax in an eighteenth-century atmosphere.

The Greenwoode Inn ✪
104 WOODMONT PLACE, WILLIAMSBURG, VIRGINIA 23188

Tel: **(804) 566-8800**
Best Time to Call: **8 AM–10 PM**
Hosts: **Dr. and Mrs. James Stam**
Location: **40 mi. E of Richmond**
No. of Rooms: **4**
No. of Private Baths: **4**
Suites: **$95–$105**

Open: **All year**
Breakfast: **Full**
Pets: **No**
Children: **Welcome, over 12**
Smoking: **No**
Social Drinking: **Permitted**

This B&B, in a three-story Georgian home, is especially noted for warm hospitality, good conversation, interesting antiques, beautiful accommodations, and a delicious breakfast—all the things one looks for in a bed and breakfast. Your hosts, Jim and Priscilla, who have retired from academia, love travel and people. They previously owned Miss Malley's Inn and The Little Traveller Inn, both on Chincoteague Island.

The Homestay Bed & Breakfast ✪
517 RICHMOND ROAD, WILLIAMSBURG, VIRGINIA 23185

Tel: **(804) 229-7468; (800) 836-7468**	Breakfast: **Full**
Best Time to Call: **10 AM–9 PM**	Credit Cards: **MC, VISA**
Hosts: **Barbara and Jim Thomassen**	Pets: **No**
Location: **3 mi. from Rte. I-64, Exit 238**	Children: **Welcome, over 10**
No. of Rooms: **3**	Smoking: **No**
No. of Private Baths: **3**	Social Drinking: **Permitted**
Double/pb: **$70–$85**	Minimum Stay: **2 nights, weekends,**
Single/pb: **$60–$75**	**holidays, and special events**
Open: **All year**	Airport/Station Pickup: **Yes**
Reduced Rates: **15% less Jan. 1–**	
Mar. 31	

Cozy and convenient! Enjoy the comfort of a lovely Colonial Revival home furnished with turn-of-the-century family antiques and country charm. Rooms with a Victorian double bed, king-size bed, or twin beds are available. The rooms are accented with an attention to detail. You may relax in the second floor sitting room or by the fire in the living room. A full breakfast, served in the formal dining room, features homemade breads, herb jellies (made with herbs from the garden), and delicious hot dishes. You are just four blocks from Williamsburg's famed historic area, adjacent to the College of William and Mary campus, alumni house and football stadium, and minutes away from Jamestown, Yorktown, and Busch Gardens.

Legacy of Williamsburg Tavern
930 JAMESTOWN ROAD, WILLIAMSBURG, VIRGINIA 23185-3917

Tel: **(804) 220-0524; (800) 962-4722**	Open: **All year**
Hosts: **Mary Ann and Ed Lutkewich**	Breakfast: **Full**
Location: **2 mi. from Rte. 64, Exit 59**	Credit Cards: **MC, VISA**
No. of Rooms: **4**	Pets: **No**
No. of Private Baths: **4**	Children: **No**
Double/pb: **$85**	Smoking: **No**
Suites: **$130**	Social Drinking: **Permitted**

Ed and Mary Ann have furnished their 18th-century-style home with lovely antiques from that era. The suite is the ultimate in privacy, and features a canopy bed in the bedroom and a comfortable sofa facing a fireplace in the living room. Flowers, fruit, wine, and candy will make you feel welcome. You'll awaken to the aroma of freshly baked breads, just the beginning of a hearty breakfast. Afterward, stroll across the street to the campus of William and Mary College, walk to the restored area, or drive to Busch Gardens nearby.

Liberty Rose B&B ✪
1022 JAMESTOWN ROAD, WILLIAMSBURG, VIRGINIA 23185

Tel: **(804) 253-1260**	Breakfast: **Full**
Best Time to Call: **9 AM–9 PM**	Credit Cards: **MC, VISA**
Hosts: **Brad and Sandi Hirz**	Pets: **No**
No. of Rooms: **4**	Children: **Welcome, over 12**
No. of Private Baths: **4**	Smoking: **No**
Double/pb: **$105**	Social Drinking: **Permitted**
3 Suites: **$165**	Minimum Stay: **Weekends**
Open: **All year**	Airport/Station Pickup: **Yes**

This enchanting old home is one of Williamsburg's most romantic—Brad and Sandi created their B&B as a honeymoon project! Antiques from all periods fill the Liberty Rose. In the guest rooms, comfortable queen-size poster beds are draped with fringed reproduction damasks and topped with silk-covered goose-down duvets. Alongside the bed, in an old-fashioned armoire, you'll find a TV-VCR. The luxurious baths have claw-footed tubs, marble showers, and ample supplies of robes, towels, and bubble bath. And everywhere you'll notice little extras, such as a dish full of chocolates, complimentary soft drinks, freshly baked chocolate chip cookies, and a long-stemmed silk rose that's yours to keep.

War Hill ✪
4560 LONG HILL ROAD, WILLIAMSBURG, VIRGINIA 23188

Tel: **(804) 565-0248; (800) 743-0248**	Cottage: **$100–$145; sleeps 2–5**
Best Time to Call: **9 AM–9 PM**	Open: **All year**
Hosts: **Shirley, Bill, and Will Lee**	Breakfast: **Full**
Location: **2 mi. from Williamsburg**	Credit Cards: **MC, VISA**
No. of Rooms: **5**	Pets: **No**
No. of Private Baths: **5**	Children: **Welcome**
Double/pb: **$65–$85**	Smoking: **No**
Suite: **$95–$135; sleeps 2–5**	Social Drinking: **Permitted**

War Hill is situated in the center of a 32-acre working farm, just three miles from the tourist attractions. Built in 1968, this Colonial replica couples the charm of yesteryear with today's contemporary conveniences. The suite is composed of two bedrooms and a bath. The wide heart-pine floors came from an old school, the stairs from a church, the overhead beams from a barn; the oak mantel is over 200 years old. Fruits from a variety of trees in the orchard are yours to pick in season. In autumn, Shirley and Bill serve delicious homemade applesauce and cider. Angus show cattle graze in the pasture, and the sounds you'll hear are crickets, frogs, owls, and the morning crowing of the rooster.

Williamsburg Sampler Bed and Breakfast ✪
922 JAMESTOWN ROAD, WILLIAMSBURG, VIRGINIA 23185

Tel: **(800) 722-1169**	Open: **All year**
Best Time to Call: **7:30 AM–10:30 PM**	Breakfast: **Full**
Hosts: **Helen and Ike Sisane**	Pets: **No**
Location: **Heart of Williamsburg**	Children: **Welcome, over 12**
No. of Rooms: **4**	Smoking: **No**
No. of Private Baths: **4**	Social Drinking: **Permitted**
Double/pb: **$85–$90**	Airport/Station Pickup: **Yes**

Welcome to one of Williamsburg's finest 18th-century plantation-style homes. The three-story, brick Colonial B&B is richly furnished throughout with antiques, pewter, and samplers. This elegant home complements those located in the restored area and is within walking distance to historic Colonial Williamsburg. Lovely accommodations include four-poster beds in king and queen sizes, television, and your hosts' famous "skip lunch" breakfast. Personalized gift certificates are available.

Azalea House ✪
551 SOUTH MAIN STREET, WOODSTOCK, VIRGINIA 22664

Tel: **(703) 459-3500**	Breakfast: **Full**
Hosts: **Margaret and Price McDonald**	Credit Cards: **AMEX, MC, VISA**
Location: **35 mi. N of Harrisonburg**	Pets: **No**
No. of Rooms: **3**	Children: **Welcome**
No. of Private Baths: **3**	Smoking: **No**
Double/pb: **$50–$70**	Social Drinking: **Permitted**
Open: **All year**	

This spacious home, built in the early 1890s, served as a parsonage for 70 years. It has been restored following its Victorian tradition and has porches, bay windows, and a white picket fence—in spring, one hundred blooming azaleas enhance its beauty. The interior is made particularly lovely with family heirlooms and pretty color schemes. Azalea House is within walking distance of fine restaurants, antique shops, and an art gallery. It is convenient to wineries, orchards, trails, horseback riding, and fishing. Air-conditioning assures your summer comfort.

The Country Fare ✪
402 NORTH MAIN STREET, WOODSTOCK, VIRGINIA 22664

Tel: (703) 459-4828
Best Time to Call: 7–11 AM; 6–10 PM
Host: Bette Hallgren
Location: 35 mi. S of Winchester
No. of Rooms: 3
No. of Private Baths: 1
Max. No. Sharing Bath: 3
Double/pb: $65

Double/sb: $45–$55
Single/sb: $35
Open: All year
Breakfast: Continental
Pets: No
Children: Welcome, by arrangement
Smoking: No
Social Drinking: Permitted

A small cozy inn, circa 1772, The Country Fare is one of Shenandoah County's oldest homes. It is restored and carefully preserved and has wide pine floorboards upstairs, original doors and hardware, and walls hand-stenciled with original designs. Nana's Room boasts hand-painted furniture and a private bath. Two other bedrooms—one with a queen-size, the other with a full-size bed—share an old-fashioned bathroom with a claw-footed tub. Expanded Continental breakfast, served before the dining room's wood-burning stove, consists of seasonal fruits, juices, home-baked breads and muffins, and some of Nana's surprises. Your host will share information on the interesting sights and attractions of the valley.

WASHINGTON

Deer Harbor • • Anacortes

Oak Harbor • Langley • Mt. Vernon
Port Townsend •
•
• Edmonds
Port Orchard • • Seattle/Kirkland
Tacoma •   Spokane •
• Olympia   • Ritzville

• Long Beach   Clarkston •
• Cathlamet

• White Salmon

Pacific Bed & Breakfast Agency ✪
701 NORTHWEST 60TH STREET, SEATTLE, WASHINGTON 98107

Tel: **(206) 784-0539; fax (206) 782-4036**
Best Time to Call: **9 AM–5 PM**
Coordinator: **Irmgard Castleberry**
States/Regions Covered: **Statewide; Canada—Vancouver, Victoria, British Columbia**

Rates (Single/Double):
  Modest: **$45 / $45**
  Average: **$55 / $85**
  Luxury: **$85 / $200**
Credit Cards: **AMEX, MC, VISA**
Minimum Stay: **2 nights in Seattle**
Descriptive Directory: **$5**

Victorians, contemporaries, island cottages, waterfront houses, and private suites with full kitchens are available. Most are close to downtown areas, near bus lines, in fine residential neighborhoods, or within walking distance of a beach. Many extras are included, such as pickup service, free use of laundry facilities, guided tours and more. The University of Washington and the University of Puget Sound are nearby. There is a $5 surcharge for one-night stays.

A Burrow's Bay B&B
4911 MACBETH DRIVE, ANACORTES, WASHINGTON 98221

Tel: **(206) 293-4792**
Hosts: **Beverly and Winfred Stocker**
Location: **92 mi. N of Seattle**
Suites: **$95; sleep 2–6**
Open: **All year**
Breakfast: **Continental, plus**

Credit Cards: **MC, VISA**
Pets: **Sometimes**
Children: **Welcome**
Smoking: **No**
Social Drinking: **Permitted**
Airport/Station Pickup: **Yes**

Enjoy sweeping views of the San Juan Islands from this lovely contemporary Northwest home. The guest suite consists of a large sitting room with a view and a comfortable bedroom with a blue-and-tan motif and wall-to-wall carpeting. You are sure to enjoy the privacy and relaxation of having your own private deck, fireplace, TV, and a separate entrance. Beverly and Winfred offer an extensive buffet from which you may select breakfast. They are located within walking distance of Washington Park, restaurants, and ferry rides to the nearby islands. Your hosts will be glad to provide touring advice for day trips to Victoria, B.C., Deception Pass, and Port Townsend.

The Channel House ✪
2902 OAKES AVENUE, ANACORTES, WASHINGTON 98221

Tel: **(206) 293-9382**
Hosts: **Dennis and Patricia McIntyre**

Location: **65 mi. N of Seattle; 18 mi. W of I-5, Exit 230**

No. of Rooms: **6**
No. of Private Baths: **6**
Double/pb: **$69–$89**
Cottage: **$95–$190**
Open: **All year**
Breakfast: **Full**

Credit Cards: **DISC, MC, VISA**
Pets: **No**
Children: **Welcome, over 12**
Smoking: **No**
Social Drinking: **Permitted**

Built in 1902 by an Italian count, this three-story Victorian house has stained-glass windows, rare antiques, gracious ambience, and is in mint condition. The guest rooms have beautiful views of Puget Sound and the San Juan Islands. It's an ideal getaway for relaxing in the "cleanest corner of the country." Your hosts serve gourmet breakfasts in front of the fireplace. The communal hot tub is a treat after salmon fishing, tennis, or golf. And it's only minutes from the ferry for visiting Victoria, British Columbia.

Sunset Beach B&B ✪
100 SUNSET BEACH, ANACORTES, WASHINGTON 98221

Tel: **(206) 293-5428**
Best Time to Call: **8 AM–10 PM**
Hosts: **Joann and Hal Harker**
Location: **80 mi. NW of Seattle**
No. of Rooms: **3**
No. of Private Baths: **1**
Max. No. Sharing Bath: **4**
Double/pb: **$79**
Double/sb: **$69**

Open: **All year**
Reduced Rates: **Available**
Breakfast: **Full**
Credit Cards: **MC, VISA**
Pets: **No**
Children: **No**
Smoking: **No**
Social Drinking: **Permitted**

This B&B is located on exciting Rosario Straits. Relax and enjoy the view of seven major islands from the decks, stroll on the beach or walk in the beautiful Washington Park, adjacent to the private gardens. Guests have private entry, bathrooms, and TV. Full breakfast is served. It's only five minutes to San Juan Ferries, fine restaurants, marina, and convenience store nearby. The sunsets are outstanding.

The Country Keeper Bed & Breakfast Inn
61 MAIN STREET, CATHLAMET, WASHINGTON 98612

Tel: **(206) 795-3030**
Hosts: **Barbara and Tony West**
Location: **70 mi. NW of Portland, Ore.**
No. of Rooms: **4**
No. of Private Baths: **2**
Max. No. Sharing Bath: **3**
Double/pb: **$75–$85**
Single/pb: **$65–$80**
Double/sb: **$65–$75**

Single/sb: **$55–$65**
Open: **All year**
Reduced Rates: **3 days or more**
Breakfast: **Full**
Credit Cards: **MC, VISA**
Pets: **No**
Children: **Welcome, over 10**
Smoking: **No**
Social Drinking: **Permitted**

Cathlamet is a scenic, quiet place on the Columbia River, within an easy drive of the Mount St. Helens National Monument. It is a fishing and farming community with a strong sense of history. The inn was built in 1907 from local timber; the fine work of craftsmen is seen in the inlaid floors and stained-glass windows. Breakfast is a romantic affair served in the handsome dining room. Afterward, cycle the game refuge, play a round of golf or a set of tennis, fish, sail, or windsurf.

The Cliff House ✪
2000 WESTLAKE DRIVE, CLARKSTON, WASHINGTON 99403

Tel: **(509) 758-1267**	Breakfast: **Full**
Best Time to Call: **8 AM–8 PM**	Other Meals: **Available**
Hosts: **Doug and Sonia Smith**	Credit Cards: **MC, VISA**
Location: **8 mi. W of Clarkston**	Pets: **No**
No. of Rooms: **2**	Children: **Welcome, over 10**
No. of Private Baths: **2**	Smoking: **No**
Double/pb: **$65–$75**	Social Drinking: **Permitted**
Single/pb: **$60–$70**	Minimum Stay: **2 nights on weekends**
Open: **All year**	**and holidays**
Reduced Rates: **10% seniors; weekly**	Airport/Station Pickup: **Yes**

Breathtaking is one of the best ways to describe The Cliff House's view of the Snake River, 500 feet below. Chief Timothy State Park, named for the Nez Percé Indian leader, lies along the river. Depending on the season, you may see geese, ducks, pheasant, deer, even an occasional bald eagle in the area. White-water rafting and jet boat trips along North America's deepest gorge, Hells Canyon, can be arranged. Your hosts set out different breakfasts each day; apple pancakes, waffles, and stratas are among the typical offerings.

Palmer's Chart House ✪
P.O. BOX 51, ORCAS ISLAND, DEER HARBOR, WASHINGTON 98243

Tel: **(206) 376-4231**	Open: **All year**
Hosts: **Majean and Don Palmer**	Breakfast: **Full**
Location: **50 mi. N of Seattle**	Pets: **No**
No. of Rooms: **2**	Children: **Welcome, over 10**
No. of Private Baths: **2**	Smoking: **No**
Double/pb: **$60–$70**	Social Drinking: **Permitted**
Single/pb: **$45**	Foreign Languages: **Spanish**

It's just an hour's ride on the Washington State ferry from Anacortes to Orcas Island. Seasoned travelers, Majean and Don know how to make your stay special. Each guest room has a private deck from which to view the harbor scene. Blueberry pancakes are a breakfast specialty. *Amante*, the 33-foot sloop, is available for sailing with Don, the skipper.

Aardvark House ✪

7219 LAKE BALLINGER WAY, EDMONDS, WASHINGTON 98026

Tel: (206) 778-7866
Best Time to Call: **Anytime**
Hosts: **Jim and Arline Fahey**
Location: **13 mi. N of Seattle**
No. of Rooms: **3**
Max. No. Sharing Bath: **4**
Double/sb: **$55**

Single/sb: **$45**
Open: **All year**
Breakfast: **Full**
Pets: **No**
Children: **Welcome (crib, high chair)**
Smoking: **No**
Social Drinking: **Permitted**

This lovely lakefront home is within walking distance of a four-star restaurant and a city bus. Your hosts, a well-traveled retired Air Force couple, enjoy square dancing, outdoor living, gardening, and swimming. They'll be glad to take you on a cruise around Lake Ballinger on their barge. Breakfasts are varied, with home-grown raspberries, blueberries, and plums, and entrées like coddled eggs, omelets, and the house specialty, sourdough waffles cooked outdoors over a wood fire.

Driftwood Lane Bed and Breakfast

724 DRIFTWOOD LANE, EDMONDS, WASHINGTON 98020

Tel: (206) 776-2686
Best Time to Call: **8–10 AM; 6–9 PM**
Hosts: **Ed and Lois Schaeffer**
Location: **15 mi. N of Seattle**
No. of Rooms: **1**
No. of Private Baths: **1**
Double/pb: **$50**

Single/pb: **$45**
Open: **All year**
Breakfast: **Continental**
Pets: **No**
Children: **No**
Smoking: **No**
Social Drinking: **Permitted**

This contemporary home in the heart of Edmonds reflects the relaxed life-style of the town, where you can take in Puget Sound and the snowcapped Olympic Mountains. Listen to the cry of sea gulls and watch nearby ferryboats as you walk along the beach or savor the excellent cuisine in town. Or catch a lingering sunset from the Schaeffers' deck. Their newly decorated guest room has a queen-size bed and an adjoining private bath. Continental breakfast is highlighted by fresh fruits, applesauce, and preserves from your hosts' own trees.

The Harrison House ✪

210 SUNSET AVENUE, EDMONDS, WASHINGTON 98020

Tel: (206) 776-4748
Hosts: **Jody and Harve Harrison**
Location: **15 mi. N of Seattle**
No. of Rooms: **2**
No. of Private Baths: **2**
Double/pb: **$55–$65**
Single/pb: **$45–$55**

Open: **All year**
Breakfast: **Continental**
Pets: **No**
Children: **No**
Smoking: **No**
Social Drinking: **Permitted**

This new, informal, waterfront home has a sweeping view of Puget Sound and the Olympic Mountains. It is a block north of the ferry dock and two blocks from the center of this historic town. Many fine restaurants are within walking distance. Your spacious room has a private deck, TV, wet bar, telephone, and king-size bed. The University of Washington is nearby.

Heather House ✪
1011 "B" AVENUE, EDMONDS, WASHINGTON 98020

Tel: (206) 778-7233	Single/pb: $50
Best Time to Call: 5–6:30 PM	Open: All year
Hosts: Harry and Joy Whitcutt	Breakfast: Continental, plus
Location: 15 mi. N of Seattle	Pets: No
No. of Rooms: 1	Children: No
No. of Private Baths: 1	Smoking: No
Double/pb: $55	Social Drinking: Permitted

This contemporary home has a spectacular view of Puget Sound and the Olympic Mountains. The guest room has a comfortable king-size bed and opens onto a private deck. Joy and Harry are world travelers and enjoy their guests. The homemade jams, jellies, and marmalades are delicious. You can work off breakfast by walking a mile to the shops, beaches, and fishing pier.

Hudgens Haven ✪
9313 190 SOUTH WEST, EDMONDS, WASHINGTON 98020

Tel: (206) 776-2202	Single/pb: $40
Best Time to Call: 4–8 PM	Open: All year
Hosts: Lorna and Edward Hudgens	Breakfast: Continental
Location: 20 min. from downtown Seattle	Pets: No
	Children: Welcome, over 10
No. of Rooms: 1	Smoking: No
No. of Private Baths: 1	Social Drinking: Permitted
Double/pb: $45	

Hudgens Haven is located in a picture postcard town on Puget Sound. Windows on the west side boast a lovely view of the waterfront. The guest room is furnished with antiques as well as a queen-size bed, rocker, and plenty of drawer space. Edmonds, located 20 minutes from downtown Seattle, is a former lumber town with interesting old houses and an abundance of small shops and excellent restaurants. Continental breakfast is included in the room rate, but for an additional $3.50 per person, Lorna will gladly prepare her hearty woodsman's breakfast.

The Maple Tree **○**
18313 OLYMPIC VIEW DRIVE, EDMONDS, WASHINGTON 98020

Tel: **(206) 774-8420**
Hosts: **Marion and Hellon Wilkerson**
Location: **15 mi. N of Seattle**
No. of Rooms: **1**
No. of Private Baths: **1**
Double/pb: **$45**
Single/pb: **$40**

Open: **All year**
Breakfast: **Continental**
Pets: **No**
Children: **Welcome, over 5**
Smoking: **No**
Social Drinking: **Permitted**

The Maple Tree is a beautifully restored older home with landscaped grounds. Located across the street from Puget Sound, it commands a stunning view of the Olympic Mountains. You're welcome to watch the activity on Puget Sound through the telescope in the solarium. Lounge on the brick patio or watch the sun set over the snowcapped mountains as you sip a glass of Washington State wine. Hellon and Marion enjoy having guests and exchanging travel experiences with them. Hellon loves to cook; both like to work in their rose garden.

Shumway Mansion **○**
11410-99 PLACE NORTH EAST, KIRKLAND, WASHINGTON 98033

Tel: **(206) 823-2303**; fax: **822-0421**
Best Time to Call: **9 AM–7 PM**
Hosts: **Richard and Sallie Harris, and Julie and Marshall Blakemore**
Location: **5 mi. NE of Seattle**
No. of Rooms: **8**
No. of Private Baths: **8**
Double/pb: **$65–$82**

Suites: **$95; sleeps 4**
Open: **All year**
Breakfast: **Full**
Credit Cards: **AMEX, MC, VISA**
Pets: **No**
Children: **Welcome, over 12**
Smoking: **No**
Social Drinking: **Permitted**

This stately 24-room mansion, built in 1909, has a regal presence overlooking Lake Washington. The eight antique-filled guest rooms, including a charming corner suite, pair today's comforts with intricately carved pieces from yesteryear. Richard and Sallie will indulge your palate with variety-filled breakfasts that always feature homemade scones and jams. Within a short distance are water and snow recreation, an athletic club, downtown Seattle, and lots of shopping. After a busy day, return "home" and relax in front of the fire with a seasonal treat.

Log Castle Bed & Breakfast **○**
3273 EAST SARATOGA ROAD, LANGLEY, WASHINGTON 98260

Tel: **(206) 221-5483**
Best Time to Call: **8 AM–9 PM**
Hosts: **Jack and Norma Metcalf**
Location: **40 mi. N of Seattle**

No. of Rooms: **1**
No. of Private Baths: **1**
Double/pb: **$80**
Open: **All year**

Breakfast: **Full**
Credit Cards: **MC, VISA**
Pets: **No**
Children: **Welcome, over 11**

Smoking: **No**
Social Drinking: **No**
Airport/Station Pickup: **Yes**

You don't have to build your castle on the sand on Whidbey Island, because one already awaits you. The imaginative design of this log lodge includes an eight-sided tower where any modern-day princess would feel at home. Taredo wood stairways, leaded and stained-glass motifs, and comfortable furnishings create a rustic yet sophisticated atmosphere. The four guest rooms all offer beautiful views of the surrounding mountains and water. Relax beside a large stone fireplace, take a rowboat ride, or a long walk on the beach. Your hosts offer breads and cinnamon rolls right from the oven as part of a hearty breakfast served on a big, round, log table. Host Jack Metcalf is a state senator and also loves to entertain when he is not working at the legislature. For those of you who don't mind paying a higher rate, 3 rooms are available.

Boreas Bed and Breakfast ✪
607 NORTH BOULEVARD, P.O. BOX 1344, LONG BEACH, WASHINGTON 98631

Tel: **(206) 642-8069**
Best Time to Call: **9 AM–9 PM**
Hosts: **Sally Davis and Coleman White**
Location: **100 mi. W of Portland, Oregon**
No. of Rooms: **4**
No. of Private Baths: **2**
Max. No. Sharing Bath: **4**
Double/pb: **$85**
Single/pb: **$75**
Double/sb: **$65–$75**
Single/sb: **$55–$65**

Open: **All year**
Reduced Rates: **Available**
Breakfast: **Full**
Credit Cards: **MC, VISA**
Pets: **Sometimes**
Children: **Welcome, 6 and over**
Smoking: **No**
Social Drinking: **Permitted**
Minimum Stay: **2 nights on weekends, May 15–Sept 15**
Airport/Station Pickup: **Yes**

Located 20 minutes north of the Columbia River, this 1920s beach home is remodeled in an eclectic style, mixing art and antiques with comfort and casualness. The house sits on the primary dunes with only an expanse of sand and grasses between it and the Pacific. A stone fireplace dominates the two large living rooms which face the ocean, a lovely path winds through the dunes to the surf. From this quiet residential area, it is still only a short walk to shopping, the boardwalk, and restaurants. The twenty-eight mile stretch of wild Pacific coast is a hiking and cycling paradise complete with bird sanctuaries, lighthouses and panoramic vistas. Your hosts enjoy travel and outdoor activities as well as sharing ideas and experiences with their guests.

Maple Valley Bed & Breakfast ✪

20020 SOUTHEAST 228, MAPLE VALLEY, WASHINGTON 98038

Tel: **(206) 432-1409**
Best Time to Call: **9 AM–9 PM**
Hosts: **Jayne and Clarke Hurlbut**
Location: **26 mi. SE of Seattle**
No. of Rooms: **2**
Max. No. Sharing Bath: **4**
Double/sb: **$50–$65**
Single/sb: **$45–$60**

Open: **All year**
Reduced Rates: **Families**
Breakfast: **Full**
Pets: **Sometimes**
Children: **Welcome**
Smoking: **No**
Social Drinking: **Permitted**
Airport Pickup: **Yes**

After a good night's sleep in either of the B&B's guest rooms—one with a four-poster log bed and the other complete with a pink rosebud tea set, you'll come down to breakfast at a table that overlooks the lawn, the Hurlbuts' resident peacocks, and a wildlife pond teeming with a variety of northwestern birds. If the morning is cool, you'll be warmed by a stone fireplace and you won't go away hungry after orange juice, lemon-blueberry muffins, a plate-size hootenanny pancake (served with whipped cream, strawberries, slivered almonds, and syrup), ham, sausage or bacon, fresh-ground coffee, tea, or hot chocolate.

The White Swan Guest House ✪

1388 MOORE ROAD, MT. VERNON, WASHINGTON 98273

Tel: **(360) 445-6805**
Best Time to Call: **Mornings; evenings**
Host: **Peter Goldfarb**
Location: **60 mi. N of Seattle, 6 mi. SE of La Conner**
No. of Rooms: **3**
Max. No. Sharing Bath: **3**
Double/sb: **$75**
Single/sb: **$65**

Guest Cottage: **$125–$165; sleeps 4**
Open: **All year**
Reduced Rates: **Weekly in cottage**
Breakfast: **Continental**
Credit Cards: **MC, VISA**
Pets: **No**
Children: **Welcome (in cottage)**
Smoking: **No**
Social Drinking: **Permitted**

Surrounded by farmland and country roads, this storybook Victorian farmhouse, built in 1898, is painted crayon yellow and framed by English-style gardens. There's a wood stove in the parlor, wicker chairs on the porch, books for browsing, and a unique collection of old samplers. A platter of homemade chocolate chip cookies is waiting for you on the sideboard. It's only 6 miles to LaConner, a delightful fishing village brimful of interesting art galleries, shops, waterfront restaurants, and antique stores. The San Juan ferries are a half hour away.

North Island B&B ○

1589 NORTH WEST BEACH ROAD, OAK HARBOR, WASHINGTON 98277

Tel: **(206) 675-7080**	Open: **All year**
Best Time to Call: **Weekdays**	Breakfast: **Continental**
Hosts: **Jim and Maryvern Loomis**	Credit Cards: **AMEX, DISC, MC, VISA**
Location: **65 mi. NW of Seattle**	Pets: **No**
No. of Rooms: **2**	Children: **No**
No. of Private Baths: **2**	Smoking: **No**
Double/pb: **$90**	Social Drinking: **No**
Single/pb: **$85**	

Ships of all kinds sail by as the sound of ocean waves lulls you to sleep at night at North Island Bed and Breakfast. Located on the west shore of historic and picturesque Whidbey Island, this is a newly constructed home on 175 feet of private beach. Ample parking, king-size beds and a fireplace combine to give guests the very best in accommodations. Guests have access to the beach, yard and living room. Breakfast, served between 8:30 and 9:30 AM, features fresh fruit in season, juice, homemade breads and muffins, cereals, and freshly ground coffee or tea.

Puget View Guesthouse ○

7924 61ST NORTHEAST, OLYMPIA, WASHINGTON 98516

Tel: **(360) 459-1676**	Reduced Rates: **Families; weekly; off-season**
Best Time to Call: **Evenings**	Breakfast: **Continental, plus**
Hosts: **Dick and Barbara Yunker**	Credit Cards: **MC, VISA**
Location: **4½ mi. from I-5, Exit 111**	Pets: **Sometimes**
No. of Rooms: **1 cottage**	Children: **Welcome**
No. of Private Baths: **1**	Smoking: **No**
Guest Cottage: **$72–$102; sleeps 4**	Social Drinking: **Permitted**
Open: **All year**	

This charming waterfront guest cottage is located next to Tolmie State Park and adjacent to Dick and Barbara's log home. The panoramic Puget Sound setting makes it a popular, romantic getaway. You are apt to discover simple pleasures such as beachcombing or birdwatching and activities such as kayaking or scuba diving. Your breakfast, an elegant repast, is brought to the cottage. You are welcome to use the beachside campfire for an evening cookout or to barbecue on your deck.

"Reflections"—A Bed and Breakfast Inn ✪
3878 REFLECTION LANE EAST, PORT ORCHARD, WASHINGTON 98366

Tel: **(206) 871-5582**	Single/sb: **$55**
Best Time to Call: **Anytime**	Suites: **$90**
Hosts: **Jim and Cathy Hall**	Open: **All year**
Location: **15 mi. W of Seattle**	Breakfast: **Full**
No. of Rooms: **4**	Credit Cards: **MC, VISA**
No. of Private Baths: **2**	Pets: **No**
Max. No. Sharing Bath: **4**	Children: **Welcome, over 15**
Double/pb: **$65**	Smoking: **No**
Single/pb: **$65**	Social Drinking: **Permitted**
Double/sb: **$55**	

This sprawling Colonial home stands majestically on a bluff overlooking Puget Sound and Bainbridge Island. Each cheerful guest room, furnished with New England antiques, affords superb views of the water and ever-changing scenery. Port Orchard offers a variety of diversions, from small shops filled with antiques and crafts, to marinas, parks, and boat excursions around the peninsula.

The English Inn ✪
718 "F" STREET, PORT TOWNSEND, WASHINGTON 98368

Tel: **(206) 385-5302**	Open: **All year**
Best Time to Call: **10 AM**	Breakfast: **Full**
Host: **Juliette Swenson**	Credit Cards: **MC, VISA**
Location: **60 mi. W of Seattle; 25 mi.**	Pets: **No**
from Rt. 103, Exit 20	Children: **Welcome, over 10**
No. of Rooms: **5**	Smoking: **No**
No. of Private Baths: **5**	Social Drinking: **Permitted**
Double/pb: **$75–$95**	

Built in 1885, this Italianate Victorian house has five large bedrooms decorated mostly in antiques, with modern comfort in mind. The full breakfast usually includes freshly baked scones and homemade marmalade. There is a beautiful lounge and dining room for guests to enjoy, as well as a hot tub and gazebo in the garden. The inn is situated just a few minutes from downtown and close to several good restaurants. Port Townsend, a Victorian seaport, is set between the Olympic Mountains to the west and the Cascades to the east. It makes a great spot to tour from; close by are ferries to the San Juan Islands, and Victoria, British Columbia.

Holly Hill House ○
611 POLK, PORT TOWNSEND, WASHINGTON 98368

Tel: **(206) 385-5619**
Best Time to Call: **After 11 AM**
Hosts: **Lynne Sterling and Phyllis Olson**
Location: **60 mi. NW of Seattle**
No. of Rooms: **5**
No. of Private Baths: **5**
Double/pb: **$72–$86**
Suite: **$125**
Open: **All year**

Breakfast: **Full**
Credit Cards: **MC, VISA**
Pets: **No**
Children: **Welcome, over 12**
Smoking: **No**
Social Drinking: **Permitted**
Minimum Stay: **2 nights festival weekends**

Built in 1872, Holly Hill House is the former residence of R. C. Hill, who served variously as mayor, state representative, and the first banker of Port Townsend. Each room, lavishly furnished with Victorian antiques, is lovingly maintained down to the stippled woodwork. The grounds feature distinctive plantings, including holly trees and two unusual Camperdown elms known as upside-down trees. Nearby are marinas, golf courses, fishing sites, beaches, and many fine restaurants for your dining pleasure.

The Portico ○
502 SOUTH ADAMS STREET, RITZVILLE, WASHINGTON 99169

Tel: **(509) 659-0800**
Best Time to Call: **Days; evenings**
Hosts: **Mary Anne and Bill Phipps**
Location: **60 mi. SW of Spokane**
No. of Rooms: **2**
No. of Private Baths: **2**
Double/pb: **$56–$68**
Single/pb: **$50–$62**
Open: **All year**

Reduced Rates: **10% Mar.–Apr.; 10% seniors; 20% after 5th night**
Breakfast: **Full**
Other Meals: **Available**
Credit Cards: **AMEX, DISC, MC, VISA**
Pets: **No**
Children: **Welcome**
Smoking: **No**
Social Drinking: **Permitted**

This stately 1902 mansion, listed on the National Register of Historic Places, combines Queen Anne and Classical Revival architecture. The interior is distinguished by gleaming oak woodwork, wood-spindled screens and columns, a grand entry staircase, and antique furnishings. In season, the grounds are resplendent with flowers, wild berries, fruit trees, and a vegetable garden, making for some tasty treats. Bill, a retired air force officer, and his wife, Mary Anne, provide a romantic setting that lets guests experience the serenity of this rural eastern Washington community.

Chelsea Station B&B Inn ○
4915 LINDEN AVENUE NORTH, SEATTLE, WASHINGTON 98103

Tel: **(206) 547-6077**
Best Time to Call: **10 AM–1 PM**
Hosts: **Dick and Marylou Jones**

Location: **2 mi. N of downtown Seattle**
No. of Rooms: **6**
No. of Private Baths: **6**

Double/pb: **$99–$109**
Open: **All year**
Reduced Rates: **Off-season**
Breakfast: **Full**
Credit Cards: **AMEX, DC, DISC, MC, VISA**

Pets: **No**
Children: **Welcome, over 12**
Smoking: **No**
Social Drinking: **Permitted**

Just five minutes from Seattle's downtown bustle, Chelsea Station consistently provides the peaceful surroundings travelers appreciate. Lace curtains, ample breakfasts, comfy king-size beds, and antique furnishings recreate the warmth of grandma's time. This 1920 Federal Colonial is an outstanding example of the bricklayer's art. The nearby Seattle Rose Gardens contribute beauty to the surroundings. With a cup of tea in the afternoon, you will find Chelsea Station is a perfect place for relaxation and renewal. Full-time innkeepers Dick and Marylou bring their backgrounds in health care to the nurturing spirit of their B&B. Early reservations are recommended.

Mildred's Bed & Breakfast ✪
1202 15TH AVENUE EAST, SEATTLE, WASHINGTON 98112

Tel: **(206) 325-6072**
Best Time to Call: **Mornings**
Hosts: **Mildred and Melodee Sarver**
Location: **5 mi. NE of City Center**
No. of Rooms: **3**
No. of Private Baths: **3**
Double/pb: **$85**
Single/pb: **$75**

Open: **All year**
Breakfast: **Full**
Credit Cards: **AMEX, DC, MC, VISA**
Pets: **No**
Children: **Welcome**
Smoking: **No**
Social Drinking: **Permitted**
Airport/Station Pickup: **Yes**

Mildred's is the ultimate trip-to-Grandmother's fantasy come true. A large white 1890 Victorian, it's the perfect setting for traditional, caring B&B hospitality. Guest rooms on the second floor have sitting alcoves, lace curtains, and antiques. Mildred's special touches, like coffee and juice delivered to your room one half hour before breakfast, and tea and cookies on arrival, make her guests feel truly pampered. Across the street is historic 44-acre Volunteer Park with its art museum, flower conservatory, and tennis courts. An electric trolley stops at the front door and there is ample street parking. It is just minutes to the city center, freeways, and all points of interest.

Prince of Wales ✪
133 THIRTEENTH AVENUE EAST, SEATTLE, WASHINGTON 98102

Tel: **(206) 325-9692; (800) 327-9692**	Open: **All year**
Best Time to Call: **10 AM–9 PM**	Reduced Rates: **10% weekly**
Host: **Carol Norton**	Breakfast: **Full**
Location: **In heart of Seattle**	Credit Cards: **AMEX, MC, VISA**
No. of Rooms: **4**	Pets: **No**
No. of Private Baths: **2**	Children: **Welcome**
Max. No. Sharing Bath: **4**	Smoking: **No**
Double/sb: **$60–$70**	Social Drinking: **Permitted**
Suites: **$75–$90**	Foreign Languages: **Italian, Spanish**

From this convenient address, it's just a brief walk to the Convention Center and a short bus ride to the Space Needle, Pikes Place Market, and downtown Seattle's many other attractions. In the evening, you're sure to be tempted by the menus of neighborhood restaurants. Carol serves a delicious breakfast. The guest rooms have great views; the suites have queen-size beds, sitting room, and private baths.

Roberta's Bed and Breakfast
1147 SIXTEENTH AVENUE EAST, SEATTLE, WASHINGTON 98112

Tel: **(206) 329-3326; fax: (206) 324-2149**	Breakfast: **Full**
	Credit Cards: **MC, VISA**
Host: **Roberta Barry**	Pets: **No**
No. of Rooms: **5**	Children: **Sometimes**
Single/pb: **$75–$85**	Smoking: **No**
Open: **All year**	Social Drinking: **Permitted**

Roberta's is a 1903 frame Victorian with a large, old-fashioned front porch. The house is located in a quiet, historic neighborhood near the heart of the city. The cheerful rooms all boast queen-size beds. The Peach Room has bay windows, oak furniture, and Grandma's fancy desk; the Rosewood Room has a window seat and built-in oak bookcase; all five rooms are filled with books. In the morning you'll smell a pot of coffee right beside your door. That's just a warm-up for the large breakfast to come. The specialty of the house is Dutch Babies, a local dish, served with powdered sugar or fresh berries. For your convenience the *New York Times* and local newspapers are available every morning. For those of you who don't mind paying a higher rate, 4 rooms are available.

Seattle Bed & Breakfast **O**
2442 N.W. MARKET # 300, SEATTLE, WASHINGTON 98107

Tel: **(206) 783-2169**
Host: **Inge Pokrandt**
Location: **1 mi. from I-5**
No. of Rooms: **4**
No. of Private Baths: **2**
Suite: **$45**
Guest Cottage: **$75 for 2**
Open: **All year**

Breakfast: **Continental**
Credit Cards: **AMEX, MC, VISA**
Pets: **No**
Children: **Welcome (crib)**
Smoking: **No**
Social Drinking: **Permitted**
Foreign Languages: **German**

Built in 1925, this charming two-bedroom cottage is close to downtown, the University of Washington, fine beaches and all sightseeing. Enjoy the privacy, the fine oak furniture, the fireplace, and all the little touches that make you feel welcome. The private suite in Inge's home has a full kitchen, and some breakfast food is provided. Fresh flowers, fruits, and candy all spell out a warm welcome. The cedar deck in the sunny backyard is most enjoyable.

Spokane Bed & Breakfast Reservation Service **O**
627 EAST 25TH, SPOKANE, WASHINGTON 99203

Tel: **(509) 624-3776**
Best Time to Call: **8 AM–7 PM**
Coordinator: **Pat Conley**
States/Regions Covered:
  Canada—British Columbia, Vancouver, Victoria; Idaho—Coeur d'Alene, LaClede, Sandpoint; Washington—Seattle, Spokane, Yakima

Descriptive Directory: **Free**
Rates (Single/Double):
  Modest: **$40 / $45**
  Average: **$45 / $50**
  Luxury: **$62 / $92**
Credit Cards: **AMEX, MC, VISA**
Minimum Stay: **Only on 3-day weekends**

You can't beat the attractions of the Spokane area: excellent skiing and snowmobiling, perfect lakes for waterfront sports, large family-oriented parks, museums, symphonies, opera, and theater. This service will put you in touch with all manner of guest houses, from charming riverfront contemporaries to elegant, turn-of-the-century homes.

Marianna Stoltz House **O**
427 EAST INDIANA, SPOKANE, WASHINGTON 99207

Tel: **(509) 483-4316**
Hosts: **James and Phyllis Maguire**
No. of Rooms: **4**

No. of Private Baths: **2**
Max. No. Sharing Bath: **4**
Double/pb: **$65–70**

Single/pb: **$55–$60**
Open: **All year**
Breakfast: **Full**
Credit Cards: **AMEX, DC, DISC, MC, VISA**

Pets: **No**
Children: **Welcome, over 12**
Smoking: **No**
Social Drinking: **Permitted**
Airport/Station Pickup: **Yes**

The Marianna Stoltz House, a Spokane landmark, is a classic American Foursquare home built in 1908. Period furnishings complement the house's woodwork, tile fireplace, and leaded glass bookshelves and cupboards. The bedroom quilts are heirlooms from Phyllis' mother, the B&B's namesake. The Maguires are Spokane natives—Phyllis grew up in this very house—and can tell you about local theaters, museums, and parks. Full breakfasts consist of juice, fruit, muffins, and main dishes such as sausage-cheese strata and puffy Dutch pancakes with homemade syrup.

Greater Tacoma B&B Reservations ○
3312 NORTH UNION AVENUE, TACOMA, WASHINGTON 98407

Tel: **(206) 759-4088**
Best Time to Call: **After 10 AM**
Coordinator: **Sharon Kaufmann**
States/Regions Covered: **Bremerton, Enumclaw, Fox Island, Gig Harbor, Olalla, Olympia, Puyallup, Silverdale, Tacoma**

Descriptive Directory: **Free**
Rates (Single/Double):
 Modest **$65 / $65**
 Average **85 / $85**
 Luxury **$165 / $165**
Credit Cards: **AMEX, MC, VISA**

Greater Tacoma B&B Reservations offers more than fourteen inspected and licensed accommodations. Prefer full or Continental breakfast? Shared or private bath? Have your choice at homes that range from a cozy cottage to a historic waterfront mansion. Some sites have extra amenities like hot tubs and romantic Jacuzzis.

Commencement Bay B&B ○
3312 NORTH UNION AVENUE, TACOMA, WASHINGTON 98407

Tel: **(206) 752-8175**
Best Time to Call: **10 AM–1 PM**
Hosts: **Bill and Sheri Kaufmann**
Location: **1 mi. N of Tacoma**
No. of Rooms: **3**
No. of Private Baths: **1**
Max. No. Sharing Bath: **4**
Double/pb: **$90–$105**
Double/sb: **$70–$95**

Open: **All year**
Reduced Rates: **Available**
Breakfast: **Full**
Credit Cards: **AMEX, MC, VISA**
Pets: **No**
Children: **Welcome, over 12**
Smoking: **No**
Social Drinking: **Permitted**
Airport/Station Pickup: **Yes**

An elegantly decorated Colonial home overlooking scenic north end Tacoma, this B&B has dramatic bay and mountain views from both the rooms and the common areas. Guests can enjoy a quiet, relaxing fireside reading area, an outdoor hot tub in a lovely garden, a casual game room with large-screen TV, microwave, and refrigerator—even an office for business travelers (with a fax/modem available). The B&B offers guests cable TV, VCR, or telephone in select rooms, an early businessman's breakfast on weekdays, and transportation to nearby universities or downtown business areas. It is close to several water-front parks, jogging/hiking trails, great restaurants, quaint shops (including antiques), and easy freeway access. A delicious breakfast and different gourmet coffees are served daily.

Inge's Place ✪
6809 LAKE GROVE SW, TACOMA, WASHINGTON 98499

Tel: **(206) 584-4514**	Suites: **$60**
Host: **Ingeborg Deatherage**	Open: **All year**
Location: **3 mi. from I-5**	Reduced Rates: **Available**
No. of Rooms: **3**	Breakfast: **Full**
No. of Private Baths: **1**	Pets: **No**
Max. No. Sharing Bath: **4**	Children: **Welcome**
Double/pb: **$50**	Smoking: **No**
Single/pb: **$40**	Social Drinking: **Permitted**
Double/sb: **$45**	Airport/Station Pickup: **Yes**
Single/sb: **$35**	Foreign Languages: **German**

This spic-and-span home is in a lovely Tacoma suburb called Lake-wood. Feel welcome to use the hot tub, large backyard, and patio. There are many restaurants and shopping centers within walking distance, and several nearby lakes where fishing is excellent. Tacoma is the gateway to Mount Rainier. Inge is a world traveler, teacher, and enthusiast about B&Bs.

Keenan House ✪
2610 NORTH WARNER, TACOMA, WASHINGTON 98407

Tel: **(206) 752-0702**	Double/sb: **$50**
Best Time to Call: **Evenings**	Single/sb: **$45**
Host: **Lenore Keenan**	Open: **All year**
Location: **2½ mi. from I-5**	Breakfast: **Full**
No. of Rooms: **4**	Pets: **No**
No. of Private Baths: **2**	Children: **Welcome**
Max. No. Sharing Bath: **4**	Smoking: **No**
Double/pb: **$60**	Social Drinking: **Permitted**
Single/pb: **$50**	

This spacious Victorian house is located in the historic district near Puget Sound. It is furnished in antiques and period pieces. Afternoon tea is served, and ice is available for cocktails; fruit and croissants are served with breakfast. Local possibilities include Puget Sound, Vashon

Island, the state park, zoo, and ferry. It's only five blocks to the University of Puget Sound.

Llama Ranch Bed & Breakfast ☉
1980 HIGHWAY 141, WHITE SALMON, WASHINGTON 98672

Tel: **(509) 395-2786; (800) 800-LAMA
[5262]**
Hosts: **Jerry and Rebeka Stone**
Location: **50 mi. E of Portland, Oreg.**
No. of Rooms: **5**
Max. No. Sharing Bath: **4**
Double/sb: **$55**
Single/sb: **$45**
Open: **All year**

Reduced Rates: **$5 less Dec.–Mar.;
15% weekly**
Breakfast: **Full**
Credit Cards: **DISC, MC, VISA**
Pets: **Sometimes**
Children: **Welcome**
Smoking: **No**
Social Drinking: **Permitted**

Jerry and Rebeka enjoy sharing their love of llamas with their guests, and it is a rare person who can resist a llama's charm. Their B&B commands stunning views of Mt. Adams and Mt. Hood. The guest rooms are unpretentious and comfortable. Llama Ranch is located on 97 acres at the base of the Mt. Adams Wilderness Area. Nearby activities include horseback riding, white-water rafting, plane trips over Mount St. Helens, water sports, and cave exploration. The less adventurous are certain to enjoy learning about the ranch's serene animals.

WEST VIRGINIA

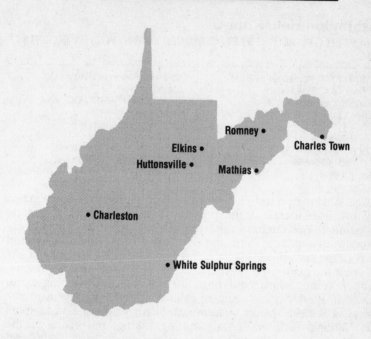

Romney •

Elkins •

Huttonsville •

Mathias •

• Charleston

Charles Town •

• White Sulphur Springs

Historic Charleston Bed & Breakfast ☉
114 ELIZABETH STREET, CHARLESTON, WEST VIRGINIA 25311

Tel: **(304) 345-8156; (800) CALL-WVA**
Best Time to Call: **8 AM–11 PM**
Hosts: **Bob and Jean Lambert**
Location: **½ mi. from I-77, I-64, Exit 99**
No. of Rooms: **3**
No. of Private Baths: **3**
Double/pb: **$65**
Single/pb: **$60**

Open: **All year**
Reduced Rates: **6% seniors, families**
Breakfast: **Full**
Credit Cards: **MC, VISA**
Children: **Welcome**
Smoking: **No**
Airport Pickup: **Yes**

The exterior of this 1905 American Foursquare home is painted gray clapboard with white trim. Most of the interior woodwork is the original natural oak. Guest accommodations are spacious—each room has a fireplace, private sitting area, and central heating and air conditioning. The entrance hall is furnished with a Victorian loveseat, candle table, and a claw-footed desk, setting the tone for the rest of the house, which is decorated with antiques, collectibles, and handicrafts. Breakfast is served in the dining room, on an early 1930s dining suite. Then you can explore the area, starting with the state capitol and cultural center one block away.

Washington House Inn ✪
216 SOUTH GEORGE STREET, CHARLES TOWN, WEST VIRGINIA 25414

Tel: (304) 725-7923; (800) 297-6957	Reduced Rates: Available
Best Time to Call: Anytime	Breakfast: Full
Hosts: Nina and Mel Vogel	Credit Cards: AMEX, MC, VISA
Location: 60 mi. NW of Washington, D.C.	Pets: No
	Children: Welcome, over 6
No. of Rooms: 6	Smoking: No
No. of Private Baths: 6	Social Drinking: Permitted
Double/pb: $70–$95	Airport/Station Pickup: Yes
Open: All year	

George Washington didn't sleep here—but his relatives did. Built in 1899 by descendants of the president's brothers, John Augustine and Samuel, Washington House Inn is a wonderful example of Late Victorian architecture. From the three-story turret and wraparound porch to the carved oak mantels, this home echoes a bygone era. As you enter the main foyer, period antiques help you step back in time. In the morning, a hearty full breakfast is served in the dining room. Located in West Virginia's eastern gateway, the inn is convenient to a host of activities. Within a ten-minute drive you will find Harpers Ferry National Park, white-water rafting, biking, and hiking on the restored C&O Canal towpath, thoroughbred horse racing, and Grand Prix-style sports car racing.

The Retreat at Buffalo Run ✪
214 HARPERTOWN ROAD, ELKINS, WEST VIRGINIA 26241

Tel: (304) 636-2960	Open: All year
Best Time to Call: 8 AM–9 PM	Reduced Rates: Weekly
Hosts: Kathleen, Bertha, and Earl Rhoad	Breakfast: Full
	Pets: Sometimes
Location: 160 mi. S of Pittsburgh	Children: Welcome
No. of Rooms: 6	Smoking: No
Max. No. Sharing Bath: 4	Social Drinking: Permitted
Double/sb: $49	Airport Pickup: Yes
Single/sb: $39	

This gracious turn-of-the-century home is located at the gateway to the 840,000-acre Monongahela National Forest, within walking distance of downtown Elkins and Davis and Elkins College. The home is warmly decorated with antiques, art, and contemporary furnishings. Wide

porches, tall shade trees, evergreens, and rhododendron groves surround the house. Close by are wilderness areas for hiking, biking, fishing, cross-country skiing; country auctions; and the Augusta Heritage Arts Festival. Breakfasts receive rave reviews. Bertha and Earl are avid bird-watchers; their daughter Kathleen is a college career counselor who collects cookbooks.

Gerrardstown's Prospect Hill
BOX 135, GERRARDSTOWN, WEST VIRGINIA 25420

Tel: **(304) 229-3346**	Guest Cottage: **$95 for 2; $135 for 4**
Best Time to Call: **Evenings**	Open: **All year**
Hosts: **Hazel and Charles Hudock**	Breakfast: **Full**
Location: **4 miles from Route 81**	Pets: **No**
No. of Rooms: **3**	Children: **Welcome in cottage**
No. of Private Baths: **3**	Smoking: **Permitted**
Double/pb: **$85**	Social Drinking: **Permitted**
Single/pb: **$75–$85**	

Prospect Hill is a Georgian mansion set on 225 acres. The house dates back to the 1790s, and is listed on the National Register of Historic Places. One can see that this was a well-to-do gentleman's home, with permanent Franklin fireplaces, antiques, and a half mural depicting life in the days of the early Republic. Guests may choose one of the beautifully appointed rooms in the main house or the former servants' quarters, complete with country kitchen and a fireplace in the living room. There is much to do on this working farm, including visiting the antebellum outbuildings, fishing, biking, and exploring the vast grounds. Near historic Harpers Ferry, Martinsburg, and Winchester, the area offers fine sightseeing and splendid restaurants.

The Hutton House ✪
ROUTES 219 AND 250, HUTTONSVILLE, WEST VIRGINIA 26273

Tel: **(800) 234-6701**	Open: **All year**
Best Time to Call: **Anytime**	Reduced Rates: **Available**
Hosts: **Dean and Loretta Murray**	Breakfast: **Full**
Location: **17 mi. S of Elkins**	Other Meals: **Available**
No. of Rooms: **7**	Credit Cards: **MC, VISA**
No. of Private Baths: **3**	Pets: **No**
Max. No. Sharing Bath: **4**	Children: **Welcome**
Double/pb: **$65–$70**	Smoking: **No**
Single/pb: **$55–$65**	Social Drinking: **Permitted**
Double/sb: **$55**	Airport/Station Pickup: **Yes**
Single/sb: **$48**	

Built in 1899 by a scion of Huttonsville's founder, Hutton House commands a broad view of the Tygart Valley and Laurel Mountain ridges. This ornate Queen Anne mansion, with its extraordinary woodwork and windows, is listed on the National Register of Historic Places. Travelers come here to ski at Snowshoe, visit Cass Railroad, and hike in the Monongahela National Forest. Civil War buffs will find plenty of battle sites to study, and the Augusta Heritage Arts Festival, in nearby Elkins, also merits a detour. For breakfast, your hosts dish out cantaloupe sorbet and whole wheat pancakes drizzled with maple syrup made from their own trees.

Mr. Richard's Olde Country Inn ✪
U.S. 219, ROUTE 1, BOX 11-A1, HUTTONSVILLE, WEST VIRGINIA 26273

Tel: **(304) 335-6659**	Open: **All year**
Best Time to Call: **AM**	Reduced Rates: **10% seniors**
Host: **Richard S. Brown**	Breakfast: **Full**
Location: **21 mi. S of Elkins**	Other Meals: **Available**
No. of Rooms: **13**	Credit Cards: **MC, VISA**
No. of Private Baths: **8**	Pets: **Sometimes**
Max. No. Sharing Bath: **4**	Children: **Welcome**
Double/pb: **$60**	Smoking: **Permitted**
Single/pb: **$35**	Social Drinking: **Permitted**
Double/sb: **$50**	Minimum Stay: **2 nights on 3-day**
Single/sb: **$35**	**weekends**
Guest Cottage: **$135; sleeps 6**	

Built in 1835, this antebellum mansion has been restored to its original splendor, with a full-service bar and restaurant. Some rooms have fireplaces, some have verandas. Guests dine on a robust West Virginia breakfast with specialties like stuffed French toast, omelets, and fresh fruit. The restaurant is open daily for light lunches and dinners of seafood, charbroiled steaks, and family meals. The great outdoors is the big attraction here; local activities run the gamut from white-water rafting, hiking, mountain biking, skiing, hunting, and fishing, to the tamer sports of golfing and antiquing. Amateur astonomers will want to pull up at Greenbank Observatory, the largest telescope in the U.S.

Valley View Farm ✪
ROUTE 1, BOX 467, MATHIAS, WEST VIRGINIA 26812

Tel: (304) 897-5229	Reduced Rates: **Weekly**
Best Time to Call: **Evenings, 8–10PM**	Breakfast: **Full**
Host: **Edna Shipe**	Other Meals: **Available**
Location: **130 mi. SW of D.C.**	Pets: **Welcome**
No. of Rooms: **4**	Children: **Welcome (crib)**
Max. No. Sharing Bath: **4**	Smoking: **Permitted**
Double/sb: **$40**	Social Drinking: **Permitted**
Single/sb: **$20**	Airport/Station Pickup: **Yes**
Open: **All year**	

This 1920s farmhouse is decorated with comfortable Early American–style furniture and family mementos, and there's a nice porch for relaxed visiting. This is no place to diet because Edna is a good cook. Seasonal recreational activities are available in nearby Lost River State Park and on Rock Cliff Lake. You are certain to enjoy the local festivals, house tours, and interesting craft shops. Bryces Ski Resort is less than an hour away.

Hampshire House 1884 ✪
165 NORTH GRAFTON STREET, ROMNEY, WEST VIRGINIA 26757

Tel: (304) 822-7171	Breakfast: **Full**
Hosts: **Jane and Scott Simmons**	Credit Cards: **AMEX, DC, DISC, MC, VISA**
Location: **35 mi. W of Winchester, Va.**	Pets: **No**
No. of Rooms: **5**	Children: **Welcome**
No. of Private Baths: **5**	Smoking: **No**
Double/pb: **$60–$80**	Social Drinking: **Permitted**
Single/pb: **$50–$60**	Airport/Station Pickup: **Yes**
Open: **All year**	
Reduced Rates: **Available**	

Only two and one half hours west of Washington, D.C., via Route 50 lies Romney, the oldest town in West Virginia. Surrounded by beautiful rolling hills, Hampshire House is conveniently located to the downtown area. Bicycles are ready for touring the town, with its quaint shops and historic buildings. Trail rides and hayrides are available at the local equestrian center, and winery tours are nearby. The bedrooms are attractively furnished with old-fashioned furniture and wallpapers and kept comfortable with central heating and air-conditioning. Jane and Scott graciously offer complimentary snacks and invite you to enjoy the old pump organ, television, VCR, or a variety of games.

The James Wylie House ✪
208 EAST MAIN STREET, WHITE SULPHUR SPRINGS, WEST VIRGINIA 24986

Tel: **(304) 536-9444; (800) 870-1613**
Hosts: **Cheryl and Joe Griffith**
Location: **100 mi. SE of Charleston**
No. of Rooms: **4**
No. of Private Baths: **4**
Double/pb: **$55–$65**
Single/pb: **$50–$55**
Open: **All year**

Reduced Rates: **10% after 3rd night**
Breakfast: **Full or Continental**
Credit Cards: **AMEX, MC, VISA**
Pets: **No**
Children: **Welcome**
Smoking: **No**
Social Drinking: **Permitted**
Airport/Station Pickup: **Yes**

This three-story Georgian Colonial-style dwelling dating back to 1819 features large, airy rooms that are comfortably furnished and accented with antiques. Pretty quilts, iron beds, old toys, and select period pieces enhance the bedrooms' decor. Specialties such as apple pudding, homemade coffee cake, and a delicious egg-and-sausage casserole are often part of the breakfast fare. The world-famous Greenbrier Resort is less than one mile away and historic Lewisburg is less than nine miles away. Recreational opportunities abound in the nearby state parks and ski resorts.

WISCONSIN

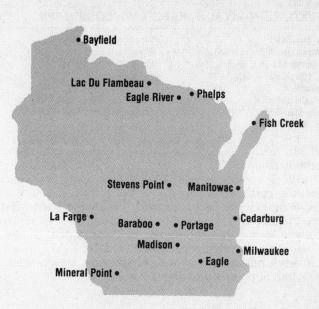

• Bayfield

Lac Du Flambeau •
Eagle River • • Phelps

• Fish Creek

Stevens Point •   Manitowac •

La Farge •
Baraboo • • Portage   • Cedarburg

Madison •
• Milwaukee
• Eagle

Mineral Point •

Baraboo's Gollmar Guest House
422 3RD STREET, BARABOO, WISCONSIN 53913

Tel: **(608) 356-9432**
Best Time to Call: **10 AM–10 PM**
Hosts: **Tom and Linda Luck**
Location: **200 mi. NW of Chicago**
No. of Rooms: **3**
No. of Private Baths: **3**
Double/pb: **$75**
Open: **All year**

Breakfast: **Full**
Credit Cards: **MC, VISA**
Pets: **No**
Children: **Welcome, over 7**
Smoking: **No**
Social Drinking: **Permitted**
Station Pickup: **Yes**

Built in 1889 by the Gollmars, a renowned Victorian circus family, this handsome home contains its original chandeliers, beveled glass windows, oak woodwork, hardwood floors, and beautiful hand-painted murals. All bedrooms have queen-size beds. A special guest parlor leads to an outdoor patio, and the grounds include flower gardens and a picnic area. Before heading out for the local sights, which range from Circus World Museum to the world famous Crane Foundation, you'll dine on breakfast dishes like decadent French toast and turkey bacon and sausage.

Pinehaven ❂
E13083 STATE HIGHWAY 33, BARABOO, WISCONSIN 53913

Tel: **(608) 356-3489**
Best Time to Call: **5 PM–10 AM**
Hosts: **Lyle and Marge Getschman**
Location: **10 mi. from I-90**
No. of Rooms: **4**
No. of Private Baths: **4**
Double/pb: **$65–$75**
Single/pb: **$60–$70**

Open: **All year**
Breakfast: **Full**
Credit Cards: **MC, VISA**
Pets: **No**
Children: **Welcome, over 5**
Smoking: **No**
Social Drinking: **Permitted**

Lyle and Marge's home is nestled in a pine grove with a beautiful view of the Baraboo Bluffs and a small private lake. Guest rooms are all new, with air-conditioning. The full breakfast may include fresh-baked muffins, coffee cakes, egg dishes, meat, fruit, and juice. Eat in the dining room, on the deck, or on the screened-in porch. Play the baby grand piano. Feel free to take a leisurely stroll in these inviting surroundings. A tour to see your hosts' Belgian draft horses and antique wagons and sleighs on the farm side of the highway, and wagon or sleigh rides pulled by the Belgians, may be arranged. Fine restaurants and numerous activities abound in the area.

The Victorian Rose ❂
423 THIRD AVENUE, BARABOO, WISCONSIN 53913

Tel: **(608) 356-7828**
Hosts: **Bob and Carolyn Stearns**
Location: **40 mi. N of Madison**
No. of Rooms: **3**
No. of Private Baths: **3**
Double/pb: **$65–$75**

Open: **All year**
Breakfast: **Full**
Pets: **No**
Children: **No**
Smoking: **No**
Social Drinking: **Permitted**

The Victorian Rose is located on a large corner lot, surrounded by sugar maples and pine trees, within walking distance of Baraboo's historical sites, speciality shops, and galleries. The Stearns family welcomes you to their beautifully restored nineteenth-century "Painted Lady," furnished with roses, lace, antiques, and heirloom collectibles. Guests can enjoy a game or book in the library parlor or watch old classic movies by the fireplace with a cup of tea and sweet treats. Appropriately enough, guest rooms are decorated in Victorian decor. A full gourmet candlelight breakfast awaits guests in the morning.

Lakeside Lodging
ROUTE 1, BOX 253, BAYFIELD, WISCONSIN 54814

Tel: (715) 779-5545
Best Time to Call: Mornings; evenings
Hosts: Mr. and Mrs. Wallace Nordin
Location: ½ mi. from Bayfield
No. of Rooms: 1
No. of Private Baths: 1
Double/pb: $45

Open: May 1–Nov. 15
Reduced Rates: Available
Breakfast: Continental
Pets: No
Children: Welcome, over 12
Smoking: Restricted
Social Drinking: Permitted

The Nordins invite you to their home about a quarter mile from town. Thanks to a rollaway bed, three can stay in the guest room, which has a private entrance, a patio overlooking the lake, air-conditioning and cable TV. Breakfast includes juice, tea, coffee, assorted muffins, and cereal.

Stagecoach Inn Bed & Breakfast ✪
W61 N520 WASHINGTON AVENUE, CEDARBURG, WISCONSIN 53012

Tel: (414) 375-0208
Hosts: Brook and Liz Brown
Location: 17 mi. N of Milwaukee
No. of Rooms: 13
No. of Private Baths: 12
Double/pb: $65
Suites: $95

Open: All year
Breakfast: Continental
Credit Cards: AMEX, MC, VISA
Pets: No
Children: Welcome, over 12
Smoking: No
Social Drinking: Permitted

The inn, listed on the National Register of Historic Places, is housed in a completely restored 1853 stone building in downtown historic Cedarburg. The rooms, air-conditioned for summer comfort, combine antique charm with modern conveniences. Each bedroom is decorated with antiques and trimmed with wall stenciling. A candy shop and a pub that is a popular gathering place for guests occupy the first floor. Specialty stores, antique shops, a winery, a woolen mill, and a variety of fine restaurants are within walking distance.

Eagle Centre House B&B ✪
W370 S9590 HIGHWAY 67, EAGLE, WISCONSIN 53119

Tel: (414) 363-4700
Best Time to Call: 7 AM–10 PM
Hosts: Riene Wells Herriges and Dean
  Herriges
Location: 30 mi. SW of Milwaukee
No. of Rooms: 5
No. of Private Baths: 5
Double/pb: $85
Single/pb: $85
Suites: $125

Open: All year; closed Christmas Eve
  and Christmas Day
Reduced Rates: Available
Breakfast: Full
Credit Cards: AMEX, MC, VISA
Pets: No
Children: Welcome, over 12
Smoking: No
Social Drinking: Permitted

Eagle Centre House is an authentic replica of an 1846 Greek Revival stagecoach inn built on 20 secluded acres. From the front parlor to the third-floor bedrooms, you will admire the splendid collection of antiques. Take a seat on the porch or in the parlor and browse through period publications. Even the breakfast specialties are inspired by the 19th century. There are hiking and cross-country ski trails in both Kettle Moraine State Forest and Old World Wisconsin, an unusual outdoor museum. Other athletic options include downhill skiing, sledding, biking, golfing, horseback riding, and waterfront sports.

Brennan Manor, Old World Bed and Breakfast ✪
1079 EVERETT ROAD, EAGLE RIVER, WISCONSIN 54521

Tel: (715) 479-7353
Best Time to Call: **Days**
Hosts: **Connie and Bob Lawton**
Location: **3 mi. E of Eagle River**
No. of Rooms: **4**
No. of Private Baths: **4**
Double/pb: **$69–$85**
Single/pb: **$59–$79**
Guest Cottage: **$650 weekly; sleeps 6**
Open: **All year**

Reduced Rates: **10% seniors; 15% weekly**
Breakfast: **Full**
Credit Cards: **MC, VISA**
Pets: **No**
Children: **No**
Smoking: **No**
Social Drinking: **Permitted**
Airport/Station Pickup: **Yes**

Built in the 1920s, the era of the great lumber barons, this lakeside country estate combines a relaxed atmosphere and old-world charm. With its 30-foot timbered ceiling, large arched windows, massive stone fireplace, and hand-hewn woodwork, the great room may conjure up King Arthur's Camelot. For summer fun, there's boating, golfing, biking, water skiing, canoeing, fishing, and more. Winter sports enthusiasts will enjoy cross-country and downhill skiing, as well as the 500 miles of marked snowmobile trails that begin at the B&B's front door.

Thorp House Inn & Cottages
4135 BLUFF ROAD, P.O. BOX 490, FISH CREEK, WISCONSIN 54212

Tel: (414) 868-2444
Best Time to Call: **8 AM–10 PM**
Hosts: **Christine and Sverre Falck-Pedersen**
No. of Rooms: **3**
No. of Private Baths: **3**
Double/pb: **$90**
Cottages: **$75–$125**
Open: **All year**

Reduced Rates: **Weekly**
Breakfast: **Continental**
Pets: **No**
Children: **Welcome, in cottages**
Smoking: **Yes, in cottages**
Social Drinking: **Permitted**
Minimum Stay: **3 nights summer and holiday weekends**
Foreign Languages: **Norwegian**

Thorp House is a turn-of-the-century country Victorian inn perched on a wooded hill overlooking Green Bay. The beach, shops, restau-

The Thorp House – Fish Creek, WI

rants, and Peninsula State Park are just a stroll away. Four elegant guest rooms recreate romantic periods of the past with fine antiques and accessories, documentary wall coverings, and European lace. Each room has a private bath (one with a whirlpool), central air-conditioning, and ceiling fans. Guests have their own parlor with its original granite fireplace. A delicious home-baked breakfast is included. Also available: country cottages with wood-burning fireplaces, full kitchens and baths (some with whirlpools), decks, and views of the bay. For those of you who don't mind paying a higher rate, 1 room is available.

Trillium ✪
ROUTE 2, BOX 121, LA FARGE, WISCONSIN 54639

Tel: **(608) 625-4492**
Best Time to Call: **Mornings; evenings**
Hosts: **Joe Swanson and Rosanne Boyett**
Location: **40 mi. SE of La Crosse**
Guest Cottage: **$70 for 2**
Open: **All year**
Breakfast: **Full**

Reduced Rates: **Single guest; weekly; winter, after first night**
Pets: **No**
Children: **Welcome (crib)**
Smoking: **Permitted**
Social Drinking: **Permitted**
Airport/Station Pickup: **Yes**

This private cottage is on a working farm located in the heart of a thriving Amish community. It has a large porch and is surrounded by an orchard, garden, and a lovely tree-shaded yard. There's a path beside the stream that winds through woods and fields. The cottage is light and airy, with comfortable wicker furniture. Nearby attractions include the Elroy-Sparta Bike Trail, Mississippi River, trout streams, and cheese factories.

Ty Bach B&B ⊙
3104 SIMPSON LANE, LAC DU FLAMBEAU, WISCONSIN 54538

Tel: **(715) 588-7851**	Single/pb: **$45–$55**
Best Time to Call: **8 AM–10 PM**	Open: **All year**
Hosts: **Janet and Kermit Bekkum**	Breakfast: **Full**
Location: **70 mi. N of Wausau**	Pets: **Sometimes**
No. of Rooms: **2**	Children: **No**
No. of Private Baths: **2**	Smoking: **No**
Double/pb: **$50–$60**	Social Drinking: **Permitted**

In Welsh, *ty-bach* means "little house." Located on an Indian reservation in Lac du Flambeau, this modern little house overlooks a small, picturesque Northwoods lake. Sit back on the deck and enjoy the beautiful fall colors, the call of the loons, and the tranquility of this out-of-the-way spot. Choose from two comfortable rooms: one features a brass bed, the other opens onto a private deck. Your hosts offer oven-fresh coffee cakes, homemade jams, and plenty of fresh coffee along with hearty main entrées.

Annie's Bed & Breakfast
2117 SHERIDAN DRIVE, MADISON, WISCONSIN 53704

Tel: **(608) 244-2224**	Breakfast: **Full**
Hosts: **Anne and Larry Stuart**	Credit Cards: **AMEX, MC, VISA**
No. of Rooms: **2 suites**	Pets: **No**
No. of Private Baths: **2**	Children: **Welcome, over 12**
Suites: **$84–$100 for 2; $144–$160 for 4**	Smoking: **No**
	Social Drinking: **Permitted**
Open: **All year**	Minimum Stay: **2 nights**
Reduced Rates: **Available**	Airport/Station Pickup: **Yes**

When you want the world to go away, come to Annie's, a quiet inn with a beautiful view of meadows, water, and woods. This charming, fully air-conditioned cedar shake home has been a getaway for travelers since 1985. The house is a block from a large lake and directly adjoining Warner Park, allowing guests a broad selection of activities, including swimming, boating, tennis, hiking, and biking during summer, and cross-country skiing and skating in winter. The four antique-filled guest rooms are full of surprises and unusual amenities. There is a great-hall dining room, pine-paneled library with a well-stocked

wood stove, and a soothing double whirlpool surrounded by plants. The unusually lovely gardens, with romantic gazebo and pond, have been selected for the annual Madison Garden Tours.

Arbor Manor Bed and Breakfast ✪
1304 MICHIGAN AVENUE, MANITOWOC, WISCONSIN 54220

Tel: **(414) 684-6095**
Best Time to Call: **Evenings**
Hosts: Jay and Lou Ann Spaanem
Location: 60 mi. N of Milwaukee
No. of Rooms: 3
No. of Private Baths: 3
Double/pb: $85
Open: All year

Reduced Rates: **Available**
Breakfast: **Full, Continental**
Credit Cards: **MC, VISA**
Pets: **No**
Children: **Welcome, over 12**
Smoking: **No**
Social Drinking: **Permitted**
Airport/Station Pickup: **Yes**

Arbor Manor is located in an area of historic houses on Lake Michigan. This Greek Revival-style home has luxurious accommodations— antiques and king- and queen-size beds furnish the spacious rooms. Despite its small-town atmosphere, Manitowoc has museums, a theater, and golfing facilities, plus hiking trails, and Lake Michigan fishing. A short trip will take you to Wisconsin's famous Door County peninsula. Your hosts Lou Ann, a former teacher, and Jay, an accountant, promise to make your stay as pleasant as possible.

Marie's Bed & Breakfast ✪
346 EAST WILSON STREET, MILWAUKEE, WISCONSIN 53207

Tel: (414) 483-1512
Best Time to Call: 8 AM–8 PM
Host: Marie M. Mahan
No. of Rooms: 4
Max. No. Sharing Bath: 4
Double/sb: $55–$70
Open: All year

Breakfast: Full
Credit Cards: MC, VISA
Pets: No
Children: Welcome
Smoking: No
Social Drinking: Permitted
Airport/Station Pickup: Yes

Your hostess has decorated this turn-of-the-century Victorian with an eclectic mixture of antiques, collectibles, and her own original artwork. Give yourself time to walk around the historic Bay View neighborhood, with its many architectural styles. Downtown Milwaukee is just six minutes away. Breakfast, served in the garden when weather permits, is highlighted by homemade breads, pastries, and a variety of locally prepared sausages.

Ogden House ✪
2237 NORTH LAKE DRIVE, MILWAUKEE, WISCONSIN 53202

Tel: (414) 272-2740
Hosts: Mary Jane and John Moss
No. of Rooms: 2
No. of Private Baths: 2
Double/pb: $75
Single/pb: $75
Suites: $85

Open: All year
Breakfast: Continental
Pets: No
Children: Welcome
Smoking: Permitted
Social Drinking: Permitted

The Ogden House is a white-brick Federal-style home listed on the National Register of Historic Places. It is located in the North Point–South historic district, a neighborhood shared by venerable mansions overlooking Lake Michigan. Miss Ogden herself would feel at home here having homemade butterhorns for breakfast. You are sure to feel at home, too, whether you're relaxing on the sun deck, sitting by the fire, or retiring to your four-poster bed. Ogden House is convenient to theaters, the botanical garden, the Brewers' Stadium, the breweries, and many fine restaurants.

The Wilson House Inn ✪
110 DODGE STREET, MINERAL POINT, WISCONSIN 53565

Tel: (608) 987-3600
Best Time to Call: Evenings
Hosts: Bev and Jim Harris
Location: 50 mi. SW of Madison
No. of Rooms: 4
No. of Private Baths: 2

Max. No. Sharing Bath: 4
Double/pb: $55–$60
Single/pb: $50–$55
Double/sb: $45–$55
Single/sb: $40–$50
Open: All year

Breakfast: **Full**
Credit Cards: **MC, VISA**
Pets: **Sometimes**

Children: **Welcome (crib)**
Smoking: **No**
Social Drinking: **Permitted**

The Wilson House Inn is located in the heart of the beautiful uplands area. This red-brick Federal mansion was built in 1853 by Alexander Wilson, who became one of the state's first attorneys general. A veranda was added later, and it is where guests are welcomed with lemonade. The rooms are airy, comfortable, and furnished in antiques. Mineral Point was a mining and political center in the 1880s, and it is filled with many historic sites. Fishing, golfing, swimming, skiing, and the House on the Rock are all nearby.

The Limberlost Inn
HIGHWAY 17, #2483, PHELPS, WISCONSIN 54554

Tel: **(715) 545-2685**
Hosts: **Bill and Phoebe McElroy**
No. of Rooms: **2**
Max. No. Sharing Bath: **4**
Double/sb: **$47**
Open: **All year**

Reduced Rates: **10% weekly**
Breakfast: **Full**
Pets: **No**
Children: **Welcome, over 10**
Smoking: **No**
Social Drinking: **Permitted**

The inn was designed and constructed by Bill and Phoebe McElroy. They picked a fine spot for their log home, just a minute from one of the best fishing lakes and largest national forests in the state. Each guest room is decorated with antiques, and the beds all have cozy down pillows and hand-stitched coverlets. Breakfast is served on the screened porch, by the fieldstone fireplace, in the dining room, or in your room. Stroll through the garden, rock on the porch swing, or take a picnic lunch and explore the streams and hiking trails. When you return, a Finnish sauna and a glass of wine or a mug of beer await.

Country Aire ✪
N4452 COUNTY U, BOX 175, PORTAGE, WISCONSIN 53901

Tel: (608) 742-5716	Suites: $75
Best Time to Call: Evenings	Open: All year
Hosts: Bob and Rita Reif	Breakfast: Continental
Location: 37 mi. N of Madison	Pets: No
No. of Rooms: 3	Children: Welcome
No. of Private Baths: 2	Smoking: No
Double/pb: $60	Social Drinking: Permitted
Single/pb: $50	

Forty acres of woods and meadows surround this spacious country home, built into a hillside overlooking the Wisconsin River. The house has open cathedral ceilings and a beautiful view from every room. Choose from comfortable bedrooms with queen-size or twin beds; the kids will enjoy the room with bunk beds. Guests are welcome to use the tennis court or go canoeing on the river. In the winter, skating can be enjoyed on the pond, and the area is perfect for cross-country skiing. Devil's Head and Cascade Mountain are close by for downhill skiing. Bob and Rita are minutes away from the Wisconsin Dells, Baraboo, and Devil's Lake State Park. Relax at the end of the day in the serenity of this beautiful country setting.

Dreams of Yesteryear Bed & Breakfast ✪
1100 BRAWLEY STREET, STEVENS POINT, WISCONSIN 54481

Tel: (715) 341-4525	Open: All year
Best Time to Call: After 4 PM	Breakfast: Full
Hosts: Bonnie and Bill Maher	Credit Cards: MC, VISA
Location: 30 mi. S of Wausau	Pets: No
No. of Rooms: 4	Children: Welcome, over 12
No. of Private Baths: 2	Smoking: No
Double/pb: $55–$75	Social Drinking: Permitted
Single/pb: $50–$70	Airport/Station Pickup: Yes

Dreams, listed on the National Register of Historic Places and featured in *Victorian Homes* magazine, was designed by architect J. H. Jeffers, who also designed the Wisconsin Building at the St. Louis World's Fair of 1904. Lavish in Victorian detail, the home is handsomely decorated, with floral wallpapers and period furniture. One bathroom has a claw-footed tub and a pedestal sink. Bonnie, a University of

Wisconsin secretary and square dance caller, and Bill, owner of a water-conditioning business, love to talk about the house and its furnishings. Skiing, canoeing, shopping, and university theater, among other activities, are in close proximity.

For key to listings, see inside front or back cover.

○ This star means that rates are guaranteed through December 31, 1995, to any guest making a reservation as a result of reading about the B&B in *Bed & Breakfast U.S.A.*—1995 edition.

Important! To avoid misunderstandings, always ask about cancellation policies when booking.

Please enclose a self-addressed, stamped, business-size envelope when contacting reservation services.

For more details on what you can expect in a B&B, see Chapter 1.

Always mention *Bed & Breakfast U.S.A.* when making reservations!

If no B&B is listed in the area you'll be visiting, use the form on page 743 to order a copy of our "List of New B&Bs."

We want to hear from you! Use the form on page 745.

WYOMING

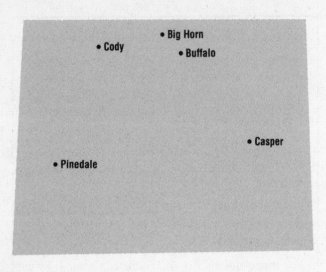

Spahn's Big Horn Mountain Bed and Breakfast
P.O. BOX 579, BIG HORN, WYOMING 82833

Tel: **(307) 674-8150**
Hosts: **Ron and Bobbie Spahn**
Location: **15 mi. SW of Sheridan**
No. of Rooms: **2**
No. of Private Baths: **2**
Double/pb: **$65–$95**
Open: **All year**

Cabins: **$65–$100**
Breakfast: **Full**
Pets: **No**
Children: **Welcome (baby-sitter)**
Smoking: **No**
Social Drinking: **Permitted**
Airport/Station Pickup: **Yes**

Ron and Bobbie Spahn and their two children built their home and this authentic log cabin. The house is set on 40 acres of whispering pines, and borders the Big Horn Mountain forestland, which stretches for over a million acres. The main house has two guest bedrooms with private baths, a three-story living room, and an outside deck. The cabin is secluded from the main house and features a queen-size bed, a shower bath, and an old-fashioned front porch. You are invited to sip a drink beside the wood stove, or take in the 100-mile view from an old porch rocker. Ron Spahn is a geologist and former Yellowstone Ranger. He can direct you to nearby fishing and hunting and can also tell you where to find the best walking and cross-country skiing trails.

Cloud Peak Inn ✪
590 NORTH BURRITT AVENUE, BUFFALO, WYOMING 82834

Tel: (307) 684-5794
Best Time to Call: Anytime
Hosts: Rick and Kathy Brus
Location: 115 mi. N of Casper
No. of Rooms: 5
No. of Private Baths: 3
Max. No. Sharing Bath: 4
Double/pb: $55–$75
Single/pb: $50–$65
Double/sb: $45–$55
Single/sb: $40–$50

Open: All year
Reduced Rates: Available
Breakfast: Full
Other Meals: Available
Credit Cards: AMEX, MC, VISA
Pets: No
Children: Welcome
Smoking: No
Social Drinking: Permitted
Airport/Station Pickup: Yes

Built in 1912, this home is an expanded bungalow with a generous front porch. The grand curved staircase leads to spacious guest rooms decorated with period antiques. In the parlor and dining room, ten-foot wood-beamed ceilings enhance the feeling of luxury. Guests are encouraged to relax by the fossilized fireplace or in the Jacuzzi sun room. You'll wake up to a three-course breakfast ranging from full country entrees to gourmet delights. The Big Horn Mountains offer something for everyone, including fishing, hiking, sightseeing, horseback riding, and boating. During spring, the wildflower display is unrivaled. Come and see what the west is all about.

Bessemer Bend Bed & Breakfast ✪
5120 ALCOVA ROUTE, BOX 40, CASPER, WYOMING 82604

Tel: (307) 265-6819
Hosts: Opal and Stan McInroy
Location: 10 mi. SW of Casper
No. of Rooms: 3
Max. No. Sharing Bath: 4
Double/sb: $45
Single/sb: $35
Open: All year

Reduced Rates: $5 less after 1st night
Breakfast: Full
Credit Cards: MC, VISA
Pets: Sometimes
Children: Welcome
Smoking: No
Social Drinking: Permitted
Airport/Station Pickup: Yes

This two-level ranch house offers great views of the North Platte River and Bessemer Mountain; the McInroys' property was once part of the Goose Egg Ranch, as commemorated in Owen Wister's *The Virginian*. Western history buffs will want to visit other points of interest, such as the site of the Red Butte Pony Express Station. In Casper you'll find a wealth of museums, parks, and restaurants. The sports-minded will be challenged by local options ranging from rock climbing and hang gliding to fishing and skiing. For indoor diversions, the McInroys' recreation room is equipped with a Ping-Pong table, an exercise bike, and plenty of books and games. Breakfasts feature coffee, fresh fruit or juice, toast, sourdough pancakes, and an egg casserole.

Durbin St. Inn Bed & Breakfast ⊙
843 SOUTH DURBIN, CASPER, WYOMING 82601

Tel: **(307) 577-5774**
Best Time to Call: **9 AM–9 PM**
Hosts: **Don and Sherry Frigon**
No. of Rooms: **5**
Max. No. Sharing Bath: **4**
Double/sb: **$70**
Single/pb: **$60**
Open: **All year**
Reduced Rates: **Available**

Breakfast: **Full**
Other Meals: **Available**
Credit Cards: **AMEX, DC, DISC, MC, VISA**
Pets: **No**
Children: **Welcome, over 14**
Smoking: **Restricted**
Social Drinking: **Permitted**
Airport Pickup: **Yes**

The Frigons' home, built in 1917 and located in the historic "Big Tree" area, has been lovingly refurbished and decorated. Soft colors, warm woods, antique and contemporary furniture, and romantic furnishings create a quiet, relaxed atmosphere. All the rooms are sunny and cheerful. The fireplaces are cozy on cold winter nights and the side deck is delightful on warm summer nights. Sherry enjoys cooking for you and making you feel at home. Don would love to take you to visit a secluded waterfall and hand-feed deer at the foot of Casper Mountain. Business travelers welcome. Make this your home away from home.

The Lockhart Inn ⊙
109 WEST YELLOWSTONE AVENUE, CODY, WYOMING 82414

Tel: **(307) 587-6074; (800) 377-7255**
Best Time to Call: **After noon**

Host: **Cindy Baldwin**
No. of Rooms: **7**

No. of Private Baths: **7**
Double/pb: **$55–$82**
Open: **All year**
Breakfast: **Full**
Other Meals: **Available**
Credit Cards: **AMEX, CB, DISC, MC, VISA**

Pets: **No**
Children: **Welcome, over 4**
Smoking: **No**
Social Drinking: **Permitted**
Airport/Station Pickup: **Yes**

Once the home of Cody's famous turn-of-the-century novelist, Caroline Lockhart, Cindy's historic frontier home has been beautifully restored while retaining the flavor of the Old West. The old-fashioned decor is combined with such modern amenities as cable TV, phones, and individually controlled heat. Breakfast is graciously served on fine china in the dining room. The house is located 50 miles from the eastern entrance to Yellowstone National Park, and there's plenty to do in addition to relaxing on the front porch. The Trail Town Museum, Buffalo Bill Historical Center, and the Cody Nightly Rodeo are just some of the attractions.

Window on the Winds ✪
10151 HIGHWAY 191, P.O. BOX 135, PINEDALE, WYOMING 82941

Tel: **(307) 367-2600**
Hosts: **Doug and Leanne McKay**
Location: **75 mi. S of Jackson**
No. of Rooms: **4**
Max. No. Sharing Bath: **4**
Double/sb: **$60**
Single/sb: **$50**
Open: **All year**

Reduced Rates: **Available**
Breakfast: **Full**
Other Meals: **Available**
Credit Cards: **MC, VISA**
Pets: **Welcome**
Children: **Welcome**
Smoking: **No**
Social Drinking: **Permitted**

Pinedale, at the base of the Wind River Mountains in western Wyoming, is on one of the major routes to Grand Teton and Yellowstone National Parks. The Winds offers world-class hiking and fishing in the summer and snowmobiling and Nordic skiing in the winter. Or, go exploring with your hosts' self-guided driving tour of historic Sublette County and Oregon Trail sites. The comfortable log home, decorated in striking Western and Plains Indians themes, is a rustic retreat—the perfect base for your Wyoming vacation. There is room for pets and kids and a large garage to store extra gear. Hosts Leanne and Doug are archaeologists who enjoy sharing their unique perspective on the cultural heritage of the area.

6

Canada

ALBERTA

Note: All prices listed in this section are quoted in Canadian dollars.

Alberta Bed & Breakfast ✪
P.O. BOX 15477, M.P.O., VANCOUVER, BRITISH COLUMBIA, CANADA V6B 5B2 (FORMERLY EDMONTON, ALBERTA)

Tel: **(604) 944-1793**
Best Time to Call: **8 AM–2 PM**
Coordinator: **June Brown**
Provinces/Regions Covered:
  Alberta—Banff, Calgary, Canmore, Edmonton, Jasper; British Columbia—Kamloops, Vancouver, Victoria, Whistler

Rates (Single/Double):
  Modest: **$30 / $40**
  Average: **$35 / $45**
  Luxury: **$45–$90 / $50–$95**
Credit Cards: **No**

Try a bit of Canadian western hospitality by choosing from June's variety of lovely homes in Alberta and British Columbia. Make a circle tour of Calgary, Banff, Lake Louise, the Columbia Icefields, Jasper, and Edmonton, and stay in B&Bs all the way. Send two dollars for a descriptive list of the cordial hosts on her roster, make your selections, and June will do the rest. The agency is closed on Canadian holidays and October through March. There's a $5 surcharge for each Banff, Jasper, and Victoria reservation.

Brink Bed and Breakfast
79 SINCLAIR CRESCENT S.W., CALGARY, ALBERTA, CANADA T2W 0M1

Tel: **(403) 255-4523**
Best Time to Call: **Mornings**
Host: **Helen G. Scrimgeour-Brink**
Location: **In Calgary**

No. of Rooms: **3**
No. of Private Baths: **1**
Max. No. Sharing Bath: **4**
Double/pb: **$65**

Double/sb: **$50**
Single/sb: **$40**
Open: **All year**
Breakfast: **Full**
Other Meals: **Available**

Pets: **Sometimes**
Children: **Welcome**
Smoking: **Permitted**
Social Drinking: **Permitted**
Airport/Station Pickup: **Yes**

Helen is a native Calgarian and a retired registered nurse who decided to open a bed and breakfast. Each bedroom is tastefully decorated. The ensuite "Sarah's Garden" is a private retreat with a queen-size bed, TV, loveseat, and complete bath. The "Teddy Bear" room is a single room across the hall from a full bathroom. The "Bed of Roses" room, on another level, has a comfortable double bed and is adjacent to a half-bath and a family room with a TV and a wide collection of books. Breakfast, served in a sunny dining room, features specialties like homemade scones, muffins, French toast, pancakes, fruit compote, and freshly squeezed juice. There is a large deck and well-landscaped private backyard. A traditional British afternoon tea, picnic baskets, or an evening meal are offered at an additional cost.

Harrison's B&B Home ✪
6016 THORNBURN DRIVE NORTHWEST, CALGARY, ALBERTA, CANADA T2K 3P7

Tel: **(403) 274-7281**
Best Time to Call: **7–8 AM; 4–7 PM**
Host: **Susan Harrison**
Location: **In Calgary, ¼ mi. from Hwy. 2**
No. of Rooms: **2**
Max. No. Sharing Bath: **4**
Double/sb: **$50**

Single/sb: **$30**
Open: **All year**
Breakfast: **Full**
Pets: **No**
Children: **Welcome, over 10**
Smoking: **Restricted**
Social Drinking: **Permitted**

Sound environmental practices are followed at this cozy bungalow in a well-treed, quiet residential neighborhood where birds and squirrels are regular visitors. Your host's interests are gardening to attract birds, walking Calgary's extensive pathway and park system, hiking and cross-country skiing in Kananaskis Country and Banff (in the Canadian Rockies, one-hour drive west), art exhibitions, and secondhand shopping. The B&B is within ten miles of Calgary Exhibition and Stampede, the Calgary Zoo and Prehistoric Park, and the University of Calgary. Nose Hill Park, shopping, and restaurants are in walking distance.

BRITISH COLUMBIA

Note: All prices listed in this section are quoted in Canadian dollars.

Canada-West Accommodations ✪

P.O. BOX 86607, NORTH VANCOUVER, BRITISH COLUMBIA, CANADA V7L 4L2

Tel: **(604) 929-1424; (800) 561-3223;**
   fax: **(604) 929-6692**
Best Time to Call: **Daily to 10 PM**
Coordinator: **Ellison Massey**
Regions Covered: **Greater Vancouver,**
   Victoria, Kelowna, Whistler

Rates (Single/Double):
   Average: **$45–$65 / $65–$85**
Credit Cards: **AMEX, MC, VISA**

This registry has over 100 hosts with comfortable bed-and-breakfast accommodations. All serve a full breakfast, and most have a private bath for guest use. When traveling through British Columbia, visitors should note that B&Bs are available within a day's drive of one another. Canada-West features friendly host families eager to share their knowledge of cultural and scenic attractions.

Deep Cove Bed & Breakfast ✪

2590 SHELLEY ROAD, NORTH VANCOUVER, BRITISH COLUMBIA, CANADA V7H 1J9

Tel: **(604) 929-3932; fax: (604) 929-**
   9330
Hosts: **Diane and Wayne Moore**
Location: **8 mi. NE of Vancouver**
No. of Rooms: **2**
No. of Private Baths: **2**
Double/pb: **$75**
Single/pb: **$65**

Open: **All year**
Reduced Rates: **Available**
Breakfast: **Full**
Credit Cards: **MC**
Pets: **No**
Smoking: **No**
Social Drinking: **Permitted**

Only 15 minutes from downtown Vancouver, Deep Cove Bed & Breakfast combines the privacy of a large secluded property and easy access to all points of interest. A separate guest cottage offers the visitor a choice of a twin or queen bedroom with a private bath. Guests are invited to relax in the red cedar hot tub on the terrace or in the lounge room with its billiard table, wood-burning fireplace, TV, and VCR. Hearty breakfasts—served either in the morning room or on the patio—feature French toast, freshly baked breads, and muffins topped with homemade jams and jellies or Quebec maple syrup.

Diane will be happy to direct you to all the special places that make this city so exciting.

Poole's Bed & Breakfast ✪

**421 WEST ST. JAMES ROAD, NORTH VANCOUVER,
BRITISH COLUMBIA, CANADA V7N 2P6**

Tel: **(604) 987-4594**
Best Time to Call: **9 AM–9 PM**
Hosts: **Doreen and Arthur Poole**
Location: **5 mi. S of Vancouver**
No. of Rooms: **2**
Max. No. Sharing Bath: **4**
Double/sb: **$55**
Single/sb: **$40**

Open: **All year**
Reduced Rates: **Available**
Breakfast: **Full**
Pets: **No**
Children: **Welcome**
Smoking: **No**
Social Drinking: **Permitted**
Station Pickup: **Yes**

On a lovely tree-lined street near the Northerner Mountains sits this quiet, Colonial home. The Pooles' residential neighborhood is close to the bus, restaurants, downtown Vancouver, Stanley Park, Capilano Suspension Bridge, Grouse Mountain Skyride, and Vancouver Island Ferry. Doreen and Arthur are retirees who are happy to assist you with information and directions. They'll serve you an abundant candlelight breakfast in the dining room.

Weston Lake Inn ✪

**813 BEAVER POINT ROAD, SALT SPRING ISLAND,
BRITISH COLUMBIA, CANADA V8K 1X9**

Tel: **(604) 653-4311**
Hosts: **Susan Evans and Ted Harrison**
Location: **30 mi. N of Victoria**
No. of Rooms: **3**
No. of Private Baths: **3**
Double/pb: **$85–$105**
Single/pb: **$70–$90**
Open: **All year**
Reduced Rates: **10% weekly
Sept.–June; 5% July–Aug.**

Breakfast: **Full**
Credit Cards: **MC, VISA**
Pets: **Sometimes**
Children: **Welcome, over 14**
Smoking: **No**
Social Drinking: **Permitted**
Foreign Languages: **French**

Nestled on a knoll of flowering trees and shrubs overlooking Weston Lake, the inn offers old-world charm in a comfortable new home. The house is on a 10-acre farm on Salt Spring Island, the largest of British Columbia's Gulf Islands. Each guest room overlooks the countryside and has a down comforter. The rooms all have different finishing touches. Throughout the house there are a number of original Canadian art pieces and intricate petit-point needlework crafted by your host, Ted. Breakfast is a full-course meal served to the sounds of classical music in the antique-filled dining room. Eggs Benedict, quiche, homemade muffins, and jams are specialties of the house.

Fresh eggs from the chickens and produce from the organic vegetable garden. Guests can relax in the hot tub, on the garden terrace, or enjoy a book in the lounge beside a wood-burning stove. It's just a few steps to swimming, boating, and fishing. You can also follow forest trails or take to a bicycle and explore this quaint island with its country roads, pastoral beauty, and talented artisans. Ask your hosts about the sailing charters they are now offering.

The Grahams Cedar House B&B ✪

1825 LANDSEND ROAD, RR3, SIDNEY, BRITISH COLUMBIA, CANADA V8L 5J2

Tel: **(604) 655-3699**; fax: **(604) 655-1422**	Open: **All year**
Best Time to Call: **Anytime**	Reduced Rates: **Weekly**
Hosts: **Kay and Dennis Graham**	Breakfast: **Full**
Location: **15 mi. N of Victoria**	Pets: **No**
No. of Rooms: **3**	Children: **Welcome, over 10**
No. of Private Baths: **2**	Smoking: **No**
Max. No. Sharing Bath: **4**	Social Drinking: **Permitted**
Double/pb: **$65–$95**	Airport Pickup: **Yes**

This modern chalet rests in a woodsy setting of tall pines and green ferns, minutes from the Swartz Bay and Anacortes ferries. Parks, marinas, and the beach are all nearby. A spacious guest room with two double beds, a private entrance, a deck, and a full kitchen/family room can be rented on its own, or as part of a suite with an adjoining bedroom sleeping an additional two people. Between June 1 and September 30, a master bedroom that opens onto a private deck and patio is also available.

Beautiful Bed & Breakfast ✪

428 WEST 40 AVENUE, VANCOUVER, BRITISH COLUMBIA, CANADA V5Y 2R4

Tel: **(604) 327-1102**	Open: **All year**
Best Time to Call: **Evenings**	Reduced Rates: **10% less weekly**
Hosts: **Corinne and Ian Sanderson**	Breakfast: **Full, Continental**
Location: **In Vancouver**	Pets: **No**
No. of Rooms: **4**	Children: **Welcome, over 14**
No. of Private Baths: **1**	Smoking: **No**
Max. No. Sharing Bath: **4**	Social Drinking: **Permitted**
Double/sb: **$75–$85**	Foreign Languages: **French**
Single/sb: **$60–$70**	

Relax in elegance in a gorgeous new Colonial home furnished with antiques, views, and fresh flowers. This is a great central location on a quiet residential street, just five minutes from downtown and within walking distance of Queen Elizabeth Park, Van Dusen Gardens, tennis, golf, three cinemas, wonderful restaurants, swimming, and a major shopping center. It's one block from bus to downtown, ferries, airport, and United British Columbia. Enjoy a view of the north shore mountain peaks or Vancouver Island and Mount Baker, comfortable beds, a large attractive backyard—and friendly helpful hosts who will assist you with your travel plans.

Johnson House Bed & Breakfast
2278 WEST 34TH AVENUE, VANCOUVER, BRITISH COLUMBIA, CANADA V6M 1G6

Tel: **(604) 266-4175**
Best Time to Call: **10:30 AM–9:30 PM**
Hosts: **Sandy and Ron Johnson**
Location: **1½ mi. from Rte. 99, Oak St. Exit**
No. of Rooms: **3**
No. of Private Baths: **1**
Max. No. Sharing Bath: **4**
Double/pb: **$85–$105**
Single/pb: **$75–$95**

Double/sb: **$60–$75**
Single/sb: **$50–$65**
Open: **All year**
Reduced Rates: **Long stays, winter**
Breakfast: **Full**
Pets: **No**
Children: **Welcome, over 8**
Smoking: **No**
Social Drinking: **Permitted**

Sandy and Ron invite you to their charming home on a quiet tree-lined avenue in Vancouver's lovely Kerrisdale district. Outside, a rock garden and sculpture catch the visitor's eye; inside, wooden carousel animals add to the homey decor. After a good night's rest on brass beds, you'll be treated to homemade muffins, breads, and jams. Then it's time to explore downtown Vancouver—a good selection of shops, restaurants, and city bus stops are only a few blocks away.

Kenya Court Guest House At-the-Beach ○
2230 CORNWALL AVENUE, VANCOUVER, BRITISH COLUMBIA, CANADA V6K 1B5

Tel: **(604) 738-7085**
Hosts: **The Williams**
Location: **20 mi. from the U.S. border**
Suites: **$85 up**
Open: **All year**
Breakfast: **Full**

Pets: **No**
Children: **Welcome, over 8**
Smoking: **No**
Social Drinking: **Permitted**
Foreign Languages: **French, German, Italian**

There is an unobstructed view of the park, ocean, mountains, and downtown Vancouver from this heritage building on the waterfront. Across the street are tennis courts, a large heated outdoor saltwater pool, and walking and jogging paths along the water's edge. Just minutes from downtown, it's an easy walk to Granville Market, the Planetarium, and interesting shops and restaurants. All the rooms are large and tastefully furnished. Breakfast is served in a glass solarium with a spectacular view of English Bay.

Penny Farthing Inn ✪
2855 WEST 6TH AVENUE, VANCOUVER, BRITISH COLUMBIA, CANADA V6K 1X2

Tel: (604) 739-9002; fax: (604) 739-9004
Host: Lyn Hainstock
Location: In Vancouver
No. of Rooms: 2
Nax. No. Sharing Bath: 4
Double/sb: $75
Single/sb: $65
Suites: $135–$155

Open: All year
Reduced Rates: Winter
Breakfast: Full
Pets: No
Children: Welcome, over 12
Smoking: No
Social Drinking: Permitted
Airport/Station Pickup: Yes

Lyn welcomes you with warm hospitality to this 1912 Heritage House filled with antiques and stained glass. Enjoy a delicious breakfast served on the brick patio in the English country garden with its fragrant flowers. Penny Farthing Inn is located on a quiet street, only ten minutes from downtown and a short walk to the beach, restaurants, and shops; bus service runs one block away. There are bikes for your use, and several nearby parks, some with tennis courts. This B&B is a smoke-free environment, but for the pleasure and comfort of smokers (and the resident cats) wicker chairs are placed on the front porch.

Town & Country Bed & Breakfast in B.C. ✪
BOX 74542, 2803 WEST 4TH AVENUE, VANCOUVER, BRITISH COLUMBIA V6K 1K2

Tel: (604) 731-5942
Coordinator: Helen Burich
States/Regions Covered: Vancouver, Vancouver Island, Victoria

Rates (Single/Double):
Modest: $35–$45 / $45–$55
Average: $40–$50 / $55–$65
Luxury: $55–$90 / $65–$160
Minimum Stay: 2 nights

Helen has the oldest reservation service in British Columbia. She has dozens of host homes, many of which have been accommodating guests for ten years. Ranging from modest homes to lovely heritage homes, they are a 15–20-minute drive to Stanley Park, beaches, Capilano and Lynn Canyons, Grouse Mountain Skyride, museums, and galleries; neighborhood restaurants and shopping areas are usually within walking distance. There are also a couple of cottages and self-contained suites. There is a $5 surcharge for Victoria and Vancouver Island reservations. In addition to normal business hours, Helen is often available evenings and weekends.

Sunnymeade House Inn ✪
1002 FENN AVENUE, VICTORIA, BRITISH COLUMBIA, CANADA V8Y 1P3

Tel: **(604) 658-1414;** fax: **(604) 658-1414**
Best Time to Call: **Mid-mornings; evenings**
Hosts: **Jack and Nancy Thompson**
Location: **1½ mi. from Rte. 17**
No. of Rooms: **6**
No. of Private Baths: **4**
Max. No. Sharing Bath: **4**

Double/pb: **$79–$149**
Double/sb: **$79–$149**
Open: **All year**
Breakfast: **Full**
Pets: **No**
Children: **No**
Smoking: **No**
Social Drinking: **Permitted**

Take the scenic route into Victoria and discover this inn on a winding country road by the sea. The Thompsons designed, built, decorated, and custom furnished the English-style house. Nancy, a former professional cook, will prepare your breakfast from a choice of seven. You'll be steps away from the beach and within walking distance of tennis courts and restaurants. All bedrooms have vanity sinks and mirrors for makeup and shaving.

Beachside Bed and Breakfast Registry
4208 EVERGREEN AVENUE, WEST VANCOUVER, BRITISH COLUMBIA, CANADA V7V 1H1

Tel: **(604) 922-7773; (800) 563-3311;** fax: **(604) 926-8073**
Coordinators: **Gordon and Joan Gibbs**
Regions Covered: **Chemainus, Nanaimo, North Shore, Parksville,**

Vancouver, Victoria, Whistler Mountain Area
Rates (Single/Double):
Average: **$40/$50–$80**
Luxury: **$75/$85–$180**

This newly organized B&B network emphasizes exceptional properties. Experience warm Canadian hospitality in well-maintained, tastefully decorated homes. Hosts offer everything from romantic luxury locations to quiet peaceful retreats. Gordon and Joan are world travelers who have run their own B&B for ten years; Gordon is also a certified tour guide.

Beachside Bed and Breakfast
4208 EVERGREEN AVENUE, WEST VANCOUVER, BRITISH COLUMBIA, CANADA V7V 1H1

Tel: **(604) 922-7773;** fax: **(604) 926-8073**
Hosts: **Gordon and Joan Gibbs**
Location: **4 mi. NW of Vancouver**

No. of Rooms: **3**
No. of Private Baths: **3**
Double/pb: **$100**
Open: **All year**

Breakfast: **Full**	Children: **Welcome**
Credit Cards: **MC, VISA**	Smoking: **No**
Pets: **No**	Social Drinking: **Permitted**

Guests are welcomed to this beautiful waterfront home with a fruit basket and fresh flowers. The house is a Spanish-style structure, with stained-glass windows, located at the end of a quiet cul-de-sac. Its southern exposure affords a panoramic view of Vancouver. A sandy beach is just steps from the door. You can watch the waves from the patio or spend the afternoon fishing or sailing. The hearty breakfast features homemade muffins, French toast, and Canadian maple syrup. Gordon and Joan are knowledgeable about local history, and can gladly direct you to Stanley Park, hiking, skiing, and much more.

NOVA SCOTIA

Note: All prices listed in this section are quoted in Canadian dollars.

Fairfield Farm Inn ✪
10 MAIN STREET, BOX 1287, MIDDLETON, NOVA SCOTIA, CANADA B0S 1P0

Tel: **(902) 825-6989; (800) 341-6096** (USA); **(800) 565-0000** (Canada)	Open: **All year**
Best Time to Call: **9 AM–9 PM**	Breakfast: **Full, Continental**
Hosts: **Richard and Shae Griffith**	Credit Cards: **AMEX, MC, VISA**
Location: **90 mi. W of Halifax**	Pets: **No**
No. of Rooms: **5**	Children: **Welcome, over 16**
No. of Private Baths: **5**	Smoking: **No**
Double/pb: **$50–$60**	Social Drinking: **Permitted**
Single/pb: **$45–$55**	Airport/Station Pickup: **Yes**

Built in 1886, this Annapolis Valley farmhouse has been completely restored and furnished in period antiques to enhance its original charm. Museums, recreational facilities, boutiques, and restaurants are a short walk from the inn. Fairfield Farm is a 75-acre fruit and vegetable farm with an apple orchard and melon patch. The Annapolis River and Slocum Brook are on the property, as are birding and

walking trails. Innkeepers Richard and Shae take pride in offering maritime hospitality and wholesome country breakfasts.

ONTARIO

Note: All prices listed in this section are quoted in Canadian dollars.

Bed and Breakfast Homes of Toronto ⊙
P.O. BOX 46093, COLLEGE PARK POST OFFICE, 444 YONGE STREET, TORONTO, ONTARIO, CANADA M5B 2L8

Tel: **(416) 363-6362**
Coordinator: **Rob Dallimore**
Regions Covered: **Toronto, Mississauga**

Rates (Single/Double):
Modest: **$40–$50**
Average: **$55–$65**
Luxury: **$75–$95**

Bed and Breakfast Homes of Toronto is a group of independent, quality B&Bs located in many prime locations spread over the city, near Toronto's excellent public transit. Send for a free brochure then contact the home of your choice directly.

Limestone City Bed & Breakfast Registry ✪
39 GLENAIRE MEWS, KINGSTON, ONTARIO, CANADA K7M 7L3

Tel: **(613) 545-1741**
Best Time to Call: **After 3 PM**
Coordinator: **Mary O'Brien**
States/Regions Covered: **Kingston, Ontario**

Rates (Single/Double):
Modest: **$38–$48**
Average: **$38–$48**
Luxury: **$50–$65**
Credit Cards: **MC, VISA**

Mary's unique listings, all of them smoke-free environments, are priced according to the location and type of accommodation. Kingston has many historic sites, museums, theaters, and parks, plus a rich assortment of restaurants and shops. The city is also famous for its boat tours and its important local landmark, Fort Henry.

Cozy Corner ✪
2 MORTON CRESCENT, BARRIE, ONTARIO, CANADA L4N 7T3

Tel: **(705) 739-0157**
Best Time to Call: **10 AM–9 PM**
Hosts: **Charita and Harry Kirby**
Location: **36 mi. N of Toronto**
No. of Rooms: **3**
No. of Private Baths: **1**
Max. No. Sharing Bath: **3**
Double/sb: **$55**
Single/sb: **$45**
Suites: **$85**
Open: **All year**

Breakfast: **Full**
Other Meals: **Available**
Credit Cards: **VISA**
Pets: **No**
Children: **No**
Smoking: **No**
Social Drinking: **Permitted**
Minimum Stay: **2 nights**
Airport/Station Pickup: **Yes**
Foreign Languages: **Spanish, German**

A warm welcome awaits you at this contemporary two-story brick home. Choose from three lavishly appointed rooms. Amenities include a Jacuzzi, central air-conditioning, TV, and a sunny greenhouse. Charita, a former schoolteacher, spent four years as governess to Julio Iglesias's three children prior to moving to Canada; her English-born husband completed three years of culinary training in Germany before working at the Savoy Hotel London. Thanks to Harry's expertise, you'll wake to a superb British-style breakfast featuring imported Lincolnshire pork, sausage, bacon, grilled tomato, fried bread, and scrambled eggs. German coffee cake, muffins, or toast with marmalade will appeal to the guest with a sweet tooth.

Windmere Bed & Breakfast ✪
SELWYN, RR 3, LAKEFIELD, ONTARIO, CANADA K0L 2H0

Tel: **(705) 652-6290; (800) 465-6237;**
fax: **(705) 652-6949**
Hosts: **Joan and Wally Wilkins**
Location: **12 mi. NE of Peterborough**
No. of Rooms: **3**

No. of Private Baths: **2**
Max. No. Sharing Bath: **4**
Double/pb: **$60**
Double/sb: **$50**
Single/sb: **$40**

We wish we could share with you the many letters of reference attesting to "the cleanliness," "the warm Mennonite hospitality," "the delicious food," "the friendliness of the Hieberts." Their air-conditioned home is 10 miles from Niagara Falls, Ontario, and the U.S. border. The Shaw Festival Theatre and all of the area's points of interest are within walking distance. The breakfast muffins, served with homemade jams, are a special treat.

The Turner House ✪
P.O. BOX 1509, 293 REGENT STREET, NIAGARA-ON-THE-LAKE, ONTARIO, CANADA L0S 1J0

Tel: **(905) 468-4440**
Best Time to Call: **9 AM–9 PM**
Hosts: **Donna and Larry Turner**
Location: **20 mi. N of Niagara Falls**
No. of Rooms: **3**
No. of Private Baths: **1**
Max. No. Sharing Bath: **4**
Double/pb: **$85**
Double/sb: **$75**

Open: **All year**
Reduced Rates: **Jan.–Apr.**
Breakfast: **Full**
Credit Cards: **MC, VISA**
Pets: **No**
Children: **Welcome, over 12**
Smoking: **No**
Social Drinking: **No**

Located in a historic town near Niagara Falls, this 1880s Victorian home provides a quiet base for your tour of the battlefields and forts of the War of 1812, Niagara Falls, the Welland Ship canal, and local vineyards and wineries. Then attend one of the many plays at the Shaw Festival Theatre. Turner House is within walking distance of shops, dining, and three theaters. Enjoy your hosts' fine home, full breakfast, and knowledge of the area. Sit in the parlor, the upstairs sitting room, by the pool, or on the porch and relax before your next activity in this scenic and historic area.

Ottawa Bed & Breakfast ✪
488 COOPER STREET, OTTAWA, ONTARIO, CANADA K1R 5H9

Tel: **(613) 563-0161; (800) 461-7889**
Best Time to Call: **10 AM–10 PM**
Coordinators: **Robert Rivoire and R. G. Simmens**

Regions Covered: **Ontario—Ottawa**
Rates (Single/Double):
  Average: **$45 / $55**
Credit Cards: **No**

If you are seeking an interesting but inexpensive holiday, then Canada's capital, Ottawa, is the place for you. The city is packed with free activities including museums, the House of Parliament, art galleries, and historic sites. You can skate on the Rideau Canal or bike on miles of parkways and trails.

Australis Guest House ✪
35 MARLBOROUGH AVENUE, OTTAWA, ONTARIO, CANADA K1N 8E6

Tel: **(613) 235-8461**
Best Time to Call: **After 4 PM**
Hosts: **Brian, Carol, and Olivia Waters**
Location: **1 mi. from Parliament**
No. of Rooms: **3**
No. of Private Baths: **1**
Max. No. Sharing Bath: **4**
Double/pb: **$58**
Single/pb: **$48**
Double/sb: **$50**
Single/sb: **$35**

Open: **All year**
Reduced Rates: **10% seniors; 10% less Nov.–Mar.**
Breakfast: **Full**
Pets: **No**
Children: **Welcome, over 6**
Smoking: **Yes**
Social Drinking: **No**
Station Pickup: **Yes**
Foreign Languages: **French**

Located on a quiet tree-lined street in Sandy Hill, one of Ottawa's first residential areas, Australis House is next to the Rideau River and Strathcona Park. It is but a twenty-minute walk to the Parliament buildings, museums, and the art gallery. This handsome brick house boasts leaded windows, fireplaces, oak floors, and eight-foot stained-glass windows overlooking the hall. Your hosts have lived in Africa, Asia, and Latin America, and mementos from their travels are displayed throughout. Hearty, delicious breakfasts, with fruit salads and home-baked breads and pastries, ensure that guests start the day in the right way.

The Turn of the Century ✪
RR #1, SOUTH MOUNTAIN, ONTARIO, CANADA K0E IW0

Tel: **(613) 989-3220**
Best Time to Call: **9 AM–9 PM**
Hosts: **Michel Corriveau and Lola McEvoy**
Location: **30 mi. S of Ottawa**
No. of Rooms: **2**
Max. No. Sharing Bath: **4**
Double/sb: **$45**
Single/sb: **$35**

Open: **All year**
Breakfast: **Full**
Credit Cards: **VISA**
Pets: **Sometimes**
Children: **Welcome**
Smoking: **No**
Social Drinking: **Permitted**
Foreign Languages: **French**

Delight in breakfast cooked on a wood-burning stove. Savor home-made bread and cheese, goat's milk, farm-fresh eggs, and homegrown vegetables and herbs. Or learn a new craft, like milking a goat or playing a pump organ. In the morning, nestled in muslin sheets and one of Grandmother's quilts, you'll wake up to fresh air. This turn-of-the-century home opens its doors, barn, and large warm kitchen to you. For our hearing-impaired friends, Michel knows sign language.

the room with twin beds, decorated in rose tones. If weather permits, breakfast is served on the deck; specialties include apple puff pancakes, omelets, and waffles.

Beaconsfield B&B ✪

38 BEACONSFIELD AVENUE, TORONTO, ONTARIO, CANADA M6J 3H9

Tel: **(416) 535-3338**; fax: **(416) 535-3338**	Single/sb: **$55**
	Suites: **$95**
Best Time to Call: **Anytime**	Open: **All year**
Hosts: **Bernie and Katya McLoughlin**	Breakfast: **Full**
No. of Rooms: **4**	Pets: **No**
No. of Private Baths: **1**	Children: **Welcome**
Max. No. Sharing Bath: **4**	Smoking: **No**
Double/pb: **$95**	Social Drinking: **Permitted**
Single/pb: **$85**	Foreign Languages: **Spanish, Russian**
Double/sb: **$65**	

Bernie and Katya, an artist-actress couple, invite you to their colorful 1882 Victorian home full of fun and sun, art, and heart. Beaconsfield is in a quiet, multicultural downtown neighborhood just beyond the commercial center. A short trolley ride takes you to major theaters, CN Tower, SkyDome, Chinatown, and Eaton Centre. Choose between imaginatively decorated rooms or the very private Mexican honeymoon suite with its treetop terrace. All come with top-of-the-line beds and full, creative breakfasts presented musically in an eclectic dining room. Parking, TV, air-conditioning, sundecks, refrigerator, and microwave are among the amenities at guests' disposal.

Broadleaves ✪

67 ORCHARD VIEW BOULEVARD, TORONTO, ONTARIO, CANADA M4R 1C1

Tel: **(416) 486-5252**	Open: **All year**
Best Time to Call: **Anytime**	Breakfast: **Continental**
Hosts: **Cavelle and Peter Davis**	Pets: **No**
Location: **In Toronto**	Children: **Welcome, over 12**
No. of Rooms: **2**	Smoking: **No**
Max. No. Sharing Bath: **4**	Social Drinking: **Permitted**
Double/sb: **$60–$65**	Foreign Languages: **French, German**
Single/sb: **$50–$55**	

Welcome to Broadleaves, an uptown home surrounded by maple, linden, and ash trees. This detached, two-story brick home, built in 1911, is conveniently located at Yonge-Eglinton, just minutes from the subway entrance. Cavelle and Peter offer two rooms—a double with original oak trim and working fireplace and a twin with French doors to a sun room. Guest accommodation is apart from hosts', with exclusive use of the treetop deck and separate kitchen for light snacks.

A generous Continental breakfast includes freshly baked croissants with homemade preserves, muffins, cereal, toast, fruit, and freshly ground coffee or tea.

PRINCE EDWARD ISLAND

Note: All prices listed in this section are quoted in Canadian dollars.

Woodington's Country Inn ✪

RR 2, KENSINGTON, PRINCE EDWARD ISLAND, CANADA C0B 1M0

Tel: **(902) 836-5518**
Best Time to Call: **Noon**
Hosts: **Marion and Claude "Woody" Woodington**
No. of Rooms: **5**
Max. No. Sharing Bath: **4**
Double/sb: **$44**
Single/sb: **$22**

Open: **All year**
Reduced Rates: **10% after Sept. 15**
Breakfast: **Full**
Other Meals: **Available**
Pets: **Welcome**
Children: **Welcome**
Smoking: **Permitted**
Social Drinking: **Permitted**

Relax on the spacious lawns surrounding this immaculate Victorian farmhouse or stroll to the private beach. You'll feel at home immediately. Marion is a fabulous cook and her table reflects all that is fresh and wholesome. Woody hand-carves the most realistic duck decoys you've ever seen. Marion's spare time is spent making gorgeous quilts. A wood carving or quilt would make a memorable souvenir to take home.

Smallman's Bed and Breakfast

KNUTSFORD, O'LEARY, RR 1, PRINCE EDWARD ISLAND, CANADA C0B 1V0

Tel: **(902) 859-3469**
Best Time to Call: **10 AM–noon; 6–10 PM**
Hosts: **Arnold and Eileen Smallman**
Location: **7½ mi. from Rte. 2**
No. of Rooms: **4**
Max. No. Sharing Bath: **6**
Double/sb: **$25–$35**
Single/sb: **$25**

Suites: **$35**
Open: **All year**
Breakfast: **Full**
Other Meals: **Available**
Pets: **Sometimes**
Children: **Welcome**
Smoking: **Restricted**
Social Drinking: **No**
Airport/Station Pickup: **Yes**

made muffins and jam, and fresh seasonal fruit from their own gardens and orchards. Additional light meals are offered at moderate cost.

Gîte de Campagne ✪
1028 PRINCIPALE, PRÉVOST, QUÉBEC, CANADA J0R 1T0

Tel: **(514) 224-7631**	Reduced Rates: **10% 3 nights and**
Best Time to Call: **Days and evenings**	**longer**
Host: **François Laroche**	Breakfast: **Full**
Location: **35 mi. N of Montreal**	Pets: **Sometimes**
No. of Rooms: **3**	Children: **Welcome**
Max. No. Sharing Bath: **4**	Smoking: **Permitted**
Double/sb: **$50**	Social Drinking: **Permitted**
Single/sb: **$26**	Foreign Languages: **French**
Open: **All year**	

Experience warmth, comfort, and magic at this B&B. The Gîte de Campagne is a hundred-year-old house on the outskirts of a wooded park where a river runs; hiking, bicycle, and ski trails abound. In the backyard, during the summer, one can find a vegetable garden, a small forest, and adjacent golf course. The house is situated in a quiet village in the heart of all the cultural and outdoor acivities of the Laurentian area. Your hostess is a university graduate in advertising, and currently studying photography.

Appendix:
UNITED STATES AND CANADIAN TOURIST OFFICES

Listed here are the addresses and telephone numbers for the tourist offices of every U.S. state and Canadian province. When you write or call one of these offices, be sure to request a map of the state and a calendar of events. If you will be visiting a particular city or region, or if you have any special interests, be sure to specify them as well.

State Tourist Offices

Alabama Bureau of Tourism and
  Travel
401 Adams Ave.
Montgomery, Alabama 36103
(800) 252-2262

Alaska Division of Tourism
P.O. Box 110801
Juneau, Alaska 99811-0801
(907) 465-2010

Arizona Office of Tourism
1100 W. Washington Street
Phoenix, Arizona 85007
(602) 542-8687

Arkansas Department of Park and
  Tourism
1 Capitol Mall
Little Rock, Arkansas 72201
(501) 682-7777 or (800) 643-8383 or
  (800) 828-8974

California Office of Tourism
801 K Street, Suite 1600
Sacramento, California 95814
(800) 862-2543 or (916) 322-2881

Colorado Dept. of Tourism
1625 Broadway
Suite 1700
Denver, Colorado 80202
(303) 592-5510 or (800) 255-5550

Connecticut Department of Economic
  Development—Vacations
865 Brook Street
Rocky Hill, Connecticut 06067-3405
(203) 258-4355 or (800) CT-BOUND

Delaware Tourism Office
99 Kings Highway, P.O. Box 1401
Dover, Delaware 19903
(302) 739-4271 or (800) 441-8846

Washington, D.C. Convention and
  Visitors' Association
1212 New York Avenue N.W.
Suite 600
Washington, D.C. 20005
(202) 789-7000

Florida Division of Tourism
126 W. Van Buren Street
Tallahassee, Florida 32399-2000
(904) 487-1462

Georgia Tourist Division
Box 1776
Atlanta, Georgia 30301
(404) 656-3590 or (800) 847-4842

Hawaii Visitors Bureau
2270 Kalakaua Avenue
Suite 801
Honolulu, Hawaii 96815
(808) 923-1811

Idaho Travel Council
700 W. State Street
P.O. Box 83720
Hall of Mirrors, 2nd floor
Boise, Idaho 83720-0093
(800) 635-7820 or (208) 334-2470

Illinois Office of Tourism
310 South Michigan Avenue
Suite 108
Chicago, Illinois 60604
(312) 744-2400 or (312) 814-4732 or
   (800) 487-2446 (within Illinois) or
   (800) 223-0121 (out of state)

Indiana Tourism Development
   Division
1 North Capitol, Suite 100
Indianapolis, Indiana 46204-2288
(317) 232-8860 or (800) 289-6646

Iowa Tourism Office
200 East Grand Ave.
Des Moines, Iowa 50309
(515) 242-4705

Kansas Department of Economic
   Development—Travel and Tourism
   Division
700 SW Harrison Street, Suite 1300
Topeka, Kansas 66603-3712
(913) 296-2009 or (800) 252-6727

Kentucky Department of Travel
   Development
Capitol Plaza Tower, 22nd floor
500 Mero Street
Frankfort, Kentucky 40601-1974
(502) 564-4930 or (800) 225-8747
   (out of state)

Louisiana Office of Tourism
P.O. Box 94291
Baton Rouge, Louisiana 70804-9291
(504) 342-8119 or (800) 334-8626
   (within Louisiana)
   (800) 633-6970 (out of state)

Maine Publicity Bureau
P.O. Box 2300
97 Winthrop Street
Hallwell, Maine 04347
(207) 623-0363 or (800) 533-9595

Maryland Office of Tourist
   Development
217 E. Redwood Street
Baltimore, Maryland 21202
(410) 333-6611 or (800) 543-1036

Massachusetts Division of Tourism
100 Cambridge Street—13th Floor
Boston, Massachusetts 02202
(617) 727-3201 or (800) 447-MASS
   [6277] (out of state)

Michigan Travel Bureau
Department of Commerce
P.O. Box 30226
Lansing, Michigan 48909
(517) 373-0670 or (800) 543-2YES

Minnesota Tourist Information Center
121 7th Place East
#100 Metro Square
St. Paul, Minnesota 55101-2112
(612) 296-5029 or (800) 657-3700
   (out of state)

Mississippi Division of Tourism
P.O. Box 1705
Ocean Springs, Mississippi 39566-1705
(601) 359-3297 or (800) 927-6378

Missouri Division of Tourism
P.O. Box 1055
Jefferson City, Missouri 65102
(314) 751-1912 or (800) 877-1234

Montana Promotion Division
1424 9th Avenue
Helena, Montana 59620
(406) 444-2654 or (800) 548-3390

Nebraska Division of Travel and
   Tourism
P.O. Box 94666
Lincoln, Nebraska 68509
(402) 471-3796 or (800) 228-4307 (out of
   state) or (800) 742-7595 (within
   Nebraska)

Nevada Commission on Tourism
Capitol Complex
Carson City, Nevada 89710
(702) 687-4322 or (800) NEVADA 8
[638-2328]

New Hampshire Office of Travel and
   Tourism Development
P.O. Box 1856
Concord, New Hampshire 03302-1856
(603) 271-2343 or (603) 271-2666

New Jersey Division of Travel and
   Tourism
C.N. 826
Trenton, New Jersey 08625
(609) 292-2470 or (800) 537-7397

New Mexico Department of Tourism
491 Old Santa Fe Trail
Santa Fe, New Mexico 87503
(505) 827-7400, (800) 545-2040, or (800) 545-2070 (out of state), (505) 827-7402 (FAX)

New York State Division of Tourism
1 Commerce Plaza
Albany, New York 12245
(518) 474-4116 or (800) 225-5697
  (in the Northeast except Maine)

North Carolina Travel and Tourism
  Division
430 North Salisbury Street
Raleigh, North Carolina 27611
(919) 733-4171 or (800) VISIT NC
  [847-4862]

North Dakota Tourism Promotion
Liberty Memorial Building
604 E. Boulevard
Bismarck, North Dakota 58505
(701) 224-2525 or (800) HELLO ND
  [435-5663]

Ohio Division of Travel and Tourism
77 South High Street, 29th Floor
P.O. Box 1001
Columbus, Ohio 43266
(800) 282-5393

Oklahoma Division of Tourism
P.O. Box 60,000
Oklahoma City, Oklahoma 73146
(405) 521-2409 or (800) 652-6552
  (in neighboring states) or
  (800) 522-8565 (within Oklahoma)

Oregon Economic Development
  Tourism Division
775 Summer Street N.E.
Salem, Oregon 97310
(503) 378-3451 or (800) 547-7842

Pennsylvania Bureau of Travel
  Marketing
Department of Commerce
453 Forum Building
Harrisburg, Pennsylvania 17120
(717) 787-5453 or (800) 847-4872

Puerto Rico Tourism Company
23rd Floor
575 Fifth Avenue
New York, New York 10017
(212) 599-6262 or (800) 223-6530
  or (800) 866-STAR [7827]

Rhode Island Department of
  Economic Development
Tourism and Promotion Division
7 Jackson Walkway
Providence, Rhode Island 02903
(401) 277-2601 or (800) 556-2484
  (East Coast from Maine to Virginia,
  also West Virginia and Ohio)

South Carolina Division of Tourism
1205 Pendleton St.
Columbia, South Carolina 29201
(803) 734-0122

South Dakota Division of Tourism
Capitol Lake Plaza
711 East Wells Avenue
Pierre, South Dakota 57501
(605) 773-3301 or (800) 732-5682
  (out of state) or (800) 952-2217
  (within South Dakota)

Tennessee Tourist Development
P.O. Box 23170
Nashville, Tennessee 37202-3170
(615) 741-2158

Texas Dept. of Commerce
Division of Tourism
P.O. Box 12728
Austin, Texas 78711-2728
(512) 462-9191 or (800) 888-8839

Utah Travel Council
Council Hall
Capitol Hill
Salt Lake City, Utah 84114
(801) 538-1030 or (800) 200-1160

Vermont Department of Travel and
  Tourism
134 State Street
Montpelier, Vermont 05602
(802) 828-3236 or (800) VERMONT

Virginia Division of Tourism
202 North 9th Street
Suite 500
Richmond, Virginia 23219
(804) 786-4484 or (800) 847-4882

Washington State Tourism
  Development Division
P.O. Box 42500
101 General Administration Building
Olympia, Washington 98504
(206) 586-2088 or 586-2102
  or (800) 544-1800 (out of state)

Travel West Virginia
2101 E. Washington Street
Charleston, West Virginia 25305
(800) CALL WVA [225-5982]

Wisconsin Division of Tourism
P.O. Box 7606
Madison, Wisconsin 53707-7606
(608) 266-2161 or (800) 372-2737
   (within Wisconsin and neighboring
   states) or (800) 432-8747 (out of
   state)

Wyoming Travel Commission
I-25 and College Drive
Cheyenne, Wyoming 82002
(307) 777-7777 or (800) 225-5996
   (out of state)

Canadian Province Tourist Offices

Alberta Tourism, Parks, and
   Recreation
City Center Building
10155 102 Street
Edmonton, Alberta, Canada T5J 4L6
(403) 427-4321 (from Edmonton area)
   or 800-222-6501 (from Alberta) or
   800-661-8888 (from the U.S. and
   Canada)

Tourism British Columbia
1117 Wharf Street
Victoria, British Columbia, Canada
   V8W 2Z2
(604) 387-1642 or (800) 663-6000

Travel Manitoba
Department 6020
7th Floor
155 Carlton Street
Winnipeg, Manitoba, Canada
   R3C 3H8
(204) 945-3777 or (800) 665-0040 (from
   mainland U.S. and Canada)

Tourism New Brunswick
P.O. Box 12345
Fredericton, New Brunswick, Canada
   E3B 5C3
(506) 453-8745 or (800) 561-0123 (from
   mainland U.S. and Canada)

Newfoundland/Labrador Tourism
   Branch
Department of Tourism & Culture
P.O. Box 8730
St. John's, Newfoundland, Canada
   A1B 4K2
(709) 729-2830 (from St. John's area)
   or (800) 563-6353 (from mainland
   U.S. and Canada)

The Department of Economic
   Development and Tourism
Government of N.W. Territories
Yellow Knife Box 1320
Northwest Territories, Canada
   X1A 2L9
(403) 873-7200 or (800) 661-0788

Nova Scotia Tourism
P.O. Box 456
Halifax, Nova Scotia, Canada B3J 2R5
(902) 424-4247 or (800) 341-6096
   (mainland U.S.) or
   (800) 565-0000 (Canada)

Ontario Ministry of Tourism and
   Recreation
Customer Service
Queens Park
Toronto, Ontario, Canada M7A 2E5
(410) 965-4008 (within Canada) or
   (800) 668-2746 (from mainland U.S.
   and Canada, except Yukon & N.W.
   Territories)

Department of Economic
   Development and Tourism
Quality Services
P.O. Box 940
Charlottetown, Prince Edward Island,
   Canada C1A 7M5
(902) 368-4444 or (800) 565-7421 (from
   New Brunswick and Nova
   Scotia—May 15 to October 31) or
   (800) 565-0267

Tourisme Quebec
C.P. 979
Montreal, Quebec H3C QW3
(800) 363-7777 (from 26 eastern states)
   or (514) 873-2015 (collect from all
   other U.S. locations)

Tourism Saskatchewan
1919 Saskatchewan Drive

Regina, Saskatchewan, Canada
   S4P 3V7
(306) 787-2300 or (800) 667-7191
   (from Canada and mainland U.S.,
   except Alaska)

Tourism Yukon
P.O. Box 2703
Whitehorse, Yukon, Canada Y1A 2C6
(403) 667-5340

BED AND BREAKFAST RESERVATION REQUEST FORM

read about your home in _____ (___) and would
be interested in making reservations to stay with you.

My name: _____

Address: _____

_____

Telephone: _____

Business address/telephone: _____

Number of adult guests: _____

Number and ages of children: _____

Desired date and time of arrival: _____

Desired length of stay: _____

Mode of transportation: _____
(car, bus, train, plane)

Additional information and special requests: _____

_____

_____

_____

_____

I look forward to hearing from you soon.

Sincerely,

APPLICATION FOR MEMBERSHIP
(Please type or print)
(Please refer to Preface, pages xxxix–xl for our membership criteria.)

Name of Bed & Breakfast: _____

Address: _____

City: _____ State: _____ Zip: _____ Phone: ( ) _____

Best Time to Call: _____

Host(s): _____

Located: No. of miles _____ compass direction _____ of Major

City _____ Geographic region _____

No. of miles _____ from major route _____ Exit: _____

No. of guest bedrooms with private bath: _____

No. of guest bedrooms that share a bath: _____

How many people (including *your* family) must use the shared
bath? _____

How many bedrooms, if any, have a sink in them? _____

Room Rates:
$ _____ Double—private bath $ _____ Double—shared bath
$ _____ Single—private bath $ _____ Single—shared bath
$ _____ Suites
Separate Guest Cottage $ _____ Sleeps _____

Are you open year-round? ☐ Yes   ☐ No
If "No," specify when you are open: _____

How many rooms are wheelchair-accessible? _____

Do you require a minimum stay? _____

Do you discount rates at any time? ☐ No   ☐ Yes

Do you offer a discount to senior citizens? ☐ No   ☐ Yes: _____ %

Do you offer a discount for families? ☐ No   ☐ Yes: _____ %

Please supply the name, address, and phone number of three personal references from people not related to you (please use a separate sheet).

Please enclose a copy of your brochure along with color photos including exterior, guest bedrooms, baths, and breakfast area. Bedroom photos should include view of the headboard(s), bedside lamps and night tables. Please show us a typical breakfast setting. Use a label to identify the name of your B&B *on each*. If you have a black-and-white line drawing, send it along. If you have an original breakfast recipe that you'd like to share, send it along, too. (Of course, credit will be given to your B&B.) **Nobody can describe your B&B better than you. Limit your description to 100 words and submit it typed, double spaced, on a separate sheet of paper. We will of course reserve the right to edit.** As a member of the Tourist House Association of America, your B&B will be described in the next edition of our book, *Bed & Breakfast U.S.A.*, published by Plume, an imprint of New American Library, a division of Penguin USA, and distributed to bookstores and libraries throughout the U.S. The book is also used as a reference for B&Bs in our country by major offices of tourism throughout the world.

Note: The following will NOT be considered for inclusion in *Bed & Breakfast, U.S.A.*: B&Bs having more than 15 guest rooms. Rental properties or properties where the host doesn't reside on the premises. Rates over $85 for double occupancy. (This does not include reservation services, suites, cottages, apartments; or qualified B&Bs.) Rates exceeding $35 where 6 people share a bath. Rates exceeding $40 where 5 people share a bath, or rooms are without night tables or adequate bedside reading lamps.

Note: If the publisher or authors receive negative reports from your guests regarding a deficiency in our standards of CLEANLINESS, COMFORT, and CORDIALITY, and/or failure to honor the rate guarantee, we reserve the right to cancel your membership.

This membership application has been prepared by:

_____

(Signature)

Please enclose your $35 membership dues.   Date: _____

Yes! ☐ I'm interested in Group Liability Insurance.

No ☐ I am insured by _____ .

Return to:
Tourist House Association of America
RD 1, Box 12A
Greentown, Pennsylvania 18426

To assure that your listing will be considered for the 1996 edition of *Bed & Breakfast U.S.A.*, we MUST receive your completed application by March 31, 1995. Thereafter, listings will be considered only for the semiannual supplement. (See page 743.)

APPLICATION FOR MEMBERSHIP FOR A
BED & BREAKFAST RESERVATION SERVICE

NAME OF BED & BREAKFAST SERVICE: _____

ADDRESS: _____

CITY: _____ STATE: _____ ZIP: _____ PHONE:(   ) _____

COORDINATOR: _____

BEST TIME TO CALL: _____

Do you have a telephone answering ☐ machine?   ☐ service?

Names of state(s), cities, and towns where you have hosts (in alphabetical order, please, and limit to 10):

Number of hosts on your roster: _____

THINGS OF HISTORIC, SCENIC, CULTURAL, OR GENERAL INTEREST IN THE AREA(S) YOU SERVE:

Range of Rates:
    Modest: Single $ _____   Double $ _____
    Average: Single $ _____   Double $ _____
    Luxury: Single $ _____   Double $ _____

Will you GUARANTEE your rates through December 1996?
☐ Yes   ☐ No

How often do you reinspect listings? _____
Do you require a minimum stay? _____
Surcharges for one-night stay? _____
Do you accept credit cards? ☐ No   ☐ Yes:
☐ AMEX ☐ DINERS ☐ DISCOVER ☐ MASTERCARD
☐ VISA

Is the guest required to pay a fee to use your service?
☐ No   ☐ Yes—The fee is $ _____

Do you publish a directory of your B&B listings?
☐ No   ☐ Yes—The fee is $ _____

Are any of your B&Bs within 10 miles of a university? Which? ____

Briefly describe a sample host home in each of the previous categories: e.g., a cozy farmhouse where the host weaves rugs; a restored 1800 Victorian where the host is a retired general; a contemporary mansion with a sauna and swimming pool.

Please supply the name, address, and phone number of three personal references from people not related to you (please use a separate sheet of paper). Please enclose a copy of your brochure.

This membership application has been prepared by:

_____
(Signature)

Please enclose your $35 membership dues.   Date: _____

If you have a special breakfast recipe that you'd like to share, send it along. (Of course, credit will be given to your B&B agency.) As a member of the Tourist House Association of America, your B&B agency will be described in the next edition of our book, *Bed & Breakfast U.S.A.*, published by Plume, an imprint of New American Library, a division of Penguin USA. Return to: Tourist House Association, RD 1, Box 12A, Greentown, PA 18426.

To ensure that your listing will be considered for the 1996 edition, we must receive your completed application by March 31, 1995. Thereafter, listings will be considered only for the semiannual supplement. (See next page.)

INFORMATION ORDER FORM

We are constantly expanding our roster to include new members in the Tourist House Association of America. Their facilities will be fully described in the next edition of *Bed & Breakfast U.S.A.* In the meantime, we will be happy to send you a list including the name, address, telephone number, etc.

For those of you who would like to order additional copies of the book, and perhaps send one to a friend as a gift, we will be happy to fill mail orders. If it is a gift, let us know and we'll enclose a special gift card from you.

ORDER FORM

To:
Tourist House
Association—
Book Dept.
RD 1, Box 12A
Greentown, PA
18426

From: _____

Address: _____
(Print your name)

_____
City   State   Zip

Date: _____

Please send:

☐ List of new B&Bs ($3.00), available July to December.

☐ _____ copies of *Bed & Breakfast U.S.A.* @ $15.00 each (includes 4th class mail)

Send to: _____

Address: _____

_____
City   State   Zip

☐ Enclose a gift card from:

Please make check or money order payable to Tourist House Association.